AF621254

A Separate Authority (He Mana Motuhake), *Volume I*

Steven Webster

A Separate Authority (He Mana Motuhake), *Volume I*

Establishing the Tūhoe Māori Sanctuary in New Zealand, 1894–1915

palgrave macmillan

Steven Webster
Social Anthropology
The University of Auckland
Auckland, New Zealand

ISBN 978-3-030-41041-4 ISBN 978-3-030-41042-1 (eBook)
https://doi.org/10.1007/978-3-030-41042-1

© The Editor(s) (if applicable) and The Author(s), under exclusive licence to Springer Nature Switzerland AG 2020
This work is subject to copyright. All rights are solely and exclusively licensed by the Publisher, whether the whole or part of the material is concerned, specifically the rights of translation, reprinting, reuse of illustrations, recitation, broadcasting, reproduction on microfilms or in any other physical way, and transmission or information storage and retrieval, electronic adaptation, computer software, or by similar or dissimilar methodology now known or hereafter developed.
The use of general descriptive names, registered names, trademarks, service marks, etc. in this publication does not imply, even in the absence of a specific statement, that such names are exempt from the relevant protective laws and regulations and therefore free for general use.
The publisher, the authors and the editors are safe to assume that the advice and information in this book are believed to be true and accurate at the date of publication. Neither the publisher nor the authors or the editors give a warranty, expressed or implied, with respect to the material contained herein or for any errors or omissions that may have been made. The publisher remains neutral with regard to jurisdictional claims in published maps and institutional affiliations.

Cover illustration: John Steele / Alamy Stock Photo

The author and his family have identified the old home in the cover photo as that of Hikawera Te Kurapa, the *tohunga whakapono* ('expert on truth or faith') of Te Urewera hapū in the 1970–1980s. It was in Papueru, Heipipi, located on the road just south of Ruatāhuna (Fig. 1.1). Hikawera himself died in the 1980s. His name appears in the indexes of both volumes.

This Palgrave Macmillan imprint is published by the registered company Springer Nature Switzerland AG.
The registered company address is: Gewerbestrasse 11, 6330 Cham, Switzerland

Preface

E te atua
tahuri mai ōu taringa ki tā mātou īnoi
hei whakangaro atu koe inā tangi atu mātou.
Anga mai, titiro mai hoki koe
ki a mātou e pokaikaha noa nei,
tangi nei hoki,
koi mātou e whakakorōria nei
ki tōu ingoa tapu.
Āmine[1]

('O Lord
turn your ear to our prayer
lest our cries be lost to you.
Turn to us, look at us
see our turmoils,
our cries of anguish,
so that we may glorify
your sacred name.
Amen')

Getting to Know Ngāi Tūhoe

My personal interest in Urewera lands and Tūhoe kinship began with treks into these mountains in the 1970s soon after my family and I had immigrated to New Zealand from the USA to teach social anthropology and Māori studies at the University of Auckland. We had been taken in as visiting *kaupoi* ('cowboys', Tūhoe jargon for Americans or 'yankees') by Tūhoe *hapū* (descent group or 'sub-tribe') in Ruatāhuna and Ruātoki with which we became increasingly involved in the following years (Fig. 1.1). One of the strongest charms of Māori society is their sincere embrace of *tauiwi* ('strangers') as well as *hoariri* (enemies, opponents; lit., 'angry friends', details of which emerge in Parts II and III of this book). I soon realized that there were surviving blocks of largely unoccupied Māori land scattered throughout the huge and heavily forested Urewera National Park surrounding us, often belonging to Tūhoe descent groups my family and I were coming to know. Old meetinghouses, *marae* ('courtyards'), orchards, and signs of old homesteads survived on these lands, ancestors were buried in them, and ties of kinship extended across them to opposite ends of the Urewera mountain ranges.

At that time, I sensed that a kinship history still lay in these blocks of land, but I had no idea that these remnants themselves obscured a previous colonial history of earlier surveyed blocks and still deeper ancestral roots. It turned out that those earlier ancestors had struggled successfully at the turn of the century to consolidate their sanctuary in the Urewera in *he mana motuhake* ('an independent authority'), an exclusive dominion underwritten by a special statute, but then had to survive a predatory purchase campaign and imposed reorganization of the lands they managed to retain into entirely new blocks in radically different locations. All this chaos of hope, success, and desolation had happened between 1894 and 1926. Many had died in WWI, the flu epidemic, and poverty or been left landless and itinerant by the time of the historic anticlimax. All traces of the previous hard-fought boundaries of the UDNR (Urewera District Native Reserve) disappeared from the new maps, and often survived only in Tūhoe memories and stories. Often it survived, albeit confusedly, only in the colonial archives. Indeed, many aspects of the UDNR, and especially those intrinsic to the organization of *hapū*, had become a lost history—as had been explicitly intended by the Crown in 1921.[2]

In Part III, the Conclusion of this Volume I, I will expand on some of the personal implications of my and my family's early years with the Tūhoe as *tauiwi* or *kaupois*, and subsequent births, marriages, and deaths over the intervening years. The surprises and ironies, loneliness and companionship, tragedies and joys of social anthropological 'participant observation' know no bounds, particularly when one's whole family is involved. However, here in this primarily ethno*historical* work the contemporary and often personal implications will remain in the background until they emerge somewhat 'reborn' in the Conclusion. Unlike most historical research, my family's *ethnographic* research with the Tūhoe in the 1970–1980s was based on many years of frequent visits to their homes (and they to ours in Auckland) and continuing *whānau* ('extended family') connections. It would have been somewhat the same for the earliest traders and settlers taken in as *mokai* ('pets') by Māori *rangatira* ('chiefs') and their *whānau*. One of the ironies of our personal experience with the Tūhoe is that it was my later ethnohistorical research that has joined us irrevocably to them through their deep ancestral roots in Te Urewera. As will be described in the Conclusion, it is as if they knew even in the 1970s that this would happen.

In 1984 I made my first foray into the archival history of this dramatic Urewera era at the turn of the century, and distributed among Tūhoe leaders an unpublished manuscript on my findings, including the onset of the Crown's betrayal of their sanctuary in the UDNR (Webster n.d. (1984–5)). In 2002 this preliminary effort prompted the Waitangi Tribunal to recruit me to research comprehensively and report on the Urewera Consolidation Scheme 1921–1925 (Webster 2004), here the subject of Volume II. Since the 1980s, the Tribunal has been investigating and attempting to settle violations of Treaty rights with the Māori recognized in New Zealand law until the 1870s but disregarded for most of the next century. The surprising opportunity to work for the Tribunal threw me willy-nilly back into the research I had first glimpsed in the 1970s, and I still see no end to the information that can be extracted from the deluge of archive records assembled especially with the insightful and determined help of Himaima Tumoana, herself a Tūhoe and member of the Ruatāhuna-Ruātoki *whānau* that had originally taken us in. In the 1980s I had been urged by another young Tūhoe scholar (now one of their leaders) to pursue research in Tūhoe land history as recorded in archives throughout the country, in order to complement Tūhoe elders' and scholars' own oral history and private papers. These two volumes on *He Mana Motuhake* are the result.

I initially saw my research for the Tribunal as requiring neutral scholarship that could mediate between Tūhoe claimants and the Crown's defense. However, I was soon encouraged by the Tribunal to follow the evidence and express my conclusions freely. My earlier 1984–1985 research had exposed the initial Crown betrayals of the Tūhoe and UDNR (Urewera District Native Reserve) which began soon after their sanctuary had finally been established in 1907. The further evidence I was able to uncover of the subsequent predatory purchasing campaign and duplicitous intentions of the Crown in the UCS (Urewera Consolidation Scheme) clearly strengthened the grounds of the Tūhoe claim. The contributions of many historians, especially that of Judith Binney, were crucial, but as a social anthropologist I was fortunate to have benefitted from years of intermittent participation in their ordinary lives, an advantage not usually integral to historical research methods. In July 2004 I was able to present my findings before the Tribunal in Te Whaiatemotu meetinghouse on the Te Urewera hapū marae near Ruatāhuna where my family and I had first been hosted in the 1970s. I was again hosted and surrounded supportively by the younger members of the hapū (children when we had first met them!), and able to visit and mourn in the nearby ***urupā*** 'cemetery' where others of them had been buried with their predecessors. Judge Savage, heading the Tribunal's inquiry, understandably looked askance at this 'American' academic's ***kaupoi*** manner, but the locals knew better.

My research for the present book grew directly out of my work for the Waitangi Tribunal and presentation of that report. Volume I of *He Mana Motuhake* describes the unique manner in which the Tūhoe and Crown had, in good faith and accordance with Tūhoe wishes, investigated and established their sanctuary as the Urewera District Native Reserve between 1894 and 1913. It was my Tribunal report on the subsequent era, revised and augmented here in Volume II, that had described how the same Crown soon proceeded to subvert and undo that entire achievement and the promise of the 1896 UDNR Act. Just as my study of the 1921 UCS had drawn me back into the preceding Crown purchase campaign that led to it, this whole era drew me further back into the preceding UDNR that the UCS had dismantled. Whereas my report for the Tribunal had described *how* all this was lost, this volume seeks to describe in detail, relying on the transcribed words of the Tūhoe ancestors themselves, *what* was lost. Now, almost a century later, the promise of the 2014 settlement is that some of what was lost by 1926 might eventually be regained.

I started my research on the UDNR soon after presenting my report on the UCS, but was inspired by the Tribunal's prodigious effort and findings in their final report (20 chapters) released in 2009–2015 strongly supporting the Tūhoe claims, and especially by the settlement with the Crown in 2014. Regardless of these Tūhoe victories, my leading motivation in continuing this research was to set the record straight on two key issues that had been largely overlooked by the Tribunal itself and perhaps underplayed by the Tūhoe in their negotiations with the Crown for the 2014 settlement.

As the Tūhoe know well but have learned the hard way since the 1850s, given the fickleness of governments and reversals of power, it is important to maintain vigilance and let no gain by the disempowered slip by.

One leading motive in this ethnohistory is to follow up on my argument that the 1896 Act largely reflected the *mana motuhake* goals of the Tūhoe themselves and, most importantly, their control over its investigation 1899–1903 in practice (Webster 2004: 20; 27–31; 2017). My position on this key issue is now supported by contemporary Tūhoe leaders but contrary to most of the other reports to the Tribunal and specifically those by Judith Binney and Jeffrey Sissons, although both strong protagonists of the Tūhoe. My own position in 2004 (and that of present Tūhoe leaders) and elaborated in the present volume was that the Crown's betrayal of the UDNR was grievously aggravated by the fact that it had been enacted and established largely in good faith with the Tūhoe and under their practical control by that same Crown. Ironically, the other researcher who impressively mounted this argument was not Binney, Sissons, or other supporters of the Tūhoe claims but Cecilia Edwards, the solicitor defending the Crown. Perhaps she had anticipated that whether the claimants' case for the injustice of the later purchase campaign and Urewera Consolidation Act was weak or strong, if it was argued that the UDNR was unjust to begin with, she could respond that its subsequent undoing was an insignificant loss or even a gain for the Tūhoe. In the event, the deciding factor may have been that the Crown did not attempt to respond to the evidence that I marshaled regarding the Crown's undoing of the UDNR through sustained and predatory injustices in both its purchase campaign and Urewera Consolidation Scheme.

My other main motive to pursue this research into the investigation and establishment of the UDNR was to emphasize the key structural and organizational role of Tūhoe *hapū* in the resulting land titles of their sanctuary. As I have documented here and in my previous publications with regard to Māori in general (Webster 1975, 1990, 1997, 1998a, b, 2002, 2011) and Tūhoe specifically (Webster 2010, 2013, 2017, 2019), misunderstanding of the social organization of *hapū* has been persistent since earliest colonization. It is sometimes even despairingly indulged by Māori in the seriously misleading (but, for the Crown) administratively advantageous image of 'whānau, hapū, and iwi' ('extended family', 'sub-tribe', and 'tribe', respectively) as hierarchically and even territorially organized. Until 1975 it had been widely assumed even among social anthropologists that all Māori hapū were long defunct. My effort to rectify this oversight in 1975 coincided with the resurgence of popular awareness of hapū in the Māori renaissance, but my article in defense of their continuing vitality and historical adaptation to land-loss was not seriously challenged until Jeffrey Sissons' important alternative interpretation was published in 2010. Because Sissons also drew much of his information from his own early social anthropological field research among the Tūhoe, I think I was able to defend my understanding of hapū effectively with specific regard to Tūhoe hapū as well as Māori in general (Webster 2013).

Given even Elsdon Best's ethnological but nevertheless superficial understanding of Tūhoe hapū organization as secretary for the UDNR commission (argued in Part I here), the explicit hope of the UCS to eradicate it, and the long-established popular and administrative misunderstanding of Māori hapū in general, perhaps it should not be surprising that the Tribunal findings regarding the purchase campaign and consolidation scheme in the Urewera tended to overlook major implications of hapū control of Urewera lands that I had emphasized in my 2004 report.

Volume II of *He Mana Motuhake* details some underplayed implications of the Tribunal's oversights regarding the structure and organization of hapū. These include (i) the Tūhoe tactics for resisting the Crown purchasing strategies; (ii) the UCS demand that *pupuri whenua* ('land-withholders', derogatorily publicized by the Crown as 'non-sellers') be broken down into small-farming 'families'; and (iii), despite Tūhoe resistance to this demand (by reorganizing descent groups around siblings), (iv) the grave loss or dislocation of ancestral rights caused by Crown pre-emptions and evacuations, false promise of roads, reduction of the size of each new block for its costs (to be paid in land) of survey and access to the promised roads, and resulting relocation of remaining ancestral rights of the stripped-down consolidation groups to over 200 small blocks. For the next several decades, these relocated *mōrehu* ('remnants' or 'survivors') of the ancestral UDNR lay scattered, "*whakamoana-ed*" ('adrift'), often isolated and consequently deserted and faced again by Crown threats, throughout what was to become the vast and rugged Urewera National Park. Although the Tribunal's report addressed most of these injustices, the crucial implications for the damage potentially done to hapū organization were usually overlooked. As well as weakening the Tūhoe case, this compromised the Tribunal's invaluable historical record for future use by others, most tragically perhaps for Tūhoe themselves.

In this volume I will return in the Conclusion to some of these implications and the resulting difficulties for Tūhoe descendants who wish to recover more of what was lost from their hapū by the Crown's dismantling of the UDNR in 1921 than was returned in its 2014 apologies and settlement.

Indigeneity in New Zealand

At the risk of stretching the reader's patience with apparently theoretical but actually practical and even global issues, a wider but important New Zealand context in which I and my family are still getting to know *Ngāi Tūhoe* needs to be briefly examined here.

My credentials in support of the Tūhoe that I hope to have outlined above may not be sufficient if challenged in the name of indigeneity. As will be discussed in the Introduction, the Tūhoe themselves have often been considered to be icons of New Zealand indigeneity, even by other Māori iwi. This concept is the most recent in a history of popular but often justifiable moral or legal claims that have emerged globally since the 1960s (Webster 1997; 1998b). In New Zealand, similar issues began nearly a century ago in the 1920s with the anthropological but patronizing and racially tinged concept of Māori 'culture loss' or, by the 1950s, cultural-deficit theory—in both cases, urged by Māori as well as Pākehā ('European' or 'white' New Zealander) scholars. In the 1970s, about the time that I and my family started to get to know the Tūhoe, similar claims emerged in the Māori cultural renaissance in terms of *Māoritanga* ('Māori-ness'), *te reo* (Māori language), racism versus anti-racism, assimilation versus multi-culturalism or bi-culturalism, or treaty rights. By the 1990s such issues were being expressed in terms of 'cultural safety' in government or public services and, at least in the universities, 'post-colonial' decolonization or 'postmodernist' disenchantment. The social and intellectual heritage of these concepts in New Zealand are among the historical conditions of their current replacement by notions of indigeneity. Here in this preface is the best place for me to attempt briefly to outline the wide range of positions taken by prominent scholars, Māori as well as Pākehā, in what would now usually be seen as support for indigeneity, and to situate my own position relative to them.

1. Ameria Salmond proposes a recursively ontological ethnography of cultural otherness (other 'being' or existence) that defers to the creativity as well as radical otherness of Māori culture, describing one iwi's development of their *whakapapa* ('genealogy') extended

digitally as well as cosmologically that she contends escapes both traditionalist and strategic cultural constructionist understandings of Māori indigeneity (Salmond 2013–4; Webster 2019).

2. Much earlier in the development of the current issue of indigeneity and probably influenced by Linda Smith's work (see below), Lynette Carter described the bureaucratic incorporation of *whakapapa* and contrasted this with ordinary traditional understandings of it, cautiously defending the latter while accepting that it had to modernize in the legal and corporate terms of contemporary society (Carter 2003).
3. Paulette Regan, generalizing her experience of indigeneity claims in Canada to New Zealand and Australia, proposes a revised truth-and-reconciliation story-telling procedure that can overcome subtle 'post-colonial' barriers to reconciliation, obscured in liberal forms of denial, guilt, or empathy, with the goal of transforming unconscious colonizers into activist allies of indigeneity (2010).
4. Avril Bell examines indigeneity in several of Britain's settler societies, including New Zealand, excavating historical layers of settler ideology, semiology, and repressive tolerance that often distort indigenous persons' concepts of what is possible, similarly proposing an ethics or "a new, relational imaginary" that can nurture settler acceptance of the profound autonomy demanded by "indigenous ontologies and ways of life" (Bell 2014).
5. Roger Maaka, following Mason Durie's as well as Augie Fleras' earlier works, examines "the politics of indigeneity" in New Zealand and concludes that regardless of bureaucratic "offloading [of] government responsibility to indigenous communities ... with minimal transfer of power or authority," Māori indigeneity is being influentially "mainstreamed" for the better in society (Maaka and Fleras 2009).
6. Linda Tuhiwai Smith's influential polemic *Decolonising Methodologies* used the image of decolonization before that of indigeneity had developed, but relies on established radical sociological critique influenced by Paulo Friere's form of Marxism to promote Māori "oppositional ways of knowing" or resistance against racial oppression and marginalization including the subtle forms of compromise more acceptable to Carter, Maaka, and Durie (Smith 2012; first edition 1999).

7. In straightforwardly Marxist terms, Elizabeth Rata analyses "the ways in which a particular and influential concept of indigeneity was established by the circumstances which led to neotribal capitalism and then subverted by the emergence of that regime" in the Māori renaissance since the 1970s (Rata 2000, 2002: 174).
8. Over a decade earlier, in less scholarly but more readable yet bluntly Marxist terms suspicious of the liberal government's "devolution" of "iwi authority", Dun Mihaka's frankly working-class critique of effete 'traditional' Māori *tangihanga* (funeral ceremonies), religiosity, and other customs urged a potentially revolutionary *Māoritanga* in support of *te ao mārama* (a more informed, lucid world) (Mihaka 1989: 72).
9. Paul Moon, similarly to John Rangihau's 1975 assertion of *Tūhoetanga* ('Tūhoe-ness') against a generalized form of Māoritanga and following Said's critique of 'orientalism', defends multipolar forms of indigeneity, including the distinctiveness of different Māori *iwi*, 'tribes' against reductionist globalizing or hegemonic neocolonial policies promoting a hybrid indigeneity at international as well as national levels (Moon 2015).
10. Marama Muru-Lanning analyzes the position of Māori contending for control over water resources and business enterprises in terms of appropriation of material forces and commodification of social relations as well as ideology obscuring these processes, but defends the practical necessity of Māori cooperation with established power structures when necessary to gain leverage (Muru-Lanning 2016; 2018).
11. Jeffrey Paparoa Holman analyzes the influence of Elsdon Best and his primary informant Tutakangahau in Best's extended fieldwork among the Tūhoe on metaphysical concepts that have come to be assumed by Māori as well as other authorities to be central in the indigenous Māori worldview. Holman argues that far from being traditional these concepts must be understood in terms of the late 1890s ideological context common to both of them (Holman 2010; as will be seen, both were also deeply involved in establishing the UDNR).
12. Miranda Johnson analyzes the rising influence of indigeneity movements historically in the settler societies of New Zealand as well as Canada and Australia in the concurrent global rise of neoliberal governance, concluding that political reaction to retain control

over material forces such as land has often compromised these indigenous movements in ways that exploit class inequality within them. In 2017 she extended this approach to the legal establishment of the Wanganui River in New Zealand as a "person" in indigenous terms, arguing that this beguiling metaphor obscured a much more important material and ideological history of conflict (Johnson 2016; 2017).

13. Fiona McCormack analyzes Māori indigeneity in terms of gifts and commodity theory, examining relative control over fisheries, land, cultural venues, and conflict settlement in the face of subtle appropriation under neoliberal governance, emphasizing that despite the risk of greater losses of control over such resources, the results of Māori initiatives remain essentially unpredictable and sometimes retain or even gain control (several of her articles since 2011 are reviewed in Webster 2016).

I have tried to arrange these advocates of indigeneity roughly in sequence from weaker to stronger theoretical positions in terms that I myself consider more effectively supportive of Māori indigeneity. Although in New Zealand a few Māori have always been accepted in positions of national leadership at least since the 1870s, the relatively high proportion of these scholars who probably identify as Māori (six of the thirteen: Carter, Maaka, Smith, Mihaka, Moon, and Muru-Lanning) displays the increasing opportunity for social mobility since the Māori cultural renaissance began in the 1970s. Indeed, signals in the names used by some authorities suggest indigeneity is valued by others who would identify, or be identified by others, as Pākehā.

Interestingly, this array also suggests that the range of theoretical positions regarding indigeneity (at least in terms of my own preferences in social and historical theory) is nearly as wide between Māori as Pākehā scholars. Insofar as my preferences reflect theoretical differences more generally, this suggests wide disagreement between scholars, Māori as well as Pākehā, all of whom advocate Māori indigeneity but in different ways. Although I have tried to characterize each of their positions neutrally, many would identify the criteria I have implicitly used as dogmatically historical materialist and disagree or invert my prioritization or even my judgment that they are all supporters or advocates of indigeneity.

For instance, Salmond might dismiss Johnson's critique of the Whanganui River legal personhood as reducing ontological otherness to "strategic cultural identity construction" by an overseas academic who talks about rather than to Māori. Similarly, Johnson might demur (as have I: Webster 2019) that Salmond's perhaps romanticized 'two-worlds' approach to Māori culture has overlooked or essentialized the specific history of the Māori concept of *whakapapa* from a culturalist and even patronizingly nativist point of view. Although Holman's profession has been literary and his scholarship in Māori language and history well-established, some other advocates of indigeneity assuming the primordial authenticity of Māori concepts whose colonial history he has exposed may indignantly reject his thesis as presumptuous and hostile. Mihaka and Rata both assert frankly Marxist approaches to Māori indigeneity, but while Mihaka defends it as a working-class tradition, Rata attacks it as a threat to democracy.

Ironically, Rata's Marxist critique has precipitated criticisms from defenders of Māori indigeneity as a right-wing reaction against it. To the contrary, I would argue that her quietly emotional first-hand account of families torn apart in the confrontation between Muriwhenua tribes of the Far North reveals a commitment to indigeneity in the form of a Māori working-class that parallels Mihaka's in a more academic register (Rata 2000: 155–97; 2002: 185–94)]. Nevertheless, on two key issues, hapū and capitalist class structure, Rata's careful critique of Māori indigeneity reverts to an ahistorical form of two-worlds biculturalism that subverts her Marxist orthodoxy. Her actual support for Māori indigeneity is the baby thrown out with the bathwater.

First, the structural difference between whānau, hapū, and iwi that I have been at pains to clarify (even for the Waitangi Tribunal) is collapsed by Rata in her otherwise important critique of iwi corporatization under neoliberal capitalism since the 1980s. Her analysis mentions neither hapū nor the misleading synonym 'subtribes', confounding hapū with either 'families' or iwi in the ideological hierarchy that has served government as well as popular misunderstanding for so long. At least since earliest colonization, iwi ('tribes') have often been an opportunist reorganization of ancestral genealogies and of particular administrative interest to government, and at least since the 1840s hapū have usually been a more or less successful form of resistance against iwi as well as capitalist class structures, always causing enough trouble to be abjured if not suppressed by government (Webster 1998a; 2002). Second, Rata's argument for such a collapse of Māori indigeneity into neoliberal capitalism apparently assumes the separate formation of a Māori capitalist class structure paralleling that of the long-established Pākehā capitalist class structure, with a class of elite Māori appropriating the labor of their own captured Māori working class (2000: 225–32; 2002: 195).

A more historical approach to New Zealand as a settler colony (such as Bell's, Regan's, and Johnson's) would have to admit that Māori have been an ethnic sector of the Pākehā working class at least since the 1840s and an ethnic sector of the Pākehā elite if not capitalist class at least since the 1890s. Nor has the much longer struggle between them ever been as predictable as Rata assumes it was. The illusion of a wholesale sell-out by a separate Māori class hierarchy led by its Māori capitalists into neoliberal governance in the space of a decade or two is itself misled by the two-worlds biculturalist ideology of the 1980s–1990s. The Marxist orthodoxy Rata applies appears to be ahistorical, disregarding its major transformation in 1930s critical theory, let alone the contemporary transformation required in the face of neoliberal capitalism such as I outlined above regarding Johnson and McCormack.

Behind all the divergent positions outlined above there is the unspoken premise of all approaches to indigeneity whether supportive, indifferent, or hostile: the legal (i.e., political-economic and historical) issue of treaty rights. Most of the supporters of Māori indigeneity above set this issue aside, but would recognize its crucial bearing on their position. After all, not just any kind of racial, ethnic, or minority assumption of difference qualifies one as 'indigenous' to a country. Being accepted as indigenous in a nation state is only a start: next may come the question of a treaty, and then the legitimacy of a so-called treaty. As outlined by Bell, Johnson, and Regan, the history of these implications has arisen or been hidden differently in most settler colonies, dogged in historically different way[s] in the USA, Canada, New Zealand, and Australia, for instance, by the question of recognition of the ancient European legal precedent of native or aboriginal title to their traditional lands (McHugh 1991; Brookfield 1999). Whether a supporter or critic of indigenous rights, one's defense may stand or fall on this particular history of the judicial premises and precedents of national power.

How would I characterize my own criteria for more insightful or effective theoretical critique in support of Māori indigeneity? The touchstone must be, of course, justice. My leading criteria to find this touchstone would be the degree of consideration regarding the historical conditions of the specific situation, and the priority given to material over ideological sources of power that can be mobilized under those conditions. These factors are crucial in distinguishing between understandings that effectively challenge a hierarchy of power unjustly maintaining a particular social situation or, instead, are appropriated by, inadvertently reinforce, or opportunistically comply with that power hierarchy. When such details have been more or less worked out, we may be ready to touch the touchstone.

Of course, ideology, imaginary, semiology, or 'discourse' can be a material force, but if these are confounded with manifold other forms of material force, the critique is incapacitated. If an enthusiast of indigeneity relies too much on the rhetorical power of the word or merely moralistic appeals in pursuit of justice, the power of a lawyer or a law easily trumps that even out of court, as the shifting history of treaty rights has shown in each settler state. And behind the subaltern power of a judiciary maze-way lie other less obvious official powers. Meanwhile, racist or subtler forces trump indigeneity in the streets or national institutions every day regardless of the official situation.

I have been guided in my own research by two appropriate warnings, both learned in the 1980s. It was at this time that my social theory began to be transformed by political-economic practice in the not-so-ivory tower of the University of Auckland. As Marx had said regarding history:

> Hegel remarks somewhere that all facts and personages of great importance in world history occur, as it were, twice. He forgot to add: the first time as tragedy, the second as farce…. Men make their own history, but they do not make it just as they please; they do not make it under circumstances chosen by themselves, but under circumstances directly encountered, given, and transmitted from the past. (McLellan 1977: 300)

It is not merely ironic that both the Crown and the Tūhoe have each lived this particular Urewera history at least twice.

It was a bit earlier in the 1980s in the Urewera mountains that I came to appreciate a similarly trenchant insight into the material forces of history and truth (even in those days the Urewera was no less a political-economic hot-bed than the University). Hikawera Te Kurapa, the Tūhoe ***rangatira*** and ***tohunga whakapono*** (expert in matters of truth and belief) of Te Urewera hapū in Ruatāhuna, in answer to a serious question put to him whether or not it mattered that tourists were told true stories about the history of Tūhoe and their mountain sanctuary, thought it over for a moment and then replied:

> *Ka kore e tika e pono tō tuku i te kōrero, ka hoki mai ki te ngau i tō tou* ('if you don't speak the truth, it will come back and bite you on your ass'). (Rongonui Tahi, personal communication)

Of course, I have had to accept that my attempt to follow these warnings in my advocacy of Tūhoe indigeneity sometimes leads to my having to relive my own history ignominiously or get my own ass bitten, by Tūhoe as well as by their adversaries or supporters.

Indigeneity and Tūhoetanga

I mentioned above that in 1975 John Rangihau, a Tūhoe leader and government official, contributed commentaries on "being Māori" to a collection edited by historian Michael King (1975: 12–4; 183–90). This was in the early years of the Māori cultural renaissance, and Rangihau was characteristically tactful but frank in his criticism of patronizing Pākehā racism and 'bandwagon' support of the new Māoritanga. Instead, he asserted *Tūhoetanga* because

> I have a faint suspicion that Maoritanga is a term coined by the Pakeha to bring the tribes together. Because if you cannot divide and rule, then for a tribal people all you can do is unite them and rule. Because then they lose everything by losing their own tribal histories and traditions that give them their identity. (in King 1975: 190)

As outlined above, this suspicion was similarly stated by Paul Moon in 2015, and put in terms of the subtleties of neoliberal government obeisance toward Māori by Fiona McCormack. Indeed, this patronizing approach to Māori culture had first been advocated by the national Māori leader Apirana Ngata as well as Raymond Firth in the 1920s (Webster 1998b: 88–102). Felix Keesing, another anthropologist of that era, recommended a pacified and generalized form of Māori 'race pride' against an early form of *Tūhoetanga* that he saw arising threateningly from working-class values, as reported by the Presbyterian Church:

> One thing we have to contend with is the communistic social habits of the Maori. Nowhere does the ancient communism of the Maori maintain to-day as in Tuhoe. These people still think and move *en masse*. The most private domestic affairs are brought to the meeting-house and discussed and settled by the tribe. Everyone is a member of the tribe rather than a separate entity, and anyone who refused to go the way of the tribe is considered a bad Maori. (Keesing 1928: 93–4, quoted in Webster 1998b: 93)

Although this defiance with social class undertones happened in the bitter wake of the UCS, it had deeper roots and can be seen to continue in the stubborn *Tūhoetanga* that finally recovered their Te Urewera sanctuary in 2014.

I am reassured that some Tūhoe leaders view the historical era that I have examined here in Volume I in ways that confirm my own regarding the crucial role of hapū and the stubborn defiance of some leaders in the face of neoliberal governance as well as colonization. In 2003 the Tūhoe *rangatira* Paora Kruger and Hori Thrupp clearly understood that while the UDNR was a triumph for the *mana motuhake* of the Tūhoe sanctuary, in the UCS the Crown, as well as taking most of their land, attempted to weaken the mana of their hapū as well:

> *Kare tonu te kaihoro o te kawana ki te whenua e ngata, tona hiahia kia riro ki te ia te katoa.... ma tenei ka whakakorea, whakaititia te mana o nga hapu a rangatira hoki* ('the greed of the government for the land was not yet satisfied; they desired that it all be gone.... so that the mana of the hapū and their leaders as well might be abolished or minimised'). (Paora Kruger and Hori Thrupp 20–22 August 2003; personal communication with Himaima Tumoana; my translation of her transcript)

In 2015 the younger Tūhoe *rangatira* Rongonui Tahi mentioned above recounted how in the 1940s he had been sent by his Rūātoki grandparents to be brought up by adoptive grandparents in the old settlement of Ohāua in order to maintain the *ahi kaa* ('burning hearth-fires') and *mauri* ('life force') of ancestral and occupational rights of Ngāti Rongo hapū in Ōhāua (Tahi 2015). In the 1970s Tahi was a member of our host *whānau* in Mātaatua, and I will return to the ethnohistory of Ohāua te Rangi in Chap. 6 and again in Part III. Although Tahi's account followed the Tūhoe recovery of their Te Urewera sanctuary in 2014, he does not mention this, instead emphasizing that his elders in Ōhāua had never accepted Crown ownership or the National Park surrounding them. In this context, the characteristic defiance of *Tūhoetanga* was expressed by ignoring the results of the whole UCS. On the other hand, Tahi ruefully joked that while in the old days it was Pākehā hunters or tourists who got lost, nowadays it was Tūhoe who should have known better. So, in his turn, Tahi was making sure that his grandchildren were kept in touch with the history of Te Urewera and especially Ōhāua, where they were building a *wharekai* ('dining hall') beside the beloved old *kauta* ('cook-houses') and *wharenui* (ceremonial 'meetinghouse') to encourage continuing hapū activities in this part of Te Urewera.

The following year Tama Iti, another Tūhoe leader related to our host *whānau*, also stated a similar challenge in terms of *mana motuhake*. Even before Dun Mihaka and even more theatrically, Iti began notoriously to confront government with working-class defiance (*kanohi ki te kanohi*, 'face to face') in the 1970s occupation of Parliament grounds and later land march protesting the loss of Māori land. In 2003, in commemoration of the Crown's confiscations of Tūhoe land in the 1860s, he stage-organized a spectacular mock battle including the burning of car-wrecks confronting the arrival of the Waitangi Tribunal in Ruātoki, his home town. In 2007 Tama Iti was a target of an 'anti-terrorist' national police raid that included Ruātoki as well as some other New Zealand communities. He was prosecuted and, for lack of more serious evidence, jailed for two years on a ludicrous charge of possessing an unlicensed firearm (as do many Tūhoe as subsistence hunters of wild pig and deer). This punishment appeared to be a vindictive retaliation for his years of defiance as well as to cover the embarrassment of the Ministry of Justice for its clumsy and fruitless national mobilization against "terrorism" (Sluka 2010).

In 2010 the government found itself under criticism for what many conservatives thought was an indulgent policy toward Māori claims. Although then in the middle of prolonged negotiation with Tūhoe, the Prime Minister spoke out in an effort to reassure the public that the Urewera National Park would definitely remain in Crown hands. The negotiations quietly persisted behind the scenes, and the release of Waitangi Tribunal reports showed mounting evidence of the Crown's indefensible position. The government's predicament was probably also aggravated because the Tribunal's reports carry more than merely recommendatory weight where the lands in question are held by the Crown rather than in private ownership. By 2011 the government had joined in a compact with the Tūhoe to continue negotiations in good faith regarding the status of Te Urewera (Higgens 2014: 10–11). Reflecting the caution for intramural consensus with which Tūhoe negotiators proceeded, this compact was signed by the many representatives of Tūhoe hapū rather than the iwi leadership.

The issue of ownership of Te Urewera was finally avoided in negotiations by emphasizing the Tūhoe wisdom and popular environmentalist conviction that the land 'owns' the people rather than vice versa, and implying such a precedent in the legislation. Reflecting this compact in all sincerity, by 2014 the Te Urewera Act explicitly stated that

> [t]he purpose of this Act is to establish and preserve in perpetuity *a legal identity and protected status* for Te Urewera for its intrinsic worth, its distinctive natural and cultural values, the integrity of those values, and for its national importance. (in Ruru 2014: 18–9; my italics)

Nevertheless, when the settlement Acts and their manifold apologies were finally passed by Parliament in 2014, the government still found itself faced by the same 'communistic social habits' whereby Tūhoe 'still think and move *en masse*' that the Presbyterian Church had to 'contend with' in 1928. With appropriate *whakaiti* ('humility') the chief negotiator Tamati Kruger let his deference to the will of the Tūhoe be widely known by emphasizing that 'my work is finished', quietly dramatizing that ratification and acceptance of the government's apologies by a Tūhoe consensus was still required.

Kruger's realism fortifies his traditionalism and the defiant idealism of *Tūhoetanga*. In the 1980s he was the young Tūhoe scholar who had suggested I begin to explore the colonial archives to complement their own historical knowledge of their ancestors and Te Urewera lands. His leadership of Tūhoe under the new Te Urewera Acts remains explicitly and confidently hostile toward the business interests to which his senior relatives had often committed the Tūhoe-Waikaremoana Trust Board in the 1980s. At that time, visiting him and his family in the Ōhāua meetinghouse in the middle of those mountains, I remember him expressing this same conviction in terms of what he already saw as the 'irreconcilability of money and mana'.

He also continues to hold Tūhoe as well as government to account (Kruger 2017; 2018). Kruger emphasizes that although the negotiations to recover their Te Urewera sanctuary had taken 20 years, the battle to regain the *mana motuhake* of the Tūhoe had just begun. He lamented that many Tūhoe had drifted away from the ideals upon which it had been built, and that many of their youth were unfamiliar with Tūhoe hapū, iwi, or their history. (A trek was organized in February 2019 from Rūātoki to the interior of Te Urewera in the Ōhāua te Rangi blocks (Chaps. 6 and 11), and it is true that few of its participants knew details of what had happened there as recently as the 1920s.) During the negotiations for return of Te Urewera, Kruger had investigated some overseas precedents in returning lands to indigenous peoples, and been advised by them of shortcomings and disappointments. He remains on guard against the blandishments of neoliberal governance as well as the reversible policies of government such as those that had previously won Te Urewera for his ancestors but soon took it back from them.

In the context of global environmental concerns as well as Tūhoe demand for return of the National Park, negotiations with government had coupled popular concern for the natural environment closely to Tūhoe *mana motuhake*. The Te Urewera settlement had even become a United Nations model for settlement of indigenous claims in settler colonies, and indigenous claimants in other countries were viewing it "more as a legal sword than a resolution of the relationship with nature" (Kruger 2018). Kruger's own manner in the successful negotiations probably wisely avoided such confrontation, but all parties knew that Tūhoe defiance and insistence on consensus among hapū stood behind him.

Following the settlement of Te Urewera as a "legal identity and protected status" in 2014, it is likely that bipartisan support developed in Parliament gained by 2017, on this precedent and its recognition in the UN, the legal status of "personhood" for the Whanganui River that was examined, as outlined above, by Miranda Johnson (2017). Two influential anthropological commentaries on Māori fresh-water rights also appeared in the interim: Anne Salmond hopefully adapted her two-worlds ontology of Māori culture to support the "…weaving [of] distinct, even incommensurable vocabularies together in legal frameworks" (2014: 305). Also as outlined above, Marama Muru-Lanning, similarly hopeful but assuming no such ontological cultural difference, less innocently explored "the impact of the recent wave of neoliberal privatization on Māori…resources in their ancestral territories," including rivers as "integrated, living, whole river system[s]" (2016: 193, 8–9).

Although Johnson did not mention it in her 2017 commentary, in 2011 she had already traced in social-historical detail the 'postcolonial incorporation of Indigenous concepts of ecological spirituality and interdependency with nature' emphasized in the findings of the Waitangi Tribunal's review of the long history of the Whanganui River case. The scholarly restraint displayed by Johnson in 2017 by 'leaving a space' for the unfolding of the complex social and juridical history hidden behind the enthusiasm of the legal precedent of personhood for a river (or a mountain, or Lake Waikaremoana, or Urewera National Park) supports Kruger's patience with Tūhoe recovery of *mana motuhake* as well as the Crown's apparent relaxation of its unilateral sovereignty. However, more pointedly in the conclusion of her 2011 article, Johnson emphasizes the potentially neoliberal implications of the hopefully 'postcolonial' reformation: the Tribunal's statement, postcolonial in intention and effect, conceals a profound irony. In the reorientation from colony to postcolony, Māori, who as claimants to *the* law of the land cannot anticipate sovereign independence from the extant nation-state, must 'contribute' to their own reparation. (Johnson 2011: 111)

As outlined above, Fiona McCormack's understanding of Māori options under neoliberal governance parallels Johnson's. Such a potentially subversive legal implication of the assumed postcolonial reconceptualization also "echoes older colonial and racist tropes of natives mistaking Europeans for gods" (Johnson 2017). Kruger and other Tūhoe leaders are certainly aware that the 'legal sword' behind the beguiling image of ecological and spiritual personhood is double-edged.

Notes

1. A Ringatū liturgy by Te Kooti, adapted from Judith Binney's *Redemption Songs: A Life of Te Kooti Arikirangi Te Turuki* (2012: 297–8; fn 118; Bridget Williams Books, Wellington, New Zealand). See further details on sources and my translation in endnote for this same liturgy repeated at close of the last chapter.
2. The notion of 'the Crown' needs some unpacking for readers unfamiliar with the British Commonwealth tradition, particularly in the context of settler colonies, treaty rights and claims, and indigenous peoples which is the focus of *He Mana Motuhake*. In the USA, for instance, the rough equivalent of the Crown is the federal government. The notion of sovereignty has developed historically between Commonwealth and other countries, especially the USA. A recent social anthropological approach to the Crown in New Zealand (by a British and a Māori scholar) is Shore and Kawharu (2014).

References

Bell, Avril. 2014. *Relating Indigenous and Settler Identities; Beyond Domination*. Identity Studies in the Social Sciences; Hampshire, England: Palgrave Macmillan.

Binney, Judith. 2012. *Redemption Songs: A Life of Te Kooti Arikirangi Te Turuki*. (First edition, 1995.) Bridget Williams Books, Wellington, New Zealand.

Brown, Wendy. 2015. "The End of the Corporate University: What We are Now." https://www.youtube.com/watch?v=Z5EWYohECRQ.

Brookfield, Jock. 1999. *Waitangi and Indigenous Rights: Revolution, Law and Legitimation*. Auckland, Auckland University Press.

Carter, Lynette. 2003. *Whakapapa and the State: Some Case Studies of the Impact of central government on traditionally organized Māori groups*. PhD thesis, The University of Auckland.

Higgens, Rawinia. 2014. "Te Wharehou o Tūhoe: The house that 'we' built". *Maori Law Review*, Special Issue–The Tūhoe-Crown Settlement October 2014, pp. 7–13.

Holman, Jeffrey. 2010. *Best of Both Worlds: The Story of Elsdon Best and Tutakangahau*. Penguin Books.

Iti, Tama. 2016. "Kanohi ki te kanohi…" Sir Paul Reeves Memorial Lecture. https://www.leadershipnz.co.nz/blog/latest-news/2016/11/17/sir-paul-reeves-memorial-lecture-2016.

Johnson, Miranda. 2011. "The Burdens of Belonging: Indigeneity and the Refounding of Aotearoa/New Zealand." New Zealand Journal of History, 45, 1.

Johnson, Miranda. 2016. *The Land is Our History: Indigeneity, Law and the Settler State*. New York: Oxford University Press.

Johnson, Miranda. 2017. "The river is not a person: Indigeneity and the sacred in Aotearoa New Zealand." Posted by The Immanent Frame, Social Science Research Council, June 14, 2017.

King, Michael. 1975. *Te Ao Hurihuri; the world moves on: aspects of Maoritanga. Wellington, Hicks-Smith.*

Kruger, Tamati. Tamati Kruger 2017 https://e-tangata.co.nz/identity/tamati-kruger-we-are-not-who-we-should-be-as-tuhoe-people/; also 2018: https://e-tangata.co.nz/korero/tamati-kruger-down-that-way-glory-waits/.

McHugh, Paul. 1991. *The Maori Magna Carta: New Zealand Law and the Treaty of Waitangi*. Auckland, Oxford University Press.

McLellan, D. (ed.). 1987. Karl Marx; Selected Writings. Oxford: Oxford University Press.

Mihaka, Dun. 1989. *Ki te Whei-Ao…Ki te Ao-Marama…*. Edited by Marama Laurenson. Te Ringa Mangu Ltd., p.o. Box 3662, Wellington, N.Z.

Moon, Paul. 2015. "The Impression of Hybridised Indigeneity: A History of the United Nations' Permanent Forum on Indigenous Issues and the Emergence of a Globalised Construction of Indigeneity." *International Journal of Critical Indigenous Studies*, Volume 8, Number 1.

Muru-Lanning, Marama. 2016. *Tupuna Awa: People and Politics of the Waikato River*. The University of Auckland Press, Auckland, N.Z.

Muru-Lanning, Marama. 2018. "Vision Matauranga, Eclectic Anthropology and the Fading Empire". Anthropology Seminar Series, 13 September 2008.

Rangihau, John. 1975. "Being Māori," in Michael King (ed.) *Te Ao Hurihuri: the world moves on: aspects of Maoritanga*. Wellington: Hicks Smith.

Rata, Elizabeth. 2000. *A Political Economy of Neotribal Capitalism*. Lanham: Lexington Books.

Rata, Elizabeth. 2002. "The Transformation of Indigeneity." Research Foundation of State University of New York Fernand Braudel Center *Review*, Vol. 25, No. 2 (2002), pp. 173–195.

Regan, Paulette. 2010. *Unsettling the Settler Within: Indian Residential Schools, Truth Telling, and Reconciliation in Canada*. University of British Columbia Press, Vancouver.

Ruru, Jacinda. 2014. "Te Wharehou o Tūhoe: The house that 'we' built". *Maori Law Review*, Special Issue–The Tūhoe-Crown Settlement October 2014, pp. 16–21.

Salmond, Anne. 2014. "Tears of Rangi: Water, Power, and People in New Zealand." *Hau: Journal of Ethnographic Theory* 4 (3): 285–309.

Salmond, Amiria. 2013. 'Transforming translations (part 1) "The owner of these bones"'. *Hau: Journal of Ethnographic Theory* 3 (3): 1–32.

Salmond, Amiria. 2014. 'Transforming translations (part 2) Addressing ontological alterity'. *Hau: Journal of Ethnographic Theory* 4 (1): 155–187.

Shore, Cris and M. Kawharu, 2014. The Crown in New Zealand; Anthropological Perspectives on an Imagined Sovereign. *Sites*, vol 11 no 1.2

Sluka, Jeffrey. 2010. "The Ruātoki Valley 'Antiterrorism' Police Raids: Losing 'Hearts and Minds" in Te Urewera." *Sites, a Journal of Social Anthropology and Cultural Studies*, (new series) Vol 7 No 1: 44–64.

Smith, Linda. 2012. Decolonizing Methodologies: Research and Indigenous Peoples. Second edition, London: Zed Books.

Tahi, Rongonui. 2015. "Ron Tahi, quintessential horseman who's dedicated his life to Ohāua Marae, Te Urewera." Waka Huia, N.Z. https://www.youtube.com/watch?v=Fo6TNr-2YeA.

Webster, Steven. n.d. (1984–5) "Urewera Land 1895–1926; a tentative historical survey of Government and Tuhoe relations as reflected in official records." Unpublished manuscript, 50 pp. Held in the University of Auckland Library. Auckland, N.Z.

Webster, Steven. 1997. "Maori hapuu and their history" in *The Australian Journal of Anthropology* 8:3:307–335. University of Sydney, Sydney, Australia.

Webster, Steven. 1998a. "Maori Hapuu as a Whole Way of Struggle; 1840s-50s before the Land Wars" in *Oceania*, 69 (1) 4–35. University of Sydney, Sydney, Australia.

Webster, Steven. 1998b. Patrons of Maori Culture: Power, Theory, and Ideology in the Maori Renaissance. Dunedin, N.Z.: Otago University Press.

Webster, Steven. 2002. "Maori retribalization and Treaty Rights to the New Zealand Fisheries" in *The Contemporary Pacific*, 14 (2):341–376. University of Hawaii.

Webster, Steven. 2016. "Maori Indigeneity and Commodity Fetishism", *Sites, a Journal of Social Anthropology and Cultural Studies* (new series) Vol 13 no 2: 1–18.

Webster, Steven. 2017. "Māori Kinship and Power: Ngāi Tūhoe 1894–1912." *Journal of the Polynesian Society* 126 (2): 145–180.

Webster, Steven. 2019. "Māori indigeneity and the ontological turn in ethnography." *Sites, N.S.* 16 (2): 11–36.

Acknowledgments

As always, my leading debt, for food, rest, and indulgence as well as clearer thinking and better anthropological fieldwork skills, is to my partner Lois of over half-a-century and our children, now all grown but still taking care of us. Although Volume II is a major revision of my 2004 report to the Waitangi Tribunal, my commentary here continues to owe alot to the personnel of the Tribunal whose heroic historical work amassing and distributing supporting papers as well as earlier reports left me in awe. Their patient encouragement of my own efforts as an anthropologist new to these skills propelled one of my own early excursions into serious ethnohistory. The Tribunal also set me up with two keen research assistants, Himaima Tumoana and Clementine Fraser, whose expertise, respectively, in breaching derelict archives and collation of reams of confusing records laid the foundation of hard data that enables Volume II to rise above the narrow but rich primary sources on which this Volume I must rest. Among the many historians from whose earlier work on the Tribunal's Urewera Enquiry I have benefitted are Judith Binney (further acknowledged in Chap. 1 of Vol. II), Vincent O'Malley, S.K.L. Campbell, Anita Miles, Heather Bassett and Richard Kay, R.P. Boast, Brian Murton, Brenda Tahi, and social anthropologist and colleague in Tūhoe research Jeffrey Sissons. Antedating them, a foundation for all our work was laid by Tūhoe scholars Jim Te Wharehuia Milroy and Sidney Melbourne, working with geographer Evelyn Stokes. All these works are cited in the chapter references or concluding bibliography.

Contents

About the Author

Steven Webster immigrated with his family from the USA to New Zealand in 1972 and taught courses in social anthropology and Māori studies at the University of Auckland until retiring in 1998. He continues there as an honorary research fellow.

His PhD thesis from the University of Washington, Seattle, was on kinship, ecology, and ethnicity of an indigenous community in the Peruvian Andes, but in New Zealand he took up research among Māori in the Urewera and the university. His courses developed from kinship, ethos and worldview, ethnicity, history of anthropology, and Māori land history in colonial New Zealand to political-economic critique of ideologies. After retiring, he taught as a visitor at the Northwest Indian College in Tacoma, Washington, and at Princeton University. He completed research for the Waitangi Tribunal on the Urewera District Native Reserve, Crown purchase campaign, and Consolidation Scheme 1894–1926, and continues ethnohistorical and other research regarding the Māori.

A Note on Sources

Urewera Minutebooks series, 1899–1926

These are cited by acronym and arranged alphabetically in references. Copies are held in various archives noted (NA Wgtn: National Archives, Wellington, N.Z.; NA Ak: National Archives, Auckland, N.Z.; Waiariki MLC: Waiariki Māori Land Court Archives, Rotorua, N.Z. (also holds most copies and some originals); Univ.Auck.Lib: The University of Auckland Library (also holds many on microfilm).

A Note on Translations From Māori

All words in Māori are italicized and followed in their early appearances by brief glosses appropriate to the context, which also appear in the index with that Māori word. Exceptions are proper nouns in Māori and *hapū*, the ancestral descent group, because it appears frequently. The author has often relied on Tūhoe Himaima Tumoana and other native speakers for these translations or glosses. However, in the case of many common words or expressions, translations of Urewera District Native Reserve Commission minute book 1 (UMB 1), and other occasions the author has relied on Māori dictionaries and his own limited familiarity with *te reo* Māori. If no other source is cited, the author takes full responsibility for translations or glosses.

Previous Publication

An earlier version of Chap. 4 was published in 2010 as "He kaawai hapuu Tuuhoe no te ao o mua: An ethnohistorical reconstruction of one hapuu branch of Ngai Tuuhoe in the Urewera District Native Reserve 1899–1903" in *Sites* (N.S.), 7(1): 1–43. 'Theoretical approaches to Volume I and II details were published in 2017 as "Māori Kinship and Power: Ngāi Tūhoe 1894–1912" in the *Journal of the Polynesian Society* 126 (2): 145–180, and in 2019 as "Ōhāua te Rangi and Reconciliation in Te Urewera 1913–1983" in the *Journal of the Polynesian Society* 128 (2): 191–224.'

List of Figures

CHAPTER 1

Introduction

1 A Brief Historical Overview

The following chapters attempt to reconstruct the struggle of *Ngāi Tūhoe* or the Tūhoe people, an indigenous *iwi* ('tribe') of Māori, to consolidate their mountain sanctuary in the Urewera under their own authority—*he mana motuhake*, an independent dominion—protected from the incursions of colonization in New Zealand.[1] This part of my account is focused narrowly upon a few years, especially 1899 through 1907, during which the Tūhoe were relatively successful in negotiating a settlement with the Crown and achieving their goal. Their less successful struggle against the Crown's betrayal of this settlement between 1915 and 1925 has been available as my report to the Waitangi Tribunal (Webster 2004), now revised as a sequel Volume II accompanying this Volume I.

The 2014 Te Urewera settlement negotiated with the New Zealand government returned most control over the vast Urewera National Park to the Tūhoe. In terms of New Zealand's history of hostility toward what in other nations has long been recognized as some form of 'internal' sovereignty or 'home-rule' of their indigenous peoples, this 2014 settlement was a reversal of the earlier reversal of the epochal 1896 Urewera District Native Reserve Act. Probably for the first time since British sovereignty was assumed in 1840, the 1896 Act established virtual home-rule for a Māori iwi over their ancestral lands. By

© The Author(s) 2020

S. Webster, *A Separate Authority (He Mana Motuhake)*, Volume I,
https://doi.org/10.1007/978-3-030-41042-1_1

1907 the 1896 Act established the Urewera District Native Reserve (UDNR) for Tūhoe self-governance over the Urewera, but this statute began to be systematically subverted by 1908. By 1926 the huge reserve had been completely dismantled with over 70% of it taken over by the Crown. By the 1950s most of this Crown land became the Urewera National Park. The 2014 settlement may have finally reversed this embittered history.

The 2014 Tūhoe Claims Settlement and Te Urewera Acts formally settled Tūhoe claims to the Waitangi Tribunal pursued since the 1980s, and along with the earlier Service Management Plan intend to redress the Crown's detailed acknowledgment and apology for 40 historical wrongs it did to the Tūhoe since 1840, including the confiscation of their best lands during the 1860s land wars (Tūhoe Claims Settlement Act 2014: 23–4; Te Urewera Act 2014). The details are unsparingly abject and the apology is eloquent; my abiding impression is that the Tribunal inquiry had been thorough and the government settlement sincere. In the 2004 hearings, I had been disappointed that, unlike many of the other reports for the Tribunal, the Crown decided not to present a counter-case to mine regarding the Crown's subversion of the UDNR 1915–1926. However, in returning virtually the whole reserve to Tūhoe control in the 2014 Act, it went much further in redress than I had hoped.

Nevertheless, despite the laborious effort of Tūhoe leaders and government, understandably given this bitter history, many Tūhoe remain skeptical of the sincerity of the government's long-term intentions. The major betrayals of the past had often been led by reversals of previous policies and even disregard of previous laws. Tūhoe research of similar settlements overseas was not encouraging. The recent re-runs of Crown dishonor in the 2007 'anti-terrorism' raids in the Rūātoki valley of the Urewera and imprisonment of key leaders on spurious charges (Sluka 2010), and the Prime Minister's public refusal in 2010 of any such settlement involving the Urewera National Park, of course, reinforced Tūhoe doubts. Perhaps it is true that *Ngāi Tūhoe*'s long battle to maintain their ***mana motuhake*** has in many ways just begun again.

The four figures included here will orient this introduction, but can also serve as an overview of major historical developments through to the Te Urewera settlement in 2014.

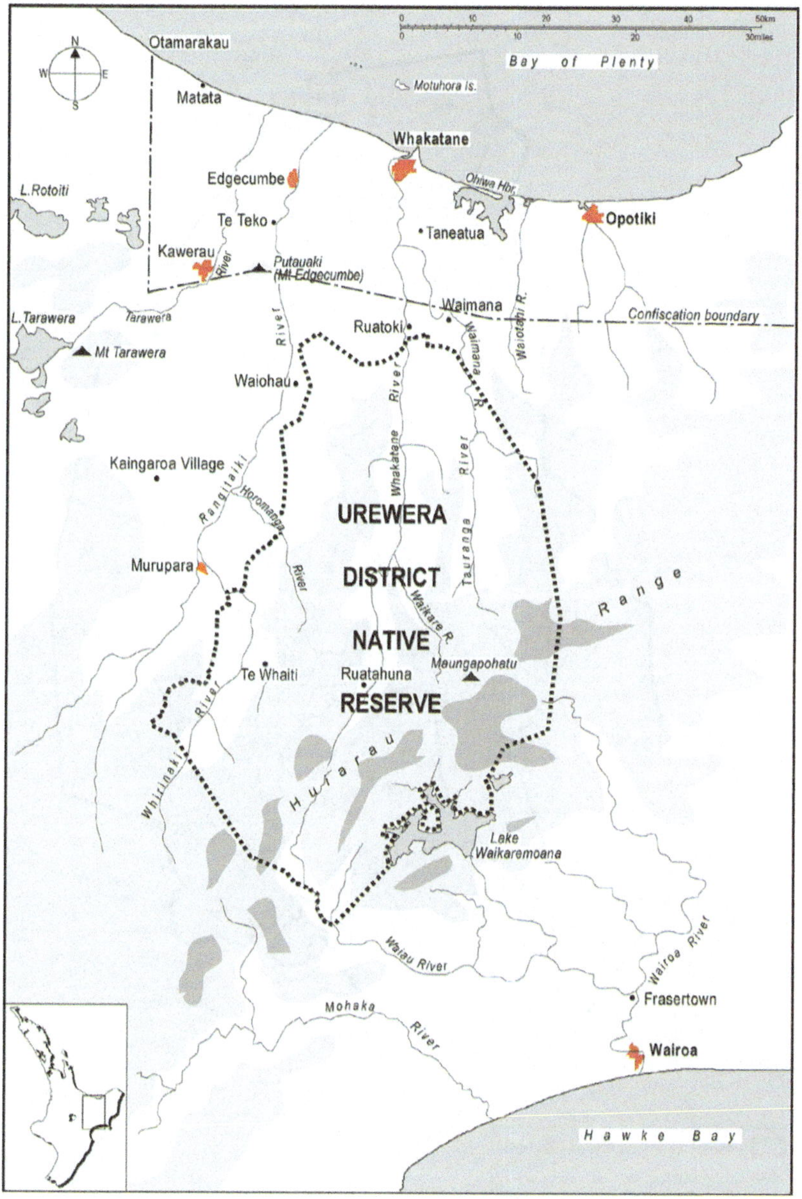

Fig. 1.1 Location of Urewera District Native Reserve (1907) and its vicinity, the North Island, New Zealand. (Webster 2004: 13)

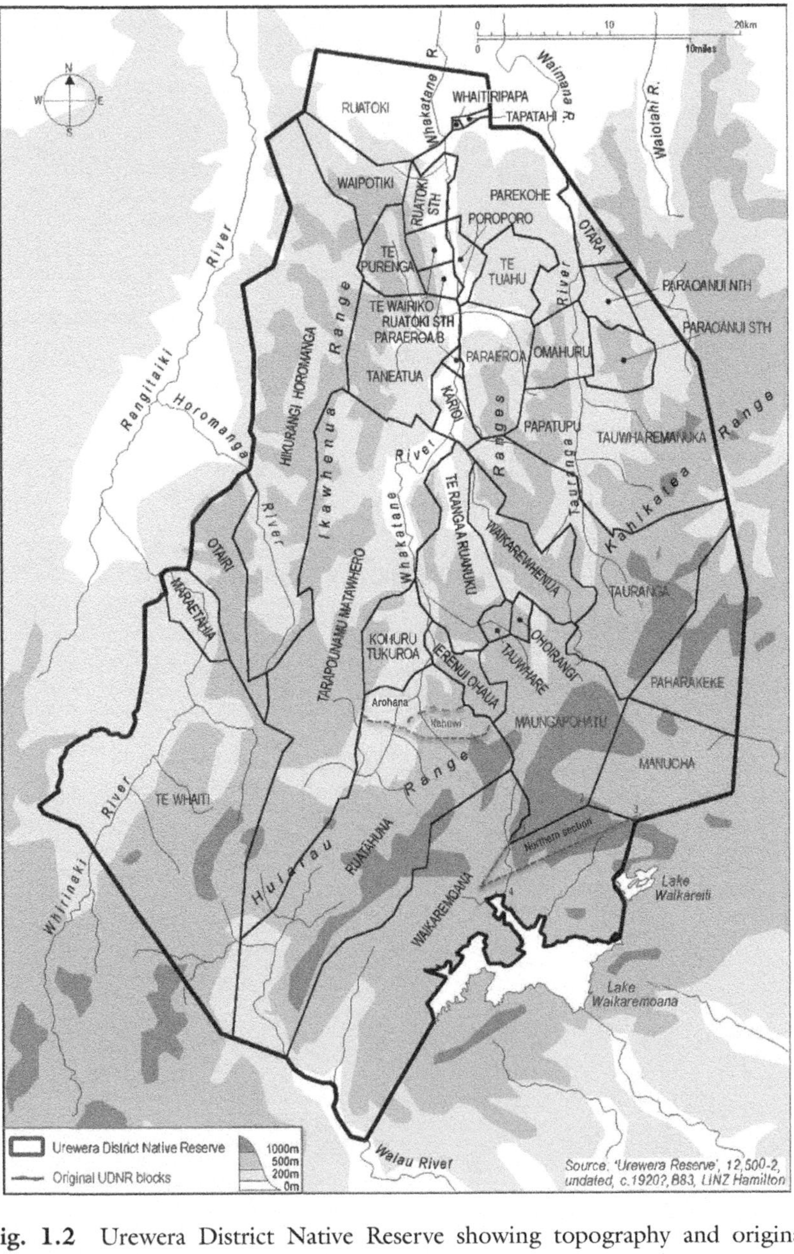

Fig. 1.2 Urewera District Native Reserve showing topography and original blocks, 1907. (Webster 2004: 331)

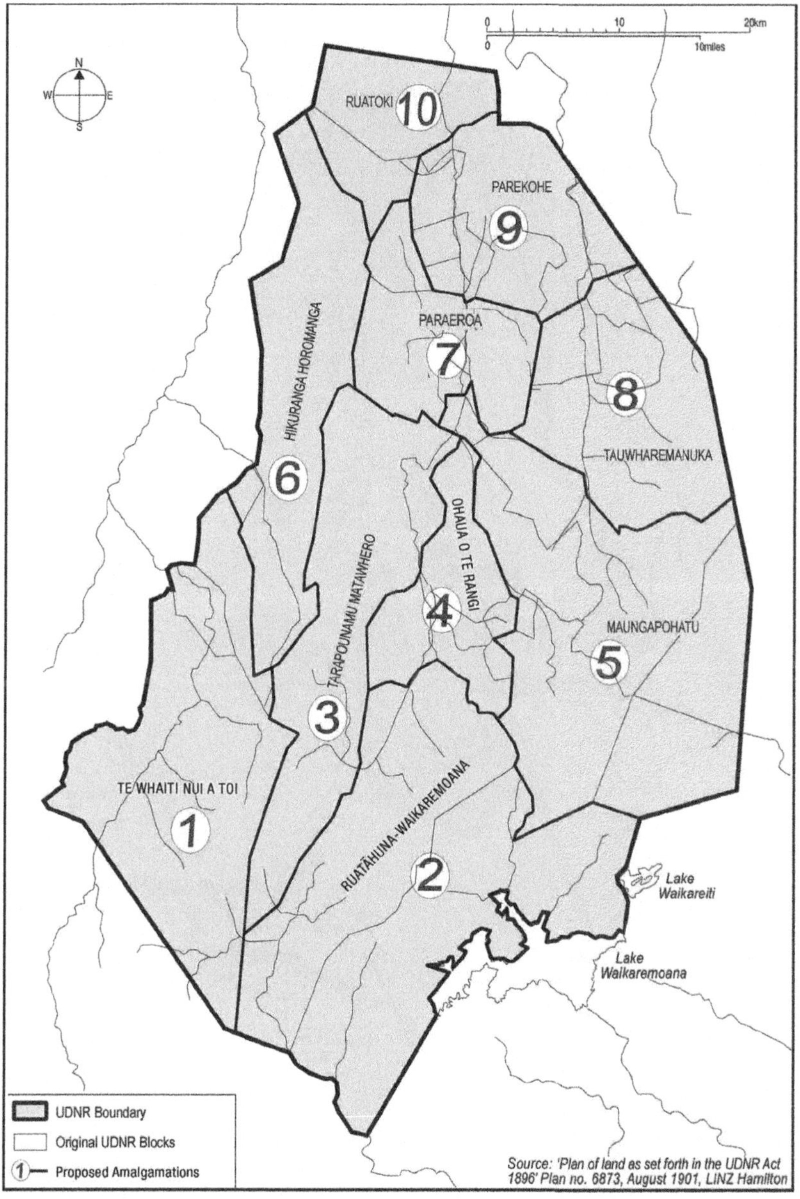

Fig. 1.3 Proposed amalgamation of 35 blocks into 10 titles, May 1902. (Webster 2004: 17)

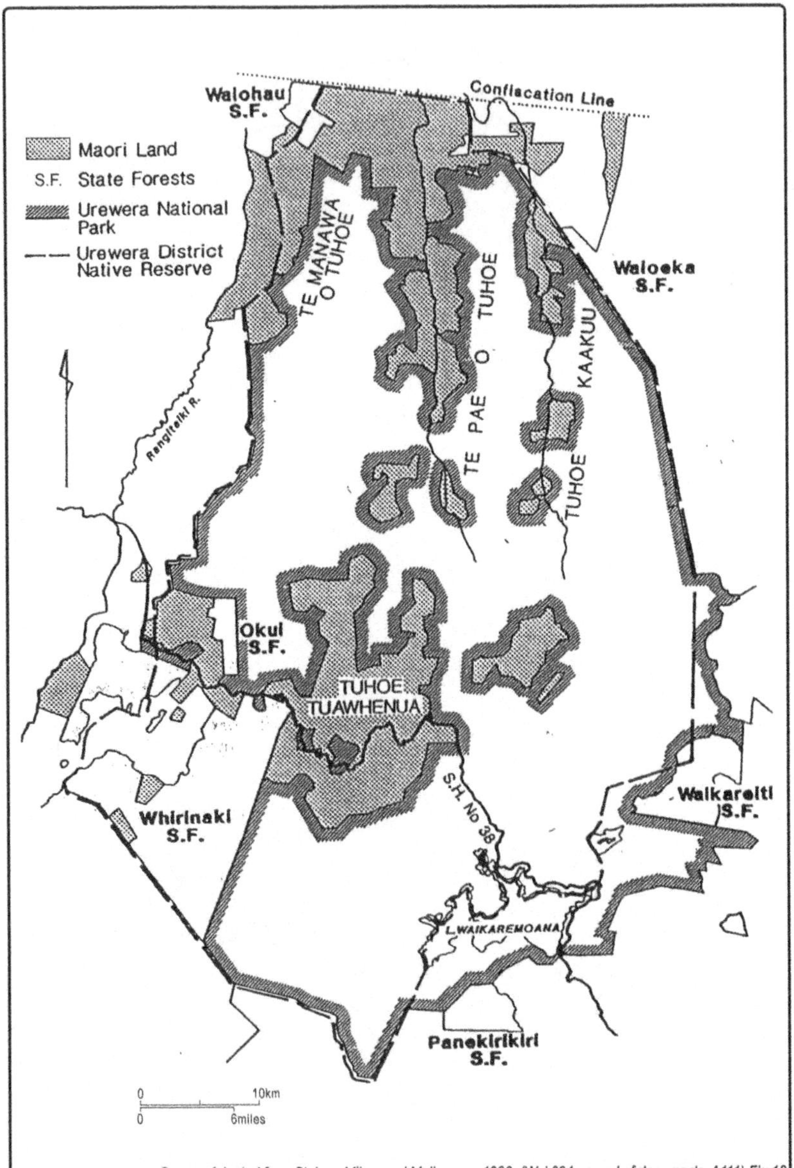

Fig. 1.4 *Pupuri whenua* (non-sellers) surviving shares of Urewera District Native Reserve as relocated in the Urewera Consolidation Scheme 1921–1926. (Webster 2004: 18)

Figure 1.1 depicts the general locality of the original Urewera District Native Reserve (UDNR) in the contemporary North Island of New Zealand, and the main details of the area between the Bay of Plenty and Hawke's Bay. This area includes the northern coastal lands confiscated by the Crown in the 1860s land wars and Lake Waikaremoana on the southern boundary. The Urewera Mountains are shown in shading rising from the Bay of Plenty coast to their southern-most crest in the Huiarau Range. The three main river valleys running from south to north out of the mountains to the Bay of Plenty coast are also shown, with the Whakatane (originally Ohinemataroa) River and Tauranga/Waimana River and their major tributaries centered in the UDNR.

Figure 1.2 depicts about 38 blocks of the UDNR when it was formally established in 1907. This map also displays useful details of ranges, elevations, rivers, and tributaries. The investigation and provisional titles of these blocks are the main subject of the first few chapters, focusing primarily on the records of the 1899–1903 commission which, I argue, was dominated by Tūhoe leaders. For reasons that will be explained, these records are far more reliable than those of the appeals commission, which did not meet until 1906–1907. Some blocks were later partitioned in the Native Land Court between 1907 and 1913.

Figure 1.3 is a simplified version of the most detailed map of the UDNR that I have discovered. The version here depicts an obscure proposal in May 1902 to amalgamate 35 blocks of the UDNR into only 10 titles, but which was aborted when hearings resumed the following October. The original blocks as approved in 1907 are outlined within each amalgamation and can be identified by reference to Fig. 1.2. The amalgamation proposal was only briefly explained in the records, but was apparently supported by all five Tūhoe commissioners (and probably most other Tūhoe leaders) as well as the two Pākehā ('white' or 'European') commissioners who were the chairman and a Native Land Court judge. Because of its rich implications for research of Tūhoe *hapū* (descent group or 'sub-tribe') organization and the relative *mana* ('prestige' or 'authority') of *hapū* leaders, two amalgamations are analyzed in Chap. 6. The entire Part II of this volume (Chaps. 7, 8, 9, and 10) is devoted to a detailed reconstruction of the proposed Ruatāhuna-Waikaremoana amalgamation, an extensive marriage alliance, and related political alliances between *hapū* leaders during the period 1900–1913.

Figure 1.4 depicts the major developments from the establishment of the UDNR in 1907, through its several decades as the Urewera National Park surrounding remnant Tūhoe lands, to the 2014 Te Urewera settlement acts returning most control of the national park to the Tūhoe. Comprehensively, this map outlines the largely congruent boundaries of the

(i) UDNR 1907–1921; Already by 1908 the Crown was circumventing the intentions of the 1896 Act and arranging purchases of individual shares in hopes of buying out entire blocks;
(ii) the four customary Tūhoe regions into which over 200 blocks owned by Tūhoe refusing to sell their shares in the old blocks were relocated in the reserve by the Urewera Consolidation Scheme of 1921–1926 (relative extent is exaggerated; in reality, it is less than 30% of the UDNR); and
(iii) the Urewera National Park that was established in the 1950s on the Crown's 1925 award to itself of over 70% of the UDNR obtained in its purchase campaign along with more taken for surveying and road costs.

The sequel Volume II of this ethnohistory examines details of the Crown purchase campaign and following Urewera Consolidation Scheme 1915–1926 which repealed the UDNR and its intended virtual home-rule (Webster 2004). The promised roads were never built, resulting in continuing impoverishment, and by the 1930s, pressure was again being applied to owners of the new blocks to sell to the Crown. Nevertheless, almost all of the over 200 new blocks held by the Tūhoe 'non-sellers' throughout the national park remained defiantly in their descendants' ownership for nearly another century, importantly backing up their negotiations for the return of Te Urewera in the 2014 settlement.

Since the global ethnic revivals of the 1970s, and in some reports for the Waitangi Tribunal over the last two decades, a romantic assumption that the history of colonization is a history of victimization has often been led to a further assumption of passive acceptance by the colonized. Such assumptions are rarely supported by the facts of an actual colonial history and are furthermore damaging to efforts to redress an unjust history. To the contrary, examination of a specific history usually shows, as it does with the Tūhoe, that although the colonized may have lost much in the long run, they did not do so without a struggle, often maintained control of events at least for the short run, and in this way ensured that part of that history was made on their own terms. I argue that the era of investigation and establishment of the Urewera District Native Reserve 1894–1912, although it would soon pass, must be seen in these terms. In Volume II, with regard to the following Crown purchase campaign and Urewera

Consolidation Scheme 1915–1926, I again substantiate this perspective. The Tūhoe accomplishment in regaining control of their Urewera sanctuary in 2014, nearly a century later, speaks for itself.

2 Ngāi Tūhoe and Te Urewera

One might well ask who *are* 'the Tūhoe' and what *is* 'the Urewera' (or 'the Ureweras')? Both terms are laden with popular assumptions and ambiguous use historically. The Tūhoe have long been notorious in New Zealand's imagination for their defiant isolation and independence, and closely associated with the rugged wilderness of the Urewera ranges. In the musket wars before the 1840 Treaty of Waitangi, the Urewera had often been their retreat from marauding Māori better armed than they, and this continued through the 1860s land wars with the Crown and the following confiscations of their more arable lands nearer the coast (now admitted to have been unjustified). Especially since the Māori cultural renaissance of the 1970s, the Tūhoe and some of their more outspoken leaders have become a popular symbol of Māori radicalism. They are also often admired among other Māori *hapū* and *iwi* as the most 'traditional' and stalwart of contemporary Māori peoples. It is true that, unlike most other Māori populations, many of the youth, as well as all of the elders of some of the Urewera communities, still speak Māori as their 'first' language, that is, continue to use it ordinarily in their community as well as in their homes. On the other hand, like the romantic Pākehā stereotype of the Tūhoe as 'traditional', the popular Māori stereotype of them is readily inverted to view them as primitive or uncivilized.

Angela Ballara, the leading authority on the general history of Māori iwi 1769–1945, summarized her information on the Tūhoe as "the development of a modern tribe" (1998: 290–301). In line with her general conclusion regarding the historical dynamics of Māori iwi and *hapū*, she describes an overlapping and shifting history of independent *hapū* or *iwi* across the Urewera and surrounding areas, but nevertheless concludes that "the concept of Tūhoe as one tribe – one corporate group to confront the outside world" tended to endure (1998: 301). Originally settling and intermarrying in the central part of the Urewera, by the 1850s the Tūhoe expanded through war with the surrounding tribes to control all of the Urewera and contest its northern margins on the Bay of Plenty. During the 1860s land war, some of their *hapū* joined with other *iwi* against colonial forces, and in 1868–1872 some of their *hapū* confronted the government forces and *kupapa* (loyal Māori) throughout the Urewera, either in their own defense or in support of 'the rebel' Te Kooti's forces, which had taken refuge there. Ballara reports that for a time after the 1860s, the Tūhoe were known by the "names 'Te Urewera' and 'Urewera tribe' [that] were adopted enthusiastically by Europeans and retained long after the Tūhoe themselves had reverted to their ancestral name" (Ballara 1998: 296). Ballara's history of the *iwi* name confirms one report by the eminent Tūhoe *rangatira* ('chief') Tamaikoha in 1900 that

> this tribe was formerly called N[gati] Awa [the iwi to the west of the Urewera with whom Tuhoe had fought but later settled a peace]. After that this tribe was named Tuhoe....That mana was conferred upon all. They are now called Te Urewera. (UMB 4: 55 (in Māori, UMB 2: 46))

Tamaikoha's understanding of what Ngāi Tūhoe had been called was also confirmed by Mehaka Tokopounamu (UMB 4: 75).

The government documents of the UDNR 1899–1907, and even those of the Urewera Consolidation Scheme in 1921, still referred to the Tūhoe as 'the Urewera'. (As will later be explained, this situation is further confused for outsiders by reference to certain *hapū* ('subtribe') of the Tūhoe *iwi* ('tribe') as 'Tūhoe' and, later, as 'Te Urewera'!). Regardless of their enduring common identification as Tūhoe or 'the Urewera' tribe or *iwi*, Ballara emphasizes that the many Tūhoe *hapū* usually pursued divergent or independent goals in trade, missionization, resistance and messianic movements, and conflict with the Crown. Tūhoe leaders arose and attempted in 1864 and again in 1874 to form wider alliances with adjacent *iwi* or *hapū* known as Mātaatua and Te Whitu Tekau, but these were too ambitious actually to hold together. In the early 1890s, many but not all Tūhoe *hapū* resisted leasing of Urewera lands and the government's initiation of surveys and roads, precipitating Seddon's visit in 1894 and subsequent negotiation of plans for the UDNR. As will be described in Chap. 3, the commission's investigation of the UDNR in 1899 precipitated identification of anywhere from 24 to 126 different *hapū* laying claims to particular Urewera lands! This apparent insurgence may have been only an intensification of the usual relative independence of Tūhoe *hapū* admitted by Ballara regardless of their enduring general identity as Tūhoe (or 'the Urewera').

Except for brief accounts by early missionaries and first visits by government officials during and after the land wars, the Tūhoe were first described by the well-known ethnologist Elsdon Best in 1925 in his exhaustive *Tuhoe, Children of the Mist*. (His use of 'Tuhoe' rather than 'the Urewera' in the title at this time probably helped popularize this term.) The title reflects the already-established popular image of the Tūhoe as reclusive *tūrehu*, ghosts or fairies shrouded in the mountain mists. Jeffrey Paparoa Holman has recently argued that Best and Tutakangahau (among the Tūhoe leaders described in Part II) together worked out key metaphysical notions in late nineteenth-century terms that have come to be taken as autochthonous Māori concepts by Māori as well as Pākehā experts (Holman 2010). Best's 1925 ethnography has become a classic regardless of his often arrogantly jocular and racial asides, reflecting the usual assumptions of his time even among anthropologists. This tome was actually the culmination of his extensive research and participation as secretary to the Urewera Commission that investigated Tūhoe claims to the Urewera 1899–1903 under the 1896 UDNR Act. More will be said later about his important role in this investigation. The richness of Best's careful genealogical fieldwork and his fluency in Māori enabled him to assist the Pākehā chairman and judge on the commission to understand some of the fundamentals of Tūhoe social organization. However, as will be shown, the manifold details were often beyond Best's understanding or interest, yet were negotiated between the five Tūhoe commissioners and other leaders outside hearings, carefully recorded in the block lists, and routinely approved in deference to the home-rule intentions of the UDNR Act.

The old but often resurrected Tūhoe expression for 'Te Urewera' is *Te Rohe Pōtae o (Ngāi) Tūhoe*, 'the sanctuary of the Tūhoe people' (my translation), extending from the 1860s confiscation boundary to include all of the proposed UDNR by 1896 (Binney 2002: 2–10; Fig. 1.1). These words and their meaning were sanctified in their use by the Ringatū prophet Te Kooti in 1883, upon his return to the Urewera from his own refuge in the King Country on the western side of North Island (for instance, in his *waiata tohetohe*, 'song of warning') *Kaore te pō nei mōrikarika noa*... (below). In 1868 following the land wars, Te Kooti had escaped from exile in the Chatham Islands and charismatically led successful reprisals and ambushes throughout the Urewera against government troops and *kūpapa*, loyalist East Coast Māori militia. Demonized by the settlers and an increasingly vindictive campaign by *kūpapa*, in 1872 he finally escaped to the protection of the King Country, where the term *rohe pōtae* had originated in reference to the postwar refuge of the Maniapoto people.[2] Although to avoid government retribution it had to be dissimulated, some Tūhoe war leaders were involved or even allied with Te Kooti during his refuge in the King Country as well as the Urewera. During the land wars, Te Whenuanui I and his war party had joined Tainui forces in the battle against British regulars at Orākau. The war leader Tamaikoha (described in Chaps. 4 and 5) may also have cooperated with Te Kooti during his refuge in the Urewera (Sissons 1991). Later in 1883, welcoming the return of Te Kooti to the Urewera, Te Whenuanui I built one of the biggest meeting houses in New Zealand in Te Kooti's honor at Mātaatua marae in Ruatāhuna, naming it *Te Whai a te Motu* ('pursuit of independence/separateness'); Binney translates it as "pursuit across the land" and presents Te Kooti's song of warning (2002: 16–23)[3]:

Kaaore te poo nei moorikarika noa!
Te ohunga ki te ao, rapu kau noa ahau.
Ko te mana tuatahi ko te Tiriti o Waitangi,
Ko te mana tuarua ko te Kooti Whenua,
Ko te mana tuatoru ko te Mana Motuhake;
Ka kiia i reira ko te Rohe Pootae o Tuuhoe,
He rongo ka houhia ki a Ngaati Awa.
He kino anoo raa ka aata kitea iho
Ngaa mana Maaori ka mahue kei muri!
Ka uru nei au ki te ture Kaunihera
E rua aku mahi e noho nei au:
Ko te hanga i ngaa roori, ko te hanga i ngaa tiriti!
Puukohu taairi ki Pooneke raa,
Ki te kaainga raa i noho ai te Minita.
Ki taku whaakaro ka tae mai te Poari
Hai noho i te whenua o Kootitia nei;
Paa rawa te mamae ki te tau o taku ate.
E te iwi nui, tuu ake ki runga raa,
Tirohia mai raa te hee o aku mahi!
Maaku e kii atu, 'noohia, noohia!'
Noo mua iho anoo, noo ngaa kaumaatua!
Naa taku ngaakau i kimi ai ki te Ture,
Noo konei hoki au i kino ai ki te hoko!
Hii! Hai aha te hoko! ee

Alas for this unhappy night!
Waking to the world I search about in vain.
The first mana is the Treaty of Waitangi,
The second mana is the Land Court,
The third mana is the Separate Mana;
Hence the Rohe Pōtae of Tūhoe,
And peace made with Ngāti Awa.

It would indeed be an evil thing
To abandon the mana of the Māori!
If I submitted to the law of the Council,
Two things I would do:
Building roads, and building streets!
Yonder the mist hangs over Wellington,
The home of the Minister.
I fear that the [Land] Board will come
To dwell in this land of Kootitia,
And I am sick at heart.
All my people, be watchful,
See the evil of these things!
I say to you, 'Remain, remain [on your land]!'
It is from former ages, from your ancestors!
Because my heart has searched out the Law,
For this reason I abhor selling!
Hi! Why sell!

As shown in Fig. 1.1, the old UDNR reserve, the Urewera National Park that replaced it, and now (since the 2014 settlement) the Tūhoe *iwi's* recovered Te Urewera sanctuary is located about 20 kilometers inland from the Bay of Plenty coast and extends about 60 further kilometers into the interior of the mountains. The original reserve covered about 656,000 acres in 1921 when it was dismantled. The Urewera Mountains are old and relatively low but steeply worn and still heavily forested. (Some areas became state forest, but Tūhoe were usually prevented from gaining income by selling timber from their new blocks within the National Park.) As shown in Fig. 1.2, the interior valleys descend northwards to the coast from about 300 meters altitude and the ridgelines rise to 700 meters and occasionally to over 1200 meters altitude. The fabled mists of Elsdon Best's book still often pour in over the ridgelines and enfold the valley bottoms, obscuring the steep precipices above. Visiting Maungapōhatu (Fig. 1.1) with my family and wife's mother in 1972, a Tūhoe whom we queried along the road advised us (with a playful wink) that the only way to clear the mists from that fabled summit was to do a *whakapohane* toward it (disdainfully to show one's buttocks, nowadays by raising skirt or dropping trousers)!

As shown in Fig. 1.1 but best detailed in Fig. 1.2, the Whakatane (originally Ohinemataroa) River and its several large tributaries run down the center of the Urewera, and the Tauranga/Waimana River and its tributaries bisect the eastern half. The western areas of the Urewera overlook but do not include most of the Whiranaki/Rangataiki River valley, which by the 1890s had already been lost by the Tūhoe and other *iwi* through the Native Land Court, often illegitimately (Binney 2002). Due to the coastal confiscations of the lower reaches of the Urewera, the only cultivable land in the old UDNR was river bottoms and limited benches above them, more extensive in the Waimana, Ruātoki, and Ruatāhuna settlement areas but generally of poor horticultural capacity even along the river bottoms. During the Urewera Consolidation Scheme 1921–1926, anticipating the promised roads along the Whakatane and Tauranga/Waimana rivers (which they paid for inland but which were never built), the Tūhoe 'non-sellers' relocated their remaining shares in these hopefully more cultivable areas in blocks that might have become small 'family farms' (as the Scheme's organizer Apirana Ngata misleadingly urged) if the roads had been built. These relocations were doubly or triply misled insofar as Crown pre-emptions of favored areas in anticipation of Pākehā settlement radically narrowed their choices, and the assumed agricultural potential even of the Crown's areas, let alone those that were left, was exaggerated (Webster 2004: 214–316).

As depicted in Fig. 1.4, the over 200 'non-sellers' blocks relocated in the Urewera Consolidation Scheme from the old blocks of the UDNR tended to be grouped into four customary areas of the Urewera: *Te Pae o Tūhoe* ('the bench' of hosting Tūhoe) and *Tūhoe Kākū* ('rough flax cape' of Tūhoe?) running down the middle of the park, straddling the intermediate and lower northern reaches of the Whakatane and Tauranga/Waimana Rivers, respectively; *Te Manawa o Tūhoe* ('the heart (or stomach) of Tūhoe') overlooking the Rangataiki River along the northwestern boundary of the park; and *Tūhoe Tuawhenua* (the 'interior' or 'mainland' of Tūhoe) straddling the southern upper reaches of the Whirinaki, Whakatane, Waikare, and Tauranga Rivers. Although the Tūhoe used many traditional names for general regions of the Urewera (for instance, *Ruatāhuna kākahu mauku* referring to the dwellers of that region as 'all dressed in rain-soaked cloaks'), these four descriptions were widely used 1950–1980s probably because the non-sellers' new blocks scattered through the interior of the National Park tended to be grouped in these four regions. By the early 1960s these "Māori enclaves" in the National Park were being threatened with expropriation for tax arrears, while at the same time the government was preventing their owners from gaining income from their timber resources in order to pay these taxes (Stokes et al. 1986: 103–4).

3 Historical Background of the Urewera District Native Reserve

Although there were no comprehensive accounts of the Tūhoe between Elsdon Best's 1925 classic and the excellent social and economic overview in 1986 by Stokes, Milroy, and Melbourne (the latter two authors are Tūhoe), several more recent general studies of the colonial and contemporary history of the Urewera and the Tūhoe are now available as reports for the Urewera Inquiry of the Waitangi Tribunal. Here in an endnote I have listed my selection of them from the concluding bibliography.[4] These and many more specialized reports to the Tribunal were the basis for its final report and the Tūhoe negotiations with government that led to the 2014 settlement. In 2014 Vincent O'Malley provided a synopsis of key nineteenth-century developments in Tūhoe and Te Urewera history leading to the settlement (2014).

The overview below cites some of these sources, and others will be cited in the chapters that follow. However, my debt is greatest to the historian Judith Binney's careful original research untangling some of the complications especially of the 1890s (Binney 2002). The skills shown in Binney's research are admirably *ethno*historical, and a model for Tūhoe and other researchers in Te Urewera history. However, as will be discussed in Chaps. 2 and 3, Binney and Jeffrey Sissons (a social anthropologist with field research experience among the Tūhoe; Sissons 1991, 2002) argue the general conclusion that the UDNR Act and implementation was stacked against the Tūhoe from the beginning. To the contrary, I hope to demonstrate that the Crown's investigation and establishment of the UDNR sincerely intended home-rule, and its subversion of the reserve did not start until 1908.

As a result of general protests among Māori in the 1890s against the methods of the Native Land Court, and losses of land to the Court or government on several sides of the Urewera, Tūhoe resistance to any surveying for roading or boundaries within their *Rohe Pōtae* grew steadily. In response to these problems, Prime Minister Seddon visited several Māori districts including the Urewera in April 1894 to explain and negotiate the general need for land surveys. In the Urewera for over a week, along with his Native Minister James Carroll (a 'half-caste' Māori of the adjacent East Coast), Seddon visited Ruātoki, Te Houhi (located between Waiohau and Te Whaiti), Te Whaiti, Ruatāhuna, and Te Kuha (near contemporary Tuai at the southeastern corner of Lake Waikaremoana), touring the length of the region (see Fig. 1.1; Binney 2002: 131–159).

Although particularly in Ruātoki and Ruatāhuna the Tūhoe stood firmly against surveys and road plans, Seddon nevertheless insisted that surveys were necessary for the government's protection of Tūhoe lands, but at the same time he confirmed government recognition of Tūhoe's autonomous control over their *rohe pōtae* and assured them this would continue to be respected (Binney 2002: 131–159). Nevertheless, the following year government insistence on beginning surveys for roads in the interior of the Urewera resulted in armed confrontations and tense negotiations with Tūhoe in both Ruātoki and Te Whaiti that continued for months, finally leading Seddon to receive a series of Tūhoe delegations in Wellington (2002: 165–210). By 1896, these negotiations resulted in the Urewera District Native Reserve Act, which in return for Tūhoe cooperation with internal magnetic surveys at government expense, assured them virtual home-rule over the Urewera.

I would argue that the 1896 Act was the *Tūhoe* treaty, as a separate settlement with the Tūhoe and distinguishable from the Treaty of Waitangi which has come to be accepted as a pact with all Māori (as it happened, along with many other Māori iwi, the Tūhoe had no opportunity to sign it). Indeed, in his 1904 visit to the Urewera, the British Governor Lord Ranfurly saw the 1896 Act as a 'treaty' confirming the Urewera District Native Reserve as a self-governing enclave within the nation (Binney 2002: 299). Binney similarly suggests that the Tūhoe settlement with the Crown in 1871 could be viewed as such a treaty, and that the 1896 UDNR Act confirmed it (2002: 1, 3, 206). However, she nevertheless concludes that Prime Minister Seddon's personal commitment to Tūhoe was ambivalent and the final legislation was "a betrayal of Tūhoe aspirations for internal local autonomy" (2002: 206–221). To the contrary, as I will argue in Chap. 2, the 1896 Act and the establishment of the Native Reserve were carried out by the Crown and the investigative commission in good faith, and are therefore better taken as the Tūhoe treaty, the official realization of the long-promised compact. On the other hand, I agree with Binney that by 1908 the original Act was being systematically betrayed by government, and substantiated this through 1926 in my report to the Waitangi Tribunal (Webster 2004).

I have attempted to correct Binney's excellent research in one other regard: the Tūhoe population at the turn of the century. In 1903, the Urewera District Native Reserve Commission published provisional titles and comprehensive lists of owners for 35 blocks of the UDNR that they had been investigating since 1899. As I will explain in Chaps. 4 and 5, these important records reveal much more than superficial study might suppose and probably even more than the Pākehā commissioners and even Elsdon Best fully appreciated.

First of all, the total number of persons in the Native Reserve turns out to be many more than has been previously calculated. Anita Miles and, later, Judith Binney examined censuses of the time, tracing an apparent steady decline in population from a high of 1650 persons in 1886, to 1421 in 1896, to 1094 in 1901 (Miles 1999: 85–94; Binney 2002: 480–497). Binney concludes that the marked decline by 1901 resulted from crop failure, famine, and increasing poverty beginning especially in 1898. However, examination of the provisional block list titles drawn up 1899–1902 and published in 1903 show that the population was probably much higher than the censuses would lead one to suppose. The number of persons named in 35 block lists ranges from 44 to over 900, and averages 420 persons per block. Although together the lists total 14,712 names, this is misleading because most Tūhoe had rights in many Urewera blocks (some as many as 24). My tabulation of the 1903 block lists by surnames shows that about 1993 different persons were named. This is a far higher number than any of the censuses indicate and, quite contrary to Miles and Binney, may actually reflect a population increase well underway by the turn of the century.

However, it must be kept in mind that the block lists figure of 1993 represented persons found to have land rights, not necessarily resident in the Urewera or even in the district. Insofar as land rights devolved through descent from both parents regardless of residence at least for a few generations, it is likely that some of these persons in the block lists lived outside the area, for example, married into other Māori communities, or working in towns or cities or in itinerant labor. Binney reports non-resident Tūhoe ranging from 2% to 10% recorded in the censuses from 1886 through 1901. In 1901, about 8% of the official census of 1094 were reported to be living outside Whakatane County, in which the Urewera District was located. The commissioners discouraged inclusion of Tūhoe who were reported to have left the Urewera permanently, but Tūhoe probably ignored this if non-residents continued to visit and sustained some active support. Nevertheless, even if the proportion of Tūhoe with recognized land rights living outside the *rohe pōtae* in 1901 was granted to be 10% of my count from the block lists (say, 200 persons), the actual number of

Tūhoe resident in the Native Reserve may have been as much as 60% higher than the 1901 census indicated.

This does not necessarily imply the Tūhoe had been thriving despite the 1890s depression and famines emphasized by Binney, but it may mean that the birth rate was outstripping a high mortality rate. High birth and mortality rates are common among impoverished peoples. The 1903 block lists and the descent group examined in Chaps. 4 and 5 suggest that a high birth rate had been established for some years and continued into the 1920s despite the high mortality of the war years, the influenza epidemic of 1918, and another depression. Generally throughout New Zealand, it was belatedly discovered that while colonial policies were still 'smoothing the pillow of a dying race', by the turn of the century the Māori population was already recovering from the epidemics that accompanied colonization. Indeed, by 1920, one of the factors pressing the government to gain Tūhoe cooperation for the Urewera Consolidation Scheme was that, despite their strenuous decade-long campaign to purchase the UDNR, succession orders were showing that there were 20% more '*non-sellers*' (about 2342) than there were total *owners* of the reserve in 1903 (Webster 2004: 179).

The following chapters will examine in detail how the UDNR was established, but the introductory outline offered above with Figs. 1.1, 1.2, 1.3, and 1.4 can be expanded somewhat here and, as a preview of Volume II, followed through to the 1920s and the Urewera Consolidation Scheme.

Under the 1896 Act, between 1899 and 1902 the Urewera was investigated by a commission with a majority of elected Tūhoe leaders (five of seven commissioners) and surveyed into 35 blocks intended to be 'hapu blocks'. In 1903, provisional titles were issued for each of these blocks, to be finalized under the UDNR Act by a separate appeals commission. The extraordinary intention of the Act to establish home-rule for the Tūhoe was treated by the investigative commission as an opportunity to research and record traditional organization of one of the more notorious tribes of what was then assumed to be 'a dying race', and the ambitious ethnologists S. Percy Smith and Elsdon Best were appointed as chairperson and secretary of the commission, respectively. In accord with the Act, the commission intended the block titles to function primarily as an internal electoral system supporting home-rule, quite differently from the usual colonial intention to facilitate Native land alienation.

An appeals commission with no Tūhoe representatives met in 1906–1907 and finalized titles to 38 blocks including additions or partitions concluded since 1903. As I will argue in later chapters, this commission was in some ways careless and even incompetent, and Binney points out convincing evidence for systematic bias (2002: 247–249). Nevertheless, by 1908 a provisional representative government of the UDNR had been formed under the Act comprised of 35 'hapu' committees and a *Komiti Nui*/General Committee with exclusive control over the disposition of Tūhoe lands under the Act, although alienations could be made (only) to the Crown. The investigation of land rights had prompted the emergence of many new *hapū* and the decline of others, but it had also consolidated Tūhoe leadership with the prospect of *mana motuhake* or independence protected in perpetuity by the Crown.

Although the main concern of these chapters is to lay out the degree of control maintained by Tūhoe leadership 1899–1903 over the realization of their goal of *mana motuhake* protected under the UDNR Act, there is no doubt that by 1908 this control and the Act itself was being actively undermined by the government. I think that in my unpublished essay (1984–1985) I may have been the first person to report that it was the eminent Māori leader Apirana Ngata, rapidly rising in influence in the new Liberal government, who by 1910 broke the control of the elected General Committee (*Komiti Nui*) under the UDNR Act by forcing the elected chairman Numia Kererū to accept supporters of the prophet Rua Kenena on the committee. I concluded that Ngata realized his goal to gain alienations of UDNR lands was being frustrated by Numia, and that Rua Kenana was able to convince his followers to sell (Webster n.d. (1984–5)). Numia (Kererū) Te Ruakariata's role in establishing the UDNR and his relationship with other Tūhoe leaders is examined in detail especially in Part II.

Judith Binney's thorough archival research later guided me to Numia's earlier report of the election of the *Komiti Nui* in 1908 and intentional exclusion of Rua and his supporters for having departed from "the law of the Government" (2002: 390–1). Binney also noted that the 1908 list of committee members had been annotated—'almost certainly by Ngata'—scribbling Rua's name alongside Numia's in pencil. I furthermore found on the same copy that while pencil dots probably marked the approval of most of the 32 General Committee members who were properly representing the 32 blocks of the UDNR, pencil Xs had been made alongside the names of five of them. At least four of these five were probably close allies of Numia Kererū (including his eminent nephew Tupaea Rapaera, Seddon's escort in his 1894 tour). Whether or not Ngata made these marks, it is clear that he sought to circumvent Numia's mana and legitimate control over alienations of Urewera lands by using Rua Kenana. Binney's assessment of Ngata's role in the Crown's purchase campaign and Urewera Consolidation Scheme is even more critical than my own (Binney 2002: 442–445; Webster 2004). Surprisingly, given this history, I myself have encountered few criticisms of Ngata's role from Tūhoe themselves, perhaps because his daughter is said to have married into Tūhoe.

By 1910 popular demands to 'open up the Ureweras' for settlement, forestry, and mining had moved the Liberal government to undermine the 1896 Act. Within a few years, Rua and his followers had sold extensive shares of the Reserve to the Crown especially in the eastern blocks of the Tauranga/Waimana River valley. By 1916 the Crown, illegally at first and finally by circumventing the Act, had mounted a highly organized campaign purchasing individual undivided interests which was sustained until 1921, finally acquiring a majority of shares in value in most blocks (Webster 2004: 60–213). However, the Crown had been unable entirely to buy out any one of the 35 blocks, so that in every block its shares remained inseparably held in common with increasingly stubborn Tūhoe 'non-sellers' or, as the Tūhoe termed them, *pupuri whenua* ('land-keepers'). Furthermore, although many Tūhoe were left landless or had retained only token shares of their most significant ancestral lands, the number of 'non-sellers' was actually increasing through succession of children or relatives to the many shareholders who died in the war and flu epidemic as well as natural causes.

In order to resolve this predicament, in 1921 the Crown decided to use Apirana Ngata's scheme for the consolidation of Native land shares in similar situations. Although the scheme had been designed to consolidate scattered Native land rights for the benefit of Māori kin groups or families, in the case of the Ureweras it was used to enable the Crown to extract its own shares from those of the non-sellers and consolidate them in favored locations for its own benefit (Webster 2004: 214–632). With Ngata's crucial help, ministers nevertheless convinced dubious Tūhoe leaders that the scheme was to resolve *their* predicament rather than the Crown's. Furthermore, for the location of its own shares, the Crown imposed preemptions across many of the agriculturally most-promising old blocks regardless of where it had actually purchased shares, and deducted further payments in land for the cost of surveys and roading amounting to 40% of each new block allocated to non-sellers in the areas which remained available to them. In the end, rather than cutting out its own shares and leaving the remainder of the Reserve for the non-selling Tūhoe, the Crown actually cut out the Tūhoe shares and awarded itself the remainder of the land. Including a windfall surplus of 46,000 acres from resurveying, the Crown's own award totaled about 75% of the original Native Reserve.

As will be shown in Volume II, the Tūhoe were not passive victims in the face of the Crown's newly predatory policies. Although their resistance had to take radically different forms and the losses to their *mana* as well as their lands were often crushing, it actually strengthened among some *hapū* and in certain areas of their sanctuary. While opportunism and internal conflict caused the compromise of some leaders and breakdown of some descent groups, as in the establishment of the UDNR the deployment of kin-based solidarity and power against the threatening policies continued to develop new forms of resistance. It will be argued in Volume II that the cooperation and consolidation of certain clusters of *hapū*, and the organization of widespread opposition to the Urewera Consolidation Scheme that became notorious as the *Apitihana* ('oppositionists'), was sometimes able to stall the Crown's increasingly divisive retaliations.

The Crown's promise of roading into the interior along the length of both major rivers had led many Tūhoe 'non-sellers' to accept allocation of their retained shares in new blocks along this proposed route, often giving up more favored ancestral lands elsewhere in the old blocks of the Native Reserve. Crown demands for smaller 'family farms' led to over 200 of these new blocks along the major rivers where the roads were planned, but in restricted areas on relatively rugged and agriculturally unpromising land. Nevertheless, the roads were never built, and in the 1950s Tūhoe protests over the land lost for that purpose finally resulted in a small government annuity that supported the Tūhoe tribal trust board.

Almost all new blocks resulting from the consolidation scheme survived scattered throughout the Crown award, which in the 1950s became the Urewera National Park. However, due to their limited size, cultivability, and isolation as well as employment and schooling necessities, most of the interior blocks were uninhabited by then, and remain so. Many Tūhoe nevertheless know these remnants of their ancestral lands well through hunting and other visits as well as family histories. In the 1970s the blocks in each of these four traditional regions shown in Fig. 1.4 were grouped into four amalgamations with these traditional names, intended primarily for development of forestry resources to be managed by the Tūhoe Tribal

Trust Board (Murton 2004: 824–842). However, this comprehensive 'new' amalgamation plan (if the aborted plan of 1902 be remembered) was delayed by divergent goals among different *hapū*, initiation of separate trusts or schemes, and by the late 1980s the plan itself was finally found to be administratively faulty and had to be quashed.

Since the 'new' amalgamations of the 1970s have been aborted, and the old Urewera National Park that surrounds many of them has been returned to the Tūhoe by the 2014 Te Urewera Act, what is the status of these hundreds of 'new' blocks carefully relocated by the *pupuri whenua* in 1921–1926? Have these *new* old blocks disappeared in this confused and involuted history somewhat like the original old blocks carefully established in the UDNR by 1907? By 1926 most of the new blocks had become 'Māori land' legally held in the name of particular descent groups and *whānau* numbering from a few to over 100 owners under the jurisdiction of the Māori Land Court (Webster 2004). Over the intervening years most probably remained in the name of these original owners. Each new generation raised elsewhere was likely to forget more of this tangled history. Furthermore, the legal statuses of many of these blocks have been changed by their owners over the intervening years, especially by the aborted plan for the new amalgamations and reactions to it in the 1970–1980s, including the formations of incorporations, trusts, and manifold protective arrangements available under the reformed Māori Land Act of the 1970s.

Untangling the legal history of each block would be difficult, but necessary if its legal status were to be changed. This was probably a major reason behind the resistance against the Te Urewera settlement by Tama Nikora, one of the most respected Tūhoe elders and by far the most knowledgeable regarding Urewera surveying, registration, and legal history. According to my reading of the 2014 Te Urewera Act, the legal status of all these blocks, and any change of their status since 1926, remains unchanged by the new Act—although many are now surrounded by 'Te Urewera' land controlled by all Tūhoe rather than the Urewera National Park. Sections 91, 92, and 101 of the 2014 Act appear to recognize the legal status of 'adjacent land' to the new Te Urewera, emphasize that it is not changed by the Act, and foresee the possibility of eventually adding them to Te Urewera. It is clear that the status of these 'adjacent' blocks would have been a central issue in the negotiations among Tūhoe *hapū* and adjacent *iwi* as well as between Tūhoe and the Crown, and carefully if quietly provided for in the Act.

As Ballara documented, *Ngāi Tūhoe* have always been a fractious lot regardless of their solidarity in the face of a common threat. After all, these blocks originated since 1908 in the hard-fought efforts of the *pupuri whenua* ('non-seller') ancestors to retain their ancestral lands as earlier established in the UDNR against the Crown's predatory campaign to take over all of their hard-won homeland. The surviving *mōrehu* ('remnants') were furthermore retained for decades by the descendants of these now-illustrious ancestors against often-hostile Crown and National Park authorities and, finally, sometimes against their own Trust Board's plan to amalgamate them in the 1970s. The status of many of these blocks actually remains unchanged since 1926 and—with succession orders often purposely left in abeyance—in the names of the original owners, now great-great-great-grandparents of the most recent generation. Their *mana* lies restive in these lands.

It is bitterly ironic that the Crown had actually intended the 1921 Urewera Consolidation Scheme to break down 'old tribal ways', and the much fuller ancestral history of the old blocks of the UDNR has often been obscured by the resulting relocation of new blocks. The Crown itself was often utterly confused in dogged pursuit of its purchase campaign, and again confused and often careless in pursuit of its Consolidation Scheme, so it is no surprise that many Tūhoe have lost track of the details of their ancestral rights as established by their own ancestors in the UDNR. On the other hand, personal documents, as well as rich oral histories, have been passed on among Tūhoe through generations. The following chapters hope to add to and guide further understanding and research in the rich archival records. It remains to be seen whether the Crown's settlement with the Tūhoe in 2014 can restore some of this tangled history and the resources needed to unravel and benefit economically from it.

4 A Preview of the Following Chapters

Chapter 2, 'The Tūhoe *rohe pōtae* and the Urewera District Native Reserve Commission', describes the investigative commission and examines the issue of its legitimacy among the Tūhoe with regard to the reliability of its record for an ethnohistorical reconstruction. The first part of the chapter summarizes the statutory brief, organization, and general procedures of the commission, and previews its findings with regard to the blocks into which the reserve was surveyed, the rights of particular *hapū* to these blocks, and the leaders who would represent each block. The second part assesses the legitimacy of the commission through a reconsideration of the grounds on which the Tūhoe commissioners were elected, evidence of the sincerity of commission's intentions and its deference to Tūhoe deliberations, and examination of several confrontations that developed early in its investigations.

Chapter 3, 'Difficulties of the Commission Defining Urewera Blocks by *hapū*', examines the major problem the commission had fulfilling the statutory assumption that the land blocks of the reserve could be laid out in accord with *hapū* organization. The resulting contradictions clarify the actual structure and dynamics of Māori *hapū*, at least in this historical context and among Tūhoe. Specific difficulties examined include changes in the number and identification of *hapū* over several years, procedural compromises and precedents set in the first block investigation, the following resolution to expedite hearings, and an aborted plan to amalgamate the 35 blocks into which the reserve had been divided into only 10 larger blocks.

Chapter 4, 'The Tamaikoha *hapū* Branch: Internal Social Organization', describes in detail a descent group of about 60 persons spanning four generations as an example of a *hapū* branch during these years. This *hapū* branch was headed by an old war leader whose dealings with the commission were described in Chap. 2. Displaying the ethnohistorical method used, a 1903 title and official block list of owners including this *hapū* branch are analyzed in order to explicate the significance of sibling groups and surnames, identify spouses, mothers, marriages, and land rights. The notion of a *kāwai* or *hapū* branch is introduced in relation to wider *hapū* organization, the analysis of which is undertaken in Chap. 5.

Chapter 5,'The Tamaikoha *hapū* Branch: *hapū* Affiliations', approaches the fundamental role of *hapū* in Tūhoe social and political organization during these years. The special difficulty of identifying *hapū* affiliations, which in cognatic descent systems are inherently multiple and ambiguous, is explored in specific terms. Data from Best's and the commission's records that bear on the question of the Tamaikoha *hapū* branch's affiliations are extracted and examined for evidence. First, potential *hapū* affiliations are reconstructed from genealogical records. Second, active affiliations of the *hapū* branch are identified and assessed from records of claims, block investigations, and committee memberships. The special problem of Tamaikoha's prestige, ambivalent relation to the commission, and sometimes informal claims are also examined.

Chapter 6, 'Tūhoe *hapū* Organization and the Amalgamation Plan', returns to an overview of Tūhoe *hapū* throughout the Urewera District Native Reserve by way of a belated plan of the commission in 1902, introduced in Chap. 3, to group the 35 blocks that they had investigated and approved into just 10 larger blocks. The various motives behind the plan and the last-minute decision to abort it are considered, concluding that it was primarily an initiative of Tūhoe leaders themselves. Analysis of the blocks that would have been grouped together in each amalgamated block offers insights into ecological subsystems of the Urewera, alliances between *hapū*, dominant sibling groups, and leaders of particular *hapū*, and the possibility of *hapū* 'clusters' dominated by one or two *hapū*. Two of the ten proposed amalgamations are examined to explore these implications, in both cases revealing political-economic alliances at different stages of development based on extensive intermarriage between descent groups.

Part II, 'Kinship and power in Ruatāhuna and Waikaremoana, 1899–1925' (Chaps. 7, 8, 9, and 10), pursues more intensively the approach developed in Chap. 6 to analyze a third proposed amalgamation of two large blocks at the southeastern end of the reserve (Fig. 1.3, amalgamation 2). These chapters reconstruct in detail the development of a prolonged confrontation especially between a marriage alliance among migrants, three important *hapū*, and their leaders over several decades.

Chapter 7, 'The Ruatāhuna-Waikaremoana Migrant Marriage Alliance by 1898', follows the intensive intermarriage between five descent groups that had developed since the early 1800s, arguing that it had originated in the Tūhoe 'conquest' or assimilation of friendly *hapū* of Ngāti Kahungunu *iwi* in Waikaremoana. The descent groups involved had rights in Waikaremoana and Ruatāhuna but, as relatively recent migrants between these areas, had developed few rights elsewhere in the Urewera. The kinship and political activities of key leaders in the five descent groups of this migrant marriage alliance are traced during the years 1899–1913.

Chapter 8, 'Confrontations Over Waikaremoana and Ruatāhuna, 1899–1907', examines the role of the migrant marriage alliance in otherwise apparently unrelated confrontations between claimants for each of these two blocks. In the case of Waikaremoana, leaders of the alliance were confronted by leaders of Tamakaimoana and other *hapū* in adjacent Maungapōhatu over a 4000-acre section of land between them supposed by Tūhoe to have been taken in conquest from Ngāti Kahungunu *iwi* along with the rest of Waikaremoana. In the case of Ruatāhuna, Te Urewera *hapū* led by Te Whenuanui II was confronted by Ngāti Rongo *hapū* led by Numia Kererū and Numia's claim to rights in Manawarū, the northern portion of the block. Te Whenuanui I had closely intermarried with the migrant marriage alliance and, by 1903, was supported by them in this confrontation. Nevertheless, unresolved aspects of both confrontations were left obscured before the appeals commission in 1907 and were either pre-empted by it or remained unsettled.

Chapter 9, 'The Ruatāhuna Partition, 1912', traces details of the confrontation between the Te Whenuanui II's supporters in the migrant marriage alliance and Numia Kererū's demand for rights in the Manawarū section of Ruatāhuna that arose in 1902 but remained silent and unaddressed in the 1907 appeals. Te Whenuanui II had died in 1907, and increases of shares that the appeals commissioners had left up to Numia may have mollified his supporters in the migrant marriage alliance. Te Whenuanui III made no appearance in the 1912 case, and only the most prestigious of the five alliance descent groups continued to oppose Numia's appeal to partition Manawarū between descendants of Arohana for Te Urewera *hapū*, and descendants of Kahuwī for Ngāti Rongo *hapū*. The arguments they raised were found to be much weaker than Numia's, and his arrangements for all five partitions of Ruatāhuna block including Kahuwī were successful.

Chapter 10, 'Some Plausible Explanations', is my attempt to understand what was going on behind the scenes of the Ruatāhuna-Waikaremoana *hapū* cluster. The apparent inconsistencies revealed in the previous three chapters regarding the Ruatāhuna-Waikaremoana migrant marriage alliance, Te Urewera, Ngāti Rongo, and Tamakaimoana *hapū*, and their respective leaders Te Haka Te Whenuanui II, Numia Kererū Te Ruakariata, and Tutakangahau Tapui are re-examined. The strategy and final triumph of Numia Kererū emerges in the context of his rising influence as a UDNR commissioner as well as *rangatira*, Te Whenuanui II's unexpected death and Numia's exploitation of the opportunity to influence his successor and overcome his support in the migrant marriage alliance, and his uncompromising control of the Ruatāhuna partition.

Part III, Conclusion (Chap. 11, 'A Contemporary Retrospect: Getting to Know *Ngāi Tūhoe*'), describes in personal terms the way in which I and my family got to know, and are still getting to know, *Ngāi Tūhoe* and especially some hapū of both the Manawarū and Ohāua te Rangi regions.

Photographs of the village of Ohāua in 1924 by the renowned social anthropologist Raymond Firth become the vehicle for my recapitulation of several decades of important marriage alliances between Ngāti Rongo and Te Urewera hapū that dramatically clarify the ancestry and relationships of the Ruatāhuna and Ruātoki *whānau* that hosted us in the 1970–1980s. Finally, I describe a confrontation we witnessed in Ohāua in 1983 between these two hapū that appeared to continue those decades earlier that I described in Part II. Can the promise of a *tatau pounamu* reconciliation between these two hapū, repeatedly renewed in the ancestral series of marriage alliances between them, be renewed yet again?

Notes

1. *Mana motuhake* is currently sometimes translated by Tūhoe as 'maximum sovereignty', apparently intending to challenge the Crown's assumption of paramount sovereignty.
2. *Rohe pōtae* literally means 'hat-boundary', and refers to the way the Māori king Tawhiao was said to have laid down the boundary of his people's refuge in the King Country of the west central North Island by setting his hat down on the map and declaring the land reserved from sales. Because his head was *tapu*, this gesture declared what came to be called the King Country *tapu* as well. Te Kooti's *waiata* emphasized the same status for Tūhoe control of Te Urewera.
3. (Binney 1997: 118–119, 2002: 17–18, citing McLean and Orbell 1975; this translation appears in Binney 1997, but is discussed and somewhat modified by her in 2002: 18 fn28).
4. Stokes, E., J.W. Milroy, and H. Melbourne 1986; Campbell 1997; Miles 1999; Binney 2002; Marr 2002; Edwards 2004; Murton 2004. Stokes et al., Miles, and Binney's Volume I also survey the traditional and early colonial history of the Urewera, including its role in the land wars, the Crown's land confiscations, and the refuge of Te Kooti's rebellion through to the 1870s. The Urewera Inquiry of the Waitangi Tribunal, and supporting research by the Crown Forestry Rental Trust and the Crown Law Office, have also resulted in many more specialized studies of Urewera history published by these institutions. The Waitangi Tribunal's *Urewera Record of Inquiry, July 2005*, compiles these sources.

References

Ballara, Angela. 1998. *Iwi: The dynamics of Māori tribal organization from c.1769 to c.1945.* Wellington, N.Z.: Victoria University Press.

Binney, Judith. 1997. "He Mana Tuatoru: the Rohe Pōtae of Tūhoe." *New Zealand Journal of History* 31(1): 117–131.

Binney, Judith. 2002. *Encircled Lands; Part Two: A History of the Urewera 1878–1912.* An Overview Report on the Urewera for the Waitangi Tribunal. WAI 894, A15. Wellington, N.Z.: Waitangi Tribunal.

Campbell, S.K.L. 1997. *Urewera Overview Project: Land Alienation, Consolidation, and Development in the Urewera 1912–1950.* A report commissioned by the Crown Forestry Rental Trust. WAI 894, A55. Wellington, N.Z.: Waitangi Tribunal.

Edwards, Cecilia. 2004. *The Urewera District Native Reserve Act 1896, a report for the Crown Law Office.* Parts I-III. WAI 894, #D7. Wellington, N.Z.: Waitangi Tribunal.

Holman Jeffrey. 2010. *Best of both worlds: the story of Elsdon Best and Tutakangahau.* Auckland, N.Z.: Penguin.

Marr, Cathy. 2002. *The Urewera District Native Reserve Act 1896 and Amendments.* A report commissioned by the Waitangi Tribunal. WAI 894, A 21. Wellington, N.Z.: Waitangi Tribunal.

Miles, Anita. 1999. *Te Urewera.* A report for the Waitangi Tribunal Rangahaua Whanui Series. WAI 894, A 11. Wellington, N.Z.: Waitangi Tribunal.

Murton, Brian. 2004. *The Crown and the People of Te Urewera, 1860-c2000: The Economic and Social Experience of a People.* Research report commissioned by the Crown Forestry Rental Trust. 2 vols., 1,791 pages. Wai 894 H12, Te Urewera inquiry. Wellington, N.Z.: Waitangi Tribunal.

O'Malley, Vincent. 2014. "Historical background". Special Issue – Tūhoe-Crown Settlement, Māori Law Review, October 2014 Whiringa-ā-nuku (māorilawreview.co.nz).

Sissons, Jeffrey. 1991. *Te Waimana, The Spring of Mana: Tuhoe History and the Colonial Encounter.* Dunedin, N.Z.: Otago University Press.

Sissons, Jeffrey. 2002. "Waimana Kaaku: A History of the Waimana Block." A report commissioned by the Crown Forestry Rental Trust, June 2002. Wellington, N.Z.: Waitangi Tribunal.

Sluka, Jeffrey. 2010. "The Ruātoki Valley 'Antiterrorism' Police Raids: Losing 'Hearts and Minds' in Te Urewera." *Sites, a Journal of Social Anthropology and Cultural Studies,* (new series) Vol 7 No 1: 44–64.

Stokes, Evelyn, J. Te Wharehuia Milroy, and Hirini Melbourne. 1986. *Te Urewera; nga iwi, te Whenua, te Ngahere; People, Land and Forests of Te Urewera.* Hamilton, N.Z., University of Waikato. WAI 894 record of inquiry, doc A11. Wellington, N.Z.: Waitangi Tribunal

Te Urewera Act 2014. Public Act 2014 No 51. Date of assent 27 July 2014. N.Z. Parliament. http://www.legislation.govt.nz/act/public/2014/0051/latest/whole.html

Tūhoe Claims Settlement Act 2014. Public Act 2014 No 50. Date of assent 27 July 2014. N.Z. Parliament. http://www.legislation.govt.nz/act/public/2014/0050/latest/whole.html.

UMB 2. Urewera District Native Reserve Commission minute book 2, Smith, Butler, et al., (8Mar1900–20Feb1901), in Māori, Index, 350 pp. NA Wgtn: Urewera MB 2, MLC 13,W3518, CD2, Vol. 2, 358 pp.; NA Ak: AREPRO 4711/1442. Acronym: UMB 2.

UMB 4. Urewera District Native Reserve Commission minute book 4 (English translation of UMB 2), Butler, Scannell, et al, (9Mar1900–May1900), index 12 pp., 344pp.; NA Wgtn: Urewera MB 4, MLC 13, W3518, CD 2, Vol. 4, 357 pp.; NA Ak: AREPRO 4711/1446. Acronym: UMB 4.

Webster, Steven. n.d. (1984–5) "Urewera Land 1895–1926; a tentative historical survey of Government and Tuhoe relations as reflected in official records." Unpublished manuscript, 50pp. Held in the University of Auckland Library. Auckland, N.Z.

Webster, Steven. 2004. *The Urewera Consolidation Scheme: Confrontations between Tuhoe and the Crown, 1915–1925.* Vols I, II. Report commissioned by the Waitangi Tribunal. WAI 894 #D8. Wellington, N.Z.: Waitangi Tribunal.

PART I

Tūhoe *Hapū* and the Establishment of the Urewera District Native Reserve

CHAPTER 2

The Tūhoe *Rohe Pōtae* and the Urewera District Native Reserve Commission

1 The General Procedures and Findings of the Commission

Under the 1896 Urewera District Native Reserve Act, the investigative commission was finally formed in 1899, held hearings through 1902, and submitted the provisional block orders and lists of owners in 1903. The latter were subject to appeals and an appeals commission which did not meet until 1906. The sittings of the investigative commission were held from February through May for four consecutive summers, circuiting through Rūātoki, Waimana, Te Houhi (located between Waiohau and Te Whaiti; see Fig. 1.1), Te Whaiti, Ruatāhuna, Maungapohatu, and Waikaremoana settlements, usually setting up a camp and holding the hearings in a *wharenui* ('meetinghouse'). In accord with the statute, the investigative commission was composed of two Pākehā commissioners, one of whom was to be the chairman, and a majority of five Tūhoe commissioners. The Pākehā members were the surveyor general and prominent amateur ethnologist S. Percy Smith, who was the chairman, and William J. Butler, a Native Land Court judge. After Smith stood down in March 1901, David Scannell, another judge of the Native Land Court who had heard earlier cases on the Rūātoki block, took his place as the second Pākehā commissioner and chairman, although Butler often took the chair and submitted the final report in late 1902. The five Tūhoe commissioners remained the same persons throughout the four years of investigation and were all prominent *rangatira* ('chiefs' or leaders): Numia

© The Author(s) 2020
S. Webster, *A Separate Authority (He Mana Motuhake)*, Volume I,
https://doi.org/10.1007/978-3-030-41042-1_2

Kererū Te Ruakariata, Hurae Puketapu, Te Pou Papaka, Mehaka Tokopounamu, and Tutakangahau Tapui. Following an early amendment to the Act, any one of these Tūhoe commissioners would formally step down when official decisions were to be made on claims to a land block in which they were an interested party, although their participation in the extensive informal proceedings probably continued.

In practice, the ethnic distinction and Tūhoe bias built into the commission was probably redressed and bridged somewhat by the addition of the rising (and later famous) amateur ethnologist Elsdon Best as secretary, and no doubt interpreter and often advisor, certainly to the Pākehā and probably also to the Tūhoe commissioners. Best had already been resident among the Tūhoe for several years (at Te Whaiti and later, Rūātoki) and had extensive research underway there, was fluent in Māori, and had the chairman Percy Smith, also an amateur ethnologist, as his established patron. He had the confidence of some Tūhoe leaders including the influential commissioner Tutakangahau (Holman 2010), but Best's manner was arrogant and abrasive, and other leaders including the commissioner Numia Kererū probably only tolerated him. Although other clerks later assisted Best, he remained the Commission's secretary throughout its four-year investigation, keeping extensive files of its complex proceedings which by 1907 he was to revise into his classic tome *Tuhoe, The Children of the Mist* (1973 [1925]). Although his (or Smith's) racial and evolutionist prejudices seriously distorted much of Tūhoe history (Sissons 1991), his hundreds of pages of versions of oral history, whakapapa, comments, and indexes on specific ancestors make his work indispensable though annoying for many contemporary Tūhoe. Binney (2002) has most thoroughly examined Best's voluminous archived papers.

The first two of seven (actually, nine) minutebooks of the commission were written in Māori by Best, and mostly translated (not by Best, but by a clerk) in two others of the seven.[1] These will be cited here as UMB (Urewera minutebook). These documents and the location of copies are listed in the references to each chapter here (and comprehensively in Webster 2004). For more than half of the four years of investigation during the summer months (1 February 1899 through 20 February 1901), the commission's minutes were kept in Māori. Surprisingly, most of UMB 1 was never translated. This procedure probably reflects the home-rule intention of the 1896 Act and deference to the Tūhoe majority of commissioners who, although more or less fluent in English, would need to have continual access to the complex official details of the proceedings in their first language. In the following section of this chapter I argue that the 1896 Act was sincere in its intention to establish home-rule in the UDNR and that the commission was generally accepted as legitimate by the Tūhoe. The official role of Māori in the investigation supports my argument.

The official brief of the commission was to "divide the Urewera district into blocks, adopting as far a possible hapu boundaries, and to investigate the ownership of each block" (Butler in AJHR 1902: 1). The extent to which the commission was able to do this will be more fully considered in Chap. 3, but details in (Fig. 2.1) in conjunction with (Fig. 1.2) raise doubts. Many of the 35 blocks were awarded to several hapū usually with no distinction in the block list, and no hapū at all were ever specified as owners of the three Rūātoki blocks. Although final awards of 16 blocks were made in the name of single hapū, 12 were made in the name of two or three hapū, and three were made in the name of *seven* hapū. The jump to seven hapū in these three blocks (Ruatāhuna, Taneatua, and Maungapōhatu) suggests that the maximum number of representatives allowed on the block committees (seven) might have become a rationale for limiting hapū claims in cases where the large number of hapū claiming rights to a block could not be further reduced even by the commission (this may explain the case of Rūātoki blocks 1, 2, and 3). Nor does the wide variation in the number of persons listed as owners for each block have any clear correlation with the size of a block or number of hapū found to have rights to it. As was noted in recalculation of the Tūhoe population in Chap. 1, the persons named as owners in the block lists overlap to a very large extent, as do the block or hapū committees. Nevertheless, perhaps in deference to the expectations of Parliament, the chairman's final report in 1902 termed these blocks 'hapu blocks', and the 1907 appeals commission referred to the block committees as 'hapu' committees. Moreover, neither the investigative nor the appeals commission named any hapū at all in their official block orders.

A general procedure was developed by the commission at each stage of its investigation. Probably with an eye to their official brief, the first season in 1899 was devoted to drawing up a list of 49 hapū in the Reserve, holding initial sittings in each of the selected centers of settlement, discussing boundaries and the areas to be surveyed into blocks, and receiving lists of claimants for these blocks. These lists were submitted in the name of a specific hapū, usually by hapū or hapū branch leaders, but were mentioned only by identification letter or number in the minutebooks. (These lists would be helpful in reconstructing the membership of hapū and hapū branches but, unfortunately, have not been located in the archives and may have been lost.) Strikingly, many of the Tūhoe hapū carefully listed at the start of the 1899 season do not appear as claimant hapū later that same year, while many others not listed do lay claims. Final awards in 1902, furthermore, named yet other hapū, totaling over 120 different hapū—which is quite unlikely in a population of about 2000 persons. This situation will be analyzed in Chap. 3.

The boundaries of many blocks were stubbornly contested and had to be negotiated and changed in later hearings or were continued as appeals. The Crown had agreed to bear the entire cost of surveys, and for the limited purpose of the Native Reserve and home-rule as well as the saving of costs, these were carried out by approximate magnetic, chain, and landmark methods. Despite these delays, survey of about 35 blocks and a rough compiled plan of the Reserve were completed for sittings in the 1900 season. So far as I have been able to determine, the earliest surviving survey or compiled plan of the Reserve is one dated August 1901, which is held in LINZ, Hamilton, as Urewera plan number 6873 (Figs. 1.3 and 6.1). Although the lines of the proposed amalgamations are drawn over some details, it is nevertheless the most carefully detailed plan I have encountered. Most subsequent plans through 1921 were probably drawn from this one. The 35 individual block plans from which it was compiled are listed on the original, but I have examined only a few of these. The original surveyors' notebooks and correspondence are also archived and would reveal still more details (including the names of guides and informants) if sorted and examined carefully.

The general procedure pursued in the 1900–1902 seasons was to investigate rights of (i) ancestry, (ii) occupation, and (iii) relative shares for each block, in that order. When delays were encountered in some blocks, investigation of others was resumed at the point where they had been postponed; thus the minutebooks proceeded sequentially through each season but were usually indexed by block so entries regarding a previous case could be located and reviewed by claimants as well as the commissioners. The first stage of investigation for each block sought to identify the founding ancestors from whom the claimants traced their rights to a block, and test the *whakapapa* (genealogy) whereby descent was claimed by hearing objections. The second stage examined the extent to which claimants with demonstrated ancestral rights had also maintained legitimate occupation on the block for at least the three most recent generations, that is, occupation or use by parents, grandparents, and great-grandparents of the oldest living claimant. An at least preliminary formal decision of the commission announcing the successful claimants was made on the basis of these two stages of investigation. Finally in the UDNR commission's procedure, unsuccessful claimants lists were set aside and relative shares of ownership were apportioned between successful claimants. This entire procedure but especially this third stage will be more fully examined in Chap. 3. Although in deference to Tūhoe criticisms the 1896 Act and the commission chairman were at pains to avoid association with the Native Land Court, the general criteria of land rights were adopted from the investigative procedure into Māori custom law that court had developed since 1865 (Firth 1959: 383–388; Webster 1975: 134; Sorrenson 2015).

The 1900 season began with the investigation of the Te Waipotiki, Te Purenga, and adjacent blocks just south of the Rūātoki blocks (see Fig. 1.2). Several weeks and over 200 pages of minutes were devoted to the Te Waipotiki block alone, mostly to cross-examination of witnesses. Despite a resolution to expedite hearings thereafter, the area tentatively laid out for Te Purenga was much more extensive than shown in Fig. 1.2 and, for the sake of resolving some conflicting hapū claims, needed breaking down into several other blocks. For each block, claimants' representatives were continually urged to negotiate differences outside formal session, merge similar claims together to save time, and bring before the commission hearings only matters they had failed to resolve among themselves. The arrangements settled outside formal sessions are usually not mentioned in the minutebooks, rather appearing in perfunctory entries as approvals or taken for granted. A few blocks appear to have been settled largely on this informal basis outside of hearings, and boundaries, ancestry, or occupation of claimants were simply recorded as approved when no formal objections were raised. The commission's reliance on these informal procedures reflect its brief to establish the reserve on the basis of Tūhoe custom, but also suggest that the role of the Tūhoe commissioners, along with other Tūhoe leaders, was pervasive whether formally stood down or not.

In the usual case, where contending claims remained unresolved outside the formal hearings, *kaiwhakahaere* (conductors) were named for each block to organize the formal examination of witnesses for each outstanding claimant, usually representing one or a few hapū. Kaiwhakahaere were usually claimants to the block themselves, but the frequency with which certain leaders (including recused commissioners) conducted cases suggests they were favored by the commissioners for their skills.

Cross-examination of witnesses was used for the first case, but usually avoided thereafter in order to expedite hearings, relying on less formal methods of confirmation or objection from other witnesses or the public and following up unresolved objections later. It is clear that wide discussion outside the hearings often resulted in the emergence of further issues in subsequent hearings, and this was usually welcomed by the chairperson. As was mentioned above, the three stages of investigation of a block (rights of ancestry, occupation, and relative shares) were usually staggered with other blocks in different stages of investigation. The allocation of shares among successful claimants often resolved continuing opposition and ambiguity of rights between them. As will be explained in the following chapters, the 'relativity' of rights expressed in 'shares' actually developed by the Tūhoe commissioners and other leaders thus extended to important status discriminations considerably beyond mere generational differences and, in all probability, beyond the expertise or interest of the Pākehā commissioners.

Ideally, a formal decision announcing successful claimants lists was made before undertaking the final investigative stage of allocating relative shares among individuals on these lists. However, in practice these early decisions were often tentative and had to later deal with amended and even additional lists. The final formal decisions on a block were often delayed for months, sometimes without any explanation recorded in the minutes. Most of them were finalized between January and March in 1902 in Rūātoki, and a specific date and location for each block was reported in the official preliminary block orders published in 1903 (and included here in Fig. 2.1). In some cases, no formal decision was actually recorded at the reported time, but instead merely a perfunctory remark referring to earlier resolutions in the case. In all cases, reconstruction of the deliberations regarding a particular block requires piecing together successive entries throughout several of the minutebooks, often with only fragmentary explanation of what had happened and sometimes not indexed.

In October 1902 the commission reconvened to conclude its four seasons of investigations of the 35 blocks into which they had divided the Reserve. All the members of the commission met together to confirm their previous decisions regarding each block, consider any alterations necessary, and list the provisional block committees in accord with the Act. In accord with a later amendment to the Act, only the Tūhoe commissioners who claimed no interest in a block were recorded as acting in the confirmation of a block. Some minor changes were made to the lists and some appeals were announced. Crucially at this time, the one to several hapū that had been recognized to have rightful claim to each block in terms of ancestry and occupation were recorded for all blocks except Rūātoki 1, 2, and 3. Significantly, the names of the hapū emerging in the October 1902 confirmation of decisions were largely different from those listed in 1899 at the beginning of investigations. The following year, in 1903, 255 pages of block orders were published, in Māori as well as English, listing over 14,000 names as owners of the entire reserve (Scannell in AJHR 1903: 1–256). However, interestingly, no hapū at all were named in these official provisional block orders, nor later in the final orders. As will become clear later, this was probably to allay appeals from hapū that had been implicitly subordinated to others found to have dominant rights in a block.

Below (Fig. 2.1) are the conclusions of the commission in 1902, with the blocks in the order addressed and, where more than one hapū of block owners was recognized, in the order listed. The date and place of the commission's decision, and total number of persons named, follow the list of hapū. After confirmation of their decisions, the commissioners named provisional block committees for each block including the Rūātoki blocks, and this list is also shown in the order recorded.

I take this information, along with the official block lists resulting from four years of investigation the legitimacy and reliability of which is next argued, as foundational for ethnohistorical analysis. An appeals commission was finally formed in 1906 under the 1896 Act to hear the appeals, but there were only a few important modifications of the 1903 block orders. Most of the modifications were superficial compromises adding further shareholders, sometimes arbitrarily for the sake of expedience, and the legitimacy of the appeals commission is far more dubious primarily because there were no Tūhoe members.[2] As mentioned in the Introduction, Binney was highly critical of the impartiality of the appeals commission.

The provisional block committees appointed in 1902 were revised in 1907 after appeals were decided upon. Although again no hapū were named in the final block orders of 1907, the revised committees were called 'hapū' rather than 'block' committees. For comparison, both committees are listed in Fig. 2.1 in the order recorded. These committee lists, along with the actual naming in October 1902 of the hapū awarded block ownership, are probably among the most important documentary records available regarding hapū organization of the Tūhoe during these years.

	UDNR Block (in order of Oct 1902 confirmations)	Hapū Rights Recognised (in order named)	Provisional Block Committee (Oct 1902)	Committee revision 1907(* indicates cont'd from 1902)
1	Otairi	Ngai Te Au (1903 order cites decision 20 March 1902, in Rūātoki; names 133 persons)	Tihema Te Hau Peraniko Kapeta Erueti Mauri (Uauri?) Tahatu Te Whatu Harehare Ahuriri	*Tihema te Hau Raka Mehaka Hahona Heemi *Peraniko Kapeta Haare Haare Manuka Puritia
2	Maraetahia	Ngai Tawha (1903 order cites decision [same date, location?]; names 252 persons)	Tihema Te Hau Peraniko Kapeta Te Manihera Pahiri Pihopa Tamehana Matoru (?) Mehaka	Tihema te Hau *Peraniko Kapeta *Manihera Pahiri *Pihopa Tamehana Tureti Mehaka Tane Hauraki Harehare Atarea
3	Te Whaiti Nui a Toi	Tuhoe [Te Urewera?], N. Whare, N. Manawa (1903 order cites decision 26 March 1902, in Rūātoki; names 424 persons)	Akuhata Te Kaha Paitini Wi Tapeka Te Tuhi Pihopa Te Wharekotua Pahiri Teepa Mohi Wharepapa Whatanui Teneti Rakuraku	*Wharepapa Whatanui *Te Tuhi Pihopa Matakuare te Hira Te Matahaere Whatanui Hohepa Poia Wirimu Tamati Te Warunui Rawiri
4	Ierenui-Ohaua	N. Rongo, N. Rakei (1903 order cites decision 13 March 1902, in Rūātoki; names 401 persons)	Te Pouwhare Te Roau Paparutu Matiu Mika Te Tawhao Numia Te Ruakariata Pekahinau Wi Taikete Paora Rangiaho Tauru Tuhua	*Numia te Ruakariata *Te Pouwhare te Roau Te Whetu te Paerata Te Wharekiri Paparatu *Mika te Tawhao Akuhata te Kaha Hohia te Ahikaiata
5	Karioi	Ngamaihi, N. Te Kahu (1903 order cites decision 21 February 1902, in Rūātoki; names 285 persons)	Akuhata Te Hiko Turei Tiakiwai Hauwai Tiakiwai Te Raukaraka Ereatara Tangira Te Hira	*Turei Tiakiwai Te Wharau Tapuae *Akuhata te Hiko *Tangira te Hira *Hauwai Tiakiwai Hohia te Ahikaiata
6	Tauranga	N. Maihi, N. Te Kahu, N. Tamaroki. (1903 order cites decision 17 February 1902, in Rūātoki; names 547 persons)	Te Wharau Tapuae Te Pou Papaka Te Mai Te Maipi Paiaka Rakuraku Paora Kingi Paora Rangimonoa (?) Tuari Hakeke Tamaikoha D [sic]	*Te Wharau Tapuae *Paiaka Rakuraku *Paora Kingi Paora Te Paoro Tangohau Tupaea Rapaera *Te Pou Papaka Tupara Kaaho
7	Kohuru-Tukuroa	N.Rongo, N.Tamariwai, N.Korokaipapa (1903 order cites decision 17 March 1902, in Rūātoki; names 377 persons)	Te Pouwhare Te Roau Te Korowhiti Hira Te Waewae Te Roau Heremia Heremia Heurea Tamehana Te Hira Piri o Rehua Haki Matika	*Te Pouwhare te Roau Te Wakaunua Houpepe Paora Rangiaho Numia te Ruakariata Timi Tamehana Hohia te Ahikaiata Tupara Kaaho
8	Omahuru	Ngai Tatua (1903 order cites decision 11 March 1902, in Rūātoki; names 237 persons)	Te Pairi Tu Te Rangi Te Tawhi Tapuae Mohomoho Waretini Te Hue Hopa Tuhukia Te Hiko	*Te Pairi Tuterangi *Te Tawhi Tapuwae *Mohomoho Waretini Taihakoa Poniwahio *Tuhukia te Hiko Te Ahu Hopa
9	Parekohe	N.Turanga, Te Urewera, N. Te Kapo (1903 order cites decision 27 March 1902, in Rūātoki; names 703 persons)	Te Wharetuna Heremia Te Whetu Paerata Te Rewiti Rutane (?) Te Whiu Maraki Wati Wakaunua Tamehana Te Puia Taahu Hirawanu	Numia te Ruakariata *Te Whetu Paerata Te Pouwhare te Roau Mika te Tawhao Haturini Papaka Te Wharao Tapuae *Wati te Wakaunua
10	Ruatahuna	Te Urewera, N. Te Riu, N. Kuri, N.Tu, N.Manunui, N.Kakahutapiki, N.Ruatahuna (1903 order cites decision 10 March 1902, in Rūātoki; names 884 persons)	Te Haka Te Whenuanui Te Iriwhiro Te Wiremu Paraki Wereta Te Mapu Te Pukeiotu Noho Taratoa Numia Te Ruakariata Hiraka Paora	Te Wharepouri te Amo *Te Iriwhiro te Wiremu *Paraki Wereta Mihaka Matika *Numia te Ruakariata *Hiraka Paora Te Waka Hatata

Fig. 2.1 Urewera District Native Reserve Blocks, Hapū, and Committees

	UDNR Block (in order of Oct 1902 confirmations)	Hapū Rights Recognised (in order named)	Provisional Block Committee (Oct 1902)	Committee revision 1907(* indicates cont'd from 1902)
11	Te Ranga-a-Ruanuku	N. Ha (1903 order cites decision 14 March 1902, in Rūātoki; names 563 persons)	Te Wharekiri Paparatu Taihakoa Poniwahio Te Pouwhare Te Roau Wharetuna Heremia Tupaea Rapaera Mika Te Tawhao Hiki Natanahira	Numia te Ruakariata *Te Pouwhare te Roau Te Whetu te Paerata *Mika te Tawhao *Hiki Natanahira Te Pairi Tuterangi Hori Atarea
12	Pukepohatu [Papatupu Land?]	N. Tokotuai (1903 order cites decision 21 February 1902, in Rūātoki; names 44 persons)	Tiopira Tamaikoha Hakeke Tamaikoha Noho Te Wharau Taupae Karaka	declared ininvestigated (confused with Papatipu Land?)
13	Paraoanui	N. Taumata (1903 order cites decision 14 March 1902, in Rūātoki; names 115 persons)	Tuhukia Te Hiko Te Pairi Tu Te Rangi Te Hue Hopa Te Tawhi Tapuae Te Hauwaho Tamaikoha Takao Tamaikoha Mohomoho Waretini	*Tuhukia te Hiko Taihakoa Poniwahio *Te Pairi Tuterangi *Te Hauwaho Tamaikoha *Takao Tamaikoha Netana te Whakaari
14	Paraeroa	N.Hinekura, N.Mura (1903 order cites decision [date? location?]; names 213 persons)	Anania Te Ahikaiata Te Hira Waikite Te Hira Pira o Rehua Mahika Matika Ru Hoani Kanuehi Te Waara Mika Te Tawhao	Tupara Kaaho Paora Rangiaho *Anania te Ahikaiata Tamehana te Puia *Te Hira Waikite *Mika te Tawhao *Mihaka Matika
15	Tapatahi	N. Takiri (1903 order cites decision 21 January 1902, in Rūātoki; names 132 persons)	Te Rahui Hoera Heurea Tamehana Rangiteremauri Mihaka Paora Kingi Paora Heremia Heremia	*Heremia Heremia *Te Rahui Haora *Rangiteremauri Mihaka Tamehana te Puia *Paora Kingi Paora Kiriahuru te Whenuanui
16	Te Waipotiki	N. Rongo, Mahurehure (1903 order cites decision 24 January 1902, in Rūātoki; names 527 persons)	Numia Kereru Teepa Mohi Te Iwikino Hairuha Akuhata Te Kaha Te Paoro Tangohau Te Wakaunua Houpepe	*Numia te Ruakariata Te Whetu te Paerata Te Pouwhare te Roau *Akuhata te Kaha *Te Wakaunua Houpepe *Te Paoro Tangohau Hohia te Ahikaiata
17	Te Poroporo	N. Maruhakapua [N.Maru?] (1903 order cites decision 21 January 1902, in Rūātoki; names 237 persons)	Te Mataku Papita Wharetuna Heremia Heremia Heremia Wharepouri Te Amo Taihakoa Poniwahio	*Te Mataku Papita *Wharetuna Heremia *Heremia Heremia *Te Wharepour te Amo *Taihakoa Poniwahio Puihi Marutawhao
18	Taneatua	N.Whakateke, N.Manutohikura, Te Urewera, N. Ruatahuna, N.Ha, N. Tokotuwai, N. Tamakaimoana (1903 order cites decision 18 February 1902, in Rūātoki; names 911 persons)	Te Amo Kokouri Tawera Moko Tupara Kaaho Puihi Marutawhao Teepa Mohi Heurea Tamahana Turei Tiakiwai	Te Wharepouri te Amo *Tawera Moko *Tupara Kaaho *Puihi Marutawhao Timi Tamehana Mihaka Matika Hori Atarea
19	Te Purenga	N. Koura (1903 order cites decision 17 February 1902, in Rūātoki; names 297 persons)	Mehaka Ruka Heurea Tamehana Mika Wikiriwhi Taihakoa Poniwahio Hori Aterea Takurua Tamarau	*Hori Atarea Mehaka Ruka Timi Tamehana *Mika Wikiriwhi Tamehana te Puia *Takurua Tamarau
20	Te Wairiko	Te Aitanga o Tanemoeahi (1903 order cites decision 20 January 1902, in Rūātoki; names 238 persons)	Haami Taupo Kiekie Mikaere Toko Te Mataku Mika Te Tawhao Wharetuna Heremia	*Kiekie Mikaera *Haami Taupo *Toko te Mataku *Mika te Tawhao *Wharetuna Heremia Taihakoa Poniwahio

Fig. 2.1 (continued)

	UDNR Block (in order of Oct 1902 confirmations)	Hapū Rights Recognised (in order named)	Provisional Block Committee (Oct 1902)	Committee revision 1907(* indicates cont'd from 1902)
21	Whaitiripapa	Te Urewera (1903 order cites decision 27 January 1902, in Rūātoki; names 289 persons)	Tupaea Rapaera Tupara Kaaho Akuhata Te Kaha Puria [Turia] Rongokataia Tamaikoha Te Ariari	Numia Ruakariata Te Pouwhare te Roau *Akuhata te Kaha *Te Wakaunua Houpepe Hohia te Ahikaiata Tiopira Tamaikoha
22	Rūātoki South	N. Muriwai (1903 order cites decision 2 February 1902, in Rūātoki; names 280 persons)	Te Wakaunua Houpepe Utiera Tuau Te Amo Kokouri Paparutu Matiu Tawera Moko Tupara Kaaho Wharetuna Heremia	Numia te Ruakariata Mika te Tawhao Taihakoa Poniwahio *Wharetuna Heremia *Tupara Kaaho Te Wharepouri te Amo
23	Hikurangi-Horomanga	Patuheuheu, N.Haka, N.Hiki (1903 order cites decision 27 March 1901, in Te Houhi; names 374 persons)	Mika Te Tawhao Te Ao Te Rangi Rihipeti Hahona Hemi Te Whaiti Paora Tukino Te Mumuhu Te Hiro Tangohau Waihua Waihua	Te Wharepapa Peita *Mika te Tawhao Te Ao-o-terangi Rihipeti *Hahona Hemi Tihema te Hau Natana Koura *Te Hira Tangohau
24	Waikaremoana	Tuhoe [inclu N.Manunui, N.Hinekura], Ruapani (1903 order cites decision 20 February 1902, in Rūātoki; names 729 persons)	Hori Te Mataa Te Wao Ihimaera Mahaki Tapiki Wi Mutu Matiaha (?) Rawaho Te Winitana Te Kaaho Te Kaaho Matamua Whakamoe	Te Waipatu te Winitana Hurae Puketapu Wahia Paraki *Matamua Whakamoe Tuahine Noa Mei Erueti Hape Te Wao
25	Ohiorangi	Ngai Tama (1903 order cites decision 17 February 1902, in Rūātoki; names 413 persons)	Te Wharekiri Paparatu Akuhata Te Hiko Mohomoho Waretini Te Tawhi Poniwahio Hikihiki Te Taniwha	*Te Wharekiri Paparatu *Akuhata te Hiko *Mohomoho Waretini *Te Tawhi Poniwahio Te Wharau Tapuae
26	Tauwhare	N. Mura (1903 order cites decision 17 February 1902, in Rūātoki; names 199 persons)	Ereatara Heremia Te Wara Tamaro Tamati Rautao Noho Te Wharau Haami Taupo	Kiekie Mikaere Kanuwehi te Waara Te Tawhi Poniwahio *Noho te Wharau *Hami Taupo Taihakoa Poniwahio Mika te Tawhao
27	Otara	Ngai Turanga (1903 order cites decision 27 January 1902, in Rūātoki; names 253 persons)	Paiaka Rakuraku Te Tawhi Tapuae Tuhukia Te Hiko Te Ahu Hopa Te Whetu Paerata Turei Te Hawiki	*Te Whetu te Paerata Te Wharau te Tapuae *Turei Te Hawiki Te Pairi Tuterangi Nika te Paerata *Paiaka Rakuraku Tamehana te Puia
28	Tarapounamu-Matawhero	N.Tawhaki, N. Te Wehi (1903 order cites decision 17 March 1902, in Rūātoki; names 883 persons)	Rawiri Te Kokau Taiwera Rawiri Tuku a Te Rangi Tutakangahau Te Whatu Moihi Toki Pirini Mihaera Tangohau Te Hata Waewae	*Rawiri te Kokau Te Manihera Pahiri *Taiwera Rawiri Eruera Pirihita Te Wharepouri te Amo Te Hira Tangohau Wepiha te Whatanui
29	Waikare-whenua	Ngaitama (1903 order cites decision 4 February 1902, in Rūātoki; names 505 persons)	Taihakoa Poniwahio Te Rewiti Ruta Mohomoho Waretini Te Pairi Tu Te Rangi Turei Tiakiwai Te Wharekiri Paparatu Wiremu Te Purewa	Hori Atarea *Te Pairi Tuterangi Te Pouwhare te Roau *Turei Tiakiwai *Taihakoa Poniwahio *Te Wharekiri Paparatu Tamehana te Puia
30	Te Tuahu	Hamua (1903 order cites decision 11 February 1902, in Rūātoki; names 351 persons)	Ereatara Heremia Mika Te Tawhao Tuhukia Te Hiko Taihakoa Poniwahio Te Rewiti ? [sic]	No revision?

Fig. 2.1 (continued)

	UDNR Block (in order of Oct 1902 confirmations)	Hapū Rights Recognised (in order named)	Provisional Block Committee (Oct 1902)	Committee revision 1907(* indicates cont'd from 1902)
31	Tauwhare-Manuka	Whakatane, N.Tokotuai, N.Tamariwai (1903 order cites decision 14 February 1902, in Rūātoki; names 339 persons)	Tupaea Rapaera Tiopira Tamaikoha Netana Te Whakaari Paiaka Rakuraku Te Maipi Te Whiu Taupae Karaka Te Kahu o Rangi i Te Rika who? [sic]	*Netana te Whakaari Numia te Ruakariata *Tiopira Tamaikoha Tupara Tamana Takao Tamaikoha
32	Maungapohatu	Tamakaimoana, Ngapotiki, Ngai Tumatawha, Ngai Tatua, N.Maru, N.Te Ao [Te Au], N.Pou (Eria's list) (1903 order cites decision 13 May 1901, in Te Houhi; names 919 persons)	Te Whare Te Taniwha Te Iwikino Hairuha Te Waaka Te Rihi Tupaea Rapaera Tauaki Te Hou Te Wharepapa Wi Taikete Rangimonoa Tuari	Numia te Ruakariata Te Whetu te Paerata Te Wakaunua Houpepe Rakuraku Rehua Te Tuhi Pihopa Te Paoro Tangohau Akuhata te Kaha
33	Rūātoki No.1	(lists and cmte ordered, but no hapuu named) (1903 order cites decision 14 October 1902, in Whakatane; names 497 persons)	Numia Kereru Te Pouwhare Te Roau Te Whetu Paerata Te Iwikino Hairuha Te Wakaunua Houpepe Te Amo Kokouri Akuhata Te Kaha	*Numia te Ruakariata *Te Pouwhare te Roau *Te Whetu te Paerata *Akuhata te Kaha Hohia te Ahikaiata Wati te Wakaunua Te Paoro Tangohau
34	Rūātoki No.2	(lists and cmte ordered, but no hapuu named) (1903 order cites decision 14 October 1902, in Whakatane; names 558 persons)	Teepa Mohi Pihi Te Peeti Te Paoro Tangohau Te Iwikino Hairuha Te Wakaunua Houpepe Akuhata Te Kaha Mika Wikiriwhi	Numia te Ruakariata Te Pouwhare te Roau Te Whetu te Paerata *Akuhata te Kaha Hohia te Ahikaiata Wati te Wakaunua *Te Paoro Tangohau
35	Rūātoki No.3	(lists and cmte ordered, but no hapuu named) (1903 order cites decision 14 October 1902, in Whakatane; names 603 persons)	Numia Kereru Te Korohiti Hira Akuhata Te Kaha Te Walti Kepa Te Paoro Tangohau Hohia Te Ahikaiata Paora Rangiaho	*Numia te Ruakariata Te Pouwhare te Roau Te Whetu te Paerata *Akuhata te Kaha *Hohia te Ahikaiata Wati te Wakaunua *Te Paoro Tangohau

Fig. 2.1 (continued)

The committee memberships were revised in 1902 and again in 1907 under specific circumstances and will be examined in Chaps. 5 and 6. The overlap of membership between different block committees at the same time, as well as in the same committee between 1902 and 1907, like the extensive overlap in the lists of block owners, reflects the overlapping structure of hapū alliances and affiliations and the relative influence of hapū leaders. Although the 1896 Act intended these 'provisional' committees to become permanent through popular election by the shareholders of each block as electors, Binney's crucial research confirms my own earlier evidence that by 1908 the government was intending to subvert the statutory home-rule authority of these committees and their representation on the Komiti Nui or General Committee of the UDNR in order to facilitate land sales by Rua Kenana and mining exploration (Binney 2002: 388–98; Webster n.d. [1984–5]).

Nevertheless, the Tūhoe probably treated both the provisional and final block committees as permanent from the time they were first listed. As in most other decisions of the commission, the committee members were certainly selected by the Tūhoe commissioners in close negotiation with other Tūhoe leaders of all the hapū concerned. Although in some cases the persons named may have only been proxies in the direct control of leading elders who preferred to remain less obvious, inspection shows that the majority were persons of leading *mana* in their own right, that is, authoritative influence arising from—or withdrawn by—a consensus of other members of the hapū for which they spoke.

2 The Legitimacy of the Commission Among Tūhoe

Historian Judith Binney and social anthropologist Jeff Sissons, two leading Pākehā scholars whose field research among the Tūhoe has earned the respect of many of them, are skeptical that the 'first' Urewera Commission (1899–1903), in their investigation and arrangement of provisional block orders of the Urewera District Native Reserve, fairly represented the Tūhoe at large and remained independent of its Pākehā chairmen (Binney 2002: 213–221, 235–47; Sissons 2002: 64–9). Before examining the evidence that might support Binney and Sissons' skepticism, a prima facie case can be made to the contrary that the investigative commission (perhaps quite unlike the 'second' or appeals commission) was generally accepted as legitimate among the Tūhoe and that the Tūhoe commissioners usually retained control over its results.

The most compelling general evidence supporting the legitimacy of the investigative commission among the Tūhoe is the coherence and integrity of the principles of social organization revealed in almost all the block order lists. As will be shown in Chap. 4, the organization of these lists could only have been the result of painstaking supervision by the Tūhoe commissioners outside the commission's formal sittings, on the basis of their personal expertise in such matters, of claimants lists which themselves had been worked out in terms of the same principles of social organization by leaders of the hapū and hapū branches concerned, probably in close consultation with other leaders. Although the land court judges and Best were broadly familiar with the social organization of Māori hapū, and Smith as well as Best were driven partly by their ethnological interests, the Tūhoe commissioners appear to have pursued these principles of their social organization considerably beyond the interest and perhaps understanding of their Pākehā colleagues. There is little indication even in Best's professional publications that he had more than a superficial understanding of these principles.

It should also be emphasized that the 1896 Act was importantly the result of Tūhoe negotiations and probably represented sincere intentions for 'home-rule' on the part of Seddon, Carroll, Smith, Best, and some benevolent parliamentarians. After Seddon's dramatic tour of the Urewera in March 1894, he appears to have harbored a certain sentimental loyalty to Tūhoe and particularly to Kererū Te Pukenui (Numia's older brother, soon deceased) and his nephew Tupaea Rapaera.[3] As late as 1904, Native Minister Carroll accompanied Britain's Lord Ranfurly in a tour of the UDNR and appeared committed to the sincere intentions of the 1896 Act and the investigative commission. Carroll's arrogant but righteous rebuttal of the suspicions of some Tūhoe *rangatira* at Te Whai a Te Motu *marae* in Ruatāhuna (probably Te Whenuanui II) implies these intentions remained unchanged at that time, as does Lord Ranfurly's understanding of the 1896 Act as a 'treaty' confirming the reserve as a self-governing enclave, expressed in Carroll's company (Binney 2002: 299, 303). Smith and Best, furthermore, clearly had their ethnological motives for 'preserving' Tūhoe customs and traditions insofar as possible, and their appointment to the commission probably reflected this.[4]

Until the 1896 Act began to be actively undermined about 1908 (as Binney shows), its provisions ensured a representative General Committee of Tūhoe *rangatira* virtually complete control over 656,000 acres of land within the Tūhoe *rohe pōtae* despite popular and commercial demands for access to it. Even after Apirana Ngata broke down the solidarity of the General Committee in 1910, and through the following decade of Crown purchasing in disregard of it, this statute continued to be a rallying point for defiant Tūhoe.

The general relaxation of commission procedures also indicated some deference to Tūhoe control beyond merely their majority on the commission. It is fairly clear in the minutebooks that the Pākehā commissioners saw themselves as facilitators and officiators of arrangements to be made by the Tūhoe themselves, requiring their formal intervention in details only when conflicts arose that could not be resolved outside the hearings. It is clear that the Tūhoe commissioners were expected to work closely with other Tūhoe leaders as well as each other in the organization and preparation of cases, and there is furthermore little doubt that informally they all continued to influence decisions even when formally recused as having an interest in a particular block. The commission actively pressed all claimants to settle all aspects of a case including contending claims, boundaries, lists of owners, and relative shares outside of the hearings, routinely approved proposals to which there were no objections, and even neglected to record some deliberations and decisions, apparently because they were accepted without objection among the Tūhoe leaders. On the other hand, exhaustive detail was usually recorded as evidence when contentions reached the formal hearings, and by 1900 Chairman Smith was expressing exasperation with delays. In all these ways the investigation and its findings can be seen to be largely a Tūhoe procedure—as was probably intended by Smith and Best as well as Seddon and authors of the legislation.

Judith Binney examined the correspondence recording the selection of the five Tūhoe commissioners (2002: 222, 231). She reports that in November 1896 'local elections' were held and (according to Tūhoe reports to the Crown) *te poti* (the vote) resulted in the selection of Numia Kererū for the Rūātoki region; Te Pou Papaka for the Waimana region; Mehaka Tokopounamu for the Galatea and Te Houhi region (located between Waiohau and Te Whaiti; see Fig. 1.1); Hurae Puketapu for the Waikaremoana region; and 'Kutu' for the Ruatāhuna region. She deduced that Kutu was Kutu Te Kikiwa (2002: 222 fn18). Under the Act, these commissioners were intended to 'represent' these regions or localities of the Urewera, and the 'voting' was apparently assumed to have taken place within each of these five regions.

The actual mode of 'election' was probably quite different, and largely under the control of the Tūhoe leaders. Binney reports that by 1899 Kutu had been replaced by Tutakangahau for the Maungapōhatu and Ruatāhuna regions, probably due to Kutu's agedness, and Te Pou Papaka's election for Waimana, Tawhana, and Ohiwi had over-ridden the influential leader Te Whiu Maraki's original election for Waimana, due to the insistence of two other influential leaders, Tamaikoha and Rakuraku. These changes reveal the ambiguity of the notion of regional or local representation, as well as the influence of some leaders over an election, and suggest that the Tūhoe were making an effort to approximate electoral 'regions' in the sense intended in the Act.

Whereas Tutakangahau was a Tūhoe *rangatira* of established *mana*, there was no "Kutu Te Kikiwa" in Best's 1898 genealogical census of Tūhoe, which is the most comprehensive archival record available and includes a few deceased generations (Best 1898: 28, 62). However, there was a Kutu Huta, who may have been the same person (*te kikiwa* means 'the black/dark one', and may have been a nick-name). Kutu Huta's daughter Te Uru was the second wife of Hakeke, the *rangatira* war leader Tamaikoha's *mātāmua* ('first-born') and eldest son (see Chap. 4), so Kutu may have been another Tūhoe leader and favored by Tamaikoha. However, there is little archival evidence of any other leadership positions held by Kutu Huta: in 1899, he submitted no claims in the name of any hapū, nor was he named to any of the 1902 or 1907 block committees. Although by 1903 he had been recognized to hold leading shares in Te Waipotiki and Te Whaiti blocks, they were only weak shares and his rights were recognized in only six other blocks, suggesting that his predecessors were immigrants to the Urewera.

As will be more fully discussed in Part II, the leading *rangatira* of the Ruatāhuna area was Te Whenuanui I until his death in 1894, and thereafter his son Te Haka, Te Whenuanui II. An intriguing possibility (that I will not pursue in this work) is that in the wake of Te Whenuanui I's death Tamaikoha's influence was sufficiently dominant in Te Urewera hapū (his as well as Te Whenuanui I's primary affiliation) to promote his first-born son Hakeke's father-in-law to represent the Ruatāhuna region on the Commission despite Kutu's limited *mana* in other respects. Insofar a Kutu was soon replaced, this possibility is consistent with Tamaikoha's indignant appeal in 1906 for increased shares in Ruatāhuna where, as a *rangatira* of Ngāti Kurī as well as Te Urewera hapū, one would expect he would hold leading shares. The replacement of Kuta Hutu by Tutakangahau, representing Ruatāhuna as well as Maungapōhatu regions may have been some quid pro quo balancing Tamaikoha's favor of Te Pou Papaka over Te Whiu Maraki in the Waimana region: Maungapōhatu was the center of Tutakangahau's primary hapū Tamakaimoana, but he had no leading *mana* in the Ruatāhuna area, receiving only token recognition of rights in the block. In any case, the apparent absence of Te Haka Te Whenuanui II, who succeeded Te Whenuanui I in 1894 and in other respects held the leading *mana* of the Ruatāhuna area, from consideration as the representative of that region raises further important but unanswered questions.

I suggest that the election or nomination of Tūhoe commissioners, reflecting actual Tūhoe social organization more than the preconceptions of the legislation, represented dominant hapū more than it did these supposed electoral regions. It is true that the legislation was as preoccupied with hapū as it was with electoral regions, but insofar as it sought to 'divide the Urewera district into blocks, adopting as far a possible hapu boundaries…' it was naively assumed that hapū actually were local or regional and that the two would more or less coincide. As will become clear later, this popular misconception of hapū was the source of many of the problems of the commission.

At the first formal meeting of the commission on 1 February 1899 in Whakatane, a list of "the hapu of Te Urewera" was drawn up in such a way that each was spoken for by only one Tūhoe commissioner (UMB 1: 4–7; reproduced in Fig. 2.2 as recorded by Best). Although the five supposed electoral regions or districts were prominent in the listing, and were listed primarily under the name of the commissioner apparently representing them, hapū were the leading concern and nine different settlement areas were actually named. Another of the considerations of the Commission at this meeting was the Urewera locations at which they would hold their sittings, but, again, seven not five settlements were proposed the following day (Rūātoki, Waimana, Te Houhi, Te Whaiti, Ruatāhuna, Maungapōhatu, and Waikaremoana).

On this signal occasion of the commission's first meeting, 45 hapū of the Tūhoe or 'Te Urewera' were named. Ten hapū were named by Numia at five locations, including Te Houhi, Ruatāhuna, Te Waimana, and Ohāua as well as Rūātoki, the region he supposedly represented; fifteen hapū were named by Tutakangahau at six locations, including Rūātoki, Waimana, Tawhana, and Te Waiiti as well Ruatāhuna and Maungapōhatu, the regions he supposedly represented; four hapū were named by Te Pou at two locations, including Tawhana as well as Te Waimana, the region he supposedly represented when first elected; six hapū were named by Hurae Puketapu at three locations, including Te Whaiti and Ruatāhuna as well as Waikaremoana, the region he supposedly represented; and ten hapū were named by Mehaka Tokopounamu at four locations, including Rūātoki and Te Whaiti as well as Galatea and Te Houhi, the regions he supposedly represented. Nine different settlement areas or localities were actually named for the 45 hapū, with 34 hapū located 'at' one locality, nine hapū located 'at' two localities, and two hapū located 'at' three localities.

This information is one of the few places in the minutebooks where a hapū is associated with a particular locality. Even when a hapū was recorded to be located at one place, although most members and some land rights may have been relatively centralized there, it is likely that both were actually more scattered. Definite settlements or homesteads were small but numerous in the Urewera, and even the *primary* residences of Tūhoe at this time were probably quite scattered and only notionally reducible to

Fig. 2.2 Hapū and locations listed by Tūhoe commissioners in the first meeting of commission

Given by Numia:

N. Rongo	at Ruatoki, Te Houhi, and Ohaua
N. Koura	at Ruatoki, Ruatahuna, and Te Waimana
N. Ha	at Ruatoki and Ohaua
Hamua	at Ruatoki
N. Muriwai	at Ruatoki
N. Kumara	at Ruatoki
N. Turanga	at Ruatoki and Waimana
Mahurehure	at Ruatoki
N.Te Kapo	at Ruatoki
N. Mura karehe	at Ruatoki

Given by Tu takana hau:

N. Te Kahu	at Tawhana
N. Maru	at Maunga pohatu
N. Potiki	at Maunga pohatu
Tama kai moana	at Maungapohatu
N. Tu mata wha	at Maungapohatu
N. Tatua	at Waimana
N. Kuri	at Maungapohatu and Te Wai iti
N. Te Riu	at Ruatahuna
N. Kakahu Tapiki	at Ruatahuna
N. Ruatahuna	at Ruatahuna
N. Tawhaki	at Ruatahuna and Ruatoki
N. Koro kai Whenua	at Ruatoki
N. Tamakere	at Maungapohatu and Ruatahuna
N. Wehi o te Rangi	at Ruatahuna
N. Tuhaere	at Ruatahuna

Given by Te Pou:

Whakatane	at Te Waimana
Ngamaihi	at Te Waimana and Tawhana
N. Tamaroki	at Te Waimana
N. Tama	at Te Waimana

Given by Hurae Puketapu:

Maarakoho	at Te Whaiti
N. Manunui	at Ruatahuna and Waikare
N. Pa ki tua	at Waikare
N. Hinekura	at Waikare
Te Whanaupani	at Waikare
N. Taraparoa	[left blank]

Given by Mihaka:

Patuheuheu	at Te Houhi
N. Hiki	at Te Houhi
N. Manawa	at Te Houhi and Galatea
N. Hui	at Galatea
N. Te Au	at Galatea
N. Whare	at Te Whaiti
N. Te Koraha [Karaka?]	at Te Whaiti
N. Hape	at Galatea
N. Mahanga	at Galatea
N. Rakei	at Ruatoki and Te Houhi

nine settlements. Seasonal cultivation, gathering, and use of other resources, as rights of members of a particular hapū, probably always involved temporary or seasonal residences for each *whānau* ('extended family') or part of a *whānau*, often far from their primary residence.[5] Although the primary residence of hapū leaders might be so generalized, the 'location' of any given hapū was certainly even more notional than that of *whānau* or individuals. The Tūhoe, always relatively reliant on gathering and hunting—and confined to the Urewera mountains ever since the loss of their best agricultural lands in the 1860s confiscations—were probably more transient than any time in their earlier history.

The formality, publicity, and probably prepared coordination of this naming and location of hapū in the commission's first meeting were significant. Although the meeting was held in Whakatane (outside their *Rohe Pōtae*) rather than Rūātoki, it is likely that it was attended by some other leaders (the minutes did not usually note whether other Tūhoe were present at hearings, but approvals and objections make it clear that they were widely attended at least by prominent leaders). It is significant that no hapū was named by more than one commissioner. Tūhoe and Māori in general carefully avoid speaking for or about other hapū unless they are acknowledged to be affiliated with that hapū, and even then are careful to defer to others whose affiliation is stronger or more senior. Especially in such a formal context, heard by other Tūhoe leaders as well as the other commissioners, the naming of a hapū certainly implied acknowledged affiliation and perhaps leadership of that hapū, as well as representation of it as an electoral 'region'. This is also a reasonable assumption considering that (as will be shown in Chap. 4) by 1902 many Urewera leaders' land rights were confirmed in at least 10 and as many as 24 of the 35 Urewera blocks, reflecting at least weak and sometimes strong membership rights in several hapū.

Thus the Tūhoe commissioners could stand as representatives and publicly name the many hapū that they did because they had sufficient *mana* in each hapū named. It is furthermore likely that by prior agreement, with other hapū leaders as well as among themselves, the Tūhoe commissioners had arranged or implicitly acknowledged that only the one among them who had the strongest right to speak for a particular hapū would list it, and be deferred to by other commissioners who had a weaker or no acknowledged right.

Contrary to continuing preconceptions, scholarly as well as popular, contemporary Māori hapū are not localized or regional kin groups, and probably never were even before European contact (Webster 1975, 1998). Although hapū may maintain loyalty to ancestrally symbolic localities (such as a primary residence of a founding ancestor), and may maintain a core membership living in such a locality, because land rights as well as ancestral descent are traced cognatically (through both parents), their social organization is ***inherently*** scattered geographically and overlapping in membership with other hapū.

As will become clear in the following chapters, the hapū organization of Tūhoe was in this general form during these years. Yet hapū were clearly the keystone of their political organization. For this reason, although compromises may have been made to maintain the appearances of the electoral regions expected in the legislation, the actual political representation of the commissioners was almost certainly based primarily on hapū affiliations and leadership. Their 'election' in this context was probably through selection by the consensus of leaders in accord with relative status rank (from ***mātāmua*** (first-born) through ***kaumātua*** ('elders' of both genders) to ***rangatira*** ('chiefs')) in each hapū they represented in this situation, as much for their ability to deal with the Crown as the strength of affiliation and seniority of descent in that hapū. Insofar as hapū leadership was primarily based on popular consensus among all members of a hapū as expressed by their elders, the commissioners had indeed been popularly 'elected'. It is furthermore likely that the Tūhoe had become aware of the misleading Pākehā assumption that hapū were localized or regional, and decided that it would be easier for them to navigate this ambiguity than reform the Parliament's preconception of electoral regions.

While the preceding arguments may establish a prima facie case for the legitimacy of the commission among Tūhoe at large, there are also good reasons supporting Binney's and Sissons' doubts about this that must be assessed. First, there was an element of coercion to survey and establish Crown titles in the Urewera that echoed coercive procedures in the Native Land Court and was carried over into the commission.

Prime Minister Seddon's visit to the Urewera in 1894 had been prompted by confrontations over the government's efforts to initiate surveys in the Rūātoki and the Te Whaiti regions of the *Rohe Pōtae a Tūhoe*. In his discussions in Rūātoki and the several other settlements he visited, Seddon emphasized to the Tūhoe that the Crown could not defend their lands from settlers without official surveys and titles. The Tūhoe would not have failed to see this caution as a subtle threat that they would be on their own if they continued to be uncooperative with the Crown. Similarly, ever since the founding of the Native Land Court in 1865, the law had enabled 'any Māori' to apply for a survey and submit a claim for any land without regard to the settled customary rights of other Māori, which would then be for the Court to investigate and decide. While maintaining the appearances of neutrality, this policy had the intended effect of forcing Māori to appear in court and file counter-claims in order to defend their legitimate rights against opportunists (Sorrenson 1956). There is no doubt that a similar coercive dynamic operated to some extent in the 1899 hearings of the commission, when the number of claims laid escalated rapidly by the time of the Ruatāhuna hearings and eventually numbered more than 200 for the 35 blocks of the reserve. This situation will be examined later, but breakaway leaders and hapū were probably taking advantage of the entirely new opportunity to establish independence.

Second, the enforcement of individual ownership in common upon customary communal tenure by hapū does appear to have found its way into the 1896 Act. The commission's requirement that each individual be assigned relative shares of ownership in common within what was nevertheless assumed to be 'hapū blocks', that is, blocks found by the commission to be customarily owned by a hapū, was probably a late addition to the 1896 Act and not clearly negotiated with Tūhoe (Marr 2002: 99–100). Indeed, in 1907 the final block orders dropped all mention of 'families' or 'whānau', specifying only 'persons' as 'owners' of the shares. Notoriously among Māori since the 1860s, the Native Land Court had undermined Māori control of their lands first by naming a limited number of trustees but treating them as exclusive owners of the land ('the ten-owner rule') and, when that tactic was finally stopped, by listing all owners individually (the 'memorial of ownership'), thus encouraging faction, partition, and alienation. Hapū themselves could be named as owners in common, but this was very rarely done under the Court. In the case of the 1896 Act, the listing of individual shareholders was intended for electoral purposes, but potentially individualized land ownership as well. Indeed, by 1910 and the onset of the Crown purchasing campaign, this provision was to be the undoing of the Urewera District Native Reserve and the *Rohe Pōtae a Tūhoe*. Finally, if these notoriously threatening policies were implicit in the operation of the UDNR commission, how could it be claimed that its statutory role was any different from that of the Native Land Court?

Binney's and Sissons' arguments and the preliminary evidence above can be taken further. The question of the legitimacy of the commission needs to be more fully assessed with regard to four specific situations that emerged before the commission in 1899 and 1900:

(i) the apparent reluctance of at least one important Tūhoe *rangatira*, Tamaikoha, to cooperate with the commission;
(ii) his and several other leaders' demands that land blocks be awarded in the name of trustees or hapū rather than a list of individuals;
(iii) the charge that the commission operated in the manner of the Native Land Court and thus weakened Tūhoe control over their lands; and
(iv) an apparent effort by some Tūhoe leaders to force resignations among the Tūhoe commissioners.

The remainder of this chapter will be devoted to an examination of each of these situations in turn.

Tamaikoha Te Ariari and his extensive hapū branch are the subject of Chaps. 4 and 5. Sissions concludes that by the end of the March 1899 hearings the influential leaders "Tamaikoha, Rakuraku, Te Whiu and others from Te Waimana remained reluctant participants in a process over which they had little control", initially finding the commission's procedures so deeply disturbing that the first two agreed not to place their Tauranga valley lands before it (Sissons 2002: 104–107). These three elders had been war leaders, and their attitude toward the commission would have been very influential indeed. However, although the secretary Elsdon Best did record such protests among some Tūhoe leaders, I interpret their positions to be much more ambiguous. Unfortunately, Best's minutes were detailed when he considered the proceedings important evidence for the case at hand (or for his ethnological interests), but otherwise they were often brief and elliptic, even where discussions were central to the procedures of the commission itself.

Tamaikoha was first recorded to participate in a discussion of the boundaries of Te Ranga a Ruanuku block on 20 February 1899 in Rūātoki at Tauarau marae, joining in several routine objections to boundaries and lists of claimants (UMB 1: 49). However, on 23 February at the beginning of the first hearing in Waimana, Tamaikoha stood to ask if he could address the commission, and said that "the Māori are not content to submit their lists for the Waimana blocks at the present time" (UMB 1: 59). When the chairman asked if this was the consensus of all the people rather than just his own and Rakuraku's idea, eight others expressed support for his position. However, probably indicating that Tamaikoha and Rakuraku were considering a less passive boycott of the commission, these supporters also said they would be against withdrawing their lands entirely from the *rohe pōtae*, that is, from the commission's jurisdiction. This public reservation, probably from other elders, suggests that the three old war leaders were not backed by a wide consensus. In response, Tamaikoha clarified that he and Rakuraku were merely being careful, wishing to observe the procedure of the commission before submitting claims and lists.

Nonetheless, immediately on the following day 24 February, Tamaikoha handed in his first claim list (A19), probably in the name of Whakatane hapū for Te Hukanui, a part of Parekohe block (UMB 1: 66; also 1: 78). Can his doubts have been mollified so soon? Earlier that day he had expressed conditional support for other lists (and was later joined in this by Rakuraku), and stated a whakapapa showing that Ngāti Hinekura and Ngāti Taumata hapū were 'one people', both within Ngāi Te Riu hapū. At this time, some influential support appears to have fallen away from him: the *rangatira* Te Amo Kokouri, whose primary influence was in Ruatāhuna, stood to clarify that he no longer agreed with Tamaikoha and Rakuraku (that the lists of hapū claimants should be withheld), and felt that it was well that the commission would come to Ruatāhuna. It appears that other leaders were also observing the procedure of the commission before deciding whether or not to cooperate with it.

In the following two seasons of commission hearings Tamaikoha participated in claims and lists of several hapū for at least 13 different blocks of the 35 being formed in the Native Reserve (see Fig. 1.2): Te Hukanui (later the southern extension of Parekohe), Whaitiripapa (a tiny block appearing in Rūātoki No. 3), Te Purenga, Taneatua, Paraoanui, Papatupu (Pukepohatu), Tauwhare-Manuka, Ohāua o te Rangi, Paraeroa, Pukepohatu (later part of Paraeroa), and Rūātoki 1, 2, and 3. Far from having no control over the commissions' proceedings, I would suggest that perhaps more than any of the other *rangatira* who were closely consulted by the Tūhoe commissioners, he was able to influence decisions made outside of the formal sessions and place fait accompli before them. Sissons' own analysis shows that several of the blocks which were awarded (i.e., confirmed) to hapū in which Tamaikoha was a prominent leader were uncontested and virtually rubber-stamped by the commission.

Tamaikoha did later protest that his submission of a list for the Tauwhare-Manuka block was coerced because others were laying claims to it while it was well known to be rightfully his (Sissons 2002: 105–6). As explained above, one of the primary causes of widespread hostility toward the Native Land Court was the coercion of owners to submit a claim in order to prevent the award of their land to interlopers. Probably relying on deference by others to his predominant *mana* in several blocks, Tamaikoha submitted no formal claims for them, and this may have been his intention for Tauwhare-Manuka block until these challenges to his *mana* obtruded. On the other hand, Tamaikoha apparently did not raise this complaint with regard to any of his many other formal claims.

The process of laying claims for blocks during 1899 was probably felt to be coercive in some cases. There was a rapid and perhaps competitive increase in the submission of claims in the name of specific hapū by the time the commission sat in Ruatāhuna. However, I will argue later that this was due to an acceleration in the splits and mergers normal among hapū asserting relative independence, rather than subversion of hapū solidarity by opportunists intending to sell, as was promoted in the Native Land Court. It must be emphasized that while some degree of coercion and individualization of title was implicit in the 1896 Act, it was on the whole radically unlike the Land Court procedure insofar as it was explicitly devoted to claims and awards in the name of hapū holding the land in common, intended individual shareholding to function as an electoral role rather than promote partition and alienation of land, and reserved the power to alienate to the *Komiti Nui* or General Committee, which was composed of representatives from each hapū block.

Another form of challenge to the commission that emerged a month later in late March 1899 may have been associated with Tamaikoha and Rakurakus' early threat to withdraw the Tauranga/Waimana lands from its jurisdiction, at least temporarily. The new challenge took the form of insisting that the land blocks be established under the names of *tiake* (*kai-tiake*; caretakers or trustees) or entire hapū rather than the individual members of hapū. The demand that the block orders be in the name of caretakers appears to have arisen on the first day of the hearing at Toreatai (Toreatau?) *marae* at Maungapōhatu on 28 March 1899 (UMB 1: 169–70). The hearings through the previous month since Te Waimana had been held at Te Houhi, Te Whaiti, and Ruatāhuna, consecutively, and already more than 175 claim lists had been submitted in the name of about 40 different hapū.

The Tūhoe commissioner Tutakangahau, a prominent *rangatira*, had stood down from the commission to make a claim, and spoke first regarding a delay in submission of his list in the name of the Tamakaimoana hapū. The second speaker was the *rangatira* Te Wharau (probably Te

Wharau Tapuae, not Te Wharau Tamaro; (Best 1898: 7, 8)), who led off by remarking trenchantly that '*kua mutu te unuunu e nga tangata nga whenua o roto i te raina a Tamaikowha raua ko Rakuraku*' (the people have finished taking apart the lands at the center of Tamaikoha and Rakurakus' lineage). Te Wharau was probably referring to a block considered at the hearing in the Waimana area, perhaps Te Hukanui or Paraoanui. He went on to ask if the commissioners had appointed Tamaikoha and Rakuraku as caretakers of these lands, stating that if they had done so he would object and insist on adding six additional caretakers representing other hapū. He would also accept it if the commissioners were to name (entire) hapū as caretakers of the block, but cited a case where the land was lost to its owners because only a single caretaker had been named.

Although Te Wharau appears to have been unclear regarding the commission's procedure, his demand was subtle and well-informed. It appears that in order to safeguard their land from alienation, he was opposed to leaving it in the hands of a single trustee, instead insisting on a distribution of trusteeship among several hapū leaders or naming the hapū itself (or several) as owner. However, it is significant that he may also have been rejecting the alternative of naming individually all the members of a hapū, or all persons found to be legitimate owners of a block ('the people have finished *taking apart* the land…'). He also seems to have been aware of the earlier Native Land Court strategies of limiting trustees and treating them as owners. He may furthermore have been laying responsibility for the 'taking apart' of Tamaikoha and Rakurakus' lands at the feet of their 'people' (i.e., the members of their hapū) as much as the commission.

The implications raised by Te Wharau's challenge turn out to be crucial for the reserve, both for the moment and in the coming years, but unfortunately Best's minutes do not clarify them without further interpretation. Te Wharau was supported in his demand by three other leaders: Taihakoa, Paora Kingi, and Tamaikoha himself. Paora Kingi explained that if Te Wharau's demand for additional caretakers was not met, he would withdraw his part of the land from the block because he was presently in conflict with Tamaikoha, who he said insisted that Paora's part of the claim remain within Tamaikoha's boundary and hapū. This confrontation probably reflected claims for independence of new or included hapū from previously dominant ones, and the assertions of relative mana between hapū leaders. Taihakoa's position was probably similar to or allied to Paora Kingi's, and implies that the Paraoanui block was indeed the one 'taken apart' in the Waimana hearing because Taihakoa continued to confront

Tamaikoha over the rights to that block until finally it was partitioned in 1907 by the appeals commission.

The issues raised by the supporters of Te Wharau's demand therefore clarify some ambiguities: the demand that block ownership be in the name of trustees or hapū themselves was often a demand that the rights of several hapū to a given block be recognized. This in turn implied that simply naming as owners all the individual members of descent groups found to be rightful claimants of a given block was unacceptable to some leaders—probably because such a merger implied subordination of the hapū rights or independent leadership being pressed.

However, the commission appeared to foreclose on Te Wharau's demands. The chairman (Percy Smith) responded to Te Wharau by pointing out that they all had copies of the 1896 Act and it allowed neither for appointment of caretakers for such large blocks as these, nor for hapū to stand in the place of the owners as shareholders. Te Wharau immediately responded that this being the case, their land would be left quiet (i.e., withheld from the commission) and no claim lists would be submitted. The chairman then said that decision was up to them, but they should not later complain that the commission had not called for claims; they had been invited both at Waimana and at Maungapōhatu. So, in this confrontation, the threat of awarding land to other claimants had again been invoked. Finally, in support of Te Wharau, Tamaikoha warned that he would go to Wellington to find whether or not Tūhoe had the authority to act as caretakers for their lands. In response to Te Wharau's suspicion regarding the Waimana hearing, Tamaikoha clarified that '*E mohio ana ahau kaore aku mana ki te tiaki i aua whenua*' ('I know that the authority as caretaker of our lands is not ours'—that is to say, he and Rakuraku had not been appointed by the commission as caretakers for the Hukanui or Paraoanui block).

Although Te Wharau appears to have remained uncompromising in his protest, he actually submitted four claim lists the following day, 29 March 1899: for Paraoanui block in the name of Ngāti Hinekura hapū, Paraoanui block in the name of Ngāi Te Riu hapū, Ohiorangi block in the name of Ngāti Tama and Tūhoe hapū, and Paraoanui block in the name of Te Whakatane hapū. Furthermore, he had already submitted four other claims lists for other blocks at the Rūātoki and Ruatāhuna hearings. Thus it appears that, like Tamaikoha and his supporters the Waimana hearings, Te Wharau either gave in to the threat that others with less right would be recognized as owners of the block, or had made his demands primarily to assert his authority and register his doubts.

The demand for caretakers of blocks rather than individual shareholders emerged again in the following sitting 4 April 1899 at Waikaremoana on Waimako marae (UMB 1: 187–192, 197). Judge Butler, who had been absent from the hearing at Maungapōhatu, was present at Waikaremoana, and Percy Smith's responses appeared less self-assured and more revealing, arguing at length against Hori Wharerangi's articulate and informed doubts. Wharerangi was supported by 20 others at the hearing. He insisted that, like their rights to the Waipaoa block (just outside the Native Reserve to the north of Lake Waikaremoana) the previous decade, their lands would be lost if they could not withdraw them from the jurisdiction of the commission or leave them in the name of caretakers. Their fears were clearly centered on the individualization of shares of ownership. Smith repeatedly assured Wharerangi and his supporters that under the Act their lands could never be sold or leased; in response, Wharerangi pointed out that many laws had been made for Māori lands and new laws might lead to alienations; Smith responded that the Act had the full support of parliament and would not be changed unless the Tūhoe themselves were successful in changing it. None of this reassured Wharerangi—and within two decades all his doubts would prove to be well-founded, most completely with regard to the Waikaremoana lands.

Although this challenge to the commission was here put most strongly, it appears to have come mainly from Ngāti Ruapani who sometimes considered themselves to be an independent *iwi* separate from Tūhoe. This separate status may have implied disadvantage to Ngāti Ruapani: in his refusal to let Wharerangi withdraw his hapū lands from the Native Reserve, the chairman attempted to convince him it was only in 'Pākehā thinking' that all hapū within the *rohe* were considered to be hapū of the Tūhoe iwi, and that he should not let that worry him. Nevertheless, Wharerangi clearly saw himself as defending Tūhoe lands as a whole: '*kua oti te hoatu i tenei whenua e Tūhoe ki to ringa. Ko te mate tuatahi tenei i mahia nei e koe. Ki muri ko te ruri, i muri i tena ko the whakawa…*' (the giving over of these lands of the Tūhoe into your hands is finished. This is only the first step. Next will be the surveying, and then will come the investigating…) (UMB 1: 189).

Again, contrary to his informed and uncompromising position, the following day Wharerangi is recorded to have submitted a claim list of individuals for the Waikaremoana block in behalf of Ngāti Ruapani and four hapū, at least two of which were clearly part of the Tūhoe *iwi*. He also submitted another claim list in the name of four hapū including Ruapani, perhaps a few weeks later. The block was finally awarded to members of Ngāti Ruapani as well as Tūhoe (the Tūhoe *hapū*, later known as Te Urewera *hapū*). However, neither Wharerangi nor 9 of his 20 supporters appear at all in the final 1903 block lists, and most of the remaining twelve supporters were recognized to hold shares in only a few blocks, mainly Waikaremoana, Ruatāhuna, and Maungapōhatu. As he had said, he and many other Ngāti Ruapani might have truly been left *whenua rawakore* (landless) by the earlier loss of their rights in the Waipaoa block outside the reserve.

Considering these early objections to the commission, the balance of evidence suggests that they did not generally act under a sense of compulsion, but instead intended to assess the fairness of its procedures and soon offered cooperation by laying their claims and arguing their cases. Tūhoe leaders had, after all, negotiated the terms of the 1896 Act and considered its implications for several years, and their selected leaders were a majority when the commission was finally formed. Tūhoe notoriously follow the political ideal of carefully forming a consensus and then acting upon it in solidarity, and these objectors appear to be conforming, albeit reluctantly, with this ideal. A further explanation might be that some leaders who continued to harbor doubts intended to assert their *mana* and register them publicly, but proceeded to cooperate with the commission once this had been done.

The Waikaremoana hearing was the commission's last in the 1899 season. At the beginning of the commission's following season in February 1900 a third form of challenge to its legitimacy emerged at Rūātoki: the charge that the commission was proceeding in much the same way as the Native Land Court. The earlier challenges threatening to withdraw lands from the jurisdiction of the commission, refusing to submit claims lists, and demanding that the blocks be left in the care of trustees or hapū, reflected specific criticisms of the Court's routine procedure; now the more general charge explicitly emerged.

It was in this context that the provision of the 1896 Act to list individual owners in each block as an electoral role was made explicit by the commission itself. Although it was argued above that non-regional hapū constituencies were the actual basis, from the point of view of the Act, regional electoral roles had also been the fundamental assumption guiding the election of the Tūhoe commissioners in 1896–1899. In his 1899 report for the commission, Chairman Smith described the two objects of the 1896 Act to be the ascertainment of the owners of the Urewera district, and the division of "the country into areas which are to serve as the basis for the local government of the tribes" (Smith in AJHR 1899: x–xi). Judith Binney doubts that the government sincerely intended this electoral purpose, suspecting that individualized ownership was actually intended to facilitate alienation of the Urewera lands much as it had been in the Native Land Court (Binney 2002: 230–234). However, the following evidence suggests to the contrary that at least Chairman Smith took the statutory provision of electoral roles seriously.

The chairman's remarks on 6 February 1900 suggest that the criticism of the commission as no better than the Court had been in the air the preceding year. He explained the general procedure for their first block investigation (to be the Te Waipotiki block) in contrast to the procedure of the Court (UMB 1: 209). He emphasized that unlike the Court the Natives were to conduct their own cases before the commission, that they selected their own guides for the surveyors, and that relatives of these guides could conduct their own cases (he meant that for each block, each contending hapū would select surveyor guides and conductors). The Waipotiki case was to show the Natives that contentions over boundaries or rights would be worked out on the spot to their own satisfaction as the investigation of each block was worked through.

As it turned out, after an exhaustive 3 weeks and over 100 dense pages of minutes investigating boundaries and rights to Te Waipotiki block alone, and faced with the prospect of more than 30 more block investigations, Chairman Smith and Judge Butler urgently pressed for an expedited procedure. Gaining the support of most of the Tūhoe commissioners, they contended that the problem with the procedure for Te Waipotiki was that it took as long as it would before the Native Land Court (26 February 1900; UMB 3: 136–140; Judge Butler claimed it had taken even longer). Reinforcing his remarks earlier that month, Chairman Smith pointed out that the Act

> said there should not be any connection of the Native Land Court with this land. The Commissioners will undertake the best method of proceeding with this land so that the said land will be investigated easily and without adhering to Native Land Court's Acts as these acts are executed with great difficulty. We are not to investigate these land[s] so that they may be sold or lease[d] but we are here to ascertain the electoral localities in this land. (UMB 3: 136–7)

Smith's emphasis here on the electoral purposes of the commission in accord with the Act, contrasted to the admitted alienation purposes of the Native Land Court, is significant. The previous year he had raised these electoral purposes quite spontaneously when discussing how inadvertent omissions from the claimant lists might later be added. In the context of commissioner Tutakangahau's concern that members of his hapū claiming shares in Tarapounamu block were very widely scattered, Smith had emphasized

> *Ko te tino hiahia kia homai katoa nga ingoa o nga tangata katoa o roto i te rohe potae... mehemea kaore ratau e whakaatu i o ratau nei ingoa ki a koe akuanei pea kaore ratau e whai pooti* (the main desire is to have all the names of all the people in the Rohe Potae a Tūhoe... if they do not give their names to you now perhaps later they will not be able to vote/count). (UMB 1: 165)

Smith was clearly referring to the establishment of a system of representative home-rule by committees as mandated by the Urewera District Native Reserve Act. These several comments in different contexts imply that his own commitment to the ideals avowed by the Act was sincere. His position as chairman renders it the more unlikely that he was cynically concealing a real intention to alienate Tūhoe lands, and this reasoning can probably be extended to the original intentions of the Act as well as to his protégé Elsdon Best and to Judge Butler. Although such sincerity could be attributed to Smith and Bests' enthusiasm and naiveté as amateur ethnologists, Smith's usual role as Surveyor General renders this unlikely. The reversal of Parliament's original intention and the subversion of the Act by 1910 were under another administration, and in any case not uncommon in the history of Māori land legislation.

The last of the four sorts of early challenges to the commission to be assessed is an apparent effort by some Tūhoe to purge some or all of the Tūhoe commissioners between June and August 1900, during the commission's first winter adjournment.[6] This development again involved the Tūhoe *rangatira* Tamaikoha Te Ariari. If the initiative reflected significant popular discontent with the Tūhoe commissioners regardless of their appropriate representation of hapū as argued earlier, it would indeed compromise the legitimacy of the commission.

On 25 June the commissioner Hurae Puketapu wrote to Chairman Smith reporting that Tamaikoha had approached him to say that some hapū of Tūhoe objected strongly to the commission's decisions on the lands and wanted him (Hurae), Tutakangahau, and Te Pou Papaka to be removed from the commission (Hurae represented the hapū of settlements in the Waikaremoana and Te Whaiti areas; Tutakangahau the hapū of Maungapohatu and Ruatāhuna areas; and Te Pou the hapū of the Tauranga/Waimana basin). Hurae reported that Tamaikoha had refused to explain why, but he felt it was merely jealousy.

Several weeks later on 9 August 1900 the commissioner Numia Kererū wrote Smith to inform him that it was the commissioners Hurae Puketapu and Mehaka Tokopounamu (representative for Te Houhi and Galatea) themselves who proposed that the Tūhoe commissioners be dispensed with and that Māori commissioners from other localities (i.e., outside the *rohe pōtae o Tūhoe*) be appointed in their place. Numia reported that Makarini Tamarau, Mehaka, and Tupara Temana were taking a petition on the issue to Wellington from a meeting held at Ruatāhuna. Numia himself felt that 'if they wish to resign, well and good' and others should be appointed in their place. Although he did not specify it in the message, Numia probably meant that the replacements should be Tūhoe leaders rather than outsiders. Smith replied to Numia that he doubted that the government would accept any changes of the commissioners, and this turned out to be correct.

In order to assess the possible bearing of these accusations and counter-accusations on the legitimacy of the commission, further evidence can be examined. The apparent conflicts may have been rooted in the major factions among Tūhoe hapū which arose February 1897–March 1898, the records of which were discovered and analyzed by Judith Binney (2002: 223–234). Binney attributes the splits to Tūhoe frustration at delays and the failure of the Crown to support their efforts to organize in implementation of the UDNR Act that lay neglected since its passage in 1896. Mehaka, Makarini Tamarau, and Hurae Puketapu (the same three involved in the complaints about the Tūhoe commissioners between June and August 1900) were leaders in the establishment of a 'council' which split the February 1897 meeting held at Ruatāhuna, causing the walkout by the other major faction, which was led by Tamaikoha and his senior son Hakeke, Numia Kererū, Te Whiu Miraka, Rakuraku, and Paora Kingi. The faction including Tamaikoha and Numia appears to have been led by prominent *rangatira* mainly of the Tauranga/Waimana basin and some of Rūātoki, and was characterized as 'Ngāti Rongo' (Numia's primary hapū, based in Rūātoki) by Mehaka's faction. Mehaka's faction was characterized as centered in Ruatāhuna by Tamaikoha, Numia, and their faction, and both claimed to represent 20–34 hapū throughout the Urewera. The total number of hapū reported for the Urewera or Tūhoe *iwi* at this time varied from 24 (Best 1896, in Binney 2002: 498) to 45 (the Tūhoe commissioners 1899).

So far as the records indicate, both major factions supported the 1896 Act, albeit with some reservations. Binney is inclined to accept the claims of some senior leaders that the disaffections were overcome and unity re-achieved by March 1898 at the final of a series of meetings that were held at Waimana. Nevertheless, the re-emergence of Mehaka Tokopounamu as central in the attempted purge of the Tūhoe commissioners in 1900, confronted by Tamaikoha and probably Numia, suggests that the 1897 factions had not been fully unified by the Waimana meeting in February 1898. The alignment of these two factions also echoes another conflict that may have developed by 1899 over control of the relatively valuable timber and (rumored) gold resources in Te Whaiti Nui a Toi block on the western side of the Urewera. Although awarded by the commission to three hapū in 1902, the leading Tūhoe or Te Urewera *hapū* (distinguished from the Tūhoe or Urewera *iwi*) was thrown out by the appeals commission in 1907, leaving the entire block in the control of the two remaining hapū, Ngāti Whare and Ngāti Manawa, represented on the original commission by Mehaka Tokopounamu. A brief confrontation recorded in the minute-books in March 1899 suggests that at that time some claimants in the Te Whaiti block were set against Mehaka for not "adhering to the agreements made with the people" (UMB 1: 132). This charge may have originated from the Tūhoe (or Te Urewera) hapū with rights in that block, foreseeing Mehaka's strategy to exclude them contrary to earlier agreements.

The intervention of Tamaikoha in the original appointments of the five Tūhoe commissioners discussed above, and the possibility raised there that he was behind the initial appointment of Kuta Hutu with the intention of circumventing Te Whenuanui II's *mana* in the Ruatāhuna region, may also have been involved in the 1897 confrontation. In any case, the apparent efforts to purge some or all of the Tūhoe commissioners in 1900 was probably rooted in these earlier confrontations rather than factions resisting the 1896 Act or the investigative commission.

The concern of some leaders that the general procedure of the commission was potentially as damaging as that of the Native Land Court may have also been put to rest by the end of 1900, the second summer season of hearings. Chairman Percy Smith resigned the following summer season, probably in March 1901, and on 18 March on Judge Butler's motion Native Land Court Judge David Scannell was elected chairman by all the commissioners (UMB 4: 1). If there was still significant suspicion regarding the sincerity or fairness of the commission's procedures, Smith's replacement by a second Land Court judge would probably have been objected to by at least some of the Tūhoe commissioners. Scannell had heard extensive Tūhoe cases in the Native Land Court, notably the Rūātoki cases of the early 1890s, and would recuse himself from future hearings when this case was raised. Butler frequently acted as chairman thereafter and submitted the final report of the commission at the end of 1902.

The first part of this chapter summarized the procedure and findings of the UDNR commission 1899–1903. In the second part it has been argued that the balance of evidence indicates the commission was generally accepted as legitimate among Tūhoe leaders and people at large: the Tūhoe played a central role in the prolonged negotiation of the 1896 Act; the Tūhoe commissioners fairly represented the actual organization of hapū rather than an artificial division of electoral regions; the commission generally deferred in its procedures to the customs and extramural deliberations of the Tūhoe; some Tūhoe leaders who remained skeptical nevertheless reluctantly cooperated with the commission after publicly displaying the grounds of their objections; the Pākehā commissioners were sincerely committed to the electoral rather than the potentially disruptive effect of individualized shares of owners in the block lists; an apparent effort to purge the Tūhoe commissioners was rooted in earlier Tūhoe conflicts rather than factions resisting the Act; and, finally, the rich sociological content of the block lists would be shown in Chap. 4 to be the work of the Tūhoe commissioners themselves, probably largely unappreciated by their Pākehā colleagues who were content to be facilitating Tūhoe home-rule.

Notes

1. Most of the first minutebook has not been translated, but has been glossed in English by Himaima Tumoana (herself a Tūhoe) for the Tribunal. However, while I have been indispensably guided by her glosses, the translations of this minutebook which I quote, or rely on for interpretation, are my own. It is significant that the two minutebooks in Māori were probably rewritten by Best from his detailed and extensive notes, which apparently were originally taken in English and some shorthand (Best Urewera notes MS-Papers 1187-034, 293, 294, ATL). I have not yet examined these notes to see if there are important differences from the official minutebooks.

2. My approach differs in this important regard from that of Tama Nikora, a leading Tūhoe *rangatira* who has been central in the Tūhoe-Waikaremoana Trustboard for many years and helped to lead its most influential claim to the Waitangi Tribunal. Nikora is probably the most knowledgeable Tūhoe elder on historical matters. Rather than the 1903 provisional block lists, he has taken the final block lists published by the appeals commission in 1907 as foundational for a reconstruction of contemporary *iwi* membership, probably because it became the legal basis of shareholding in the Native Reserve. However, I argue that the legitimacy of the original commission, and the questionable impartiality of the appeals commission, makes the records of the former more reliable, at least ethnohistorically. Furthermore, due to the apparent loss of the original claims lists, the appeals commission's frequent addition of further owners in each block, usually merely to achieve closure after several years, would increase the difficulty of reconstructing hapū affiliations.
3. Kererū Te Pukenui Te Ruakariata was among the *rangatira* who hosted Seddon in his visit to Rūātoki in April 1894, first among the Urewera settlements visited on his tour (AJHR 1895: G-1, Vol II p. 48–79). Te Pukenui was the elder brother of Numia Kererū Te Ruakariata, who took on his brother's name after the elder's death in 1896, and was to become one of the more influential commissioners by 1899. Te Pukenui was repeatedly named by Seddon to his hosts in the other Urewera settlements, and after an apparently traumatic crossing of Lake Waikaremoana Seddon expressed gratitude for a safe passage to Tupaea Rapaera, who had been sent by Te Pukenui to personally accompany Seddon. Tupaea was actually *tuakana* or senior in birth to Pukenui and Numia, being the son of their sister Turaki, the mātāmua or eldest among the Te Ruakariata siblings (Best 1898: 33). Probably because of this *whakapapa raarangi* (genealogy of first-born), Tupaea was personally greeted by speaking *rangatira* in other Urewera settlements, even in Waikaremoana by Kahungunu leaders. When the bill was enacted, Seddon expressed regret to Parliament that Te Pukenui had died and was unable to witness the fruition of his work.
4. On the other hand, in the postscript to his *Tuhoe* … Best saw this work as a funereal epitaph, preserving a record of the Tūhoe as they had been traditionally, before fading away as a dying race. Reflecting the ahistorical understanding of culture of his time, he was even dismissive of the contemporary Tūhoe among whom he lived as authentic in his racial sense.
5. This was traditionally the case among many Māori, and most fully documented for the Ngāi Tahu of South Island (Anderson 1980), whose general ecological situation was comparable to the Urewera.
6. MS paper 1187 folder 297, Polynesian Society collection, Alexander Turnbull Library, Wellington, NZ.

References

AJHR 1895. The Prime Minister's visit to the Ureweras. Undated. Appendices to the Journal of the House of Representatives 1895, G-1, Vol II: 48–79.

AJHR 1899. Smith, S. Percy. "The Urewera District Native Reserve Act, 1896." Undated. Appendices to the Journal of the House of Representatives 1899, C-1: x–xi. Wellington, N.Z.

AJHR 1902. Butler, WK. "The Urewera District Native Reserve Act, 1896." 6 August 1902. Appendices to the Journal of the House of Representatives 1902, G-6: 1. Wellington, N.Z.

AJHR 1903. D. Scannell. 'Commissioners' Orders Under the "Urewera District Native Reserves Act, 1896."' Undated. Appendices to the Journal of the House of Representatives 1903, G-6: 1–256. Wellington, N.Z.

Anderson, A.J. 1980. "Towards an explanation of protohistoric social organisation and settlement patterns amongst the southern Ngai Tahu." *New Zealand Journal of Archaeology* 2: 3–23.

Best, Elsdon. 1898. "Tuhoe genealogies 1898" (spine title); "Genealogies of the Tuhoe tribe. Also includes all living members of the tribe in 1898, as given before the Urewera Commission set up under the act of 1896." Manuscript qMS [172]. Wellington, N.Z.: Alexander Turnbull Library. [NB: the author can supply a digital index for this resource.]

Best, Elsdon. 1973. *Tuhoe, Children of the Mist.* Vols. I and II (genealogies). Second edition. Wellington, N.Z.: A.H. and A.W. Reed Ltd. (first published 1925 as Vol VI of the Memoirs of the Polynesian Society).

Binney, Judith. 2002. *Encircled Lands; Part Two: A History of the Urewera 1878–1912.* An Overview Report on the Urewera for the Waitangi Tribunal. WAI 894, A15. Wellington, N.Z.: Waitangi Tribunal.

Firth, Raymond. 1959. *The Economics of the New Zealand Maori.* Second edition. Wellington, New Zealand: Government Printer. (1st edition 1929).

Holman, Jeffrey Paparoa. 2010. *Best of both worlds: the story of Elsdon Best and Tutakangahau.* Auckland, N.Z.: Penguin. 4,

Marr, Cathy. 2002. *The Urewera District Native Reserve Act 1896 and Amendments.* A report commissioned by the Waitangi Tribunal. WAI 894, A 21. Wellington, N.Z.: Waitangi Tribunal.

Sissons, Jeffrey. 1991. *Te Waimana, The Spring of Mana: Tuhoe History and the Colonial Encounter.* Dunedin, N.Z.: Otago University Press.

Sissons, Jeffrey. 2002. "Waimana Kaaku: A History of the Waimana Block." A report commissioned by the Crown Forestry Rental Trust, June 2002. Wellington, N.Z.: Waitangi Tribunal.

Sorrenson, M.P.K. 1956. "Land purchase methods and their effect on Māori population 1865–1901." *Journal of the Polynesian Society* 65 (3): 183–199.

Sorrenson, M.P.K. 2015. "The lore of the judges: Native land court judges' interpretations of Māori custom law." *Journal of the Polynesian Society* 124 (3): 223–242.

UMB 1. Urewera District Native Reserve Commission minute book 1 (identified as Urewera Commission minute book '3'), Smith, Butler, et al, (1Feb1899–8Mar1900), in Māori, Index 22pp., 382pp. NA Wgtn: Urewera MB 3, MLC 13, W3518, CD2, Vol 3, 397 pp.; NA Ak: AREPRO 4711/1445. Acronym: UMB 1.

UMB 3. Urewera District Native Reserve Commission minute book 3 (identified as '3A'; English translation of last part of UMB 1), Smith, Butler, et al, (9Feb1900–8Mar1900). 189 pp., index, NA Wgtn: Urewera MB 3A, MLC 13, W3518, CD 2, Vol 3A, 191 pp.; NA Ak: AREPRO 4711/1444. Acronym: UMB 3.

UMB 4. Urewera District Native Reserve Commission minute book 4 (English translation of UMB 2), Butler, Scannell, et al, (9Mar1900–May1900), index 12 pp., 344pp.; NA Wgtn: Urewera MB 4, MLC 13, W3518, CD 2, Vol. 4, 357 pp.; NA Ak: AREPRO 4711/1446. Acronym: UMB 4.

Webster, Steven. 1975. "Cognatic Descent Groups and the Contemporary Māori: a Preliminary Reassessment." *The Journal of the Polynesian Society* Vol. 84(2): 121–152, 1975.

Webster, Steven. n.d. (1984–5) "Urewera Land 1895–1926; a tentative historical survey of Government and Tuhoe relations as reflected in official records." Unpublished manuscript, 50pp. Held in the University of Auckland Library. Auckland, N.Z.

Webster, Steven. 1998, "Maori Hapu as a Whole Way of Struggle: 1840–50s Before the Land Wars." *Oceania* 69(1): 4–35.

Webster, Steven. 2004. *The Urewera Consolidation Scheme: Confrontations between Tuhoe and the Crown, 1915–1925.* Vols I, II. Report commissioned by the Waitangi Tribunal. WAI 894 #D8. Wellington, N.Z.: Waitangi Tribunal.

CHAPTER 3

Difficulties of the Commission Defining Urewera Blocks by *Hapū*

1 Introduction

The discussions in the previous chapter summarized the procedures and findings of the Urewera District Native Reserve commission between 1899 and 1903, and examined issues bearing on the legitimacy of the commission among the Tūhoe. Some of the apparent ambiguities of the Tūhoe organization of *hapū*, and the consequent difficulties of the commission dividing the Urewera district 'into blocks, adopting as far a possible hapu boundaries' (Butler in AJHR 1902: 1) have been briefly mentioned, but can now be addressed more fully. Insofar as *hapū* were and continue to be the most important feature of Māori social organization, this inquiry may also further our understanding of them.

The 1896 Act had recognized the central importance of hapū for home-rule of the reserve, but assumed they were tidy groups of kin coterminous with regions of land which could be surveyed into blocks the owners of which could be treated as electoral roles. To the contrary, hapū kin were scattered and overlapping rather than grouped locally, and the Tūhoe commissioners were more representative of hapū in this way than of discrete electoral regions. The blocks which were finally laid out were often awarded to more than one hapū, and their lists of owners overlapped extensively, as did the membership of their block or 'hapu' committees. The number, names, and organization of the hapū in the reserve, furthermore, went through major changes even during the commission's investigation.

© The Author(s) 2020

S. Webster, *A Separate Authority (He Mana Motuhake)*, Volume I,
https://doi.org/10.1007/978-3-030-41042-1_3

The specific difficulties of squaring the surveyed blocks of the Urewera with Tūhoe hapū will be examined below. In more general (and national) terms, the difficulty is best understood as resulting from the colonial imposition of a system of abstract line boundaries upon a system of highly specific narrative histories of land occupation and use. In addition, a system of exclusive ownership of land in a similarly abstract sense was imposed upon a system of distinctive rights to particular resources of particular areas of land, rivers, streams, forests, and even forest canopies (see Anderson 1980). Finally, the specificity of the narrative history thus overridden by line boundaries and private freehold ownership lay in a core of *whakapapa* (genealogy) connecting ancestors who had lived on or used these resources, embellished with events recorded in names, songs, and stories.

More fundamentally still, while the established system of land tenure was founded upon use values in specific social and historical contexts, the new tenure was intended to transform these into abstract exchange or commodity values, thus 'freeing' the values for the purposes of capital from these restraining contexts. In an earlier era, the Doomsday Book of Old England and enclosures of the commons had underwritten a parallel transformation in Britain, individualizing and privatizing what had been rights held in common and passed down through families. This earlier transformation in Britain lay the groundwork for the capitalist political economy which was just beginning to flower there by the time of the Treaty of Waitangi, and quite consciously became the colonizing basis of New Zealand (Webster 1998).

These political economic ideologies were further complicated by assumptions regarding Māori kinship organization which had also been entrenched since earliest colonization. These assumptions remain entrenched today in policies as well as popular misunderstanding, regardless of better practical understanding handed down by such institutions as the Native Land Court, some early commentators and later scholars and, of course, Māori themselves. At the most spontaneous and naive level, Māori society has conventionally been seen to be organized in three levels of what are assumed to be kin groups: *whānau* (extended 'families'), *hapū* ('subtribes'), and *iwi* ('tribes'). Often a fourth most inclusive level is added: *waka* ('canoes'). Numbers vary widely, but in the early 1900s Best characterized Tūhoe *whānau* as being composed of about 50 persons; among contemporary hapū, membership usually ranges from fewer than 50 to several hundred persons.

Most misleadingly, these three or four levels of Māori social organization are assumed to be organized hierarchically, that is, *iwi* ('tribes') are divided into *hapū* ('subtribes'), and hapū are divided into *whānau* ('extended families'). This entire hierarchy is furthermore assumed to be based on kinship by descent: each hapū is distinguished by descent from a common ancestor, all of which are in turn descendants of the *iwi* ancestor. Each group is often assumed to be headed by an authority, also organized hierarchically into *kaumātua* ('elder') for each *whānau*, *rangatira* ('chief') for each hapū, and an *ariki* as paramount authority for the iwi. These divisions have long been assumed to occur through ordinary 'growth' of the society and 'fission' of larger into smaller groupings of kin. Similarly, complications of the tidy hierarchy have long been assumed to be the result of 'intermarriage' and implicitly viewed as confusing some more natural or autochthonous order.

Contrary to this simplistic model of Māori kinship, some contemporary commentators have argued that whereas hapū are kin groups in the strict sense of cognatic descent groups recognizing a common ancestor, *whānau* and *iwi* are descent groups only in loose senses (Metge 1967; Webster 1975, 1997, 1998; Ballara 1998). Unlike hapū, *whānau* include spouses, adopted, and others who often do not affiliate with the same ancestor and belong to other hapū; thus they are not descent groups at all. *Iwi*, also unlike hapū, are usually not descent groups in any strict sense but rather confederations of hapū which might historically or even temporarily set up a common *iwi* ancestor for political reasons. The evidence from Ballara (1998) and Webster (1998) shows that these basic differences obtained in early colonial times as well as among contemporary Māori.

The founding ancestor of a hapū is much less likely to be changed, and is often the basis of the name of the hapū. Being a member of or belonging to a hapū necessarily means that one can trace genealogical descent or *whakapapa* down through a line of predecessors—either male or female in each generation—from an ancestor who is considered to be the founder of the hapū (anthropologically, this is termed 'cognatic descent'). In addition to this minimum requirement, for stronger rights to hapū land as well as membership, one must show that residence on or use of the particular land claimed in the name of that hapū, or at least active participation in the hapū affairs of that particular land, has been maintained at least since the generation of the great-grandparent through whom one traces the ancestral right. That is to say, a parent of either gender can pass on full or partial rights, although these can lapse through disuse or be renewed through reoccupation. Most importantly, hapū membership is rarely exclusive because marriage is usually outside third cousins and is often with members of other hapū, some rights of both parents are maintained for at least a few generations, and some even token rights can be maintained for many generations.

This 'overlapping' of kinship groups is inherent in the structure of cognatic descent groups wherever they may be found, which is commonly throughout the Pacific and Southeast Asia. Such overlapping or 'mixing' through intermarriage is not some deterioration of a primordial integrity and exclusivity of 'clans' or 'tribes', such as is supposed for patri- or matrilineal groups like the Old Testament Jews or many African and Asian societies where children are affiliated exclusively with the kin of one parent (and even these cases rarely live up to their unilineal ideology). The assumption that such apparently tidy systems of kinship and land rights associated with other parts of the world was also the case in New Zealand continues to confound official and popular understanding of Māori society.

2 Changes in Identification of Urewera Hapū, 1896–1907

Despite the vague sense of doubt suggested by the phrase 'adopting as far as possible hapu boundaries', the full difficulties of squaring the Urewera land blocks with hapū organization were not anticipated in the 1896 legislation. Surprisingly, although the Native Land Court had struggled with some implications of this problem for decades, Seddon, Carroll, and the Tūhoe leaders had negotiated for over a year, and the commission chairperson and secretary were leading ethnologists, it is clear that the drafters of the legislation were only vaguely aware that there would be such difficulties. However, by the time of his first annual report to parliament in 1899, Smith had come to understand the problem fairly well, and could not help but voice some despair.

> It was soon found that practically there are no such things as [areas of land with] defined hapu boundaries such as were acknowledged by the people as belonging to any given hapu to the exclusion of others. As a matter of fact, nearly the whole area is subject to overlapping claims, sometimes three or

> four claims one on top of the other with discordant boundaries; and the hapus are so mixed by inter-marriage that it is difficult to say to what hapu any particular individual of the tribe belongs. As the work progressed it became apparent that the title to the whole area would require investigation before any boundaries could be determined suitable for a division into districts. (Smith in AJHR 1899: x–xi)

Although frustrated, Smith's complaint was (and still is) a rather lucid description of traditional rights to land as well as the organization of hapū and hapū land rights among Māori generally, not just Tūhoe. He saw clearly that each hapū had no *exclusive* control over any specific area definable as a block, and that individual affiliations to hapū were multiple and even ambiguous. A persistent confusion lay in his assumption that these ambiguities were the result of hapū being 'mixed by intermarriage'. This is still a common and misleading understanding of what was really the normal social organization of hapū as cognatic descent groups. Hapū have probably *always* been 'mixed' by intermarriage insofar as some marriages (not just by 'nobility') always occurred between persons whose primary affiliation was with different hapū, and in such cases the children held membership rights in both hapū. Actually, as will be seen with regard to the Tūhoe, they were recognized to hold rights in any of the hapū lands to which either one of their parents had maintained affiliation. They could, furthermore, hold at least weak rights to hapū lands in which their parents' grandparents had maintained active affiliation regardless of lapsed affiliations since then. This situation will be more fully examined below with regard to relative shares recognized in the block owner lists.

Although the minutebooks do not remark upon what must have been a difficulty even for the ethnologists and Land Court judges on the commission, there was a striking inconsistency in the number and names of hapū which were recorded at various times during their investigations. For comparison, Fig. 3.1 tabulates the hapū named in six successive contexts between 1896 and 1907:

1. Elsdon Best's report to Percy Smith in March 1896 "Hapus of the Urewera Tribe ... Tuturu and allied" (in Binney 2002: 498);
2. the list of hapū and localities drawn up by the commissioners in their first formal meeting 1 February 1899 (Fig. 2.2; UMB 1: 4–13);

3. the hapū recorded for lists of claimants submitted to the commission during the 1899 hearings, which circuited throughout the Urewera (tabulated from UMB 1 and 2);
4. the hapū recorded in the commission's final confirmation of block awards in October 1902 (Fig. 2.1; UMB 7: 42–58);
5. the hapū named in the minutes of the appeals commission 1906–1907 (UAMB 1–3), derived from the Urewera Minutebooks Index (Laurie 1995);
6. the hapū and subdivisions published by Elsdon Best (Best 1973 [1925]: 214–5), probably on the basis of records kept between 1896 and 1907.

I have attempted no comparison with a list of 25 hapū "of Nga Pōtiki" drawn up in 2004 for the Waitangi Tribunal's Urewera inquiry (Kruger 2004). However, illustrating that hapū identification has changed historically among Tūhoe, this list distinguishes between hapū names ***ōnamata*** ('in ancient or old times') and ***anamata*** ('hereafter' or contemporary; 24 different names are given).

While the raw numbers of Urewera or Tūhoe hapū named in these different contexts vary widely, those listed by the commission itself in 1899 and 1902, at the beginning and end of its investigation, might be taken as most significant. In both contexts the situation was relatively formal, and all Tūhoe commissioners were present. Yet, without any recorded explanation, 45 were listed in 1899 while 50 were listed in 1902. More confusingly, while the 1899 list named 13 hapū which did not appear in the 1902 list, the 1902 list named 17 hapū which did not appear in the 1899 list. There were only 29 hapū which appeared in both lists. Best himself had reported only 25 hapū a few years earlier in 1896, but then reported 56 hapū in 1925, probably on the basis of information gathered by 1903 only a few years later than his earlier report. Both of Best's lists furthermore purported to be total counts, including hapū 'allied' with or 'subdivisions' of others as well as ***tūturu*** (true or 'real') hapū which were not subdivisions of others (whereas the 1925 list named them separately, the 1896 list did not).

Hapuu (totals at the bottom of each column)	Best 1896	Comm-ission 1899	Claim lists 1899	Awards 1902-3	Appeals 1906-7	Best 1925
Aitanga a Haeora			x			
Aitanga a Mahuki (cf Te Aitanga...)			x			
Apa, N.			x		x	
Awa, N.			x		x	
Ha, N.	x	x	x	x	x	x
Haka, N.			x	x	x	x *
Hapuamatotoru, N.			x			
Hamua	x	x	x	x		x
Hape, N.		x	x		x	
Hika, N.(N.Hiki?)			x			
Hiki, N.		x	x	x	x	x *
Hine, N.			x			
Hinekahu, N.			x			
Hinekura, N. (Best: or N. Te Riu)	x	x	x	x	x	
Hinekura, N. of Waikaremoana						x
Hinemanga, N.			x			
Hinemuri, N.			x			
Hineuru, N.			x			
Hinewhakrau, N.			x			
Hoa, N.(N. Ha?)					x	
Hore, N.			x			
Hui, N.		x	x			
Hingaanga, N.			x			
Horaaruhe, N.			x		x	x **
Hore, N.			x			
Kahina, N.			x			
Kahungunu, N.			x			
Kaira, N.						x
Kakahu Tapiki, N.(Kahutapiki…)	x	x	x	x		x
Kapuru, N.			x			
Karetehe, N.					x	x
Kauae, N.			x			
Kohatu, N.			x			
Kohiwi, N.			x			
Koro, N.			x		x	
Korokaipapa, N.(see N.Korokaiwhenua, Papa)			x	x		
Korokai Whenua, N.		x	x			x ***
Kotore, N.			x			
Koura, N.	x	x	x	x	x	x
Kumara, N.		x	x			x
Kumete, N.			x			
Kuri, N.	x	x	x	x		x
Maarakoho		x				
Marokoko			x			
Mahanga, N.		x	x		x	
Mahurehure	x	x	x	x	x	x
Maihi, Nga	x	x	x	x	x	x
Manawa, N.		x	x	x		
Manunui, N.	x	x	x	x		x
Manutohikura, N.			x	x		x
Maru, N. (N.Maruhakapua? not likely)	x	x	x	x		x

Fig. 3.1 Tūhoe hapū named in various sources, 1896–1907

Maruhakapua, N.			x	x		
Maruiwi, N. (N.Tamapokere)			x			
Mura N.	x		x	x	x	x
Murahioi, N.					x	
Mura karehe, N.(N.Murekareke)		x	x			
Muriwai, N.		x	x	x	x	x ****
Pa ki tua, N.		x	x			
Pakoko, N.			x			
Patuheuheu	x	x	x	x	x	x *****
Papa, N. (Korokaipapa?)			x			
Pareheka, N.			x			
Porouara, N.			x			
Potiki, N.	x	x	x	x	x	x
Pou, N. ('Eria's list')				x		
Puhi, N.			x		x	
Pukeko, N.			x			
Raka, N.			x			
Rakei, N.		x	x	x		x *
Rakeinui, N. (N.Rakei?)			x			
Rangitihi, N.					x	
Rangiwewehi, N.			x			
Raoa, N.			x			
Raotao, N. (N.Ruatao? cf. Kruger)			x			
Rawa, N.						x #
Rerekahika, N.	x					x
Rohe, N.						x **
Rongo, N.(..karae)	x	x	x	x	x	x
Rongotauro, N. (Rongotauaroa? cf Kruger)			x			
Rongowhakaata			x			
Ruapani, N.			x	x		
Rua, N.			x			
Ruatahuna, N		x	x	x		x
Ruatore, N.						x *
Tahu, N.					x	
Tahupo, N.(?)			x			
Taione, N.			x			
Takiri, N.			x	x	x	
Takotorepo, N.			x			x
Tama kai moana	x	x	x	x	x	x ##
Tama, N.	x	x	x	x	x	x *
Tamakere, N.	x	x	x			x ***
Tamariwai, N.			x	x		
Tamaroki, N.		x	x	x		
Tanemoeahi (cf Te Aitanga a...)						
Taokaki, N.						x ***
Tapa, N.			x			
Tapu, N.			x			
Taraparoa, N.	x	x	x			x
Tararehe, N.			x			
Tatua, N. (=N. Te Atua?)		x	x	x	x	x ###
Taua, Ngai				x		
Tauaiti, N.			x			
Taumahaora, N.			x			
Taumata, N.			x	x		x #
Tawha, Ngai			x	x	x	
Tawhaki, N.	x	x	x	x	x	x

Fig. 3.1 (continued)

Te Au, N.		x	x	x		x ###
Te Aitanga a Pou, N. (see w/o Te, and w/o Aitanga)			x			
Te Aitanga o Tanemoeahi/-ahu			x	x	x	
Te Hapuoneone, N.			x			
Te Hina, N.			x			
Te Kaho, N.			x			
Te Kahu, N.		x	x	x		
Te Kahutupuni?			x			
Te Kapa, N.			x			
Te Kapo, N.		x	x	x	x	x
Te Karaka, N. (N.Te Karaha)		x	x		x	
Te Kehu, N.			x			
Te Riu, N. (N. Te Rurehe)		x	x	x	x	x ####
Te Rurehe, N			x			x **
Te Ua, N.						x **
Te Uaha, N.			x			
Te Umuiti, N.	x					x **
Te Wehi, Ngai (Te Wehi o te Rangi)		x		x		
Tira, N.					x	
Tokotuai, N.			x	x		x
Tokowaru, N.			x		x	
Tu, N.			x	x		
Tuahau, N.			x			
Tu mata wha, N.	x	x	x	x		x ####
Tuhaere, N.		x				x ***#####
Tuhoe (=Te Urewera?)			x	x		
Tuhoe-potiki, N. (=Tuhoe?)	x		x			x
Turipona, N.			x			
Tumatawhero, N. (also cf. Kruger)			x			x
Turanga, N.	x	x	x	x		x
Upukorehe, Te	x					
Urewera, Te (=N.Tuhoe? Tuhoe-Potiki?)			x	x	x	x
Warahoe			x			x
Whakairi, N.						x #
Whakapuru, N.						x *
Whakarau, N.			x			
Whakatane (Te)		x	x	x	x	x
Whakateke, N.			x	x		x
Whakatohea			x			
Whanau a Tamapokai			x			
Whanaupani, Te		x	x			x
Whare, N.		x	x	x	x	
Whatupe, N.			x			
150	25	45	126	50	39	56

Best's annotations of 1925 list:

* subdivision of Patuheuheu hapuu.
** subdivision of N. Te Riu hapuu.
*** subdivision of N. Tawhaki hapuu.
**** formerly N. Hamua; division of N.Turanga.
***** largely N. Rongo.

connected to N. Te Riu.
or N. Huri.
subdivision of Tamakaimoana hapuu
or N. Hinekura
alternate spellings N.Tuhea or N.Tuhaiereao

Fig. 3.1 (continued)

A total of 150 different hapū names appear in the six successive contexts, for an Urewera population of about 2000 persons at this time. What are we to make of this wide variation over no more than a decade? To begin with, clearly there are in the lists some mere misspellings resulting in spurious duplication, and some hapū or *iwi* often considered outside or only partly Tūhoe (such as Ruapani, Whakatohea, Rongowhakāta, Rangatihi, Ngā Puhi, Ngāti Pukeko, Ngāti Whare, Ngāti Manawa, Te Upukorehe, and probably several others). There were also at least some abbreviations or aliases so well known even to the Pākehā commissioners that using both, even in formal lists, was assumed to cause no confusion (such as Korokaiwhenua and Korokaipapa, Ngāi Te Riu and Ngāi Te Rurehe, and perhaps Tūhoe and Tūhoe-Pōtiki). In some cases there were also probably two different hapū names, or a change of name being established, for virtually the same group of people (said to be so for Ngāti Rongo and Māhurehure, and apparently so for the Tūhoe *hapū* and Te Urewera *hapū*), but in this case one could suppose that use of both names in the same context implied some significant differences, at least ideological, rather than simple identity. Finally, as noted by Best in 1925, many hapū were 'subdivisions' or 'connected to' other, presumably dominant, hapū.

In any case, such subordinations, duplications, extraneous or peripheral groups, and virtual identities would probably leave at least 100 of the 150 apparently different hapū names referring to substantially different hapū identities if not different groups of people. How could over 100 such hapū be reduced to Best's early list of 25 or even his later list of 56 hapū?

Some explanation of this striking variation may be suggested by developments immediately following the commission's careful listing of 45 hapū in their first sitting on 1 February 1899. Over the next two months, the commission circuited through the main centers of the Urewera to consider block boundaries and accept claims. As mentioned earlier, during that time about 260 claimants lists were submitted in the name of 126 different hapū, almost a tripling of the 'official' count only a few weeks before. Although none of these lists have been located and even their tabulation in the minutebooks is fragmentary, a rapid acceleration of submissions is discernable in the five hearings between Rūātoki and Ruatāhuna. The list is inflated somewhat by a disproportionate number of claims for only 1 of the 50-some blocks being defined (24 of the 260 claim lists were for the Waikaremoana block, often in the name of hapū that appear nowhere else in the record), but the increase is nevertheless extraordinary.

As concluded earlier, some sense of compulsion comparable to that used in the Native Land Court was probably intended by the Act and even by Chairman Smith in order to bring all rightful claimants forward expediently. However, insofar as such rights were often long-settled in most of the blocks among most Tūhoe leaders, this factor probably cannot account for such a disparity between hapū named in these different contexts and the acceleration of claims.

In his classic studies of traditional Māori hapū and other cognatic descent groups in Polynesia, Raymond Firth perceptively characterized them as "waxing" or "waning", flourishing or declining, according to changing circumstances (Firth 1959: 114; Webster 1975: 124). It would not be surprising to find such a normal process accelerated or intensified among Tūhoe hapū under the circumstances of the 1896 Act. This major change also came on top of the 1860s confiscation of coastal lands that had made refugees of many influential hapū affiliated with Tūhoe, some of which were taken in by others better established in the Urewera. A dramatic account of patronage and subordination between hapū was revealed later in the investigation of Maungapōhatu block at the southeastern end of the UDNR (UMB 1: 179; see Fig. 1.2). The *rangatira* (and commissioner) Tutakangahau, asserting the claim of Tamakaimoana hapū to the entire Maungapōhatu block, stated that Ngāti Tatua, Ngāti Maru, Ngāti Ru, and Ngāi Te Au hapū were 'all mine' because the Crown's 1860s confiscation of their lands north of the Urewera district had left them landless and destitute. By claiming these hapū as 'mine', he meant that they were dependent and under the patronage of Tamakaimoana hapū, and probably gifted land rights expressed in terms of *aroha* or compassion. A further likely example of this result of the Crown's confiscation will be examined in Chap. 6 with regard to the proposed Parekohe amalgamation of blocks (Fig. 1.3).

It is likely that in 1899 the UDNR process of identifying significant boundaries and accepting claims in the name of hapū rapidly came to be seen as an opportunity for previously dependent hapū, or sectors of established hapū aspiring to independence, to assert independence from their parent or other hapū that had previously maintained some seniority or dominance over them. Eight of the apparently new hapū named in the claimants lists of 1899, but not the formal listing earlier that year, survived the commission's investigations to be recognized in 1902 as having rights in various blocks. Nine others had emerged, or changed their name, since the claimants lists were closed. The opportunity for independence might have long been anticipated, at least since the negotiations between Tūhoe and the Crown had begun in 1895 and the principles of the Native Reserve had been laid out, published, and (as Binney showed) argued over subsequent to 1896. The hopes of aspirants to hapū independence may have been raised as confidence in the promise of home-rule increased.

These situations of hapū dominance and subordination were inherently ambiguous, and might have been seen, for instance, by the dominant hapū as leaving the claims process to its subordinate branches while maintaining its *mana* above the fray. At the same time as some hapū were breaking up, others may have been merging. Previously independent hapū left weaker in the confiscations or later struggle to exploit the new opportunities, or declining due to previous breakaways, may have merged with others or resurrected earlier identities from ancestors recognized in common. Meanwhile, as will be examined below, the commission's later investigations reinforced these internal developments with its own ambiguous procedure: discriminating between stronger and weaker claims by different hapū, while urging 'minor' claims to unite with 'major' ones in more inclusive blocks wherever possible.

This hypothetical explanation of the disparities of hapū names and numbers is generally consistent with the shifts in total numbers of hapū recorded throughout these years: 25 in 1896; 45 by early in 1899; 126 later in 1899 when most claims had been received; 50 by 1902 when final decisions had been taken; 39 in appeals by 1906; 56 probably after appeals had been heard and some partitions arranged. Thus it is fairly clear that the total number of 100–150 different hapū names which appear in the records over these years represented many merely aspiring or notional hapū or hapū branches that finally fell short of the relative independence, acceptance, and *mana* expected of established hapū, or (for these or bureaucratic reasons) the commissions' reluctance to lay out more blocks than necessary.

Tūhoe aligned with these aspiring but unsuccessful hapū could nevertheless be found to hold land rights in particular blocks, but only as members of other hapū, implicitly accepting their *mana*. On the other hand, the discrimination between '*tūturu*' and 'allied' hapū or hapū 'subdivisions' within both of Best's lists, and implicit in the deliberations and final awards of the commission, also make it clear that no line could be drawn between established hapū and those that in the end were not formally recognized.

3 Procedural Precedents and Compromises in the Te Waipotiki Case

The general procedure of the commission for the investigation of each block was outlined in Chap. 2, describing the three stages of inquiry into ancestry, occupation, and relative shares of successful claimants. Hapū claims were submitted, block boundaries negotiated, and surveys begun for the entire reserve during the 1899 season. The hearings of full evidence for each block started early the following February 1900 with the Te Waipotiki block, situated just south of Rūātoki block west of the Whakatane River (Fig. 1.2). In many ways Te Waipotiki was a test case for the commission, and a study of it reveals procedural precedents and compromises that guided the investigation of the remaining blocks of the reserve.

Because the block boundaries were unsettled and surveys incomplete, the investigation was long and arduous (taking most of February and March and some of April) and the minutebook record confused, but it is nevertheless the most detailed of all the blocks. The record for Te Waipotiki is also confusing because several minutebooks are involved with sometimes scattered entries totaling over 200 pages. The original minutebooks (UMB 1 and 2) were translations into Māori by Best from his notes in English and shorthand, and later translated back into English as UMB 3 ('3A') and 4 (but also apparently partly rearranged or revised). The following analysis draws primarily from the English translation UMB 3: 1–142 but some of UMB 4 as well; the Māori version (in which I was assisted by Himaima Tumoana's abstracts in English) is UMB 1: 211–382 and extensive additions in UMB 2.

The typical multiplicity of claims and ambiguity of hapū rights and identities over which Smith despaired in his report, described in general terms in the previous section, are recorded with relative candor as well as detail for the Te Waipotiki case. At the first sitting of the commission for its second season of hearings, on 6 February 1900 at Tauarau marae in Rūātoki, the commissioners examined the completed maps and decided to begin their hearings with the Waipotiki block (UMB 1: 209). Again, the chairman emphasized key differences between their procedures and those of the Native Land Court, pointing out that the Tūhoe were able to appoint their own conductors and present their own cases, appoint their own relatives as guides for the surveyors, and were relieved by the government of the expenses of these surveys.

Initial claims for the Te Waipotiki block were laid during the summer of 1899 in the name of Ngāti Rongo, Nga Pōtiki, and Tūhoe-Pōtiki hapū, the latter claiming the western portion of the block, known as Raungaehe and including Owhakatoro. However, the investigation of Te Waipotiki block the following year dealt with claims by Numia Kererū for Ngāti Rongo hapū, Akuhata Te Kaha for Te Māhurehure hapū and Ngāti Tāwhaki hapū, and further claims in the name of Tūhoe, Ngāti Koura, Ngāti Raka, and still other hapū. How were the new claims of these other hapū related to those laid the previous summer, and what happened to the claims in the name of Ngā Pōtiki and Tūhoe-Pōtiki? Ngā Pōtiki was a very old and inclusive hapū from which most contemporary hapū of the Tūhoe *iwi* can trace descent (Kruger 2004: 30). Tūhoe-Pōtiki was probably also called Tūhoe hapū (which was later called Te Urewera hapū). Some of the other new claimant hapū were probably 'subdivisions' or affiliates of Ngā Pōtiki that may have decided to pursue independent claims.

Early in the hearings the commissioners had decided in closed session (and the absence of Numia Kererū and Mehaka Tokopounamu as claimants for Te Waipotiki) that there was no practical difference between Te Māhurehure and Ngāti Rongo hapū: "It would appear that we are deciding as to a hapu name, not as to ownership of the land.... We cannot say who are N.Rongo or who are Te Mahurehure. They must decide that themselves" (UMB 4: 17–19). While Ngāti Rongo claimed the whole block exclusively, Te Māhurehure apparently broke away from Ngāti Rongo to claim the block along with Ngāti Tāwhaki hapū.

After hearing the evidence regarding occupation, the commission announced that the minimum continuous occupation required for successful claimants would include at least the three previous generations on the block, that is (as outlined above), the parents, grandparents, and great-grandparents through whom the oldest living claimants had successfully demonstrated descent from the accepted founding ancestor of the block (UMB 4: 83–86). This was a 'minimum' pre-requisite for a successful claim in the sense that even though still earlier occupation by appropriate ancestors may have lapsed entirely, if occupation had been resumed and not been successfully *challenged* by other claimants throughout these three recent generations, its legitimacy among Tūhoe was accepted as established. On this criterion of occupation the commission found that both the lists submitted for Ngāti Rongo hapū and those submitted by Te Māhurehure hapū were entitled to the whole block with the exception of the western portion (Raungaehe). There, lists submitted from Te

Māhurehure, Ngāti Tāwhaki, and Tūhoe-Pōtiki, except for some names struck out because they fell short of this minimum requirement of continuous occupation, were found to be entitled.

The history of changing hapū names often reflects shifting alliances between hapū, in this case at least between Ngāti Rongo, Te Māhurehure, and Ngāti Tāwhaki. Similarly, spontaneous exchange in this case revealed that Tūhoe-Pōtiki hapū's claim to the western portion of Te Waipotiki block may have been a move for independence from Ngāti Rongo: one claimant for Tūhoe-Pōtiki, cross-examined by Numia Kererū for Ngāti Rongo, asserted that Numia had prevailed upon him to include their claim as part of Ngāti Rongo, but that he had been offended and refused to subordinate himself to them (UMB 4: 167–8). Numia responded disdainfully that Ngāti Rongo had only taken his people in as orphans—'*he kai na taku patu*' ('food from my war-club', but translated as 'remnants of my victory over their tribe').

The naming of Te Māhurehure hapū along with Ngāti Rongo in the confirmation of the Te Waipotiki block award, despite the conclusion that they were practically identical, suggests that branches of Ngāti Tāwhaki and perhaps Tūhoe-Pōtiki hapū accepted the *mana* of Māhurehure but not that of Ngāti Rongo, and in this way were included but not named separately in the award. Such compromises combining sectors of other hapū under the name of a successful claimant hapū, from whose ancestor they could also trace descent and demonstrate recent occupation, were probably common in the commission's awards. The implied subordination of *mana* to that of the explicitly named hapū was a trade-off for recognition of land rights as part of the named hapū, but perhaps also the beginning of an alliance with another hapū. In any case, it is clear that such subordination was a very sensitive issue, probably explaining the rarity of any final formal record of it. While the final confirmation of awards in October 1902 for all blocks in the reserve named (and implicitly prioritized) specific hapū in closed session, no hapū at all were named in the contentious block orders for Rūātoki, nor in the official provisional block orders for all the UDNR blocks published in 1903, nor in the permanent orders published after settlement of appeals in 1907.

Such relationships of dependency or subordination among an integrated group of hapū with overlapping memberships and rights in a particular territory was probably typical of Māori hapū organization in many regions of New Zealand. Quite apart from the occasional confederation of hapū as "subtribes" of an *iwi* or "tribe", there is now considerable evidence that in pre- and early colonial eras 1760–1860 Māori hapū were organized in "communities" or "clusters" of hapū structured in this way (Ballara 1995, 1998; Webster 1998: 10–11). While ecological factors such as food resources and complementary exchange with other regions tended to define the territory of such a 'hapū cluster' (Anderson presents the most detailed evidence of this), social and historical factors such as duration of occupation, migrant and refugee movements, political alliances, genealogical seniority, key marriages, and the relative *mana* of leaders derived from these factors defined the relationships between constituent hapū. Specific examples of such hapū clusters as constituent parts of the wider Tūhoe or Te Urewera *iwi* will be examined in Chap. 6 and Part II.

4 Establishing a System for Assignment of Relative Shares

The deliberations over the assignment of relative shares in the Te Waipotiki block set a precedent that was later to be developed in careful discriminations for all UDNR blocks within *and between* block lists. This procedure was probably developed by the Tūhoe leaders well beyond the interest or understanding of secretary Best as well as the Pākehā commissioners. The English translation and rearrangement of UMB 1 and 2 in UMB 3 and 4 are difficult to follow but a coherent account can be reconstructed here. In Chaps. 4 and 5 details of the developed relative shares system will be pursued with regard to one hapū branch in the Tauwhare Manuka block.

Although Tūhoe hostility toward procedures of the Native Land Court was respected in the 1896 Act and by the commission chairman, many of the basic procedures established in the Te Waipotiki case were nevertheless adapted from those established in that court since the 1860s. Guidance of the Tūhoe in these procedures, most of whom had only indirect experience with the Court, was probably the purpose of the one Native Land Court judge appointed to the commission of seven members (two when Chairman Smith was replaced by Judge Scannell in the 1901 season). However, in addition to the agreed avoidance of most Native Land Court procedures, it must be kept in mind that the situation in the UDNR differed from the usual situation before that court in at least three major ways: (i) rather than a piecemeal approach to each claim, the manner and intention of the investigation of the entire area and its very numerous claimants had been settled by Tūhoe negotiation with the government in advance and set down in special legislation; (ii) relative rights over many blocks of a very large area was being determined for many hapū (i.e., the whole 'iwi') simultaneously; and (iii) most importantly, the Tūhoe commissioners were largely in control of the procedures and the findings. Generally, the formal hearings of the commission intervened only to deliberate and decide on disagreements that the Tūhoe leaders—including the Tūhoe commissioners whether or not they were formally stood down—could not settle between themselves outside the sittings.

While the Native Land Court was set up primarily to facilitate alienation of Māori land (Webster 1975: 133–7), UDNR commission policy and practice intended to settle titles on individuals as an electoral role representing kin groups, ideally hapū, that were expected to continue their customary rights in perpetuity and, on the principle of home-rule, could alienate their shares in common only through a General Committee composed of elected representatives from each of the blocks of the UDNR. Consequently, the investigative commission of the UDNR encouraged adherence to what had become widely accepted as customary criteria of land rights by Māori as well as the Court. Although somewhat different terminology was used by the commission, these criteria had come to be known in the Native Land Court as *take kite hou*, *take tuupuna*, *take raupatu*, and *take tuku* (land rights by reason of discovery, ancestry, conquest, or gift, respectively). Most importantly, each of these bases of claim required demonstration of more or less continuous *noho* ('sit', 'stay', or 'dwell'), occupation or use over the three previous generations through whom the oldest living claimants traced their claim. Evidence of this occupation or use was tested in court to assess its degree of public acceptance or recognition. In the Native Land Court the relative intensity, weakness, or lapse of occupation was often described in terms of *ahi kā*, *ahi tere*, and *ahi mātaotao* (burning, flickering, cold hearth-fires, respectively).

Although this three-generation rule had been developed in the Native Land Court, as the *sin qua non* of investigation of original titles, it was probably firmly based in widespread Māori 'custom law' for the sake of establishing quiet title (that could then be peacefully alienated by the Court). The customary criteria of such occupation or use had become recognized as widely variable from permanent residence (*noho tūturu*) through maintenance of unattended cultivations, gathering birds, rats, eels, plants; evidence of temporary encampments, fences, traps, or cultivation; symbolic acts by persons of *mana* (e.g., dropping a feather from a head-dress or leaving some other *tohu whenua* or *tapatapa whenua* (symbolic sign or mark of a land claim) on the land, receiving prestations of food from the block, even continuing burials upon it); such acts surreptitiously undertaken just inside the margins of the block and remaining unchallenged; and marriages or adoptions into the kin group that was maintaining more active occupation. Reoccupation of land to which all ancestral rights had lapsed might be allowed to re-establish those rights if invited or unchallenged by legitimate occupants and maintained. These activities were also implicitly recognized as varying widely in intensity, duration, or lapse. These and many other criteria of general Māori custom law had been recognized since earliest colonial times (Firth 1959: 383–388; Webster 1975: 134; Sorrenson 2015).

Similarly to the Native Land Court, most UDNR commission cases were concerned with founding ancestors, subsequent descendants, and occupation or use, but issues of gifting and conquest frequently emerged. In UMB 1 and 2, Best systematically indexed the proceedings, in the margins and by page at the beginning of the volume, using several key Māori terms including *rohe* ('boundaries'), *tohu* ('marks' or 'placenames'), *pa* (fortifications, settlements, buildings, fences, etc), *tupuna* ('ancestors'), *noho* (occupation or use), *kimi panga* ('searching out shares'), and *panga tangata* ('individual shares'). The UDNR cases were especially concerned with issues of *noho* or occupation in the sense of regular *use*, due to the importance of hunting and gathering in the rough Urewera terrain but also the loss of their best agricultural lands in the 1860s confiscations.

On 20 March 1900 the commission announced the decision for Te Waipotiki block in terms of hapū, specifically justifying their reasoning in terms of the descent of claimants lists or portions of them from founding ancestors of the block (UMB 4: 19; 80–86). With regard to the requirement of continuous occupation, it is significant that in addition to *noho* the last two terms regarding relative shares (*kimi panga* and *panga tangata*) were raised for the first time with regard to Te Waipotiki block and the Raungaehe portion of it (UMB 2: 72–3 [3 times, 20 March 1900; translated at UMB 4: 83–5]; and UMB 2: 88 [once, 26 March 1900; translated at UMB 4: 103]). The repeated emphasis in the minutes probably reflects the care being taken by the commission and participants to express customary occupational *rights* in the ambiguous terms of 'shares' for the first time. Tūhoe with experience in the Native Land Court would have been wary, understanding it in terms of alienable shares of ownership in land, but its numerous meanings in Māori ranged from traditional *panga* ("throw", "aim", "guess at") to contemporary *pānga* ("contact points", "relations (maths)", "share", "apparatus") (Williams 1957: 257; Ryan 1995: 170).

The definition of 'continuous occupation' so carefully repeated in the Te Waipotiki case, explicitly indexed at UMB 2: 88 as *kimi panga* or 'searching out shares', was fullest in the decision regarding the rights of Rongokarae or his wives in Te Waipotiki block. These rights

> … *a i heke iho hoki ana take ki era o a ratau uri i roto i nga rarangi, i mahi ki runga i te whenua i nga whakatuturanga tangata e toru[, ara i nga whakatupuranga e rua i mua atu i tenei,] a kaore hoki i haere ki wahi ke noho tuturu ai, haunga ia nga haere i te wehi i te taua, kaore he tikanga o era.* (UMB 2: 72)

This was translated as:

> …would descend to their joint offspring who are named in their lists *and who can be proved to have exercised rights of ownership for three generations back from adults living at the present day* [*, even so, in the two generations before this,*] and have not permanently left the district. Temporary absence due to outside warlike expeditions that did not themselves occupy the country – do not count. (UMB 4: 83; my italics; brackets mark a phrase in Māori left out of the translation)

The phrase overlooked in the translation was probably intended to emphasize that three generations of continuous occupation was the minimum requirement for recognition of rights in terms of relative shares, and that actual occupation might be proven, for instance, for five generations. Presumably, occupation proven beyond the minimum, like more intensive occupation than regular use of resources by absentees, might merit more 'shares' than others whose occupation of the block was only three generations or less intensive.

Given its statutory role, the general intention of the commission would probably have been to express customary hapū rights in specific areas of land in terms of an electoral roll for each block, and then annotate this list of names in terms similar to the relative shares of individual ownership, held *in common* and undivided, awarded in Native Land Court investigations. (Section 8 of the 1896 UDNR Act put this in terms of the relative share of 'entitlement' of each 'family' and each member of each 'family', again confusing *whānau* with hapū descent groups.)

On 2–3 April 1900 the commission invited the conductors of the Te Waipotiki case to "define the shares of each individual" on the lists of accepted claimants (UMB 2: 142–3; UMB 4: 171–3). The way in which this was then done was unique: it appeared only once again in the minute-books, for the immediately following Tapatahi case. Probably because conductors Numia Kererū for Ngāti Rongo hapū and Akuhata Te Kaha for Te Māhurehure hapū had already agreed to cooperate upon a joint list, the chairman invited them simply to assign shares to each individual in the compiled list as either 'B' for a *panga nui* ('big share') or 'S' for a *panga iti* ('small share'), allowing them to differ in their judgment with regard to the minimum requirement of continuous occupation in the block. The two conductors proceeded to do this with regard to single persons, siblings, or whole descent groups ranging from a few to over 50 persons, working through a total of 794 individuals. In each case, first Akuhata assigned either a B or an S (only four of the latter) to 29 individuals or sibling groups. In each case, Numia apparently either agreed (no entry) or differed (six S's, one 'no claim', and one 'nil' against Akuhata's B's; two B's against Akuhata's S's). It is likely that the relatively few differences in their assignments reflected the early conclusion of the commission that the name of the hapū was the real point of contention between them rather than its membership, which was virtually the same. Presumably the few differences that emerged in this trial run were renegotiated between the two conductors outside the hearing, because the list was not brought up again in the minutes. Prefiguring the formal confirmation by the commission in October 1902 to award the block in Ngāti Rongo's name with Māhurehure named second but no other hapū, the chairman's final comments on 9 April made it clear that Akuhata was to defer to Numia in agreements for further changes in the lists.

As will be exemplified in Chap. 4, the distribution of relative shares in all blocks was soon refined from the crude 'B', 'S', or 'nil' *panga* for each individual first used in the Te Waipotiki case to numbers usually ranging from 1 to 20 for each individual, generally in values of 5, 10, 15, and 20 but in lower parts of this range sometimes interpolated to intermediate numbers between 1 and 11. As well as reflecting the relative intensity and duration of their occupational rights beyond the minimum formally approved by the commission, manifold other social rank distinctions were made in terms of these share allocations, most basically between generations of the same descent group and their rights in different blocks relative to the rights of other descent groups in the same block.

Some revealing regularities in the assignment of relative rights or shares can be summarized here before closer analysis of one example is undertaken in the next chapter. Sibling groups (usually with the same surname, misleadingly termed 'family groups' in the block order as well as the 1896 Act) usually all receive the same number of shares, although the recognition of seniority between *mātāmua* ('first-born'), *tuakana* ('senior sibling' or cousin), and *teina* ('junior sibling' or cousin) is a strong custom among Tūhoe and generally among Māori. This is probably primarily because occupational rights are customarily viewed among Māori as ancestral *birth*-rights equally succeeded to by each offspring at birth, but also because these rights of descent are traced equally through either gender (Webster 1975: 124–6).

While full siblings in each generation received equal shares regardless of age or gender, UDNR commission practice with regard to different generations of a descent group recognized greater rights in terms of larger share proportions for older generations. Sibling groups or individuals of each successive generation of offspring from the oldest living generation in a descent group usually received half as many shares as sibling groups or individuals in their parents' generation. This was shown in the typical regular reduction of (leading) shares in a block from 20 to 10 to 5 if there were three living generations, or 20 to 15 to 10 to 5 if there were four living generations, or 20 to 10 if there were only two living generations. This declension was probably primarily because the *mana* or customary respect due each older generation over-rides the simple equality of birthrights by descent. The typical allocation of higher values (20 for the senior generation) for stronger occupational rights in the first part of a block list and lower values (15, 10, or less for the senior generation) for weaker rights in the last half also suggests a consistent recognition of the 'leading' descent groups of a block due to the relatively greater duration or intensity of their continuous occupation. This implication will be also be examined in Chap. 4.

Finally, refinement of the big/small/nil shares system also extended the relativity of shares within each block to relativity of shares allocated to the same descent group in *other* blocks. While in any particular block allocation of shares to different descent groups differed according to their occupational rights relative to one another in that block, and as described above were usually ranked earlier or later in the block list, these allocations were also relative to those made to the same descent group in other blocks. Comparison of different block lists reveals that while the senior generation of a particular descent group was allocated 20 shares in one block, it was allocated only 10 in another and 5 in yet another block (and accordingly the next younger generation 10, 5, or 2–3, respectively, in some cases resulting in no shares at all for the youngest generation). Given their descent from the appropriate ancestor found for that block, and meeting the minimum requirement of continuous occupation there, the different allocations of shares to the same descent group in different blocks would have reflected their relatively stronger or weaker occupational rights in those blocks. The very wide differences of rights in different blocks for the same descent group, clearest in the case of prestigious lines (including shares extended to them on the basis of *aroha* even though minimal occupation had not been demonstrated before the commission) vividly displays the extension of relative rights between as well as within blocks.

If one is not aware of what was going on here between different blocks, the superficial appearance of similarity between the regular declension of rights for successive generations in the same descent group is easily confused with the very different significance of the regular declension of rights of whole descent groups relative to one another in the same block. Overlooking this fundamental significance leads to disregard of significant differences of occupational rights for the same descent group in different blocks as well as the differences between different descent groups in the same block. These and other confusions are likely if one does not recognize the continuities of rights that unfold in descent groups over generations, and effects on relative rights by the marriages between them.

All these implications, of course, follow from the unusual situation of investigation of the UDNR, which necessarily involved identification of the rights of many different hapū in many different blocks, virtually simultaneously. The despair of Chairman Smith, and the relief the Pākehā commissioners as well as Best must have been felt to leave these details to the Tūhoe leaders outside the hearings, is easy to understand. The manifold dimensions in which the Tūhoe commissioners and other leaders were able to do all this, matching the new convention of relative 'shares' to the statutory requirement of electoral roles by 'family' in such discriminating detail, revealed their simple mastery of their own customs.

5 The Resolution to Expedite Hearings and Merge Claims

Hearings on Te Waipotiki block ran for over two months early in 1900, already the second season of investigation. As mentioned earlier, Chairman Smith was alarmed at the time being consumed for just one block and already on 26 February, after over two weeks of hearings on this case alone, proposed that the commissioners consider a more expedient procedure (UMB 1: 312 ff; UMB 3: 135 ff). Although his proposal was soon carried, as seen above the case continued to be heard for most of March and into April.

In order to expedite their investigations, Smith proposed that each *kai-whakahaere* (conductor) representing hapū claims to a particular block give their whole case themselves rather than bringing in additional witnesses, asserting that the questioning of witnesses took up too much time and did not bear much on the judgment of the cases. He reinforced his recommendation with the advice that if the claimants resorted to the Native Land Court's procedure and the consequent delays, the government was likely to reconsider its resolution to bear the costs of the investigation and require of the natives (i.e., of the Tūhoe claimants) the same fees as would the Court. Although Judge Butler waited until each of the five Tūhoe commissioners had responded to the chairman's proposal, he reinforced it by asserting their procedure was actually taking longer than would the Native Land Court, and emphasized that the government had enacted the legislation because the Natives objected to the Court. Although Smith invited his colleagues' responses by concluding that 'this is my own point of view', he had introduced his proposal as 'our suggestion' (*ta maua whakāro*), implying inclusion of Butler but some deference to the opinions of the Tūhoe commissioners.

Smith or Butler may have earlier raised the need to expedite procedure individually with some of the Tūhoe commissioners, most of whom immediately agreed with the proposal voicing only minor doubts. Mehaka Tokopounamu and Hurae Puketapu spoke first, supporting the chairman's recommendation and even augmenting it with the idea that lesser or minor claims should be 'united under one case'—the notion which was to become adopted. Mehaka also seemed to clear the way for a policy settling as much as possible informally outside the commission hearings:

> Let the conductors of the various cases [for each block] consider the matter of uniting these cases, outside the Commission. But if this step cannot be favourably be [sic] settled, let them explain to the Commission the impediment to such union. (UMB 3: 138)

Smith and Butlers' suggestion that conductors for claimants and counterclaimants present their entire case without cross-examination of witnesses would minimize having to deal with further counterclaims in the hearings, effectively requiring that such complications be settled between Tūhoe leaders 'outside the Commission'. Although their ready support of Smith and Butler's proposal may be unrelated, it will be remembered that by August after that season's hearings had been adjourned Mehaka and Hurae, according to Numia, were pressing to replace all the Tūhoe commissioners including themselves with other Māori.

Finally, speaking last and probably most influentially, Tutakangahau also supported the chairman's recommendation, pointing out that expedience was required if their most knowledgeable old people were not to die off first. Smith felt that "we all consent to this suggestion" and concluded that "the minor cases of the opposing parties will be brought together to make up one case" (UMB 3: 140). However, Numia Kererū's 'consent' was certainly ambiguous, and could even be taken as a warning. To his earlier trenchant objection that "I do not wish that my work should be shortened" (UMB 3: 136), he added:

> Yes, it takes much time to proceed with these cases under the present system but to bring cases which have different claims together under one case may be difficult indeed. Let them see to their cases whether they should unite them or not. If we follow up the present suggestion, the people might object. They might entertain the opinion that this method of procedure will prevent them from bringing forward all their claims. As regards the expenses, there is no trouble in that because this Commission will finally investigate the whole of the land. The opposing parties may arrange as to whether they should unite their cases or not. I suggest that you (the European commissioners) should consider the best system of procedure in this land. (UMB 3: 138–9; my italics)

In addition to the explicit expressions of doubt, Numia's final remark here may actually be considered a warning, much more strongly worded than its translation: *'Ma korua, ma nga komihana Pākehā e whakatakoto he tikanga ma matau, koinei taku whakaaro'* (UMB 1: 313; my translation of this would be: 'perhaps you two, the Pākehā commissioners, ought to lay down a procedure which is in accord with our truth [Tūhoe custom], this is my opinion'). Tutakangahau furthermore appeared to support Numia's reference to *he tikanga ma matau*, stating that the Act required that 'this land should be investigated according to Māori customs'. Nevertheless over-riding these concerns, perhaps as a concession to Numia, Smith cautiously qualified his regulation with the proviso that the "conductor will give the whole account of the land in question. Should the conductor forget anything *another person* may complete that description" (UMB 4: 140; my italics).

Thus the way was left open for corrections or augmentations of conductors' evidence, apparently even from the floor, if not to more direct confrontation of witnesses in cross-examination. However, it is clear that Numia's main concern was that 'minor' or 'lesser' cases, or protests, would not get a fair hearing, instead being forced to 'unite' with what someone deemed to be the 'major' case—that is, to subordinate their claim to it. From the point of view of hapū organization, this was tantamount to ignoring legitimate protests or even to denying autonomy to an accepted or aspiring hapū.

Judge Butler's final report in 1902 was able to announce the reduction of 58 original "hapū block" claims to 34 blocks (AJHR 1902). Whereas investigation of the Te Waipotiki block took two months, investigation of the remaining 34 blocks (there were actually 35 in total) was completed in about 12 more months through three seasons of sittings concluded in October 1902, so it appears that the new procedures were relatively more expedient. Cases were certainly expedited by continual encouragement to settle as many differences as possible (i.e., 'unite them under one case') outside of formal hearings, and this was probably the main factor in reducing over 260 separate claims registered in 1899 to a notional 58 blocks, and these to a final 35 blocks. On the other hand, the supposed 58 blocks gazetted at the conclusion of the 1899 season obscured many overlapping and even redundant areas which in any case would have been reconciled (UMB 1: 204, citing Gazette 8 June 1899). It is also doubtful that the resolution to forego cross-examination was a major factor in the expedience achieved. Conductors often continued to rely on witnesses to back up the claim of each hapū, and although there was little formal cross-examination, in their presentation witnesses as well as conductors continued to challenge each other's evidence in detail. Objections from the floor were usually invited and considered. Once again, it can be argued that despite the effort of the Pākehā commissioners to expedite investigations, the Tūhoe retained considerable control over the commission and its investigations.

Nevertheless, as Numia had warned, this procedure was clearly sometimes a suppression of conflicting claims for the sake of official appearances, concealing these within a single somewhat arbitrary block boundary. The resulting disputes or discontents may have been seen by the commissioners as manageable under home-rule, that is, under the authority of the hapū committees and the representative General Committee instituted under the Act. However, the suppression of 'minor' claims was probably the cause of many appeals faced by the appeals commission in 1906. As will be seen in Part II, in 1900 Numia himself was already pressing a claim for part of Ruatāhuna. By 1912, it may have also been the cause behind a general problem identified by the chief judge of the Native Land Court in his effort to resolve continuing Tūhoe demands to partition several blocks of the reserve.

During 1912–1913 Chief Judge Jackson Palmer heard at length several appeals in the Native Appeals Court and sought to clarify the problem in a memo.[1] He explained that if the Urewera commission had made every piece of land with distinct hapū boundaries into a distinct block, the blocks would have been too numerous and interests too scattered. He remarked that traditional hapū boundaries 'had been maintained down to the present day, and were well-defined' in Rūātoki 1, 2, 3, Te Whaiti, Taneatua, Ruatāhuna, and perhaps in Waikaremoana blocks. Consequently, he pointed out, the blocks laid out by the commission frequently contained three or more 'distinct' areas having defined hapū boundaries belonging to a 'distinct' group of people who had 'gotten into the block title' through rights to only one or another portion of the whole block. Yet when the block orders were drawn up, in the absence of an explicit record to the contrary in the judgment upon which it was based, their relative interests were mistakenly extended to the whole block rather than being explicitly limited to the portion over which their rights had been recognized.

So it appears that at least in some blocks, original claims for specific portions could have been recognized by the commission as separate claims and awarded separate blocks, but were instead viewed as 'minor' and merged with adjoining claims in a larger block. This predicament was probably clearest in the claims for Taneatua block, which were sufficiently clear and uncontested so that the minutes of investigation were perfunctory, although the block had to be awarded to seven different hapū. Evidence emerged in the investigation of an adjacent block that in Taneatua shares had actually been allotted by hapū, "so many to each ancestor" (UMB 6: 14) and then divided among the successful claimants claiming under that ancestor. However, as happened in most such cases in the UDNR, neither the different hapū branches nor the different parts of the block were recorded in the title, presumably leaving this to enforcement under the organization of home-rule authority established by the 1896 Act. Yet, as was clearest in the case of Ruatāhuna block, discontent regarding the merger of adjoining claims persisted until partitioning was achieved in 1913. It turned out that it was Numia Kererū who conducted the appeals for both of these blocks before the chief judge, who commented favorably upon the integrity and reliability of his efforts. This situation will be examined more fully in Part II.

On the other hand, the chief judge may have overdrawn the point that shares awarded to some owners on the understanding that they were limited to a portion of a block had come to be taken as extending over the entire block. While this had clearly occurred in some cases he had identified, as argued in the previous section, the Tūhoe commissioners, working with the conductors outside the hearings, were systematically careful to allocate shares in ways which discriminated between relatively strong and weak occupational rights of whole descent groups between as well as within each block. As it happened, the range of shares for this crucial discrimination appeared superficially similar to the range of shares distinguishing between successive generations of each descent group. Like his predecessors, the chief judge may not have clearly appreciated the difference between these two superficially similar ways of recognizing differential rights in a block.

Thus, in most cases, the allocation of relatively fewer shares in a block to a particular descent group may have intentionally reflected the limitation of their rights to only a portion of that block. These extramural but ongoing efforts on the part of the Tūhoe commissioners and conductors suggest that while the merging of minor cases caused some major problems in particular blocks, they had on their own worked out general methods to maintain fairness in terms of (as Numia and Tutakangahau had put it) 'our truth'. Insofar as the 1896 Act guaranteed the continuing home-rule control of these leaders over their lands, they would be able to oversee and enforce the variation of rights signified in their distributions of relative shares.

6 The Aborted Plan for Radical Block Amalgamations

As mentioned in Chap. 2, Percy Smith resigned from chairmanship in March 1901 and was replaced by Judge D. Scannell, who, along with the other Pākehā member Judge W.J. Butler (and Secretary Elsdon Best), saw the investigation through to the publication of the provisional orders in 1903. Scannell had been in charge of earlier cases in the Native Land Court throughout the district including those dealing with the contentious Rūātoki and nearby Whaitiripapa blocks, and officially became the commission chairman, signing all the orders in 1903 except those for the Rūātoki block.[2] However, he apparently stood down for the hearing on Rūātoki block which began 15 April 1902 and Butler was elected chairman for the remaining sessions through early May, writing the 1902 annual report to the Native Minister and reconvening the commission for a few final weeks in October 1902. During this time, Scannell was replaced by Captain Gilbert Mair, who in 1906–1907 was to become a member of the UDNR appeals commission (excepting the Rūātoki case, appeals for which were heard separately by the other two members of that commission—neither of them Tūhoe). While the five Tūhoe commissioners remained the same throughout the investigation of the reserve, Judge Butler (and Secretary Best) was thus the only Pākehā member of the commission who had worked continually with them.

By May 1902 the commission had finally completed investigation of all cases for the Reserve and had drawn up draft orders for all blocks excepting Rūātoki. After closing the case for Rūātoki, the minutes perfunctorily record two extraordinary sessions in which, without reporting any apparent earlier intentions or further explanation, a radical plan was approved to amalgamate (or 'regroup' under one title) all 35 blocks of the Reserve into only 10 large blocks.[3] The minutes need to be quoted in full (compare Figs. 1.2 and 1.3):

> Friday, May 2nd 1902.
> The Commission opened at 9.a.m.
> Engaged all morning inspecting disputed boundaries [of the Ruatoki block].
> - 2.p.m. -
> After some discussion, it was decided by the commission to include each of the following groups of blocks in separate Orders:
>
> 1. To be called Te Whaiti Nui a Toi:
>   Te Whaiti Nui a Toi
>   Otairi
>   Maraetahia

2. To be called Ruatahuna – Waikaremoana:
    Ruatahuna
    Waikaremoana
3. To be called Maungapohatu:
    Maungapohatu
    Tauranga
    Waikare-whenua
    Karioi
    Ohiorangi
    [Manuoha]
    [Paharakeke]
4. To be called Ohaua te Rangi:
    Te Ranga-a-Ruanuku
    Tauwhare
    Tukuroa Kohuru [sic]
    Ierenui Ohaua
5. To be called Tauwharemanuka:
    Tauwharemanuka
    Pukepohatu
    Paraoanui
    Omahuru
6. To be called Parekohe:
    Parekohe
    Te Tuahu
    Poroporo
    Ruatoki South
    Wairiko
    Otara
    [Whaitiripapa]
7. To be called Paraeroa:
    Paraeroa
    Tane Atua [sic]
    Te Purenga
8. [To be called Ruatoki:]
    Ruatoki No.1
    Ruatoki No.2
    Ruatoki No.3
    Waipotiki
    Tapatahi
9. Hikurangi Hormanga
10. Tarapounamu Matawhero

> Each group to form a division under Sec 6. Act of 1896.
> Present Orders are Interlocutory [.] power to revise is given by Sec.8 Act of 1900.
> It is clear to the Commissioners that some of the former decisions of the Commission should be reconsidered before final Orders are made.
> Captain Mair moved that decision in Ruatoki blocks be deferred till October next to enable him to peruse evidence, exact date to be fixed by Chairman.
> Motion seconded by Mehaka Tokopounamu and carried.
> Commission considered that it would not be right to reconsider former decisions without giving ample notice of intention to do so. as many of the persons interested had returned to their homes for purpose of harvesting crops etc. It was therefore decided to defer matter till sitting in October. (UMB 7: 23–25; brackets added)

Checks beside the name of each block apparently indicated care that none were left out, but three additional blocks included in the amalgamations as outlined on the 1901 survey plan (Fig. 1.3) have been inserted above in brackets. Whaitiripapa (a tiny block on the southeastern boundary of Rūātoki but included in Parekohe amalgamation) may have been left out because the Rūātoki partitions remained unsettled, and Manuoha and Paharakeke (both on the eastern boundary) because they were being claimed by east coast *iwi* (and were removed from the UDNR by the appeals commission in 1907; Berghan 2001: 62). The compiled Urewera survey plan 6873, dated August 1901 (Fig. 1.3), nevertheless clearly marks these blocks as within the proposed amalgamations, to be called Rūātoki and Maungapōhatu, respectively.

Although finalization of the proposal was deferred to the following spring for possible objections from those who 'had returned to their homes for purpose of harvesting crops etc.', the commission nevertheless appeared to anticipate final approval from Tūhoe as well as the Native Ministry. They stayed through the weekend to meet the following Monday 5 May to name provisional block committees for the ten ***amalgamated*** blocks (except the Rūātoki amalgamation) before adjourning for the winter (UMB 7: 26–29). Either at this time or during the recess, the new boundaries were furthermore carefully superimposed over the 1901 survey plan.

Nevertheless, when the commission was reconvened in Whakatane on 3 October 1902, again without further explanation, the minutes perfunctorily recorded that

> [t]here being some doubt as to the jurisdiction of the commissioners to group blocks together under one title (vide f 23 ante) as was proposed at last sitting it is decided to issue separate titles for each division [i.e., each of the 35 blocks, as originally planned] and to appoint provisional local committees for each. (UMB 7: 43)

Between 3 and 12 October the commissioners then proceeded to consider any necessary revisions and confirm the draft orders drawn up for each of 31 blocks, excepting Rūātoki 1, 2, and 3 and adjacent Te Waipotiki (UMB 7: 42–66). Following this, the commission also approved lists of members of the provisional block committees for each of these blocks. The boundaries, lists of owners, shares, and provisional block committees for the Rūātoki partitions and Te Waipotiki block were approved and ordered on the following two days, and the commission adjourned with "the title to the whole reserve complete" (UMB 7: 70).

It is significant that the confirmations of the original 35 blocks all apparently occurred in open hearings with all Tūhoe commissioners present, although in the case of each block only those commissioners who had no interest in the case were listed as 'acting'. Even before the above announcement of 'some doubt' regarding the amalgamation plan, Chairman Butler had opened the first session simply by announcing

> that the commissioners had been called together to give their decision in the Ruatoki blocks and to revise any of the Orders already made that commissioners consider need revision – each block would be called on separately and the European commissioners together with the Maori members of Commission who took part in the investigation of title would consider any reasonable requests for revision of Orders of any of the blocks included in the reserve. (UMB 7: 42–3)

Although confirmation of Rūātoki and Te Waipotiki were delayed a few days, objections or requests were raised in only 15 of the 31 other blocks, and these were all settled in two days, usually by adding a few names to the block list, and several times by declining the request or objection as not having been raised at the proper time. In only a few cases did the objector announce plans to appeal the confirmation. This was all accomplished in only three days of hearings (3, 6, and 7 October), all committees for the 32 blocks were submitted and approved on 8 October, and the held-over confirmations of Rūātoki and Te Waipotiki blocks were completed on 13 October. It is all the more significant that, as described in Chap. 2 and Fig. 2.1, the one to several hapū declared to have rights to each of the 31 blocks (32 when Te Waipotiki was completed) were explicitly named and implicitly prioritized—an inherently sensitive issue that was avoided in the preliminary as well as final block orders. As will be seen below, Judge Butler in his 1902 report nevertheless referred to the block committees as 'hapu committees', either reflecting the way they were habitually referred to in the commission's investigations or to conform with the naive assumption of the UDNR Act.

However, the minutes recording the October 1902 sessions were very brief, and one suspects a great deal of discussion was either not recorded or happened outside the hearings. In any case, it again appears that there was considerable agreement, at least between both Tūhoe and Pākehā commissioners, regarding the final confirmations of the original 35 blocks as well as the planning and abortion of the amalgamation plan immediately preceding these confirmations. The wide participation of most other Tūhoe leaders was made the more likely by the concurrent attention to the contentious partitions and many hapū claimants of the Rūātoki block. What was hidden behind the scant record of both these major developments?

Aside from the minutes regarding the amalgamation plan quoted above, the amalgamated block outlines depicted on Fig. 1.3, and an indirect reference in Butler's 1902 report for the commission, there appears to be no other evidence clarifying the sudden plan for a major reorganization of the Reserve just as the investigation neared completion, and its equally sudden abortion a few months later. The thinness of the evidence may suggest that the initiative for the amalgamations came primarily from the Tūhoe themselves through their commissioners, and gained the support of the Pākehā commission members, perhaps including Scannell (who would preside after consideration of Rūātoki but apparently was not present) as well as Butler, Mair, and Secretary Best. Officially, only Hurae Puketapu and Te Pou Papaka had not been stood down on the Rūātoki case, but it is certain that the other three Tūhoe commissioners would have been fully included in such a momentous proposal.

On the one hand, that the commission first decided that afternoon in May that 'some of the former decisions of the Commission should be reconsidered', and only as an afterthought decided 'that it would not be right to reconsider former decisions without giving ample notice', suggests an arrogant autonomy that neither the Act nor the commission's mode of operation would support. On the other hand, in view of the issues of ***mana*** fought out between hapū and their leaders in most of the 35 blocks over the last several years, the proposal needed to have ***already*** decided (i) which blocks to group together in each amalgamation, (ii) what to name each amalgamation, and—even more significantly, (iii) which leaders to appoint as representatives in the committee for each amalgamation. Each of these issues almost certainly required wide knowledge, discussion, and approval at least among most other Tūhoe leaders before the proposal was reported the way it was in the minutes. None of these issues would have been taken lightly among the Tūhoe at large, let alone among the five Tūhoe commissioners.

Whether or not the proposal originated from the Tūhoe commissioners and other leaders, what motive might explain the support of the Pākehā commissioners for it? They might have welcomed it insofar as their continual effort since the Te Waipotiki case had been to unify minor with major claims in fewer and larger blocks. They may also have been embarrassed by the increasing number of appeals that would have to be dealt with later by an appeals commission despite their continual efforts to settle unresolved differences formally in hearings as well as informally outside them. Appeals had already begun to mount, and totaled over 222 by 1906 when that commission finally met (Binney 2002: 247). The Pākehā commissioners might also have realized that likely reduction of the extensive duplication of names across many block lists of owners would present the amalgamated block lists more convincingly as the electoral roles which the 1896 Act expected of the titles. The proposal may also have been supported or even prompted by comments from the temporary commissioner Captain Gilbert Mair while 'inspecting disputed boundaries' of Rūātoki that same morning. Mair's reputation for having led campaigns against the Tūhoe during the 1860s incursions into the Urewera may have still resonated among important Tūhoe leaders, and the contentious Rūātoki hearings had involved many of them.

A few months later in August 1902 Judge Butler briefly summarized the progress of the commission since 1899 in a report to the Native Minister, almost certainly referring to the amalgamation plan and attributing it to Tūhoe other than the commissioners. He concluded that

> [s]everal applications were made to the Commissioners to revise some of their earlier decisions; but many of the persons whose interests might have been affected by such revision had left for their homes to harvest crops, and it was thought that they were entitled to notice before cases were reopened. For this reason and because winter was approaching, the Commissioners decided to adjourn to a day in October to be fixed by the Chairman. This sitting, which will be the last as regards the ascertainment of title to the Urewera district, will occupy a few days only. Decision will then be given in the Ruatoki case, and final orders made for all the hapu blocks. (AJHR 1902, G-6)

It is also significant that Butler assumed all outstanding matters including the amalgamation would 'occupy a few days only', suggesting that all the commissioners anticipated few objections from other leaders and even the Tūhoe at large regarding the amalgamation plan. That is to say, the 'several applications' probably represented a consensus among at least some important Tūhoe leaders. Although the postponement of further consideration of the plan to October may have responded to some doubts expressed among the five Tūhoe commissioners, the fait accompli of blocks already grouped together in one name for amalgamated orders, and committee members already named to a smaller and far more centralized structure of authority, certainly reflects their general approval and probably support from other key leaders.

The perfunctory reason given in October for summarily dropping the amalgamation plan, that there was 'some doubt as to the jurisdiction of commissioners to group blocks together under one title', is strangely at odds with Butler's August report as well as the commission's position as it had been stated in May. At that time, it was clear that the 1896 Act and its amendments had been studied, at least by Butler and Mair but also probably by Scannell. They apparently found sufficient authority to treat the decisions and draft orders on 35 blocks as merely interlocutory or provisional, and simply to revise—that is, merge—them into orders for the ten amalgamations anticipated. The new doubts about jurisdiction probably masked a ministerial decision not to risk reopening any of the cases but instead wrap up the commission as soon as possible, insofar as it had already been working for four years to implement an Act by then six years old.

An examination of the block committees elected or appointed by Tūhoe between 1902 and 1908 suggests a Tūhoe motive for proposing or supporting the amalgamation proposal. These 'local', 'hapū', or block committees were discussed in Chap. 2 and members of the 35 committees in 1902 and 1907 are listed in Fig. 2.1 for comparison. As pointed out there, although the Act envisioned 'provisional' committees that would be made permanent in elections by the owners of each block after appeals were settled, the Tūhoe probably treated these committees as permanent from the outset. Seven members was the usual number for each committee. Although in 1902 the members may have been appointed by the Tūhoe commissioners, because of the importance of relative rights and representation of more than one hapū in each block, it is obvious that this would have proceeded only if it had already been settled among the leaders of each hapū with influence or *mana* in the block. Those leaders in turn, in most cases, would have had to confer with other leaders of the hapū concerned.

These block committees actually went through at least three elections or selections: the committee members of each of the 10 amalgamated blocks (except Rūātoki, because still in hearings) were listed by the commissioners in May 1902 and replaced by committees for each of the 35 blocks in October 1902 when the amalgamation proposal was aborted. Then finally in March 1907 at the completion of the long-delayed appeals hearings, that commission listed the members of the (permanent) committees, reporting that they had been "selected by the owners of the land [the blocks finally approved] from amongst their number and proposed by them to be the members for the Hapu [sic] Committee for this block, and agreed to by all the owners present before this commission..." (AJHR 1907 G-4: 1–29). In March 1908, in accordance with the Act, this was followed by the election of the *Komiti Nui* or General Committee, composed of a representative from each of these 35 "hapū" committees (Binney 2002: 388–393).[4]

A comparison of the three sets of block committees described above and the Komiti Nui reveals a significant continuity of the same committee members 1902–1908. Tūhoe leaders had probably foreseen that with block committees of seven for each of the blocks, there would be as many as 245 possible positions for 35 blocks, and 35 representatives of these block committees on the Komiti Nui. Insofar as previous efforts to bring divergent hapū interests together into a consensus-based Tūhoe *iwi* had been unsuccessful (Ballara 1998, discussed in the Introduction), some ambitious Tūhoe leaders were probably quick to realize that amalgamation into fewer blocks would facilitate control over divergent hapū interests, especially in controlling possible further alienation of Urewera lands. A Komiti Nui of only 10 members representing 10 amalgamated blocks offered a big advantage in terms of gaining consensus among divergent hapū interests.

The goal of centralizing Tūhoe authority appears to have been pursued even when the amalgamation proposal was aborted. Unsurprisingly, 54 of the members appointed to the amalgamation committees in May 1902 were re-appointed in October to the 35 block committees. Suggesting established leadership roles continuing since 1899, 21 of them had represented hapū laying the original claims. In October 1902 many of them sat on not one but several of the 35 block committees, occupying 111 of the 245 positions. Of the remaining 134 positions filled by different persons from those named to the amalgamation committees, 58 had also represented hapū submitting claims in 1899. Out of the 134, 42 represented from two to six different blocks, reflecting their wider individual influence. Moreover, at least 50 of the 134 persons also had siblings, fathers, or sons appointed to these committees.

If a goal of centralizing authority over the 35 blocks was continued in 1906–1907, progress was made regardless of the numerous appeals being fought out. While about 119 of the 1907 committee positions were filled by different persons, 101 members of the 1902 committees were re-elected, and ranked highly in the 7 positions for each block. Again reflecting continuing leadership or *mana*, 55 of the persons filling these positions had been members of the amalgamated block committees in May 1902.

Of the 33 persons elected in 1908 from the 1907 'hapū' (block) committees as representatives on the Komiti Nui, all were sent as representatives of only one block committee. However, many sat on more than one of the block committees at the same time, and this proportion increased significantly between 1902 and 1907. Thirteen of the 33 Komiti Nui representatives had sat on more than two block committees at the same time since 1902, and 15 had sat on more than two committees at the same time since 1907. Furthermore, while only one representative on the Komiti Nui had sat on more than six committees since 1902, five had sat on more than six committees at the same time since 1907, and two of these had been a member on ten committees, while one had been a member on 14 committees at the same time. Finally, 18 of the representatives on the Komiti Nui had held one of the three leading positions on seven of the 1907 committees. As mentioned in Chap. 2, although some of the 33 may have been proxies for *rangatira* who preferred to remain in the background, most were probably proven leaders of mana.

Even with this extensive overlap of the 1907 committee memberships, their 33 representatives in the Komiti Nui would be much less ready to form a consensus than 10, had the amalgamation proposal been successful. Nevertheless, Numia Kererū was elected chairperson by 26 out of 28 votes. Their cooperation went further: the Komiti had "expressly excluded from selection the members of the block committee[s] who had left 'the law of the Government and have taken to the practices of Te Rua...'" (Binney 2002: 391). Numia and other leaders certainly knew by then that the increasingly influential Tūhoe prophet Rua Kenana was offering to sell parts of the UDNR to the Crown. Nevertheless, working for the Native Ministry, by 1910 Apirana Ngata had forced Numia to accept Rua's representatives on the Komiti Nui (Webster n.d. [1984–5]).

One final implication of the amalgamation proposal will be pursued in the following chapters. Support among Tūhoe for the amalgamation proposal may also have been prompted by alignment of the amalgamations with long-established 'clusters' of hapū, described above in connection with compromises worked out between hapū claims to the Te Waipotiki block. Historically and socially entrenched alliances and patronages, arising in ecological integrity or complementarity of a set of streams and ridges as well as the social and historical relationships of several hapū, may have underlain some amalgamations as 'natural' Tūhoe units in the UDNR. Ballara's ethnohistorical example on the Wairarapa Coast (1995) was probably more extensive than any of the amalgamations but otherwise consistent with the Urewera situation: it involved 500–1000 persons in eight hapū, three of which were dominant over the others, controlling the resources of a territory some 40 kilometers across. The constituent hapū of a cluster changed continuously over decades. In the case of the proposed Urewera amalgamations, a more rugged and compartmentalized topography and smaller hapū, as well as an increasingly intensive colonial history, could explain the differences.

The possibility that some amalgamations grouped lands controlled by a hapū cluster raises several more specific questions. Did the intended amalgamations group together blocks which were controlled by the same or more closely related hapū? Were leaders or leading sibling groups in these hapū less likely to act independently or opportunistically? Was the overlap of block committees significantly increased? Did the shareholders of these blocks tend to have rights in other blocks of the same amalgamation? Would the disparity of relative strength and weakness of rights increase rather than ease problems of cooperation? These questions will be returned to in Chap. 6, in which analysis of two amalgamation proposals will throw further light on the organization of Tūhoe hapū 1899–1903.

This chapter has been devoted to some of the problems confronted and approaches taken by the UDNR investigative commission in their effort to align blocks of land with the ancestral land rights claimed by Tūhoe hapū. After a brief introduction, the extensive changes in identification of a rapidly increasing number of descent groups claiming hapū status in the UDNR between 1896 and 1907 were tabulated and discussed in general terms. This was followed by a study of Te Waipotiki, the first block investigated, with an eye to the procedural precedents and compromises regarding hapū rights that emerged during these prolonged hearings. The next section was devoted to close analysis of the distribution of relative shares among successful claimants that was developed in the Te Waipotiki block investigation, arguing that the refinement of this procedure was largely under the control of Tūhoe leaders outside formal hearings and came to represent important details of hapū social organization. The following section of the chapter described the only partly successful effort of the commission to expedite the investigation of the remaining blocks of the UDNR by merging minor with major hapū claims and reducing the total number of blocks to be laid out in the reserve. The final section discussed the motives and implications of a largely unexplained but widely supported (nevertheless, soon aborted) proposal at the end of the last full season of investigations to amalgamate into only ten titles the 35 blocks that had been exhaustively investigated and finally approved in the preceding four years.

* * *

Notes

1. Chief Judge Jackson Palmer, 'Decisions under Sect 50 affecting the Urewera Native Reserve', 9 October 1912. National Archives, Wellington: Department of Māori Affairs (MA series) *Blocks of Land (special files)* MA 13/90 Special File 227.
2. For a history of Rūātoki block, which at different times set it apart from the rest of the Urewera Native Reserve, see Oliver (2002), Fraser (2002), and Kruger (2004). The background for Whaitiripapa block will be reviewed in Chap. 5.

3. While the commission saw themselves as 'grouping' blocks, I use the term 'amalgamation' to emphasize the virtually completed form of the block orders. The term has also become established with this meaning regarding Māori land reorganization since the 1960s and, as mentioned in the Introduction, in the 1970–1980s major amalgamations were problematically carried out on the remnants of Tūhoe lands in the Urewera.
4. Binney's discovery of new evidence is very important and confirms my own earlier conclusions that Apirana Ngata, against the will of the General Committee and its chairperson Numia Kererū, forced the inclusion of Rua Kenana and his supporters onto the committee so that with his influence the government could begin to purchase UDNR lands through it (Webster n.d. [1984–5]). Also see Binney 1997: 127; 125 fn 37. By 1915 the government illegitimately began its campaign to purchase from individual owners. The resulting wound between Tūhoe supporting Rua's Iharaira and those against them still festers.

References

AJHR 1899. Smith, S. Percy. "The Urewera District Native Reserve Act, 1896." Undated. Appendices to the Journal of the House of Representatives 1899, C-1: x–xi. Wellington, N.Z.

AJHR 1902. Butler, W.J. "The Urewera District Native Reserve Act, 1896." 6 August 1902. Appendices to the Journal of the House of Representatives 1902, G-6: 1. Wellington, N.Z.

AJHR 1907. G. Mair, D.F.G. Barclay, Paratene Ngata. "The Urewera District Native Reserve: reports of the commissioners appointed ...." Report and orders. Undated. Appendices to the Journal of the House of Representatives 1907 G-4: 1–190. Wellington, N.Z.

Anderson, A.J. 1980. "Towards an explanation of protohistoric social organisation and settlement patterns amongst the southern Ngai Tahu." *New Zealand Journal of Archaeology* 2: 3–23.

Ballara, Angela. 1995. "Porangahau: The Formation of an Eighteenth Century Community in Southern Hawke's Bay." *New Zealand Journal of History* 29(1):3–18.

Ballara, Angela. 1998. *Iwi: The dynamics of Māori tribal organisation from c.1769 to c.1945.* Wellington, N.Z.: Victoria University Press.

Berghan, Paula. 2001. "Block Research Narratives of the Urewera, 1870–1930; A resource document for Urewera District Treaty Issues." WAI 894 #A86. Wellington, N.Z.: Waitangi Tribunal..

Best, Elsdon. 1973. *Tuhoe, Children of the Mist.* Vols. I and II (genealogies). Second edition. Wellington, N.Z.: A.H. and A.W. Reed Ltd. (first published 1925 as Vol VI of the Memoirs of the Polynesian Society).

Binney, Judith. 1997. "He Mana Tuatoru: the Rohe Pōtae of Tūhoe." *New Zealand Journal of History* 31(1): 117–131.

Binney, Judith. 2002. *Encircled Lands; Part Two: A History of the Urewera 1878–1912*. An Overview Report on the Urewera for the Waitangi Tribunal. WAI 894, A15. Wellington, N.Z.: Waitangi Tribunal.

Firth, Raymond. 1959. *The Economics of the New Zealand Maori*. Second edition. Wellington, New Zealand: Government Printer. (1st edition 1929).

Fraser, Clementine. 2002. *Report on Tuhoe and Native Land Court 1866 to 1896*. WAI 894, #A103. Wellington, N.Z.: Waitangi Tribunal.

Kruger, Tamati. 2004. "Ngā Hapū ō Ngā Pōtiki." Appendix to Final Report *Ruātoki; Ngā Rauru ō Ngā Pōtiki*. Anamata College, Taneātua, N.Z. 10 January 2004. Urewera Enquiry WAI 894. Wellington, N.Z.: Waitangi Tribunal.

Laurie, John. 1995. "Annotated index of Urewera and Whakatane Minutebooks." University of Auckland Library. Auckland, N.Z.

Metge, Joan. 1967. *The Maoris of New Zealand*. London: Routledge & Kegan Paul.

Oliver, Steven. 2002. "Ruatoki Block Report." A report commissioned by the Waitangi Tribunal. WAI 894 record of inquiry, doc A6. Wellington, N.Z.: Waitangi Tribunal.

Ryan, P.M. 1995. *The Reed Dictionary of Modern Māori*. Auckland, N.Z.: Reed Books.

Sorrenson, M.P.K. 2015. "The lore of the judges: Native land court judges' interpretations of Māori custom law." *Journal of the Polynesian Society* 124 (3): 223–242.

UMB 1. Urewera District Native Reserve Commission minute book 1 (identified as Urewera Commission minute book '3'), Smith, Butler, et al, (1Feb1899–8Mar1900), in Māori, Index 22pp., 382pp. NA Wgtn: Urewera MB 3, MLC 13, W3518, CD2, Vol 3, 397 pp.; NA Ak: AREPRO 4711/1445. Acronym: UMB 1.

UMB 2. Urewera District Native Reserve Commission minute book 2, Smith, Butler, et al., (8Mar1900–20Feb1901), in Māori, Index, 350 pp. NA Wgtn: Urewera MB 2, MLC 13,W3518, CD2, Vol. 2, 358 pp.; NA Ak: AREPRO 4711/1442. Acronym: UMB 2.

UMB 3. Urewera District Native Reserve Commission minute book 3 (identified as '3A'; English translation of last part of UMB 1), Smith, Butler, et al, (9Feb1900–Mar1900). 189 pp., index, NA Wgtn: Urewera MB 3A, MLC 13, W3518, CD 2, Vol 3A, 191 pp.; NA Ak: AREPRO 4711/1444. Acronym: UMB 3.

UMB 4. Urewera District Native Reserve Commission minute book 4 (English translation of UMB 2), Butler, Scannell, et al, (9Mar1900–May1900), index 12 pp., 344pp.; NA Wgtn: Urewera MB 4, MLC 13, W3518, CD 2, Vol. 4, 357 pp.; NA Ak: AREPRO 4711/1446. Acronym: UMB 4.

UMB 7. Urewera District Native Reserve Commission minute book 7, Butler, Mair, et al. (28Apr1902–14Oct02), in English, 70 pp.; NA Wgtn: Waiariki, Urewera MB 7, CD, W3518/2, 63 pp.; NA Ak: AREPRO 4711/1449. Acronym: UMB 7.

Webster, Steven. 1975. "Cognatic Descent Groups and the Contemporary Māori: a Preliminary Reassessment." *The Journal of the Polynesian Society* Vol. 84(2): 121–152, 1975.

Webster, Steven. n.d. (1984–5) "Urewera Land 1895–1926; a tentative historical survey of Government and Tuhoe relations as reflected in official records." Unpublished manuscript, 50pp. Held in the University of Auckland Library. Auckland, N.Z.

Webster, Steven. 1997. "Maori hapuu and their history" in *The Australian Journal of Anthropology* 8:3:307–335. University of Sydney, Sydney, Australia.

Webster, Steven. 1998, "Maori Hapu as a Whole Way of Struggle: 1840–50s Before the Land Wars." *Oceania* 69(1):4–35.

Williams, H.W. 1957. *A Dictionary of the Maori Language*. Sixth edition. Wellington, N.Z.: Government Printer.

CHAPTER 4

The Tamaikoha *Hapū* Branch: Internal Social Organization

1 Introduction: The Tamaikoha Kāwai or Hapū Branch

The previous chapters introduced the *rohe pōtae o Tūhoe* and the Urewera District Native Reserve commission 1899–1903, considered the legitimacy of the commission among the Tūhoe, and examined the difficulties the commission encountered squaring the land blocks into which they divided the reserve with the array of Tūhoe hapū. It is now appropriate to describe in detail a particular example of a Tūhoe hapū descent group as it was organized during these years. Chapters 4 and 5 will be devoted to this end, the first concerned with the internal social organization of a particular hapū branch, and the second with its various hapū affiliations.

The following ethnohistorical reconstruction focuses upon one relatively small descent group for several reasons. First, although smaller than most hapū, it was a spectacularly extensive descent group already spanning four living generations and over 60 persons by 1903 (see Fig. 4.1; the successive generations depicted are genealogically reorganized in Fig. 4.2 and will be explained later). In social anthropology, such cognatic descent groups have been variously referred to as a 'ramage', 'stock', or 'lineage'. However, the first two terms are not in ordinary usage, and 'lineage' more properly refers to part of a unilineal (patri- or matrilineal) clan as distinct from a cognatic descent group. For these reasons, I have decided to use the ordinary English word 'branch' or, in Māori, *kāwai* to refer to a more delimited descent group that is part of a cognatic descent group, that is, affiliated with one or

© The Author(s) 2020
S. Webster, *A Separate Authority (He Mana Motuhake)*, Volume I,
https://doi.org/10.1007/978-3-030-41042-1_4

more hapū by descent through either gender from a common ancestor. Māori language is replete with metaphors of branching growth and 'shoots' such as *kāwai* and, reflecting the central role of ancestral descent in Māori society, such terms often refer to *whakapapa* or genealogy.

The Tamaikoha hapū branch was furthermore an influential descent group, affiliated with many hapū, controlling land in many blocks, and closely connected to important Tūhoe leaders including Te Whiu Maraki, Tupaea Rapaera, and Numia Kererū. For nearly the entire period 1896–1921, from the negotiation of the Urewera District Native Reserve Act through the establishment of the reserve to its dismantling in the Urewera Consolidation Scheme, this hapū branch (and probably several entire hapū) was led by Tamaikoha Te Ariari, one of the most famous *rangatira toa* ('warrior chiefs') of the Tūhoe. As became clear in Chap. 2, Tamaikoha (often called Eru Tamaikoha in the records) was a leading figure in the early investigations of the commission. Considerable information about him has also already been made public (Sissons 1991; Oliver 2007). For all these reasons I hoped that my own further study, also drawing almost entirely on public records, brings no offense to his descendants or other Tūhoe, but rather encourages further research.

Tamaikoha Te Ariari's hapū branch appears in other block lists but is most inclusive and coherent in the Tauwhare Manuka block, including at least those persons numbered 93 through 151 in that block list (Fig. 4.1). It was in the Tauwhare Manuka block that many of them retained some shares even after the Crown purchase campaign 1910–1921, which had especially disastrous results among the previously extensive land rights of Tamaikoha's many descendants. In 1902, Tamaikoha and his wives had about ten living children, all over 18 years old by 1903 (when the lists were published and ages, which were recorded only for those 18 or under, were updated). His *mātāmua* or oldest child Hakeke, a son, had about 16 living children by three wives, the youngest of which was about 11 years old, but Hakeke himself had died by 1907. Two of Tamaikoha's other children were also relatively prolific: his second child, his oldest daughter Pihitahi, had six living children the youngest of which was eight years old; Tamaikoha's third son, Tiopira, had ten living children the youngest of which was five. In addition to these large sibling groups, the *kāwai* included about 13 smaller sibling groups or individuals appearing in this and other block lists who were Tamaikoha's other grandchildren or great-grandchildren. In 1902, when he was probably only in his 60s, he already had at least 60 living offspring. Insofar as high infant mortality is typical of such populations in such times, at least half again as many may have already died.

"The Urewera District Native Reserve Act, 1896."

TAUWHARE-MANUKA.

BEFORE THE COMMISSIONERS
APPOINTED UNDER THE SAID ACT.

In the matter of the land called or heretofore known as "Tauwhare-Manuka," being part of the land described in the First Schedule to the said Act; and in the matter of the investigation of the title to such land.—At a sitting of the Commissioners held at Ruatoki on the 14th day of February, 1902, before David Scannell, William James Butler, Mehaka Tokopounamu, and Te Pou.

IT is hereby ordered that the persons whose names appear in family groups in the first column of the Schedule attached hereto, and therein numbered respectively from 1 to 339, both inclusive, are, and are hereby declared to be, the owners of the parcel of land to be called or known as "Tauwhare-Manuka," containing 28,860 acres, more or less, and delineated on the plan indorsed hereon.

And it is further ordered that the relative shares of the said families and individuals shall be as set out opposite the name of each of them respectively in the second column of the said Schedule; and it is hereby declared that the share of each family and individual shall be inalienable except to His Majesty.

As witness the hands of the above-named Commissioners.

D. SCANNELL, Chairman.
W. J. BUTLER.
MEHAKA TOKOPOUNAMU.
TE POU.

SCHEDULE.

TAUWHARE-MANUKA.

First Column.	Second Column.	
1 Tauarau te Wiremu, m	10	
2 Te Iriwhiro te Wiremu, m	10	
	—	20
3 Ngataua Tauarau, f	5	
4 Ripeka Tauarau, f	5	
5 Himiona Tauarau, m	5	
6 Katerina Tauarau, f	5	
	—	20
7 Nuku te Ratana, m, 6	2	
8 Tarei te Ratana, m, 5	2	
	—	4
9 Hieke Himiona, m, 1	..	2
10 Matehaere Tarei, f	..	10
11 Mihi Tarei, f	10	
12 Hera Tarei, f, 16	10	
13 Ramarihi Tarei, f, 7	10	
	—	30
14 Puhata Tauaki, f	..	5
15 Te Hiko te Tatana, m, 11	2	
16 Wera te Tatana, f, 8	2	
17 Hinehou te Tatana, f, 5	2	
	—	6
18 Te Mai te Maipi, m	5	
19 Karawhira te Maipi, f	5	
20 Reremoana te Maipi, f	5	
21 Hinemotu te Maipi, f	5	
	—	20
22 Kohuka te Mai, m	2	
23 Harete te Mai, f, 16	2	
	—	4
24 More Tutarakauika, f, 8	..	5
25 Paraone Orupe, m, 12	2	
26 Te Rangi Orupe, m, 10	2	
27 Te Wairama Orupe, f, 7	2	
28 Te Kere Orupe, m, 2	2	
	—	8
29 Tuhua te Ahuru, m	1	
30 Te Ruakahukura te Ahuru, m, 17	2	
31 Te Ao te Ahuru, m, 10	2	
32 Te Ataibaea te Ahuru, f, 6	2	
33 Te Aroha te Ahuru, m, 1	2	
	—	9
34 Te Naha te Kauru, m	2	
35 Kiwhakiwha te Kauru, m	2	
36 Puru te Kauru, f	2	
37 Tangira te Kauru, m	2	
	—	8

First Column.	Second Column.	
38 Horopapera Tatu, m, 7	1	
39 Te Uruna Tatu, f, 1	1	
	—	2
40 Peata te Iriwhiro, f	2	
41 Tikareti te Iriwhiro, m, 16	2	
42 Marara te Iriwhiro, f, 14	2	
43 Moa te Iriwhiro, f, 12	2	
44 Hinewairangi te Iriwhiro, f, 7	2	
45 Te Ao te Iriwhiro, f, 5	2	
	—	12
46 Te Rika Mikaera, m	2	
47 Mekita Mikaera, f	2	
48 Make Mikaera, m	2	
49 Hiki Mikaera, m	2	
	—	8
50 Te Whatu Rua, m, 17	1	
51 Toko Rua, m, 14	1	
52 Whakaataata Rua, f, 12	1	
	—	3
53 Te Ahuru te Rika, m	1	
54 Kahuorangi te Rika, m	1	
55 Pine te Rika, f	1	
56 Te Katene te Rika, f	1	
	—	4
57 Tawhara Kahuorangi, m	1	
58 Hoani Kahuorangi, m, 10	1	
59 Hinehou Kahuorangi, f, 8	1	
60 Te Umuariki Kahuorangi, m, 6	1	
61 Roka Kahuorangi, f, 5	1	
	—	5
62 Tatai te Kaawa, f, 12	1	
63 Te Wahataua te Kaawa, m, 10	1	
64 Kaari te Kaawa, f, 8	1	
65 Kanara te Kaawa, m, 5	1	
66 Riaka te Kaawa, m, 1	1	
	—	5
67 Hohepa Manahi, m, 5	..	1
68 Tiwa te Poukohe, m, 5	..	1
69 Te Horohau Make, m	1	
70 Te Wharewi Make, m	1	
71 Te Taniwha Make, m	1	
72 Mahia Make, m, 16	1	
73 Ratika Make, f, 13	1	
74 Tukumaru Make, m, 11	1	
75 Raha Make, f, 9	1	
76 Hori Make, m, 2	1	
	—	8
77 Wikiriwhi te Horohau, m, 16	1	
78 Iti te Horohau, m, 16	1	
	—	2

Fig. 4.1 The Tamaikoha hapū branch (numbered 93–151) as it appeared in the Tauwhare Manuka block owners list (AJHR 1903: 101–102). (Adapted from *Sites*, New Series, Vol. 7 No. 1 (2010))

TAUWHARE-MANUKA—*continued.*

First Column.	Second Column.	
79 Moewaka Tamaruru, f	..	1
80 Rapaera Tahuri, m, 5	1	
81 Hinekoti Tahuri, f, 3	1	
82 Huriana Tahuri, f, 2	1	
83 Miini Tahuri, f, 1	1	
	—	[illegible]
84 Tiena Hiki, f	1	
85 Raiba Hiki, f, 8	1	
86 Heripo Hiki, m, 6	1	
	—	3
87 Noho te Wharau, m	10	
88 Te Ngahuru te Wharau, m	10	
89 Reha te Wharau, m	10	
	—	30
90 Te Awhena Reha, m, 6	5	
91 Ana Reha, f, 2	5	
	—	10
92 Tamaikoha te Ariari, m	..	20
93 Hakeke Tamaikoha, m	10	
94 Pihitahi Tamaikoha, f	10	
95 Pohe Tamaikoha, f	10	
96 Te Hauwaho Tamaikoha, m	10	
97 Tiopira Tamaikoha, m	10	
98 Te Unupo Tamaikoha, f	10	
99 Wharetutu Tamaikoha, f	10	
100 Paruru Tamaikoha, m	10	
101 Takao Tamaikoha, m	10	
102 Te Ahi Tamaikoha, m	10	
	—	100
103 Hinehou Konoro, f, 13	..	2
104 Hinehou Tori, f, 8	2	
105 Pita Tori, m, 7	2	
106 Moe Tori, f, 5	2	
	—	6
107 Konoro Hakeke, m	5	
108 Reihana Hakeke, f	5	
109 Kawehi Hakeke, f	5	
110 Mahia Hakeke, m	5	
111 Mariana Hakeke, f	5	
112 Hineitarewa Hakeke, f, 14	5	
113 Kete Hakeke, m, 13	5	
114 Te Wairawaho Hakeke, m, 12	5	
115 Te Otawa Hakeke, f, 11	5	
116 Kahuwi Hakeke, m	5	
117 Marakihau Hakeke, m	5	
118 Hopaea Hakeke, f	5	
119 Noti Hakeke, f, 18	5	
120 Te Kohi Hakeke, m, 17	5	
121 Wharewhakawa Hakeke, f, 16	5	
	—	75
122 Miria Tupaea, f	5	
123 Te Urupa Tupaea, f	5	
124 Te Kohunui Tupaea, m, 17	5	
125 Hariata Tupaea, f, 16	5	
126 Whata Tupaea, f, 10	5	
127 Turaki Tupaea, f, 8	5	
	—	30
128 Poniu Tumoana, m, 5	..	2
129 Te Haka Wi, m	5	
130 Te Hiko Wi, m, 14	5	
	—	10
131 Te Wharenikau Timi, f, 14	5	
132 Te Koherangi Timi, f, 12	5	
133 Rangiaohia Timi, f, 11	5	
	—	15
134 Taheke te Hauwaho, f, 1	..	5
135 Rangiaho Paora, m, 10	5	
136 Hinehou Paora, f, 8	5	
137 Ngatapa Paora, f, 6	5	
138 Neera Paora, f, 5	5	
	—	20
139 Teko Tiopira, f	5	
140 Paraha Tiopira, f, 14	5	
141 Ruru Tiopira, m, 12	5	
142 Taahu Tiopira, m, 10	5	
143 Te Karetu Tiopira, f, 8	5	
144 Tureiti Tiopira, m, 6	5	
145 Toheroa Tiopira, m, 5	5	
	—	35
146 Meto Teko (H.C.), f, 5	..	2
147 Maramena te Hata, f, 15	..	5
148 Tuirina Tawera, m, 8	5	
149 Hinekirunga Tawera, f, 6	5	
150 Ira Tawera, f, 5	5	
	—	15
151 Karaka Takao, m, 6	..	5
152 Te Uru Kutu, f	..	2
153 Moko Tupaea, m	..	20
154 Tawera Moko, m	10	
155 Takoto Moko, f	10	
156 Takahiao Moko, f	10	
	—	30
157 Puhata Mahia, f	..	20
158 Taupae te Karaka, m	..	10
159 Whaitiri Taupae, f, 10	5	
160 Ramari Taupae, f, 6	5	
161 Tumanako Taupae, m, 2	5	
	—	15
162 Rautipu te Haunui, f	20	
163 Raumiria te Haunui, f	20	
	—	40
164 Te Atamea te Whiu, m	10	
165 Te Maipi te Whiu, m	10	
166 Wari te Whiu, f	10	
167 Te Wahanga te Whiu, f, 13	10	
	—	40
168 Harehare Eparaima, f, 12	5	
169 Te Koro Eparaima, m, 10	5	
170 Heu Eparaima, f, 8	5	
171 Monumonu Eparaima, f, 2	5	
	—	20
172 Te Whaiaipo te Maipi, m, 2	5	
173 Noho te Maipi, f, 1	5	
	—	10
174 Makarangi Kamaua, f, 6	5	
175 Rereata Kamaua, f, 3	5	
	—	10
176 Patu Ru, f, 9	..	[illegible]
177 Te Whakaruku Horopapera, f	2	
178 Kiri Horopapera, f	2	
179 Te Heuheu Horopapera, m	2	
180 Tatu Horopapera, m	2	
	—	8
181 Rangitiriao te Heuheu, f, 18	..	1
182 Heeni te Whioi, f	1	
183 Oneone te Whioi, m, 10	1	
	—	2
184 Te Whanoke Rakuraku, m	15	
185 Teneti Rakuraku, m	15	
186 Taua Rakuraku, m	15	
187 Te Hiwera Rakuraku, f	15	
188 Te Hau Rakuraku, f	15	
189 Paiaka Rakuraku, m	15	
	—	90
190 Wi Teneti, m, 7	5	
191 Eraihia Teneti, m, 6	5	
192 Kaakaa Teneti, m, 5	5	
	—	15
193 Wairini Taua, f	5	
194 Hena Taua, m, 12	5	
195 Te Poono Taua, m, 9	5	
196 Mahuika Taua, m, 7	5	
197 Tiaare Taua, m, 6	5	
198 Maraea Taua, f, 3	5	
	—	30
199 Tarei Paiaka, f, 11	5	
200 Ria Paiaka, f, 8	5	
201 Raho Paiaka, m, 6	5	
202 Mero Paiaka, f, 5	5	
	—	20
203 Whaku te Awhekaihe, f, 13	5	
204 Wei te Awhekaihe, f, 10	5	
205 Herehere te Awhekaihe, f, 8	5	
	—	15
206 Maui te Tawhi, m	..	5
207 Te Herekau Maui, m, 2	..	2
208 Te Amorakau Kepa, f	2	
209 Te Naiti Kepa, m	2	
210 Te Wharetenetí Kepa, m	2	
	—	6
211 Turanga Tairi, m, 9	1	
212 Hapaiariki Tairi, m, 7	1	
213 Tairi Tairi, m, 1	1	
	—	3
214 Netana te Whakaari, m	..	20

Fig. 4.1 (continued)

The Tauwhare Manuka block order list runs three double-columned pages of persons found by the commission to be owners. At the head of the list of owners, as seen in (Fig. 4.1), the formal block order of the commissioners notes that there were 339 owners and the block covered 28,860 acres. Compared with the other 34 blocks of the Reserve, both these figures fall in the middle range. The block was located in the Urewera District Native Reserve (Fig. 1.2) on the eastern bank of the Tauranga/Waimana River in its middle reaches between 300 and 1000 meters altitude. Three or four smaller blocks north of it appear to have been separated off from a larger area extending along this bank, and the Wai-iti River, the major tributary of the Tauranga/Waimana River, drains south from the upper reaches of Tauwhare Manuka through the middle of them. Like most of the UDNR except for small areas along the river bottoms, the land was steeply ridged and covered in dense forest, non-arable except for difficult development of very limited pasture capacity.[1] Correspondence suggests by 1918 this block was the primary *kāinga* ('settlement', residence) of Tamaikoha and at least two of his older sons.

Tamaikoha was a prominent leader in the late 1860s land war in the Bay of Plenty and Urewera. From Sissons' information regarding the other Tūhoe war leader Te Whiu Maraki (whose sister was one of Tamaikoha's wives), it appears that Tamaikoha was born between 1826 and 1832, so he would have been in his 30s during the war. Although he was listed in the 1921 Urewera Consolidation Scheme, he died in 1915 and (as will be described in Volume II) many of his offspring died in the war and flu epidemic soon thereafter. Some of Tamaikoha's predecessors have been included in the genealogy depicted in Fig. 4.2. Supposing an average of at least 20 years between first-born children of each generation, his parents Te Ariari, and Tiramate were probably born before 1810, and his grandparents Rangipa and Urunga were probably born before 1790. Te Ramahaki, Urunga's parent, would have been born in the time of Cook's voyages. Tamaikoha's oldest child Hakeke, himself father of 16 living children and still living at the time the UDNR was investigated, was probably a young teenager during the land wars and perhaps in his 50s by 1906, when he died.

Tamaikoha's role in the land wars continued through 1870 but remains unclear. He was clearly associated with the long *te whai a te motu* (pursuit of separateness or independence) of the famous 'rebel' Te Kooti throughout the Urewera (the huge meetinghouse of this name at Mātaatua outside

Ruatāhuna was dedicated to Te Kooti by the Urewera hapū and war leader Te Whenuanui I in 1883). Oliver's comments (Oliver 2007) regarding Tamaikoha are made in a biographical account of the *kūpapa* (Crown loyalist) leader Rapata Wahawaha from the East Coast Ngāti Porou *iwi* ('tribe'), but reflect the popular assumption that Tamaikoha was a member of the rebel 'Hauhau' cult, Crown propaganda against Māori resistance which was extended loosely to Te Kooti. Oliver reports that Tamaikoha remained 'undefeated' in 1866, but by 1870 'made peace' with the Crown loyalist leader Te Keepa (who fought alongside Wahawaha against the Tūhoe resistance) and in 1871 acted as an 'intermediary' between Te Wahawaha and Tūhoe in securing peace and the withdrawal of Wahawaha's garrison from the Urewera.[2]

Sissons' account of Tamaikoha's role in the war is much fuller and more sympathetic toward Te Kooti and possible Tūhoe supporters. He emphasizes his leadership in resistance against the incursion of the Crown into Urewera lands on the pretexts of harboring 'Hauhau' and participating in the execution of the missionary spy Volkner. Sissons concludes that while Tamaikoha's resistance to these incursions may have coincided with Te Kooti's evasion of them, even his occasional role as an intermediary was only ambiguously aligned with the Crown. He reports that Tamaikoha is buried where he was said to have usually lived, at Tauanui on the left bank of the Waimana River just above its junction with the Whakatane River (1991: 236). Tauanui or Tawanui is in the part of the Waimana block sold by the 1890s and was outside the northeast boundary of the Urewera District Native Reserve. Although it was some of the best agricultural land remaining after the Crown's confiscations in the 1860s, Tamaikoha's most extensive land rights were in the interior of the Urewera district up the Whakatane but especially the Tauranga/Waimana river valleys. Sissons also reports that in 1897 Tamaikoha's senior sons Hakeke and Tiopira both owned general stores in the vicinity of Whakarae (1991: 167); this was located just below the junction of the Wai-iti and Tauranga/Waimana River, well inside the northeast boundary of the UDNR and on lands still retained by the hapū branch after the disastrous Crown purchase campaign and the 1921 consolidation scheme.

The extent of early alienation by the hapū branch of land in the lower reaches of the Waimana River, and the entrepreneurial effort of Hakeke and Tiopira as storekeepers, reflects the extent to which Tamaikoha and his offspring had adapted to Pākehā (European) culture within a few decades after the land wars. Nevertheless, Tamaikoha struggled to retain control of their remaining lands in Waimana block and, as discussed in Chap. 2, was highly skeptical of the motives of the UDNR commission in its first year of operation and at least for a while led the resistance against it (Sissons 2002 Appendix 1: 64–69). Whether his and others' skepticism was sustained or not, the later betrayals by the Crown proved it well-founded, and radically reduced the landholdings of Tamaikoha's many offspring as well as many other Tūhoe. In terms of the *mana* of the *mātāmua* line (first-born among siblings) in Tamaikoha's hapū branch, it can be noted that he himself was apparently without living siblings, and that the senior line from him ran down through his son Hakeke Tamaikoha and his grandson Konoro Hakeke to his great-granddaughter Hinehou Konoro, aged 13 in 1903. Consolidation Scheme records show she was still living in 1921, holding small shares in Maungapōhatu but in no other blocks of the Urewera Native Reserve. By that time, most of her numerous cousins were among the Tūhoe *kore whenua*, 'those without land'.

The format of these block lists, as legal orders or 'block *owner* lists', can be misleading with regard to a clearer conceptualization of hapū as well as the electoral roles that they were intended to represent under the 1896 Act. Hapū are ancestral descent groups, which is to say that most of the generations that comprise a hapū are deceased. Yet a hapū branch such as the four generations of Tamaikoha's offspring depicted in the Tauwhare Manuka block list represents only its *living* generations. The deceased generations that link this hapū branch to others in the same list and ultimately to the founding ancestor of one or more hapū are not included, although these are the source of their rights to this block. As legal orders, such lists assume alienable ownership of the living generations rather than the inalienable birthrights that derive from these deceased generations and their founding ancestor. Furthermore, as has been explained in previous chapters and will be analyzed in Chap. 5 in terms of Tamaikoha's descendants, a hapū branch can be affiliated with several different hapū, although one or two are usually given priority over the others by its descendants in their claim to rights in a particular area of land.

While the predecessors connecting several living hapū branches in a block list may be invisible to an outsider, they are obvious or assumed by many members of these living descent groups who see each other as 'cousins' and even as continuing an ancestral *tuakana/teina* or senior/junior sibling relationship between each other. Although the deceased generations and the living hapū branches they link together would probably not be seen from an outsider's point of view as a social 'group' in a face-to-face sense, they are often assumed to be concretely 'present' by the living members. As is the case in many other kinship systems based on ancestral descent, living members of a hapū or their leaders are often viewed as personifications, bodily extensions of, or even identical to a long-dead founding ancestor. By 1900 the UDNR commission, following the usage of the Tūhoe claimants, was routinely referring to the common ancestor in whose name a hapū had claimed a block as 'the claimant', even though he (or she) had been dead for many generations. Witnesses made such statements as "In regard to [the claim of Te Urewera hapū for the block] Whaitiripapa, Te Whanapeke and his descendants *are the claimants.* They lived together at Ohae fortification…" (UMB 3: 177, italics added). As will be discussed in Chap. 5, the Whaitiripapa block was claimed by Tamaikoha Te Ariari in the name of his ancestor Whanapeke, yet Whanapeke lived nine generations before Tamaikoha. Similarly, in this same case, Tamaikoha referred to the counter-claimant Numia Kererū, who was speaking for the hapū Ngāti Rongo, as though Numia were the personal recipient of a gift of land that had been given to that hapū by a descendant of Whanapeke several generations earlier.

The implications of the block lists for understanding Tūhoe social organization are manifold but obscured in other ways. The Tamaikoha *kāwai* or hapū branch is depicted in this chapter in three forms: as it appeared in the Tauwhare Manuka block order list of owners published in 1903 (Fig. 4.1, above); a reorganization of selected sibling groups of this hapū branch in a genealogical form, adding certain ancestors and spouses (Fig. 4.2, below); and a tabulation of the land rights of senior persons in this genealogical sketch from which hapū affiliations can be inferred (Fig. 4.3). Analysis guided by Figs. 4.1 and 4.2 will show how the block lists of the Urewera District Native Reserve have been interpreted to exemplify central principles of Tūhoe social organization and the internal social organization of the hapū branch as it was 1899–1903. Analysis guided by Figs. 4.2 and 4.3 will then reconstruct details of spouses and mothers, marriages, and half-siblings in conjunction with land rights recognized among the blocks of the Native Reserve. In Chap. 5, following the evidence summarized in Fig. 4.3, identification of the several hapū affiliations maintained by the Tamaikoha hapū branch during these years will be attempted.

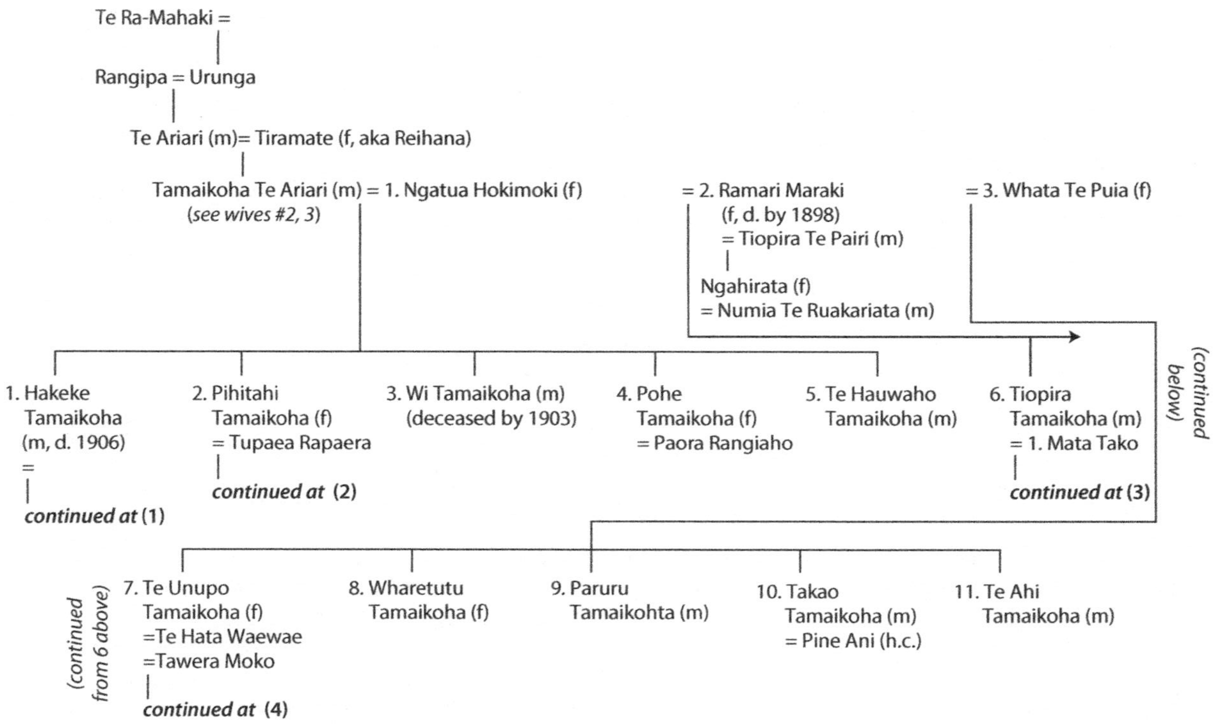

Fig. 4.2 Tamaikoha hapū branch, 1903 (selected, augmented, and genealogically arranged). (Source: Sites, New Series, Vol. 7 No. 1 (2010))

Legend:

Some spouses have been added to the descent group in order to trace land rights, or due to their importance in alliance with other descent groups. Note that the first three generations were deceased, while all the other persons included were

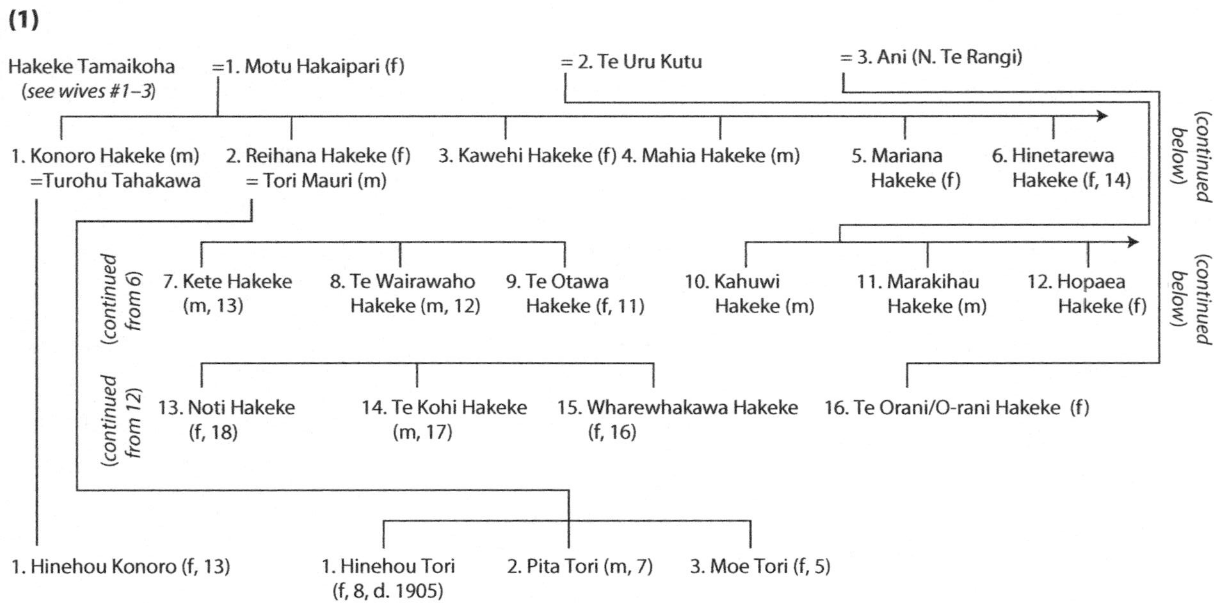

Fig. 4.2 (continued) alive 1899–1903 unless specifically noted as deceased (d.). The offspring of only 4 of Tamaikoha's 10 living children have been selected, depicted separately in continuations (1) through (4)

Symbols: = means marriage; = 1, = 2 mean priority of marriages; horizontal lines connect siblings (numbered in birth order), continued on the next line if necessary; vertical lines connect parents and children (including distinctions between additional spouses and half-siblings); gender (m or f), age (in 1903), and date of birth (b.) or death (d.) follow names in parentheses

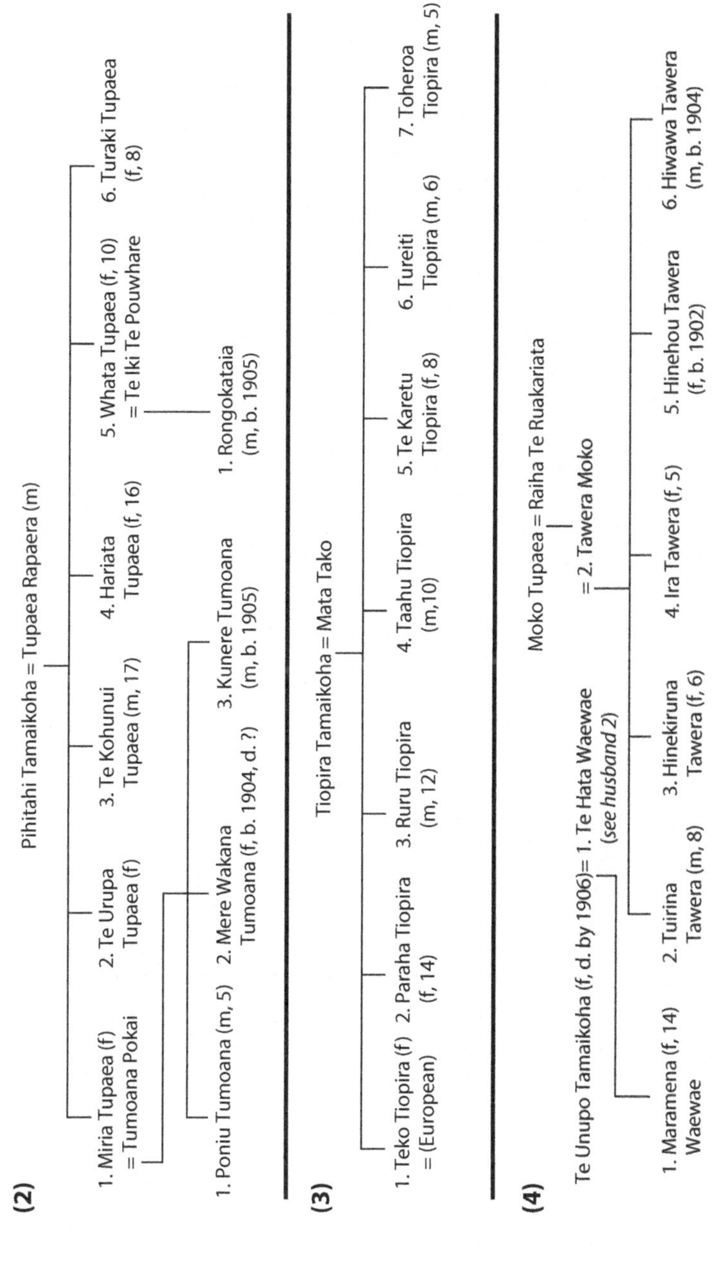

Fig. 4.2 (continued)

2 Sibling Groups and Surnames

The selected genealogy of Fig. 4.2 has been derived primarily from the Tauwhare Manuka block list of Fig. 4.1, but this may not be obvious. The legal order heading each block list misleadingly characterized the groupings of persons as 'families', and this crucial misunderstanding is reinforced by the apparent surname or 'family name' consistently carried by everyone in the group. It is important to realize that each grouping is not a 'family' but instead a *sibling group*, and that the second name is not an ordinary 'surname'. The parents of these sibling groups both bear different second names from those of their children and appear elsewhere in the list, or in other lists, usually grouped with *their* siblings. Individuals who are listed alone probably had no living siblings or only siblings without rights in this block; one example in the hapū branch being examined is Tamaikoha himself, who apparently had no living siblings. Therefore, without either parents or spouses included, these sibling groups are neither 'families' nor *whānau*. As will be seen, far from being domestic groups of any kind, these sibling groups represent successive generations of a *descent* group or hapū branch in which all share a common progenitor (in this case, Tamaikoha) or, along with other hapū branches, a common ancestor.

Furthermore, the 'surnames' appearing in these sibling groups were actually the *first* name of the *father*, so, quite unlike the European surname, change with each generation. This requires some explanation: persons listed in Māori whakapapa (genealogies), including those of Tūhoe recorded by Best, are conventionally identified by only a 'first' name, that is, one name only. As the European convention of a surname or "family name" became accepted by Māori, it was the father's "first" (or only) name, which was used (Metge 1967: 131). However, unlike in the European custom of continuing the surname in each generation, for a few generations Māori continued to adopt the father's first name rather than his 'surname'—which was seen instead as a grandparent's (only) name. Tūhoe did not generally begin to continue their 'surname' until the 1930s, and one still encounters individuals whose first name, having been taken in honor of a grandparent, is the same as their surname (which originated from the same person). A further complication is that many Tūhoe also adopted Māori transliterations of Pākehā surnames, or entirely different Pākehā surnames, although their previous Māori surname remains common knowledge several generations later.

As mentioned in the previous chapter, the use of surnames appears to have first been required of Tūhoe during the investigation of the Te Waipotiki block. In March 1900, the earliest such instruction I have found, the chairman Percy Smith actually directed that *maternal* names be cancelled and replaced by father's names. Apparently, some Tūhoe were adding the (first or only) name of the mother rather than the father. It is significant that the commission had to remind claimants of this European convention in later hearings. This suggests that untutored Tūhoe addition of a surname, contrary to the patrilateral bias of European culture, was 'cognatic', that is, did not distinguish on the basis of parents' gender but rather on the basis of other factors such as land rights, hapū membership, or *mana* (as some European conventions such as hyphenation or double surnames also illustrate). The block lists show that in the case of 'half-caste' (denoted 'h.c.') children of a Tūhoe mother and Pākehā father, the children were consistently allowed to be given their mother's first name as their surname. This exception to the paternal first-name rule was probably allowed because the children derived no such Tūhoe statuses from their Pākehā father, but did from their mother. (Interestingly, there were apparently no 'half-caste' children of Tūhoe men and Pākehā women, or they were not identified as 'h.c.' in the block lists.)

Sibling groups were actually central in Tūhoe social organization, being minimal descent groups, usually descendants of the same parents and thus the same ancestors, and sharing the same ancestral land and hapū rights. Half-siblings shared at least half of the same ancestors and, where they were offspring of the same father by different mothers (paternal half-siblings), were usually grouped together in the block lists. The separate grouping of offspring of the same mother by different fathers was probably merely the result of the patronymic 'surname' system imposed, and reflected no less sibling solidarity than paternal half-siblings. In the face of Crown policy hostile to larger non-seller kin groups in 1921, full- or half-sibling groups nevertheless persisted as the core of most new groups (often hapū branches) formed under the Urewera Consolidation Scheme. Characteristic of cognatic kinship systems, among Tūhoe of this time, the central social role of shared land and hapū rights devolved through females was no less important than that devolved through males; contrary to some academic as well as popular assumption, this is generally the case among contemporary Māori (Webster 1975: 125–6).

The block lists are comprised of sibling groups organized in *kāwai* or hapū branches, often displaying several successive living generations. As in the case of the Tamaikoha hapū branch, the descent line between these generations can be traced, using the patronymic surname to identify the father and a process of elimination and other methods to identify the mother. As well as the gender of each individual, age was recorded if 18 years old or less. It also turns out that each sibling group is consistently ordered by birth from the eldest to the youngest sibling. Relative seniority among siblings is a fundamental principle of Māori kinship, well documented in contemporary as well as traditional society. General terms for siblings still in common use are *mātāmua* (eldest sibling, regardless of gender), *tuakana* (older sibling of the same gender), and *teina* (younger sibling of the same gender). Although some gender discrimination is suggested in the strict usage of the latter two terms (i.e., they are not properly applied between a brother and sister), in ordinary usage they simply mean 'senior' and 'junior', respectively, regardless of gender.

All three of these terms marking relative seniority are furthermore extended through generations and applied to the most distant cousins regardless of the gender of intervening ancestors. Successive generations in the UDNR block lists are also often (but not always) ordered in accordance with the principle of relative seniority, offering additional clues for the reconstruction of the descent line. The principle is clear in Fig. 4.1, where a third and even a fourth generation of Tamaikoha's offspring are ranked more highly than their parents or even grandparents. Commonly in the block lists, in accord with this principle of seniority the grandchildren as well as the children of relatively senior siblings are given priority, often being listed *before* the offspring of the senior's teina or junior siblings (regardless of gender). This is shown in the case of Tamaikoha's first-born child (a son) Hakeke and second-born child (a daughter) Pihitahi, whose first-born grandchildren Hinehou (number 104) and Poniu (number 128), respectively, were listed before Tamaikoha's third-born son's two children (numbers 129, 130) and all the rest of his offspring. Indeed, as Tamaikoha's great-granddaughter in the *mātāmua* (first-born) line, Hinehou is even listed before her own father (Konoro Hakeke, number 107).

Although the 'first' name of mothers of sibling groups is rarely carried over as their children's surname, they can nevertheless be identified using these principles of social organization evident in the block lists along with UMB 8, an important surviving record of the commission discussed in Chap. 3. When Elsdon Best drew up this draft of the final block lists late in 1902, he furthermore annotated most sibling groups in about half of the block lists with the names of their mother (or mothers). While the imposed patronyms in the block lists indicated the father's side of each sibling group's genealogy, this information recorded the mother's side and reflected any birthrights to land or hapū membership devolved through her. Although this invaluable record could have been made by Best to check on the proportion of shares allocated to the children, it was probably intended for his own use in genealogical research because it apparently resulted in no changes of shares.

Tamaikoha Te Ariari (m) (*wives 1–3 follow*)	=1. Ngatua Hokimoki (f)	=2. Ramari Maraki (f)	=3. Whata Te Puia (f)
30: Pukepohatu. 20: Whaitiripapa, Tauwhare Manuka, Ohiorangi, Taneatua, Paraoanui (N). 10: Paraoanui (S), Karioi, Tawhaiti Nui, Parekohe, Ruatahuna (1903). 5: Waikarewhenua, Tauranga, Waikaremoana. 1: Tarapounamu-Matawhero.	20: Karioi, *Tauranga* 10: Taneatua 5: Tauwhare Manuka (*see children 1–5 below*)	20: Waikarewhenua, Otara, *Te Ranga Ruanuku*, Parakohe. 5: Karioi. 4: Maungapohatu. (*see child 6 below*)	20: Waikarewhenua, Otara. 15: Parekohe. 10: Tapatahi, *Te Purenga*. 5: Taneatua, Tarapounamu-Matawhero. (*see children 7–11 below*)
1. Hakeke Tamaikoha (m)	2. Pihitahi Tamaikoha (f), (= Tupaea Rapaera)	4. Pohe Tamaikoha (f), (= Paora Rangiaho)	5. Te Hauwaho Tamaikoha (m)
20: Pukepohatu 10: Whaitiripapa, Tauwhare Manuka, Tauranga, Taneatua, Paraoanui (N), Ohiorangi. 5: Paraoanui (S), Karioi, Ruatahuna, Karioi, Te Whaiti Nui. 4: Waikarewhenua. 3: Ruatoki (S). 2: Maungapohatu, Waikaremoana. 1: Tarapounamu-Matawhero.	20: Pukepohatu. 10: Whaitiripapa, Tauwhare Manuka, Tauranga, Taneatua, Paraoanui (N), Ruatoki 1, 2. 5: Karioi, Paraoanui (S), Ruatahuna, Te Whaiti Nui. 4: Waikarewhenua. 3: Ruatoki (S). 2: Maungapohatu, Waikaremoana. 1: Tarapounamu-Matawhero.	20: Pukepohatu. 10: Whaitiripapa, Tauwhare Manuka, Tauranga, Taneatua, Paraoanui (N), Ruatoki 1. 5: Karioi, Paraoanui (S) Ruatahuna. 4: Waikarewhenua. 3: Ruatoki South. 2: Maungapohatu, Waikaremoana. 1: Tarapounamu-Matawhero.	20: Pukepohatu. 10: Whaitiripapa, Tauwhare Manuka, Tauranga, Taneatua, Paraoanui (N). 5: Karioi, Paraoanui (S), Ruatahuna. 4: Waikarewhenua. 3: Ruatoki South. 2: Maungapohatu, Waikaremoana. 1: Tarapounamu-Matawhero.

Fig. 4.3 Parents and extension of land rights in the Tamaikoha hapū branch. (Source: Sites, New Series, Vol. 7 No. 1 (2010))
Legend:
Figure 4.3 shows only a few parents and sibling groups selected from Fig. 4.2, which details the genealogical relationships more fully. Of the third generation, only Hakeke's numerous offspring are shown here, and none of the fourth generation.

6. Tiopira Tamaikoha (m)	7. Te Unupo Tamaikoha (f)	8. Wharetutu Tamaikoha (f)	9. Paruru Tamaikoha (m)
20: Otara, Waikarewhenua, Pukepohatu, Parekohe. 15: Te Ranga a Ruanuku, Te Tuahu. 10: Tauwhare Manuka, Taneatua, Paraoanui (N), Whaitiripapa, Ruatahuna. 5: Karioi, Paraoanui (S), Te Whaiti Nui. 2: Maungapohatu, Waikaremoana. 1: Tarapounamu-Matawhero.	20: Waikarewhenua, Te Purenga, Pukepohatu. 15: Kohuru Tukuroa. 10: Whaitiripapa, Tauwhare Manuka, Taneatua, Paraoanui (N), Otara, Ruatahuna, Te Ranga a Ruanuku, Parekohe, Ruatoki 1. 5: Karioi, Paraoanui (S). 3: Ruatoki South. 2: Maungapohatu, Tauranga, Waikaremoana, Ruatoki 3. 1: Taraponamu-Matawhero.	20: Waikarewhenua, Te Purenga, Pukepohatu. 15: Kohuru Tukuroa. 10: Whaitiripapa, Tauwhare Manuka, Taneatua, Paraoanui (N), Otara, Ruatahuna, Te Ranga a Ruanuku, Parekohe. 5: Karioi, Paraoanui (S). 3: Ruatoki South. 2: Maungapohatu, Tauranga, Waikaremoana, Ruatoki 3. 1: Tarapounamu-Matawhero.	20: Waikarewhenua, Te Purenga, Pukepohatu. 15: Kohuru Tukuroa. 10: Whaitiripapa, Tauwhare Manuka, Taneatua, Paraoanui (N), Otara, Ruatahuna, Te Ranga a Ruanuku, Parekohe. 5: Karioi, Paraoanui (S). 3: Ruatoki South. 2: Maungapohatu, Tauranga, Waikaremoana, Ruatoki 3. 1: Tarapounamu Matawhero.

10. Takao Tamaikoha (m)	11. Te Ahi Tamaikoha (m)
20: Waikarewhenua, Te Purenga, Pukepohatu. 15: Kohuru Tukuroa. 10: Whaitiripapa, Tauwhare Manuka, Taneatua, Paraoanui (N), Otara, Ruatahuna, Te Ranga a Ruanuku, Parekohe. 5: Karioi, Paraoanui (S). 3: Ruatoki South. 2: Maungapohatu, Tauranga, Waikaremoana, Ruatoki 3. 1: Tarapounamu-Matawhero.	20: Waikarewhenua, Te Purenga, Pukepohatu. 15: Kohuru Tukuroa. 10: Whaitiripapa, Tauwhare Manuka, Taneatua, Paraoanui (N), Otara, Ruatahuna, Te Ranga a Ruanuku, Parekohe. 5: Karioi, Paraoanui (S). 3: Ruatoki South. 2: Maungapohatu, Tauranga, Waikaremoana, Ruatoki 3. 1: Tarapounamu-Matawhero.

Fig. 4.3 (continued) Note that members of each sibling group are numbered in their birth order, and that notes in italics refer to wives and offspring. Land rights of each person are depicted here in relative shares held in each land block (20, 10, 5, etc.,), as they were awarded in the 1903 orders. For distinctions of relative status in a block,

1. Hakeke Tamaikoha (m), (d. 1906)	= 1. Motu Hakaipari (f)	= 2. Te Uru Kutu (f)	= 3. Ani (N. Te Rangi)
(*see land rights above; wives 1–3 follow here*)	20:Waikarewhenua, Te Tuahu, Omahuru. 10: Paraoanui (S) (*see children 1–9 below*)	20:Kohuru Tukuroa, Paraeroa. 10: Whaitiripapa, Tauwhare Manuka. 5: Te Waipotiki, Tauranga, Taneatua, Ruatahuna, Tarapounamu Matawhero, Te Whaiti Nui. (*see children 10–15 below*)	(probably from N. Te Rangi iwi, with no Tuhoe land rights) (*see child 16 below*)
1. Konoro Hakeke (m)	2. Reihana Hakeke (f)	3. Kawehi Hakeke (f)	4. Mahia Hakeke (m)
10: Waikarewhenua, Te Tuahu, Omahuru. 5: Karioi, Whaitiripapa, Tauwhare Manuka, Ohiorangi, Tauranga, Paraoanui (N). 3: Paraoanui (S). 2: Ruatoki South, Ruatahuna. 1: Tarapounamu-Matawhero.	10: Waikarewhenua, Te Tuahu, Omahuru. 5: Karioi, Whaitiripapa, Tauwhare Manuka, Ohiorangi, Tauranga, Paraoanui (N). 3: Paraoanui (S). 2: Ruatoki South, Ruatahuna. 1: Tarapounamu-Matawhero.	10: Waikarewhenua, Te Tuahu, Omahuru. 5: Karioi, Whaitiripapa, Tauwhare Manuka, Ohiorangi, Tauranga, Paraoanui (N). 3: Paraoanui (S). 2: Ruatoki South, Ruatahuna. 1: Tarapounamu-Matawhero.	10: Waikarewhenua, Te Tuahu, Omahuru. 5: Karioi, Whaitiripapa, Tauwhare Manuka, Ohiorangi, Tauranga, Paraoanui (N). 3: Paraoanui (S). 2: Ruatoki South, Ruatahuna. 1: Tarapounamu-Matawhero.

Fig. 4.3 (continued) 15 or more shares held in the senior living generation (and proportionally fewer in the succeeding generations) are nominated 'strong' shares, and strong shares listed among the first 100 shareholders of a block list are nominated 'leading' shares in that block. Leading shares are underlined in this table. Shares in a block that are distinctive for purposes of matching mothers with offspring appear in italics

5. Mariana Hakeke (f)	6. Hinetarewa Hakeke (f), (14)	7. Kete Hakeke (m), (13)	8. Te Wairawaho Hakeke (m), (12)
10: Waikarewhenua, Te Tuahu, Omahuru. 5: Karioi, Whaitiripapa, Tauwhare Manuka, Ohiorangi, Tauranga, Paraoanui (N). 3: Paraoanui (S). 2: Ruatoki South, Ruatahuna. 1: Tarapounamu-Matawhero.	10: Waikarewhenua, Te Tuahu, Omahuru. 5: Karioi, Whaitiripapa, Tauwhare Manuka, Ohiorangi, Tauranga, Paraoanui (N). 3: Paraoanui (S). 2: Ruatoki South, Ruatahuna. 1: Tarapounamu-Matawhero.	10: Waikarewhenua, Te Tuahu, Omahuru. 5: Karioi, Whaitiripapa, Tauwhare Manuka, Ohiorangi, Tauranga, Paraoanui (N). 3: Paraoanui (S). 2: Ruatoki South, Ruatahuna. 1: Tarapounamu-Matawhero.	10: Waikarewhenua, Te Tuahu, Omahuru. 5: Karioi, Whaitiripapa, Tauwhare Manuka, Ohiorangi, Tauranga, Paraoanui (N). 3: Paraoanui (S). 2: Ruatahuna. 1: Tarapounamu-Matawhero.
9. Te Otawa Hakeke (f), (11)	10. Kahuwi Hakeke (m)	11. Marakihau Hakeke (m)	12. Hopaea Hakeke (f)
10: Waikarewhenua. 5: Karioi, Whaitiripapa, Tauwhare Manuka, Ohiorangi, Tauranga, Paraoanui (N), Ruatahuna. 3: Te Waipotiki, Paraoanui (S). 2: Ruatoki South. 1: Tarapounamu-Matawhero.	10: Kohuru-Tukuroa, Paraeroa. 9: Taneatua. 5: Karioi, Whaitiripapa, Tauwhare Manuka, Ohiorangi, Tauranga, Paraoanui (N), Ruatahuna. 3: Te Waipotiki, Paraoanui (S). 2: Ruatoki South, Waikarewhenua. 1: Tarapounamu-Matawhero.	10: Kohuru-Tukuroa, Paraeroa. 9: Taneatua. 5: Karioi, Whaitiripapa, Tauwhare Manuka, Ohiorangi, Tauranga, Paraoanui (N), Ruatahuna. 3: Te Waipotiki, Paraoanui (S). 2: Ruatoki South, Waikarewhenua. 1: Tarapounamu-Matawhero.	10: Kohuru-Tukuroa, Paraeroa. 9: Taneatua. 5: Karioi, Whaitiripapa, Tauwhare Manuka, Ohiorangi, Tauranga, Paraoanui (N), Ruatahuna. 3: Te Waipotiki, Paraoanui (S). 2: Ruatoki South, Waikarewhenua. 1: Tarapounamu-Matawhero.

Fig. 4.3 (continued)

13. Noti Hakeke (f), (18)	14. Te Kohi Hakeke (m), (17)	15. Wharewhakawa (aka Materoa?) Hakeke (f), (16)	16. Te Orani / O-rani Hakeke (f)
10: Kohuru-Tukuroa, Paraeroa. 9: Taneatua. 5: Karioi, Whaitiripapa, Tauwhare Manuka, Ohiorangi, Tauranga, Paraoanui (N), Ruatahuna. 3: Te Waipotiki, Paraoanui (S). 2: Waikarewhenua. 1: Tarapounamu-Matawhero.	10: Kohuru-Tukuroa, Paraeroa. 9: Taneatua. 5: Karioi, Whaitiripapa, Tauwhare Manuka, Ohiorangi, Tauranga, Paraoanui (N), Ruatahuna. 3: Te Waipotiki, Paraoanui (S). 2: Ruatoki South, Waikarewhenua. 1: Tarapounamu-Matawhero.	10: Kohuru-Tukuroa, Paraeroa. 9: Taneatua. 5: Karioi, Whaitiripapa, Tauwhare Manuka, Ohiorangi, Tauranga, Paraoanui (N), Ruatahuna. 3: Te Waipotiki, Paraoanui (S). 1: Tarapounamu-Matawhero.	9: Taneatua. 5: Tauranga, Karioi.

Fig. 4.3 (continued)

The information in Figs. 4.2 and 4.3 can now be approached. Two additional sources were important in the genealogical depiction of selected sibling groups of the Tamaikoha hapū branch in Fig. 4.2: Best's 1898 genealogical census and his collected genealogies of the Tūhoe (Best 1973: Vol 2). With this information it was possible to identify and add to Fig. 4.2 a few of the apparently most significant ancestors, check and augment the number and order of the sibling groups, identify several of their spouses, and confirm the order of marriages. Land rights recognized by the commission are tabulated in Fig. 4.3 for most of the leading members of the hapū branch. As will be detailed later, the spouses which have been added to the Fig. 4.2 genealogy are, as the other parent(s) of a sibling group, additional sources of ancestral hapū as well as land rights. The information in Fig. 4.3 will also be drawn upon in confirming the order of marriages and distinguishing half- from full siblings.

3 Spouses, Mothers, Marriages, and Land Rights

Examination of the portions of Tamaikoha's hapū branch included in Fig. 4.2, in conjunction with available archival information, clarifies some aspects of Tūhoe social organization and family history during this era. Here below, Tamaikoha's children and those of his oldest child Hakeke, by far the most extensive sibling groups of the branch and both sprung from more than one marriage, will be examined with regard to their mothers and their associated land rights. This enables distinctions to be drawn between full- and half-siblings, and clarifies the possibility of concurrent as well as the priority of marriages. Three further children of Tamaikoha's, Pihitahi, Tiopira, and Unupo will be commented on with regard to their marriages (see genealogical extensions 1–3 in Fig. 4.2, but not pursued in Fig. 4.3).

The large sibling group representing Tamaikoha Te Ariari's children in the Tauwhare Manuka block list are actually three sets of paternal half-siblings. The mothers of his eleven living children (in 1898, ten by 1902) were three different women, most reliably reported in Best's genealogical census (1898: 28) and partly confirmed by Sissons (1991: 164). As laid out in Fig. 4.2, his census clearly depicts children 1 through 5 (Hakeke through Te Hauwaho) as born by Ngatua Hokimoki, child 6 (Tiopira) as born by Ramari Maraki, and children 7 through 11 as born by Whata Te Puia. The relative seniority of these three wives is also made clear in Best's 1898 census, although a reversal between Whata and Ramari had to be corrected by later annotations as "3d wife" and "2d wife", respectively. However, Best's 1902 annotations of the mothers of Tamaikoha's children in the draft block lists of UMB 8 distinguished between half-siblings at very different points, and overlooked Ramari's birth of Tiopira entirely. Generally, he recorded children 1 through 4 as born by Ngatua and 5 through 11 as born by Whata, that is, drawing the half-siblings distinction between Pohe and Te Hauwaho, including the latter as well as Tiopira (whose mother was actually Ramari) among Whata's children. On the Taneatua block list, Best even recorded all siblings 2–10 as Whata's children, with only Hakeke as the child of Ngatua.

The award of land rights and relative shares among Tamaikoha's children, abstracted from all the block lists in which the hapū branch held rights and depicted in Fig. 4.3 under their names, can clarify inconsistencies between Best's records. The procedures for allocation of relative shares examined in the previous chapter guide the following analysis in identification of mothers, marriages, and half-siblings. The allocation of relative shares, and especially those reflecting relative rights of the same individual or sibling group in different blocks, will be examined more closely in the following chapter with regard to other aspects of social status and especially hapū affiliations.

Generally, all members of a sibling group were allocated an equal number of shares regardless of seniority. Insofar as individuals of the sibling group held different shares, the most likely source of this disparity was different parents, through whom different land rights had devolved. The most distinctive land rights of the three wives, relative to Tamaikoha and to each other, have been marked in italic type in Fig. 4.3. The apparent differential extension of these land rights to Tamaikoha's children tends to confirm different mothers at the points laid out in Fig. 4.2, which is as Best detailed it in his 1898 census. The comparison is not conclusive, primarily because Tamaikoha's and his wives' land rights overlapped considerably, and some of their children's land rights appear to have originated not from any of these parents but rather as *aroha* (compassion, in this case, gifts) from other relatives, or as restored ancestral rights due to renewed occupation which had lapsed for their parents. Regardless of equivocal data, the evidence laid out below fairly clearly outweighs alternative conclusions regarding maternal filiation in the sibling group.

Ngatua Hokimoki's much stronger rights to Tauranga block (20 shares rather than the 5 held by Tamaikoha) were extended in appropriate shares (10) only to children 1 through 5, while 6 (Tiopira) held none and children 7 through 11 held only 2 shares each, probably in virtue of their father's shares. Tiopira is the only child to have held shares in Te Ranga a Ruanuku block, where his probable mother Ramari held 20 shares (Tiopira held 15, more than would be expected, and also strong shares in Te Tuahu block, of unexplained origin). Ramari's distinctive shares in Maungapōhatu block do not reinforce this evidence, because a small share in this block was extended to all Tamaikoha's children, apparently in *aroha*. Whata's distinctive shares in Te Purenga block were extended only to children 7 through 11 while children 1 through 6 (Tiopira) held none; however, it remains unexplained why Whata's children held 20 shares each in this block, while she held only 10 shares, the reverse of the usual proportional difference between parent and child. Other distinctive shares among Tamaikoha's children remain unexplained, but are not inconsistent with the conclusions indicated by the above evidence regarding which children were the paternal half-siblings.

When a sibling group (all bearing the first name of their father as their 'surname') is apparently born of more than one mother, and the father thus appears to have had more than one wife, several important sociological or cultural issues arise. One of the first is, did such a 'wife' constitute a 'marriage' (*moe* or *moenga*, literally to sleep or a sleeping place) in the eyes of the Tūhoe? While some liaisons resulting in children were probably not considered a 'marriage', any recorded by the Tūhoe commissioners in the block lists as extending rights in land almost certainly were marriages in a publicly accepted sense. Divorce was probably not uncommon, but the extension or succession to land rights was a birth-right determined by descent and filiation, so would remain unaffected (at least one apparent instance in Tamaikoha's hapū branch is his daughter Te Unupo's first marriage and child born to Te Hata Waewae; both later had several children by other spouses).

Insofar as polygyny (concurrent wives) was probably still common among leading Tūhoe men, the question also arises whether the wives which Best denoted as Tamaikoha's first, second, and third might have been concurrent to some extent. Fair evidence of this might be the relative ages of his children. If Tamaikoha's wives were having his children concurrently, it is possible that their consistent ordering in most block lists did not simply reflect their ages from eldest to youngest, but rather the relative seniority of their mothers while some of their ages overlapped. Drawing on Bruce Biggs' work *Māori Marriage*, Joan Metge reported that traditionally the "wife of highest rank – usually the first – took precedence over other wives, and her children over theirs, regardless of age" (1967: 27). While none of the ages of Tamaikoha's children was recorded (all being over 18), many of those of his eldest child Hakeke were recorded, and so at least in his case can help to clarify the possibility of concurrent marriages.

However, seniority among concurrent marriages is far more ambiguous than seniority of birth order, being determined by possibly ambiguous marriage sequence (in terms of public recognition), wives' rank (*mana*, and thus ancestral reputations as well as birth orders), politically sensitive issues such as ancestral *tuakana* and *teina*, and many other contingencies as well as imperfect memory. These ambiguities were probably often a matter of contention—and continue to be in certain hapū among Tūhoe.[3] Best's correction of the seniority between Tamaikoha's wives may have reflected such ambiguity and contention regarding concurrent marriages.

The living members of Tamaikoha's hapū *kāwai* or branch were unusually extensive because of his numerous children, but especially because his eldest child Hakeke, the *mātāmua* among all his children, had even more. Analysis of Hakeke's 16 living children and their mothers is again clarified by the data on land rights extended to them from their parents, and again Best's reports are inconsistent though indispensable. On the balance of documentary evidence, I have concluded that Hakeke's wives and their children were as they are laid out in Fig. 4.2: his wives, in their order of seniority, were Motu Hakaipari, Te Uru Kutu, and an 'Ani' whose 'surname' remains unidentified. However, Best noted in his genealogical census that Ani was "N. te Rangi"(1898: 28), probably meaning that she was from another *iwi* Ngāi Terangi of Tauranga to the west on the Bay of Plenty. Although there are some ambiguities of mothers among Hakeke's children, it can be concluded that children 1 through 9 (Konoro through Te Otawa) were probably born by Motu Hakaipari, children 10 through

15 were probably born by Te Uru Kutu, and child 16 was probably born by Ani.

After Hakeke's wives and children, the other children of Tamaikoha in Fig. 4.2 whose marriages and children are selected for study are child 2, Pihitahi, child 6 Tiopira, and child 7, Te Unupo. Each of these persons represented important political alliances with other hapū or hapū branches, and probably contributed to the consolidation of Tūhoe leadership during these years. Hakeke's sister Pihitahi, second-born of her sibling group, married another prominent Tūhoe *rangatira*, Tupaea Rapaera. Te Unupo was first-born of Tamaikoha's third marriage with Whata Te Puia, and herself also had children by marriages to two other important Tūhoe leaders, Te Hata Waewae and Tawera Moko. The political alliances represented by Tiopira will be outlined below, after further analysis of the principle of sibling seniority exemplified by Wi, Tamaikoha's third child.

According to Best's 1898 census, Pihitahi was followed by Tamaikoha and Ngatuas' second son Wi, who had two children aged 14 and probably 22 by 1903 but who himself had died by then. His children Te Haka Wi and Te Hiko Wi are listed in Tamaikoha's hapū branch as shareholders 129 and 130 in the Tauwhare Manuka block list (see Fig. 4.1). Because the block lists include only living members, without Best's earlier census it would have been more difficult to identify them as the children of a dead son of Tamaikoha. Their position in the list is a good demonstration of the principle of sibling group birth order that generally determines it (unless overruled by seniority among wives and mothers). They are listed after *all* the living offspring of siblings senior to them (193–228), but before the offspring of siblings junior to them (even great-grandchildren, such as Poniu Tumoana, Pihitahi's grandson through her daughter Miria Tupaea, are given priority over their 'uncles'). It is significant that this trans-generational principle of seniority was not restricted to siblings of the same gender, as the traditional meaning of the terms *tuakana* and *teina* was generally taken to be.

In accord with the gender-neutral sense of tuakana and teina, the guiding principle of the order of the block lists thus appears to be to extend seniority between siblings through all their offspring generations regardless of the gender of intervening progenitors. Where block lists include many branches or an entire hapū, this is probably the principle ideally ordering the branches. Many block lists fall far short or even disregard this ideal (notably Maungapōhatu block), but it is clearly the fundamental basis of order in most lists. As shown by the example of Hakeke's marriages, the principle of order that may occasionally over-ride seniority among siblings is seniority among their mothers where marriages are concurrent. An interesting exaggeration of the principle of seniority among siblings may occur in Fig. 4.1: children 103–106 are listed even before their parents Konoro and his sister Reihana Hakeke. This may be because the latter are the *mātāmua*/first-born and second-born of Hakeke, Tamaikoha's first-born, that is, a four-generation line of *mātāmua* from Tamaikoha. These children might be given an *honorific* priority over their parents because they are succeeding to this *mātāmua* or primogenitive line. Presumably reflecting Tūhoe practice, Best's extended genealogies (1973: Vol II) consistently list siblings of each generation in what he concluded to be their birth order, usually recording the most recent generation with the name of the *mātāmua* child born to the line, no matter what gender or how young.

Tiopira Tamaikoha, Tamaikoha's child 6 and Ramari Maraki's only child (by Tamaikoha), evidently married only Mata Tako (Fig. 4.2). Tiopira and Mata had seven living children in 1903, the oldest of whom was over 18 and married to a Pākehā (European), and the other six of whom were aged from 14 down to five years old. Among Tamaikoha's children, Tiopira alone represented the prestigious marriage between the *rangatira* Tamaikoha and the older sister of the rangatira Te Whiu Maraki, Tamaikoha's colleague in the land wars. Ramari Maraki was second-born and Te Whiu Maraki seventh and last-born of the sibling group (Best 1898: 22), so she was very senior to Te Whiu, famous as he was. Although she appears to have died by 1898, Ramari apparently had several children by at least two other men beside Tamaikoha (1898: 22 at 1). An interesting issue would be whether these marriages of Ramari could be considered concurrent, that is, polyandrous in the same way as many male Tūhoe leaders of the time were polygynous. Whether or not these marriages were recognized, her high social status would have made it important to distinguish between her children by different men, and thus the children's land and hapū rights extended through her (see Fig. 4.3; e.g., she had leading as well as strong shares in both Otara and Waikarewhenua blocks). Tiopira Tamaikoha might have been named after another husband of Ramari, Tiopira Te Pairi. Apparently the only living child of Ramari Maraki and Tiopira Te Pairi in 1903 was Ngahirata Tiopira, who represented yet another significant political alliance between leading Tūhoe. Ngahirata was the only wife of Tūhoe *rangatira* Numia Kererū Te Ruakariata, one of the five Urewera commissioners, and chairman of the Tūhoe General Committee under the Urewera District Native Reserve Act 1896 until he died in 1916. Numia's major influence in the establishment of the UDNR will be traced in Part II.

This section of the chapter has attempted to reconstruct some of the details of social organization embedded by Tūhoe leaders in the block lists, especially their arrangement of descent groups by seniority of generations and wives and their allocation of relative shares. It was concluded in the previous chapters that neither the Pākehā commissioners nor even Elsdon Best had a significant role in these refinements. After all, the above examination suggested that subtleties of relative shares showed land rights extending from ancestry to gifts and other unexplained sources, as well as that most allocations confirmed each other in the intricacies of rights between half-siblings and the vagueries of multiple marriages. Only leaders intimately familiar with each block would know these things as well as the birth order of ancestral sibling groups and consequent status differences between each generation of sibling groups descended from them.

4 Difficulties Determining Hapū Affiliations of the Tamaikoha Hapū Branch

The general social structure and organization of Tūhoe hapū as cognatic descent groups was explored in Chap. 3. The affiliation of a hapū branch such as the Tamaikoha *kāwai* to one or more hapū is difficult to reconstruct from the block lists in which the branch appears. As explained above at the end of the first section, the primary problem is that while the block lists depict only the living members of one or more hapū as though they were freehold 'owners' of the block, the rights of a hapū to that land are birthrights devolved through deceased ancestors who are immediately identified with the living generations but do not appear in the block list. Although most or all of the branches of the wider hapū might be shown in a block list, their descent lines from a common ancestor are truncated and remain unclear without additional genealogical information. The commission had indeed organized their investigation of each block in this way, first identifying a founding ancestor who had originally held *mana* over the land in question, and then confirming or rejecting the genealogical descent of claimants from this ancestor and, finally, examining the extent to which they had maintained occupation. With the help of Best's 1898 genealogical census, a few generations of the deceased links between hapū branches in a particular block list can be reconstructed, but hapū affiliations would remain unidentified.

Study of a block investigation as recorded in the minutebooks can identify the hapū involved and some of the missing descent links, but these remain fragmentary for several other reasons some of which were outlined in Chap. 3 with regard to the investigation of the Te Waipotiki block. Due to cognatic descent and the overlapping nature of hapū, block lists often include branches primarily affiliated with other hapū which could nevertheless claim recent occupational rights and trace descent from the ancestor found to hold mana over the block. By the same token, block lists often exclude branches of a hapū awarded ownership because they could not demonstrate recent occupation. The separate claims of Ngāti Rongo and Māhurehure hapū for Te Waipotiki block regardless of the near identity of their membership also illustrated the fractious nature of hapū branches aspiring to recognition as independent hapū.

Second, although key whakapapa (genealogies) were often recorded in the minutes, much information assumed between the commissioners was left out of the often perfunctory record; furthermore, because the intention of the enquiry was to establish home-rule, many basic understandings and arrangements were left for Tūhoe leaders to settle before they were brought in to the official hearings, and in the hearings much was probably simply accepted without full understanding by the Pākehā members. Finally, and most unfortunately for the purposes of fuller reconstruction of hapū organization, the numerous lists of claimants from which the commissioners worked to settle the final block lists—and which were submitted in the name of a particular hapū—have apparently all been lost. On the other hand, much of the detail assumed between knowledgeable leaders in informal negotiation would also have be left out of these lists.

From the point of view of the Pākehā commissioners and even Best, perhaps the most fundamental impediment to their fuller understanding of the manifold status discriminations carried out by the Tūhoe commissioners and other leaders was the sheer number of blocks and hapū being investigated simultaneously. Such a situation was rarely confronted in the Native Land Court. Ironically, the resulting complexity of ownership later became the primary impediment to the Crown purchase campaign culminating in the Urewera Consolidation Scheme (Webster 2004: 167–187). The necessary corollary of overlapping hapū and land rights within blocks was the extension of the land rights of a given hapū across several blocks of the Native Reserve. Insofar as there were over 14,000 names on the 35 block lists of owners but only about 2000 different persons claiming rights in the Reserve, it is evident that a given individual or sibling group was usually recognized to hold land rights in many blocks. Insofar as these blocks were awarded to different hapū, it follows that an individual or sibling group appearing in different block lists often had some affiliation with several different hapū. Tamaikoha himself was awarded shares in 16 of the 35 blocks, and his children were awarded shares in as many as 24 blocks (usually due to additional rights held through their mothers). Although many of these blocks were controlled by the same or closely related hapū, the number of hapū affiliations potentially held by the members of the hapū branch was nevertheless numerous.

The context of extensive historical change among Tūhoe during these years raises a further more general difficulty in identification of hapū affiliations. Discussions in previous chapters have sometimes assumed that rights in particular blocks of the reserve straightforwardly reflected affiliation or rights of membership in particular hapū, although which hapū remained unclear. But are land rights simply equivalent to hapū rights? If not, what is their relation? Might their conflation be misleading, or obscure important issues?

Hapū affiliations were traditionally, and continue to be, closely associated with land rights of groups and individuals. From early colonial days, hapū tended to be assumed by officials, and presented by Māori, as the land-holding group. Rights to the use of land derived primarily from hapū membership, and only hapū leaders of pre-eminent ***mana*** had the prerogative to alienate those rights by gift or, later, lease or sale. Significantly, the recognition of full ownership and protection of their lands assured the Māori 'tribes' by the Crown in the 1840 Treaty of Waitangi was addressed to hapū rather than *iwi*.

However, assumptions that hapū membership rights and land rights are always congruent or coextensive are liable to obscure important differences and changes between them. Changes of affiliation within hapū must also be considered at several levels, from individual through group levels to historical changes of individuals and groups. No consistent direction can be assumed of historical, let alone individual or group, change of affiliation. Firth's insight that hapū 'wax' and 'wane', although better than the old dogma that *whānau* 'grow' into hapū and hapū 'grow' into *iwi*, are both naturalistic metaphors and so liable to obscure the unpredictability of historical change.

For instance, there is evidence that by 1861 in Northland and Auckland, due to the rising commodity value of land, Māori distinguished between hapū rights and land rights, treating the latter more restrictively if defending them and more broadly if pressing them against other hapū (Webster 1998: 28–9). After the 1860s, Native Land Court policy perversely identified land rights with unrestricted descent, extending them far beyond the limits of hapū membership from an original owner to all descendants in perpetuity if not abrogated by a will (Webster 1975: 135). Although Māori have always resisted such a policy, individuals have always taken advantage of the legal opportunity to partition and alienate shares of hapū land to which their moral right as active hapū members may have lapsed (and this was probably the intention of the policy). With regard to contemporary hapū, in the current Māori Renaissance a case can be made that claims to hapū membership, and their acceptance, are extended well beyond legitimate rights to what little land remains (see Metge 1967: 86). All these situations show that conflation of land rights and hapū rights may obscure significant historical processes.

On the other hand, at least at the time of the commission's investigation 1899–1903, Tūhoe appear to have extended land rights considerably beyond active hapū membership. While leaders of *mana* may have exercised active membership in several hapū, their rights to land were often recognized in so many blocks that even where some of these blocks were awarded to the same or closely allied hapū, their rights as hapū members must have been merely a gesture of *aroha* or respect. Because cognatic descent from a common ancestor implies multiple or overlapping kin group memberships, it implies prioritization among members by hapū leaders as well as prioritization among hapū affiliations by members. In the establishment of the UDNR, it is unlikely that the range of active hapū membership was as extensive as the land rights recognized by the commissioners.

One important factor in the apparent extension of land rights beyond hapū rights was the confidence, prevailing among enough Tūhoe leaders, that the 1896 Act did protect their control over their own lands. As has been discussed in Chap. 3, this confidence appears to have resulted in claims to independence by many hapū previously dependent on or part of other hapū, thereby often increasing the proportion of competing claims for the same areas of land. Early in the commission's investigations a revealing issue emerged: some Tūhoe charged that others were extending their land claims too widely, protesting that "people cannot sit in two claims in hope that if one fails they can jump to the other side" (UMB 1: 130). The commission was probably unable effectively to discourage such proliferation of claims.

Resulting tensions between hapū may have frequently been eased by the generous recognition of claims of at least nominal shares of land in blocks where these rights, along with some degree of active affiliation with the hapū awarded the block, would otherwise have been seen as lapsed. Requests were also frequently made by hapū leaders awarded a block to extend some shares in *aroha* (compassion) to some excluded claimants, even after a case was closed and routine denial certainly anticipated. The gesture would nevertheless be important. Importantly, the most common resolution of appeals decided by the 1906–1907 appeals commission was to extend shares to appellants, perhaps further weakening the principle of hapū solidarity in control of its lands and rendering them vulnerable to the later Crown purchasing campaign.

The following Chaps. 5 and 6 explore the array, range, and prioritization of hapū affiliations among Tūhoe during this era. However, the cautions raised above must be kept in mind. The intricate structure of hapū so well understood by the Tūhoe commissioners was itself changing in new ways. Although most of the arable land of the Tūhoe had been confiscated by the 1870s, a new form of land tenure in the Urewera backed by the Crown, and the minute individualization of shares, appear to have prompted an illusion of land wealth among them which to some extent out-ran active hapū rights. By 1925, any such illusion of wealth was to be shattered and most of the Urewera lost to the Tūhoe. Between 1910 and 1921 the extension of shares beyond solidary hapū membership, as well as individualization of shares on the well-meaning model of an electoral role, had been ruthlessly exploited by the Crown. Despite their extensive holdings established under the reserve by 1903, many of the Tamaikoha *kāwai* had been left *whenua rawakore*, landless, by the time of the Urewera Consolidation Scheme.

Notes

1. This block was among those targeted early in purchasing and pre-empted in the 1921 consolidation scheme, because the public and the Crown entertained an exaggerated impression of its agricultural promise until 1922.
2. Oliver's revision in 2013 reports only that Tamaikoha acted as intermediary in 1871, but adds that Tūhoe helped to capture Kereopa (a Māori from Taranaki accused of murdering Volkner) so that the war would end. I have been told by Tūhoe that Tamaikoha's colleague Te Whiu Maraki 'ran Kereopa down' on the ridgeline near Ō hāua te Rangi. This suggests Tūhoe were giving him refuge there. Tamaikoha had influence with Ngāti Rongo through several marriages of his children (Fig. 6.3), and Ngāti Rongo controlled the Ō hāua area.

3. In at least two cases, the priority of meeting houses or dining halls named after wives of an ancestor is seriously contested, sometimes to the amusement of other hapū.

References

AJHR 1903. D. Scannell. 'Commissioners' Orders Under the "Urewera District Native Reserves Act, 1896."' Undated. Appendices to the Journal of the House of Representatives 1903, G-6: 1–256. Wellington, N.Z.

Best, Elsdon. 1898. "Tuhoe genealogies 1898" (spine title); "Genealogies of the Tuhoe tribe. Also includes all living members of the tribe in 1898, as given before the Urewera Commission set up under the act of 1896." Manuscript qMS [172]. Wellington, N.Z.: Alexander Turnbull Library. [NB: the author can supply a digital index for this resource.]

Best, Elsdon, 1973. *Tuhoe, Children of the Mist.* Vols. I and II (genealogies). Second edition. Wellington, N.Z.: A.H. and A.W. Reed Ltd. (first published 1925 as Vol VI of the Memoirs of the Polynesian Society).

Metge, Joan. 1967. *The Maoris of New Zealand.* London: Routledge & Kegan Paul.

Sissons, Jeffrey. 1991. *Te Waimana, The Spring of Mana: Tuhoe History and the Colonial Encounter.* Dunedin, N.Z.: Otago University Press.

Sissons, Jeffrey. 2002. "Waimana Kaaku: A History of the Waimana Block." A report commissioned by the Crown Forestry Rental Trust, June 2002. Wellington, N.Z.: Waitangi Tribunal.

Oliver, Steven. 2007. "Wahawaha, Rapata? -1897." Dictionary of New Zealand Biography, updated 22 June 2007. URL: http://www.dnzb.govt.nz/

UMB 1. Urewera District Native Reserve Commission minute book 1 (identified as Urewera Commission minute book '3'), Smith, Butler, et al, (1Feb1899–8Mar1900), in Māori, Index 22pp., 382pp. NA Wgtn: Urewera MB 3, MLC 13, W3518, CD2, Vol 3, 397 pp.; NA Ak: AREPRO 4711/1445. Acronym: UMB 1.

UMB 3. Urewera District Native Reserve Commission minute book 3 (identified as '3A'; English translation of last part of UMB 1), Smith, Butler, et al, (9Feb1900–8Mar1900). 189 pp., index, NA Wgtn: Urewera MB 3A, MLC 13, W3518, CD 2, Vol 3A, 191 pp.; NA Ak: AREPRO 4711/1444. Acronym: UMB 3.

Webster, Steven. 1975. "Cognatic Descent Groups and the Contemporary Māori: a Preliminary Reassessment." *The Journal of the Polynesian Society* Vol.84(2): 121–152.

Webster, Steven. 1998, "Maori Hapu as a Whole Way of Struggle: 1840–50s Before the Land Wars." *Oceania* 69(1):4–35.

Webster, Steven. 2004. *The Urewera Consolidation Scheme: Confrontations between Tuhoe and the Crown, 1915–1925.* Vols I, II. Report commissioned by the Waitangi Tribunal. WAI 894 #D8. Wellington, N.Z.: Waitangi Tribunal.

CHAPTER 5

The Tamaikoha *Hapū* Branch: *Hapū* Affiliations

1 Introduction

Chapter 4 analyzed several aspects of the internal social organization in the Tamaikoha hapū branch, and concluded with a review of the difficulties facing identification of the wider hapū affiliations of such groups. Relying primarily on the 1903 block lists and finally on the allocation of relative shares enumerated in them, the analysis extracted implications regarding surnames, sibling groups and generations, principles of seniority, marriages, and half-siblings, and attempted to reconstruct these aspects of the Tamaikoha *kāwai*.

Given the difficulties reviewed, can wider implications of social status such as hapū affiliations be similarly derived from this data? The distinction between relative rights between generations and relative rights between descent groups in different blocks turned out to be a rich source of information on such status differences. Especially the difficult reconstruction of multiple marriages and half-siblings relied upon the allocations of relative rights to the same individual or sibling group in different blocks. This information reveals the most about the varying land rights of a given hapū branch in the context of different blocks, furthermore relative to other hapū branches in each block. Insofar as the blocks were confirmed in 1902 in the name of one or more hapū, one can suppose that this information might reflect the hapū affiliations of a given hapū branch.

With regard to the Tamaikoha *kāwai*, this data was laid out for the first few living generations in Fig. 4.3. Shares in certain blocks were italicized

© The Author(s) 2020

S. Webster, *A Separate Authority (He Mana Motuhake)*, Volume I,
https://doi.org/10.1007/978-3-030-41042-1_5

for the purpose of identifying half-siblings and their other parent. As described in Fig. 4.3, further distinctions regarding status can now be drawn between these shares. For the purpose of a deductive ranking of relative social status or *mana* (prestige or authority) of a given *kāwai* in each block, 15 or more shares allocated to a senior generation will be considered 'strong' shares (relative to other shareholders in that block). If, in addition to holding strong shares, a senior generation of a *kāwai* is also listed among the first 100 persons in the block list, they will also be considered to hold 'leading' shares (i.e., to be influential leaders relative to other shareholders in that block). Insofar as these statuses extend from a senior generation to all their offspring, the same relative rank or *mana* can be assumed to apply to the entire *kāwai* even though their shares are reduced for each succeeding generation.

Following these deductions of social status or *mana*, it can be seen that Tamaikoha (and therefore his *kāwai*) was ranked among the first 100 persons in five of the six blocks in which he held strong shares. That is to say, the *kāwai* held not merely strong but also leading shares in five of the many blocks in which they held some shares. One can suspect that these leading shares reflected active affiliations in the hapū that were found to control, or hold *mana* over, these blocks.

The following sections of this chapter draw conclusions regarding the hapū affiliations of Tamaikoha's *kāwai* on the basis of the information on their land rights summarized in Fig. 4.3 supplemented by other data from the records of the UDNR commission. First, the most likely potential affiliations succeeded to from Tamaikoha's parents and certain ancestors are identified, drawing upon Elsdon Best's genealogies of the Tūhoe, derived primarily from evidence placed before the commission. The potential hapū affiliations drawn from these genealogies are then narrowed down to a list of relatively active affiliations by examination of (i) the *kāwai*'s shares in each block as shown in Fig. 4.3; (ii) the claims made in the name of particular hapū for the various blocks at the outset of the commission's investigations in 1899; (iii) details recorded in the minutes of the subsequent investigations 1899–1902; and (iv) the appointments of *kāwai* members to block or hapū committees in 1902. Finally, with an eye to the effects of particular historical conditions, identification of changes in hapū affiliation and an estimate of divergence between the extent of land rights and hapū rights can be attempted.

2 Potential and Active Hapū Affiliations

Elsdon Best's genealogy plates 5, 6, 10, 15, 17, 20, 21, and 27 all locate Tamaikoha in the context of different *whakapapa* (genealogies), recording founding ancestors, 'tribes' (*iwi* or hapū), and hapū of the Urewera district (Best 1973: Vol II). Drawing on these genealogies, five of Tamaikoha's predecessors have been included in Fig. 4.2, the selected genealogy showing many of the hapū branch members listed in the Tauwhare Manuka block list (Fig. 4.1). Closer comparison of Best's genealogies could identify other ancestors of Tamaikoha (because these may be doubled in number each generation and, theoretically, include all the predecessors of each ancestor!). In principle or *potentially*, Tamaikoha might have claimed some membership rights and perhaps corresponding land rights in any of the hapū or *iwi* Best's genealogies identify as including any of these ancestors.

However, as explained in Chap. 3, in customary or traditional practice generally among Māori, this wide array of potential hapū and corresponding land rights was limited to those rights that had been actively maintained by recent descendants of the founding ancestor or (as the 1899–1903 commission applied this general rule with regard to the Tūhoe) "continuous occupation" for at least three generations before the oldest living claimant. A claim based upon *tīpuna* (or *tūpuna;* 'ancestor') or ancestry had to be backed by *noho*, continuous occupation or legitimate use of specifiable land within the block at least since the claimant's great-grandparent descended from that *tīpuna.* If in the opinion of the commission this minimum requirement was met, successful claimants for a block were then left to negotiate relative shares with regard to relative strength or weakness of occupation, before as well as throughout these three most recent generations, in terms of actual residence, regular or occasional use of resources, recognition of ancestral gifts, and other details confirmed by oral tradition as well as visual evidence. As a result of all these considerations, different hapū branches were finally recognized to have stronger or weaker rights in a particular block relative to other hapū branches (and such priorities could be reversed for the same descent group in a different block). In addition, leaders of *mana* such as Tamaikoha were probably expected as well as more able to maintain numerous hapū affiliations and thus rights to it lands, and merely symbolic ties to the land were more likely to be indulged.

Thus in Tamaikoha's case, the hapū and corresponding land rights of his hapū branch would generally have been limited to those that could be shown to have been actively sustained since the time of Te Ra Mahaki and, for stronger rights, by his predecessors as well (again, see Fig. 4.2). In principle, this claim could be tested with regard to any of Tamaikoha's other ancestors of this third preceding generation, perhaps as many as seven others. However, it can probably be assumed that those of his predecessors appearing prominently in Best's whakapapa were those through whom Tamaikoha was recognized to trace his rights: that is to say, his father's mother's father Te Ra-Mahaki, his father's father Rangipa (or either of his parents), and his mother Tiramate (or any of her grandparents). The potential hapū affiliations of the Tamaikoha *kāwai* through only these ancestors were numerous.

Moreover, in addition to potential claims through Tamaikoha from at least these five of his predecessors, all of the children of Tamaikoha could potentially claim ancestral hapū rights through their own mothers, that is, one or another of Tamaikoha's three wives. Through Tamaikoha's first wife Ngatua, all her descendants could again potentially claim the rights of Hapuoneone and Ngāti Mura-kareke (plate 5), reinforcing those rights from Te Ariari's parents. Through Tamaikoha's second wife Ramari, Tiopira and all his descendants could also potentially claim the rights of Hapuoneone and Ngāi Turanga, specifically 'Te Kareke' hapū (plates 5 and 8), which is probably an abbreviation for Ngāti Mura-kareke hapū. Thus, Ngatua and Ramaris' hapū rights both reinforced the Ngāti Murakareke hapū rights Tamaikoha held from his father. Finally, all Tamaikoha's descendants through his third wife Whata Te Puia could potentially claim rights to Ngā Maihi hapū, 'the Tūhoe or Te Urewera' hapū, and a senior line of Ngāti Koura hapū (plates 12, 27, and 33, respectively). Thus, Whata's children's potential rights to Te Urewera hapū from Rangipa through Tamaikoha were reinforced by Whata's own rights.

In summary, ancestral rights as shown in Best's whakapapa suggest that Tamaikoha or his many offspring could *potentially* (i.e., on the basis of ancestry alone, apart from the question of occupation of hapū land or *active* rights) claim rights in the following hapū:

Te Whakatane hapū (and through this, perhaps Whakatohea *iwi* and Ngā Pōtiki, Ngāi Tātua, or Tamakaimoana hapū);

Ngāti Rawa (and through this, Ngāti Rakei, Ngāti Haka, Patuheuheu, Ngā Pōtiki, or Ngā Maihi hapū);

Ngāi Te Riu hapū;
Ngāi Tama, the Tūhoe or Te Urewera hapū, Tūhoe Pōtiki hapū, and Tanemoeahi hapū (and through these, perhaps Ngāi Turanga hapū);
Ngāti Kurī hapū;
Ngāti Mura or Ngāti Mura-kareke hapū;
Ngāti Whare hapū and Ngāti Tāwhaki hapū;
Ngāti Koura hapū.

Other commission records furnish evidence of active affiliation with some of these hapū. After a summary of general issues, these records will be examined closely with regard to several blocks of the reserve. In addition to the tabulation of the *kāwai*'s shares in various blocks (Fig. 4.3), the numerous references to different blocks and hapū are best followed by using the map showing the final blocks of the UDNR (Fig. 1.2) and the list of hapū and committees of each block (Fig. 2.1).

Significantly, some of the potential hapū affiliations deduced above are independently confirmed by Jeff Sissons' informants, who in 1978 provided various details regarding Tamaikoha (Sissons 1991: 10, 62, 142, 68, 89, 91, 105, 155). During the land wars and probably through 1871, he was said to have been the leader of three of these hapū: Ngāi Tama (along with another war leader Te Whiu Maraki), Te Whakatane, and Ngāi Tātua, all hapū of Te Urewera *iwi* (which later came to be known as Ngāi Tūhoe *iwi*). He was said to also have claimed affiliation with two others listed above: Ngāi Turanga and especially Te Urewera hapū, which in the NLC (Native Land Court) in the 1880s was awarded the Waimana blocks of the lower Waimana basin (and under his leadership sold much of them, against the wishes of the other leading *rangatira* Te Whiu and Rakuraku). Sissons also reported that Tamaikoha 'perhaps' affiliated with Ngāti Kurī; this apparently confirms Best's 1896 report that he was the 'leading chief' of this hapū, located at Te Waiiti in what was to become the Ruatāhuna block. Furthermore, this information from Sissons' informants implies *active* hapū affiliations, at least through 1871. Insofar as these affiliations were still recounted in the 1980s, they may have been sustained by Tamaikoha's *kāwai* well into the twentieth century.

The first evidence to be considered is about 264 claimant lists for the 35 blocks which were submitted to the commission in 1899 as it circuited through the main settlements of the Native Reserve. These were discussed in Chap. 3 in terms of the emergence of many hapū that had not been named elsewhere. Although the original lists are apparently lost, a fairly complete record of the person and hapū in whose name they were submitted was kept in the minutebooks, demonstrating at least that person's probably active hapū affiliation with regard to the block of land claimed, whether or not the claim was successful.

A perhaps unique difficulty arises with regard to determining the active or significant hapū affiliations of Tamaikoha's *kāwai*. As argued in Chap. 2 assessing his and others' early resistance to the commission, in exchange for his cooperation Tamaikoha probably relied on his considerable *mana* to lay and win several claims outside the formal procedures of the investigation. Following Sissons' insight that several land claims in which Tamaikoha was certainly closely involved were settled with only a perfunctory record of them (Sissons 2002: Appendix 1), I concluded that informal deals with the commission, a virtual rubber-stamping of Tamaikoha's demand, played a part in some cases. For the purposes of determining the active hapū affiliations of his *kāwai*, an unfortunate implication of this is that these 'informal' claims, as will be seen, furnish less information.

However, several of Tamaikoha's claims were investigated (or recorded) more fully. As described in Chap. 2, soon after announcing his intention to withhold his claimant lists for "the Waimana blocks" (probably meaning the lower Tauranga/Waimana basin within the *rohe pōtae*; UMB 1: 59, 23 February 1899) and merely observe the operations of the commission, he nevertheless began to submit formal claims for some of these blocks. These were among the first 40 claim lists submitted in Rūātoki and Waimana, and the block name, claimant hapū, and *kaihomai* ('deliverer', or person submitting the claim) were often not clearly recorded. However, the information recorded together with the subsequent hearings show that three claimant lists submitted by Tamaikoha were probably for Waimahe and Hukanui (later included as the southeastern part of Parekohe block) and probably all in the name of Ngāi Te Riu hapū (lists A 19 and A 51 in Rūātoki hearings, and B 2 in Waimana hearings). In the Rūātoki hearings Tamaikoha had also formally submitted two other claimant lists: A 21 for areas which probably came to be defined as Paraeroa (including Pukepohatu) and Te Purenga blocks, probably in the name of Ngāi Tokotuai hapū, and A 25 for Whaitiripapa block, probably in the name of Te Urewera hapū. Some weeks later in the Ruatāhuna hearings he also submitted claimant list D 24 for the large Tarapounamu-Matawhero block in the name of Ngāti Tāwhaki hapū.

Thus the claimants lists furnish significant evidence of Tamaikoha and his descendants' active affiliation with Ngāi Te Riu, Te Urewera, Ngāti Tāwhaki, and Ngāi Tokotuai hapū, all but the last of which are among the potential affiliations deduced above from Best's whakapapa plates. The implications of each of these claims will be examined below.

There is also evidence that other leaders in or close to Tamaikoha's hapū branch did lay further formal claims: his *mātāmua* son Hakeke submitted the successful claim for Paraoanui block in the name of Te Whakatane hapū. His eldest daughter Pihitahi's husband, Tupaea Rapaera, submitted four claims: another for Whaitiripapa block, also in the name of Te Urewera hapū, and three claims for the Ruatāhuna block in the name of Kakahutapiki hapū. Although these claims might be seen as competing with Tamaikoha's rights, it is more likely that they reinforced or complemented his own formal or informal claims, probably by prior arrangement.

Finally, Tamaikoha and Hakeke's early claims for the Parekohe and Paraoanui region of the lower Tauranga River, which included the settlements of Matahi and Whakarae, was more disputed than the other blocks in the valley (Sissons 2002: 110) and is best set aside for further research. It appears that despite his mana and persistent confrontation, compromises, and the delay of commission decisions, Tamaikoha's claims made little progress against those of Taihakoa Poniwahio in this area, and even his rights in Paraoanui block eventually suffered partition. Nevertheless, these cases suggest that his hapū branch had some degree of active affiliation with Ngāi Taumata, Ngāi Te Riu, and Te Whakatane hapū.

3 Ngāi Tokotuai Hapū and Claims to Tauwhare Manuka and Pukepohatu Blocks

In 1899 neither Tamaikoha nor anyone else put in a formal claim for the Tauwhare Manuka block. The award and his belated claim in 1902 were probably pre-arranged with other leaders outside of formal hearings, and perhaps with the commission itself (UMB 6: 114, 198–9). According to Sissons, in 1899 Tamaikoha had intended to hold Tauwhare Manuka and probably other blocks out of the commission's jurisdiction, but he felt forced to submit his claim to fend off encroachment by claimants of surrounding blocks (2002: 111). As well as Te Whakatane hapū, Tamaikoha stated that part of the Tauwhare Manuka block belonged to Ngāi Tokotuai hapū (Best sometimes spelled this Tokotuwai), but to no others. There were no objections and the commission immediately awarded the block to these two hapū. There were some objections to the list of owners drawn up by Tamaikoha, but a statement by Hakeke suggests that these were caused by additions made to the list in the hearing after agreement had been reached outside the hearing, and all objections were then withdrawn or dismissed. Although the case was then declared closed, at least part of a claim for Tamariwai hapū (by Hekerangi Mahaki) was later added to the block list.

Tamaikoha's extensive *kāwai* represented in the Tauwhare Manuka block list (Fig. 4.1) is thus again shown to have maintained active affiliation with Te Whakatane hapū and, implicitly, its parent hapū Ngāi Tātua. We can assume that they were not affiliated with Tamariwai hapū, but insofar as Tamaikoha claimed part of the block for Ngāi Tokotuai, they may have been affiliated with that hapū as well. Ngāi Tokotuai had probably gained general recognition only recently; although Best cited it among 39 hapū of Tūhoe after 1907 (Best 1973 Vol 1: 215), it had not been recorded in his 1896 list nor in the list drawn up by the Tūhoe commissioners in 1899. However, their investigation also awarded Ngāi Tokotuai exclusive control of Pukepohatu block across the Tauranga/Waimana River from Tauwhare Manuka, and it was among the several hapū awarded the Taneatua block due west of the Whakatane River (see Fig. 1.2). These awards may have arisen from Tamaikoha's early formal claim A 21, probably in the name of Ngāi Tokotuai hapū, for lands in the lower middle Whakatane River basin then defined loosely as Te Purenga and later distinguished into several other blocks probably including Paraeroa, Taneatua, and Pukepohatu. The question of if and how Tamaikoha's hapū branch affiliated with Ngāi Tokotuai can be explored with regard to these cases.

Giving evidence in these investigations, Tamaikoha simply traced the hapū from the ancestor Tokotuai, implying he (or she) was well known, and his evidence was not challenged by other claimants (UMB 4: 98). However, the whakapapa did not trace descent to himself, nor to any of his relatives identified previously from commission records, so it remains unclear from this evidence how his hapū branch was ancestrally affiliated with Ngāi Tokotuai. Nor is the ancestor Tokotuai indexed or located in Best's genealogies, so descendants cannot be identified from this source. This situation again suggests that the hapū was a branch of Te Whakatane hapū that had recently gained independence.[1]

The role of Ngāi Tokotuai in Tamaikoha's hapū branch's rights in Taneatua block also remains unclear. The successful claims of Ngāi Tokotuai and five other hapū to Taneatua block originally sought separate blocks, specifying different land areas over which their lists of claimants held ancestral and occupational rights. Although the commission decided to join these claims together and award the block to all six hapū, neither the block order nor final list of owners recorded the distinctions between hapū and their respective land areas. Again, the commission and Tūhoe leaders appear to have been relying on the promised self-government and traditional leadership of the Native Reserve to manage any resulting conflicts. However, as explained in Chap. 3, the precedent of recognizing different claims but joining them within a single block was extended to several other blocks of the Reserve, and by 1912–1913 had led to contention and applications to partition requiring review and settlement by the chief judge of the Native Land Court.

Less ambiguous information regarding Ngāi Tokotuai hapū should be available from the record of the Pukepohatu block because it was awarded exclusive rights there. However, the emergence and fate of this block are extraordinary and itself must be unraveled. Although this background is complex, it clarifies aspects of Tamaikoha's claims strategy as well as the hapū branch's land rights through Ngāi Tokotuai hapū.

The Pukepohatu block was located directly across the middle Tauranga/Waimana River from Tauwhare Manuka block, extending west to the Paraeroa block on the east bank of the Whakatane River (Fig. 1.2). While the 1901 survey plan relied upon by the commission names this block of approximately 7488 acres 'Pukepohatu', the version published in the 1907 AJHR and again in 1921 for the Urewera Consolidation Scheme named the same block 'Papatipu Land'. A yet more fundamental confusion probably arose in the early claims for what was to become Paraeroa block immediately to the west, the southern part of which is dominated by a mountain named 'Pukepohatu' (800 m altitude). On 24 February 1899 Tamaikoha claimed this latter piece of land, specifying that it was part of Paraeroa, in the name of Ngāi Tokotuai hapū (probably claim A 21; UMB 1: 68–9). Then, nearly three years later on 11 February 1902, he also claimed the 7488-acre block between Paraeroa and the Tauranga/Waimana River, again for Ngāi Tokotuai hapū (UMB 6: 178). On both occasions, these adjacent but different pieces of land were named 'Pukepohatu' in the minutebooks, and we can suppose that Tamaikoha accepted this name and extended it over both areas. There were three objections to his claim to the southern part Paraeroa block (in which the mountain Pukepohatu stood) but none to his claim for the separate Pukepohatu block of 7488 acres, and the commission immediately awarded it to Ngāi Tokotuai.

Tamaikoha eventually withdrew his claim for the southern part of Paraeroa block as well as another in the northern part, apparently indignant regarding the collapse of negotiations between what he described as his 'committee' and Tupara Te Kaaho, who was later listed first among all owners and probably held pre-eminent *mana* over the block (UMB 6: 310–11). The only members of Tamaikoha's hapū branch receiving any shares in Paraeroa block were Hakeke's children by Uru Kutu, who held leading shares there.[2]

However, his claim for the *other* 'Pukepohatu' block (of 7488 acres) in the name of the same hapū was unopposed and accepted. On 21 February 1902 the commission received Tamaikoha's list of names of members of Ngāi Tokotuai with rights in this Pukepohatu block, and stated that "the majority have stood out voluntarily. They do so it is stated to facilitate leasing... [sic] so as to contribute toward the cost of survey" (UMB 6: 210). This may explain the unusually short and clearly truncated form of the block list. Insofar as the cost of surveys for the Native Reserve was all borne by the Crown (as agreed in negotiations for the 1896 Act), the survey foreseen was probably for partitioning of Tauwhare Manuka block, which took place soon after the 1906–1907 appeals commission finalized the orders for the Native Reserve.

Although the unopposed award of the Pukepohatu block of 7488 acres to Ngāi Tokotuai was clear enough, the presumably careful arrangements and decisions were later ignored by the Crown. The 1906–1907 appeals commission concluded that it was "perfectly clear" this block had "never been investigated" and its title was "issued in error", leaving resolution of this problem to the Native Minister (AJHR 1907, G-4: 28). The block was subsequently merged with Tauwhare Manuka block and subdivided into nine partitions, rendering the huge expanse of these two blocks especially vulnerable to the Crown purchase campaign that began by 1908 and by 1921 acquired the majority of shares. The situation is tragic insofar as it appears that the appeals commission, far from being perfectly clear, overlooked Tamaikoha's withdrawal of his claims in Paraeroa block and themselves confused the 1899 claim list A 21 for its southern portion (which was dominated by the mountain Pukepohatu and had been recorded with that name) with the 1902 award of the Pukepohatu block.

Crucial evidence of the appeals commission's own confusion is the statement of Tupara Kaaho, the key counter-claimant for the southern portion of Paraeroa, on 11 February 1902, that his 1899 objection to Tamaikoha's claim in Paraeroa had 'nothing to do with the present claim', that is, with the Pukepohatu block of 7488 acres. Tamaikoha's claim to that block was therefore unopposed and awarded immediately to Ngāi Tokotuai hapū (UMB 6: 178). The appeals commission instead jumped to the conclusion that it had never been investigated, ignoring the obvious fact that the commission frequently left routine investigations to Tūhoe leaders deliberating outside its formal hearings and, after settling any objections, recorded the results without elaboration—as it had for the Tauwhare Manuka as well as the Pukepohatu case.

4 Te Urewera Hapū and the Claims to Whaitiripapa Block

In addition to his formal claims in the name of Ngāi Te Riu and Ngāi Tokotuai hapū made in Rūātoki in February 1899, Tamaikoha also laid claim to the small (about 167 acres) but coveted Whaitiripapa block just south of Rūātoki partition 1 near the east bank of the Whakatane River (Fig. 1.2; claim A 25, UMB 1: 70). Although the hapū in whose name he lay the claim was not recorded, records of the investigation show it to have been Te Urewera hapū, earlier known as Tūhoe Pōtiki or the Tūhoe hapū. (Again, this *hapū* is not to be confused with what at this time was called the Urewera *iwi* or confederation of hapū, of which Te Urewera hapū was one.)

The whakapapa for Te Urewera hapū is among the most extensive in Best's collection, where it was described as a hapū of the "Tūhoe or Te Urewera tribe" (1973 Vol. II, plate 27). This hapū was recognized as owners in at least five blocks awarded by the commission (some under its other name, Tūhoe), more than any other hapū of the Tūhoe iwi. Thus, Tamaikoha's claim for Whaitiripapa block implicitly asserted his and his hapū branch's active affiliation with Tūhoe (and probably Tūhoe Pōtiki) hapū, potential rights in which had come down to him from his father's father Rangipa as rights in Te Urewera hapū.

Tamaikoha's was the first claim for the block, but several others were made later in 1899 in the Ruatāhuna sitting: D 47 and D 67 by Tupara Kaaho, also in the name of Te Urewera hapū; D 66 by Tupaea Rapaera (Tamaikoha's senior daughter's husband), also for Te Urewera hapū; D 89 by Hurae Ruru in the name of Ngāti Ruatāhuna hapū, claim X by Ahikaiata for Te Māhurehure hapū, and another claim H by Tamaikoha for Te Urewera hapū (UMB 1: 318; 2: 175). Several other "new lists" were mentioned in the final judgment the following year, but apparently all were for names to be added to the earlier lists for these same three hapū: Te Urewera, Ngāti Ruatāhuna, and Māhurehure (UMB 4: 339–40).

Study of the Whaitiripapa investigation reveals overlapping rights of these three and a fourth hapū, Ngāti Rongo, to the coveted land of Whaitiripapa block. Ngāti Ruatāhuna hapū turns out to be part of Te Urewera hapū centered in the Ruatāhuna area and, as was shown in the Te Waipotiki investigation, Māhurehure hapū was virtually identical to Ngāti Rongo hapū. It turns out that Tamaikoha was probably mediating between two other important *rangatira* who remained behind the scenes: Numia Kererū of Ngāti Rongo, and Te Whenuanui II, son of an old war leader of Te Urewera hapū like Tamaikoha himself, as well as head of Ngāti Ruatāhuna hapū (Best 1973 Vol. I: 232). It will be remembered from Chap. 3 that Akuhata Te Kaha represented Māhurehure hapū in opposition (in name if not membership) to Ngāti Rongo's claim for Te Waipotiki block. Mahurehure's proxy role for Ngāti Rongo in the Whaitiripapa block may have been arranged in the compromise between Akuhata and Numia in the Te Waipotiki block case, which was finally being concluded by the commission when it took up the Whaitiripapa case in late February 1900.

As well as clarifying the dynamics of hapū affiliations, some understanding of what was going on behind the scenes between Tamaikoha, Numia Kererū, and Te Whenuanui II becomes important again in Part II. Although rights to Ruatāhuna lands at the opposite end of the Urewera were not yet at issue, the investigation of Whaitiripapa may have prompted a dramatic confrontation between Numia Kererū and Te Whenuanui II that would continue for over a decade.

The involvement of both of these *rangatira* in the Whaitiripapa case remained behind the scenes, but may have been given away at the start by Tupaea Rapaera, another *rangatira* whose unquestioned *mana* extended across more blocks than any other, including Ruatāhuna as well as

Whaitiripapa, and who ranked highly in both Te Urewera and Ngāti Rongo hapū. Tupaea was also Numia Kererū's nephew, the son of Numia's eldest sibling and *mātāmua* Turaki Te Ruakariata, long deceased. Early in the Whaitiripapa case when conductors were being considered, Tupaea is recorded to have announced that "my claim list and that of Whenua [sic] may be conducted *by Kereru*" (UMB 3: 180 7 March 1900; my emphasis). 'Whenua' was probably not Te Whenuanui II himself, the leader of both Ngāti Ruatāhuna and Te Urewera hapū in the Ruatāhuna area, but rather Whenua Tahakawa, whose uncle's son Mihaka Matika was married to Te Whenuanui I's daughter Hinepau (see Fig. 8.1). As will be described in Part II, by 1903 the influential Taratoa sibling group were close supporters of Te Whenuanui II against Numia Kererū, and their children, including Mihaka, Whenua, and Paora, would confront him in the 1912 partition of Ruatāhuna.

It turned out that neither Numia Kererū nor Te Whenuanui II nor Whenua officially participated in the Whaitiripapa case. Probably as a nominally neutral representative, Akuhata Te Kaha was leading conductor for the Ngāti Ruatāhuna as well as Māhurehure claims, the proxies for Ngāti Rongo and Te Urewera hapū, respectively. Negotiations regarding conduct of the case by Numia Kererū himself may have failed because Te Whenuanui II had become suspicious of his motives with regard to Ruatāhuna lands. With regard to Whaitiripapa, it turns out that Tamaikoha probably adroitly side-stepped the confrontation by accommodating most claimants.

As will also be explored more fully in Part II (see Fig. 8.1), many commentators including myself have confused Te Whenuanui II with his father Te Whenuanui I. Judith Binney's meticulous historical research argues convincingly that the old war leader Te Whenuanui (I) died in 1894 and his chiefly title was succeeded to by his son Te Haka Te Whenuanui (who thereby became known as Te Whenuanui II), and furthermore that when the latter died in 1907, this title was passed on to Te Haka's full-sister's son (Binney 2002: 20–23). Binney's conclusion is further substantiated by the 1903 provisional block orders, which list Te Whenuanui Te Umuariki (Te Whenuanui I) only for the Manuoha and Paharakeke blocks (probably by mistake insofar as these were added belatedly to the UDNR). Only his living children (Te Mauniko, Te Haka, and Kiriahuru) are listed in the 17 other blocks in which he or their mother were found to have rights, with shares appropriate to the eldest living generation.

Beside myself, the difference between father and son has often been confused, even by commentators close to the hapū concerned such as Pou Temara, biographer of Te Whenuanui, and Brenda Tahi, historian of Ruatāhuna.[3] Although Bassett and Kays' report on Ruatāhuna to the Waitangi Tribunal notes Te Whenuanui's death in 1907 (2002: 72), they appear not to distinguish between Te Whenuanui I and II. The immediate, even trans-substantial identification of important leaders with their ancestors by Tūhoe themselves has often led to such confusion. Best was aware of the difference between Te Whenuanui I and II, recording the father of Te Haka as "Te Whenuanui I" in his 1898 genealogical census (1898: 5) and noting that "Te Whenua-nui (also known as Te Haka) is the principle man" of the hapū Tūhoe-Pōtiki (later known as Te Urewera hapū) in his 1925 Tūhoe (1973 Vol. I: 223). However, in his 1898 census he neglected to note that Te Whenuanui I had died and recorded his son simply as 'Te Haka' without noting that he had become Te Whenuanui II. Best also nowhere recorded Te Whenuanui I's father (Te Umuariki) or mother (Tikina), and consistently contributed to the later confusion by recording Te Whenuanui II's frequent evidence before the Urewera commission as given by 'Te Whenuanui', failing to note either that it was Te Haka or Te Whenuanui II. The appeals commission similarly made no distinction. (On the other hand, in overlooking the generational difference between Te Whenuanui I, II, and III, Best may have only been following a Tūhoe custom of substantive identification.) Some further implications of this confusion and the facts discovered by Binney will also be discussed in Part II.[4]

Tamaikoha introduced his case for Te Urewera hapū's rights to Whaitiripapa block on 27 February 1900, and continued it on 6 and 15 March (UMB 3: 146–7, 177–9; UMB 4: 55–6; 339–40 [in Māori, UMB 1: 320, 337–341, 354–5; UMB 2: 46–7]). His commentaries appear to be disjunct in crucial places, but Best's record in Māori fails to clarify ambiguities in the translation, so one suspects Best rather than Tamaikoha was having trouble following the details. Tamaikoha and Numia had taken their counterclaims to the Native Land Court and Native Appellate Court a few years before where the first decision had gone to Numia but its reversal on appeal to Tamaikoha, and Tamaikoha may have been attempting to review those arguments. The case before the commission was also heard at the same time as other still-undefined blocks all of which were approached at that time as parts of a much larger 'Te Purenga' block, and evidence was often given by the same claimants for what became different blocks.

In his introductory commentary for Te Urewera hapū's claim on 27 February, Tamaikoha stated that the founding ancestor of Whaitiripapa (which he translated as 'a thunder above') was Te Whanapeke, and that his permanently occupying descendants could be traced down through himself and daughter Pihitahi (who married Tupaea Rapaera) and son Wi (who was buried there) and their families. Tamaikoha's brief commentary was followed immediately by Akuhata Te Kaha for Māhurehure hapū's claim. Significantly, Akuhata announced that 'Tamaikoha will conduct Whaitiripapa under one claim' and that although he himself had not made a claim, he would 'watch the proceeding and according to their account, I will either act as conductor or not'. Because Akuhata was clearly representing the main opposition—implicitly Ngāti Rongo hapū and Numia Kererū as well as Māhurehure hapū—this statement implied that they might be willing to accept Tamaikoha's conduct of the case 'under one claim', but that with due caution they wanted first to see how he would present it. After summarizing Tamaikoha's presentation of his case over three days, I will return to summarize Akuhata's and the other claimants' responses.

Tamaikoha submitted a strikingly extensive whakapapa for Whaitiripapa block on 2 March (UMB 1: 337–341; Fig. 5.1). It is included here for its clarity as a classic example of whakapapa in its emphasis on *mātāmua* lines of the first-born, and its disregard of gender, marriages, and, usually, siblings. However, in this case Tamaikoha's inclusion of some sibling groups is notable. He traced the descendants of the founding ancestor Whanapeke through 10–11 generations to Tamaikoha's own time, but included several sibling groups and their descendants extending across five pages of the minutebook. Five brothers and sisters of Tawhakamoe (who was Te Whanapeke's great-grandson) were included in the fourth generation; three children of Tamawhai (who was Tawhakamoe's younger brother) were included in the fifth generation; and six children of Kahuwī (who was Tawhakamoe's son) were included in the sixth generation. Tamaikoha furthermore included a selection of descendants from these sibling groups that within 4–6 generations included a current leader or prominent member from most or all of the other claimant lists.

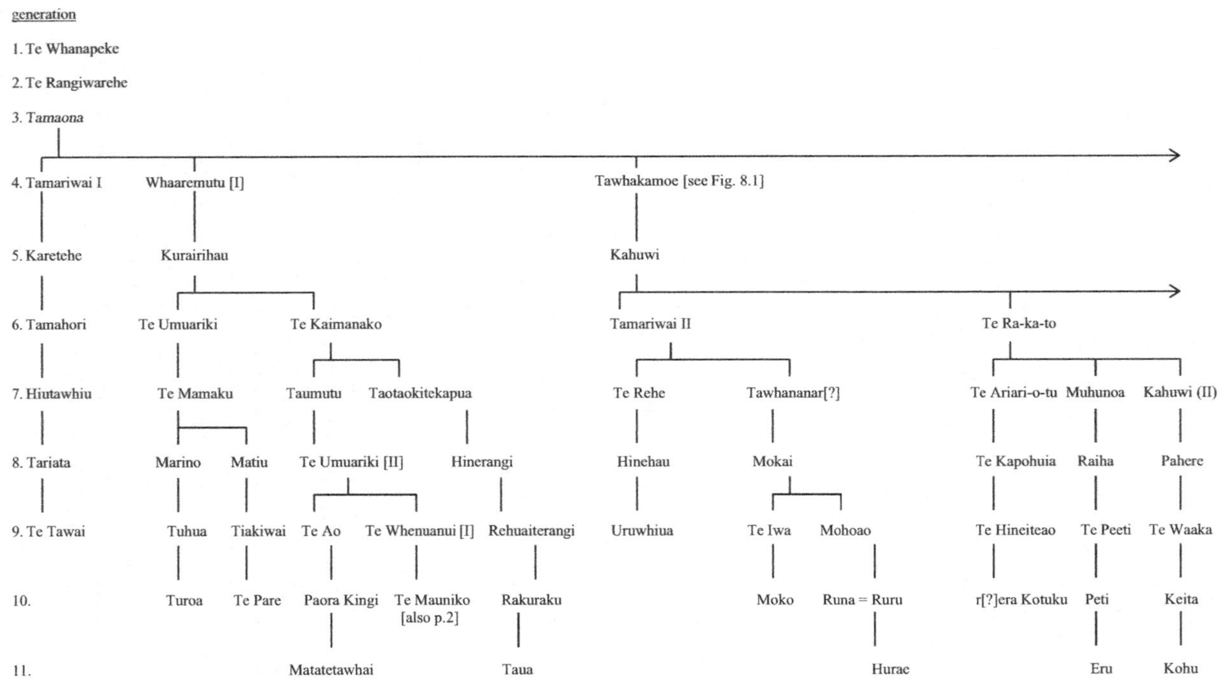

Fig. 5.1 Tamaikoha's whakapapa in support of his claim for Whaitiripapa block, 2 March 1900. (Source: UMB 1: 337–341 (2 March 1900))
Legend:
Note emphasis on *mātāmua* line and disregard of siblings, gender, and marriages typical of whakapapa rarangi; author's additions to original details are in brackets. Tamaikoha himself appears in generation 9, p. 2. His senior wife Ngatua and *mātāmua* son Hakeke are in the nearby descent line. Te Whenuanui I and his *mātāmua* daughter Te Mauniko also of Te

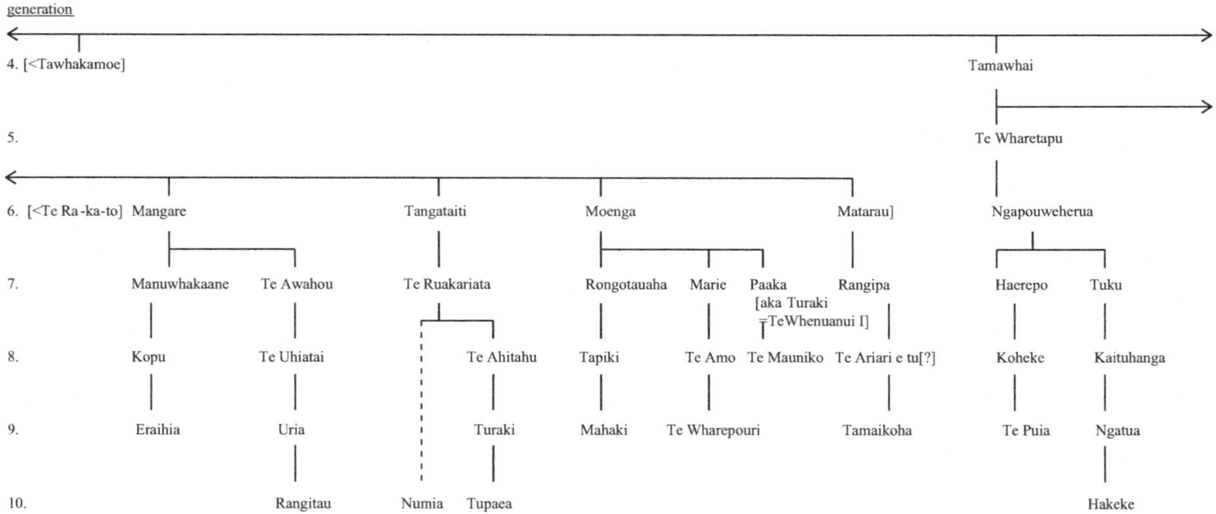

Fig. 5.1 (continued) Urewera hapuu appear in generation 9, p. 1 and generation 7, p. 2. Numia Kereru of Ngati Rongo hapuu was apparently an afterthought noted in generation 10, p. 2, and has been added by author as husband of Tuhiwai Tiopira, generation 10, p. 3. As noted at Tawhakamoe, generation 4, p. 1, this whakapapa overlaps with Fig. 8.1, which is discussed in detail in Chaps. 8 and 9

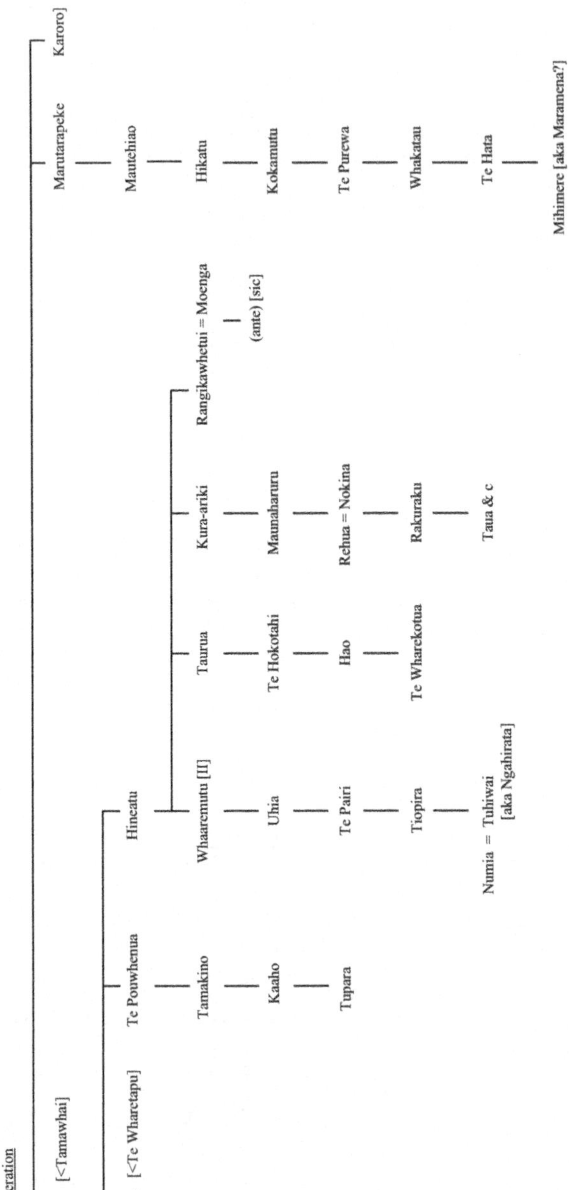

Fig. 5.1 (continued)

In this way Tamaikoha was apparently admitting their rights to Whaitiripapa if, in addition to this ancestry, sufficient occupation could be demonstrated. Explicitly listed were Te Whenuanui (I), Hurae Ruru, Tupaea Rapaera, Te Amo Kokouri and Te Mauniko (Te Whenuanui I's nephew and daughter, respectively), and Tamaikoha himself and his wife Ngatua (descendants of Kahuwī's sister Matarau and uncle Tamawhai, respectively). In addition to its inclusivity, this spectacular whakapapa also displayed the *tuakana/teina* (seniority) relationship between the Te Urewera descent lines and, with appropriate *whakaiti rangatiratanga* (chiefly humility), bowed to Te Whenuanui I as the *mātāmua* (senior) line while taking the *pōtiki* (youngest) line for himself. Tamaikoha's masterful presentation may have nevertheless gently demeaned the leader of the real opposition and adversary in the earlier NLC decisions: while Ngāti Rongo was represented by the ancestor emphasized by Akuhata Te Hata's testimony (Te Purewa) and his descendant Te Hata Waewae, Numia Kererū himself appeared only as a cousin of Tupaea Rapaera (Fig. 5.1 p. 2, where his name may have been added as an afterthought, or even by Best himself, and in any case inaccurately) and later (Fig. 5.1 p. 3) as only the husband of a descendant, Tuhiwai (Ngahirata) Tiopira.

On the other hand, with regard to the impending confrontation between Numia Kererū and Te Whenuanui II that will be pursued in Part II, it was the key position of Kahuwī that, while including Numia's claim to Whaitiripapa, may have opened an opportunity for him to extend his claims against Te Urewera hapū to Ruatāhuna block and so constitute a threat to Te Whenuanui II (see Te Whenuanui I, Fig. 5.1). In such a case, it would be significant that Te Whenuanui II's ancestral claim, stemming from Whāremutu I, an uncle of Kahuwī rather than Kahuwī himself, might have to defer to Numia's rights in Ruatāhuna. As will be seen in Part II, Numia was to claim these rights directly from Kahuwī as a favored, although adopted, son of Arohana (see Fig. 8.1).

Tamaikoha's following commentary on 6 March again emphasized the significance of Kahuwī by describing the origin of his name (after the battle of Rotoiti, his father Tawhakamoe's dead body was found covered in rushes—*Kahuwī*, a cloak of rushes); his mother's subsequent remarriage to Arohana (another important ancestor of Te Urewera hapū in Ruatāhuna—see Fig. 8.1); the continuous permanent occupation of Whaitiripapa by his grandfather along with his older brother, his father Te Ariari, and himself for two years at his grandfather Rangipa's request, as well as his daughter and son Pihitahi and Wi and their children; and

Rangipa's dramatic burning down of a large house built by a Ngāti Rongo 'inside' Whaitiripapa land and even named 'Whaitiripapa', sometime before the 1860s conflicts with the Crown. Tamaikoha explicitly rejected a previous claim that certain drainage ditches were the boundary, reporting that a stake was shifted to the proper boundary 'where it remains undisputed', and adding that 'this boundary was decided by the Appellate Court' (reversing the earlier NLC decision that had awarded Whaitiripapa to Numia Kererū). On the other hand, Tamaikoha admitted that 'I lived upon the [Whaitiripapa] boundary but my plantation is on Ngāti Rongo's land' apparently adjacent to it. Probably with regard to Ngāti Rongo and other claims of established occupation on or use of Whaitiripapa land, Tamaikoha simply said: 'I am not able to give explanation in regard to others occupation'. Finally, near the end of this testimony, he apparently stated that '*[m]y ancestor sold Moenga [Kahuwī's youngest sister; Fig. 5.1 p.2] for a bundle of fern-roots*'.

This last comment may have been referring to the marriage of Moenga to a distant cousin (apparently shown in Fig. 5.1, pp. 2 and 3). However, whether in regard to this marriage or another, in fuller context it might have been intended to deride a Ngāti Rongo claim that their hapū's right to Whaitiripapa derived from a *pākūhā* or marriage gift. Tamaikoha brought this event up in his third and closing testimony on 15 March, but apparently made several other important points in the same context that are obscure in both the translation and Best's Māori. Below is the translation, with some of Best's original Māori inserted in brackets for comparison with some crucial phrases.[5]

> Just at that time [during the 1860s war] a N. Rongo woman was secretly married in consequence of which a land was given away privately ie Whaitiripapa was given away as a gift. N. Ruatāhuna occupied Kahuwi [*No taua wa ka moea tetahi wahine o N.Rongo ka tukuna tahaetia a Whaitiripapa. No N.Ruatāhuna te iwi o Kahuwi.*] Tamawhai's "mana" was not taken away. In my father's time, no one came to disturb him. I had three kaaingas there yet there was no quarrel or dispute about them. Kererū's boundary cut through a portion of Whaitiripapa. Kererū claimed the land from Rongokarae and Kahuwi….The land was awarded to me [in his appeal against the first NLC decision]…. It was afterwards handed to Numia – who lived after my father. It was handed to him as a gift through Kahuwi [*I muri ka whakahokia ki nga morehu o toku papa, ki a Numia, kaore kia katoa. He hoatu na waho i runga a Kahuwi*]. (UMB 4: 55–6; 1: 46–7; my brackets)

Regarding the marriage gift, Tamaikoha's point to the commission was apparently that any such gift of Whaitiripapa to Ngāti Rongo was *tahaetia* or stealthy, that is, not done with public approval, permission, or authority, perhaps obscured in the tumult of war.

But what was implied in his following comment that it was Ngāti Ruatāhuna people who occupied Kahuwī (or 'are the people of Kahuwī')? As will be seen in Part II, Te Whenuanui II's hapū Ngāti Ruatāhuna did occupy the northern part of Ruatāhuna block in an area that may have already been named after the same Kahuwī and his adoptive father Arohana, who had married his mother after his father Tawhakamoe's death in the battle of Rotoiti (Fig. 8.1). Arohana had indeed received that area as a gift, although not in marriage, but from another widow (not Tawhakamoe's widow) for avenging the death of her husband. So Tamaikoha may have been playing on the irony that Te Whenuanui II and Hurae Rurus' hapū were already occupying Kahuwī's land in distant Ruatāhuna. In any case, the reference to Kahuwī's possible rights to land in Ruatāhuna may have alerted Numia Kererū—and alarmed Te Whenuanui II.

There are further possible implications in the disjunct minutebook record above. Although Tamaikoha rejected any rights by way of a marriage gift, he appears to admit that Numia Kererū and Ngāti Rongo hapū had some rights to Whaitiripapa but that the *mana* over the land was still held by him (i.e., by Te Urewera hapū). He traces this dominant *mana* through descendants in undisputed occupation from the time of Te Whanapeke, through Tawhakamoe's younger brother Tamawhai and his son Kahuwī, to Tamaikoha's grandfather Rangipa and his father Te Ariari, to his own *whānau*'s continued occupation at the latter's request. In the earlier testimony Tamaikoha had admitted that Ngāti Rongo had rights to the adjacent land, and implied some undisputed occupation of Whaitiripapa that he was 'unable to explain' (although it was a very small block and Akuhata gave detailed evidence of continuous occupation by Ngāti Rongo). Although 'Tamawhai's [that is, Tawhakamoe's surviving younger brother] *mana* was not taken away', Tamaikoha appears to admit that a gift of Whaitiripapa land was made to Ngāti Rongo through their ancestor Kahuwī, if not in Kererū's own time then to his Ngāti Rongo predecessors. A better translation of the last sentence quoted above might be 'Afterwards [after my father's death in the 1860s] his remnants [that is, his rights to Whaitiripapa] were restored to Numia, but not entirely! The gift was restored upon the *mana* of Kahuwī [although the *mana* of the land remains with Te Urewera, Ngāti Rongo can continue to use the land]'. Finally, when the commissioners were later discussing the case in April 1900, Tutakangahau asserted that Tamawhai (whose *mana* Tamaikoha appeared to be relying upon as "not taken away") "had only a small claim in the land" compared to his deceased older brother Tawhakamoe and his son Kahuwī (UMB 4: 190; my brackets). This would have lent support to Ngāti Rongo's claim.

After cautiously watching how Tamaikoha presented his case 'under one claim' after the 27 February hearing, although Akuhata Te Kaha proceeded to mount an opposing claim for Māhurehure (i.e., for Ngāti Rongo), contrary to Tupaea's announcement, neither he nor Numia Kererū appeared in the following hearings. As a tactful leader of *mana*, perhaps Numia was deferring to the success of Tamaikoha's appeal and reversal of the earlier NLC award of Whaitiripapa to Numia. However, as a strategically ambitious *rangatira*, he may also have been planning unobtrusive access to Te Urewera land in Ruatāhuna as well as Whaitiripapa—and in the latter case was able to use Ngāti Ruatāhuna's own ancestral claim through Kahuwī to do so.

It is significant that while Akuhata's claim was submitted in the name of Māhurehure (and Ngāti Rongo), and on grounds of occupation his case boldly confronted Tamaikoha's case for Te Urewera hapū, Tupara's lists were submitted in the name of Te Urewera hapū and in this way accepted the *mana* of Te Urewera over Ngāti Koura in Whaitiripapa block. Although Akuhata (and Numia Kererū) apparently refused such deference, the commission's 1902 confirmation of their decision on Whaitiripapa block awarded it exclusively to Te Urewera hapū and did not mention Ngāti Rongo or Māhurehure. Given the inclusiveness of Tamaikoha's whakapapa for his case, the commission had no trouble deciding to include almost all of the claims lists under the *mana* of Tamaikoha and Te Urewera hapū (UMB 4: 339–40).

5 Ngāti Tāwhaki Hapū and the Claims to Tarapounamu-Matawhero Block

Tamaikoha's final formal claim list laid before the commission in 1899 was D 24 for Tarapounamu-Matawhero block in the name of Ngāti Tāwhaki hapū, presented in the Ruatāhuna hearing 22 March (UMB 1: 145, 150–53). Tarapounamu-Matawhero is one of two very large blocks situated in the western Urewera which together stretch nearly its entire length south to north (the other is Hikurangi-Horomanga block; see Fig. 1.2). Tarapounamu-Matawhero dominates most of the western tributaries of the Whakatane River between Ruatāhuna and Taneatua blocks, but includes the river itself only in its northern portion at Honoi, on a spectacular switchback which remained obscured on many maps. As discussed earlier, Tamaikoha's ancestral rights and potential hapū affiliation for this claim probably devolved from Tiramate, Tamaikoha's mother and wife of his father Te Ariari. Ngāti Tāwhaki was part of the extensive old Ngā Pōtiki hapū, and Tiramate also apparently had rights in Ngāti Whare hapū (or iwi), to whom a major portion of the adjacent Te Whaiti Nui a Toi block was awarded.

Best reported that Ngāti Tāwhaki included several "subdivisions", subordinate hapū or hapū branches still dependent (or which had become dependent) on Ngāti Tāwhaki: Ngāti Tamakere, Ngāti Korokaiwhenua, Ngāti Taokaki, and Ngāti Tuhea or Tuhaereao (1973 Vol. I: 214). In addition to Tamaikoha's claim, there were 17 others made for Tarapounamu-Matawhero block, mostly at the Ruatāhuna hearing, and mostly also in the name of Ngāti Tāwhaki hapū. There were apparently difficulties only hinted at in the minutes, and concluding hearings were not until January and March 1902. When these decisions were reviewed for confirmation in October of that year, the block was awarded in the names of Ngāti Tāwhaki and Ngāi Te Wehi hapū (probably also called "Wehi o te Rangi"), a subdivision of Ngāti Tāwhaki, with a total of 883 persons listed (UMB 6: 48–58, 311–12).

One might suspect that many of the large number of claims in the name of Ngāti Tāwhaki were actually claims by one of its dependent hapū branches aspiring to independence or independent control over a locality in the block. The discussion in the minutebooks also indicates that while some claims from other hapū or *iwi* were rejected, several others (Warahoe, Ngāti Whare and Ngāi Te Riu) may have accepted the dominant *mana* of Ngāti Tāwhaki over the block and the inclusion of some part of their members under its name. Ngāi Te Wehi was probably separately named in the award because Tutakangahau, a commissioner (recused for this case) and leader in Ngāti Tāwhaki, accepted that it enjoyed some independence from Ngāti Tāwhaki within the block (UMB 6: 45). The high number of owners in the title also suggests the extension of the Ngāti Tāwhaki hapū mana or 'umbrella' over sectors of other hapū as well as its many branches.

In January 1902 the claimants proposed that Ngāti Tāwhaki settle conflicting claims in "the Matawhero end" (north end) of the block by allotting "shares in Tarapounamu as was done in Taneatua, so many to each ancestor" (UMB 6: 14). Apparently, each hapū or hapū branch which had demonstrated occupational as well as ancestral rights from the common ancestor of Ngāti Tāwhaki as a whole, but claiming some independence through their own chosen ancestor (presumably as a descendant of Tāwhaki), would receive an appropriate proportion of the total shares implicitly in the name of their own ancestor. In Taneatua and some other blocks the limitation of such a sector of shares to a particular part of a block was not formally defined in the title and thus, as was described in Chap. 3, ambiguous in relative shares. However, this may have been avoided in the Tarapounamu-Matawhero block. Although the shares awarded in many cases ranged from 20 to 10 or 5 shares as was usual, this was the only block in which the majority of the large number of shareholders were awarded only one share. Such widespread token recognition may have represented rights limited to a relatively small area of the large block, as well as weak occupational or ancestral rights. This solution to disparate claims may have avoided the troubles in other blocks but, as it turned out, like disregard of minor claims, it also left these blocks more vulnerable to the Crown purchase campaign 1915–1921.

Although most members of Tamaikoha's hapū branch as it appears in the Tauwhare Manuka block list were included in Tarapounamu-Matawhero block list, they received only such token shares and were ranked far from the head of the list (numbers 579–631). Tamaikoha himself was awarded only one share and, presumably because a person granted a right of membership could hold no less (even an infant), each of his offspring listed also received one share although they spanned four generations. On the other hand, many other sibling groups in the block list were awarded the usual 10 or 20 shares, and thus stand out clearly as the leading descent groups in Ngāti Tāwhaki hapū.

Why, considering that he was the first to lay the claim for the block in the name of Ngāti Tāwhaki, was Tamaikoha not among them? Although no formal claim was laid in his name for the adjacent Te Whaiti Nui a Toi block, Tiramate's potential rights there in Ngāti Whare hapū were recognized with significant shares (ten shares for Tamaikoha, five to each of his children, and so on). As well as the issue of Tiramate's claim to occupation in the two blocks, quite different weight may have been attributed to Tamaikoha's personal *mana* and especially to an important marriage alliance between Te Urewera and Ngāti Tāwhaki. His third daughter Te Unupo (and senior daughter by Whata Te Puia) had first married Te Hata Waewae, whose mother Te Hirea Pahiri was a member of one of the most influential sibling groups in Ngāti Tāwhaki and the source of Te Hata's leading shares in Tarapounamu-Matawhero block (Best 1898: 28, 2). Although the marriage apparently did not last, Te Unupo and Te Hatas' only child Maramena (recorded as 'Mihimere' in Tamaikoha's whakapapa: Fig. 5.1 p. 3) might have been an important symbol of the alliance between Te Urewera hapū, Ngāti Tāwhaki hapū, and Ngāti Rongo hapū, which will be examined in Chap. 6.

6 Further Awards Without Formal Claims

In addition to recognition of their rights in Tauwhare Manuka without anybody having made a formal claim to it, and in Taneatua, Pukepohatu, and Te Whaiti Nui a Toi blocks without himself having made a formal claim, Tamaikoha and his *kāwai* were awarded significant and sometimes strong shares in some other blocks. Two other cases were Ohiorangi block, where they received strong shares (20 to Tamaikoha, 10 to each of his children, and so on), and Ruatāhuna block, where they were awarded significant shares (10 to Tamaikoha, 5 to each of his children, and so on) and on appeal Tamaikoha's (but not his offspring's) were increased to 20 shares in 1906. Were active hapū affiliations implied in these awards even though no formal claim had been made?

Ohiorangi was one of two small blocks (about 1200 acres) in the upper Waikare River carved out from the larger blocks dominating that river in its course to join the middle Whakatane River. The block was awarded exclusively to Ngāi Tama hapū, and Tamaikoha and most of his hapū branch were awarded strong although not leading shares. Again, their potential rights in this hapū had devolved from Tamaikoha's father's father Rangipa and, according to Sissons, Tamaikoha had been a war leader for Ngāi Tama hapū (as well as for Te Whakatane, Ngāi Tatua, Te Urewera, and Ngāti Kurī hapū). The status of his *kāwai* in the block was also reinforced indirectly. One of Tamaikoha's colleagues in the war had been Te Whiu Maraki, who was probably a key leader in Ngāi Tama hapū and whose hapū branch was awarded leading shares in Ohiorangi block. It will be recalled that Tamaikoha's second wife Ramari was Te Whiu's *tuakana* sister, and mother of Tiopira, one of Tamaikoha's senior sons.

Given these credentials, the award of strong shares to the hapū branch implies that Tamaikoha could also demonstrate recent occupation of the block by one of his predecessors if he had wished. It is likely that, as in the case of Tauwhare Manuka and Pukepohatu blocks, Tamaikoha could assume that his rights in Ohiorangi block were so well-established that other Ngāi Tama leaders would look after him, and that he need not submit them to the commission for formal recognition. On the other hand, Ngāi Tama hapū was also awarded exclusive rights to the adjacent Waikarewhenua block further down the Waikare River, but Tamaikoha received only weak (5) shares there even though his colleague Te Whiu was the only claimant. The comparison shows clearly that any occupational claim he had in Waikarewhenua had probably lapsed, and the weak shares might reflect no more than his *mana* in that hapū.

Again, unless challenged, such discriminations remained unexplained in the minutes, having been decided previously in arrangement of the claims lists and negotiation outside the hearings. The minimum three-generation criterion of *noho* or recent occupation was inherently ambiguous, and may have been a determining factor in either award. For instance, rights falling short of the three-generation criteria, but nevertheless honored or indulged in particular circumstances (such as prominent *mana*) might include occupation re-established after it had lapsed; occupation by an ancestor with doubtful ancestral rights in Ngāi Tama hapū; occupation by regular use of resources in the block rather than residence in any stronger sense (a precedent established in the Te Waipotiki block case); merely symbolic occupation established, for instance, in a gift between hapū leaders (as in the marriage arrangement over Whaitiripapa block); and many other specific historical situations. Thus it can be said that, among the Māori, land rights (and thus kinship, especially whakapapa) *are* history.

The shares allocated to Tamaikoha's hapū branch in the large Ruatāhuna block were also awarded without any formal claim by them, and probably reflect similar but more dramatic ambiguities. As discussed with regard to the Whaitiripapa block, Tamaikoha's potential affiliation at least in Te Urewera hapū extended across the extremities of the Reserve to the Ruatāhuna block, and one might suspect that this hapū affiliation implicated some land rights. The block was located in the southernmost part of the Reserve, straddling the divide between the upper Whakatane tributaries and the streams running south in the opposite direction, and the western flanks of the Huiarau range, to the east of which was the even larger Waikaremoana block and the already famous lake. These two blocks will be the focus of Part II.

In 1902 the commission awarded the Ruatāhuna block to seven hapū: Te Urewera, Ngāi Te Riu, Ngāti Kurī, Ngāti Tu, Ngāti Manunui, Ngāti Kakahutapiki, and Ngāti Ruatāhuna, in that order of precedence. (As will be described in Chap. 9, the legal ambiguity of implicit limitation of shares to certain internal localities, as had been done in Taneatua block, led to the later partitioning of Ruatāhuna.) There are several possible grounds for the rights of Tamaikoha's *kāwai* in the block. Successful claims in other blocks showed that the *kāwai* had at least ancestral rights in two of these hapū: Te Urewera and Ngāi Te Riu hapū. Rights may have been implied in Tamaikoha's whakapapa for Whaitiripapa insofar as both he and Te Whenuanui II, the leader of Te Urewera in that area, were both descendants of Te Whanapeke (Fig. 5.1). Best and Sissons' report his leadership in Ngāti Kurī hapū as recently as the 1890s. Furthermore, it was earlier pointed out that Tupaea Rapaera, another leader of *mana* who although not himself a member of Tamaikoha's hapū branch had married his senior daughter Pihitahi, had laid three claims for Ruatāhuna block in the name of Kakahutapiki hapū. A leading ancestor of this hapū was Ruruhe (Kruger 2004: 30), who was also the founding ancestor of Ngāi Te Riu hapū in which name Tamaikoha had formally claimed parts of Parekohe and Paraoanui blocks.

Given the extent of the Ruatāhuna block, the large number of hapū found to have rights there, and Tamaikoha's probably active rights in at least three of them, it seems likely that he would have been able to demonstrate occupational rights through at least one of his several ancestors at three generations remove. So again it appears that he may have relied upon his manifest rights and *mana*, and perhaps indirect representation through the claims of relatives and other prominent leaders in the block such as Tupaea Rapaera and Te Whenuanui II, to secure rightful shares in the block for himself and his hapū branch. This supposition is borne out dramatically by his appeal in 1906 against his award of only moderate shares in the block (10 for himself, 5 for his children, and so on). His action probably showed that in at least some blocks where he had laid no claim, he nevertheless expected recognition of his prominent status by other claimants. Unfortunately, as was often the case, no details of the appeal were recorded, probably because it was in large part settled among Tūhoe leaders outside the appeals hearing. Tamaikoha's own strong shares (20) were recognized in 1906 on his appeal, but one supposes he remained galled that none of the shares of his offspring were proportionally increased. The apparent reluctance of other leaders *[to support his claim]* suggests that Tamaikoha's occupational rights were indeed nil or lapsed. Insofar as Ngāti Kurī was named in the award of no other block, Tamaikoha's recent leadership of that hapū may have been the crucial consideration.

7 Block Committee Appointments

The block committees were discussed briefly in Chaps. 2 and 3. In addition to Tamaikoha's formal and informal land claims in 1899, and details emerging in the investigations, some further evidence of active hapū affiliations of his hapū branch is offered by the commissions' 1902 appointments to the block committees (Fig. 2.1). While the 1899–1903 commission's term 'block committees' implicitly recognized the difficulty of meeting the naive statutory expectation that the blocks be 'hapū blocks', it may be significant that the 1906–1907 appeals commission nevertheless termed these committees *hapū* committees. Like the block claims, appointment to these committees certainly reflected general support of the hapū concerned if not leadership, and thus reliable evidence of active affiliation. On the other hand, when the blocks were awarded to more than one hapū (and, as previous discussions have shown, even then) which and how many hapū were being represented by the appointee may remain ambiguous.

Tamaikoha himself was appointed to only the block committee of Whaitiripapa, again confirming the active affiliation of his hapū branch with Te Urewera hapū. However, several of his mature children were appointed to other block committees, certainly as representatives of their father. The general custom would have been that such official positions cannot be undertaken while the father or a *tuakana* is still alive and able, but in this case several of his sons took other committee seats, probably spreading the *kāwai* authority as widely as possible. Hakeke was appointed to the block committee of Pukepohatu/Papatupu Land block, confirming his (and the entire hapū branch's) active affiliation with Ngāi Tokotuai hapū. Te Hauwaho and Takao were both appointed to the Paraoanui block committee, confirming active affiliation of the hapū branch with Ngāi Taumata (and thus Ngāi Te Riu) hapū. Tiopira was appointed to both the Tauwhare Manuka and Papatipu Land/Pukepohatu block committees, confirming active affiliation with Te Whakatane and, again, Ngāi Tokotuai hapū.

Hakeke was also appointed to the block committee for Tauranga block, a large block located south of Tauwhare Manuka and Pukepohatu blocks. The implications of this appointment for hapū affiliation are more difficult to determine. The Tauranga block was awarded to Ngā Maihi, Ngāi Te Kahu, and Ngāti Tamaroki hapū, none of which are among those hapū to which the hapū branch appears to have been actively affiliated. What was the basis of Hakeke's appointment to this block committee? Inspection of the block list for Tauranga suggests that his status in that block derived from his mother Ngatua Hokimoki (Tamaikoha's first wife), who was awarded strong shares in the block. The distribution of Tauranga shares within Tamaikoha's hapū branch was significant. Whereas Tamaikoha received only five shares in this block, and all his children by his second and third wives only two shares each, Hakeke and Ngatua's other three children by Tamaikoha (Pihitahi, Pohe, and Te Hauwaho) received ten shares each. Thus it is clear that Ngatua or her recent predecessors had occupied some part of the Tauranga block, as well as being descended from an ancestor in one of the three hapū awarded the block.

8 Conclusion

Although more evidence can be winnowed out of the commission records, enough has been examined above to now recapitulate the active hapū affiliations of Tamaikoha and his hapū branch 1899–1903. Among the many potential affiliations the hapū branch had succeeded to from their ancestors, a case can be made for some degree of active affiliation with 11 hapū during these years. In each case below, a few comments are added in order to review basic facts about each affiliation. Primarily on the basis of relatively positive or confirmed evidence and relatively negative or unconfirmed evidence, for simplification the list is divided into two groups distinguishing between relatively strong and relatively weak hapū affiliations.

Probably Relatively Stronger Active Affiliations

Te Whakatane hapū (ancestral right from Te Ra-Mahaki; leading shares in Tauwhare Manuka block; earlier known as Ngāi Tātua hapū);

Ngāi Te Riu hapū (ancestral right from Urunga; leading shares in Paraoanui block; comprised of Ngāti Hinekura and Ngāi Taumata hapū);

Te Urewera hapū (ancestral right from Rangipa, leading shares in Whaitiripapa and probably Taneatua blocks; earlier known as Tūhoe or Tūhoe Pōtiki hapū; other affiliations perhaps implied: Ngāti Ruatāhuna and Ngāti Rongo hapū;

Ngāi Tokotuai hapū (ancestral right undetermined, leading shares in Pukepohatu and Taneatua blocks; probably a branch of Te Whakatane hapū).

Probably Relatively Weaker Active Affiliations

Ngāi Tama hapū (ancestral right from Rangipa; strong shares in Ohiorangi and small shares in Waikarewhenua blocks);

Ngāti Kurī hapū (ancestral rights from Rangipa; moderate to strong shares in Ruatāhuna block);

Ngāti Tāwhaki hapū (ancestral right from Tiramate; symbolic or token shares in Tarapounamu-Matawhero block);

Ngāti Whare hapū (ancestral rights from Tiramate; moderate shares in Te Whaiti Nui a Toi block);

Ngāti Murakareke hapū (ancestral rights from Te Ariari; probably the basis of extension of Paraoanui into original Otara block);

Ngā Maihi and/or Ngāi Te Kahu hapū (ancestral right from Ngatua for her children; small shares in Tauranga and moderate shares in Karioi blocks).

Although this list simplifies the complexity of the foregoing analysis and reduces the plethora of potential affiliations of the hapū branch, the remaining number of apparently active affiliations may strike a student of contemporary Māori society as excessive or unmanageable. Among contemporary Māori it is not uncommon for leaders of *mana* to maintain active participation in two or more hapū, but eleven would seem beyond the reach of any. However, several considerations narrow this apparent gap.

First of all, during these years Tamaikoha probably enjoyed pre-eminent *mana* among Tūhoe hapū, shared with perhaps no more than a score of other leaders. Evidence of the several ways in which he influenced the commission's investigations furthermore suggested that his personal *mana* may have exceeded that of an old war leader and head of an unusually large hapū branch. As pointed out earlier, although he and his hapū branch were found to have rights in only a moderate number of blocks compared to other leaders with perhaps more influential ancestors, a high proportion of Tamaikoha's rights were recognized as not merely strong but also as leading shares. This high rank in so many block lists implies an unusual capacity to maintain active affiliations with several hapū. Activities of his relatively numerous senior sons and daughters would also have enabled this wide influence.

The specific historical context of the 1896 Act and the commission's prolonged investigation were certainly major factors in hapū dynamics which in several ways may further explain so many apparently active affiliations. The benevolent and even traditionalist intentions of the Act and the commission were reassuring to most Tūhoe that they would retain and in the future be protected in their control over their own lands. The manifestly new form of tenure being established also precipitated a proliferation of new hapū aspiring to independence and an even larger number of land claims to be resolved. The opportunism of individuals and sibling groups as well as the normal waxing and waning of hapū strength were probably accelerated. Given the relative size and maturity of Tamaikoha's hapū branch, it is likely that these processes led to divergent priorities of hapū affiliation among his own children, some of whom were *kaumātua* or elders in their own right. The historical reasons for divergence between rights of hapū affiliation and rights to hapū land discussed in the conclusion of Chap. 4 may also have come into play. All these forces may have resulted in the appearance of active hapū affiliations which in the longer run and under more normal circumstances would have been fewer.

Rather than analyzing hapū organization from the point of view of hapū affiliations of a specific group as was done in this chapter, Chap. 6 considers the general relationship between hapū and hapū leaders in the Urewera District Native Reserve during its establishment 1899–1903. The problem is approached through the aborted plan to reorganize the 35 blocks of the reserve into just 10 more inclusive blocks, discussed in the concluding section of Chap. 3. Following Angela Ballara's insight that hapū were often organized in 'clusters' (Chap. 3; Ballara 1998), the possibility is explored that the amalgamation plan was supported by Tūhoe because it reflected the organization of hapū in such 'clusters'.

Notes

1. A 'Tokotuai Miria' was apparently among the claimants for Taneatua block, and may have been named after this ancestor. Tupaea Rapaera, Tamaikoha's eldest daughter's (Pihitahi's) husband and found to be the leading shareholder in the block, identified Tokotuai Miria as the same person as Pita

Tumoana (UMB 4: 101). The name 'Pita Tumoana' appears nowhere else that I know of in the records of the UDNR commission nor those of the subsequent Urewera purchase campaign and consolidation scheme. However, the name of Tupaea and Pihitahis' eldest child was Miria Tupaea, and her husband was Tumoana Pokai. They are reported to have had three children, Poniu, Mere, and Kunere. The eldest, Poniu Tumoana, was about four years old in 1903, and may have had the nickname 'Pita'. Poniu died by 1921. Another possibility is that Miria had an older son by a Pākehā who (as a 'half-caste') was named Tokotuai Miria. Insofar as this child represented the *mātāmua* line (first-born child of the first-born child) of the prestigious marriage between Tupaea Rapaera and Pihitahi Tamaikoha, he may have been given the ancestral name Tokotuai by Tupaea and *also* claimed by him to be, as 'Pita Tumoana', the eldest son of Tumoana Pokai and Miria. As Tupaea's 'father-in-law', Tamaikoha's *mana* may have presided over all of these arrangements. In any case, as will be seen, the Ngāi Tokotuai hapū appears to have been established by Tamaikoha for special purposes.

2. As he promised, in 1906 Tamaikoha appealed for inclusion in the Ohora section of Paraeroa block, pointing out that he had been awarded it and alleging that the commission had nevertheless ignored his list in favor of Tupara Kaaho's list. He apparently concealed the fact that he had later withdrawn his claim for Ohora, although the commission had actually been reluctant to accept his withdrawal and instead ready to investigate it. The appeal commission neglected to discover the minute on Tamaikoha's withdrawal of the claim, instead blaming the confusion on the previous commission. However, apparently because Tamaikoha presented no evidence to support his appeal, the appeals commission decided against it—again reluctantly, and perhaps again faced by Tamaikoha's petulance or arrogance. Tupara Kaaho was also an influential leader in Ngāi Te Riu hapū, and Tamaikoha's attitude suggests he saw Tupara's counter-claim as an affront to his authority.
3. Binney herself may have confused the issue, appearing to identify Te Whenuanui II (Te Haka) as 'Te Whenuanui Umuariki' (p. 20) although it was Te Whenuanui I's *father* who was Te Umuariki (Fig. 8.1). In addition to this sort of confusion regarding generations, there are many conflicting stories, even from knowledgeable descendants, about Te Whenuanui I and even denials there was a II.
4. My preoccupation here and in Part II with succession to a 'title' suggested by the discrimination 'I', 'II', and so on in successive generations should not be taken to imply that the Tūhoe were preoccupied by 'chiefly' status. To the contrary, confrontations between Tūhoe leaders were notoriously resolved or hidden behind a solid consensus when confronted by outsiders. I have also argued that the so-called nobility among Māori was greatly exag-

gerated by colonial administrators or Māori leaders (e.g., by Apirana Ngata; Webster 1998: 100–102) seeking to emulate the British tradition of sovereigns. The respect sustained for *mātāmua* or first-born lines of descent, and generally for the discrimination of seniority between *tuakana* and *teina* and their descendant lines, discussed in Chap. 4 and vivid in the Tūhoe control of the UDNR block lists, is probably the rationale for pretenses of a Māori 'nobility'. The relaxation of Tamaikoha and Rakurakus' initial refusal to cooperate with the UNDR commission that was described in Chap. 2 is one example of the ready compliance of Tūhoe *rangatira* with a wider consensus among demands of 'their' people. Best only tentatively raised the notion of a Tūhoe '*gentes*' or aristocracy with regard to a four *rangatira*: Te Whenuanui and Rakuraku, adding that 'Kereru and Paora Kingi families were also of importance' (Best 1973 Vol. I: 223–4). As will be described in Part II, Paora Kingi was a close cousin of Te Whenuanui I and stood with Tutakangahau in his attempt to claim part of Waikaremoana. Tamaikoha's *mana* may have been too much derived from war leadership to be included. In any case, it should be kept in mind that my preoccupation with the 'title' of Te Whenuanui is only to unravel the confrontations between Tūhoe leaders that is traced in Part II.

5. Although by 1907 'Kahuwī' was being spelled 'Kahui', Best was spelling it correctly in its early occurrences (i.e., to mean 'cloak of rushes'). On the other hand, it is significant that Best's Māori orthography (unlike his oral fluency) was not sophisticated enough to distinguish the important (phonemic) difference in meaning between long and short vowels with a macron or other diacritic.

References

AJHR 1907. G. Mair, D.F.G. Barclay, Paratene Ngata. "The Urewera District Native Reserve: reports of the commissioners appointed ...." Report and orders. Undated. Appendices to the Journal of the House of Representatives 1907 G-4: 1–190. Wellington, N.Z.

Ballara, Angela. 1998. *Iwi: The dynamics of Māori tribal organisation from c.1769 to c.1945*. Wellington, N.Z.: Victoria University Press.

Bassett, Heather and R. Kay. 2002. "*Ruatāhuna: land ownership and administration c. 1896–1990.*" With Supporting Papers (S.P.) Vols 1–3. WAI 894 #A20. Wellington, N.Z.: Waitangi Tribunal.

Best, Elsdon. 1898. "Tuhoe genealogies 1898" (spine title); "Genealogies of the Tuhoe tribe. Also includes all living members of the tribe in 1898, as given before the Urewera Commission set up under the act of 1896." Manuscript qMS [172]. Wellington, N.Z.: Alexander Turnbull Library.

Best, Elsdon. 1973. *Tuhoe, Children of the Mist.* Vols. I and II (genealogies). Second edition. Wellington, N.Z.: A.H. and A.W. Reed Ltd. (first published 1925 as Vol VI of the Memoirs of the Polynesian Society).

Binney, Judith. 2002. *Encircled Lands; Part Two: A History of the Urewera 1878–1912.* An Overview Report on the Urewera for the Waitangi Tribunal. WAI 894, A15. Wellington, N.Z.: Waitangi Tribunal.

Kruger, Tamati. 2004. "Ngā Hapū ō Ngā Pōtiki." Appendix to Final Report *Ruātoki; Ngā Rauru ō Ngā Pōtiki.* Anamata College, Taneātua, N.Z. 10 January 2004. Urewera Enquiry WAI 894. Wellington, N.Z.: Waitangi Tribunal.

Sissons, Jeffrey. 1991. *Te Waimana, The Spring of Mana: Tuhoe History and the Colonial Encounter.* Dunedin, N.Z.: Otago University Press.

Sissons, Jeffrey. 2002. "Waimana Kaaku: A History of the Waimana Block." A report commissioned by the Crown Forestry Rental Trust, June 2002. Wellington, N.Z.: Waitangi Tribunal.

UMB 1. Urewera District Native Reserve Commission minute book 1 (identified as Urewera Commission minute book '3'), Smith, Butler, et al, (1Feb1899–8Mar1900), in Māori, Index 22pp., 382pp. NA Wgtn: Urewera MB 3, MLC 13, W3518, CD2, Vol 3, 397 pp.; NA Ak: AREPRO 4711/1445. Acronym: UMB 1.

UMB 2. Urewera District Native Reserve Commission minute book 2, Smith, Butler, et al., (8Mar1900–20Feb1901), in Māori, Index, 350 pp. NA Wgtn: Urewera MB 2, MLC 13,W3518, CD2, Vol.2, 358 pp.; NA Ak: AREPRO 4711/1442. Acronym: UMB 2.

UMB 3. Urewera District Native Reserve Commission minute book 3 (identified as '3A'; English translation of last part of UMB 1), Smith, Butler, et al, (9Feb1900–8Mar1900). 189 pp., index, NA Wgtn: Urewera MB 3A, MLC 13, W3518, CD 2, Vol 3A, 191 pp.; NA Ak: AREPRO 4711/1444. Acronym: UMB 3.

UMB 4. Urewera District Native Reserve Commission minute book 4 (English translation of UMB 2), Butler, Scannell, et al, (9Mar1900–May1900), index 12 pp., 344pp.; NA Wgtn: Urewera MB 4, MLC 13, W3518, CD 2, Vol. 4, 357 pp.; NA Ak: AREPRO 4711/1446. Acronym: UMB 4.

UMB 6. Urewera District Native Reserve Commission minute book 6, Butler, Scannell, et al. (16May1901–26Apr02) in English, index 9 pp., 382 pp.; NA Wgtn: Waiariki, Urewera MB 6, CD W3518/2, 398 pp.; NA Ak: AREPRO 4711/1448. Acronym: UMB 6.

Webster, Steven. 1998. *Patrons of Maori Culture: Power, Theory, and Ideology in the Maori Renaissance.* Dunedin, N.Z.: Otago University Press.

CHAPTER 6

Tūhoe *Hapū* Organization and the Amalgamation Plan

1 Introduction

The aborted 1902 plan to amalgamate all the blocks of the Native Reserve into just ten was examined in Chap. 3. Because this plan was probably instigated by Tūhoe and apparently had wide acceptance among them or at least their key leaders, it offers a promising context in which to analyze in more general terms the organization of Tūhoe hapū and leadership during the establishment of the Urewera District Native Reserve. Regardless of the motives in support of the plan, a crucial criterion upon which certain blocks were chosen to be amalgamated with others would have been the relationship of the hapū whose stronger rights over these blocks had been recognized in the awards by the commission. Under the new political organization of the Reserve, if amalgamated, these blocks and their representatives would often have to act together cooperatively. We can assume that the Tūhoe commissioners carefully considered the relationship between all the hapū involved in each proposed amalgamation, probably in terms of solidarity or compatibility such as common ancestry, relative seniority, joint leadership, and the specific history of such relationships. This wider context of hapū relations can in turn clarify the relationship of hapū rights within each constituent block of a proposed amalgamation.

© The Author(s) 2020

S. Webster, *A Separate Authority (He Mana Motuhake)*, Volume I,
https://doi.org/10.1007/978-3-030-41042-1_6

Chapter 3 concluded with a discussion of Angela Ballara's important notion of hapū "clusters" (Ballara 1995, 1998; Webster 1998: 10–11). Again, some specific questions can be explored in this regard: Did the intended amalgamations group blocks which were controlled by the same or more closely related hapū? Did the shareholders of these blocks tend to have shares or rights in other blocks of the same amalgamation? Would differences between these shares promote conflict rather than solidarity? Were leaders or leading sibling groups in amalgamated hapū less likely to act independently or opportunistically? How was the system of block committees effected? After consideration of some general issues, some of these questions will be addressed with regard to each of two different amalgamations.

With regard to the motives in support of the plan, I argued in Chap. 3 that from the point of view of the Tūhoe commissioners and other leaders the amalgamation plan may have offered more centralized control of hapū and their lands in the face of lingering doubts about the fragmenting and individualizing implications of the new form of tenure. This result would also have reassured those leading the early resistance to the commission, who feared that individual shareholding would render their lands more vulnerable to loss and demanded that the blocks be held in the name of trustees or entire hapū. The Pākehā commissioners, and perhaps the Native Minister, might furthermore have hoped that in this way many of the stubborn appeals against their decisions could be circumvented. If examination of the relationship between hapū involved in an amalgamation of certain blocks, or between their leaders, suggests an increase in solidarity or cooperation, the likelihood is increased that more centralized control of hapū and lands was a key motive for support of the plan, at least among Tūhoe leaders.

On the other hand, the amalgamation proposals might have been seen as aggravating the problems foreseen by Numia Kererū where 'minor' claims were merged with 'major' claims, sometimes imposing an arbitrary decision on legitimate aspirations for independent control of ancestral land by a hapū or hapū branch. As discussed in Chap. 3, the demands for partitioning of some blocks taken up by the Native Appellate Court in 1912 may have been responding to the problem Numia foresaw. In his initial investigation Chief Justice Jackson Palmer found that recognition of claimants' rights to a particular portion of a block might not be explicitly recorded but the relative shares of ownership awarded would nevertheless be mistakenly extended equally throughout the whole block. Presumably, the amalgamation plan foresaw amalgamating each sibling or descent group's shares in each block of an amalgamation into a single list of owners serving as a more consolidated electoral role. If so, the problem identified by the Chief Judge would be aggravated by the illegitimate extension of shares intended to be restricted to only part of a block across all the blocks of the amalgamation, including blocks in which the group may have not been recognized to hold any rights at all.

Nevertheless, as I argued in Chap. 3 and demonstrated in Chap. 4, the detailed care with which Tūhoe leaders usually laid out the rights of each descent group in ranked orders of relative shares *between* blocks as well as within each block, backed by the rising confidence of Tūhoe in the sincere intentions of home-rule of the 1896 Act would sufficiently reassure enough of their leaders to support or even propose the amalgamation plan. Their confidence would be reinforced by the prospect of a much more centralized organization of authority in 10 rather than 35 block committees, and perhaps a General Committee with only 10 rather than 35 representatives. By 1902, the confidence of the five Tūhoe commissioners in such an arrangement would also have been consolidated. The organization of these block or 'hapū' committees will be reviewed below with regard to their implications for hapū leadership.

Of probable interest especially to the Pākehā commissioners was a likely reduction of duplicated names in the amalgamated block lists so that they could better conform to the intention of the Act that they serve as electoral roles in the new self-governing organization of the Reserve. In order to test this, I collated, sorted, and culled the 1907 block lists for three of the amalgamations representing different locations in the UDNR (see Chap. 3 and Fig. 1.3): Te Whaiti Nui a Toi (three blocks) at the southern end, Parekohe (six blocks) at the northern end, and Ōhāua te Rangi (four blocks) in the middle.[1]

The three block titles of the first amalgamation example, Te Whaiti Nui a Toi, together listed 892 names, but when collated, sorted, and culled for duplicate names turned out to have only 690 different shareholders, about a 19% reduction of names. This does not appear to be a sufficient improvement in the titles viewed as electoral roles to warrant the amalgamation plan. However, in 1902 these three blocks were a uniquely early case of partition in the Reserve, and because of this, and a major change in the 1907 list of owners by the appeals commission, could be expected to show relatively little overlap of shareholders. Further consideration of the unique situation of the Te Whaiti Nui a Toi amalgamation proposal is therefore best left for Volume II, where the effects of the subsequent Crown purchase and Urewera consolidation regimes in this area of the UDNR will be discussed.

The seven blocks of the Parekohe amalgamation together listed 2078 names, but when collated, sorted, and culled for duplicate names turned out to have about 1001 different shareholders, about a 48% reduction of names. The names in the Te Tuahu block had to be added from the 1903 titles because this block did not appear among the 1907 titles, perhaps because there were no appeals before the appeals commission. Significantly, about 93% of the names in the Te Tuahu block already held shares in other blocks of the amalgamation.

Similarly, the four blocks of the Ōhāua te Rangi amalgamation together listed 1540 names, but when collated, sorted, and culled for duplicate names turned out to have about 874 different shareholders, about a 43% reduction of names. A more detailed collation showed that the range was also significant: while only 4 sibling groups held shares in all four blocks, 65 sibling groups held shares in three of the four blocks, 81 sibling groups held shares in only two of the four blocks, and 138 sibling groups held shares in only one of the four blocks. The possibility that those sibling groups holding more extensive shares in the amalgamation were leading or influential families will be examined later in closer analysis of the relationship of hapū in the amalgamation. A similar method will be used to identify leaders and hapū affiliations in the Parekohe amalgamation.

Another general issue bearing on the analysis of any amalgamated block is the organization of block or hapū committees selected to represent each block and, at the outset, each amalgamation. These committees were briefly described in Chap. 2 and laid out in Fig. 2.1. As described in Chap. 3, they were constituted three different times for the reserve: first, in May 1902 as block committees for the 10 *amalgamated* blocks of the reserve; second, in October 1902 as provisional block committees for the 35 blocks of the reserve pending appeals, and third, in 1907 as provisional 'hapu' committees for 33 blocks of the reserve. One member from each block committee constituted the Komiti Nui formed in 1908. Comparisons of these committees in Chap. 3 showed a high proportion of committee members held their seats, often on several committees at the same time, through all three selection processes. Appointment to these committees, whether by the commissioners or by leaders of the hapū involved, would generally have reflected active affiliation with and probably leadership in one or more hapū found to have strong or leading rights in the block or amalgamation. Consequently, they furnish evidence of the potential overlap of leadership and hapū affiliation between the constituent blocks of an amalgamation.

The Ōhāua Te Rangi and Parekohe amalgamations will each be examined for evidence of hapū clusters in the following sections of this chapter. This closer study of each of them will first outline their geography and, so far as can be determined from early survey plans, boundary changes that their constituent blocks had undergone; second, leading sibling or descent groups in each block will be identified in an attempt to narrow the range of potential leaders in the amalgamation; third, marriages and likely political alliances between these sibling or descent groups will be considered; fourth, their most active leaders will be identified in terms of the claims laid and committees organized for each constituent block; and finally, the hapū affiliations of these leaders will be considered for the light this may throw on the organization of hapū behind the amalgamation proposal.

2 The Ōhāua te Rangi Amalgamation

The amalgamation of Ierenui-Ōhāua, Kohuru-Tukuroa, Te Ranga a Ruanuku, and Tauwhare blocks was to be known as Ōhāua te Rangi, the name by which Ōhāua was first claimed for Ngāti Rongo hapū by Numia Kererū before it was merged with Ierenui (Figs. 1.2 and 1.3 amalgamation 4). As recorded in Fig. 2.1, the following October 1902, soon after the amalgamation proposal was aborted, the merged Ierenui-Ōhāua block was awarded to Ngāti Rongo and Ngāti Rakei hapū; Kohuru-Tukuroa block was awarded to Ngāti Rongo, Ngāti Tamariwai, and Ngāti Korokaipapa hapū; Te Ranga a Ruanuku block was awarded to Ngāti Hā hapū; and Tauwhare block was awarded to Ngāti Mura hapū.

These four blocks are located in the south-central part of the UDNR immediately north of the large Ruatāhuna block, straddling the steep ridges and valleys at intermediate altitude (Figs. 1.3 and 6.1). Did this amalgamation display the ecological coherence expected of a previously established hapū cluster? Together the four blocks straddle the confluence of two of the major interior rivers, the Whakatane River and the Waikare River, roughly forming a triangle across the high ridgelines between the right/east bank of the former and the left/west bank of the latter river. However, as will be described below, the outer boundaries drawn and redrawn on the 1901 survey plan by October 1902 suggest that this basic ecological coherence was partly over-ridden by compromises or confrontations, probably due to overlapping or shifting control over resources between the several hapū of the amalgamation and those of adjoining blocks. 'Overlaps' was the commission's general term for what in Māori was often called *whenua tohetohe* or contested lands. Nevertheless, at least in some cases, these compromises or confrontations are best understood in terms of the unique opportunity of the UDNR investigation for some hapū branches to gain independence as separate hapū.

Some of the two main rivers had to be shared with other hapū on the periphery of the amalgamation. At the south end of these blocks, Ierenui-Ōhāua occupied both banks of the Whakatane River, and the Kohuru-Tukuroa block extended from there further westward to include the eastern branches of the Pukareao River in the large Tarapounamu-Matawhero block (awarded to Ngāti Tāwhaki hapū). However, north of there along the western border of the amalgamation, the latter block occupied both banks of the Whakatane River and its huge switchback loop at Hanamahihi and Te Honoi (often overlooked on other maps). Changes made on the map along this western side reflect three 'adjustments' to the boundary with Tarapounamu-Matawhero arranged in 1902 (Fig. 6.1): one section lost the west bank of the Whakatane river from Kohuru-Tukuroa block to Ngāti Tāwhaki hapū, another section lost the west bank of that river from Te Ranga a Ruanuku block to that hapū, but a third section gained from the same hapū the east bank of the Whakatane River just above its junction with the Waikare River.

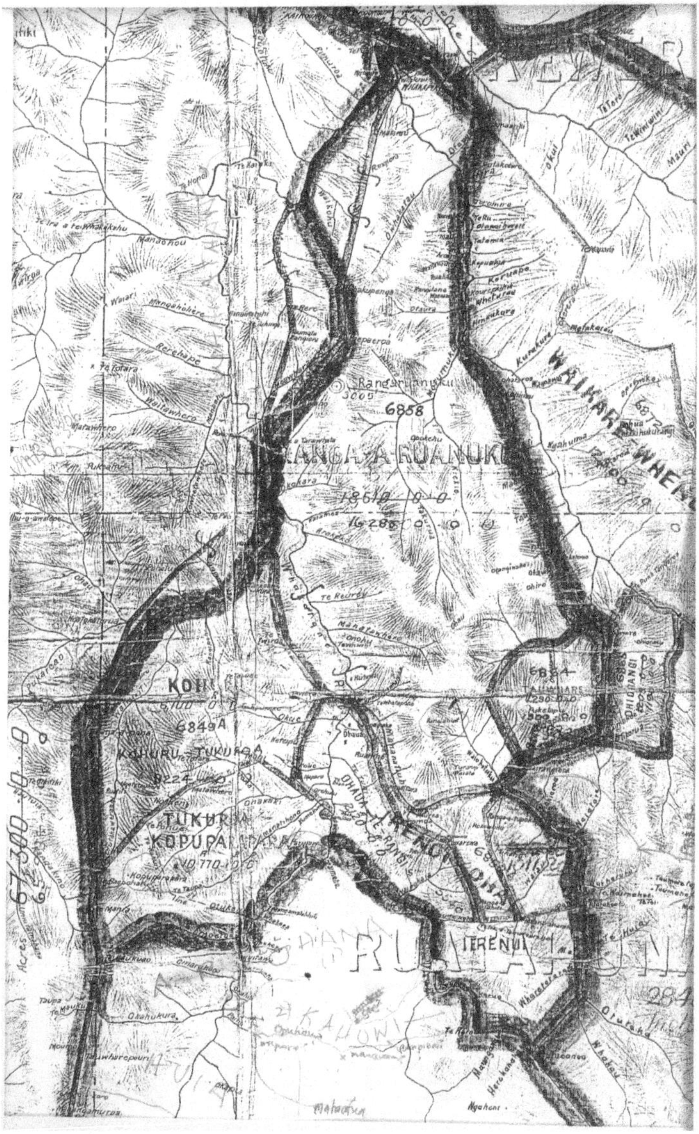

Fig. 6.1 The proposed Ōhāua te Rangi amalgamation, 1902 (enlargement from Plan No. 6873, August 1901, LINZ Hamilton)

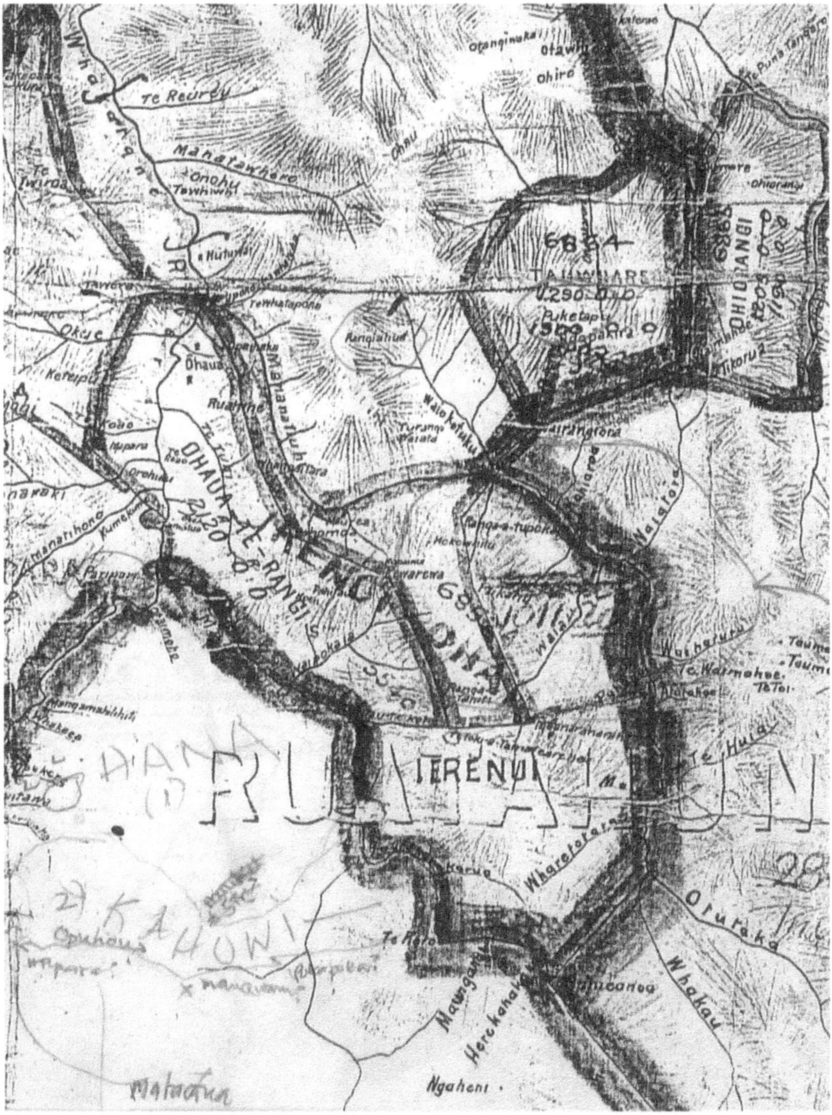

Fig. 6.2 Enlargement of Fig. 6.1 showing Ierenui-Ōhāua and adjacent blocks, 1902

On its eastern side, the proposed amalgamation shared its boundary with the Maungapōhatu, Ohiorangi, and Waikarewhenua blocks, all controlled mainly by the Tamakaimoana hapū (although the award of the last two blocks was to "Ngāi Tama" hapū, this was probably another name for Tamakaimoana hapū (UMB 1: 179)). At the amalgamation's southern end, Ierenui-Ōhāua block extended southeast far up between the Manangaatiuhi and Mahakirua streams and, along with the Te Ranga a Ruanuku block, occupied both banks of the Whakatane River in the middle of the proposed amalgamation. As will be described below, a relatively small section on the eastern boundary of Ierenui-Ōhāua, later known as 'the 1011 acre portion', was persistently contested and finally lost in appeals in 1906 and again in 1912 to Maungapōhatu block and Tamakaimoana hapū (Fig. 6.2; compare Fig. 1.3 with Fig. 1.2). Although in its middle reaches Te Ranga a Ruanuku block occupied neither bank of the Whakatane or the Waikare Rivers, it controlled one bank of the former river and both banks of the latter river in its lower (northern) end, including the junction of these two rivers and extending north up the opposite ridgeline to the boundary of Karioi block (Fig. 6.1).

Compromises and confrontations internal to the proposed amalgamation appear to have been as significant as those external to it. Within the amalgamation itself there were at least three mergers reducing what began as six into just four blocks. Early in the 1902 sittings, Kohuru and Tukuroa Kopuparapara, originally claimed and surveyed as separate blocks, were merged into Kohuru-Tukuroa. In March 1902 Ōhāua te Rangi and Ierenui, also originally claimed and surveyed as separate blocks, were merged along with a small part of the southern end of Te Ranga a Ruanuku block into Ierenui-Ōhāua block. Although it is not described in the minutes, changes on the 1901 map (6873) indicate that the addition of the small southern leg of Te Ranga a Ruanuku to the Ierenui-Ōhāua merger included a small strip along the eastern bank of the Manangaatiuhi stream that was shifted into the merger. Part of this merger was also the contentious 1011-acre portion bordering on the Manangatiuhi Stream between Ierenui, the southern leg of Te Ranga a Ruanuku, and the adjacent Maungapōhatu block (Fig. 6.2). The mergers of Kohuru-Tukuroa and Ierenui-Ōhāua were probably prompted by the commission's policy of 'unifying' 'minor' claims discussed in Chap. 3. However, the contention focused on the 1011-acre portion reflected a more persistent confrontation of the kind that Numia Kererū warned against regarding that policy, and the merger of Ōhāua te Rangi with Ierenui was also intended to settle it.

The dispute over the 1011-acre portion may have begun in 1899 and continued through 1912 (UMB 5: 344ff; UMB 6: 95–6, 107, 109, 210ff;

NACMB 1: 4–29, 2: 38–40). It was between Numia Kererū, speaking for Ngāti Rongo and Ngāti Hā hapū, and Te Iwikino Hairuha, speaking for Ngāti Rakei hapū. It may have originated in Te Iwikino's 1899 claim for Ierenui in the name of 'Ngāti Rakeinui' rather than Ngāti Rongo hapū, thereby offending Numia. Te Iwikino's claim was the only time this hapū name appeared (Fig. 3.1), perhaps indicating Te Iwikino was attempting to establish Ngāti Rakei's independence from Ngāti Rongo. This is also suggested by the commission's conclusion that Ngāti Rongo and Ngāti Rakei were "really one people but because Numia and Iwikino have fallen out this dispute has arisen" (UMB 6: 302–5). This decision was similar to their resolution of the confrontation between Ngāti Rongo and Māhurehure in the Te Waipotiki block discussed in Chap. 3. The following year (1900) in the Te Waipotiki case, Te Iwikino identified himself as a member of Ngāti Rongo and gave evidence in support of Numia's claim in opposition to Māhurehure hapū. He may have been speaking for his wife who was a granddaughter of Te Purewa I, a Ngāti Rongo war leader of great *mana* (Fig. 6.3).

Te Iwikino's status is ambiguous: he does not appear in any of the block committees of 1902 or 1907, nor did he rank highly in any of the several blocks in which he held shares except Waikaremoana, where he was ranked 11 of 729 but held only 10 shares. This ranking may have benefitted from his older siblings' marriages, which were into important descent groups two of which held high rank in that block: Waaka, Taratoa, and Wakaunua (Best 1898: 68–9, 54). His older brother Riki was deceased but had grown children by Papa Taratoa, a granddaughter of Te Purewa I. As will be described in Part II, by 1901 Numia was also confronting an influential marriage alliance centered in Waikaremoana and Ruatāhuna, in which the Taratoa descent group was a key leader. As will be explained in Chap. 7, it may be that although Te Iwikino's predecessors were stigmatized by immigrant status, he was influentially connected through his siblings and wife Ngahuia as another granddaughter of Te Purewa I. Their apparent lack of children probably aggravated Te Iwikino's doubly ambiguous status in Ngāti Rongo hapū.

Whether or not Te Iwikino's successful claim for Ierenui independent from Ōhāua Te Rangi and Ngāti Rongo hapū was the origin of the confrontation, by 1901 Numia appeared to be mounting a strategy against it. Numia's initiatives can be seen to extend the *mana* of Ngāti Hā, another hapū closely related to Ngāti Rongo, over lands adjacent to the Ierenui block. This may have also been a strategy for coopting Te Iwikino's claimants lists in the name of Ngāti Rakeinui in these areas under the *mana* of Ngāti Hā hapū instead, thereby weakening the legitimacy of Ierenui as a separate block. Te Iwikino's statement before the Native Appellate Court at a later stage of the conflict in 1912 apparently referred to such a strategy to break up and weaken Ierenui, claiming that Numia's survey had cut the block in two in order to join it and another piece to Te Ranga a Ruanuku block. He was probably referring to the 1011-acre portion and the adjacent southern leg of Te Ranga a Ruanuku, which Numia was claiming for Ngāti Hā hapū. As will be described in Chap. 8, in 1901 Numia also attempted to extend this claim to an 800-acre area of Maungapōhatu block adjacent to the 1011-acre portion of Ierenui block for Ngāti Hā hapū, probably with the goal that both areas would be joined with his claim for all of Te Ranga a Ruanuku block in the name of Ngāti Hā hapū (Fig. 6.2). Ngāti Hā was closely related to Ngāti Tāwhaki and Tamakaimoana hapū as well as Ngāti Rongo (Kruger 2004), and with this backing Numia might deprive Ierenui block of much of its size as well as undermining the independent *mana* Te Iwikino was claiming for the breakaway Ngāti Rakeinui hapū.

Although Numia's 1901 claim for Ngāti Hā was unsuccessful in Maungapōhatu block against Tamakaimoana hapū, the confrontation between Numia and Te Iwikino had become full-blown by 1902. Numia's claim for Te Ranga a Ruanuku in the name of Ngāti Hā was successful against Te Iwikino's in the name of Ngāti Rakeinui, and Numia was furthermore able to disparage Te Iwikino's several claims to occupational rights in ways that may have been drawing on his predecessors' stigmatization as immigrants (UMB 6: 95–7; 306; Ch. 7). After several weeks of hearings on Ōhāua Te Rangi, Ierenui, and nearby blocks that must have included frustrated negotiations behind the scenes, the commission finally came to a terse decision (UMB 6: 302–5). After 'clearing the court' and hearing 'outside evidence' from three *rangatira* (both rare procedures), the commission stated that it was 'utterly impossible to reconcile these two disputants', declared there was no evidence of a boundary between Ōhāua Te Rangi and Ierenui (despite Te Whenuanui II's evidence), and merged the two along with the 1011-acre portion and the southern leg of Te Ranga a Ruanuku in the name of Ngāti Rakeinui.

This decision implicitly subordinated the *mana* of Ngāti Rongo hapū to Te Iwikino's alternative and furthermore gave precedence to Ierenui in the merger's new name, Ierenui-Ōhāua. The suffix -nui ('large') was probably added to Te Iwikino's claim for Ngāti Rakei in an attempt implicitly to include Ngāti Rongo and thus mollify Numia. Although Numia's claim for Te Ranga a Ruanuku was successful, the commission's futile effort to settle the dispute by merging Ōhāua Te Rangi with Ierenui in this way must instead have galled Numia. It also frustrated his strategy to gain most of Ierenui for Ngāti Hā in Te Ranga a Ruanuku if not Maungapōhatu block. Unsurprisingly, the dispute continued with Numia's close ally in Ngāti Rongo, Te Pouwhare Te Roau, demanding that 88 persons be struck from the merged blocks, probably Te Iwikino's list that Ngāti Rongo had accepted in Ōhāua Te Rangi. However, the commission dismissed this case and instead, compounding the affront, equalized the shares allocated to Te Iwikino's claimants list with Numia's and demanded that they not interfere with each other.

As will be seen in Part II, this confrontation was a rare reversal for Numia's otherwise rapidly rising influence in the commission as well as among Tūhoe leaders. It is probably significant that by October 1902 when hapū were named in the confirmation of decisions for all blocks, Ierenui-Ōhāua was confirmed in the name of both Ngāti Rongo and Ngāti Rakei rather than 'Ngāti Rakeinui' alone, and priority was furthermore given to Ngāti Rongo.

Both Numia and Te Pouwhare pursued their appeals in 1907 and again in 1912, Numia against the inclusion of the 1011-acre portion in Ierenui-Ōhāua instead of Maungapōhatu, and Te Pouwhare against what was probably Te Iwikino's list of 88 claimants in Ierenui-Ōhāua. The latter claim continued to be unsuccessful in both appeals because, or so these tribunals claimed, there was nothing new in their arguments. In the 1912 case Numia also sought to demean Iwikino's rights in Ierenui-Ōhāua by claiming he was allotted only weak shares (10 rather than 20, presumably before the commission assigned them equal rights in an effort to settle the dispute) and that furthermore Iwikino had accepted this (NACMB 1: 15, 18). However, apparently because in 1906 Te Iwikino withdrew or did not appear to defend his opposing case, Numia's appeal to cut the 1011-acre section out of Ierenui and add it to Maungapōhatu in the name of Ngāti Hā hapū was approved in 1907, and furthermore was confirmed in 1912 when Te Iwikino did contest it. The result of shifting control of the 1011-acre portion was a peculiarly rectangular indentation in the southeastern (Ierenui) end of Ierenui-Ōhāua (compare Figs. 1.3 and 6.1 with Fig. 1.2). Although Numia appeared to have lost ground in Ierenui-Ōhāua, he had gained *mana* in the name of Ngāti Hā in Maungapōhatu where Tutakangahau, also a close ally of Numia's, was the dominant *rangatira*. As will be seen in Chap. 8, Numia's victory for Ngāti Hā in Maungapōhatu was actually *re*gaining mana that he had lost to Tamakaimoana hapū in 1901.

This bitter little victory over Te Iwikino might have also somewhat mollified Numia insofar as he had testified that Tutakangahau had tried 'to drive those [Iwikino's] people' from Maungapōhatu, and so would help stem his influence. The success of this part of Numia's strategy was probably also due to Te Iwikino's conversion by 1907 to the prophetic leadership of Rua Kenena and his 'Isrealite' followers (according to the Chief Judge in 1912), probably withdrawing his appeal with the intention of contributing the resulting shares in Maungapōhatu for Rua Kenana to sell to the Crown in order to build his community there. Numia, who was a leader of those resisting the Isrealite movement, would have found this irony satisfying. By 1908, through his rising influence and election as chairperson, he was also able to keep any of Rua's supporters off the Komiti Nui. On the other hand, Numia's animus against Rua's movement would have been frustrated by his ally Tutakangahau's apparent shift of sympathy toward Rua in 1906 well before his death the following year (Holman 2010: 196–7, 216).

Setting aside the ambiguities of boundaries within and around the Ōhāua te Rangi amalgamation, what can be said of dominant descent groups, alliances, and leaders in the amalgamation, and the possibilities of a hapū cluster? These questions can be pursued by examination of the relative shares indicated in the four block lists proposed for the amalgamation, and the several different block or hapū committees named between 1902 and 1908 for the four blocks or their amalgamation.

As described in the introduction above, there was considerable overlap between the shareholder lists for these four blocks. In this case, culling duplicated names from the lists resulted in a 43% reduction of names of sibling groups or individuals. Sorting out the extent to which sibling groups or individuals held shares across all four blocks also resulted in a hierarchy of relative rights in the amalgamation: while 138 held shares in only one of the blocks, 81 held shares in two, 65 held shares in three, and only four sibling groups or individuals held shares in all four of the blocks. In the latter case, three sibling groups (five Heremia siblings, four Te Pouwhare siblings, and two Paora siblings) and one individual (Rangi Karu, apparently with no living siblings) held shares in all four blocks. However, many were not adults, and sibling groups were often split up between the blocks. Examination of the 65 sibling groups or individuals holding shares in three of the four blocks was more promising. This category was further narrowed by considering only the leading shares in each block. Significantly, examination of the 12 sibling groups and individuals holding leading shares in at least three of the four blocks furthermore showed that together they comprised only three descent groups extending from two to four and even five living generations. The intermarriages between these descent groups suggest a growing alliance between them.

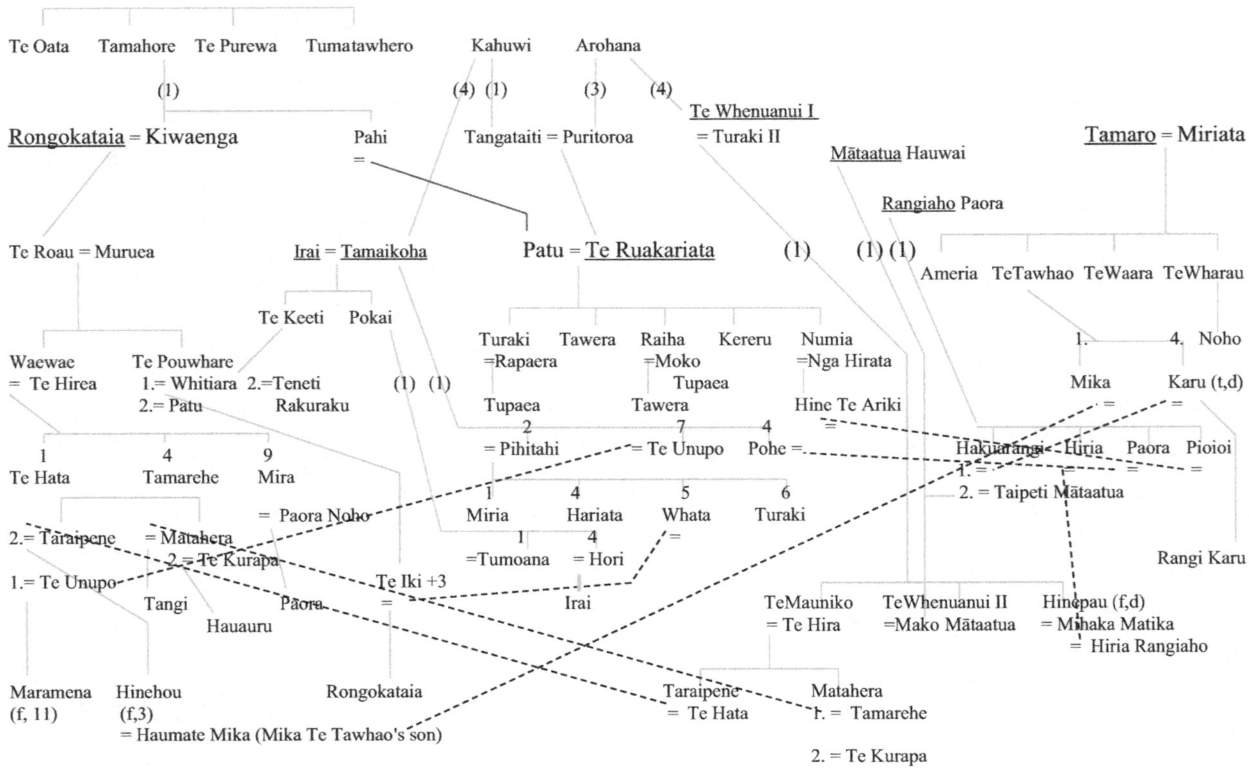

Fig. 6.3 Intermarriage of the leading descent groups of Ōhāua te Rangi amalgamation 1898–1903: Rongokataia, Ruakariata, and Tamaro

Fig. 6.3 (continued)

Legend:

1. Descent groups identified by underlined elders or predecessors (those of three leading descent groups in larger font)
2. Vertical lines denote filiation (parent to child) or descent (if numbered, this denotes the number of generations spanned)
3. Horizontal lines connect siblings (only those important to intermarriages shown; numbered by birth order)
4. = denotes marriage to person above or adjacent (numbered by priority if more than one marriage)
5. Dotted lines denote the same marriage or person connecting different descent groups
6. If notable, (f,11) denotes female gender and age; (m,d) denotes male gender and deceased

The senior generation of these three descent groups bore the patronymic 'surnames' Rongokataia, Te Ruakariata, and Tamaro—or, more accurately if the matriarch and her predecessors are not excluded, Rongokataia = Kiwaenga, Te Ruakariata = Patu, and Tamaro = Miriata. Guided by Best's 1898 genealogical census and the 1903 block lists, Fig. 6.3 displays these three descent groups in terms of the successive generations of sibling groups living at the time, including a few generations of their deceased ancestors. A bare descent line of five other groups is included (left to right: Irai, Tamaikoha, Te Whenuanui I, Mātaatua Hauwai, and Rangiaho Paora) due to significant intermarriages that will be described later. In order to focus on significant intermarriages between the three leading descent groups, Fig. 6.3 generally shows only a few key ancestors and siblings in each successive generation who have married with members of one of the other leading descent groups or, more frequently, with one of the other five descent lines. The role of these other five descent lines will be considered in relation to each of the three leading descent groups.

The Rongokataia descent group held leading shares in all four blocks, and in 1898 included at least four living generations with about 21 living members. Following Fig. 6.3 through successive generations of this leading descent group (usually using 'first' or given names only): Rongakataia's wife Kiwaenga was the daughter of Tamahore, the second of four famous warrior brothers depicted at the top of Fig. 6.3. Rongokataia and Kiwaenga gave birth to Te Roau and two other children. Although in 1907 all three of the Rongokataia siblings were probably elderly males holding leading rights in all blocks of the amalgamation except Tauwhare, apparently neither of the two younger brothers had offspring (or none with rights in the reserve). Te Roau and Muruea gave birth to the brothers Waewae and Pouwhare Te Roau, important leaders by 1903; Waewae and his wife Te Hirea Pahiri (Fig. 11.1) had nine surviving children, three of whom married significantly, but not directly with either of the other two leading descent groups of the amalgamation: most importantly, their ***mātāmua*** son Te Hata and his brother Tamarehe married Taraipene and Matahera, two ***mātāmua*** grand-daughters of Te Whenuanui I, the leader of Te Urewera hapū in the Ruatāhuna area (this descent group will be followed closely in Part II). Waewae and Te Hireas' youngest child Mira married Paora Noho, also of Te Urewera hapū.

The ***mātāmua*** Te Hata Waewae had a daughter Maramena by an earlier marriage or liaison with Te Unupo, a daughter of Tamaikoha as described in Chap. 4, and a younger daughter Hinehou by Taraipene. His brother

Tamarehe had a daughter Tangi by Matahera, but Matahera had several children by later or other husbands, Te Tuhera or Te Kurapa (Best 1898: 5, 34). Waewae's younger brother Te Pouwhare Te Roau and his wife Whitiara Ngahooro had four children, and the *mātāmua* Te Iki named his first-born after his ancestor Rongokataia and later published several Tūhoe genealogies including descendants of Tamahore and Te Purewa (Pouwhare 1959: 215–18). Te Pouwhare had another child by Patu Te Hauwaho named Nga Paki, who was the only member of the Rongokataia descent group to hold shares in Tauwhare block (through his mother). Whitiara later remarried to Teneti Rakuraku, son of another famous war-leader of Te Urewera hapū along with Tamaikoha.

The Te Ruakariata descent group held leading shares in three of the four blocks (Ierenui-Ōhāua, Kohuru-Tukuroa, and Te Ranga a Ruanuku) and in 1898 also extended four living generations with about 24 living members. As can be seen in Fig. 6.3, the marriage between Ruakariata and Patu, a daughter of Kiwaenga's sister Pahi, was apparently the beginning of an alliance in the sense that it made them all cousins of the Rongokataia descent group and descendants of Tamahore and his warrior brothers. By the 1930s the Ōhāua *marae* in the Ōhāua te Rangi block and Tauarau *marae* in Rūātoki were considered 'sister *marae*' of the Ngāti Rongo hapū, formerly led by Waewae Te Roau and Numia Kererū, respectively (Paora Kruja, personal communication 1983). The settlement of Ōhāua can be located in Fig. 6.2 at the northern end of the original Ōhāua Te Rangi block (later part of Ierenui-Ōhāua) above the eastern bank of the Whakatane River. The founding role of Tamahore and his three brothers is commemorated as the columns supporting the entryway roof of the meetinghouse Te Poho o Pōtiki in Ōhāua (see Fig. 11.2). Furthermore, after Numia's death in 1916, Waewae's younger brother Te Pouwhare Te Roau may have become a leader of Tauarau *marae* in Rūātoki until 1924, because an obelisque commemorating his death in that year stands in front of the Tauarau meetinghouse Rongokarae.

Ruakariata's ancestors Kahuwī and Arohana are included in Fig. 6.3 because they are a central issue in Part II, and because they are also ancestors of Tamaikoha and Te Whenuanui I, two of the other five descent groups intermarried with these three leading descent groups. Te Ruakariata and Patu had five children, three of whom had died by 1898. Their *mātāmua* daughter Turaki married Rapaera Taneira and had one son Tupaea Rapaera and, probably later, a daughter Raumiria by Haunui before dying. Probably as representative of the *mātāmua* line through Ruakariata, Tupaea carried the pre-eminent *mana* of the descent group, ranking highly in an unusually high proportion of the UDNR blocks (24 of 34) and, as nephew of the hosting *rangatira* Kererū Te Pukenui, escorting Prime Minister Seddon in his tour of the Urewera in 1894. Turaki, Tawera, and Kererū had all died by 1898, leaving only the youngest daughter Raiha and son, *pōtiki* ('youngest child') Numia. Already a Tūhoe leader by that time, Numia took on his older brother's name as Numia Kererū Te Ruakariata and by 1899 had been selected as one of the five Tūhoe *rangatira* serving as UDNR commissioners.

While the most significant alliance in the Rongokataia descent group was the double marriage with the Ruatāhuna branch of Te Urewera hapū led by Te Whenuanui I, the most significant alliance in the Ruakariata descent group was the double marriage with the lower Tauranga-Waimana branch of Te Urewera hapū led by Tamaikoha (Fig. 6.3). The *mātāmua* Tupaea married Tamaikoha's eldest daughter Pihitahi and had six children by her, and Raiha's *mātāmua* son Tawera Moko married Tamaikoha's younger daughter Te Unupo and had five children by her before she died (Best 1898: 28, 25). As mentioned above, Te Unupo had earlier begotten her oldest child Maramena by the *mātāmua* Te Hata Waewae in what might be seen as a precursor of these two double marriages.

The complex intermarriages of the Irai descent group can be followed in Fig. 6.3. Irai Paraheka, whose eldest daughter's daughter Whitiara had married Te Pouwhare, established a further double marriage with two of Tupaea and Pihitahis' children: their *mātāmua* daughter Miria Tupaea and younger daughter Hariata married Whitiara's first cousins Tumoana and Hori Pokai, respectively. Marriage of Irai's three grandchildren into the Ruakariata as well as the Rongokataia descent groups appears to have been quite a coup for his line: Te Keeti's and Pokai's weak rights to only two peripheral blocks of the Urewera (Waikaremoana and Hikurangi-Horomanga) probably indicate Irai and his wife were recent immigrants to the Urewera, and Pokai's wife Rakapa Mohi's strong shares in three blocks of the amalgamation was the only source of Tumoana and Hori's rights there. The Irai alliance can even be seen as a triple marriage because Miria and Hariata Tupaea's younger sister Whata soon married Te Powhare and Whitiaras' *mātāmua* son, Te Iki. In recognition of this alliance between the three descent groups, Hori and Hariatas' first-born was named after Hori's grandfather Irai, and Te Iki and Whatas' first-born was named after Te Iki's great-grandfather Rongokataia.

The Tamaro descent group held leading shares in three of the four blocks of the amalgamation (Te Ranga a Ruanuku, Tauwhare, and Ierenui-Ōhāua), and ranked highest among all leading shareholders in both of the first two blocks (top of the list in the case of the Te Tawhao sibling group). There were three living generations in 1903; as well as Tamaro and Miriata, their two oldest children Ameria and Te Tawhao had died by then, leaving their offspring holding full shares. Ameria had children by at least two different husbands, one of which (Hukanui Papita) himself had children that were probably raised by Ameria. Te Tawhao Tamaro had had five children, the *mātāmua* of which, Mika Te Tawhao, had six children. The two other Tamaro brothers younger than Te Tawhao (Te Waara and Te Wharau) were still living in 1903 and had seven children and ten grandchildren, respectively. Although some of the siblings in each generation were recorded as 'S.P.' (*sin partum*), this much higher birthrate than either the Rongokataia or Ruakariata descent group meant that the Tamaro descent group had about 45 living members in 1903.

Despite their leading role in three of the four blocks of the amalgamation, the surviving Tamaro brothers held rights in relatively few other blocks of the UDNR. While the senior living generation of the Ruakariata descent group held shares in 18 blocks, and that of the Rongokataia descent group held shares in 11 blocks, the Tamaro brothers held shares in only 8 blocks 3 of which were in the Ōhāua te Rangi amalgamation. The relatively few blocks in which the senior Tamaro sibling group held shares suggest recent immigration of their predecessors into the Urewera area. The blocks in which they held shares were all in the lower or middle river basins, suggesting their predecessors had married into the Urewera or, more likely, were refugees from northern Tūhoe hapū that had lost their lands nearer the Bay of Plenty to the 1860s *raupatu* or Crown confiscations. As mentioned earlier, Tamakaimoana hapū probably dominated all the blocks along the eastern boundary of the Ōhāua te Rangi amalgamation, and the hapū to which the Tamaro descent group may have been primarily affiliated may have been among those Tutakangahau (the leader of Tamakaimoana hapū) claimed as "mine" (Ngāti Tatua, Ngāti Maru, Ngāti Tu, and Ngā Te Au; UMB 1: 179). It may have been significant that the Tamaro descent group's leading rank was in the adjacent Tauwhare as well as Te Ranga a Ruanuku blocks, while the other two leading descent groups held few or no shares in Tauwhare block.

Another puzzling and perhaps related characteristic of the Tamaro descent group did not become apparent until I discovered that they were *also* among a few influential descent groups in the large Parekohe amalgamation planned at the northeast end of the UDNR (to be examined in the next section). These two amalgamations were not adjacent, but separated by at least ten kilometers and the entire Paraeroa amalgamation. Some branches of the Tamaro descent group furthermore appear to have established more occupational rights in either the Ierenui-Ōhāua amalgamation or the Parekohe amalgamation than other branches, or to have straddled both. Especially the first rank of the Te Tawhao sibling group in Te Ranga a Ruanuku and Tauwhare blocks, and the Hukanui sibling group following their rank in the latter block, suggests that the two eldest but deceased Tamaro siblings, the *mātāmua* Ameria and her brother Te Tawhao, had married prominent occupants of those blocks. The father of most of Ameria's own children was Hukanui, perhaps a namesake of the ancestor after whom the southern extension of Parekohe block was named.

Although the Tamaro descent group were one of the three leading shareholders in the proposed Ōhāua te Rangi amalgamation, intermarriages between them and the Rongokataia or Ruakariata descent groups were apparently only indirect or undeveloped. Significantly, Mika Te Tawhao's eldest son Haumate did marry Hinehou, the only child of the *mātāmua* couple of the double marriage between the Rongokataia and Te Whenuanui I descent groups, but that would not have been until 1910–1915.[2] It may also be significant that in 2018 John Mika, a great-grandson of Rangitane, another son of Mika Te Tawhao, was chairperson of the Te Manawa o Tūhoe Trustboard which controlled the western-most section of Urewera lands surviving the UCS (Fig. 1.4), importantly in the name of Patuheuheu hapuu—earlier identified with Ngati Rongo hapuu (Kruger 2004).

Mika's younger brother Karu Te Tawhao was probably the first to marry into the Rangiaho sibling group which was to become importantly intermarried between the Ruakariata and Te Whenuanui I descent groups. These intermarriages can be followed in Fig. 6.3. Karu married the *mātāmua* Rangiaho sibling Hakurangi, but he died soon after their only child Rangi Karu was born and Hakurangi remarried to Taipeti Mātaatua, the brother of Te Whenuanui II's wife Mako Mātaatua. As will be described in Chap. 7, Mātaatua Hauwai, the father of this brother and sister, was a leader of an extensive marriage alliance in Waikaremoana and Ruatāhuna blocks that was doubly married with two of Te Whenuanui I's children (while the daughters of their *mātāmua* sister Te Mauniko were doubly married into the Rongokarae descent group). The second Rangiaho sibling Hiria became the wife of Mihaka Matika, another leader of the Ruatāhuna-Waikaremoana marriage alliance, when Mihaka's first wife Hinepau Te Whenuanui died. Probably most importantly, the third and fourth Rangiaho siblings Paora and Pioioi married, respectively, Pohe, another daughter of Tamaikoha, and Hine te Ariki, the *mātāmua* daughter of Numia Kererū.

The Rangiaho marriages can therefore be seen as indirectly allying the Tamaro descent group with the Ruakariata as well as the Te Whenuanui I descent group and, through the latter's double marriage, with the Rongokataia descent group. Insofar as the Rangiaho sibling group as well as Tamaikoha and Te Whenuanui were primarily affiliated with Te Urewera hapū, this hapū must be seen as integral to the wider marriage alliance in the Ōhāua te Rangi amalgamation. However, as will be seen in the next section, it must be admitted that the Tamaro descent group, while holding leading land rights in the Ōhāua te Rangi amalgamation, was much more closely allied through marriages with other leading descent groups of the proposed Parekohe amalgamation.

Can key leaders of the Rongokataia, Ruakariata, and Tamaro descent groups, taken as the leading descent groups of the proposed Ōhāua te Rangi amalgamation, be identified? Finally, can the primary hapū affiliations of these descent groups be identified?

During the 1899 arrangement of boundaries and claims, 12 claimants' spokespersons submitted lists of descent groups or hapū branches claiming one or another of the four blocks of the Ōhāua te Rangi amalgamation, usually in the name of a particular hapū to which their list belonged. Five of these 1899 hapū representatives (or their brothers or sons) were later named to one or more of the 1902–1908 block or hapū committees of the amalgamation: Heremia, Paparatu, Numia, Poniwahio, and Tamehana. Two of these representatives were associated with the leading descent groups described above. Wharekiri Paparatu married one of the Waewae sisters in the Rongakataia descent group, and Numia and his older sister headed the Te Ruakariata descent group. Four Heremia brothers held leading rights in two of the blocks, and Ameria Tamaro had children by a Heremia.

Similarly, the membership of the block committees representing the four blocks of the amalgamation between 1902 and 1908 overlapped, with only 18 different persons named to 49 committee positions. The relative priority of these eighteen persons in the lists of committee members suggests that four were more influential: Te Pouwhare Te Roau, Mika Te Tawhao, Numia (Kererū) Te Ruakariata, and Paora Rangiaho. All four of these leaders appeared in the above analysis of significant marriages within and between the three leading descent groups of the amalgamation (Fig. 6.3). Two of the four (Te Pouwhare and Paora Rangiaho) were named to the amalgamation committee in May 1902. Two were named to the committees of two or three blocks of the amalgamation in both 1902 and 1907 (Te Pouwhare and Mika), while the other two (Numia and Paora) were named to the committee of at least one block in both those years (Numia to the committees of three blocks in 1907). Three were furthermore named to the 1907 committees of five to ten other blocks outside the amalgamation (Te Pouwhare, Mika, and Numia). Finally, in 1908 all four were elected to the Komiti Nui.

For comparison with these four leaders, the next most active of the 18 committee members for the blocks of the Ōhāua te Rangi amalgamation were Taihakoa Poniwahio, Te Whetu Paerata, and Hohaia Te Ahikaiata. None of these three were named to the amalgamated block committee in 1902; one was named to the committee of one block of the amalgamation in both 1902 and 1907 (Taihakoa), and the other two were named to the committees of two blocks each in 1907 but none in 1902 (Te Whetu and Hohaia); in 1908, none were named to the Komiti Nui for any of the four blocks of the amalgamation. On the other hand, all three were named to the committees of two to four other blocks *outside* the amalgamation in 1902, and six to *twelve* other blocks in 1907. These records suggest that their leadership in the blocks of the proposed Ōhāua te Rangi amalgamation, in addition to their strong rights in it, derived mainly from their wide influence in many other blocks of the reserve. Indeed, the overlaps of influence between all these leaders support the likelihood that the proposed amalgamation of all UDNR blocks in May 1902 was intended by the Tūhoe to centralize their control over their sanctuary.

In terms of claimants' spokespersons in 1899 and block committee memberships 1902–1908, the most influential leaders of the four Ōhāua te Rangi blocks were probably Te Pouwhare Te Roau, Wharekiri Paparatu, Numia (Kererū) Te Ruakariata, Paora Rangiaho, and Mika Te Tawhao. What were the primary hapū affiliations of these leaders?

The central or peripheral role of several hapū has already emerged in the previous discussion: Ngāti Rongo as the primary affiliation of the Rongokataia and Ruakariata descent groups, obvious from the location of their leadership at the two Ngāti Rongo 'sister *marae*' of Ōhāua and Tauarau, Rūātoki, respectively; Ngāti Hā and Ngāti Rakei or Rakeinui as the hapū for which Numia Kererū and Te Iwikino fought out control over Ierenui; Te Urewera hapū as the primary affiliation of Tamaikoha, Te Whenuanui I, and probably the Rangiaho sibling group in their marriage roles between the Rongokataia, Ruakariata, and Tamaro descent groups leading the four blocks of the amalgamation; Ngāti Tāwhaki and Tamakaimoana as the dominant hapū on the western and eastern sides of the amalgamation, respectively. In addition to the role of these six or seven hapū, three others in the name of which the four blocks were finally awarded in 1902 after the amalgamations were aborted might be considered: Ngāti Tamariwai and Ngāti Korokaipapa which were named for Kohuru-Tukuroa block (secondarily to Ngāti Rongo) and Ngāti Mura hapū which was named in sole control of Tauwhare block.

Te Pouwhare Te Roau's committee memberships in the four blocks of the amalgamation represented Ierenui-Ōhāua, Kohuru-Tokuroa, and Te Ranga a Ruanuku, indicating his affiliation and probably leadership in Ngāti Hā hapū (exclusively awarded the latter block), Ngāti Rongo hapū (first named in the award of both other blocks), and perhaps in Ngāti Rakei, Ngāti Tamariwai, or Ngāti Korokaipapa hapū, also named (second to Ngāti Rongo) in those awards. As pointed out earlier, the members of Ngāti Hā later came to be known as Ngāti Rongo, Ngāti Tāwhaki, and Tamakaimoana hapū (Kruger 2004: 29). Because his affiliation with Ngāti Rongo was clear, it is likely that his affiliations with Ngāti Rakei, Ngāti Tamariwai, or Ngāti Korokaipapa would be subordinated to Ngāti Rongo. His support of Numia Kererū against Te Iwikino's claim to Ierenui reinforces this. His representation of the Ierenui-Ōhāua block in the 1908 Komiti Nui also confirms the conclusion that his primary affiliation, with regard to the Ōhāua te Rangi amalgamation, was with Ngāti Rongo. On the other hand, there is evidence that Te Pouwhare's affiliation with Ngāti Rakei later came to the fore: although his death is marked by a monument on Tauarau marae and thereby his leadership in Ngāti Rongo hapū commemorated, descendants bearing his surname are nowadays affiliated with Patuheuheu hapū, one of those into which Ngāti Rakei is reported to have been assimilated (Kruger 2004: 29).

Was there further evidence of Te Pouwhare's Ngāti Rongo affiliation in his committee memberships outside the amalgamation? In 1907 he also sat on the hapū committees of Te Waipotiki, all three Rūātoki blocks, Whaitiripapa, Parekohe, and Waikarewhenua, presumably due to his leadership status in at least one of the hapū to which these blocks were awarded (Fig. 2.1). Again, his primary affiliation with Ngāti Rongo in regard to the Ōhāua te Rangi amalgamation was confirmed in the case of Te Waipotiki block, which was awarded to Ngāti Rongo and Māhurehure hapū (largely overlapped in membership).

In 1899 Paparatu Matiu submitted a claimants list for Ōhāua te Rangi in the name of Ngāti Rongo hapū, was second of seven members on the Ierenui-Ōhāua block committee in 1902, and in 1907 was replaced on that committee by his *mātāmua* son Wharekiri Paparatu. The Paparatu sibling group held leading rights in nearby Karioi block controlled by

Ngamaihi and Ngāi Te Kahu hapū, and also held rights in Ngāti Tāwhaki hapū. Wharekiri Paparatu married the third of Waewae Te Roau and Te Hirea's nine children, Hera Waewae (not shown in Fig. 6.3 for lack of space), and is said to have reinforced the Ngāti Tāwhaki affiliation of her mother Te Hirea Pahiri.

Numia Kererū also submitted a claimants list for Ōhāua te Rangi block in the name of Ngāti Rongo hapū in 1899. His assumption of leadership of the Ruakariata descent group and Ngāti Rongo hapū at Tauarau, Rūātoki after his brother Kererū Te Pukenui's death clearly implies that his primary affiliation was with that hapū. His finally successful effort to undermine Te Iwikino's challenge to Ngāti Rongo domination of the merged Ierenui-Ōhāua block by claiming parts of Ierenui for Maungapōhatu as well as Te Ranga a Ruanuku for Ngāti Hā hapū also demonstrates his leadership of that hapū, which was probably largely overlapped with Ngāti Rongo and would eventually be assimilated to it. The people of Ngāti Hā are nowadays known as Ngāti Rongo, Ngāti Tāwhaki, and Tamakaimoana. Probably reflecting his rapidly rising influence in the UDNR, Numia was named to five block committees including Ierenui-Ōhāua in 1902, thirteen block committees including Kohuru-Tukuroa and Te Ranga a Ruanuku as well as Ierenui-Ōhāua in 1907, and elected as chairman of the Komiti Nui in 1908 by 26 of 28 other block committee representatives. While he probably had wide affiliations with several other hapū, it is clear that his primary affiliation was with Ngāti Rongo.

Paora Rangiaho submitted no claims for any blocks in 1899, but was named to Ierenui-Ōhāua and Rūātoki 3 block committees in 1902 and Kohuru-Tukuroa and Paraeroa block committees in 1907. By 1908 he was the representative for Kohuru-Tukuroa on the Komiti Nui, suggesting his father Rangiaho Paora's demise and his consequent acceptance as spokesperson for his descent group. Recognition of the dominant role of Ngāti Rongo in Ierenui-Ōhāua and Kohuru-Tukuroa implies Paora's primary affiliation was probably with that hapū. However, he probably also affiliated with Te Urewera hapū through his father (Best 1973 [1925] Vol. II, plate 8: 1–2), suggesting that his representation on the Kohuru-Tukuroa, Paraeroa, and Rūātoki 3 block committees was reinforced by his representation of that hapū.

The role of the Tamaro descent group among the hapū of the Ōhāua te Rangi amalgamation remains ambiguous. It will be remembered that the rights of this descent group across the UDNR were more limited than either the Rongokataia or Ruakariata descent groups, primarily straddling the widely separated blocks of the Ōhāua te Rangi or Parekohe amalgamations. Although Mika Te Tawhao was nevertheless widely active in the UDNR, his uncles Te Waara and Te Wharau or their eldest sons Kanuehi and Noho lay no claims themselves and were named only to the Tauwhare block committee in 1902 and 1907. Kanuehi had already been named to the Ōhāua te Rangi amalgamation committee, perhaps because he was *mātāmua* of the two surviving Tamaro siblings. However, reflecting the influence of the Tamaro descent group in the proposed Parekohe amalgamation to the north, in 1899 Mika Te Tawhao submitted several claims for Parekohe and Te Tuahu (which in 1902 was included in the proposed Parekohe amalgamation) in the name of Ngāti Tūranga, Hamua, and Ngāti Muriwai hapū while laying no claims to any of the blocks in the Ōhāua te Rangi amalgamation. Then in 1902 Mika was named to six block committees including both the Ierenui-Ōhāua and Te Ranga a Ruanuku committees, and in 1907 he was named to eight block committees including Parekohe as well as Ierenui-Ōhāua, Te Ranga a Ruanuku, and Tauwhare of the Ōhāua te Rangi blocks. In 1908 he was also named as the representative for Te Ranga a Ruanuku block on the *Komite Nui* of the UDNR.

In conclusion, several considerations make it doubtful that there was an established hapū cluster behind the proposed Ōhāua te Rangi amalgamation: (i) the ambiguous role of Tauwhare block and the Tamaro descent group; (ii) the lack of direct marriage alliances between the leading Rongokataia, Ruakariata, and Tamaro descent groups; (iii) the integral role of the Tamaikoha, Te Whenuanui I, Hauwai, and Rangiaho descent groups probably more closely affiliated with Te Urewera hapū in any marriage alliance between them; (iv) the close association between these hapū and the Ngāti Tāwhake and Tamakaimoana hapū in the adjacent amalgamations; and (v) the major internal as well as external boundary compromises or mergers among its four final blocks, perhaps especially the continuing confrontation between Numia Kererū and Te Iwikino over Ierenui.

Nevertheless, the probably dominant role of Ngāti Rongo or its closely associated branch Ngāti Hā in three of the four blocks, and the integral role of Numia Kereru, Mika Te Tawhao, and a few others in most of the committees of the four blocks, suggest that a closer marriage alliance and more coherent hapū cluster across the Ōhāua te Rangi amalgamation was developing. The signal marriage some years later of Mika's son Haumate to Hinehou Te Hata, the young *mātāmua* of the Rongokataia descent group (Fig. 6.3), may have celebrated a more consolidated alliance. The subsequent developments of this hapū cluster and its leaders in the Crown's purchase campaign and Urewera Consolidation Scheme will be examined in Volume II, the sequel to this volume.

3 The Parekohe Amalgamation

The Parekohe amalgamation was to be comprised of seven blocks in the northeastern end of the reserve straddling the lower-middle reaches of both the Whakatane and the Tauranga/Waimana Rivers: Te Tuahu, Te Poroporo, Rūātoki South, Te Wairiko, Whaitiripapa, Otara, and the original Parekohe block (Figs. 1.2 and 1.3, amalgamation 9). At the end of the fourth season of the commission's investigation after the amalgamation plan had been aborted, the final block list for each of these blocks was confirmed by the commissioners in the name of one or another of six hapū (Fig. 2.1):

1. the largest block, Parekohe, was shared by three hapū named in this order: Ngāi Tūranga, Te Urewera, and Ngāi Te Kapo;
2. the three different parts of Rūātoki South block (including the northern tip of Te Poroporo) were controlled by Ngāti Muriwai hapū;
3. Te Wairiko block, situated between the parts of Rūātoki South, was controlled by Te Aitanga o Tanemoeahi hapū;
4. Te Poroporo block was controlled by Ngāti Maruhakapua hapū;
5. Te Tuahu block was controlled by Hamua hapū;
6. Otara block was controlled by Ngāi Tūranga hapū; and
7. the little Whaitiripapa block was controlled by Te Urewera hapū.

Several details of Figs. 1.2 and 1.3 need clarification: the Hukanui block, originally planned to be separate, had come to be included as the hook-shaped southeastern end of Parekohe block; the Rūātoki South block on the west side was divided into two distinct sections by the Te Wairiko block, and had come to include the northern tip of Te Poroporo block as well; the northwestern corner of the original Parekohe block included a narrow extension of land across the Whakatane River into the northern section of Rūātoki South block; and the Whaitiripapa block was the very small (67 acre) area extending north into Rūātoki 1 block at the western end of the small Te Tapatahi block (the latter was included in the proposed Rūātoki amalgamation to the east, as was the Whaitiripapa block when the amalgamation plans were aborted). As mentioned in Chap. 5, the 1901 survey plan 6378 (on which Fig. 1.3 is based) locates Whaitiripapa block on the southern bank of a bend in Oromoeroa Stream, and NZMS 170 of the Urewera National Park locates it in or near the area nowadays known as Waikirikiri.

It is important to note that while the eastern boundary of the Parekohe amalgamation straddled both banks of the lower Tauranga-Waimana River, the western boundary of the amalgamation straddled both banks of the lower Whakatane River. On the east, the Tauranga/Waimana River ran north between the Parekohe and Otara blocks. On the west, the Rūātoki South block either straddled the Whakatane River at three points or shared its banks with other blocks of the amalgamation, and a leg of the Parekohe block also extended across this river. The inclusion in this proposed amalgamation of both banks of the lower portions of both of the major rivers in the UDNR implies a strategically important relationship between the six hapū.

Culling duplicate names from the seven block lists showed there would be about 1130 owners in the Parekohe amalgamation. The relatively high proportion of duplicate names which could be dropped (48.1% compared to 43.6% in the case of the Ōhāua te Rangi amalgamation) suggests that the hapū found to have rights to the seven blocks of the amalgamation were relatively closely related, that is, considerably overlapped in membership. However, the relatively large number of blocks involved, and the apparent complexity of boundaries already apparent and further discussed below, suggests that if a 'cluster' of hapū were involved, it may have been more a matter of manifold political accommodations than ecological integrity.

Both the Parekohe and adjacent Rūātoki amalgamations at the northern end of the UDNR had lost their fuller agricultural potential in the 1860s confiscation of their richest lands further north toward the Bay of Plenty (Fig. 1.1). The Parekohe amalgamation had furthermore lost the more arable Waimana blocks just north of it through their sale in the 1880s, as mentioned in Chap. 4. Nevertheless, among the Urewera lands remaining to the Tūhoe after the confiscation, the Parekohe amalgamation would have been second only to the Rūātoki blocks in horticultural and pastoral potential. It lay across the lower-middle reaches of the Urewera ranges in their more moderate altitude, with the higher peaks at about 700 meters and the river bottoms at 150–300 meters. Most important agriculturally, unlike any other potential hapū cluster the amalgamation straddled large sections of both the lower middle Whakatane and the Tauranga/Waimana River bottoms. Although the lower Tauranga/Waimana basin was higher in altitude than the lower Whakatane basin, it was much broader and less restricted by steep ridges on each side.

The middle of the amalgamation between these two river systems was a broad plateau averaging 500 meters altitude but deeply cut by dozens of streams feeding in all directions into one or another of these two rivers. The major streams dividing this central plateau were the Ruariri and Otaneuri draining southwest into the Whakatane River, the Raroa draining north, and the Umutaoroa and Ureroa draining east into the Tauranga/Waimana River. In the center of the amalgamation at the heads of these drainages stood two dominant peaks, Ruatupapaku and Raroa, just over and just under 700 meters, respectively. This relatively low but rugged central plateau was probably intensively used in earlier days; although it remains roadless, it is still routinely crossed by Tūhoe hunters and even commuters traveling between the lower Rūātoki and lower Tauranga/Waimana valleys. The Taiarahia ridgeline above and to the east of Rūātoki was the site of an important political mobilization in the 1990s in conjunction with the Waitangi Tribunal's Te Urewera investigation, and later in 2007 of interest in so-called anti-terrorist police raids organized by the government targeting Rūātoki as well several other national locations considered to be troublesome by the National Security Intelligence Service (Sluka 2010).

The 1901 survey plan on which Fig. 1.3 is based on records several obviously problematic 'overlaps' or *whenua tohetohe* ('contested lands') and changes of block boundaries along the southern boundary of the Parekohe amalgamation. These changes were apparently settled before the amalgamation plan was drawn up, and do not appear on subsequent maps and often are not recorded in the commission's minutes. Some may have resulted from the commission's resolution to merge 'minor' with 'major' claims, as was the case in the Ōhāua Te Rangi amalgamation. From east to west, they occurred in the Otara, Te Hukanui, Te Tuahu, and Te Poroporo blocks.

The adjustment between Otara and Paraoanui blocks was mentioned in Chap. 5 with regard to the hapū affiliations of Tamaikoha's *kāwai*: sometime in 1900 the boundary between these two blocks was apparently shifted north from a line following the curves of the Okehu Stream to a straight east-west line just south of Te Rere Stream. In any case, later maps of the Reserve from 1907 to 1921 agree on the straight-line boundary. Nevertheless, when in 1902 the line for the amalgamated blocks was drawn over the 1901 map, the boundary between Otara and Paraoanui was redrawn along the Okehu Stream, appearing to revert to its earlier position. Neither position is recorded in the minutebooks. Because the straight-line boundary to the north appears to be crossed out on the 1901 survey plan 6378, it is not likely that this was merely a confusion or drafting mistake. Speculatively, it may have reflected the reversal of a previous agreement between the old war leaders Tamaikoha and Te Whiu in view of their expanded authority when Paraoanui and Otara blocks were proposed for amalgamation into the much larger Tauwhare Manuka and Parekohe amalgamations, respectively (Fig. 1.3, amalgamations 8 and 9).

The several overlaps along the northern Paraeroa boundary with Te Hukanui, Te Tuahu, and Te Poroporo blocks may also have involved counter-claims between Tamaikoha and leaders of the latter three blocks. However, a key protagonist was Tupara Kaaho, a leader in Paraeroa block but probably of limited influence in any of the blocks of the Parekohe amalgamation except Rūātoki South. The final result of this rather dramatic confrontation was a series of compromises along its southern boundary with Paraeroa block. With the exception of token shares in Parekohe block (for Te Hukanui) and his leading shares in the tiny Whaitiripapa block, Tamaikoha himself ended with no shares either in what would have been the Parekohe amalgamation or in the Paraeroa block. As mentioned in Chap. 5, expressing frustration with his 'committee' and confronted by Tupara Kaaho's intransigence, Tamaikoha dramatically withdrew all his claims for the lands in what was to become Paraeroa block (UMB 6: 177, 310–11). This may have been when the boundary across the southern end of Te Tuahu was crossed out on the 1901 plan and a roughly parallel one extending Te Tuahu was redrawn across the northern end of Paraeroa.

Another overlap between Te Tuahu and Te Poroporo blocks complicated this situation further, but was apparently settled the next day (UMB 6: 312), and is reflected in the scribbled-out boundary between the two on the 1901 plan (which suggests the settlement was a gain for Te Tuahu block). In any case, at some point a third line was struck straight across between Te Tuahu and Paraeroa from the tip of Te Hukanui to the southern end of Te Poroporo block at Otanaeuri Creek. This line was apparently the final decision of the commission and, as well as appearing on subsequent maps, a few months later was confirmed by the line drawn between the amalgamated blocks. The only other boundary adjustment recorded on the 1901 plan were two vague lines dividing the Te Wairiko block that may have indicated a change that was briefly considered but dropped.

Can some preliminary generalizations be made regarding the relationship between the six hapū later recognized to hold rights in each of the seven blocks of the amalgamation? The relatively high proportion of overlap or duplication of individual names among these blocks suggests that some of these hapū were widely overlapped in membership and perhaps closely related. Insofar as these hapū might have formed a 'cluster', a related issue would be the relative independence or dominance of some of them over others.

Ngāti Muriwai, recognized to hold exclusive rights over Rūātoki South block, was said by Best to be a division of Ngāi Tūranga (i.e., subordinate to it), which was named first of three hapū holding rights over Parekohe block and sole owners of Otara block (1973: 227; 214–5). However, he and several witnesses in hearings on these blocks suggested that Ngāti Muriwai was ephemeral or better known in terms of other hapū especially Hamua or Te Aitanga o Tanemoeahi, which were later named as owners of Te Tuahu and Te Wairiko blocks, respectively (UMB 4: 52, 181, 245). In any case, these comments are further evidence of overlaps in hapū membership between Ngāi Tūranga, Ngāti Muriwai, Hamua, and Te Aitanga o Tanemoeahi which would explain the significant reduction of duplicate names that could be achieved by amalgamating the blocks.

Ngāti Koura hapū was not formally recognized to hold rights in any blocks of the Parekohe amalgamation but nevertheless apparently overlapped with several of the hapū that were recognized there, and was later recognized to hold exclusive rights to the Te Purenga block immediately west of the Parekohe amalgamation. The evidence suggests that Ngāti Koura hapū held rights at least in Parekohe and Te Wairiko blocks under the name of Ngāi Tūranga and Te Aitanga o Tanemoeahi hapū, and probably also in Rūātoki South block under the name of Ngāti Muriwai hapū. While it had exclusive control of Te Purenga block outside the proposed amalgamation, the subordination of Ngāti Koura to these hapū in these blocks is thus implied.

Such overlapping hapū memberships may have also motivated claims by most of these hapū for many other blocks of the amalgamation. Ngāi Tūranga hapū lay claims for Parekohe, Otara, Hukanui, Te Poroporo, Rūātoki South, and Whaitiripapa blocks, and was awarded rights in the first two. Ngāti Muriwai hapū lay claims for Rūātoki South, Parekohe, Te Poroporo, Te Wairiko, and Whaitiripapa blocks, and was awarded exclusive rights to Rūātoki South. Te Aitanga o Tanemoeahi hapū lay a claim for Whaitiripapa as well as Te Wairiko block, and was awarded the latter. Hamua hapū lay claims for Rūātoki South, Te Wairiko, and Whaitiripapa as well as Te Tuahu block, and was awarded the latter. Te Urewera hapū lay claims for Te Wairiko and Rūātoki South as well as Whaitiripapa and a part of Te Purenga which was to become the Parekohe block; it was awarded exclusive rights in Whaitiripapa block and, along with two other hapū but subordinate to Ngāi Tūranga, in Parekohe block.

Among these several overlapping hapū, can leading sibling groups or descent groups be identified from the land rights they were recognized to hold in the blocks of the amalgamation? Examination of the lists for sibling groups or individuals holding shares in at least four of the seven blocks resulted in a list of about 45 different surnames. Adding the criterion of leading shares (i.e., full shares and ranked among the first 100 individuals) narrowed the list of 45 to about 21 probably influential or leading sibling groups or individuals. As displayed in Fig. 6.4 below, examination of these sibling groups and individuals showed that almost all of them were descendants of only four couples. (One of the four couples was Tamaro and Miriata, also progenitors of one of the three leading descent groups in the Ōhāua te Rangi amalgamation analyzed above.) All of the nine original progenitors appear to have died by 1902, but many of their children were still alive, and many of them had had grandchildren. In 1902, at least 200 of their descendants and their spouses were living and would have held shares in the proposed amalgamation, and many were minors. This was about 18% of the total owners in the amalgamation. Most strikingly, within the four generations depicted in Fig. 6.4, there were at least 13 intermarriages between the four original descent groups: one in the first generation, five in the second generation, four in the third generation, and three more in the fourth generation.

For the sake of clarity, Fig. 6.4 generally shows only those members of the four descent groups who married persons in one of the other descent groups, leaving out the far more numerous individuals (especially siblings) who married persons outside these descent groups or who had not yet married in 1898. A few other important leaders are included for reasons discussed later.

The rapid onset of intermarriages between the descendants of the four original progenitors suggests intentional arrangements and probably political or economic alliance. If this was the case, the declining rate of intermarriage in each successive generation after the second may reflect the increasing extent to which descendants found themselves too closely related to avoid the incest taboo. There may have been few permissible spouses among them by the time the young members of the fifth generation were ready to marry.

These and other genealogies, and several contemporary cases, have convinced me that Tūhoe recognized an incest taboo or avoided (and continue to avoid) marriage between relatives closer than fourth cousins. There was apparently one first-cousin marriage in the Tamaro descent group between Ameria's son (by an earlier marriage) and her brother Te Waara's *mātāmua* daughter (Best 1898: 8; not included in Fig. 6.4), but I have found no other instances of this among Tūhoe (I did find two

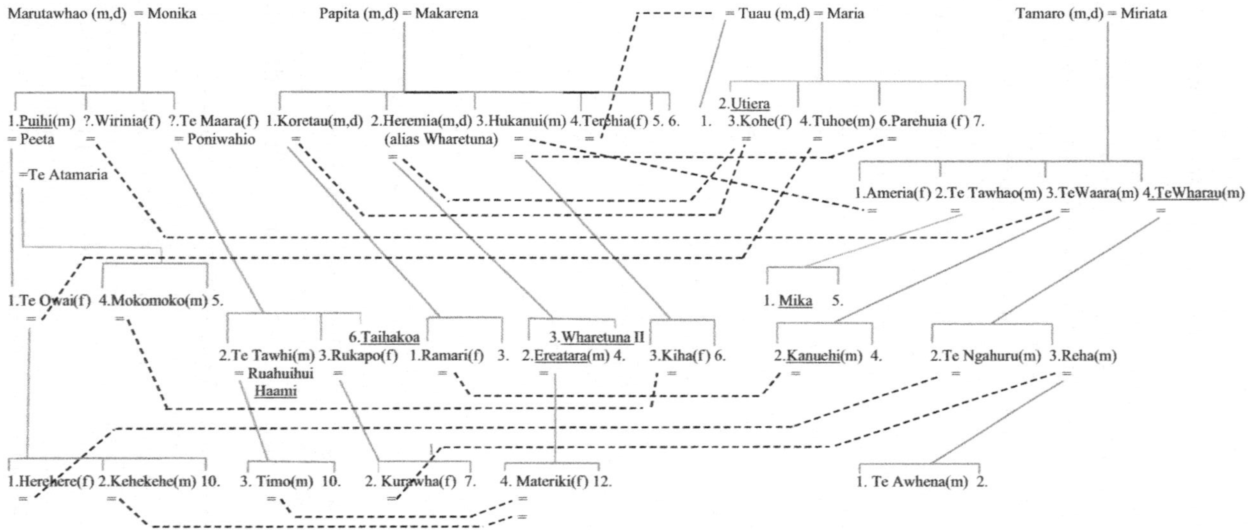

Fig. 6.4 Intermarriage of the leading descent groups of Parekohe amalgamation 1898–1903
Legend:
1. Vertical solid lines denote filiation (parent to child) or descent
2. Horizontal solid lines connect siblings (only those important to intermarriages shown; numbered by birth order)
3. = denotes marriage to person above
4. Dotted lines represent the same marriage connecting different descent groups
5. If notable, (f,11) denotes female gender and age; (m,d) denotes male gender and deceased

apparent instances of second-cousin marriage, as will be described in Chap. 7). Other commentators have found evidence of less restrictive rules generally among Māori. Joan Metge reported that "Within the *hapū*, there were strong sanctions against marriage between first and second cousins" (1967: 26). However, probably in 1929, citing his own nearby East Coast *iwi* Ngāti Porou, Apirana Ngata contested the common assumption of such a restriction, claiming that close-inbreeding, even marriage of first cousins was "extremely common" and "the rule rather than the exception" especially within "highly prized lines" of descent (Ngata n.d. [1929?]: 15). Bruce Biggs' study of traditional Māori marriage found some evidence that first-cousin marriages were disapproved (Firth 1962: 193). His finding that local descent group endogamy was encouraged to keep conflict limited to relatives may partly explain what Ngata identified as 'close in-breeding' in 'highly prized lines'.

The high number of intermarriages at the outset of the alliance show that the four descent groups were not closely related, but they may nevertheless have belonged to one or a few hapū. Best's genealogical plates index none of the four patriarchs, so no common ancestor or hapū can be readily identified between them (Best 1973 Vol II). However, a few of their children (Puihi, Korotau, Heremia, and Hukanui) and Marutawhao's wife Monika are indexed, and the genealogies in which they appear (plates 5 and 27) suggest that there may have been a distant relationship between the Marutawhao and Papita descent group (six to ten generations). Interestingly, there were no intermarriages between them in the first two generations shown in Fig. 6.4. If they did have a common ancestor, Best's genealogy suggests it was probably as part of the large Te Urewera or Tūhoe hapū, which was recognized to have rights in the Parekohe and Whaitiripapa blocks of the Parekohe amalgamation.

The conclusion that the four original progenitors and their children intended to form a political alliance reinforced by intermarriages is supported by other evidence. As earlier pointed out, since the 1860s especially the northern end of the UDNR had been deprived of its best agricultural lands in the lower valleys by the Crown's confiscations. If the second generation of descendants, most of whom were still living in 1902, averaged about 60 years old, then some of the five intermarriages among them, and all of the eight which followed, could have been a strategy undertaken by immigrants from the confiscated lands to consolidate their control over their remaining arable lands. Their consistent occupation since the 1860s, along with a legitimate ancestral claim, could explain their strong shares in some blocks of the amalgamation. As described in Chap. 5, Tutakangahau reported that five hapū had been made destitute by the confiscation and had come under his authority, probably in the upper Tauranga/Waimana basin (UMB 1: 179). The situation in the lower basins straddled by the Parekohe amalgamation may have similarly developed from a Tūhoe resettlement or accommodation of those who had lost their lands further to the north.

The differing land rights of the four descent groups are also consistent with the possibility of intermarriage for political alliance. While the leading shares of the Marutawhao and Papita descent group were strongest in Te Wairiko and Te Poroporo blocks on the west side of the amalgamation, those of the Tuau and Tamaro descent group were strongest in Parekohe and Otara blocks to the east (as well as holding lesser shares in some western blocks). The intermarriages in the first and second generation thus resulted in offspring with leading land rights straddling the lower altitudes of the Tauranga/Waimana as well as Whakatane River valleys. The intermarriages might have been a tactic to strengthen such influence or *mana* spanning these agriculturally and strategically important the valleys.

Before closer consideration of the relationships between hapū in the amalgamation, identification of the most important leaders of the Parekohe marriage alliance can be attempted through study of the 1899 claimants for, and later committee memberships of, the seven blocks of the amalgamation.

Although several of the blocks were ambiguously referred to early in the investigation as 'Te Purenga' (later applied to one smaller block immediately to the east of the amalgamation), most of the likely 1899 claimants to the seven blocks can be identified. There were about 25 persons claiming in the name of eight different hapū, five of which hapū were named in the final awards of the blocks. Only 6 of the 25 claimants were members of the four intermarried descent groups in the Parekohe marriage alliance (Fig. 6.4, underlined):

1. Puihi Marutawhao claimed Te Poroporo block for Ngāi Turanga hapū (he was misidentified in the 1899 minutes as 'Puiha'). Puihi was the matamua son of Marutawhao and Monika, progenitors of the Marutawhao descent group.
2. Taihakoa Poniwahio claimed Otara block for Ngāi Tūranga hapū. Taihakoa was the *pōtiki* (last-born child) of Te Maara, Marutawhao and Monika's daughter. Te Maara may actually have been Monika's

daughter by her sister's husband Ruka Te Waiau rather than Marutawhao (UMB 8: Te Poroporo; Best 1898: 20). Taihakoa also lay a claim for 'Te Purenga' block in the name of Ngāti Koura hapū (as will be seen later, this was probably a claim to western blocks of the amalgamation, where rights of this hapū were probably recognized under the name of other hapū). Poniwahio was an important leader in the other blocks of the UDNR and married the youngest daughter of Tutakangahau, the *rangatira* of Tamakaimoana hapū.

3. Ereatara Heremia claimed Te Tuahu block for Hamua hapū. Ereatara was the second son of Heremia Papita and Kohe Tuau, one of the several intermarriages between the Papita and Tuau descent groups. (Ereatara's younger brother Wharetuna Heremia is included in the diagram as an important leader on the block committees.)
4. Heremia claimed Te Poroporo block for Ngāti Maruhakapua hapū. He was probably Ereatara's half-brother, fathered by Heremia Papita with Kerehitina (see UMB 8: Whaitiripapa 1 and Te Poroporo 121). (Heremia is left out of the diagram for lack of space.)
5. Mika Te Tawhao claimed Parekohe block for Ngāi Tūranga hapū. Mika was the *mātāmua* son of Te Tawhao, Tamaro and Miriata's second child. It may be significant that Te Tawhao was the only Tamaro sibling who did not marry within the Parekohe marriage alliance (his wife Ewa Te Hina had leading shares in Hikurangi-Horomanga block but few others). As described with regard to the Ōhāua Te Rangi amalgamation, their *mātāmua* son Mika and the whole Tamaro descent group were also leading shareholders in that amalgamation, and Mika Te Tawhao was among the most active leaders there.
6. Finally among the 1899 claimants, Te Wharau Tamaro claimed Te Tuahu block for Hamua hapū (as Ereatara had done). Te Wharau was the *pōtiki* child of Tamaro and Miriata, progenitors of the Tamaro descent group, younger brother of Te Tawhao and uncle of Mika. It will be remembered that Te Wharau had submitted a claim for the Te Ranga a Ruanuku block of the Ōhāua te Rangi amalgamation, also in the name of Hamua hapū.

Several members of the Parekohe marriage alliance were also politically active as members of the amalgamation committees set up in 1902, the block or hapū committees set up in 1902 and revised in 1907, and the General Committee of the UDNR set up in 1908 (Fig. 2.1). Members of the four descent groups held 14 of about 40 committee seats in 1902, and

18 of about 45 committee seats in 1907. This was over one-third of the total seats for the seven blocks in both 1902 and 1907, far more than the proportion of marriage alliance members among the total owners in the Parekohe amalgamation (about 18%). The members of the marriage alliance also held two of seven positions in the committee appointed for the proposed Parekohe amalgamated block in 1902, and two of five positions elected to the General Committee representing the seven blocks of the amalgamation in 1908. Details regarding four of the six members of the marriage alliance who had submitted claimants lists in 1899, and who later also served on the committees for the blocks of the proposed Parekohe amalgamation, reflect impressive leadership activity:

1. Taihakoa Poniwahio of the Marutawhau descent group held positions on the Te Poroporo (1902, 1907), Te Tuahu (1902, 1907), Rūātoki South (1907), and Te Wairiko (1907) block committees. Outside the proposed amalgamation, he also held positions on the Te Ranga a Ruanuku (1902), Tauwhare (1907; both of the proposed Ōhāua te Rangi amalgamation), Te Purenga (1902, just west of Rūātoki South), Paraoanui (1907), Omahuru (1907), and Waikarewhenua (1902, 1907) block committees. In 1908 he was elected to the General Committee as representative of Te Poroporo block. As noted above, in 1899 Taihakoa had submitted claimants lists for Otara block in the name of Ngāi Tūranga hapū as well as for 'Te Purenga' in the name of Ngāti Koura hapū. The latter claim is probably reflected in his seats for the western blocks of the Parekohe amalgamation because, as mentioned above, Ngāti Koura rights were probably recognized under the name of other hapū in those blocks. On the other hand, his claim for Otara block and Turanga hapū raises implications that will be discussed later.
2. Ereatara Heremia of the Papita descent group in the alliance held a position only on the Te Tuahu block committee (1902) in the Parekohe amalgamation. However, he also held a position on the Tauwhare block committee (1902) in the Ōhāua te Rangi amalgamation, and his *mātāmua* son Raukaraka held a position on the Karioi block committee (1902). As noted above, in 1899 Ereatara had submitted a claimants list for Te Tuahu in the name of Hamua hapū, which was later awarded exclusive rights to this block.
3. Heremia Heremia, probably a half-brother of the other Heremia siblings by a different mother, held a position only on the Te

Poroporo block committee (1902, 1907) in the Parekohe amalgamation. However, he also held positions on the Kohuru-Tukuroa block committee (1902) in the Ōhāua te Rangi amalgamation, and on the Tapatahi block committee (1902, 1907; located just east of the Whaitiripapa block of the Parekohe amalgamation). As noted above, in 1899 Heremia Heremia had submitted a claimants list for Te Poroporo in the name of Ngāti Maruhakapua hapū, and this hapū was later recognized to have exclusive rights to the block. Probably also known as Ngāti Maru, this was one of the four hapū that had been taken in by Tutakangahau and Tamakaimoana hapū since they were left landless by the Crown confiscations to the north.

4. Mika Te Tawhao of the Tamaro descent group in the Parekohe alliance held positions on the Te Wairiko (1902, 1907), Te Tuahu (1902, 1907), Rūātoki South (1907), and Parekohe block committees in the Parekohe amalgamation. However, he was also very active in the Ōhāua te Rangi amalgamation, holding positions on the Ierenui-Ōhāua (1902, 1907), Te Ranga a Ruanuku (1902, 1907), and Tauwhare (1907) block committees there. Outside either of these proposed amalgamations, he also held positions on the Paraeroa (1902, 1907) and Hikurangi-Horomanga (1902, 1907) block committees. In 1908 he was elected to the General Committee of the UDNR representing the Te Ranga a Ruanuku block of the proposed Ōhāua te Rangi amalgamation. As noted above, in 1899 Mika had submitted a claimant list for Parekohe block in the name of Ngāi Tūranga hapū, as had Taihakoa for Otara block in the name of that hapū; again, these claims from among the Parekohe marriage alliance were rare and will be discussed later.

There were six other members of the Parekohe marriage alliance who had not submitted claims in 1899 for any blocks in the Parekohe amalgamation but who were later active on the committees for the blocks of that amalgamation:

1. Wharetuna Heremia (probably Wharetuna II, as his father Heremia was also known as Wharetuna), the third-born of four Heremia full-brothers, held positions on more block committees than either Ereatara or their half-brother Heremia Heremia. Wharetuna sat on the Parekohe (1902), Rūātoki South (1902, 1907), Te Wairiko (1902, 1907), and Te Poroporo (1902, 1907) block committees in

the proposed Parekohe amalgamation. He also sat with Mika Te Whao on the Te Ranga a Ruanuku block committee (1902) in the Ōhāua te Rangi amalgamation. Notably, in 1902 he was the only member of the Parekohe marriage alliance who held a position on the committee formed for the amalgamated block, but he was named second among seven members.

2. Te Mataku Papita, fifth son of Papita and Makarena and younger brother of Heremia (Wharetuna I), sat on the block committee for Te Poroporo in 1902 and 1907, and his son Toko Te Mataku sat on the committee for Te Wairiko in 1902 and 1907.
3. Utiera Tuau was a member of the Rūātoki South block committee in 1902. Best reported that Utiera was chief of the Hamua hapū at Waikirikiri, Rūātoki in 1896, the hapū that was found to have exclusive rights over Te Tuahu block of the Parekohe amalgamation.
4. Te Waara Tamaro's son Kanuehi Te Waara, who had married the *mātāmua* daughter of Koretau Papita, sat on the committee for Paraeroa block south of Te Tuahu in 1902, on the committee for Tauwhare block (1902, 1907) in the Ōhāua te Rangi amalgamation, and was third member of the committee for that amalgamation in 1902.
5. Haami Taupo might have married belatedly into the Parekohe alliance, insofar as his daughter Ruahuihui married Te Tawhi Poniwahio, Taihakoa's elder brother. Haami Taupo sat on the Tauwhare block committee in 1902, represented that block on the Ōhāua te Rangi amalgamation committee, sat on the Te Wairiko block committee in 1902 and 1907, and in 1908 was elected to represent that block on the General Committee.
6. Te Reweti Ruta, husband of Tuau and Marias' fifth child Taha, sat on the Parekohe and Te Tuahu block committees in 1902, and was named sixth of the seven members of the Parekohe amalgamation committee in 1902. It may be significant that except for Wharetuna Heremia, Te Rewiti was the only person with alliance connections to sit on this committee.

Before attempting to reconstruct the organization of hapū represented by the leaders whose activities are outlined above, it must be asked why these seven blocks had been proposed as an amalgamation in 1902. One would suppose that the relatively large number of blocks, hapū, and boundary modifications, and the difficulties in cooperation and unified leadership implied, would have discouraged consideration as a single amalgamated title. However, the political and economic influence to be gained by domination of the lower basins on both banks of the two major rivers of the UDNR may explain both these problems and the determination to overcome them. Hapū 'clusters' probably often came to be formed under similar circumstances. The Parekohe marriage alliance described above, apparently well-established by 1898, was probably a major factor in the formation of such a hapū cluster controlling this amalgamation. Although members of this alliance were never a majority, if they acted in concert at any time they could form a large and perhaps controlling minority across the blocks proposed for the amalgamation. The potential influence of this minority of committee seats was also balanced across the four descent groups, reducing the likelihood of division between them.

The hapū found to have exclusive rights to the four blocks largely controlled by the marriage alliance were Te Aitangi o Tanemoeahi (Te Wairiko block), Ngāti Maruhakapua (Te Poroporo block), Hamua (Te Tuahu block), and Ngāti Muriwai (Rūātoki South block). Yet the overlap of membership between these four hapū was apparently so extensive that most leaders of the marriage alliance could speak for most of them. An examination of their claims and committee positions for all blocks of the reserve shows that Ngāti Muriwai hapū was spoken for by Te Wharetuna Heremia, Taihakoa Poniwahio, Mika Te Tawhao, and Utiera Tuau; Te Aitanga o Tanemoeahi was spoken for by Te Wharetuna, Taihakoa, Mika, and Haami Taupo; Ngāti Maruhakapua hapū was spoken for by Te Wharetuna, Taihakoa, Puihi Marutawhao, and Heremia; and Hamua hapū was spoken for by Taihakoa, Mika, and Ereatara Heremia.

However, it may be significant that the marriage alliance had weaker representation in the amalgamation committee itself (only one of seven members) than in separate block committees taken together in either 1902 or 1907. If this was to be the committee with authority over the seven amalgamated blocks, why would their representation be weaker? Furthermore, they were apparently unrepresented, or only weakly represented, in the other three blocks on the eastern side of the Parekohe amalgamation. Whereas they held the majority of seats representing Te Wairiko, Te Poroporo, and Te Tuahu blocks on the western side in 1902, and in 1907 again held the majority for these blocks and also half of the seats representing Rūātoki South block, through these years they apparently held only one seat representing the Parekohe block (by far the largest block) and none representing the Otara and Whaitiripapa blocks. Although most members of the marriage alliance held no shares in Whaitiripapa, most did hold shares in Parekohe and Otara blocks and, furthermore, many held the leading shares in Parekohe. What might account for this asymmetry or striking lack of representation on some committees?

The hapū found to have exclusive or shared rights to these three blocks on the eastern side of the amalgamation were Ngāi Tūranga (exclusive rights to Otara block and first among three hapū named for Parekohe block), Te Urewera (exclusive rights to Whaitiripapa block and named second for Parekohe block), and Ngāi Te Kapo (named last for Parekohe block). If the minor role of Ngāi Te Kapo in Parekohe is discounted, it appears that the influence of the marriage alliance in the Parekohe amalgamation may have been balanced, or confronted, by two hapū: Ngāi Turanga and Te Urewera, both large and influential hapū well-established in the lower basins.

In this regard, at least, the proposed Parekohe amalgamation might be seen as divided into two halves roughly along a line running northwest from Hukanui (the southern hook of Parekohe block) to Whaitiripapa block. While on the amalgamation's western side the marriage alliance and its tightly overlapped hapū dominated both banks of the Whakatane River except for two points along northern section of Rūātoki South block, on the amalgamation's eastern side two large, established hapū dominated both banks of the Tauranga/Waimana River. In view of this split of the political-economic advantages of the proposed amalgamation, any cluster of hapū might be motivated to maintain cooperation.

It is interesting that in 1899 two leaders of the marriage alliance did submit claims for Parekohe and Otara blocks, and furthermore in the name of Ngāi Tūranga hapū: Mika Te Tawhao submitted a claim for Parekohe block, and Taihakoa Poniwahio submitted a claim for Otara block. However, in both cases their claims were confronted by lists submitted by Te Whiu Maraki (for Otara block) or Taua Rakuraku as well as Te Whiu (for Parekohe block), also in the name of Ngāi Turanga hapū. Te Whiu Maraki was a war-leader rangatira of *mana*, and Taua was the son of Rakuraku, another such war leader by then deceased. Insofar as neither Mika nor Taihakoa were named to the committees for either block in 1902, it might have been that the boldness of their early claims was rebuffed by the *mana* of these leaders, probably for Te Urewera as well as Ngāi Tūranga hapū.

Except for Reweti Ruka (who had only married into the marriage alliance, but held strong rights in Parekohe), Te Wharetuna Heremia was the only leader of the marriage alliance named to the committees of Parekohe, Otara, or Whaitiripapa blocks. Te Wharetuna was named second among the seven seats for Parekohe block, but considering the high rank and preponderance of leading shares held by the marriage alliance in that block, this was only a token representation. In 1907 Mika Te Tawhao was given a seat on the Parekohe block committee but, apparently replacing Te Wharetuna, his was again the only seat representing the marriage alliance. Most significantly, when it came to the committee that would have authority over the seven amalgamated blocks, the only member representing the marriage alliance was Te Wharetuna, outnumbered six to one by the others unless Rewiti Ruka supported him.

This apparent but perhaps easing tension between Te Aitangi o Tanemoeahi, Ngāti Maruhakapua, Hamua, and Ngāti Muriwai hapū on the western side of the proposed amalgamation, and Ngāi Tūranga and Te Urewera hapū on the eastern side, suggests a hypothetical scenario unfolding since the 1860s confiscations.

Somewhat as several other hapū had been taken in by Tamakiamoana hapū in the upper basin, Ngāi Tūranga and Te Urewera hapū may have taken in the progenitors of the Parekohe marriage alliance and settled them in areas in the lower basin that would later become the proposed amalgamation. As remnants of several landless hapū and immigrants beholden to their patrons, the refugees would seek to consolidate their position on the land by intermarrying with one another, establishing occupation and, insofar as possible, marrying advantageously among their patrons. Having gained land rights and sufficient solidarity on this basis especially along the western side by the end of the century, given the opportunities of the UDNR investigation they would seek independent hapū status and block rights. Meanwhile, their patrons might consolidate their own hapū along the eastern side against the rising influence of such a rapidly expanding marriage alliance. Yet by May of 1902 the advantages of maintaining cooperation between eastern and western sides of the several blocks might have become obvious to all of them, explaining their support for the proposed Parekohe amalgamation.

4 Conclusion

Some of the leading questions regarding amalgamations and the possibility of hapū 'clusters' listed in the introduction have been clarified. The rights of shareholders in two of the three proposed amalgamations clearly overlapped between the blocks involved, but they often extended well beyond into other blocks of the reserve. Although in each case the blocks were probably primarily controlled by one or a few hapū, there was evidence of internal as well as external confrontation between hapū. Individual leaders in these leading descent groups could be identified, although their hapū affiliation and extent of cooperation or confrontation with others often remained unclear. Insofar as hapū rights in the blocks of an amalgamation were organized as a cluster, they were in a gathering history of shifting relationships and relative rights between immigrant and settled, assimilated or emergent, and subordinate or dominant statuses consistent with Ballara's understanding of hapū clusters in nineteenth-century New Zealand. On the other hand, leading descent groups could be identified, and intermarriage between them clearly implied an alliance for political or economic purposes. While the alliance in the case of the Ōhāua te Rangi blocks was sometimes indirect involving outside hapū, the alliance in the case of Parakohe blocks was spectacularly developed, while perhaps in fragile cooperation with other hapū dominating the other side of the proposed amalgamation.

Notes

1. I used the final block orders (AJHR 1907) to do this because they were available in a form that I could sort digitally. The inclination of the appeals commission to resolve problems by extending small shares to additional owners potentially distorts the results of the following calculations, but my assumption that larger shareholders represented more influence in the block would not be significantly affected.
2. My family and I were close to their grandson, Paki Haumate, at Ruatāhuna in the 1970s; he died of pneumonia still a handsome young man in the early 1980s, and we attended his tragic funeral in Rūātoki. Paki had a learning disability, and was among the several adopted children of Rangiwhaitiri, our host in Ruatāhuna. However, although he was strikingly humble and gentle, he was well-known as a master of traditional Māori language as well as fluent in English. He would hold my hand patiently as I struggled to learn new Māori words and pronounce them properly. Only long after Paki's death and sombre *tangi* did I come to realise his *mātāmua* birth status.

References

AJHR 1907. G. Mair, D.F.G. Barclay, Paratene Ngata. "The Urewera District Native Reserve: reports of the commissioners appointed ...." Report and orders. Undated. Appendices to the Journal of the House of Representatives 1907 G-4: 1–190. Wellington, N.Z.

Ballara, Angela. 1995. "Porangahau: The Formation of an Eighteenth Century Community in Southern Hawke's Bay." *New Zealand Journal of History* 29(1): 3–18.

Ballara, Angela. 1998. Iwi: *The dynamics of Māori tribal organisation from c.1769 to c.1945.* Wellington, N.Z.: Victoria University Press.

Best, Elsdon. 1898. "Tuhoe genealogies 1898" (spine title); "Genealogies of the Tuhoe tribe. Also includes all living members of the tribe in 1898, as given before the Urewera Commission set up under the act of 1896." Manuscript qMS [172]. Wellington, N.Z.: Alexander Turnbull Library. [NB: the author can supply a digital index for this resource.]

Best, Elsdon. 1973. *Tuhoe, Children of the Mist.* Vols. I and II (genealogies). Second edition. Wellington, N.Z.: A.H. and A.W. Reed Ltd. (first published 1925 as Vol VI of the Memoirs of the Polynesian Society).

Firth, Raymond. 1962. "Book review of *Maori Marriage: An Essay in Reconstruction*" by Bruce Biggs (Polynesian Society Monographs, No. 1. Wellington, New Zealand: The Polynesian Society Incorporated, 1960). *American Anthropologist* 64: 193–4.

Holman, Jeffrey. 2010. *Best of both worlds: the story of Elsdon Best and Tutakangahau.* Auckland, N.Z.: Penguin.

Kruger, Tamati. 2004. "Ngā Hapū ō Ngā Pōtiki." Appendix to Final Report *Ruātoki; Ngā Rauru ō Ngā Pōtiki.* Anamata College, Taneātua, N.Z. 10 January 2004. Urewera Enquiry WAI 894. Wellington, N.Z.: Waitangi Tribunal.

Metge, Joan. 1967. *The Maoris of New Zealand.* London: Routledge & Kegan Paul.

NACMB 1. Native Appellate Court minute book 1, Jackson Palmer, Rawson, (13Nov1912–Feb1913), index 9 pp., 386 pp.; NA Wgtn: Waiariki, Urewera Appelate MB 1, CD 3518/2, 397pp.; NA Ak: AREPRO 4711/1450. Acronym: NACMB 1.

NACMB 2. Native Appellate Court minute book 2, Jackson Palmer, Rawson, (1Feb1913–20Aug1913), index 5 pp., 136pp.; NA Wgtn: Waiariki, Urewera Appelate MB 2, CD 3518/2, 140pp.; NA Ak: AREPRO 4711/1451. Acronym: NACMB 2.

Ngata, Apirana. n.d. MS. Not dated; probably 1929. "The genealogical method as applied to early history of New Zealand." ATL qMS NGA. Alexander Turnbull Library, Wellington. (A copy also held in Special Collections mss 2 archives A-135, University of Auckland Library, Auckland, N.Z.).

Pouwhare, Te Iki. 1959. "Genealogies from Tūhoe, by Te Iki Pouwhare." *Journal of the Polynesian Society* 68(3): 215–218.

Sluka, Jeffrey. 2010. "The Ruātoki Valley 'Antiterrorism' Police Raids: Losing 'hearts and minds' in Te Urewera." *Sites* N.S. Vol 7(1): 44–64.

UCMB 2. Urewera Consolidation minute book 2A, Carr, Knight, (27Apr1923–18Dec1926), index 33pp, 246pp.; NA Wgtn: Urewera MB 2A, MLC 13, W 3518, CD2, Vol.2, 284pp.; NA Ak: AREPRO 4711/1443. Acronym: UCMB 2A.

UMB 1. Urewera District Native Reserve Commission minute book 1 (identified as Urewera Commission minute book '3'), Smith, Butler, et al, (1Feb1899–8Mar1900), in Māori, Index 22pp., 382pp. NA Wgtn: Urewera MB 3, MLC 13, W3518, CD2, Vol 3, 397 pp.; NA Ak: AREPRO 4711/1445. Acronym: UMB 1.

UMB 4. Urewera District Native Reserve Commission minute book 4 (English translation of UMB 2), Butler, Scannell, et al, (9Mar1900–May1900), index 12 pp., 344pp.; NA Wgtn: Urewera MB 4, MLC 13, W3518, CD 2, Vol. 4, 357 pp.; NA Ak: AREPRO 4711/1446. Acronym: UMB 4.

UMB 5. Urewera District Native Reserve Commission minute book 5, Butler, Scannell, et al. (18Mar1901–16May01), in English, index 5 pp., 382 pp.; NA Wgtn: Urewera MB 5, MLC 13,W3518, CD 2, Vol.5, 388pp.; NA Ak: AREPRO 4711/1447. Acronym: UMB 5.

UMB 6. Urewera District Native Reserve Commission minute book 6, Butler, Scannell, et al. (16May1901–26Apr02) in English, index 9 pp., 382 pp.; NA Wgtn: Waiariki, Urewera MB 6, CD W3518/2, 398 pp.; NA Ak: AREPRO 4711/1448. Acronym: UMB 6.

UMB 8. Urewera District Native Reserve Commission minute book 8, ("Urewera Commission Minute Book 1896" in Waiariki MLC archives, bound xerox copy), probably by Elsdon Best. draft orders, annotated with share modifications, mothers, etc., for 20 blocks (UMB 9, covering the other blocks, appears to be lost since 1984). No copies in NA. Acronym UMB 8.

Webster, Steven. 1998. "Maori Hapu as a Whole Way of Struggle: 1840–50s Before the Land Wars." *Oceania* 69(1): 4–35.

PART II

Kinship and Power in Ruatāhuna and Waikaremoana, 1899–1913

CHAPTER 7

The Ruatāhuna-Waikaremoana Migrant Marriage Alliance by 1898

1 Introduction

The proposed amalgamation of the Ruatāhuna and Waikaremoana blocks in the southeast corner of the Urewera would have formed one of the largest blocks in the reserve, about 20% of the final 656,000 acres. Wiremu Dougherty has recently published a *waiata* ('song') that happens to dramatically straddle these two large blocks. His ancestress Mihi ki te Kapua sang a *waiata* about being left behind at Maatuahu Point on the shores of Lake Waikaremoana when her beloved returned to Ruatāhuna and the Whakatane River, about 25 kilometers overland to the northeast and separated from the lake by the relatively rugged Huiarau Range (Dougherty 2014; NZMS 170 n.d.).

According to Best's census (1898: 29, 43), Mihi's husband (perhaps this same beloved?) was Whakatipu Tokai (or Toakai), with whom she had two children and eight grandchildren by 1900. At that time their two children were probably 40–50 years old, because their oldest grandchildren were adults (over 18 years old). Significantly, nine of these ten offspring had rights in both the Waikaremoana and the Ruatāhuna blocks but in no other blocks of the Urewera. The mother of seven of the grandchildren was noted by Best to be from 'N.K.' (Ngāti Kahungunu, the extensive *iwi* to the southeast of Tūhoe). Apparently because she had no ancestral rights in Urewera blocks backed by sufficiently recent occupation, no further birthrights were added to her children's rights in Waikaremoana

© The Author(s) 2020
S. Webster, *A Separate Authority (He Mana Motuhake)*, Volume I,
https://doi.org/10.1007/978-3-030-41042-1_7

and Ruatāhuna, presumably received only from Mihi and Whakatipu. The husband of Mihi's and Whakatipu's other child held rights from only one other Urewera block, nearby Maungapōhatu, to these rights of the *mātāmua* one of their eight grandchildren (Te Hau Meiha), so this son-in-law's rights in the Urewera blocks were similarly very limited (one of his parents may also have married from Ngāti Kahungunu into Maungapōhatu, while the other parent had rights there—but none in any other Urewera blocks with sufficiently recent occupation to pass the rights on).

As will be discussed later, this pattern of narrow or limited Urewera rights probably indicates intermarriage between the Tūhoe and Ngāti Ruapani, a hapū of the Ngāti Kahungunu *iwi* that occupied the northern and western shores of Lake Waikaremoana adjacent to the Tūhoe of the Ruatāhuna area (Fig. 1.2; NZMS 170 n.d.). Maatuahu Point, from where Mihi sang her *waiata* about her beloved's departure to Ruatāhuna, is located on the northern shore west of the lake's easternmost extension (contemporary Aniwaniwa) at the mouth of the long Whanganui Inlet, which extends northwest toward Ruatāhuna.

Mihi and Whakatipus' offspring furthermore held relatively strong rights in the two blocks: although not ranked highly, their two children held senior-generation rights of 20 shares each in Waikaremoana block and 15 shares each in Ruatāhuna block, and their grandchildren 5–10 shares accordingly (AJHR 1903: Waikaremoana 370–81; Ruataahuna 635–45; Maungapōhatu 886–8). However, neither Mihi nor Whakatipu themselves appears in any of the Urewera block lists. The relative strength of their offsprings' shares shows that although the parents may have both left the Urewera lands or died, at least one had sufficient occupational rights (sustained for at least three generations before the oldest living claimant, perhaps their children in this case) as well as ancestral rights in both blocks. Mihi's waiata suggests that while she may have had rights in Waikaremoana block, the Ruatāhuna rights were perhaps Whakatipu's. On the other hand, if their children's rights to both blocks had come through only one of their parents, the other parent may have still been living in one of these blocks (probably along with their offspring) but did not appear in the block list because he or she lacked the appropriate founding ancestral rights for a rightful claim to that area. That is to say, this parent's occupation was reliant on the other parent's rights in that block (or on their children's rights).

What might be some implications of such strikingly narrow Urewera rights? The offsprings' lack of rights in any other Urewera blocks suggests that their grandparents' or parents' rights in the Urewera originated from recent ancestors who were themselves immigrants from elsewhere, probably Ngāti Kahungunu territory. Had their predecessors been resident in the Urewera for more than a few generations, marriages to longer-established Tūhoe would probably have provided wider rights to other blocks among all the descendants of that marriage. Formal recognition of Mihi and Whakatipus' offsprings' rights in the Urewera blocks, and furthermore relatively strong rights, suggests that most or all of them continued to live in one or more of the three blocks in which their rights were recognized. Nevertheless, it will be seen that their migrant origins may have held them to a stricter criterion of continuous occupation than would have been the case for long-established Tūhoe.

A complicating factor in this particular situation was the proclaimed conquest in the early 1800s (and, as will be argued later, earlier assimilation) by Ngāi Tūhoe of the Ngāti Kahungunu hapū and lands that were to become the Waikaremoana block. This situation will be examined later with regard to the commission's investigation of the block 1899–1902. Conquest, or assimilation through domination, is likely to have accelerated the normal migration and intermarriage between lands previously dominated by different hapū or *iwi*.

The Huiarau mountains, over which Mihi ki te Kapua's lover departed, are a complex of old ranges the 1000-meter crest of which runs southwest to northeast between Lake Waikaremoana and the Whakatane/Ohinemataroa and Tauranga/Waimana Rivers to the north, the two major river basins that drain north down the length of the Urewera Reserve to the Bay of Plenty (Fig. 1.2; NZMS 170 n.d.). The highest point of the Huiarau Range is the famous Maungapōhatu burial mountain (altitude 1380 meters), about 25 kilometers directly north of the main body of the lake. The crest of the Huiarau range was described to the UDNR commission as the traditional boundary between what was to become the Ruatāhuna and Waikaremoana blocks because it was earlier the boundary between the Tūhoe *iwi* and the lands of Ngāti Kahungunu *iwi*. Until the Tūhoe conquest or assimilation of what was to become the Waikaremoana block, Ngāti Kahungunu lands had extended south and east to Hawke's Bay and included the southeastern slopes of the Huiarau range as well as all of Lake Waikaremoana.

However, by the early 1800s (about five Tūhoe generations before the commission's investigation), three hapū branches of the Ngāti Ruapani hapū of the Ngāti Kahungunu *iwi* took sides with the Tūhoe against the larger part of their hapū and *iwi*. This alliance between Ngāi Tūhoe and part of Ngāti Ruapani was the basis of their proclaimed conquest and occupation of the southeastern slopes of the Huiarau range including the entire northwestern shore of Lake Waikaremoana, formerly part of the Ngāti Kahungunu territory (O'Malley 1996: 31–47; Wiri 1994). As will be described later, some Tūhoe saw the conquest as more extensive, including the southern and eastern shores of the lake as well. At least for the Tūhoe (including their Ngāti Ruapani allies) if not the Pākehā commissioners, this relatively recent political alliance and conquest was probably part of the rationale for the 1902 proposal of the Ruatāhuna-Waikaremoana amalgamation.

Many intermarriages between the Ngāti Ruapani hapū, Ngāti Kahungunu *iwi*, and Ngāi Tūhoe of adjacent areas would have occurred normally since earlier times, and would probably have increased after conquest or a more gradual shift in dominance among a cluster of hapū. The evidence of this historical process will be examined in Chap. 8. Although the earliest of these intermarriages probably long antedated the assumed conquest, and had become the basis of legitimately overlapping but contestable land rights, this point was probably lost on the 1906 appeals commission, which consequently in its confusion awarded additional shares to Ngāti Kahungunu claimants (O'Malley 1996: 44–5, citing Wiri 1994: 262–4). Ballara's seminal notion of a hapū 'cluster' and its specific history of alliances, *mana*, and relative dominance and subordination may be more clearly exemplified in the 1902 Ruatāhuna-Waikaremoana amalgamation proposal than those examined in Chap. 6.

Dougherty's recent story happens to furnish further introductory details. Mihi ki te Kapua's *waiata* supports a *whakapapa* cited by Dougherty that contains three ancestral names already mentioned in the previous chapters, and two of these names will become central to the issue examined in Chaps. 8 and 9. Strikingly in Dougherty's *whakapapa*, Murakareke is the founding ancestor, Arohana appears as the great-grandchild of Murakareke, and Kahui, Dougherty's immediate grandparent, appears as Arohana's descendant. Similarly, the composite genealogy in Fig. 8.1, referred to in Chap. 5 with regard to Whaitiripapa block and important in the following chapters, is headed by Murakareke and displays his descendants Te Arohana and Kahuwī. There, Arohana is Murakareke's great-grandson and Kahuwī (not Kahui) is Murakareke's great-great-great-grandson but by another line, descended from another of Murakareke's children. Rather than a descendant of Arohana, the Kahuwī shown in Fig. 8.1 became his adopted son after Arohana married Kahuwī's widowed mother. The origin of this Kahuwī's name was described in Chap. 5 from Tamaikoha's testimony for Whaitiripapa block (Kahuwī's father was killed in battle and his body was found covered in 'a cloak (*kahu*) of reeds (*wii*)'). The same 'Kahuwi' began to be mis-recorded as 'Kahui' in government records of the era studied here, and by 1912 when Ruatāhuna block was partitioned, partition 1 was named after the ancestor Arohana and partition 2 was named after his adopted son, mis-recorded as 'Kahui' rather than Kahuwī (Fig. 1.2).

Dougherty's *whakapapa*, as well as the Mihi ki te Kapu story, does resonate with the proposed amalgamation of Ruatāhuna and Waikaremoana. The hapū Ngāti Mura or Ngāti Murakareke (Figs. 2.1 and 3.1) was named after the ancestor Murakareke heading the *whakapapa* in Fig. 8.1, and it is likely that the Murakareke heading Dougherty's *whakapapa* is the same founding ancestor. It is also possible that the Arohana who is presented as Murakareke's great-grandchild in Dougherty's *whakapapa* is the same Arohana who is Murakareke's great-grandson in Fig. 8.1, whether or not the intervening descendants were the same. If this is the case, although Dougherty's grandparent 'Kahui' is certainly not the Kahuwī in Fig. 8.1, who preceded the former by at least five generations, he was probably named after his famous ancestor. As was described in Chap. 4, Tamaikoha's *mātāmua* grandson Kahuwi Hakeke was also probably named after his ancestor Kahuwī (follow the right side of Fig. 8.1 for the descent line). As will be seen, the struggle over the part of Ruatāhuna that by 1913 was finally named after this Kahuwī was foreseen or commemorated in these and other ways.

2 The Migrant Marriage Alliance Between Ruatāhuna and Waikaremoana Areas

The history of the Ruatāhuna and Waikaremoana blocks of the UDNR have been separately researched for the Urewera inquiry (O'Malley 1996; Bassett and Kay 2002), so in this regard an exploration of their 1902 amalgamation proposal has fuller information readily available. In addition to these sources, I took the time to work up an index for easier use of Elsdon Best's 1898 census of 'all Tūhoe' (Best 1898). This invaluable 138-page manuscript is actually composed of *whakapapa* fragments extending from most ancestors at least three generations before the senior living generation, includes marriages, spouses, and sibling groups, and was already partly cross-indexed by Best. It was almost certainly carried out by Best in preparation for the work of the commission 1899–1903 in determining land rights, which would rely on the details of such minimal genealogies, whole sibling groups, and marriages. My resulting index has enabled me to piece together lines of descent and intermarriage that were more difficult to do for the preceding chapters. I encountered very few inconsistencies in this record, and from personal experience (in Mexico and the Peruvian Andes as well as the Urewera), I know how much of Best's fieldwork effort went into it.

Nevertheless, until confirmed with contemporary *tohunga whakapapa* as well as other verifiable sources Best's work (like my own work here) is subject to his biases as well as errors. He was notoriously biased by racial dogmas of his time, but also probably by his reliance on informants whose hapū-based political bias he had come to accept. Because he does not record the sources used to compile each *whakapapa* fragment of his 1898 census, the possibility remains that he relied on only a few expert informants. However, as all Māori know well in a culture where *whakapapa* has always been a key political as well as economic principle, anyone, especially wise *tohunga whakapapa,* should avoid speaking for other hapū or descent groups unless they are very sure of their ground. It is also likely that at least some elders refused to divulge such important details of *whakapapa* to him. On the other hand, aside from the empirical consistency of his data, general cooperation with Best's effort would have been encouraged by the negotiations between Tūhoe leaders and Seddon's administration that resulted in the 1896 Act and, as argued in Chap. 2, the legitimacy gained by a commission intended to establish home-rule for the Tūhoe over the Ureweras.

In 1899 the commission held preliminary investigations of claims and boundaries in Ruatāhuna in April and, after their visit to Maungapōhatu, continued in Waimako in May. Waimako ("Waimaku" on some maps) is near the northeastern shore of Lake Waikaremoana and was also called the "Ngāti Ruapani Reserve" (O'Malley 1996: 33). As discussed in Chap. 3, the number of claims lists submitted at each sitting had accelerated rapidly, probably reflecting the opportunism of hapū aspiring to independence through demonstration of stronger ancestral rights to specific areas of land. There were a total of about 260 claims submitted for about 50 different areas of the reserve. Of these, about 28 claims were submitted for about five differently named but overlapping areas that by 1903 the commission declared under one title as the Ruatāhuna block, laid out as shown in the 1901 map (Fig. 1.2). Nevertheless, as mentioned above, by 1912 Ruatāhuna leaders pressed for a partition that eventually resulted in five separate blocks named Arohana, Kahuwī, Huiarau, Wai-iti, and Parahaki. Soon after the 28 claims for the lands that were to become Ruatāhuna were received in 1899, about 24 claims were submitted for the lands that were to become the Waikaremoana block. Although one part of this block became contentious, the Waikaremoana leaders in the investigation were determined to keep it undivided, and by 1907 it was officially established, as shown in Fig. 1.2. The apparently separate but actually interwoven histories of the establishment of each block will be examined in the following chapters.

The 28 claims for what was to become the Ruatāhuna block were made in the name of 14 hapū: Ngāi Te Ruruhe, Te Urewera, Ngāti Kakahutapiki, Ngāti Manunui, Ngāti Tāwhaki, Warahoe, Ngāi Te Riu, Tūhoe Pōtiki, Korokaipapa, Ngāti Kurī, Ngāti Tararehe, Ngāti Tokotuai, Ngā Pōtiki, and Te Aitanga o Pourangahua. By the end of the 1902 season of hearings, the hapū of successful claimants were identified as Te Urewera, Ngāi Te Riu, Ngāti Kurī, Ngāti Tu, Ngāti Manunui, Ngāti Kakahutapiki, and Ngāti Ruatāhuna—in that order.

The 24 claims for the Waikaremoana block were made in the name of 17 hapū: Ngāti Manunui, Ngāti Hinekura, Ngāi Te Riu, Ngāti Ruapani, Ngāti Ruatāhuna, Ngāti Whanaupani, Te Whanau Pani Hine Whakarau, Ngāti Pakitua, Tamakaimoana, Ngāti Taumata, Ngāti Tu, Ngāti Raoa, Ngāti Ruatāhuna, Ngāti Whakarau, Tūhoe, and Ngāti Rongo. By the end of the 1902 season of hearings, the hapū of successful claimants were identified as Tūhoe and Ngāti Ruapani. While 'Tūhoe' in this context probably meant those Urewera hapū credited with the conquest or assimilation of parts of Ngāti Ruapani hapū (of Ngāti Kahungunu *iwi*) and thus the Waikaremoana block, Best's comments on hapū of that time suggest considerable overlap with the several Ruatāhuna hapū: Ngāti Manunui was "closely related" to Ngāti Ruapani, Ngāti Tu was short for Ngāti

Tumatawhero and was "closely related" to Ngāti Manunui, and Ngāti Kakahutapiki was "a descendant" hapū of Ngāti Tumatawhero (Best 1973: 214–5).

It might also be speculated that the relatively high proportion of claimant hapū, for Ruatāhuna as well as Waikaremoana lands, reflected more strident opportunism than usual elsewhere in the UDNR. This may have been driven by what will later be argued was the high proportion of migrants in this area (including adjacent Maungapōhatu) who, as relatively recently assimilated to or conquered by Tūhoe, were not yet accepted as Tūhoe with wide ancestral rights in the Urewera and only slowing expanding occupational rights. Perhaps also reflecting the Tūhoe claim to have conquered Waikaremoana lands, a high proportion of the hapū in whose name these lands were claimed were mentioned nowhere else in the UDNR records.

At least some of the 31 individuals who in 1899 submitted claims to ancestral and occupational rights in Waikaremoana or Ruatāhuna lands, because they were speaking for one or another of these several hapū, were likely to have been influential in subsequent developments including the Ruatāhuna-Waikaremoana amalgamation proposal. A longer list of about 80 such possibly influential individuals for these two blocks was tentatively drawn up through a study of the minutebooks (investigation 1899–1903, appeals 1906–1907, and Ruatāhuna partition 1912–1913), 1903 and 1907 block lists and relative rights recognized, block committee memberships, O'Malley's and Bassett and Kays' reports, and other records of the commission. Proceeding partly on intuition, this unmanageably long list was narrowed by focusing on those individuals who, like Mihi and Whakatipus' offspring (the exemplar from Dougherty's story), appeared to have migrant origins, holding only 'narrow' rights in these two blocks and no or few others in the UDNR. This selection was sometimes augmented by Best's indications of Ngāti Kahungunu or Ngāti Ruapani origin.

Reconstruction of the recent genealogy and sibling groups of these selected individuals using Best's 1898 census soon showed evidence of marriage alliances between some of these 80 individuals. The result of these explorations is Fig. 7.1, which will be referred to as the Ruatāhuna-Waikaremoana 'migrant marriage alliance'. The comparable but probably more recent marriage alliance discovered in analysis of the proposed Parekohe amalgamation (Chap. 6, Fig. 6.4), and Ballara's conception of hapū clusters discussed in earlier contexts, were also guides for the above method.

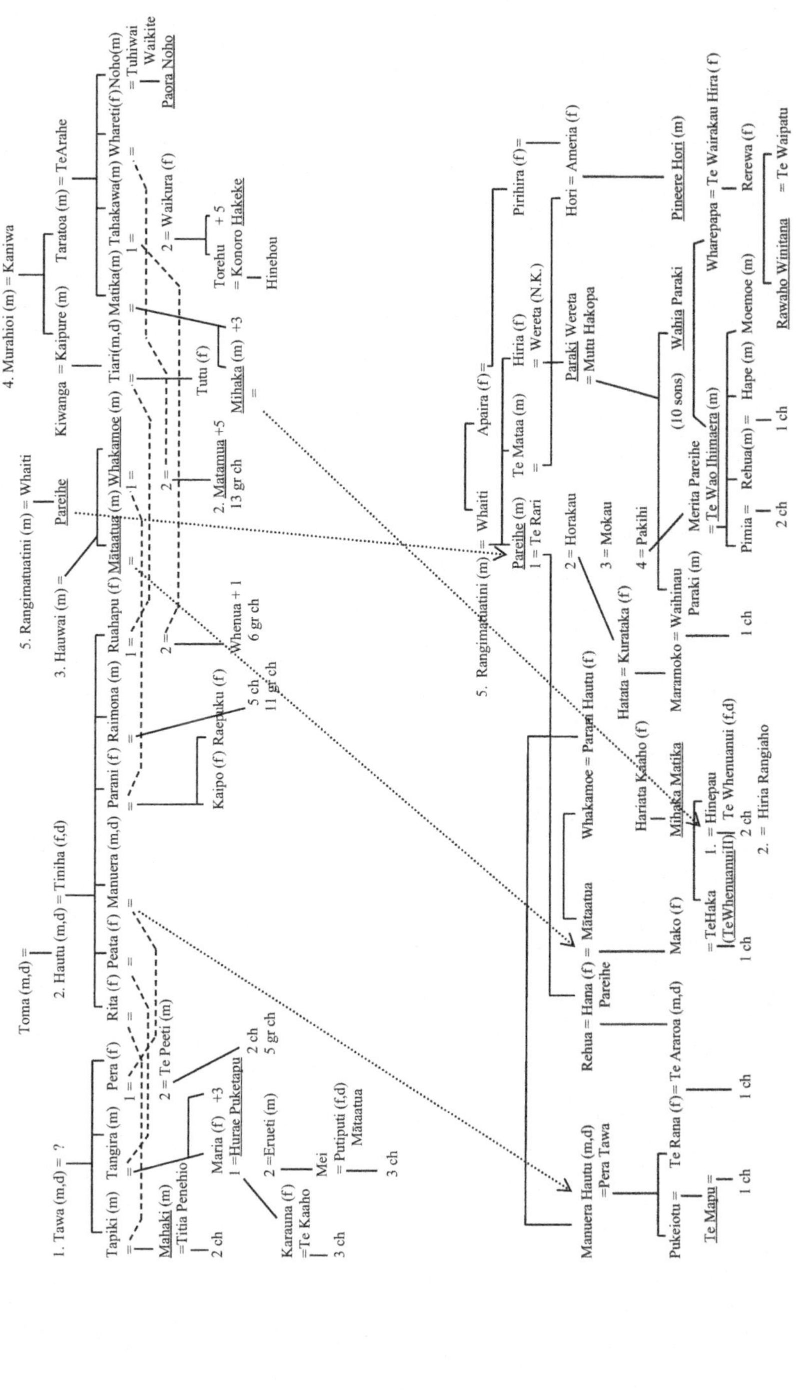

Fig. 7.1 Ruatāhuna-Waikaremoana migrant marriage alliance c. 1800–1898

Fig. 7.1 (continued)
Legend:
1. Descent groups 1. Tawa, 2. Hautu, 3. Hauwai, 4. Murahioi, and 5. Rangimatuatini
2. The long dotted-line arrows to lower section show the contemporary 5. Rangimatuatini—Pareihe descent group and its intermarriages with the other descent groups
3. Vertical solid lines depict filiation and descent lines; horizontal solid lines depict sibling groups in order of birth (some siblings not involved in intermarriage are left out, but their number sometimes show, e.g., + 3)
4. = indicates marriage to person above it (a horizontal line connecting siblings or cousins may intervene); dotted lines connect the same marriage or person. Successive marriages are numbered in order or seniority
5. Names given are 'first' names; 'surnames' usually not shown (but would be the father's 'first' name). Names of persons figuring importantly in analysis are underlined
6. Gender is marked (f)emale or (m)ale; deceased are marked (d) and, if reported by Best, Ngāti Kahungunu origin is marked 'N.K.'

Before examination of this migrant marriage alliance and influential individuals involved in it, some implications of such narrow rights in the Urewera blocks can be further explored. Tabulations of the 'surname' index of 1903 block lists revealed that a relatively high proportion of sibling groups or individuals had narrow rights to Waikaremoana and Ruatāhuna blocks but few others of the Urewera reserve. The proportion of some other block rights among those sibling groups or individuals whose rights to the Waikaremoana block were recognized might reveal patterns clarifying the history of intermarriage between this block and others of the reserve. Of the approximately 668 sibling groups or individuals in the 1903 block lists for the whole reserve, the following rough proportions were derived for comparison:

(a) about 265 or 40% were found to hold rights in Waikaremoana block;
(b) about 105 or 15–16% were found to hold narrow rights in Waikaremoana block and only a few others;
(c) about 83 or 12–13% were found to hold rights in Waikaremoana and Ruatāhuna blocks and only a few others;
(d) about 32 or 3.2% were found to hold rights in Waikaremoana and Maungapōhatu blocks and only a few others;
(e) about 19 or 2.8% were found to hold rights in Waikaremoana block only;
(f) about 13 or 1.9% were found to hold rights in Waikaremoana and Ruatāhuna blocks only.

Comparisons with Ruatāhuna and Maungapōhatu blocks were singled out above simply because they are adjacent to Waikaremoana block. Similarly, a higher proportion of 'narrow' rights is noticeable between Te Whaiti, another peripheral block on the southwestern edge of the reserve, and blocks adjacent to it, but not as striking as is the case for Waikaremoana. A similar situation appears to obtain for the long Hikurangi-Horomanga block forming the other half of the western boundary of the reserve. The difference between these three peripheral areas may have been that the Waikaremoana area was involved in a relatively recent conquest or assimilation (although Tūhoe hostilities with the Ngāti Awa, the *iwi* to the west of the reserve, were still being settled in the 1880s). Of course, the entire Urewera 'reserve' was of recent origin: as was described in the Introduction, prior to the 1870s it was more a geographic region of independent hapū or *iwi* sometimes called 'the Tūhoe' or 'the Ureweras' that attempted loose confederation as an *iwi* in the 1870s Mātaatua alliance and the 1894–1896 negotiations with Seddon that established the 1896 Act. Although since then the colonial history can be said to have consolidated Ngāi Tūhoe, subordinate as well as dominant hapū continue to assert their independence. Te Whaiti Nui a Toi region claims to have always seen itself as one or more separate *iwi*, and recently at least one leader of Ngāti Ruapani in the Waikaremoana region has protested its subordination within the 2014 statutory settlement between Ngāi Tūhoe and the Crown. On the other hand, such strains toward hapū, as well as *iwi* independence, are probably inherent in the political economy of Māori kinship.

Such narrow rights as those arising for Waikaremoana block, involving three blocks and strikingly few others of the reserve, are problematic because they stand out from the typically (and, for the Pākehā commissioners, notoriously) wide distribution of rights across the blocks of the reserve for most other Tūhoe individuals and sibling groups. Leading individuals in prestigious old descent lines often held shares in more than 20 of the 34 blocks. Insofar as 'continuous' occupation of a block by appropriate ancestors (i.e., those who were descended from a founding ancestor of the block) had to be demonstrated for three generations before the oldest living claimant to reinforce a birthright, such a wide distribution of block rights reflected sustained efforts of a descent group to *renew* lapsing occupational rights in ancestral lands, as well as the proliferation of ancestral birthrights characteristic of descent through both parents.

One might suppose that while a wider distribution of rights reflects a longer history of ancestral intermarriage and maintenance or renewals of primary residence between the Urewera blocks, the narrower distribution of rights reflects a shorter history of marriages and changes of residence. If this is a reasonable assumption, then the 40% of all Urewera sibling groups and individuals found to hold rights in Waikaremoana block as well as *many* other Urewera blocks reflects a long history of intermarriage and renewal of residence among them, probably long preceding the conquest by the Tūhoe in the early 1800s of what was later to become the Waikaremoana block. From this point of view, the alliance by Tūhoe with breakaway sections of Ngāti Ruapani, and even the 'conquest' itself, might be more accurately viewed as a relatively rapid *assimilation* of part of Ngāti Kahungunu and its territory—rapid, that is, in contrast to the much longer period of intermarriage that preceded it. This was Robert Wiri's and O'Malley's point mentioned earlier—and a key issue apparently beyond the appeal commission's (and many more recent commentators') sometimes obtuse or romanticized understanding of Māori 'conquests'.

But if the 40% proportion of all sibling groups and individuals holding rights to Waikaremoana as well as to many other blocks of the reserve implies a long history of reoccupation throughout the reserve as well as intermarriage with sections of Ngāti Ruapani or other Ngāti Kahungunu, what might be the implications of the significant 15–16% found to hold narrow rights to Waikaremoana block along with very few other Urewera blocks? Would such narrowly distributed rights indicate relatively recent migration and intermarriage between these few blocks for the descent groups involved?

That is my general conclusion, but other factors must supplement this explanation. Recent migration and intermarriage alone would not explain this relatively high proportion of narrow rights because a marriage to almost any long-established Tūhoe would devolve more than a few rights to other Urewera blocks upon the immediate next generation, and these rights could be maintained as long as occupation since a great-grandparent could be demonstrated. The most plausible explanation of such a high proportion of narrow rights is that most marriages were between descent groups *both* of which held only narrow rights. While a descent group may generally seek to widen land rights for its offspring by marrying into another descent group holding wider rights, such more privileged descent groups may be avoiding such marriages. Insofar as conquest, assimilation, or migration implies a stigma upon those dominated, these counterposed marriage strategies might be aggravated.

One way of coping with such a disadvantaged migrant status would be to form increasingly influential alliances through intermarriage with other descent groups holding only narrow rights, such as has been shown here for Waikaremoana and Ruatāhuna as well as in the case of the proposed Parekohe amalgamation (Figs. 7.1 and 6.4). These alternative migrant strategies would have been going on in both conquered or assimilated territories and the adjacent areas that tended to dominate them. Conquerors notoriously consolidated their conquest by marrying women of the vanquished, taking them back to their own lands or staying to establish occupation of the new territory. Enslaving the vanquished was another favorite theme of the British colonists, but was probably exaggerated as well as misunderstood. More importantly, if less dramatically, many early marriages were probably between Ngāti Ruapani (or other hapū of the Waikaremoana area) and Tūhoe who had immigrated into the

Waikaremoana area long before the conquest and remained long enough for their occupational rights in most other Urewera blocks to have lapsed. Some lapse of rights is also a plausible explanation of narrow rights only to Ruatāhuna or Maungapōhatu as well as Waikaremoana because these two blocks are adjacent to the latter, and occupational as well as ancestral rights would be more likely to have been sustained or re-established.

This explanation of narrow rights reinforces the conclusion that the 40% of Tūhoe found to hold rights in Waikaremoana block as well as many other Urewera blocks reflects a long history of intermarriage between the two areas. Any 'typical' migration to occupy newly conquered territory would have to be understood as overlaying the earlier long-established processes. The Waikaremoana leaders and commissioner Hurae Puketapu put the prior results of intermarriage over conquest most clearly before the appeals commission in 1906: "This was a conquest by one section of Tūhoe *over another section of Tūhoe* who had intermarried with the descendants of Ruapani" (my italics; i.e., a conquest of descent groups of Tūhoe who had earlier moved into and married members of (three) descent groups of the Ngāti Ruapani hapū of Ngāti Kahungunu). Another Waikaremoana leader Te Wao Ihimaera made the same crucial distinction from a different perspective by saying the conquest was by Ngāti Ruapani over its own hapū (UCAMB 1: 43,45). The failure of the appeals commission to understand this quite typical historical process was shown by their query of both witnesses whether or not the Ngāti Ruapani ancestral right was extinguished by the conquest, to which they both answered 'No'. Although Hurae added the clear caveat that only the right of three descent groups of Ngāti Ruapani who had *already* intermarried with Tūhoe survived the conquest, the appeals commission nevertheless took their replies as evidence that much wider Ngāti Kahungunu rights had not been extinguished and (as O'Malley documented) unjustifiably admitted many more of them to ownership in Waikaremoana block.

So a plausible explanation of the 15–16% of the Tūhoe individuals and sibling groups found in 1903 to hold narrow rights to Waikaremoana and only a few other blocks is that their descent groups accepted long periods of intermarriage with other descent groups holding similarly narrow rights while building up more extensive rights through occasional marriages into descent groups with more extensive land rights. This compromise strategy also goes some way toward explaining the lesser proportions of narrow rights in Ruatāhuna or Maungapōhatu blocks as well as Waikaremoana, shown above in proportions (c), (d), and (f). Together, these three cases constitute most of the problematic category (b). Perhaps the most puzzling case is (e), the relatively few sibling groups and individuals (2.8%) who were found to hold rights *only* to Waikaremoana block. One would suppose to the contrary that *most* of the many residents of the very large block, certainly a few hundred, would appear to have such radically limited rights insofar as their ancestral and occupational rights through their closer relatives in the vast Ngāti Kahungunu territory was ignored in their inclusion in the Urewera reserve under the 1896 Act. On the other hand, this proportion can also be seen as consistent with the compromise marrying strategy if most of the others having rights in Waikaremoana block had long since gained some rights to other Urewera areas over several generations of migration and intermarriage.

As will be seen in examination of the migrant marriage alliance below, another implication of narrow rights may need further explanation. In some of the cases of narrow rights to Waikaremoana and Ruatāhuna but few other blocks, those ancestral and occupational birthrights recognized in a younger generation appear to originate from parents who, although still probably living, were recognized to have lesser rights or not be recognized in the block lists at all. It will be argued that such cases are also best understood as continuing to hold the parents to a stricter criterion of occupation because of their migrant origin, but relieving the younger generation of this stigma. Before detailing examples of such selective recognition of occupational rights, the Ruatāhuna-Waikaremoana migrant marriage alliance in Fig. 7.1 needs to be explained in general terms.

This composite genealogy depicts a complex of marriage alliances between five descent groups over five to six generations preceding the establishment of the UDNR in 1907. The method used to derive its details was described above. The first generation of strikingly intensive intermarriage—between children of the males (from left to right) Tawa, Hautu, Hauwai, Pareihe, Kaipure, and Taratoa and their respective spouses—was probably developing at about the time of the proclaimed conquest of Waikaremoana in the early 1800s. As will be seen, participants in this intensively intermarrying generation lived about three generations before their oldest living descendants laying claims before the commission in 1899. Similarly, the conquest leaders reported by the claimants were born about three generations before this generation. The foregoing argument regarding narrow rights suggests that the migrant marriage alliance was a late example of at least several yet earlier generations of intermarriages that had long preceded the conquest, instead implying assimilation between the Tūhoe and at least three descent groups of the Ngāti Ruapani hapū of Ngāti Kahungunu *iwi*. As was the case with the Parekohe marriage alliance examined in Chap. 6, increasing common ancestors between these five descent groups and Tūhoe avoidance of marriage between cousins with a common ancestor closer than four generations probably best explains the decreasing frequency of intermarriage. In Fig. 7.1, this frequency drops from about seven in the first generation of intensive intermarriage to about five and then to two in subsequent generations.

Several other general aspects of Fig. 7.1 can be introduced here. First, there are about five different descent groups that were initially involved in the intermarriages; their leaders or *kaumātua* were (from left to right) (1) Tawa (m(ale), wife not reported); (2) Hautu and his wife Tiniha; (3) Hauwai (m, wife not reported); (4) Murahioi and his wife Kaniwa; and (5) Rangimatuatini and his wife Whaiti. Each sibling group is conventionally depicted in birth order from left to right. The generation of most intensive intermarriage was among the sons and daughters, or grandchildren, of these five 'heads of family' or *kaumatua*. It should be noted the bottom extension of the diagram in Fig. 7.1 is *contemporary* with the top section, depicting primarily the (four!) marriages, offspring, or marriage alliances of Pareihe (the son of (5) Rangimatuatini and Whaiti) with the other four descent groups (indicated by the extension of dotted-line arrows connecting the same marriage): descent group 3 through Pareihe's *mātāmua* daughter's marriage to Mātaatua Hauwai; descent groups 1 and 2 through Pareihe's grandson Te Araroa's marriage to the daughter of Manuera Hautu and Pera Tawa; and descent group 4 through his granddaughter Mako's marriage to Te Haka Te Whenuanui (Te Whenuanui II), whose sister Hinepau's husband was Mihaka Matika, *mātāmua* grandson of Taratoa and Te Arahe. Although this last marriage was only an indirect alliance for the Rangimatuatini-Pareihe descent group, in addition to this double marriage with Te Whenuanui, the Taratoa line was a very influential descent group.

As outlined in Chap. 5, Binney found that when Te Whenuanui II died in 1907, the original Te Whenuanui (I)'s name was passed on yet a third time to his sister Hinepau's son, a 'Reupene' Mihaka. Binney's important recovery of this evidence relied on two letters to the Native Ministry the details of which raise further genealogical implications of Te Whenuanui I's integration with the migrant marriage alliance. The first letter reported Te Whenuanui II's unexpected death on 2 January 1907, and was sent on

10 January by Te Wharekotua and "Mihaka Te Pouwhenua (Te Whenuanui Mihaka)" (Binney 2002: 21 fn 37). Although Wharekotua (Pahiri) appears to have no connection with the alliance, Mihaka Te Pouwhenua was probably 'Reupene' Mihaka himself. He also identified himself as 'Te Whenuanui Mihaka'—which, as son of Mihaka Matika, would be his new surname preceded by his new title as Te Whenuanui III (see Fig. 8.1). This was confirmed several weeks later in a letter from Numia Kererū to the Native Minister announcing that "the hapus of Tūhoe have set up Reupene Mihaka as successor to his uncle Te Whenuanui [II], who is now dead" (Binney 2002: 21–2). Binney notes that Numia was "a regular negotiator with government at this time", revealing "the continuing, independent bases of Tūhoe's senior leadership". Reupene's birth-name was Rangiteremauri Mihaka, the *mātāmua* son of Hinepau Te Whenuanui and Mihaka Matika, who was *mātāmua* son Matika Taratoa, *mātāmua* of the Taratoa sibling group (Fig. 8.1; Best 1898: 5; UCS 630). As can be best followed in Fig. 8.1, Hinepau was the deceased younger sister of Te Haka (Te Whenuanui II). Her and Mihaka's children Reupene or Rangiteremauri and his sister Tikina Mihaka were already adults in 1898. In the 10 January letter, Reupene appears to have also used the name Mihaka Te Pouwhenua, probably as a namesake after his mother's mother's father, Pouwhenua Rangikawhetiu (Best 1898: 106).

Further implications of Fig. 8.1 will be returned to in the following chapters. It turns out that these two marriages between two of Te Whenuanui I's children and two descent groups of the migrant marriage alliance (Fig. 7.1, groups 4 and 5) were pivotal in the resistance 1900–1907 against incursions by Tutakangahau of Tamakaimoana hapū and Numia Kererū of Ngāti Rongo hapū in both Waikaremoana and, even until 1912, Ruatāhuna.

3 Kinship, Affinity, and Political Activities of Marriage Alliance Leaders

Following the genealogy in Fig. 7.1 roughly from left to right, the kinship, marriage, and political activities of each descent group will be explained, focusing on the individuals whose names are underlined in the diagram (in some cases, as indicated by dotted-line arrows, the individual's marriage and offspring are laid out in the lower extension of descent group 5). Following the diagram closely, kinship and marriages will be described to suggest the inter-relations of alliance. Relying primarily on details as recorded in Best's 1898 census, the customarily greater ***mana*** of ***mātāmua*** (first-born) or ***tuakana*** (senior) siblings, and seniority of marriages when more than one, will be noted. In addition to outlining the recorded political activities of each leader 1899–1912, their own and their family's rights recognized in the 1903 and 1907 block lists of owners will be examined with regard to their relative rank (strong or leading; see Chap. 3), source of their rights, location of primary residence, and other implications.

3.1 Descent Groups 1 and 2

The Tawa and Hautu descent groups were pivotal, at least insofar as the first-born three children of the one group married the first-born three children of the other group. This extraordinary development almost certainly reflects an intentional alliance guided by their parents and grandparents. Two of the three remaining Hautu siblings, furthermore, married into the Hauwai and Murahioi descent groups, thereby probably laying the groundwork for the wider alliance. Parani Hautu was the senior wife of Whakamoe Hauwai, and Whakamoe's second wife was Whareti Taratoa, granddaughter of Murahioi and Kaniwa. He had children by both wives. Ruahapu Hautu, the youngest of the Hautu sibling group, married Tiare Kaipure, grandson of Murahioi and Kaniwa and first cousin of Whareti Taratoa. Ruahapu's second husband, probably after Tiare had died, was Tahakawa Taratoa, older brother of Whareti. She had children by both husbands.

In the following two generations the Tawa-Hautu triple intermarriage produced three important leaders who became prominent in the investigation of the Waikaremoana and Ruatāhuna blocks 1899–1903: Te Mapu Pukeiotu, Mahaki Tapiki, and Hurae Puketapu. Their kinship and marriage relations, and information on their influence and political activities are summarized below.

Although Te Mapu Pukeiotu was offspring of the marriage between the third-born siblings and perhaps a generation younger than the ***mātāmua*** Mahaki Tapiki (the son of the marriage of the first-born siblings), he was given the lead in the investigation of the Waikaremoana block 1899–1901. Mahaki Tapiki came into his own as ***mātāmua*** of the Tawa-Hautu alliance when Te Mapu died and he conducted the appeals cases 1906–1907. Te Mapu may have been given the earlier lead because of his better leadership skills, or because of the wide influence of his father Pukeiotu, the *mātāmua* son of Manuera Hautu and Pera Tawa. Manuera had been killed in the colonial land war (perhaps at Orakau?), leaving Pukeiotu as leader of an important family. From his parents, Pukeiotu Manuera held narrow rights in five Urewera blocks (including leading rights in Waikaremoana), and his own marriage to Meri Tamarau added rights in three more blocks to their son Te Mapu's rights.

Regardless of their expanding Urewera shares, Pukeiotu and his parents' relatively narrow rights indicate their immigrant status, at least that of their recent ancestors. Probably more importantly for the status of the family in the network of marriages shown in Fig. 7.1, Pukeiotu's younger sister Te Rana had married the son of Hana Pareihe, the *mātāmua* daughter of Pareihe Rangimatuatini and the most senior of his four wives. Finally, there is some evidence that Pukeiotu had influence among Ngāti Kahungunu who claimed rights in Waikaremoana block rejected by Tūhoe but, as explained earlier, given to them by the appeals commission on the basis of their misunderstanding the evidence. It may have been Pukeiotu the father who was sent to represent Ngāti Kahungunu interests to the 1901 investigation of Waikaremoana block that his son Te Mapu was conducting (O'Malley 1996: 39).

However, Te Mapu's own established leadership was evident in his activities before the commission. In 1899 he presented claims to the Waikaremoana block for Ngāi Te Riu hapū; to the Huiarau part of Ruatāhuna block also for Ngāi Te Riu; and to the Te Whaiti block for Ngāti Whare hapū. Ngāi Te Riu was a long-established hapū of Tūhoe, and Te Mapu clearly had the status to speak for sectors of it that had rights in Waikaremoana as well as Ruatāhuna. In 1901–1902 he conducted the case for investigation of the Waikaremoana block, and later in 1902 he became member #6 of the Ruatāhuna-Waikaremoana amalgamated block committee. In 1903 he was recognized to hold rights in seven blocks, including leading shares in Waikaremoana (#63) and strong shares (15) in Ruatāhuna. However, Te Mapu died in 1904 and Mahaki Tapiki, the customary *mātāmua* of the Tawa-Hautu alliance, took over as conductor Te Mapu's appeal regarding Waikaremoana block. It may be significant that both Te Mapu and Mahaki were assisted in their cases by Te Wao Ihimaera. Like Te Mapu's father's sister, Te Wao had married into the Rangimatuatini descent group as the husband of Pareihe's daughter by his fourth wife. As will be described later, in his own right Te Wao was also influential in both blocks.

Mahaki Tapiki was apparently the only child of Tapiki Tawa and his wife Rita Hautu, *mātāmua* son and *mātāmua* daughter of their respective sibling groups. At least in these formal terms, his *mātāmua* credentials were probably among the strongest in the migrant marriage alliance. In 1899 he was claimant to Waikaremoana block for Ngāti Ruatāhuna and Ngāti Whanaupani (hapū associated with Ruatāhuna and Waikaremoana, respectively; Ngāti Ruatāhuna was probably part of Te Urewera hapū). In 1901 he participated in the Waikaremoana investigation opposing various claimant lists. In 1902 he became member #7 of the Ruatāhuna-Waikaremoana amalgamated block committee and member #3 of the Waikaremoana block committee when the amalgamation proposal was aborted. In 1903 his rights were recognized in five Urewera blocks, including leading shares in Waikaremoana (#21) and strong shares in Ruatāhuna and Whaitiripapa blocks (the latter, again, suggests he was affiliated with Te Urewera hapū). In 1907 the appeals commission confirmed Mahaki's shares in these four blocks, and added ten shares in a fifth (Tauwhare-Manuka).

Mahaki's apparently primary affiliation with Te Urewera hapū (and Ngāti Ruatāhuna hapū, both asserted again as conductor of the 1906 appeals) is significant insofar as his Urewera rights from both parents were relatively narrow and probably immigrant in origin, and his Ngāti Ruapani (or Ngāti Kahungunu) rights were probably deeper. His wife Titia Penehio similarly held narrow (and probably immigrant) rights in both blocks, but hers along with her two older brothers were stronger and virtually leading rights in Ruatāhuna block (# 101–3, 20 shares each). Titia was the widow of Wi Tamaikoha, whose father was a leader in Te Urewera hapū in several other blocks (Chaps. 4 and 5). Titia was also a daughter of Penehio Kahuwi (Best 1898: 64), whose father was probably a descendant namesake of the key ancestor Kahuwī (aka Kahui) discussed above. Mahaki Tapiki's right to speak for these two hapū may have rested on his wife's leading rank, and may have been granted by Te Whenuanui II himself as *rangatira* of both these hapū in Ruatāhuna. In any case, at least jointly their immigrant rights in Ruatāhuna had clearly become well-established.

In 1906–1907 Mahaki Tapiki conducted the appeal for Te Whenuanui II, who, as mentioned above, had recently died. Mahaki represented Te Urewera and Ngāti Ruatāhuna hapū for Te Whenuanui II's appeals, and hapū of Waikaremoana for the appeal by Te Mapu Pukeiotu, who had also died. Te Whenuanui II's appeals had protested later changes of large and small shares in Ruatāhuna block that ignored decisions arrived at in the earlier hearings (Bassett and Kay 2002: 70–2). Mahaki's own appeal regarding Ruatāhuna block made the same point in more general terms. Te Whenuanui II had been the most influential *rangatira* in Ruatāhuna block (and others), and Mahaki's close support of his appeals probably reflected Te Whenuanui II's leadership in Te Urewera and Ngāti Ruatāhuna hapū. Regarding Waikaremoana block in his 1906 appeal, Mahaki lucidly described how in 1901 Te Mapu, supported by himself and others, had successfully opposed the inclusion of lists of certain Maungapōhatu claimants who had nevertheless been included in the final block order, and again asked that they be struck from the order. Whereas Mahaki's appeals for Te Whenuanui II regarding Ruatāhuna block were generally successful, resulting in the increased shares requested, his appeal for Te Mapu regarding the Waikaremoana block was decided against by the appeals commission. In Chap. 8 both these cases will be examined in detail for better understanding of what may have lain behind these confrontations.

Hurae Puketapu's influence and *mana* were clear in his appointment and wide acceptance among Tūhoe as one of the five Tūhoe commissioners 1899–1903. Hurae had married into the migrant marriage alliance: he was the first of two husbands of Maria Tangira, *mātāmua* daughter of Tangira Tawa and Peata Hautu (each the second-born of the intermarried sibling groups). At the commission's first meeting in 1899, Hurae spoke for five hapū associated with Waikaremoana or Ruatāhuna: Ngāti Pakitua and Ngāti Manunui (both closely associated with Ngāti Ruapani of Waikaremoana), Ngāti Hinekura (a hapū of Ngāi Te Riu hapū, as discussed in Chap. 5), and Ngāti Whanaupani. Later in 1899 he claimed Waikaremoana block for Ngāti Manunui, Ngāti Pakitua, and Ngāti Hinekura. In the 1901–1902 investigation of Waikaremoana block, he stood down as commissioner but continued to supervise it, deferring to Te Mapu as conductor and Te Wao Ihimaera regarding the contested northern boundary. In 1902 he became member #5 of the Ruatāhuna-Waikaremoana amalgamated block committee before the proposal was aborted, and in 1907 he became member #2 of the Waikaremoana hapū committee.

However, in 1903 Hurae Puketapu's Urewera rights were recognized only in Ruatāhuna and Waikaremoana blocks; while he and his three younger siblings held leading shares in Waikaremoana (#29–32, 20 shares each), he held only ten shares in Ruatāhuna block that were nevertheless highly ranked (#58). His wife Maria Tangira had rights in at least five blocks, including leading rights in Waikaremoana (#23–6) and strong rights in Ruatāhuna (#170–3) blocks. Strangely, however, their children were recognized to have rights in only one other block beside Waikaremoana and Ruatāhuna. These strikingly narrow block rights despite Hurae's influential status in several other respects remain unexplained. It may have been that he and his recent ancestors had not maintained significant occupation even in Ruatāhuna, but had usually lived in Waikaremoana block or even outside of it, perhaps in Waimako just northeast of the lake.

3.2 Descent Group 3

Marriages by Hauwai's sons Mātaatua and Whakamoe were pivotal as alliances. The ***mātāmua*** son Mātaatua married Hana Pareihe, ***mātāmua*** daughter of Pareihe Rangimatuatini by his senior wife Te Rari. Then, as described above, Mātaatua's and Hana Pareihe's daughter Mako may have established the most important alliance of the network in her marriage with Te Haka Te Whenuanui II. Mātaatua's younger brother Whakamoe married into both the Hautu and Taratoa Murahioi descent groups. He had children by both Parani Hautu and Te Whareti Taratoa, nine of which were living along with many grandchildren by 1903.

No report of Mātaatua Hauwai's political activity was found, but his younger brother Whakamoe and Whakamoe's eldest son Matamua apparently held important positions. In 1896 Best reported that "Whakamoe" was the leading chief of Ngāti Hinekura hapū in the Te Kuha area of Waikaremoana (Binney 2002: 498). Te Kuha is located in what is known as the Ngāti Ruapani reserve just south of Waimako and Tuai, but outside the area that was to become the Waikaremoana block. Assuming this chief was Whakamoe Hauwai and that his primary residence was in the Te Kuha area, and considering the more stringent requirements of occupation that were apparently applied to descendants of migrant ancestors, one wonders how far Ngāti Hinekura influence extended and where the brothers and their offspring primarily lived.

Ngāti Hinekura hapū was part of Ngāi Te Riu hapū, second to Te Urewera hapū among the several hapū named as owners of Ruatāhuna block in 1902. Although Whakamoe made no claim for either block in 1899, 13 others did for Ngāi Te Riu hapū, so some may have been deferring to him as their chief. After the 1913 partition of Ruatāhuna, Ngāi Te Riu was recognized to have major rights in Waiiti and Huiarau partitions, both of which are adjacent to Waikaremoana block. Ngāti Hinekura rights may have extended into and even beyond the Waikaremoana block as rights of the Tūhoe conquerors named in 1902 along with their Ngāti Ruapani allies as the owners of that block. Whakamoe's and Whareti Taratoa's senior son Matamua, perhaps reflecting his father's *rangatira* status in Te Kuha or his own primary residence not there but in the new block, in 1902 was member #7 of the Waikaremoana block committee and in 1907 he was continued as member #4 of that committee.

In 1903 Mātaatua Hauwai's rights were recognized by leading shares in Taneatua as well as Waikaremoana, but no other blocks. His three children by Hana Pareihe held leading shares in Ruatāhuna as well as Waikaremoana and Taneatua, indicating Hana was the source of their leading rights in Ruatāhuna. Whakamoe's two children by his senior wife Parani Hautu appear in the block lists along with and senior to his children by Te Whareti Taratoa, suggesting Parani had died and Whareti had raised them along with her seven children. Evidence given in 1912 reported that Whakamoe and Te Whareti moved (apparently from the Huiarau area of Ruatāhuna) to live in Waikaremoana where their children were born, and that after Whakamoe died Whareti had left Waikaremoana as well as the Urewera to live "with a Pakeha" in Tolaga Bay on the east coast (NACMB 2: 55]. By 1912–1913 Matamua (Whakamoe II) had succeeded to his father's name and claimed permanent homes in both Waikaremoana and Ruatāhuna blocks, and described his parents' houses and cultivations in the Huiarau partition of Ruatāhuna (NACMB 2: 58). Whakamoe (I) had apparently died before 1903, because he does not appear in any of the block lists and all his children held senior generation shares.

Most or all of Whakamoe I's numerous offspring probably continued to live with their own families in Waikaremoana, Ruatāhuna, or other blocks of the Urewera because their rights were recognized in five blocks including leading shares in Ruatāhuna (#56–64) and Taneatua (#79–89), and very strong shares in Waikaremoana (#107–15) and Paraeroa (#99–105). Had he lived, Whakamoe would have held leading rights in Waikaremoana and Taneatua (as his brother still did), but his second wife Te Whareti Taratoa's own leading rights in Ruatāhuna and Paraeroa, strong rights Waikaremoana, and rights in Taneatua reinforced his rights and added leading rights in Ruatāhuna and Paraeroa blocks to those of their children. No Hautu shares are reported in any block, but the consistent senior ranking and equal shares of Parani Hautu's two children by Whakamoe in the same sibling group as his children by Te Whareti suggest Parani also had strong rights in these blocks.

Altogether, these 1903 share allocations suggest that the rights of many offspring in the Hauwai, Pareihe, Hautu, and Murahioi-Taratoa descent groups in Ruatāhuna and Waikaremoana and even a few other Urewera blocks (in this case, Taneatua and Paraeroa) had, through advantageous marriages and continued occupation, overcome their migrant origins and become established.

3.3 Descent Group 4

Matika, Tahakawa, and Noho Taratoa (the three brothers of Whareti Taratoa, Whakamoe's second wife) or their children gained immediate influence among the Urewera blocks through their marriages. In at least two cases, these were—like Mako Mātaatua's marriage to Te Haka Te Whenuanui—into Tūhoe *rangatira* families of wide *mana*. Their father Taratoa Murahioi appears to have had only narrow immigrant rights himself, but to have been among the first in the migrant marriage alliance to marry into a Tūhoe descent group with rights in several blocks beyond Waikaremoana and Ruatāhuna. Comparison with rights through his brother Kaipure suggest that Taratoa's wife Te Arahe may have been the source of their offspring's leading rights in Paraeroa as well as reinforcing their leading rights in Ruatāhuna and Taneatua. As will be seen later, Te Arahe was a crucial *whakapapa* link from Arohana, a founding ancestor in the northern end of Ruatāhuna block (Fig. 8.1; UCAMB 1: 223, 2: 54).

Taratoa and Te Arahe's *mātāmua* son Matika married Hariata Kaaho, from an established descent group of Tūhoe, adding rights in about five other blocks to their children's' rights; although some of Taratoa's ancestral rights had lapsed (including the Rūātoki blocks), the addition included leading rights to Paraeroa block. Then in the third generation, Mihaka Matika (the *mātāmua* son of Taratoa and Te Arahes' *mātāmua* son Matika) married Te Hinepau Te Whenuanui. Hinepau was the younger sister of Te Haka Te Whenuanui (Te Whenuanui II), so in this way the Rangimatuatini and Murahioi descent groups together allied themselves with the leading family of Ruatāhuna block and Te Urewera hapū, which was also dominant in several other blocks of the reserve.

Other political activities of the Taratoa descent group developed rapidly. In 1899 Matika Taratoa claimed Ruatāhuna block for Tūhoepōtiki hapū (probably referring broadly to Te Urewera hapū), and in 1902 he was member #3 for the Paraeroa amalgamation block committee. These positions were probably in recognition of his mother Te Arahe's high rank in Ruatāhuna and Paraeroa. However, there is evidence that Matika left Ruatāhuna when his "first wife" died, and that after resettling in Waimana (just north of the reserve on the Waimana River) he himself died about 1906 and was buried there (UCAMB 2: 58, 49). The shareholding of Matika's sibling group suggests that while in 1903 they were all recognized to hold leading rights in Ruatāhuna (#35–8, probably reflecting their mother Te Arahe's rights), they were not so recognized in Waikaremoana block (#406–9). Furthermore, although in Ruatāhuna all their shares were raised from only 10 in 1903 (despite their status as a senior generation) to 20 in 1907, in Waikaremoana the shares of the two older siblings Matika and Tahakawa were only 5 compared to their younger siblings' 20 shares in 1903, and remained so in 1907. This evidence suggests that while the sibling group and their predecessors had already achieved acceptance as settled occupants probably of Ruatāhuna or Paraeroa, their rights in Waikaremoana may have weakened accordingly, especially those who had moved further away or even out of the reserve. If Matika had indeed been buried in Waimana and his body not returned to Ruatāhuna or Waikaremoana, this could well have compromised his rights there.

Whatever the status of Matika himself, his *mātāmua* son Mihaka Matika's record reflects increasing influence in several Urewera blocks. In 1902 Mihaka became member #4 on the Paraeroa block committee, and in 1907 he became member #4 on the Ruatāhuna hapū committee, #7 on the Paraeroa hapū committee, and #6 on the Taneatua hapū committee. In 1902 Mihaka's younger brother Haki Matika also became member # 7 of the Kohuru-Tukuroa block committee. As will be discussed in later chapters, in the 1912–1913 partition of Ruatāhuna block Mihaka conducted the defense for his deceased brother-in-law Te Whenuanui II against Numia Kererū's claim for part of Manawarū at the northern end of the block.

The second-born sibling Tahakawa Taratoa's first marriage to Ruahapu Hautu (widow of his cousin Tiari) was more productive of children and grandchildren than further Urewera block rights, but his second wife Waikura Himiona added rights in several blocks to their children's' rights. Their *mātāmua* daughter Torehu married Konoro Hakeke, the *mātāmua* grandson of Tamaikoha, allying the Taratoa descent group with one of the more influential *rangatira* of Te Urewera and other hapū of the middle and lower Tauranga/Waimana River valley (Chaps. 4 and 5). Augmented by rights of his two wives, in 1903 Tahakawa's children were recognized to hold leading rights in Omahuru, Karioi, and Paraeroa as well as Ruatāhuna and Waikaremoana blocks.

On the other hand, neither Tahakawa nor his offspring are recorded to have laid any claims nor become members of block committees 1899–1907. As mentioned in Chap. 5, a 'Whenua' said to have submitted a claim for Whaitiripapa block may have been Tahakawa's younger son Whenua Tahakawa, but the claim was apparently taken up by another member of Ngāti Ruatāhuna hapū. However, in 1912 Te Whenua Tahakawa did help to conduct his cousin Mihaka Matika's case in support of Te Whenuanui II in the partition of Ruatāhuna block. There was evidence given in this case that Tahakawa, as well as his elder brother Matika, had lived primarily in Paraeroa (midway down the Tauranga-Waimana River) and later Tahakawa moved even further north to live at Ohiwa on the coast, and that Whenua Tahakawa and other children were born there (NACMB 1: 240). This evidence supports the suggestion above that Matika's and Tahakawa's small shares and apparent loss of status in Waikaremoana block was due to lapse of current as well as recent ancestral occupation, perhaps aggravated by settlement outside the Urewera. Conversely, the full shares allocated to their two younger siblings Te Whareti and Noho probably reflects their renewal of occupational rights in Waikaremoana after departing Ruatāhuna with their families.

Similarly, while the Taratoa siblings' and Matika's children's shares were far from leading rank in Waikaremoana (#406–13), his younger brother Tahakawa's children's shares were all of leading rank there (#73–9) but only small (3 each) except for the two youngest (including Te Whenua Tahakawa), who received a full 20 shares each. Although this may indicate they were both borne of the senior wife and reflect her rights there, Te Whenua's later role in the 1912 partition of Ruatāhuna suggests that he and his younger sister had also moved back to renew ancestral occupation in Waikaremoana. On the other hand, all the Tahakawa children held a leading 10 shares each in Ruatāhuna block, where their father Tahakawa apparently resided and held a leading 20 shares. In any case, these striking disparities in recognition or refusal of ancestral or even current occupational rights, even within relatively well-established descent groups, probably reflect the ambivalence of migrant status in a history of conquest, assimilation, intermarriage, and shifting residence within a narrow range of Urewera blocks.

The role of the youngest sibling Noho Taratoa illustrates the same precariousness of occupational rights in descent groups of migrant origin. He married Tuhiwai Waikite of another established Tūhoe descent group holding shares in ten blocks including Ruatāhuna (but not Waikaremoana). In 1899 Noho claimed Ruatāhuna block for Te Aitanga a Pourangahua (the only time such a hapū was named before the commission), and in 1902 he became member #5 of the Ruatāhuna block committee. Although Noho Taratoa and Tuhiwai Waikite together had rights in as many as 16 blocks, their only child Paora Noho himself came to hold shares in only six of them, far fewer than his Taratoa cousins. In addition to loss of rights through lapse of recent ancestral occupation (as was probably the case for the Rūātoki blocks), it is likely that Noho Taratoa and his son Paora Noho lost or weakened their occupational rights to several blocks by returning to live in Waikaremoana block or even outside of it. Paora reports that they moved when his mother Tuhiwai died (NACMB 1: 232) and in 1912 he and his father were apparently still living in Waikaremoana rather than Ruatāhuna (NACMB 1: 291). Another report at that time indicates Paora Noho returned from Waikaremoana to Ruatāhuna about 1910 in order to maintain his parents' occupational rights there (NACMB 2: 55). As will be detailed in Chap. 9, Paora furnished the main testimony in the 1912 partition of Ruatāhuna, assisting his Taratoa first cousins Mihaka Matika and Te Whenua Tahakawa in support of Te Whenuanui II's case against the division of Manawarū at the northern end of Ruatāhuna block.

3.4 Descent Group 5

Descent group 5 from Rangimatuatini and Whaiti, depicted in the bottom section of Fig. 7.1, serves to review some of the marriage alliances of the other descent groups and exemplifies further connections between Waikaremoana and Ruatāhuna blocks. Immigrant origins may have been more far-flung. A Mataa Rangimatuatini, predecessor or namesake of Pareihe's father Rangimatuatini, may have immigrated from Taupo, probably to Waikaremoana when it was still under control of Ngāti Kahungunu *iwi* (Best 1898: 47). Also suggesting such a predecessor, Pareihe's younger brother was also named Te Mataa and had two wives both of whom had come from Taupo. As will be described below, both Te Mataa and his younger sister Hiria had grandchildren who became influential in Ruatāhuna.

Rangimatuatini's and Whaiti's *mātāmua* son Pareihe apparently fathered an extensive but only partly identified descent group intermarried with several notable Ruatāhuna families of the Tawa-Hautu-Hauwai-Murahioi immigrant network. Most strikingly, Best's 1898 census displays Pareihe's unusual number of wives (four) and at least some of their offspring. His wives' origins remain unclear, and the 1903 and 1907 block lists confuse some of them with their children as well as being mutually inconsistent. The consistency of Best's 1898 census suggests it is the more reliable source, and what appears in Fig. 7.1 is collated from five different pages of his manuscript. A rough estimation below of the time of Pareihe's marriages from the generations of their offspring suggests all four marriages occurred in the 1850s, not much later than the estimate of 1820–1840s made earlier for the most intensively intermarrying generation of the migrant marriage alliance.

However, the other records are quite inconsistent. Pareihe is not recorded to have appeared in the Urewera claims or minutes of the hearings, nor to have become a member in any of the block committees. Nor does he appear in any of the block lists, suggesting either that no appropriate recent ancestor had established occupation in Waikaremoana or any other block, or that he continued to live outside the Urewera blocks, or that he had died by 1903. Five persons bearing his 'surname' (and thus apparently his children) were recognized each to have rights in five blocks, including Ruatāhuna as well as Waikaremoana. Assuming the 1907 block list for Waikaremoana to be the most accurate (insofar as this would be their likely origin as immigrants), Pareihe's living children with rights recognized in that block (# 469–74) were Kurataka (f), Te Rari (f), Romi (f), Merita (f), Te Ururoa (m), and Ngawai (f), all adults and holding 20 shares each. However, Best's census shows Te Rari was Pareihe's senior wife, not his *mātāmua* daughter, and that Kurataka was his daughter by his second wife Horakau and Merita was his daughter by his fourth wife Pakihi. Despite such strange inconsistencies, it is significant that the same six children (or wife and five children by other wives) who had strong rights in Waikaremoana block were also recognized to have strong rights in Ruatāhuna block (20 shares each in 1907, although Te Romi was identified as a male rather than a female, and Te Ururoa was the youngest rather than Ngawai). Their shares in the other three blocks ranged only from three to five shares, and in two of them only one of the children was recognized to have any rights.

However shadowy Pareihe, his several wives, and his children might remain, they were connected by kinship or marriage to three important Ruatāhuna leaders and at least indirectly to the other four immigrant descent groups. The latter can be best reviewed following Fig. 7.1 from the point of view of the Rangimatuatini-Pareihe descent group. The key marriage was probably between Pareihe's and his first wife Te Rari's daughter Hana Pareihe to Mātaatua Hauwai, the *mātāmua* of the two Hauwai brothers. This marriage was followed in the next generation by the marriage of Hana's and Mātaatua's daughter Mako to Te Haka, who was to become Te Whenuanui II. Because Te Haka's sister Hinepau married Mihaka Matika, the Pareihe family had also gained an indirect connection with the influential Taratoa siblings though their *mātāmua*'s *mātāmua* son Mihaka. Meanwhile, Hana Pareihe's son Te Araroa (by another husband) married Manuera Hautu's and Pera Tawa's daughter Te Rana, establishing an indirect link between the Pareihe family and both the Hautu and the Tawa sibling groups. Although Hana's son Te Araroa apparently died young, he left her with a grandson Te Pou Araroa, age 19 in 1907 and Pareihe's great-grandson. Because his mother Te Rana's brother was Pukeiotu Manuera, this young man was also first cousin of Te Mapu Pukeiotu, who conducted the 1901–1902 investigation of Waikaremoana block. Meanwhile, the Pareihe family had gained another marriage connection to Te Mapu and the Hautu descent group. As mentioned earlier, upon Te Mapu's death Mahaki Tapiki, the customary *mātāmua* of the Tawa-Hautu intermarriage, took over Te Mapu's appeal in 1906 with the assistance of Te Wao Ihimaera, who had married Pareihe Rangimatuatini's daughter by his fourth wife.

Although such indirect links with other descent groups do not have the leverage of kinship or a direct marriage alliance, their consistency and mutual reinforcement, in this case, might reflect concerted political interests. In any case, Pareihe's descent group was linked directly with at least four important Ruatāhuna and Waikaremoana leaders through kinship or marriage: Te Wao Ihimaera, Rawaho Te Winitana, Pineere Hori, and Wahia Paraki. The connections of each will be examined below.

Te Wao Ihimaera married Merita Pareihe, the daughter of Pakihi who was apparently the fourth and most junior wife of Pareihe. However, in 1898 (the time of Best's census) Te Wao and Merita already had four children, the eldest two of which had married and themselves had children, indicating this fourth marriage of Pareihe's would not have been long after his first and second marriages, which had also produced grandchildren. Although Te Wao Ihimaera's land rights were narrow (in only two other blocks beside Waikaremoana and Ruatāhuna), his Ruatāhuna rights were apparently well-established (he was said by the appeals commissioners to be "partly of Tūhoe and partly of Ngāti Ruapani"; AJHR 1907 G-4: 13).

Te Wao's reputation can be explicated somewhat. In 1899 he claimed the Huiarau part of Ruatāhuna block for Ngāi Te Riu hapū and Ngāti Hinekura (a part of Ngāi Te Riu), and Waikaremoana block for Ngāti Ruapani hapū (probably only those parts of the hapū allied with Tūhoe in the conquest). In 1902 he became a member #7 of the Ruatāhuna-Waikaremoana amalgamated block committee, and then member #2 of the Waikaremoana block committee when the amalgamation was aborted. In 1907 his son Hape Te Wao became member #7 of the Waikaremoana hapū committee. In 1901 and again in the 1906 appeal Te Wao helped lead Te Mapu Pukeiotu's and later Mahaki Tapiki's cases in opposition to persistent claims for the Waikaremoana block from various Maungapōhatu hapū. Chapter 8 will be devoted to this particular development but, as will be seen, Te Wao's knowledge was deferred to with particular regard to the northern boundary of Waikaremoana. In the 1912–1913 partition of Ruatāhuna Te Wao was an important witness for the *rangatira* Numia Kererū's conduct of the case. Furthermore, in 1918 Te Wao and Rawaho Winitana (who had participated with Te Wao in the 1901 and 1906 cases) submitted well-supported but apparently ignored petitions to the Crown to exclude Waikaremoana and Ruatāhuna blocks from the Crown's purchase campaign so that they could be developed agriculturally by their owners (Webster 2004: 131–4).

In evidence given for Numia Kererū's case in 1912, Te Wao emphasized that he had "permanent homes" in both Ruatāhuna and Waikaremoana, including cultivations and houses of his own as well as his parents and his elders in the Huiarau part of Ruatāhuna (NACMB 2: 58). The implied land rights were probably the basis of his reputation as half Tūhoe and half Ngāti Ruapani. In evidence given for Te Mapu Pukeiotu in 1901, he had described his ancestral residence in Waikaremoana block to be at the head of Whanganui inlet at Te Onepu, the mouth of Te Huiarau stream (UMB 5: 372–3; this is the northeast arm of the lake up which Mihi ki te Kapua's lover had disappeared in Dougherty's *waiata*). This location was probably on the main route over the Huiarau range between Lake Waikaremoana and Ruatāhuna. He said that the settlement there belonged to Ngāi Te Riu hapū, and that his ancestor Paenahue had lived there and been killed there. Te Wao's father Ihimaera Paenahue, who was probably either the son of this ancestor or a namesake, had probably died by 1903. However, his father's younger brother Te Waiwai Paenahue was recognized to have 5 shares in Ruatāhuna, 10 shares in Tarapounamu-Matawhero, and 20 shares in Waikaremoana (#222, with 3 children). As well as occupation, the strength of these latter rights probably reflects Ngāti Ruapani hapū affiliation gained from Paenahue's or earlier marriages of Ngāi Te Riu at Onepu. In 1903 Te Wao Ihimaera and his younger brother Wharepapa were recognized to have shares in Maungapōhatu as well as these three blocks, Te Wao held strong shares in Ruatāhuna (#430), and both had strong shares in Waikaremoana (#227–8). Probably through their mother Merita Pareihe, Te Wao's four children were recognized to have shares in Taneatua and Parekohe blocks as well as the four blocks in which Te Wao held shares.

This distribution of Urewera rights over several generations again suggests the gradual recognition of immigrant rights for a younger generation with continued occupation while those of their elders' generation remained weak. Best's record of Te Wao's mother is ambiguous, but Winiata Te Kowhai was his brother Wharepapa's mother. If she was also Te Wao's mother or step-mother, and later went by another name, a 'Waipare' Kowhai holding 20 shares (contrasting with her two sisters' 5 shares) in Ruatāhuna in 1907 may have been Ihimaera Paengahue's widow and Te Wao's as well as Wharepapa's mother. If she was, the recognition of her strong shares in Ruatāhuna helps to explain the strengthening of Te Wao's rights in that block, and may indicate that his father and mother had moved from Waikaremoana (where all three Te Kowhai sisters held strong shares, but in no other blocks). Meanwhile, the apparent weakening of his brother Wharepapa's rights in Ruatāhuna may have reflected his return and re-settlement in Waikaremoana—perhaps at Onepu on the Whanganui Inlet where they both had patrimonial rights under Ngāi Te Riu hapū, or elsewhere under their Ngāti Ruapani rights. Te Wao apparently maintained his active occupation of both blocks and affiliation with both hapū; in addition, he had married into the influential Pareihe descent group.

The brothers Rawaho and Waipatu Winitana were Te Wao's nephews by marriage to his brother Wharepapa's daughter Rerewa. Their connection to the wider network of alliances needs to be examined because their leadership roles in Waikaremoana and Ruatāhuna were important at the time (and one of their probable descendants was an important participant in Ngāi Tūhoe's 2014 settlement with the Crown (Wai 2445, 3.1.3).

Rawaho Te Winitana along with Te Wao Ihimaera supported Te Mapu Pukeiotu's conduct of the 1901 opposition to claims to Waikaremoana, and its continuation before the 1906–1907 appeals commission conducted by Mahaki Tapiki. Rawaho Winitana presented no claims in 1899, but in 1902 he became member #5 of the Waikaremoana block committee, and in 1907 his younger brother Te Waipatu became member #1 of the Waikaremoana hapū committee and a member of the Komiti Nui (the General Committee of the UDNR) in 1908. Following Rawaho's opposition to Maungapōhatu claimants in the commissions' 1901 and 1906 hearings, he also appeared before the 1912–1913 court hearings on the Ruatāhuna partition, and successfully claimed increased shares for 32 persons in the Waiiti part of the block (Bassett and Kay 2002: 78,89; NACMB 2: 91–2).

As mentioned above, in 1918 both Te Wao Ihimaera and Rawaho Winitana headed petitions to the Crown to exclude Waikaremoana and Ruatāhuna blocks from the depredations of the Crown's purchase campaign so that agricultural development by its owners could be pursued. The petition headed by Rawaho had 99 signatories, was the most comprehensive plan, and asked that the Rūātoki blocks be reserved for development as well. This petition clearly reflected Rawaho's widening influence and, significantly, his rights in hapū more closely associated with the central and northern blocks of the Urewera. As will be explained more fully in Chap. 9 and Volume II, the continued leadership of the Winitana brothers in resistance to the Crown's purchase campaign 1915–1921 allied them with the wider Apitihana ('oppositionist') movement. However, in 1921 the Crown successfully pressed other Tūhoe leadership into support of its pre-emption of the entire Waikaremoana block, leaving Ngāti Ruapani virtually landless in their own ancestral area.

The range of the family's narrow shareholdings, and affiliation with hapū outside the usual Waikaremoana and Ruatāhuna ambit, needs some explanation. Rawaho and Te Waipatu were #2 and #4 among six siblings, and part of a relatively young descent group holding only narrow Urewera rights. In 1907 both their parents (Te Winitana Poututu and Te Heru Te Waaka) were still alive, and Rawaho Te Winitana had only one young child (and Te Waipatu none). The parents each held shares in only three blocks, but both held strong shares in Waikaremoana (#597 and #383, respectively). The father Te Winitana's shares were larger in Ruatāhuna than Te Heru's (10 and 3, respectively). The mother Te Heru held ten shares in

Maungapōhatu, and in 1903 one of them held leading shares in Paraoanui block (#70–3), but this was apparently lost in the partitioning of that block.

Significantly, the father Te Winitana also held ten shares in Kohuru-Tukuroa block (#241). Probably indicating the primary source of their rights, Rawaho and a sister were listed with their father in that block, and all siblings were listed with their father in Ruatāhuna. On the other hand, in Waikaremoana and Maungapōhatu blocks, all siblings were listed with their mother. In the 1906–1907 appeals case, additional information was offered by Rawaho himself regarding his residence as well as his hapū affiliation. He declared his hapū affiliations to be Ngāti Rongo, Hamua, and Ngāti Kurī, and reported that he was living in Waikaremoana (UCAMB 2: 126). Ngāti Kurī is associated with the Waiiti part of Ruatāhuna block, and Rawaho was demanding increased shares there. In this situation, it is all the more significant that he named Ngāti Rongo and Hamua hapū first, insofar as they were usually associated with Rūātoki (at the opposite end of the Ureweras). Interestingly, with the exception of one hesitant mention of Ngāti Rongo, in 1899 none of these hapū had made claims to Waikaremoana—where Rawaho said he was living in 1907. On the other hand, the implicit priority he gave these hapū in 1907 helps explain the inclusion of the Rūātoki blocks in the petition to the Crown which he led in 1918.

The distribution of 1903 block rights in this family, and its connection to the wider alliance by marriage to Te Wao Ihimaera's brother's daughter Rerewa, suggests a relatively late stage in the gathering and maintenance of occupational rights by immigrants from Waikaremoana or Ngāti Kahungunu area. Rawaho's emphasis on hapū rights probably gained through marriage and occupation in Kohuru-Tukuroa by his father's predecessors, while living in Waikaremoana where he had rights through both parents that perhaps needed restoring after ancestral occupation in Ruatāhuna and Maungapōhatu, suggests the kind of political straddling that was necessary for some generations before full acceptance was gained among descendants of other hapū with much wider rights. However, the wide support and sophistication of Rawaho's 1918 petition to the Crown also reflects the success of the descent group in gaining this influence.

The two leaders in Fig. 7.1 remaining to be discussed are Hori Te Mataa and Paraki Wereta, both close nephews of Pareihe Rangimatuatini: Hori was the son of Pareihe's younger brother Te Mataa, and Paraki was the son of Pareihe's younger sister Hiria. As noted above with regard to

Pareihe's father, Best reported in his 1898 census that Te Mataa may have been named after a predecessor who, like both of Te Mataa's wives, had immigrated from Taupo. Best also noted that Hiria's husband Wereta was 'N.K.', indicating that he was an immigrant from Ngāti Kahungunu, that is, either from that *iwi*'s lands southeast of Lake Waikaremoana or from the part of Ngāti Ruapani hapū that remained loyal to Ngāti Kahungunu.[1]

In 1902 Hori Te Mataa became member #1 on the Waikaremoana block committee, but no other political statuses were recorded. However, his son Pineere (alias Pomare) Hori became in important leader along with the prominent elder Te Amo Kokouri and others in the Apitihana opposition movement that refused cooperation with the Urewera Consolidation Scheme throughout the several years of its operation. Pineere Hori's resistance, and the attacks of the scheme's commissioners on his leadership and land resources, has been documented elsewhere (Webster 2004: 131–4; 484–5; 556–94 and will be described in Chaps. 7 and 8 of Volume II). In 1903 his father Hori Te Mataa and Hori's sister were recognized to hold strong shares (20 each, #419–20) in Waikaremoana, ten shares each in Ruatāhuna, and small shares in only two other blocks. Te Mataa's two children Pineere and his sister received the usual half as many shares in Waikaremoana and Ruatāhuna blocks, but none in the other two blocks, indicating the descent group's occupational rights had lapsed there. In 1907 the parents' and their children's' shares in Ruatāhuna were doubled; as will be discussed in the next chapter, this occurred with several other of the descent groups in the migrant marriage alliance.

Paraki Wereta was the son of Pareihe's sister and Wereta, an immigrant from Ngāti Kahungunu. Although Paraki and his wife Mutu Hakopa each held only narrow rights in the Urewera blocks (small shares in only two other blocks aside from Waikaremoana and Ruatāhuna), both held strong rights in both of the latter blocks (20 shares in 1907, #335,363 and 498,497, respectively). Furthermore, although Paraki Wereta was only a second-generation immigrant from Ngāti Kahungunu, he had apparently already achieved established *mana* in what was to become the Ruatāhuna block. In 1896 Best reported that he was the "chief" of Ngāti Manunui hapū the main settlement of which was Te Umuroa, a *marae* now located about four kilometers south of the township of Ruatāhuna (Binney 2002: 498; Binney adds that Paraki was also called 'Tiakiwhare'). Ngāti Manunui hapū was one of the seven hapū found in 1902 to have the rights to Ruatāhuna block, and one of the three hapū found to have rights to the Parahaki subdivision of the block in 1913 (see Fig. 9.1).

In 1899 Paraki Wereta claimed Ruatāhuna for Ngāti Manunui and, significantly, also submitted a claim for Te Waipotiki block (near Rūātoki) in the name of Ngāti Rongo hapū. He and Rawaho Winitana are the only leaders in this marriage alliance network to have claimed affiliation with this hapū. (Ngāti Rongo's primary block rights were further north in the middle and lower Whakatane basin but, as will be seen, it gained official rights in Ruatāhuna in 1913). In 1902 Paraki became member #4 of the Ruatāhuna-Waikaremoana amalgamated block committee and, when that plan was aborted, the Ruatāhuna block committee. In 1907 he was continued in that position, and in 1908 he also became a member of the Komiti Nui, the General Committee intended to be in control of the whole reserve. In 1907 his son Wahia Paraki became member #3 of the Waikaremoana hapū committee. It may be significant that while both (as well as the mother Mutu Hakopa) were recognized to have strong shares in Ruatāhuna as well as Waikaremoana, it appears that the father's activities were centered in the former block while the son's were in the latter block. This may have reflected their effort to maintain occupational rights in both blocks, and perhaps separate primary residences.

One source of Paraki Wereta's and Mutu Hakopa's surprisingly well-established influence in Ruatāhuna as well as Waikaremoana may have been the size and maturity of their family: by 1903 they had ten children, all of whom were adult males, and all of whom were recognized to have strong rights in both blocks. By 1907 the three oldest sons had 16 children, and the ***mātāmua*** son had 10 of them (Ruatāhuna # 497–524; Waikaremoana # 335–62). In both blocks, all of Paraki and Mutus' children were found to have ten shares and all their grandchildren five shares (i.e., strong shares of junior generations). This was an unusually consistent recognition of high status that suggests it made no difference in which block they were living, at least in the case of this expansive descent group. Their son Wahia Paraki, who aside from his father appeared most frequently in the records, was son #8 of the ten and apparently had no children by 1907. I have not yet tried to trace the political roles of the other siblings nor their wives, nor to identify Wahia's wife. However, it is probable that the relatively established influence of their mother Mutu Hakopa's immigrant family in both blocks reinforced the expanding political influence of Paraki and his son Wahia.

Paraki Wereta's status as the 'chief' (i.e., the ***rangatira***) of Ngāti Manunui hapū by 1896 might explain the other indicators of the family's influence regardless of their relatively recent immigrant status. The inclusion of his family in the extensive Pareihe Rangimatuatini descent group and its marriage alliances may also have been a factor in their prominence. However, as was pointed out in the introduction of this section, the Ngāti Manunui hapū was overlapped or closely related to at least two of the other hapū recognized to have rights to the Ruatāhuna block (Ngāti Tu and Ngāti Kakahutapiki) as well as the Ngāti Ruapani hapū of Waikaremoana block. Ngāti Manunui hapū was not recognized to have rights in any other block of the reserve except Ruatāhuna. When in early 1899 the Tūhoe commissioners named the hapū of the Urewera, Ngāti Manunui was named by Hurae Puketapu for Ruatāhuna, not by Tutakangahau who named all the other hapū for that area. Hurae was one of the Tūhoe commissioners and himself affiliated with Ngāti Ruapani. Ngāti Manunui (and Ngāti Tu or Tumatawhero) might have gained recognition only recently as independent of Ngāti Ruapani, and enjoyed only recent, and perhaps ephemeral, status as descent groups of Ngāti Ruapani that were more firmly established in Ruatāhuna than Waikaremoana. In any case, these ambiguities of hapū status attest to the long history of immigration, intermarriage, and assimilation between the two blocks.

4 Conclusion

This chapter has introduced the extensive migrant marriage alliance that was beginning to take shape in the area that was to become Waikaremoana and Ruatāhuna blocks about the time of the Tūhoe conquest of the former area in the early 1800s. It concluded with summaries of the resulting connections of kinship, affinity, and political activities of leaders in this alliance 1899–1913. Although affiliations with the several hapū involved remain unclear, the longer history of marriage alliance and expanding influence may support the notion of a hapū cluster. The complication of Tūhoe conquest or assimilation of descent groups or hapū of another *iwi* in what was to become the Waikaremoana block of the UDNR, and the possible stigmatization of migrants between nearby areas of the UDNR by longer-established Tūhoe, has emerged in the details of this longer history. In any case, the migrant marriage alliance's network of key leaders in Ruatāhuna and Waikaremoana blocks was probably a major factor in the proposal and planning of their amalgamation in May of 1902.

Chapter 8 will examine the commission's records of confrontations between the leaders of the migrant marriage alliance and other claimants in the investigation and appeals for each of these two blocks through to the establishment of the Urewera District Native Reserve in 1907. The obscured but central role of three Tūhoe *rangatira* and leaders of influential hapū begins to emerge: Te Whenuanui II of Te Urewera hapū, Tutakangahau of Tamakaimoana hapū, and Numia Kererū of Ngāti Rongo hapū.

Note

1. It is also worth noting that the only two second-cousin marriages I encountered in the rich whakapapa of Best's census were on this side of the Pareihe family: as can be seen in Fig. 16, Hori's wife was apparently his second cousin (his father's mother's sister's daughter's daughter Ameria), and Paraki's son Waihinau's wife was apparently his second cousin (his father's mother's brother's daughter's daughter Maramoko). As discussed in Chap. 5 (where another apparent exception was encountered), the usual traditional incest prohibition drawn on marriage among Tūhoe extends to third cousins, and this continues to be taken so seriously that fourth or more distant cousins (and even friends who wrongly assume they are somehow related) may consider themselves to be stigmatized insofar as they are married or having an affair.

References

AJHR 1903. D. Scannell. 'Commissioners' Orders Under the "Urewera District Native Reserves Act, 1896."' Undated. Appendices to the Journal of the House of Representatives 1903, G-6: 1–256. Wellington, N.Z.

AJHR 1907. G. Mair, D.F.G. Barclay, Paratene Ngata. "The Urewera District Native Reserve: reports of the commissioners appointed ...." Report and orders. Undated. Appendices to the Journal of the House of Representatives 1907 G-4: 1–190. Wellington, N.Z.

Bassett, Heather and R. Kay. 2002. "*Ruatāhuna: land ownership and administration c. 1896–1990.*" With Supporting Papers (S.P.) Vols 1–3. WAI 894 #A20. Wellington, N.Z.: Waitangi Tribunal.

Best, Elsdon. 1898. "Tuhoe genealogies 1898" (spine title); "Genealogies of the Tuhoe tribe. Also includes all living members of the tribe in 1898, as given before the Urewera Commission set up under the act of 1896." Manuscript qMS [172]. Wellington, N.Z.: Alexander Turnbull Library. [The author can supply a digital index for this resource.]

Best, Elsdon, 1973. *Tuhoe, Children of the Mist.* Vols. I and II (genealogies). Second edition. Wellington, N.Z.: A.H. and A.W. Reed Ltd. (first published 1925 as Vol VI of the Memoirs of the Polynesian Society).

Binney, Judith. 2002. *Encircled Lands; Part Two: A History of the Urewera 1878–1912*. An Overview Report on the Urewera for the Waitangi Tribunal. WAI 894, A15. Wellington, N.Z.: Waitangi Tribunal.

Dougherty, Wirimu. 2014. "Mātauranga ā-Iwi as it Applies to Tūhoe – Te Mātauranga o Tūhoe." *Enhancing Mātauranga Māori and Global Indigenous Knowledge*. Wellington: N.Z. Qualifications Authority/Mana Tohu Maatauranga o Aotearoa.

NACMB 1. Native Appellate Court minute book 1, Jackson Palmer, Rawson, (13Nov1912–Feb1913), index 9 pp., 386 pp.; NA Wgtn: Waiariki, Urewera Appelate MB 1, CD 3518/2, 397pp.; NA Ak: AREPRO 4711/1450. Acronym: NACMB 1.

NACMB 2. Native Appellate Court minute book 2, Jackson Palmer, Rawson, (1Feb1913–20Aug1913), index 5 pp., 136pp.; NA Wgtn: Waiariki, Urewera Appelate MB 2, CD 3518/2, 140pp.; NA Ak: AREPRO 4711/1451. Acronym: NACMB 2.

NZMS 170 n.d. "Urewera National Park" (3d Edition). New Zealand Map Service. Wellington, N.Z.: Dept. of Lands and Survey.

O'Malley, Vincent. 1996. *The Crown's Acquisition of the Waikaremoana Block 1921–25*. A report for the Panekiri Tribal Trust Board, with Supporting Papers (S.P.) Vols I–III, May 1996. WAI 894 record of inquiry, doc A50. Wellington, N.Z.: Waitangi Tribunal.

UMB 5. Urewera District Native Reserve Commission minute book 5, Butler, Scannell, et al. (18Mar1901–16May01), in English, index 5 pp., 382 pp.; NA Wgtn: Urewera MB 5, MLC 13,W3518, CD 2, Vol.5, 388pp.; NA Ak: AREPRO 4711/1447. Acronym: UMB 5.

UCAMB 1. Urewera District Native Reserve Commission Appeal minute book 1, D.F.G. Barclay, Mair, Ngata, (5Dec1906–22Jan1907). 10 pp. index, ?pp.; NA Wgtn: unable to locate; NA Ak: AREPRO 4711/1133; Univ.Auck.Lib: 333.0995 N536u. Acronym: UCAMB 1.

UCAMB 2. Urewera District Native Reserve Commission Appeal minute book 2, D.F.G. Barclay, Mair, Ngata, (23Jan1907–12Mar1907) index, 382pp.; NA Wgtn: unable to locate; NA Ak: AREPRO 4711/1134; Univ.Auck.Lib: 333.0995 N536u. Acronym UCAMB 2.

UCS closed file 630 (1921–1926). Summary of groups, alphabetical index, consolidated group lists, consolidated successions. Urewera Consolidation Scheme files, Waiariki District Māori Land Court archives, Rotorua, N.Z.

Webster, Steven. 2004. *The Urewera Consolidation Scheme: Confrontations between Tuhoe and the Crown, 1915–1925*. Vols I, II. Report commissioned by the Waitangi Tribunal. WAI 894 #D8. Wellington, N.Z.: Waitangi Tribunal.

Wiri, Robert. *Te Wai-Kaukau o Nga Matua Tipuna: Myths, Realities, and the Determination of Mana Whenua in the Waikarmoana District*, M.A. Māori Studies thesis, University of Auckland, 1994.

CHAPTER 8

Confrontations Over Waikaremoana and Ruatāhuna, 1899–1907

1 Introduction

One of the main confrontations in the Waikaremoana investigation is examined in the first section below, following it though to the 1907 appeals commission. The second section of this chapter will then deal with a particular aspect of the Ruatāhuna investigation, again following it through to the appeals commission in 1907. In both cases, the selection of a particular aspect of the investigation was initially pursued because leaders of the migrant marriage alliance described in Chap. 7 were involved, and this was the best evidence of an inter-relationship between the two areas that could explain the Ruatāhuna-Waikaremoana amalgamation proposed but aborted in 1902. However, as this possibility was pursued, the activities of the migrant marriage alliance expanded well beyond the problem of the proposed amalgamation and, as will be discussed in Chap. 9 and Volume II, continued through the Urewera Consolidation Scheme 1921–1926.

As well as the commission and court minutebooks, I have relied on O'Malley (1996: 31–47) and Bassett and Kay (2002: 58–77) for the general outline of commission's investigations 1899–1907, including the later partition of Ruatāhuna block 1912–1918 (Bassett and Kay 2002: 78–90,102–08; also Webster 2004: 116–42). Unanticipated delays during the 1899 and 1900 investigations discussed in Chaps. 2 and 3 resulted in the commission not resuming the 1899 investigation of claims to the Ruatāhuna and Waikaremoana areas until April 1901. Due to such delays and reports of low food supply for the required hosting in Ruatāhuna, it

© The Author(s) 2020

S. Webster, *A Separate Authority (He Mana Motuhake)*, Volume I,
https://doi.org/10.1007/978-3-030-41042-1_8

had been decided that the commission would not continue its circuit of the reserve but extend its sitting at Te Whaiti for the investigations of Ruatāhuna, Maungapōhatu, and Waikaremoana areas—long rugged distances further to the east (Fig. 1.1). There were protests about the difficulty of Tūhoe attendance so far from the *tangata whenua* of the lands being considered. In the event, the intended hearing in Te Whaiti of the Ruatāhuna case had to be further delayed until the following season in February 1902 when it was held even further away, far to the north in Rūātoki. Although the allocation of shares for Waikaremoana also had to be completed in Rūātoki in 1902, the claims were heard and admissions or dismissals completed in Te Whaiti 3–20 May 1901.

2 Investigation of the Waikaremoana Block, 1899–1907

The first hearing regarding the boundaries and claims of the Waikaremoana block was on 3 May 1901. Hurae Puketapu opened the discussions, although as one of the five Tūhoe commissioners he had stood down as a claimant for the block. Hurae announced that "Tuhoe" had finished their discussions regarding the block, arranging the whole boundary with only the northern part from "Taita o Makoro to Ngatapa and thence to Pukepuke" summits remaining to be approved by Te Wao Ihimaera (Fig. 1.2 ('northern portion'); UMB 5: 332). He emphasized that the Waikaremoana people were following the advice of 'our old men' that (i) their claim was to be based on conquest of the block by Tūhoe, along with 'allied hapus' of Ngāti Ruapani, over Ngāti Ruapani 'proper' (as a hapū of Ngāti Kahungunu *iwi*), and (ii) that the block was to be 'put through in this shape and not divided'.

Several aspects of Hurae Puketapu's commentary can be clarified here. First, it should be noted that both Hurae and Te Wao Ihimaera had married into the migrant marriage alliance in its third generation, and by 1898 already had grandchildren by that marriage (see Chap. 7 and Fig. 7.1). Hurae had married Maria Tangira, the *mātāmua* daughter of Tangira Tawa and Peata Hautu, the second-born siblings of the two descent groups that had each married their first three children to the first three children of the other descent group. Te Wao had married Maria Pareihe, the daughter of the most junior of Pareihe Rangimatuatini's four wives. A third leader in the alliance, Te Mapu Pukeiotu, does not take up a central role in the hearing until 13 May, but was apparently the official conductor of the case for 'the Waikaremoana people' conducted until then by Hurae and Te Wao. Te Mapu was the grandson of the marriage between the third-born siblings of the Tawa and Hautu descent groups (Fig. 7.1). His apparent absence or silence in the first few days of the hearings might be explained by the presence of his father Pukeiotu, who may have been a representative for Ngāti Kahungunu interests that were refused a hearing (O'Malley 1996: 39). A review of the commentaries on Hurae, Te Wao, and Te Mapu in Chap. 7, and on the Tawa, Hautu, and Pareihe descent groups, will further explain their leadership activities and how they were situated in the migrant marriage alliance.

The part of the northern boundary of Waikaremoana that Hurae left for Te Wao's approval was most of the common boundary between Waikaremoana, Maungapōhatu, and Manuoha blocks ('northern portion' of Fig. 1.2, which was based on survey plan 6873). In Fig. 1.2, the northern boundary of this "northern portion" runs from (1) the sharp southwestern apex of Maungapōhatu block at Taitaa o Makora (mis-spelled "Makoro" in the minutebook and "Tataemakora" on both survey plan 6873 and NZMS 170), probably located at the junction of the Hopuruahine River and the Orangitutaetutu stream; from there about 6–7 kilometers straight northeast to (2) the summit of Ngatapa, which is probably the highest peak of the Huiarau range (altitude 1416 meters; called "Manuoha" on NZMS 170) at the junction of all three blocks; from Ngatapa, the northern boundary of this "northern portion" turns southeast and runs straight for about 5 kilometers to (3) Pukepuke, the 1206-meter peak located on the eastern boundary of the reserve between the Waikaremoana and Manuoha blocks. Hurae reported that the rest of the Waikaremoana boundary (more than nine-tenths of it) had already been arranged: it was probably as shown in Fig. 1.2 (survey plan 6873) running north from Taitaa o Makora to the corner between Waikaremoana, Maungapōhatu, and Ruatāhuna blocks, and from there southwest almost the full length between Ruatāhuna and Waikaremoana blocks along the crest of the Huiarau and Pukekohu ranges, ending at the headwaters of the Waiau River along the southern end of the reserve.

Hurae's emphasis that 'Tuhoe' and 'allied hapus' of Ngāti Ruapani had agreed on this larger part of the boundary, and that their claim was based on conquest, was implicitly an exclusion of Ngāti Kahungunu *iwi* and Ngāti Ruapani 'proper' (the other sections of Ngāti Ruapani who had remained loyal to Ngāti Kahungunu) because they had been conquered in the early 1800s. In the 1907 appeals he gave more detailed evidence on this situation (UCAMB 1: 43). It was also agreed that the former boundary of Ngāti Kahungunu lands had been the crest of the Huiarau range between Ruatāhuna and Waikaremoana, and that their former lands extending from the crest of the Huiarau range south and east to the north-western shores of Lake Waikaremoana and the Waiau River had been taken from them in conquest by Tūhoe and the three descent groups of Ngāti Ruapani who had allied with the Tūhoe. Whereas the following analysis is concerned with the northern portion of the boundary contested between Waikaremoana and Maungapōhatu claimants, O'Malley's analysis is primarily concerned with the boundary between Waikaremoana and Ruatāhuna because it was contested between the Tūhoe and Ngāti Kahungunu, who despite the conquest claimed continuing rights in what was to become part of the UDNR as the Waikaremoana block.

Finally, there is also important background to Hurae's emphasis that following the advice of 'our old men' all were agreed that the block was to be 'put through in this shape and not divided'. According to later evidence given by Paora Kingi in his claim to Waikaremoana, "I proposed to Tutaka[ngahau]in 1899 when the commission sat at Waikare [that is, at Waimako] that we should divide our block. The Waikare people said to leave it [Waikaremoana] in one block. Tutaka consented [to their position]" (UMB 5: 357).[1] Tutakangahau Tapui was a *rangatira* of Tūhoe, leader of several hapū the most influential of which was Tamakaimoana, and one of the five Tūhoe commissioners. He and Paora Kingi had apparently been considering a claim in behalf of Tamakaimoana hapū that the northern portion of Waikaremoana was instead part of Maungapōhatu block (Fig. 1.2). Examination of the 1899 minutes suggests that Tutakangahau as well as Te Wao Ihimaera and other leaders of the migrant marriage alliance, threatened by Ngāti Kahungunu iwi's claims to Paharakeke block to the north, supported Hori Wharerangi's adamant distrust of the UDNR commission due to the loss of his people's lands in Waipaoa (just south of Manuoha block) in the Native Land Court (UMB 1: 197–202; see Chap. 2 on Wharerangi's objections).

It was probably in this context in 1899 that Tutakangahau decided not to press Tamakaimoana hapū's claim to the northern portion of Waikaremoana, that is, decided to close ranks with the Waikaremoana leaders against Kahungunu claims and not to divide their block. However, by the time of the 1901 hearings of Waikaremoana claims at Te Whaiti it turned out that among all the claims confronted by the Waikaremoana people, those made by Tutakangahau and Paora Kingi to be included in Waikaremoana were the most persistent. Their claims were on behalf of the hapū of the Maungapōhatu area, and when cooperation with these claims was obstructed by the Waikaremoana leaders, the commission divided the northern portion of Waikaremoana block and gave it over to Maungapōhatu block. This interpretation of the 1899 agreement and Paora Kingi's later evidence is supported by what happened in the 1901 hearings.

The Waikaremoana hearing reconvened the following Monday, 6 May 1901. Te Wao had arrived from Waikaremoana and asked for "about another week" to discuss the northern part of the boundary because it "makes a difference of about 2,000 acres" (UMB 5: 334). When this was refused by the commission he asked for "ten minutes", after which he reported that he had consulted with "Tamakaimoana, Ngāti Tu, and Ngāti Teau" hapū regarding the northern boundary and that "it has been arranged that the boundary as surveyed should stand". That was to say, the boundary between Waikaremoana, Maungapōhatu, and Manuoha as described above by Hurae and depicted in Fig. 1.2 was accepted by both Te Wao and the several Maungapōhatu hapū. Te Oti then stood for "Ngati Potiki. others representing Tamakaimoana, Ng. Te Au & etc etc" and confirmed that "all agree that *this piece of Tamakaimoana land should remain in Waikare block*" (UMB 5: 335; my emphasis). "Te Oti" was probably Tarahuru, the senior son of Tutakangahau, and conductor for the investigation of Maungapōhatu block (UMB 5: 285). Taking Te Oti's statement as direct confirmation for Tamakaimoana hapū's acceptance for Maungapōhatu as well as Te Wao's for the Waikaremoana people, the commission then confirmed this northern boundary of Waikaremoana. Te Oti's identification of the northern part of Waikaremoana as 'Tamakaimoana land' furthermore implies that Tutakangahau, who was the leader of that hapū, had again agreed with the Waikaremoana leaders not to divide the Waikaremoana block (as, according to Paora Kingi, he had at Waimako in 1899), leaving what was here assumed to be his hapū's land in that block rather than including it in the adjacent Maungapōhatu block. This northern part was probably the '2000 acres' that had concerned Te Wao (it later turned out to be more than 4000 acres or about 7% of the very large Waikaremoana block).

The commission then received claimants lists from Paora Kingi, Te Mapu Pukeiotu, Hurae Puketapu, Numia Kererū, and Te Wao Ihimaera. Although there were only five lists, they apparently included over 2000 individual names (runs of numbers but no names were recorded), and the commission announced it would accept no further lists. The readings of these lists to record objections went through two stages that same day (6 May 1901) the first of which apparently settled most differences between three representatives of "the Waikaremoana people", and the second of which reduced the remainder of claimants to those who were prepared to set up cases to press their claims against the objections of those representatives (UMB 5: 335–6). Objections to the first reading were raised only by Mahaki Tapiki, Te Wao Ihimaera, and Te Mapu Pukeiotu. It should be noted that as well as the last two, Mahaki Tapiki was also a prominent leader in the migrant marriage alliance (the *mātāmua* son of the *mātāmua* Tawa sibling). So was Hurae Puketapu, but on 3 May, having stood down as a commissioner, he had appeared anxious to remain neutral (UMB 5: 333). Fragmentary notes in the minutes indicate that many of this first stage of objections were raised against parts of the claims of the other three leaders of the alliance: Mahaki Tapiki objected to most of Te Mapu's claim, both Mahaki and Te Mapu objected to all or parts of Hurae's claim, and certain names in Te Wao's claim were objected to by Te Mapu. Perhaps significantly, the only claims list that was largely accepted by all three objectors was that submitted by Numia Kererū.

Notes in the margin of the minutebook indicate that the names of some claimants were withdrawn immediately, and remaining differences would be discussed 'outside'. Perhaps aware that these objections were an internal affair between leaders of 'the Waikaremoana people', the commission adjourned for a few hours 'to enable Te Wao's party to get the names they [all] wish to object to'. When the hearing reconvened, it was Te Mapu not Te Wao who submitted the consolidated list, now acting as conductor of their case. As a result of their deliberation outside and the previous withdrawals, the new list of claimants they objected to was still over 700 persons (again recorded in the minutebook only as runs of numbers without any names). The commission then invited claimants facing these objections to set up cases arguing for their inclusion in the block but emphasized 'that unless permanent occupation is proved they cannot be admitted'. This emphasis on 'permanent' rather than 'continuous' occupation was not typical in the Urewera investigations. In the case of Waikaremoana, it probably reflected the established Native Land Court practice that the *take* ('reason') of conquest rather than ancestry had to be followed by sustained occupation by the conquerors in order to substantiate legitimate customary rights to the conquered land. Fragmentary notes in the margin indicated that the commission's warning resulted in further withdrawals of some claims, intentions to try to settle some others outside, or announcements that cases would be set up to argue for admission of the remaining claimants before the commission.

Te Amo Kokouri was named to set up cases for five groups of widely varying sizes, Te Oti (Tutakangahau's eldest son Tarahuru) for seven such groups, Paora Kingi for two such groups, and Hurae Puketapu for one group. Along with Te Amo Kokouri, Numia Kererū and Te Oti were named to set up one case for 162 persons. Te Amo was primarily affiliated with Te Urewera hapū in Ruatāhuna where he had leading rights, and was probably also affiliated with Ngāti Rongo hapū which was led by Numia. By 13 May further confrontations and compromises had apparently resulted in further withdrawals and settlements outside the commission, reducing perhaps 15 remaining claimants lists to only two that were increasingly persistent: one to be argued by Paora Kingi, and one to be argued by Tutakangahau—the two Maungapōhatu leaders who in 1899 had considered dividing the block but then agreed with the Waikaremoana leaders not to divide it. Judging by subsequent developments, it is likely that Tutakangahau's case was initially planned to be argued by Te Oti or Te Amo, or even by Numia Kererū, rather than by Tutakangahau himself.

Despite the apparent agreement between all parties the previous morning that the northern boundary would remain as surveyed and Waikaremoana undivided, it became apparent on the morning of 7 May 1901 that the agreement was breaking down. Te Rahui (an opening claimant to Maungapōhatu for Tamakaimoana hapū in 1899) was recorded to protest:

> With regard to the portion of Maungapōhatu included in Waikaremoana agreed to by us yesterday. I agreed and others. When Te Wao and I agreed to that we understood that we would have a right *there as well as in the conquered land* and Te Wao has cut our names out. – therefore I would like to know what the commissioners think about that. I will be conductor for Tamakaimoana for that piece. (UMB 5: 337; my emphasis)

Te Oti immediately claimed that he was the conductor for Tamakaimoana, and the commission cautioned them that conductors were to be chosen by the people whose case they were conducting. The commission heard claims for Maungapōhatu over the next few days, and the apparent breakdown of the Waikaremoana agreement was not addressed in the minutes again until 10 May. However, it is significant that Te Rahui's protest implied that a distinction was generally assumed between the 'piece of Tamakaimoana land' to be left in Waikaremoana block (presumably its northern portion) and other Waikaremoana lands (probably southwest of it, closer to Lake Waikaremoana) which he described as 'the conquered land'. The distinction is important but nowhere else encountered in the minutes. Rahui's charge was apparently that he and others had assumed Tamakaimoana hapū's rights in what they considered to be their own land left in Waikaremoana block, as well as rights by conquest in Waikaremoana lands beyond it, would be recognized by the Waikaremoana leaders.

However, Te Wao Ihimaera was betraying the agreement by cutting their names out of the northern portion of land Tamakaimoana had left in Waikaremoana block.

Although provocative, Te Wao's actions could be seen to assert the rights of the three descent groups of Ngāti Ruapani, who through intermarriage had become allies of the Tūhoe, over the ***immigrant*** rights of Tamakaimoana hapū in this northern portion of Waikaremoana block. This sort of assertion of dominant ***mana*** between hapū was characteristic of hapū organization, and would force Tamakaimoana claimants to demonstrate occupational as well as ancestral rights in the northern portion of the block, as well as rights by ***take raupatu*** (conquest ***followed by*** 'permanent' occupation) beyond it. Te Wao, who (as explained in Chap. 7) affiliated with Ngāi Te Riu hapū as well as Ngāti Ruapani, had probably been deferred to by Hurae Puketapu and Te Mapu because his occupation and ***mana*** was better established in this northern area and his knowledge of its history was more detailed.

Nevertheless, by Friday 10 May Te Wao's actions disregarding the 6 May agreement appear to have back-fired in favor of the Tamakaimoana hapū claimants: all earlier agreements to avoid division of Waikaremoana and the commission's decision to confirm the boundary as surveyed were reversed. Without any record of intervening events, the commission simply announced without explanation that it had been

> agreed among all the parties interested that the northern boundary should be withdrawn south to Ngapuketurua as. shown in the plan on pencil. Leaving this area in the Maungapōhatu. That is that the dividing line at that part shall be from. Pukepuke to Ngapuketurua and thence to peg xviii at Taitamakora. Line of boundary altered accordingly. (UMB 5: 352)[2]

In Fig. 1.2, Ngapuketurua is located at (4), the southwest corner of the trapezoidal 'northern portion' of Waikaremoana block. Consequently, the new boundary between Maungapōhatu and Waikaremoana was to run from (3) Pukepuke (at the southeastern corner of the northern portion) to (4) Ngapuketurua, and from there north to (1) Taitaa o Makora. If this reversal of the earlier decision really was 'agreed among all parties', it meant that Te Wao had suddenly given up his claim to the northern section as well as the resolution of Waikaremoana's 'old men' to not divide the block and Tutakangahau's acceptance of this perhaps since 1899. It is more likely that the shifting of the Maungapōhatu boundary south to include the northern portion of Waikaremoana was imposed by the commission (Tutakangahau,

Hurae, and Numia were all formally stood down as interested parties) and intended to encourage the settlement of Tamakaimoana claims while punishing Te Wao and his supporters for undermining the 6 May agreement. At least the former intention was achieved. Although the rest the minutes for 10 May were concerned with the separate Maungapōhatu investigation, the last entry of the day reports that "the bulk of the objections [in the Waikaremoana investigation] are settled" leaving only 5 of the 15 cases still needing to be set up (UMB 5: 353).

When the commission reconvened the following Monday 13 May 1901, the confrontation between the Tamakaimoana claimants and the Waikaremoana objectors had hardened despite this major concession of over 4000 acres of land to Tamakaimoana and the Maungapōhatu block (UMB 5: 353). Before their weekend adjournment, the commission had apparently instructed Te Mapu (as conductor for the Waikaremoana block) and Tutakangahau (the dominant leader of Tamakaimoana hapū and Maungapōhatu block) to pursue discussion of the remaining claims and objections. Nevertheless, Te Mapu reported that

> Tutaka[ngahau] wished us to admit these names but we would not consent – we settled among ourselves that Tutaka should be included among. us. without an interest (with a small interest). The Waikaremoana people now wish to strike out Tutaka & all his list.

The commission's parenthetical correction of Te Mapu's 'inclusion…without interest' probably meant that only shares in *aroha* or compassion had been offered to Tutakangahau and to him alone, while the rest of his list were being entirely excluded. Tutakangahau himself responded that

> I followed Judge Butler's advice to interview these people. I asked them to withdraw their objections they said they would admit me. and the others should be withdrawn – I said I would not withdraw – I would follow out the Act – they said they would strike me out also – that was all. Therefore I ask this matter to be adjourned to Ruatoki so that I may look into the case. and point out the interests of the different families – they have rights by ancestry, by occupation, & by conquest. (UMB 5: 353)

In view of the 10 May division of Waikaremoana and loss of the northern portion to Maungapōhatu, the refusal by the Waikaremoana people to accept any Tamakaimoana claims to their reduced lands seems reasonable.

Now it was Tamakaimoana's persistence that seemed unreasonable, especially after gaining all of their claim to the northern portion by the fiat of a boundary change rather than having to argue their case for rights to it.

This is the first time that Tutakangahau himself appeared in the minutes; apparently until this time his claim or claims for Tamakaimoana hapū were being handled by Te Oti as his *mātāmua* son. Tutakangahau's intention to 'follow out the Act' in describing his response to Te Mapu may have been a reference to the statute's goal to award titles to discrete hapū. Insofar as Tamakaimoana hapū considered the northern part of Waikaremoana to be 'Tamakaimoana land', Tutakangahau's intention to claim further lands beyond it (toward the lake) exclusively for Tamakaimoana would be an appropriate riposte to Te Wao's earlier provocative intention to exclude Tamakaimoana claimants from the northern portion. In any case, it is surprising that Tutakangahau felt it necessary to adjourn the case to Rūātoki (at the far northern end of the Ureweras) to 'look into…point out the interests…' of his claimants because he was among the most knowledgeable of the *tohunga whakapapa* of the Tūhoe, and certainly the most aware of 'the interests of the different families' in his own list of claimants. He had probably organized support of others in this request to move the case to Rūātoki: both his son Te Oti and Te Wakaunua immediately seconded it. However, Te Mapu effectively undercut this proposal by more reasonably pointing out that "all Tamakaimoana are here [in Te Whaiti] and so are the Waikare people", and the commission decided to continue with the two remaining cases (Tutakangahau's and Paora Kingi's) immediately (UMB 5: 354–5).

Their cases were then heard and decided upon 13–16 May 1901 (UMB 5: 355–82). Paora Kingi also appeared unready to present a strong case for inclusion of his list in the block, and began by attempting to defer to Tutakangahau and Rakuraku, another descent group of leading *mana* in the Tauranga basin and Maungapōhatu. Significantly, Teneti Rakuraku immediately admitted that his line 'has a claim by ancestry and *mana* but not by occupation' and asked that it be struck out of Paora Kingi's list, probably weakening the latter's case at its outset. Tutakangahau's case was much more extensive and detailed, but nevertheless also relied on intermittent occupation by recent ancestors of the conquered lands or, ambiguously, relatively temporary occupation following the conquest or holding the land against renewed hostilities some decades later. Probably reflecting their insistence on the criterion of more "permanent" occupation established for the *take* of conquest, after three days of hearings the commission finally found the evidence offered "not sufficient to support the claims by occupation and therefore dismisses" both claims lists (UMB 5: 382). Given the established influence of the two claimants and the boldness of their demands despite their gains from the new boundary, this might be seen as a surprising result. Perhaps even Tutakangahau had been caught unprepared to argue his case in Te Whaiti. But why would he have been better prepared in Rūātoki?

Aspects of their arguments can be outlined. Paori Kingi credited his great-grandfather Te Umuariki and Te Umuariki's son Te Whenuanui (father of Te Haka Te Whenuanui II, the leading *rangatira* in Ruatāhuna) for leading the conquest of Waikaremoana lands with their Ngāti Ruapani allies (UMB 5: 356). These leaders lived about three generations earlier, dating the conquest in the early 1800s. (This was later supported by Akuhata Te Kaha and Rawaho Winitana for Ngāti Rongo hapū, crediting the conquest to their ancestor Te Purewa, who also lived about three generations earlier (UCAMB 2: 126–7).) Tutakangahau's evidence was focused primarily on what he presented as a later successful effort to hold the Waikaremoana area against a threatened reoccupation by the vanquished Ngāti Kahungunu *iwi* between 1860 and 1874 (UMB 5: 361). He specified the "four" Tūhoe hapū sent to hold the area to be Tamakaimoana, Ngāi Te Kahu, Ngāi Tama, and Ngāti Rongo, later adding Ngāi Te Riu and Ngāti Hinekura hapū, several of these having sprung from the old hapū Ngā Pōtiki (UMB 5: 361, 370–1).

A striking feature of Tutakangahau's case was his claim that in this way representatives of several Tūhoe hapū had each occupied specific Ngāti Kahungunu *iwi* lands beyond the Waikaremoana block, including most of the *southern* shore (opposite side from the disputed northern portion) of Lake Waikaremoana (see Fig. 1.2). He named areas around the lake clockwise from what is now the contemporary township of Tuai at the southeast end and, in response to further questions from the commissioners, claimed that these lands had actually been divided as responsibilities of specific Tūhoe hapū so that "they would not interfere with one another" (UMB 5: 361, 371). In this context he claimed that the lands "from Panekiri [the range above the southwest side of the lake] to Pukehou [a summit of that name is on the Puketukutuku peninsula on the north-central side of the lake] from there to Whanganui o Parua belongs to N. Rongo, Tamakaimoana, and Ng. Te Riu". Whanganui o Parua inlet ends at contemporary Aniwaniwa, almost all the way back east along the northern shore of the lake to Tuai, Tutakangahau's most southeastern claim. If the 'Pukehou' he named is the summit on the north side,

Tutakangahau was claiming Tūhoe occupation as well as conquest virtually surrounding the lake, well beyond what had become generally accepted as the boundaries of the Waikaremoana block. Only the far eastern shore between Aniwaniwa and Tuai seemed to be left to Ngāti Ruapani hapū, perhaps even those descent groups of it allied with the Tūhoe conquerors. In response to the commission's question whether the Waikaremoana hapū opposing his list would have any *mana* on these lands, Tutakangahau simply responded, 'No. This man who questioned me [Te Mapu] belonged to the other side'. The phrase 'other side' (and 'this man') was probably calculated to invoke the conquest and imply Te Mapu belonged among the vanquished. Although (as described above) Te Mapu's father Pukeiotu may have been affiliated with Ngāti Kahungunu *iwi* or the parts of Ngāti Ruapani that remained loyal to them, this insinuation ignored Pukeiotu's descent from the Tawa-Hautu marriage alliance.

Such bold over-reach in land rights and disdain for opponents was, of course, typical of confrontations between Tūhoe persons of *mana*, perhaps especially in formal court or tribunal procedures.[3] However, given Tutakangahau's pre-eminent *rangatiratanga*, perhaps already compromised by his pleas to adjourn his case to Rūātoki, the commissioners may have found themselves in an embarrassing position. If they had already formally given the northern part of Waikaremoana over to him, Tamakaimoana hapū, and Maungapōhatu block by altering the boundary (perhaps in over-reaction to Te Wao's provocations), what was to be done if his claim even to that part of Waikaremoana immediately adjacent to Maungapōhatu—as well as all the way around Lake Waikaremoana—fell so short of acceptable evidence of permanent occupation? To officially rescind the boundary change of 10 May might be more embarrassing than simply to ignore it.

Strangely, none of the recorded evidence worked through 13–16 May made reference to the boundary change only a few days earlier. To the contrary, the numerous references to Taita o Makoro (the key apex in the original location of the boundary confirmed on 6 May, located at the northwestern corner of the northern portion given over to Maungapōhatu on 10 May) or the Hopuruahine Stream suggest that the formal withdrawal of the boundary 4000 acres to the south on 10 May was being ignored by both parties (UMB 5: 360; 362; 368; 375–6; UCAMB 1: 22, 44). Yet if, as was apparently the case, the 10 May relocation of the northern boundary and re-designation of that land as Tamakaimoana land in Maungapōhatu had resulted in withdrawal or admission of almost all the remaining claims, one would assume that the original boundary would have to be formally rescinded or re-instated and all these claims would have to be re-heard. But instead it appears that through all the remaining investigation and even the later appeals regarding both Waikaremoana and Maungapōhatu blocks, including the final official map of the Urewera Reserve published in 1907 (Fig. 1.2), the official relocation of the boundary transferring 4000 acres from Waikaremoana into Maungapōhatu was not mentioned again and, along with all those claims (and half of the famous Ngatapa peak), left in legal limbo.[4]

The ambiguity of the northern boundary was compounded when the Waikaremoana case was reopened in January 1902 in Rūātoki to settle relative shares in the block among those admitted to the list of owners. In 1901 the remaining hearings in Te Whaiti had been concerned with other blocks, but a final entry on 20 May avoided the details but implied that the confrontation between Tamakaimoana and the Waikaremoana people had not been quelled by the 16 May decision: "The parties in this case state that they have been unable to do anything towards formulating a scheme of relative interests and ask the case to be allowed to stand over till… Ruatoki – next year" (UMB 6: 5). Apparently Tutakangahau intended to continue his demand for shares even though his (as well as Paora Kingi's) case had been dismissed as insufficient to support his claims of occupation (and therefore without any ground for rights in Waikaremoana even if conquest or appropriate ancestry were proven), and again he was holding out for this to be settled in Rūātoki.

When the new season's sitting was resumed in Rūātoki in 1902, on 16 January Hurae Puketapu asked the commission to await the arrival of the Waikaremoana people and "finish" the case in Rūātoki before adjourning to hear other cases in Whakatane due to the cold weather (UMB 6: 8). Hurae's plea again suggests a dominant faction pressing for Rūātoki as the most favorable location to resolve the confrontation. On 14 February 1902 Te Mapu finally arrived, and the commission gave him the list of names for Waikaremoana block "so that they may define the shares themselves" (UMB 6: 198). On 20 February the "lists [sic] of names [were] handed in with shares allotted" and the shares read out (UMB 6: 207). The rest of the entry is unclear, but it appears that Te Oti Tutakangahau, still representing Tamakaimoana hapū, reported that Tukuaterangi Tutakangahau (Te Oti's younger brother) had protested that he was not allotted as many shares as 'certain others' with whom he should have an equal right in Waikaremoana. Reflecting some irritation with something apparently happening behind the scenes, the commission tersely responded that

> as he and his father [Tutakangahau] set up lists of names at Te Whaiti, and these names were contested before the Commission and struck out and [nevertheless] he and his parent were included by aroha by the owners... if he is not satisfied with what they choose to give him [the] Commission will strike him out.
>
> No other objectors List closed. and block completed.

It may be significant that although the commission emphasized its 16 May decision that Tutakangahau's claimants list had been dismissed (that is, 'struck out'), its warning to Te Oti and his brother (and implicitly to their father!) instead echoed the terms of the 13 May stalemate between Te Mapu and Tutakangahau regarding token shares ('by aroha.... what they chose to give him') for Tutakangahau alone (which he had rejected). As recorded in the minutes above, the 20 February response from the commission implied that only Tutakangahau and his son Tukuaterangi had been included in the list of owners (although his son's complaint does not mention his father), and furthermore that they would be included only on the basis of *aroha* (i.e., with only token shares).

But quite to the contrary and without any record of subsequent decisions, the final list of Waikaremoana owners published in 1903 as the provisional order for the block in fact included at least 13 members in three generations of Tutakangahau's immediate descent group (probably including Te Oti as his eldest son Tarahuru, mis-spelled as "Tahuru") along with his and Tarahuru's spouses (AJHR 1903: Waikaremoana #566–80). Furthermore, judging by the appeal against this inclusion pursued by Waikaremoana leaders in 1907, probably most of the rest of Tutakangahau's extensive claimants list for Tamakaimoana hapū had been included in the block order along with his immediate family. Moreover, the shares allotted to Tutakangahau's immediate descent group, although small, were not merely token: five each for him and his wife, three for each of his children, Tukuaterangi's wife, and their children, and two for each of his other grandchildren—considerably more inclusive and generous than what the commission's warning had implied. While Tutakangahau himself may have appeared to remain above the confrontation (as well as stood down as a commissioner), at least in Rūātoki he was still able to press his claim regardless of its official dismissal.

When the appeals commission was finally convened in 1906, the confrontation between leaders of the migrant marriage alliance and the persistent Tamakaimoana claimants was pursued in Mahaki Tapiki's appeal #83, heard early in 1907. Although Te Mapu Pukeiotu had died, Mahaki took up their appeal supported by Hori Wharerangi, Te Wao Ihimaera, and Rawaho Winitana (UCAMB 1: 7–13; 2: 115–23). These same four persons had also supported Te Mapu's conduct of the case in 1901–1902 and, with the exception of Hori Wharerangi, were all leaders in the migrant marriage alliance.[5] As explained in the previous section, although Te Mapu was the grandson of one of the three marriages between the Tawa and Hautu descent groups (Manuera Hautu and Pera Tawa), Mahaki Tapiki was considerably senior in rank as well as generation, being the *mātāmua* son of the marriage between the *mātāmua* Tawa son Tapiki and the *mātāmua* Hautu daughter Rita (Fig. 7.1).

The most prominently unresolved features of the 1901–1902 investigation of Waikaremoana were the limbo in which the northern boundary was left, and the inclusion of many Tamakaimoana claimants in the final order despite the dismissal of their case. Although Mahaki Tapiki's appeal #83 lucidly presented the latter issue, the most striking features of its hearing were the appeals commission's disregard of both these unresolved issues, and the emergence of Numia Kererū's role in the submission of the original list of Tamakaimoana claimants. Like Tutakangahau, the lead claimant and Maungapōhatu *rangatira*, Numia was one of the five Tūhoe commissioners on the investigative commission. As outlined in previous chapters, the appeals commission had no Tūhoe members and, although its procedure was also to hear and decide upon only those issues the Tūhoe themselves could not settle 'outside', its procedure and decisions were sometimes uninformed, arrogant, or even biased by personal grudges or hidden agenda.

Mahaki's presentation of their appeal was straightforward: he described how they had gone over the lists handed in to the previous commission, and that some had been withdrawn after hearing their objections to them, but

> two cases were set up, one by Tutakangahau and one by Paora Kingi, for the inclusion of their lists of names to which we had objected. The Commission heard their cases and decided against them, disallowing their lists. Subsequently when the orders made by the Commission were issued we found that though some of the persons to whom we objected had been struck out of the list of owners certain others of them had been included in the orders, we therefore appealed so that the names of the persons in question be struck out of the order. (UCAMB 1: 7)

He then handed in a list of 89 persons who had been included in the 1903 publication of the provisional order for Waikaremoana block, with each of about ten descent or sibling groups annotated either 'not descendants from [founding] ancestors' or 'descendants from [founding] ancestors but no occupation'. (The following day he added three more persons who had been overlooked, for a total of 92 persons whom the appeal asked to be struck from the final block order for 729 persons.) Mahaki also named the conquering or intermarrying ancestors accepted by the commission in 1901. Finally, he asserted that 'none of the persons in the list to whom I have objected live on the land, they all live away at Whakatane, Te Whaiti, Ruatāhuna, and other places at the Northern end of the Urewera ranges'.

Mahaki and his supporters were obviously well-prepared to argue the case against founding ancestry for each of these claimant siblings or descent groups listed and, even if the claimants could demonstrate their descent from a founding or conquering ancestor of the block, to argue against their sufficiently recent or permanent occupation. However, the appeals commission seemed uninterested in the 1901 decision or the inclusion of the 92 persons in the final order regardless of the 1901 decision. Even Mahaki's effort the next day to refer them precisely to the date and minutebook pages of the original claims as well as the decision (UCAMB 1: 13) was to no avail. Instead, the commissioners repeatedly asked, "who put these persons in the list of owners.... in the first place?" (UCAMB 1: 11, 12). Finally, Mahaki claimed 'I do not know, everyone was handing in lists at the time' and instead named those who had objected to the original lists: himself, Te Wao, Te Mapu, Rawaho Winitana, and Te Kaaho Te Kaaho and his wife (note that all these names are included in Fig. 7.1)—perhaps hoping for help from others present. The appeals commissioners may have been hoping to draw out direct objections to the appeal in order to circumvent the more obvious but troublesome possibility that somehow the earlier commission had acted inconsistently with its own decisions. The ambiguous northern boundary of the block was apparently never raised by anyone.

Certainly one must wonder why no objection to the appeal was raised by Tutakangahau or Paora Kingi or their spokespersons insofar as these two persons had been explicitly named by Mahaki as having set up the unsuccessful cases to include at least some of the names whose inclusion in the order was being appealed. Even if Mahaki really did not know who had put in the original lists, his appeal had made it clear who might be suspected. Furthermore, the minutes to which Mahaki had referred record that Paora Kingi himself had put in one of five lists of claimants, although Tutakangahau apparently did not. Whatever lay behind the cooperative silence on this matter, apparently there were no objections to Mahaki's appeal at all in Wairoa where the appeals commission began its hearing, and his case was adjourned to be resumed later in Whakatane "in order to afford opportunity for those objected to [appealed against?] to appear before us if they so desired" (UCAMB 1: 13; AJHR 1907 G-4: 12). Insofar as Wairoa (on the adjacent east coast) was much closer to Waikaremoana block (and Maungapōhatu – and, presumably, the residences of Tutakangahau and Paora Kingi) than Whakatane on the coast north of the Urewera reserve, this might be seen as further avoidance of the obvious issues.[6]

When the case was resumed in Whakatane only three persons, speaking on behalf of only 12 others, raised objections against Mahaki's appeal to strike 92 persons from the provisional order. The appeals commission's previous interest in finding out who had submitted the original lists was answered by one of the objectors, who stated that Te Wao Ihimaera had put in a list in 1901 (as was also recorded at the minutebook page cited by Mahaki). In his response to the objections, Mahaki denied that any of the 12 persons had any rights in Waikaremoana and, expressing doubt that Te Wao's list had included any of them, asked for an adjournment until he could bring Te Wao and others back to the hearing from Rūātoki (UCAMB 2: 115–6). When Te Wao gave evidence the next day, he stated that "the list of 92 persons whom Mahaki Tapiki asks to be struck out under the appeal were put in by me at the previous Commission. [Numia] Kererū wrote out the list & I handed it in.... [I put in] some of the names ... [5 persons] therefore he [Mahaki] should withdraw his objection to those..." (UCAMB 2: 122).

The five persons whom Te Wao himself had added to Numia Kererū's list and wanted Mahaki to accept were the Rangiaho sibling group, and indeed appeared to have been added at the end of the list of 92 persons appealed against (UCAMB 1: 10). Te Wao went on to add that he believed Mahaki had not objected in 1901 to some included in the many lists because he had mistakenly accepted whole lists headed by rightful owners, but that Mahaki would have objected had he realized this. This part of Te Wao's statement seemed hesitant, perhaps avoiding any opposition to Mahaki's conduct of the appeal. However, Te Wao's revelation that Numia Kererū had written out the list was immediately followed by Rawaho Winitana, another of the supporters of Te Mapu's conduct of objections in 1901, who against Mahaki's appeal bluntly defended another 15 persons in the list of 92 on the grounds that they were direct descendants of Hinewaho, founder of one of the three allied Ngāti Ruapani descent groups (UCAMB 2: 122). Surprisingly, these 15 people were Tutakangahau himself and his immediate descent group, even including his own and Tarahuru's (Te Oti's) spouses (UCAMB 1: 9–10).

Considering this virtual betrayal of his support in 1901 of Te Mapu's and now Mahaki's opposition to this list, it is also surprising that the commission did not pursue Rawaho's statement, at least to insist on evidence of 'permanent' occupation required in 1901 and probably the basis of the dismissal of Tutakangahau's case. In any event, it appeared that by 1907 perhaps Te Wao's and certainly Rawaho's support of the migrant marriage alliances' opposition to Tutakanghau's (i.e., Numia's) list for Tamakaimoana hapū may have begun to waver, or even changed sides. Like Te Wao's delivery of Numia's claim list, Rawaho's proclaimed affiliation with Ngāti Rongo hapū (UCAMB 2: 126; described in Chap. 7) may have been a source of their ambivalence.

The appeals commission apparently ignored the appellant Mahaki's repeated emphasis that even where persons on the list had appropriate ancestral descent, they had "absolutely no occupation" (e.g., UCAMB 2: 116), not even asking either Rawaho or Te Wao to substantiate their approval of some on the list in the minimal terms of "permanence" required by the commission in 1901. Furthermore, the commissioners now had at least five persons apparently available to pursue their repeated concern as to who had put the original lists in: Tutakangahau, Paora Kingi, Te Wao, Rawaho Winitana, and Numia Kererū, all likely or actual objectors at least to some of the appeals before them. They had heard Te Wao's unequivocal statement that most of the list of 92, although handed in by himself, had been written out by Numia Kererū. Together with Mahaki's appeal, which explicitly associated his list of 92 persons with Tutakangahau's and Paora Kingi's persistent claims in 1901–1902, this evidence from Te Wao gave the appeals commission more than enough leads to evaluate the appeal more impartially. If Tutakangahau, Paora Kingi, and Numia were not present at the hearings, at least Numia would probably been at his home in Rūātoki, no further away than Te Wao had been. Yet none of these likely objectors to the appeal stepped forward, nor were they called upon by the commission. Yet the commissioners' decision, which followed upon Te Wao's evidence, was to dismiss the appeal because they could "not believe that any mistake was made in regard to the inclusion of these names by the last Commission.... we require very strong proof of error...before we recommend any variation of their award" (UCAMB 2: 123).

Confusion or careless disregard of the record of the 1901–1902 hearings may have been behind the appeals commission's failure to pursue these obvious questions. However, both Commissioner Captain Mair's diary and the commission's formal report suggest avoidance or obfuscation as well as misunderstanding. Most obviously, as well as ignoring the central role of Tutakangahau's and Paora Kingi's 1901 claims in Mahaki's appeal, the appeals commission's decision furthermore ignored the previous commission's *dismissal* of both their cases yet the *inclusion* in the 1903 order of at least some of the 92 persons named *regardless* of the dismissal of their cases. Captain Mair's diary furthermore betrayed an awareness of the central role of Tutakangahau's and Paora Kingi's cases in Mahaki's appeal where Mair records his version of the decision:

> After much discussion and searching up of old lists. It would appear that the persons now objected to [in Mahaki's appeal] have passed through two ordeals Already and have been found entitled to small shares. Therefor the Commission consider that they should be allowed to remain in the title. (O'Malley 1996 Vol 1 S.P.: 307)

Tutakangahau's and Paora Kingi's claims are the most likely reference here, insofar as they were the only claims to be pressed persistently through to a full hearing at Te Whaiti in May 1901. Apparently where the previous commission reported claims that first refused to compromise and then when heard out were so weak as to warrant complete dismissal on 16 May 1901, Mair saw successful passage through 'two ordeals'. Mair's impression that these claimants had 'been found entitled to small shares' also disregarded the minutes of 20 February 1902 implying that only Tukuaterangi and his father Tuta kangahau had received shares, and that those shares were merely token in *aroha*. The special sympathy of the appeals commissioners for these two claims was apparently also extended to Numia Kererū who, the commission heard (after adjourning and recalling Te Wao to inform them), had submitted the list of 92 names that nevertheless found their way into the provisional order.

The other paradox left by the commission's investigation of Waikaremoana block 1901–1902, the ambiguous status of the northern portion of Waikaremoana, was left unaddressed as well as unresolved by the appeals commission. The commission did report a prolonged review of evidence regarding the 'ancestral' or 'permanent' boundary between Ngāti Kahungunu and Tūhoe before the conquest in order to evaluate the former's claim to rights in the reserve regardless of the Tūhoe conquest of Waikaremoana. It finally decided in favor of Wi Pere that between Waikaremoana and Ruatāhuna blocks the boundary had coincided with the crest of the Huiarau range (i.e., the boundary as shown in Fig. 1.2). O'Malley, drawing on Robert Wiri's critique of their decision, convincingly shows that it was able to come to this conclusion only by misunderstanding the history of mutual assimilation between Tūhoe and Ngāti Ruapani that preceded the conquest (O'Malley 1996: 42–7). The appeals commission furthermore recommended the inclusion of sectors of Ruatāhuna and Maungapōhatu in the northernmost extension of Waikaremoana block as shown in Fig. 1.2, but careful examination of the place-names shows that these areas were not the northern portion in question here, but rather immediately to the north of its northwest apex at Taitaa o Makoro (AJHR 1907 G-4: 27). Instead of correcting the ambiguous boundary change of 10 May 1901, their descriptions of the northern portion of Waikaremoana in the 1907 report actually continued to overlook it.[7]

However, there is evidence that in 1912, sometime after Tutakangahau's death, his second son Tukuaterangi continued the persistent demand of Tamakaimoana hapū for greater shares in Waikaremoana by appealing to the Native Appellate Court to include its northern portion in Maungapōhatu block (Berghan 2001: 63–5). The irony of the 1912 situation is that apparently neither Tukuaterangi nor Chief Judge Jackson Palmer was aware that although the boundary had not been changed on the maps, the northern portion of Waikaremoana block had already been included in Maungapōhatu by the decision of 10 May 1901 and never officially rescinded. While Tukuaterangi's appeal was weak without this crucial evidence, the chief judge's similarly uninformed decision on 6 May 1912 was perhaps unfairly dismissive:

> [A]s to the Eastern portion of the [Waikaremoana block] boundary a reckless attempt was made by Tukuaterangi Tutakangahau to extend the Southern boundary of Maungpohatu so as to overlap the Waikaremoana block. In my former report I commented upon the unreliability of this man's evidence, and in this case he says that his father took him over the boundary, but, as his father did not explain its different turnings etc., he was unable to supply the names of the places where the boundary turned, or give the reason why it turned, in fact, he could not stand cross-examination. I have no hesitation in saying that an appeal or rehearing in regard to the Southern boundary [of Maungapōhatu] should not be authorised. (Berghan 2001: 64)

A few days later on 9 May 1912, the chief judge's report addressed the same appeal, elaborating that

> [t]he making of this application was a gross breach in faith, which the applicant admitted he would not have attempted while his father was alive. The father made, before the first [investigative UDNR] commission, a fair compromise in this case, and, in my opinion, obtained ample justice for his party. I have no hesitation in dismissing this application. (Berghan 2001: 63–4)

Although Tutakangahau had apparently taken his son over the boundaries of the northern portion in anticipation of a later claim, he may have neglected to emphasize the 10 May 1901 decision that would have supported his son's claim. The chief judge's 1912 misunderstanding may have been influenced by the appeals commission's similar disregard of Mahaki's appeal in 1906, and even Captain Mair's sympathy for the 'two ordeals' undergone by Tutakangahau's claimants list (despite the weakness and dismissal of his case).

It may be significant that while in 1906 the appeals commission apparently relied on their discovery that it had been Numia Kererū who had submitted Tutakangahau's list in order to conclude that they could 'not believe that any mistake was made in regard to the inclusion of these names by the last Commission', the chief judge explicitly attributed 'a fair compromise' in Tutakangahau's claim to Tutakangahau himself. This suggests that while Numia's status as a commissioner may have privileged him to over-ride the investigative commission's dismissal of Tutakangahau's list, as another commissioner Tutakangahau had the privilege of cooperating with Numia in an unofficial compromise he had denied his opponents in the migrant marriage alliance. Although such sub rosa privilege might arouse grievances among less influential Tūhoe as well as contravene the official policy that commissioners who were claimants be formally stood down, this situation supports my argument that the UDNR commission—appeals as well as investigative—quietly as well as routinely deferred to settlements arranged in Tūhoe ways by Tūhoe leaders outside of formal hearings.

In conclusion, at least two important Waikaremoana situations left in limbo by the investigative commission in 1902 remained entirely unaddressed by the appeals commission in 1907: the official division of northern Waikaremoana in favor of Tamakaimoana hapū adding some 4000 acres to Maungapōhatu that was neither rescinded nor reflected in the final maps, and the final inclusion of 92 Tamakaimoana claimants in the Waikaremoana order with small but significant shares despite dismissal of their claim. Although the latter was the explicit concern of Mahaki Tapiki's appeal, it seemed not to be taken seriously by all but 12 of those claimants who stood to lose if the appeal were approved, nor even by the commission that heard the appeal. The studied disregard of both this unjustified inclusion of shareholders and the ambiguous ownership of 4000 acres might be explained if everyone concerned accepted that the two inconsistencies canceled each other out: what Tamakaimoana got in shares in Waikaremoana compensated for what Maungapōhatu block lost on the ground and maps, and both commissions conspired to remain silent about it out of official embarrassment—or quiet deference to two Tūhoe commissioners.

3 Investigation of the Ruatāhuna Block, 1899–1907

As did the examination above of the Waikaremoana records, the following examination of the investigation and appeals for Ruatāhuna block focuses on a particular confrontation involving the migrant marriage alliance described in Chap. 7. However, in the case of Ruatāhuna this involvement does not become apparent until appeals against the results of the investigation were submitted in 1903 and finally heard in 1907. On the other hand, as will be discussed in Chap. 9, the involvement of the migrant marriage alliance remained a key factor in the partition of Ruatāhuna 1912–1913, and continued to be a significant influence in both blocks through the Crown purchase campaign and Urewera Consolidation Scheme 1915–1926.

In 1899 there were about 33 claimants lists submitted for the several areas that were to become Ruatāhuna block, some submitted in the later hearings for Maungapōhatu and Waikaremoana blocks (Bassett and Kay 2002: 53–4). Several leaders of the marriage alliance submitted nine of these claims: Te Wao Ihimaera, Paraki Wereta, Wharepapa Ihimaera, Matika Taratoa, Te Mapu Pukeiotu, and Noho Taratoa (see Fig. 7.1). Te Whenuanui II, son of the leading *rangatira* Te Whenuanui Te Umuariki, submitted three claimants lists, all in the name of Te Urewera hapū. As described in Chaps. 5 and 7, Te Whenuanui II was married to Mako Mātaatua, and his younger sister Hinepau was married to Mihaka Matika, each representing a descent group of the migrant marriage alliance. Most of the hapū in whose names the claimants lists were submitted in 1899 were finally declared among the seven hapū that were recognized to control the block in 1902.

Probably because of delays encountered in the 1901 season described in the preceding section, the commission's investigation of the claimants lists for Ruatāhuna did not begin until early in the 1902 season and all hearings were held at Rūātoki. Probably as the leading *rangatira* of the Ruatāhuna area at that time, Te Whenuanui II (misleadingly identified by Best simply as 'Whenuanui') led off by claiming the whole block for seven hapū. He then named the founding ancestors under whose *mana* each hapū could make its claim by ancestry and occupation:

1. the ancestor Arohana for Te Urewera hapū;
2. the ancestor Kuri for Ngati Kuri hapū;
3. the ancestor Te Rurehe for Ngati Hinekura or Ngai Te Rurehe hapū[8];
4. the ancestor Parahaki for Ngati Manunui hapū and Ngati Tu hapū;
5. the ancestors Te Rurehe and Parahaki for Ngati Kakahutapiki hapū. (UMB 6: 109)

This was an extraordinarily expansive claim, and that Te Whenuanui II led off with it demonstrates that he was widely accepted among the hapū of the Ruatāhuna as the leading *rangatira* of *mana* in the area. Such a statement had almost certainly been pre-arranged among most other leaders of the area. These same six hapū were named as owners of the block when the block list was finally confirmed in October 1902 (Ngāti Ruatāhuna was added as a seventh hapū, but it was part of Te Urewera hapū). The close relationship or overlapping membership between the last three hapū, and between them and Ngāti Ruapani of Waikaremoana block, was pointed out in Chap. 7 with regard to the claimants lists and the *rangatira* status of Paraki Wereta in Ngāti Manunui hapū.

The following investigation was preoccupied with defining several areas of what was to become the Ruatāhuna block (usually named as 'Ruatāhuna', 'Maioro', 'Huiarau' and 'Waiiti') but by March 1902 the commission announced that the "whole of the members of Cmsn except Tutakangahau" agreed that these areas would be treated as one block (UMB 6: 294–5). There was no further explanation of this announcement in the minutes, but it is likely that the commission's backlog of investigations prompted it. The Tūhoe commissioner Tutakangahau probably disagreed because his claim for 'Maioro' in the northern part of the block would thereby be included in the area called Huiarau or Manawarū and disadvantage his claims for Maungapōhatu block (he was later recognized to hold only token shares in the block).

It may be significant that Numia Kererū, another Tūhoe commissioner, apparently joined in the majority, although in 1900 he had been the lone protestor against expediting investigations throughout the reserve by including ‘minor’ claims in more inclusive ones (discussed in Chap. 3). His support of the resolution to treat the different areas of Ruatāhuna as one block may have been strategic: as will be explained in Chap. 9, by 1912 he successfully appealed for partition of the Ruatāhuna block in order to recognize internal “hapu boundaries” and fix relative interests accordingly (NACMB 1: 70).

As was clear from Te Whenuanui II’s 1899 submissions of claims for Ruatāhuna, his primary affiliation in that area was with Te Urewera hapū. His opening statement in the first session for the investigation of the block in Rūātoki on 3 February 1902 for so many other ancestors and hapū was extraordinary, but did not go entirely unchallenged. Although the hearings were being held in Rūātoki at the other end of the Urewera reserve, Tūhoe *kawa* (‘custom’, in this case, the ethic that hosts defer to visitors), as well as Te Whenuanui II’s pre-eminent *mana*, ensured he would be paid careful respect. Probably as a consequence of the extent and gravity in his initial proclamation, the commission immediately called for objections. It is also significant that Te Amo Kokouri and Numia Kererū immediately asked that Kahuwī be named as an ancestor along with Arohana:

> Te Amo. I object to the ancestor for [Te]Urewera. I wish to have another ancestor with Arohana – named Kahui [the correct spelling of this ancestor is Kahuwī; the mis-spelling is probably Best’s].
>
> Numia Kereru. I join with Te Amo for the Ancestor Arohana.
>
> [Commission:] Neither of these [objectors] put in a claim for this ancestor at the publishing of claims in 1899. – but the names under this ancestor are included in the list of names. And Whenuanui [sic] admits they have a claim. (UMB 6: 109–10)

This is precisely the issue that involved the migrant marriage alliance by the time of the appeals, and a confrontation between Numia and Te Whenuanui II (and, implicitly, his father) that will be traced through 1912 in the next chapter. Although it first surfaced officially here, Tupaea Rapaera’s announcement 7 March 1900 that *Numia*, rather than Te Whenuanui II’s representative, might conduct the Ngāti Ruatāhuna and Te Urewera claims to Whaitiripapa block suggests the confrontation may have emerged in that case (Chap. 5). Figure 8.1, shown below and mentioned in previous chapters, is a composite genealogy displaying the relationship between Arohana, Kahuwī, and their descendants that will be discussed in the following chapters.

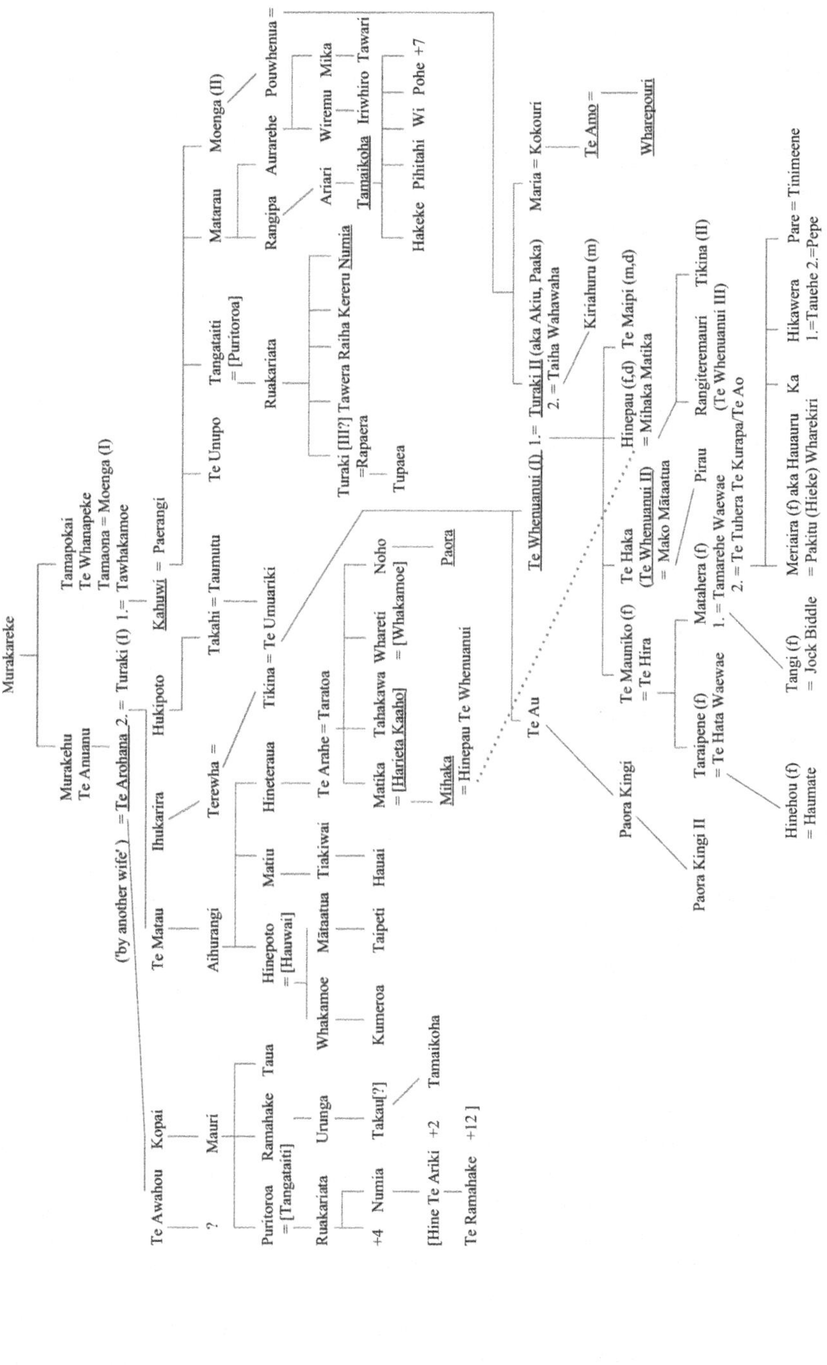

Fig. 8.1 Composite genealogy of Arohana, Kahuwī, and Te Whenuanui I, with selected predecessors and descendants.

Fig. 8.1 (continued)

(Sources: Best 1898; Paora Noho NACMB 1: 223,228,231 (1912); Numia Kereru NACMB 1: 235–6 (1912); Tamaikoha UMB 1: 337–41) (1900); Binney 2002: 20–3; Pou Temara (cited in Binney); personal communications with Rangiwhaitiri Wharekiri 1975, Paora Kruja 1983, and Tamati Kruger)
Legend:
Composite drawn from above sources, with my interpolations. Whakapapa rarangi (siblings and spouses usually not shown); bottom section contemporary with bottom part of top section; vertical lines represent filiation or descent; horizontal lines represent siblings (in order of seniority) or cousins; dotted lines connect same marriage or person; = represents marriage, seniority, or successive if numbered; persons central to my analysis are underlined

As will become apparent later from the wider context of this issue, it is also probable that Numia took care that Te Amo spoke first, and that they both respectfully linked Kahuwī with Arohana, the ancestor Te Whenuanui II had named for Te Urewera hapū. As reported, Numia actually did not mention Kahuwī by name, only joined in Te Amo's claim. This caution would have been warranted because while Numia lived in Rūātoki and was primarily affiliated with Ngāti Rongo hapū (which also hosted the commission's investigation of Ruatāhuna at Tauarau *marae*), Te Amo was Te Whenuanui I's wife's nephew as well as an important Ruatāhuna leader in his own right. It is also likely that the commission (which included Numia as a member, although officially stood down in this case) anticipated this proposal, and had received from Numia (or Te Amo) a list of claimants descended from Kahuwī: the chairman responded to the proposal by pointing out that neither Numia nor Te Amo had submitted claims for Kahuwī in 1899, and that in any case the list they had presumably furnished as descendants of Kahuwī were included in the other submissions of 1899. In this way, the commission may have been side-stepping a difficult issue. Perhaps mollified, Te Whenuanui II is reported to have accepted that those on the list had a claim, and apparently did not explicitly mention or reject the proposed ancestor Kahuwī at this time.

However, in the resumption of the Ruatāhuna hearing a few weeks later on 20 February 1902, the allocation of shares was read out and Numia Kererū himself again asked that Kahuwī be included as an ancestor (UMB 6: 208). This time Te Whenuanui II explicitly rejected Numia's proposal. Apparently he offered no explanation, but the commission noted that "this ancestor is practically included inasmuch as the descendants of this ancestor are included and full shares given them" and, again, the issue appeared to be settled. Nevertheless, yet again a few weeks later at the 3 March 1902 hearing on Ruatāhuna, Te Iriwhiro demanded the full 20 shares for (the senior generation of) nearly 100 persons whom he claimed were entitled in Manawarū and, according to Te Whenuanui II, were descendants only of Kahuwī (UMB 6: 262–3; in Fig. 1.2, Manawarū is comprised of both of the partitions named Arohana and Kahuwī in 1912). Te Iriwhiro Te Wiremu had laid claims to the Manawarū and Waiiti areas of northern Ruatāhuna in 1899, and was an influential elder of one of the several descent groups descended from Kahuwī (see Fig. 8.1, right side).

Te Iriwhiro's objection was an explicit and dramatic challenge to Te Whenuanui II's list. Numia was present in the hearing and had contributed evidence regarding the preceding claim. He may well have encouraged Te Iriwhiro's claim for increased shares or even coordinated his earlier claims with it, again avoiding direct offense of Te Whenuanui II and tactfully remaining in the background. Significantly, Te Iriwhiro's own claim apparently did not mention Kahuwī. However, Te Whenuanui II appeared to be equally well-prepared for the challenge:

> Iriwhiro – I claim 20 shares for these people. They are entitled in Manawaru.
> Whenuanui [sic:]
> These people are not descended from Arohana but from Kahui who was not one of the ancestors given, but who is practically included as his descendants are in. I have given these shares from aroha to descendants of the foster child of Arohana – these are for the part called Manawaru. they had not an exclusive right in Manawaru – we have given the desedts of Arohana double shares because he owned over the whole block.
> Iriwhiro [:]
> Manawaru was held. Partly by Arohana. and. Kahui.
> Whenuanui [sic:]
> I am descended from both– the land was not Kahui's –
> Iriwhiro:
> I admit Whenuanui [sic] is from both – whilst I am from Kahui [only]. – but he has given Te Amo who is from Kahui only. 20 shares.

The key issue that Kahuwī was a ***whāngai tamariki*** (adopted child) of Arohana, and so traditionally had no birthrights to land by descent through his adoptive parent, had finally been formally broached. Also for the first time it became explicit that it was rights to the Manawarū area in northern Ruatāhuna which were at stake, and it appears that Te Whenuanui II was already well aware of that. He probably also intended to repeat the commission's response of 20 February that 'this ancestor is practically included inasmuch as the descendants of this ancestor are included and full shares given them' (i.e., 20 shares to the senior generation of descendants able to demonstrate occupation). But he also pointedly corrected them that he had not given those in Te Iriwhiro's list full shares, but shares only from ***aroha*** (probably one or two shares) because they were descended only from Kahuwī, and Kahuwī was only a foster child: 'the land was not Kahui's' while the descendants of Arohana were given full shares 'because he owned over the whole block'. The implication was probably that while Arohana's rights of 'ownership' over Manawarū was exclusive and unrestricted, Kahuwī had no rights to any part of it. Another significant implication of this exchange was that in response to Te Whenuanui II's announcement that he was descended from both Arohana and Kahuwī, Te Iriwhiro accepted this claim and admitted that he was descended only from Kahuwī. But he then pointed out Te Whenuanui II's inconsistency in giving Te Amo Kokouri (Numia's supporter in his first attempt to gain recognition of Kahuwī) 20 shares even though he too was 'from Kahui only'. All these issues were to arise again in the 1912 partition of Ruatāhuna.

By March 1902 this emerging confrontation had considerable background already, and others present in this hearing were probably aware of it. As was described in Chap. 5 with regard to Tamaikoha's claim to Whaitiripapa block just south of Rūātoki and reviewed in Chap. 7, the ancestor Kahuwī's role in an ambiguous gift of land in that block from Te Urewera hapū to Ngāti Rongo hapū had been pivotal before. Argument through the 1890s between Tamaikoha (for Te Urewera hapū) and Numia Kererū (for Ngāti Rongo hapū) had been heard before the District Native Land Court (where Numia's case was favored); heard again before the Native Appellate Court (where Tamaikoha's case was favored and the decision reversed); and, in March of 1900, heard again before the commission. The commission awarded Whaitiripapa block officially to Te Urewera hapū, but included claimants from Ngāti Rongo hapū in the title. Ngāti Ruatāhuna hapū (which was also headed by Te Whenuanui II, and was probably a part of Te Urewera hapū) and Māhurehure hapū (which was almost indistinguishable in membership from Ngāti Rongo) were probably only proxies for the main antagonists. In the case of Whaitiripapa block, Tamaikoha had made it clear that Kahuwī and his descendants were affiliated to both Te Urewera hapū and Ngāti Rongo hapū, opening the door for a compromise settlement.

However, in the case of Ruatāhuna block, Te Whenuanui II was clearly set against any compromise with regard to Kahuwī's rights in Manawarū other than token shares extended only on the basis of *aroha*. In this case, the 'compassion' may even have been intended as patronizing. As a leader of Te Urewera hapū, Te Whenuanui II almost certainly knew all about Numia's success for Ngāti Rongo hapū in Whaitiripapa (where he and his sister Raiha were recognized to hold strong shares), and was prepared to defend Te Urewera hapū in Ruatāhuna against the same strategy. His reticence in response to Numia's two earlier efforts to obtain his recognition of Kahuwī in Manawarū is probably best understood as the disdain of an affronted *rangatira*.

The commission apparently did not ask Te Whenuanui II to elaborate on his claim regarding Kahuwī's adoption and lack of rights, nor did they ask Te Iriwhiro to elaborate on his argument. However, for better understanding of this crucial exchange, whakapapa presented by both sides to argue the same issue in 1912 can be briefly summarized here. Figure 8.1 is a composite of several whakapapa fragments presented in 1900 by Numia (for Ngāti Rongo hapū) and Tamaikoha (for Te Urewera hapū) with regard to Whaitiripapa block, and the more extensive whakapapa presented by Numia in 1912 for the partition of Ruatāhuna. Also included for comparison in Fig. 8.1 is the whakapapa presented in 1912 by Paora Noho for Te Whenuanui II's case for Te Urewera hapū. It is significant that in both cases neither side challenged the other's whakapapa, so they can be taken as relatively reliable (NACMB 1: 235–6, also 1: 228, 231; UMB 1: 337–9; UMB 5: 355, 357).

As was shown most clearly in Numia's whakapapa, Kahuwī's mother Turaki remarried after the death of his father Tawhakamoe, and her second husband was Arohana. According to the accounts given by both Numia and his opponent Paora Noho in 1912, Turaki was pregnant with Kahuwī by her first husband Tawhakamoe when he was killed, and (as recounted by Tamaikoha in 1900 for Kahuwī's role in Whaitiripapa) when her child was born he was named *kahu wii* ('cloak of reeds') to commemorate the way his father's body was found after a battle at Lake Rotoiti. Arohana then married the widow Turaki and adopted her son Kahuwī, and subsequently had three younger children by her. By the time of the commission's inquiries, Kahuwī was seen to be among the progenitors of Ngāti Rongo hapū, and Turaki's other three children by Arohana were seen to be among the progenitors of Te Urewera hapū.

In the 1900 case of Whaitiripapa block, it was Tawhakmoe's younger brother Tamawhai who was said by Numia to have gifted rights to that land from Te Urewera hapū to Ngāti Rongo via his nephew Kahuwī in exchange for a Ngāti Rongo woman in marriage (perhaps Kahuwī's wife Paerangi?). In the 1902 case of Ruatāhuna block, Te Whenuanui II was denying Kahuwī's right to transmit to his numerous offspring any of his adoptive father Arohana's rights to the Manawarū part of Ruatāhuna. This was (and generally continues to be) a customary limitation on the rights of *whāngai tamariki*/adopted children; rights to land are birthrights that come with the bloodline from both birth parents, not from an adoptive parent. If (as was argued in 1912) rights to Manawarū came only through Arohana and not through his wife and Kahuwī's mother Turaki, then

Kahuwī had no rights there. Whatever rights Kahuwī's descendants might claim in Manawarū could only be given by Arohana or his descendants as gifts or out of compassion, as tokens of their *aroha*, not as birthrights.

It is significant that a member of the immediate families of both the adversaries Te Whenuanui II and Numia Kererū bore the name of their common ancestress Turaki, birth-mother of Kahuwī and wife of Arohana, his adoptive father (Fig. 8.1). While Te Whenuanui II's mother was also named Turaki (and, to emphasize the point, referred to by Numia as 'Turaki II'), Numia's own deceased *mātāmua* sister had also been named Turaki (also mother of the *rangatira* Tupaea Rapaera), almost certainly after the same ancestress (although Numia appears not to have raised this fact himself). However, Turaki I's central role here should not obscure the fundamental difference between the Whaitiripapa and Ruatāhuna cases: while in the former case the issue was Tawhakamoe's land (having been gifted via Kahuwī to Ngāti Rongo hapū), in the latter case the issue was Arohana's land (Manawarū), and whether or not Kahuwī and his descendants had any right to it.

Te Iriwhiro's claim on 3 March 1902 that a full 20 shares should be given to (senior generations of) 96 descendants of Kahuwī, and Te Whenuanui II's uncompromising rejection, was apparently immediately followed by the commission's final decision on this issue:

> Commission decides that the descendants of a single ancestor of the two. Arohana and Kahui – will get ten shares but in the case of those coming from [both ancestors] they will [get] 20 shares. For heads. and. children and gr.children accordingly this to refer to each class of shares – for children gr children. (UMB 6: 262–3)

Superficially, this may have appeared to be a fair compromise insofar as it gave special recognition to Te Whenuanui II and his full siblings as enjoying what he had claimed (and Te Iriwhiro accepted) as his 'dual right' or descent from both Arohana and Kahuwī (through Te Whenuanui I and Turaki (II), respectively; see Fig. 8.1). Due to the restriction on marriage closer than fourth cousins (discussed in Chap. 6) and the relative recency of these two ancestors, there would have been few among the descendants of either Arohana or Kahuwī who could claim descent from both. Te Whenuanui I and his wife Turaki (II) were fourth and third cousins themselves, and apparently Te Whenuanui I's own parents were second cousins to each other (an unusual case perhaps reflecting Ngata's claim that 'highly prized lines' among the coastal Ngāti Porou iwi married close cousins in high proportion (Chap. 6).

Nevertheless, while from a more naive point of view the commission's decision may have appeared to be a fair compromise between uncompromisingly opposed parties, at least in retrospect it had misunderstood or prejudged the situation. While Te Whenuanui II insisted on giving descendants of Arohana 'double shares' *whether or not* they were also descendants of Kahuwī, the commission's decision instead treated those of them who were descendants only of Kahuwī as having equal rights (ten shares) with those who were descendants only of Arohana. Granting full rights only to those who were descendants of both further demeaned Arohana and thus Te Whenuanui II's case. The commission proposed this 'compromise' even though they apparently accepted that Kahuwī was Arohana's son only by adoption and that, in accord with the customary restriction on adoption, rights to Manawarū came only in Arohana's bloodline. One must ask why Te Whenuanui II appeared to accept such an affront to the descendants of Arohana and disregard of these facts.

There is some ambiguous evidence that Te Whenuanui II reluctantly accepted the decision. The hapū recognized to have rights to Ruatāhuna in the final confirmations of October 1902 were limited to those he had named in his opening testimony, adding only Ruatāhuna hapū, which was part of the leading hapū Te Urewera and described by Best as his 'family' hapū. However, the block committee that was named in the confirmations included both Numia Kererū and Te Irewhiro who, as well as being an acknowledged leader of Ngāti Kurī hapū, had joined with Numia in demanding recognition of Kahuwī's rights (Fig. 2.1). On the other hand, four of its seven members were leaders in the migrant marriage alliance, and Te Haka (Te Whenuanui II) led the list. It is possible that Te Whenuanui II, confronted by the pre-emptory decision of the commission, accepted a compromise whereby Numia was named to the block committee but Ngāti Rongo, for which Numia had implicitly made his demand for recognition of Kahuwī, was not named among the hapū whose rights to the block were formally recognized.

However, subsequent appeals suggest Te Whenuanui II may not have accepted the decision. Nevertheless, for some reason these later protests appeared hesitant or indirect. He submitted appeals in July 1903 and again in September 1903 against the official allocation of shares published in 1903 by the commission in the provisional order for Ruatāhuna (Bassett and Kay 2002: 72; S.P. Vol 1: 62–7). The main point in both these appeals was that although the allocation of shares that he had recommended to the commission had been accepted and confirmed, the published order had unjustifiably decreased larger shares and increased small shares. Although he mentioned the issue of descendants of Arohana and Kahuwī, and stated that those of Kahuwī had no rights to the land, this point was left unclear as well as subordinated in the appeals.

It is significant that both of Te Whenuanui II's appeals were supported primarily by leaders of the migrant marriage alliance (Fig. 7.1). He was joined in the July 1903 appeal by Turipa Manuera (Te Mapu's father's brother), Mahaki Tapiki (who would later conduct the appeal), Te Awhi (one of Tahakawa Taratoa's children), Mihaka Tamawhai (father or uncle of Te Mauniko, Te Whenuanui II's mātāmua sister), and Me Tahiatu (unidentified). In the September appeal he was joined by Noho Taratoa, Mihaka Matika, and Rahui Hoera (all in the Murahioi descent group). Te Whenuanui II's first appeal did not specify whose shares ought to be increased, but his second appeal named all 4 Taratoa siblings and 19 of their children. As can be seen in Fig. 7.1, three of the five descent groups of the marriage alliance were represented in Te Whenuanui II's two appeals: one each of the Tawa, Hautu, and Taratoa descent groups in the first appeal, and three more of the Taratoa descent group in the second appeal. Te Amo Kokouri and his son Wharepouri also supported the earlier appeal; although in 1902 Te Amo had initiated Numia Kererū's first claim for recognition of Kahuwī, here he was probably acting as Te Whenuanui I's wife's nephew (see Fig. 8.1), a resident in Manawarū, and an important leader in Te Urewera hapū. As Te Iriwhiro had pointed out in the third request for recognition of Kahuwī, Te Whenuanui II had favored Te Amo with 20 shares even though he was a descendant of Kahuwī but not of Arohana.

In October 1903 a few weeks after Te Whenuanui II's second appeal, two very similar appeals against the allocation of shares in Ruatāhuna were submitted by Te Mapu Pukeiotu and Mahaki Tapiki (Bassett and Kay 2002: 73–4; S.P. vol 1: 58–60; 68–9), leaders in the alliance and conductors, respectively, of the 1901 investigation and 1907 appeal for Waikaremoana block. Mahaki had already joined Te Whenuanui II's July appeal. However, his own October appeal was furthermore joined by Noho Taratoa (who had already joined Te Whenuanui II's September appeal), three of the Whakamoe sibling group, four of the Tangira sibling group, two of the Manuera sibling group, Hurae Puketapu, and two of the Wiremu sibling group. All of these persons except the Wiremu children were leaders of the migrant marriage alliance or their immediate offspring. Te Mapu Pukeiotu's separate appeal was joined by 11 persons; while some of these persons may have been associated with the alliance, only he himself and Wharepapa Ihimaera (Te Wao's brother) appear in (Fig. 7.1). All these appellants requested increases in shares that had been unjustifiably reduced in the 1903 orders. In 1907 Mahaki Tapiki was to conduct Te Whenuanui II's appeals for Ruatāhuna as well as his own for Waikaremoana, and Whareturoa Hoani was to conduct Te Mapu's appeal, because by then both Te Mapu and Te Whenuanui II had died.

Although the 1903 appeals clearly display mutual support between Te Whenuanui II and the migrant marriage alliance, can it also be concluded that they were protesting the 1902 decision to recognize the rights of descendants of Kahuwī as equal to those of Arohana in Manawarū?

Te Whenuanui II's July 1903 appeal protested that although his allocation of shares to his list was '20 shares for adults, 15 for children and 10 for grand-children' had been accepted and confirmed, the published order showed that 'our shares have been reduced 5 being given to adults 2 to children and 1 to grandchildren.... for we are the permanent people of this place and persons who had but small interests have had their increased by the Commissioners whereas we the descendant[s] of Te Arohana and Kahui... had our shares reduced'. His September 1903 appeal was apparently intended as a clarification of the earlier one, adding a list of those who were 'permanent people' but whose shares had been reduced, this time claiming that their ancestor was Arohana, and explicitly stating that 'the ancestor Kahui had no right to this land nor his descendants'.

There nevertheless appear to be several inconsistencies between the 1902 decision of the commission and these two appeals, as well as internal to them. The 3 March 1902 decision had been that 'descendants of single ancestor of the two. Arohana and Kahui – will get ten shares but in the case of those coming from. [both] they will [get] 20 shares. for heads...' of family. However, while Te Whenuanui II's first appeal may have ambiguously acknowledged this decision in the phrase '...descendants of Te Arohana and Kahui ancestors to whom the Ruatāhuna block was awarded...', his later clarification appears to deny it in the explicit rejection of Kahuwī's rights. Furthermore, even if Te Whenuanui II's resulting allocation of shares to his list of claimants conformed to the commission's decision, he makes no such claim; to the contrary, he appears to attribute his allocation of full shares (here, 20/15/10) to the claimants' residential status as 'permanent people' rather than as 'descendants of [both] Arohana and Kahui'. In any case, whether his final list conformed to the commission's decision or to his criterion of 'permanent people', one would suppose the list of persons attached to his second appeal whose shares had been unjustly reduced would include more than the Taratoa descent group. From Fig. 8.1 alone, it appears that at least Te Whenuanui I and Turaki IIs' several descendants (including himself) and all their offspring who had continued occupation should have been included as descendants of both ancestors and, presumably, at least some other descent groups as well.[9]

Finally, Te Whenuanui II's protest in the first appeal that those to whom he had allotted full shares had them reduced in the published order to '5 being given to adults 2 to children and 1 to grandchildren' furthermore appears inconsistent with the list of Taratoa's descendants supplied with his second appeal. Their shares in the 1903 order were actually ten shares each for the oldest living generation (the four Taratoa siblings) and five shares each for their nineteen children (AJHR 1903: Ruatāhuna #35–49, #56–63). This allocation would be consistent with descent only from Arohana, which may have been the case (Fig. 8.1 shows the siblings' mother was Te Arahe, Arohana's great-great-granddaughter).

The appeals submitted in October 1903 by Mahaki Tapiki and Te Mapu Pukeiotu were also supported by others of the migrant marriage alliance and, as had Te Whenuanui II, expressed their requests for increased shares in terms of unanticipated reductions that appeared in the official orders. However, in the case of these later two appeals, no mention at all was made of either Arohana or Kahuwī, let alone the 1902 decision of the commission. Like Te Whenuanui II's protest that "permanent people of this place" had their shares reduced while "persons who had but small interests" had their shares increased, Mahaki's appeal protested that while *nga noho tuturu* ('true occupiers' of the land) had their shares reduced, those with *paanga iti* ('small shares') or *paanga kore* ('no shares') and *tangata kore take* ('useless people' or those with no grounds for claim at all) had their shares increased or recognized (Bassett and Kay S.P. vol 1: 58–9). Similarly, Te Mapu's appeal protested that while shares awarded to *tangata noho tuturu* ('true occupiers') were small, those for *nga heke rau* ('the migrants') were large (Bassett and Kay S.P. vol 1: 68–9).

Regardless of the inconsistencies, the emphasis in all four appeals upon 'permanent people' and 'true occupiers' in contrast to 'small interests', 'no shares', 'useless people', and 'migrants' may echo the discrimination between longer-established and not-yet-accepted migrant families that was raised in Chap. 7 as an explanation for the large proportion of narrow rights-holders in Waikaremoana and Ruatāhuna but few other Urewera blocks. But what would have prompted the mutual support apparent in all four appeals between Te Whenuanui II and the migrant marriage alliance?

It might be the case that Te Whenuanui II, defending descendants of Arohana against those of Kahuwī, and the marriage alliance, defending the occupational rights of more fully accepted descendants of migrant descent groups, had found common cause by 1903. This mutual support would also have been demanded by the marriages of two of Te Whenuanui I's children that had long linked his family to several of the descent groups of the marriage alliance. As pointed out earlier, Te Haka's (Te Whenuanui II) marriage to Mako Mātaatua linked them to both the Hauwai and Pareihe descent groups, and his sister Hinepau's husband was Mihaka Matika, ***mātāmua*** of the extensive Taratoa descent group in the list accompanying Te Whenuanui II's second appeal.

The confrontation between Numia Kererū and Te Iwikino Hairuha over Ierenui-Ōhāua block examined in Chap. 6, which had also reached a crisis by 1903, may also have alerted the migrant marriage alliance to Numia's role in Waikaremoana as well as Ruatāhuna. It will be remembered that Te Iwikino's ambiguous influence within Ngāti Rongo hapū was through his siblings' and his own marriages to descendants of Taratoa Murahioi as well as Te Purewa I, leading ancestors of the migrant marriage alliance and Ngāti Rongo, respectively (Best 1898: 68–9; Figs. 8.1 and 7.1). He and his siblings also ranked very highly in their rights to Waikaremoana but not other blocks, suggesting his predecessors may have been immigrants from Ngāti Kahungunu. In his confrontation with Numia over Ōhāua, Te Iwikino may have sought support among the influential Taratoa sibling group of the alliance, which included their half-sister and his sister-in-law Papa Taratoa, a granddaughter of Te Purewa I.

But if Numia Kererū led the 1902 bid for recognition of Kahuwī's descendants' rights in Manawarū against Te Whenuanui II, what was his response to the four 1903 appeals when they were finally heard by the appeals commission in Whakatane in February 1907? Although Te Whenuanui II had died by then, his appeals still awaited a hearing and had specifically raised the issue of Arohana's and Kahuwī's rights, if not the 1902 decision itself.

Numia conducted other Ruatāhuna appeals that included one from Te Iriwhiro (Numia's likely proxy in the third challenge in behalf of Kahuwī) for increased shares that was passed with no objections, and argued at length against an appeal by Ngāti Tāwhaki hapū that was dismissed (Bassett and Kay 2002: 74). Consequently, he was likely to have been present in the hearings from the beginning when Te Whenuanui II's and his supporter's appeals were heard. Whakatane was not far from Rūātoki where he lived. As the likely instigator of the three efforts to add Kahuwī to Te Whenuanui's list of ancestors for the block, Numia would certainly have been alert with regard to the equalization of Kahuwī's with Arohana's shares required by the 1902 decision. Furthermore, as a commissioner (albeit stood down for Ruatāhuna as well as Waikaremoana cases), he would probably have known 'how it came about' that shares were apportioned (or re-apportioned) the way they finally were for publication in the provisional order.

However, when Te Whenuanui II's and Mahaki Tapiki's appeals were conducted by Mahaki on Friday 1 February 1907, Numia did not respond when objections were called for, nor even when the appeals commission announced that the case would remain open until the commission could satisfy itself as to "whether any valid cause of complaint exists against the shares awarded to these 50 persons by the previous commission" (UCAMB 2: 98–107). Nor did he respond when Mahaki explained that Te Mapu, who had been their conductor in the 1902 case but had also since died, 'did not tell me how it came about that we were given such small shares'. Mahaki added that the award of 20 shares to the senior generation, 10 for their children and 5 for their grandchildren 'was only for rightful owners of block, not for those with lesser rights', but did not mention either the 1902 decision or the issue of Arohana and Kahuwī.

Numia did finally speak up when the appeals commission gave Mahaki an opportunity to revise his list of 50 appellants and Noho Taratoa added a further 24 persons to it. Although no shortcoming of the detailed appeal was described, the commission urged Mahaki: 'will you explain? you should ask for your list back because it does not tally with your explanation'. The minutes then reported that Mahaki responded that he would like the list back for revision, and the list was returned. When Noho Taratoa requested his addition of persons to the appeals, and the commission asked for any objections to it, Numia finally broke his silence, requesting 'that this list be withdrawn to be reconsidered between us outside. I reduced their shares at time of previous cmsn'.

Surprisingly, the commission apparently did not respond to Numia's strangely tardy and apparently laconic admission that it was he who had made the mysterious reductions of shares. Instead, it only recorded that the list was "handed back accordingly [and the hearing was] adjourned until 9am Monday 4th" (NACMB 2: 104). One would suppose that this would have been the appeals commission's opportunity at least to clarify the relationship between what Te Whenuanui II had claimed was the investigative commission's acceptance and confirmation of his list of shares for the block and Numia's admitted reduction of the shares that was the very subject of these appeals.

On the following Monday, Mahaki Tapiki and Noho Taratoa each returned their revised lists for increased shares 'with the alterations we have agreed upon outside'. The commission recorded that there were no objections and on 1 February 1907 altered the lists copied into the minutebook from the appeals by crossing out 8 of the 53 persons on Mahaki's list for Te Whenuanui II's and his own original appeals, and 8 of the 24 additional persons on Noho Taratoa's list for the same original appeals. None of the requests for increased shares for each of the persons remaining on the lists had been altered, so all were apparently accepted by the commission. A few days later, Te Mapu's original 1903 appeal was presented by Whareturoa Hoani, who repeated Te Mapu's explanation that 'shares awarded to the permanent occupiers were small and those for the emigrants was large'. Again without further clarification, the commission handed the list back for resolution outside, and approved it when it was returned and there were no objections (Bassett and Kay 2002: 73). However, while Te Mapu's original 1903 appeal had named 68 persons, Whareturoa's list had already been reduced to only 22 persons when it was recorded. It is likely that Numia Kererū also facilitated the revision of this later list, either before or after it was recorded. The apparent result, then, of Te Whenuanui II's, Mahaki's, and Te Mapu's original 1903 appeals was the reduction of their lists of 103 to 99 persons, of which another 16 were dropped in revision outside the court, but approval of the requested increase of shares for all those remaining.

4 Conclusion

On the face of it, then, Te Whenuanui II and his supporters' appeals for increased shares were largely successful. It furthermore appears that the amendments to these appeals were agreed upon by all without ever raising the issue of Kahuwī's rights to Manawarū as against those of Arohana, nor the commission's 1902 decision regarding this, at least before the appeals commission. However, this sudden resolution of the impasse raises more questions than it settles. Why wasn't this issue and the commission's 1902 decision regarding it raised by the appellants (who were presumably disadvantaged by that decision) nor by Numia (who would presumably rely on it against the appeals) nor by anyone else? Why did the commission so readily grant Numia his request to settle the appeals outside hearings? Why didn't they pursue with him their concern about what had happened in finalization of the provisional order for Ruatāhuna block? Why did Numia so readily grant increased shares in apparent disregard of the 1902 decision, thereby giving up the equality of Kahuwī's right to Arohana's in Manawarū that the 1902 decision would imply?

At least with regard to the involvement of the migrant marriage alliance between Waikaremoana and Ruatāhuna, the appeal commission's apparent disregard of real and unresolved issues in each block, strangely aggravated by Tūhoe reticence or caution on these issues presumably for their own purposes, left these issues in even greater prominence in 1907 than they had been in 1903. In the case of the Waikaremoana block, these begged or unresolved issues were the location of the northern boundary between Waikaremoana and Maungapōhatu, and the inclusion in the final order of Numia's list for 92 Tamakaimoana hapū claimants regardless of the dismissal of Tutakangahau's as well as Paora Kingi's arguments. This situation remained a potential double loss for Waikaremoana, and double win for Maungapōhatu.

In the case of Ruatāhuna block, the begged or unresolved issues were the virtual silence of all parties to the appeals regarding the 1902 confrontation between the descendants of Kahuwī and those of Arohana for rights in Manawarū, the 1902 decision that granted equality between them without addressing the arguments, and the apparent readiness of Numia Kererū in 1907 to give up the advantage of that decision and increase the shares of most of the appellants. This appeared to be an empty victory for Te Whenuanui II and thus a compromise of the mana of both sides. As will be seen in the next chapter, these issues and the marriage alliance's central role in them continued to be implicated but not resolved in the partition of Ruatāhuna block 1912–3.

Notes

1. Waimako, where the commission recorded claims for Waikaremoana in 1899, is just south of Tuai on the south shore of Lake Waikaremoana.
2. O'Malley's report, focusing on the boundary issues between Tūhoe and Ngāti Kahungunu, reports only this decision regarding withdrawal of the northern boundary of Waikaremoana and apparently overlooks both the earlier agreement and the commission's own disregard of this decision the following year (1996: 37–8).
3. There may have been some grounds for Tutakangahau's claim to the southern shore of Lake Waikaremoana in a confusion arising when the commission sat at Waimako in 1899. In 1915 Rawaho Winitana and 43 others petitioned the Native Minister (Apirana Ngata) to have the eastern boundary of the reserve (which they called 'te rohe potae o te Urewera') 'moved back' to the southeastern shore of the lake because this location was understood by the investigative commission when it met at Waimako and was recorded in the 1902 sketch maps. They claimed that in 1907 the appeals commission moved the boundary back to the western shore of the lake. The petition was referred to the Native Land Court in Rotorua, where no such records could be found, and "no recommendation" was made on the petition (National Archives Le1/1915/9, pp. 362–366 in Vol 2 supporting papers to O'Malley 1996). However, even if this petition was well-founded, it would not justify Tutakangahau's claim to such extensive lands well beyond the southern shore of the lake.
4. The 1901 map (plan 6873) that has been referred to in the present analysis is apparently not the same map referred to in the quotation above as having the new boundary "shown [on] the plan [in] pencil", having no such markings visible on it. Another detailed plan that appears to derive from plan 6873 but has later details and notes upon it through to 1921, like 6873 shows the northern boundary of Waikaremoana block in the more northern position where the commission confirmed it to be on 3 and 6 May 1901 ('Urewera Native Reserve' (undated, unidentified), found in Special File 227 and moved to MA 13/91, National Archives). Most importantly, the official map announcing the formal establishment of the reserve following the appeals commission in 1907 shows this boundary in the same position ('Urewera Native Reserve', AJHR 1907 Vol III G4A, reproduced here as Figure 2). More careful detail on this 1907 map also supports the more northerly location of the boundary confirmed on 3 and 6 May, although the Ngatapa peak is named Manuoha (as it is in NZMS 170).
5. Hori Wharerangi was an important leader in defense of Waikaremoana lands and, as described in Chap. 2, an unusually well-informed and astute critic of Crown policy and practice. He may well have been an active leader in the

migrant marriage alliance, but I found no kinship or marriage information regarding him in any of the records 1899–1925. It is likely that little information was recorded regarding him because he was not recognized to have ancestral or occupational rights in any of the blocks of the UDNR. As described in Chap. 2, he had also lost his rights in the Crown's confiscation of the Waipaoa block (just outside the reserve to the north of Lake Waikaremoana).

6. Tutakangahau himself may have been ill by 1906, and he died later in 1907 (Holman 2010). A survey of the 1906–1907 minutebooks revealed no evidence given by him, nor by his *mātāmua* son Tarahuru (Te Oti). Although in the final orders of 1907 Tutakangahau was named along with his many children as shareholders in many blocks, and he led the ranking in Maungapōhatu (and none of his children held shares as a senior living generation), delayed succession such as this sometimes occurred with other leaders who had died, presumably out of respect. On the other hand, even if Tutakangahau was ill when the appeals commission convened, one would expect appropriate questions to have been put to others able to speak on his behalf on some of these key issues.
7. Another probable oversight of the appeals commission was more revealing of compromises, bias, or outright incompetence obscured in its reports. The Waikaremoana hearing had already been completed when, at the conclusion of the Ruatāhuna hearing, the commission reported almost as an afterthought that 5407 acres of southern Ruatāhuna, nearly 9% of the block, would be transferred to Waikaremoana (Bassett and Kay 2002: 76; AJHR 1907 G-4: 18). My study of several maps showed that this had nothing to do with the limbo between Maungapōhatu and Waikaremoana in which the northern portion had been left. Instead, it suggested that in their enthusiasm to support Ngāti Kahungunu's claims in Waikaremoana the commission was confused regarding the location of the southern end of the Huiarau crest boundary between Ruatāhuna and Waikaremoana, first describing it as ending near Maungataniwha to the west but later in their decision describing it as ending at Te Apiti on the Waiau River, about 8 kilometers to the east of Maungataniwha (Plans 6873 and 227). The plans show survey corrections of 5407 acres, responding to the terse recommendation of the appeals commission.
8. Te Whenuanui presented these two hapū names as alternatives, but apparently did not explicitly name Te Ruruhe as their ancestor.
9. Te Whenuanui II's final list of claimants and allocation of shares, as well as his appeals, must be assumed to refer to the whole block insofar as the commission had decided to treat the several different areas including Manawarū as one block. However, as was discussed in Chap. 3, although this led to

later partitions such as that of Ruatāhuna block in 1912, it is likely that the investigative commission deferred to Tūhoe leaders' confidence that under the home-rule assured under the UDNR they would be able to restrict the rights of particular descent groups to particular areas of blocks where their ancestral and occupational rights were limited, as well as reflecting that in the shares allocated to them.

References

AJHR 1903. D. Scannell. 'Commissioners' Orders Under the "Urewera District Native Reserves Act, 1896."' Undated. Appendices to the Journal of the House of Representatives 1903, G-6: 1–256. Wellington, N.Z.

AJHR 1907. G. Mair, D.F.G. Barclay, Paratene Ngata. "The Urewera District Native Reserve: reports of the commissioners appointed ...." Report and orders. Undated. Appendices to the Journal of the House of Representatives 1907 G-4: 1–190. Wellington, N.Z.

Bassett, Heather and R. Kay. 2002. "*Ruatāhuna: land ownership and administration c. 1896–1990.*" With Supporting Papers (S.P.) Vols 1–3. WAI 894 #A20. Wellington, N.Z.: Waitangi Tribunal.

Berghan, Paula. 2001. "Block Research Narratives of the Urewera, 1870–1930; A resource document for Urewera District Treaty Issues." WAI 894 #A86. Wellington, N.Z.: Waitangi Tribunal.

Best, Elsdon. 1898. "Tuhoe genealogies 1898" (spine title); "Genealogies of the Tuhoe tribe. Also includes all living members of the tribe in 1898, as given before the Urewera Commission set up under the act of 1896." Manuscript qMS [172]. Wellington, N.Z.: Alexander Turnbull Library. [The author can supply a digital index for this resource.]

Holman, Jeffrey. 2010. *Best of both worlds: the story of Elsdon Best and Tutakangahau.* Auckland, N.Z.: Penguin.

O'Malley, Vincent. 1996. *The Crown's Acquisition of the Waikaremoana Block 1921–25.* A report for the Panekiri Tribal Trust Board, with Supporting Papers (S.P.) Vols I-III, May 1996. WAI 894 record of inquiry, doc A50. Wellington, N.Z.: Waitangi Tribunal.

NACMB 1. Native Appellate Court minute book 1, Jackson Palmer, Rawson, (13Nov1912–Feb1913), index 9 pp., 386 pp.; NA Wgtn: Waiariki, Urewera Appelate MB 1, CD 3518/2, 397pp.; NA Ak: AREPRO 4711/1450. Acronym: NACMB 1.

NACMB 2. Native Appellate Court minute book 2, Jackson Palmer, Rawson, (1Feb1913–20Aug1913), index 5 pp., 136pp.; NA Wgtn: Waiariki, Urewera Appelate MB 2, CD 3518/2, 140pp.; NA Ak: AREPRO 4711/1451. Acronym: NACMB 2.

NZMS 170 n.d. "Urewera National Park" (3d Edition). New Zealand Map Service. Wellington, N.Z.: Dept. of Lands and Survey.

UMB 1. Urewera District Native Reserve Commission minute book 1 (identified as Urewera Commission minute book '3'), Smith, Butler, et al., (1Feb1899–8Mar1900), in Māori, Index 22 pp., 382 pp. NA Wgtn: Urewera MB 3, MLC 13, W3518, CD2, Vol 3, 397 pp.; NA Ak: AREPRO 4711/1445. Acronym: UMB 1.

UMB 5. Urewera District Native Reserve Commission minute book 5, Butler, Scannell, et al. (18Mar1901–16May01), in English, index 5 pp., 382 pp.; NA Wgtn: Urewera MB 5, MLC 13,W3518, CD 2, Vol.5, 388 pp.; NA Ak: AREPRO 4711/1447. Acronym: UMB 5.

UMB 6. Urewera District Native Reserve Commission minute book 6, Butler, Scannell, et al. (16May1901–26Apr02) in English, index 9 pp., 382 pp.; NA Wgtn: Waiariki, Urewera MB 6, CD W3518/2, 398 pp.; NA Ak: AREPRO 4711/1448. Acronym: UMB 6.

UCAMB 1. Urewera District Native Reserve Commission Appeal minute book 1, D.F.G. Barclay, Mair, Ngata, (5Dec1906–22Jan1907). 10 pp. index,? pp.; NA Wgtn: unable to locate; NA Ak: AREPRO 4711/1133; Univ.Auck.Lib: 333.0995 N536u. Acronym: UCAMB 1.

UCAMB 2. Urewera District Native Reserve Commission Appeal minute book 2, D.F.G. Barclay, Mair, Ngata, (23Jan1907–12Mar1907) index, 382 pp.; NA Wgtn: unable to locate; NA Ak: AREPRO 4711/1134; Univ.Auck.Lib: 333.0995 N536u. Acronym UCAMB 2.

Webster, Steven. 2004. *The Urewera Consolidation Scheme: Confrontations between Tuhoe and the Crown, 1915–1925*. Vols I, II. Report commissioned by the Waitangi Tribunal. WAI 894 #D8. Wellington, N.Z.: Waitangi Tribunal.

CHAPTER 9

The Ruatāhuna Partition, 1912

1 Introduction

If the confrontation between Numia Kererū and Te Whenuanui II over Kahuwī and Arohana (and, implicitly, between Te Urewera hapū and Ngāti Rongo hapū) was strangely muted in the 1907 appeals, it was back out in the open by 1912. Several years after the final establishment of the reserve in 1907, although it may have been invisible to outsiders, the confrontation was implicitly continued in Numia's appeal to the Native Appellate Court to partition the Ruatāhuna block. As described in previous chapters, by 1912 Chief Judge Jackson Palmer of the Native Land Court had become convinced that ownership of several blocks of the reserve had been left ambiguously defined because rights of particular descent groups to particular parts of a block had not been recorded, and their relative shares could be claimed to extend equally over the whole block. Perhaps Numia's lone protest in 1900 against combining 'minor' with major claims had proven well-founded (Chap. 3).

However, by 1912 it was Hori Wharerangi's bitter forecast, in 1899 before the commission, of inveterate Crown duplicity (Chap. 2) that was threatening the entire UDNR. Beginning in 1908 with Apirana Ngata's insistence against Numia and the elected members of the General Committee that Rua Kenana's *hoko whenua* ('land-selling') followers be represented, the Crown increasingly undermined its promise of home-rule. By 1915 it had retrospectively legalized a concerted campaign to circumvent the General Committee and purchase shares from individuals,

© The Author(s) 2020

S. Webster, *A Separate Authority (He Mana Motuhake)*, Volume I,
https://doi.org/10.1007/978-3-030-41042-1_9

intending eventually to buy up entire blocks (Webster 2004: 143–212). Under these ominous conditions, the merger of minor with major claims carried out in 1900–1903, and the addition of many appellants as small shareholders by the appeals commission in 1906–1907, manageable under the promised and indeed statutory terms of home-rule, had become a liability. From this point of view, by 1912 the partitions of several of the UDNR blocks including Ruatāhuna can in some cases be seen as a frantic effort to consolidate control of smaller blocks under the leadership of particular hapū. It is a bitter irony that within a decade following the 1902 proposal to amalgamate the 34 blocks of the UDNR into only 10, the confidence of many Tūhoe leaders in the 1896 Act had been betrayed.

By 1912 this wider confrontation between Tūhoe and the Crown was surely the background of the Ruatāhuna partition, and probably foremost in Numia's concern as chairman of the subverted General Committee. However, this chapter is devoted to description and analysis of the particular confrontation, since at least 1902, over the Manawarū area of Ruatāhuna described in Chaps. 7 and 8 between Numia Kererū and Te Whenuanui II along with other leaders in the migrant marriage alliance. Although Numia died in 1916, the role of the Ruatāhuna-Waikaremoana migrant marriage alliance was central to the wider confrontation and (as will be examined in Volume II) continued through the climax of the Crown's subversion of the UDNR in the Urewera Consolidation Scheme 1921–1926.

2 Manawarū: The 'Internal Boundary Dispute'

Whereas Jackson Palmer felt the problem of ambiguous relative shares had been "put right" in the partitions of Rūātoki and Te Whaiti Nui a Toi by amendment to the 1896 Act, he decided the problem should also be fixed for the Taneatua and Ruatāhuna blocks (Webster 2004: 120–1). Numia's case in preliminary hearing in 1912 was probably pivotal in the Judge's decision to hear his appeal regarding the Ruatāhuna block, and at the end of several weeks of hearings lasting through to 1913, he explicitly complimented Numia's efforts.

Numia conducted the entire investigation into subdividing Ruatāhuna block, which by 1913 resulted in its partition into five blocks, numbered from north to south: Arohana, Kahuwī, Huiarau, Te Waiiti, and Parahaki (Fig. 9.1 below).[1] At the outset of the investigation the distinction between Arohana and Kahuwī was treated as a boundary dispute internal to

Manawarū, the northernmost of the areas discussed in the 1902 proceedings. The discussion whether or not this subdivision was justified and, if so, by what internal boundary was the context in which the confrontation between Numia Kererū and the representatives of Te Whenuanui II was continued 6–10 December 1912. Although the arguments made little reference to the confrontation in terms of Ngāti Rongo and Te Urewera hapū, Numia had presented his appeal to partition the entire Ruatāhuna block in terms of "...hapu boundaries... and relative interests", probably invoking the hopeful ideals of the 1896 Act examined in Chap. 2 (NACMB 1: 70). Insofar as several other hapū were referred to in cases for the other partitions of Ruatāhuna block, one might suspect that references to Ngāti Rongo as well as Te Urewera hapū were being avoided in the arguments regarding Manawarū, perhaps to calm indignations that had festered since 1902.

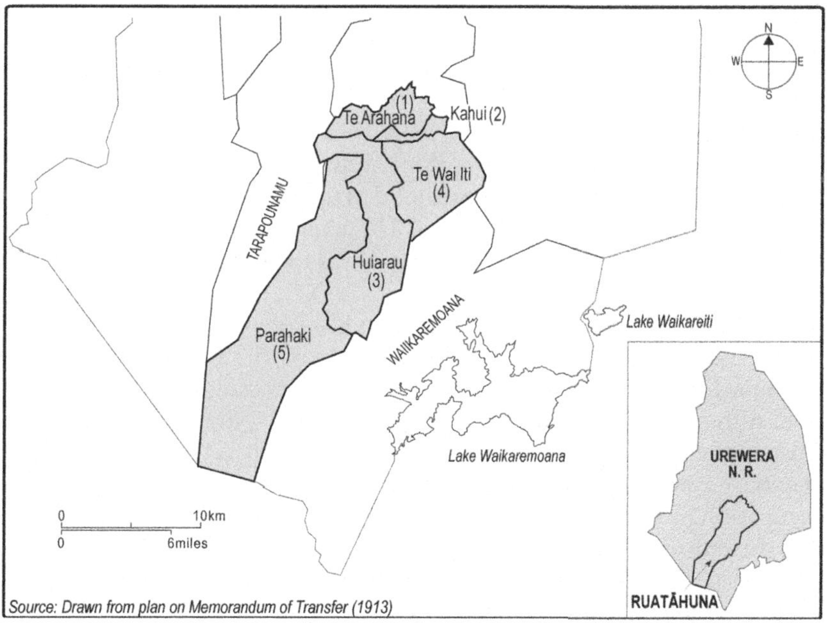

Fig. 9.1 Ruatāhuna partition 1913–1921 (note mis-spelling of Arohana and Kahuwī partitions, the latter of which became widely accepted) (Webster 2004: 117)

Numia's appeal to partition Ruatāhuna was apparently first scheduled to be heard on 5 December, but he announced that some of the boundaries of the various partitions were disputed and was readily granted further time to discuss matters out of court (NACMB 1: 191). The following day he announced that

> [a]ll boundaries agreed on except one so that matter will be fought out before the Court – one party has written out its boundary the other has not yet done so. I represent one party and Mehaka [(sic) Mihaka Matika; see Figs. 7.1 and 8.1] the other – the portions claimed under Kahuwi [(sic) later consistently misspelled Kahui] and Arawhana [(sic) later usually spelled Arohana] are the ones in dispute. (NACMB 1: 208; my brackets)

Numia then submitted boundaries and ancestors for the other three partitions (Parahaki, Huiarau, and Waiiti) and, after a 'long time spent tracing out and settling boundaries', the court noted that the only dispute was about 'the division of Manawarū into two parts – as to the dividing line'. In the following days, Mihaka Matika was to conduct the case for descendants of Arohana, and—as had Te Whenuanui II in 1902—attempt to claim the whole of Manawarū against Numia's claim to part of it for the descendants of Kahuwī. As can be seen from Fig. 9.1, after the court had made its decision on the dispute, the Kahuwī ("Kahui") partition #2 was to be the smaller southeastern portion of Manawarū bordering on Ierenui-Ohāua block as well as the Waiiti and Huiarau partitions, while the larger remainder of Manawarū to the northwest was to be designated as Arohana partition #1.

Mihaka Matika was to be supported in his case by Paora Noho (son of Noho Taratoa) and Whenua Tahakawa (son of Tahakawa Taratoa). Whenua Tahakawa also acted as conductor and cross-examiner later in the case. Although his credentials were questioned by Numia, as discussed in Chap. 7, he held leading rights in Ruatāhuna as well as Waikaremoana and may have returned to live in the latter block while his father maintained occupation in the former at least until 1907. From Fig. 7.1 it can be seen that these three claimants were sons of the three Taratoa brothers (Matika, Tahakawa, and Noho), and that Mihaka (the *mātāmua* son of the *mātāmua* sibling Matika Taratoa) was Te Whenuanui (I)'s son-in-law and Te Haka Te Whenuanui's (Te Whenuanui II) brother-in-law. Whenua Tahakawa's *mātāmua* sister Torehu was also the wife of Konoro Hakeke, the *mātāmua* grandson of Tamaikoha who, like Te Whenuanui I, was a war-leader ***rangatira*** of Te Urewera hapū in the lower Urewera valleys. Whenua Tahakawa's later role as conductor for the case was probably as second-most senior of the three cousins.

But where was Te Whenuanui III in this confrontation? As described in Chap. 7, Rangiteremauri or Reupene Mihaka had succeeded to the title soon after the 2 January 1907 death of Te Whenuanui II, and continuation of his father's defense against Numia's quest would have been his formal responsibility. Nevertheless, he is nowhere mentioned in the 1912 court record regarding the confrontation. However, this is probably simply because he was only in his 30s or younger, while his father, Mihaka Matika, ***mātāmua*** son of Matika Taratoa, ***mātāmua*** of one of the most important sibling groups in the migrant marriage alliance, was conducting the case against Numia.

So, although Te Whenuanui II himself had been dead for several years, the influential Murahioi-Taratoa descent group of the migrant marriage alliance had gathered to support his claim for all of Manawarū under the ***mana*** of Arohana against Numia Kererū's effort, since at least 1902, to establish a foothold in Ruatāhuna under the ***mana*** of Kahuwī. In addition to the Taratoa marriages to ***rangatira*** families of Te Urewera hapū, they would have been best-placed for such a claim because they all held leading shares in Ruatāhuna, and the mother of all the Taratoa siblings was Te Arahe, the great-granddaughter of Arohana's oldest ***begotten*** (biological) child by Turaki (I) (according to Paora Noho's ***whakapapa***, NACMB 1: 223 and left side of Fig. 8.1). On the other hand, Kahuwī was probably Arohana's oldest albeit ***adopted*** son and, furthermore, was referred to by Paora Noho as the ***tuakana*** (senior sibling) of Arohana's begotten children (NACMB 1: 228, Fig. 8.1).

Finally with regard to the best placement of the Taratoa siblings in the confrontation, it might be recalled that when in the 1907 appeal hearing Numia finally spoke up to admit that it was he who had reduced the shareholdings submitted to the commission by Te Whenuanui II in 1902, this was in response to Noho Taratoa's addition of 24 more appellants to Mahaki Tapiki's list of 50. Numia's main opponent in the 1912 case to partition Manawarū was Paora Noho, son and only child of Noho Taratoa. Although Numia's 1907 cooperation in the increase of most appellants' shares in Ruatāhuna may have mollified other leaders of the marriage alliance, it apparently had not done so for the Taratoa siblings and their children.

The Native Appellate Court hearing for the partition of Ruatāhuna was held in the town of Taneatua, just north of Rūātoki and the northern boundary of the reserve (Fig. 1.1). The hearing regarding Manawarū and its internal boundary ran from 6 to 10 December, and the minutebook record spans about 40 pages (NACMB 1: 208–49). Two pages in my copy (NACMB 1: 219–20) are both clearly dated several months earlier on Monday 9 August 1912, and were probably inserted from a preliminary hearing to augment the beginning of Paora Noho's December testimony regarding the original ownership of Manawarū. (The testimony of the main hearing is then continued at page 221 on 9 December 1912, also a Monday and, strangely, completes the same sentence, probably in the same hand.) However, a few other significant earlier events were recorded on these two added pages, and need to be commented upon.

According to this apparently inserted record of an earlier hearing, Numia had complained on 9 August that Mihaka's "side" (probably the Taratoa representatives of Te Whenuanui II) would not meet with "us" (him, apparently with Te Iriwhiro and perhaps others) "to discuss division of Manawarū portion although we waited all Saturday afternoon – Yesterday [Sunday] we discussed matter but could not come to any settlement" (219). Numia had then added that while 'Mihaka claims from one source Te Arohana only – My party claim from two sources Te Arohana and Kahui'. Numia also announced that settlement had been reached (apparently between Te Iriwhiro and Mihaka) that Te Iriwhiro's northern boundary of Waiiti block would be accepted as the southern boundary of Manawarū (Fig. 9.1), implying that due to this settlement the only dispute remaining to be resolved before the court was the internal division of Manawarū (between Arohana and Kahuwī). (It will be remembered that Te Iriwhiro had also supported Numia in their 1902 effort against Te Whenuanui II to gain recognition of Kahuwī as an ancestor of the block.) Mihaka is recorded to have immediately claimed that he had only consented to the Manawarū/Waiiti boundary 'under pressure' because other members of his party were not present. Then Whenua Tahakawa (apparently one who had not been present earlier) added that he did not agree with Te Iriwhiro's boundary between Manawarū and Waiiti, so the court would have to hear that case too. As conductor in the preliminary hearing, Whenua Tahakawa then called Paora Noho (his father's youngest brother's son) as a witness for the history of the ancestor Arohana's claim to Manawarū.

This August confrontation in the presumed preliminary hearing was continued before the court in similar terms at the main hearing on 7 December (210). It will be noted from Fig. 9.1 that if the Kahuwī subdivision of Manawarū were to be approved by the court, the southern boundary of Kahuwī would be the northern boundary of the Waiiti partition, and the dispute regarding the common boundary between Waiiti and Manawarū might well be obviated regardless of Whenua Tahakawa's objection. As described above, on 6 December Numia had claimed settlement of the boundaries of all five divisions of the Ruatāhuna block and submitted all boundary descriptions except one (the boundary internal to Manawarū, between Arohana and Kahuwī), emphasizing that Mihaka's party had not yet written out their boundary for Manawarū. On 7 December Te Iriwhiro opened the discussion by again announcing that the boundary between Waiiti and Manawarū had been settled. Te Amo Kokouri then claimed that it had been he, not Mihaka, who had objected to the boundary, but that he now accepted that it was settled. In later evidence it became clear that Te Amo was claiming rights under Kahuwī, and his continuing residence of the disputed land was key evidence for Numia's case (240–1). However, Mihaka then corrected Te Amo's statement, clarifying that he continued to object to the eastern portion of the boundary between Waiiti and Manawarū, correcting it in terms of the Mahakirua and Taurekarekarua streams (along the southeastern boundary of Manawarū) in such a way that Manawarū would extend all the way south to a common boundary with Waiiti, encompassing the area that had been claimed by Numia for Kahuwī (210).

Nevertheless, insofar the boundary between Waiiti and Manawarū had already been settled by Numia rather than Mihaka, Numia's case for distinguishing the intermediate area as Kahuwī was implicitly advantaged while Mihaka's case that Arohana's rights in Manawarū extended all the way to Waiiti was implicitly disadvantaged. It would have been clear to all concerned by 6 December, if not in the earlier confrontation in August, that Numia had gathered support from Te Amo as well as Te Iriwhiro for recognition of Kahuwī (both had supported him in his 1902 claims against Te Whenuanui II), and that his approach would be boldly assertive. Whereas the *mana* of Te Whenuanui II, only recently dead, had perhaps restrained Numia in 1907, now five years later it no longer did, even against the father of Te Whenuanui III, Mihaka Matika.

As was usual procedure, the evidence regarding the internal boundary of Manawarū presented by each side over the next few days was concerned to show more recent or continuous occupation by particular predecessors than the opposing party, and more detailed familiarity with place names, settlements, buildings, hunting and gathering resources, and cultivations. However, a central issue in this case was *tuku whenua* or the specific character of 'gifted land'. Whereas the issue that Kahuwī was a *tamariki whāngai* (adopted) rather than a begotten son of Arohana was raised in 1902 by Te Whenuanui II in response to Te Iriwhiro's claim, the other key issue of *tuku whenua* had not yet been raised. As Mihaka's witness, Paora Noho described both Arohana's and Kahuwī's rights to Manawarū lands in terms of gifted rights (NACMB 1: 221–2; 228–9). Paora's account has already been raised in Chap. 8 as background for analysis of the 1902 confrontation: he recounted the origin of Kahuwī's name from the way his father's body had been found cloaked in reeds (*kahu wii*) after a battle, and his subsequent adoption by Arohana, who had married Kahuwī's father's widow. This story overlapped with the one told by Tamaikoha in his claim for Whaitiripapa block in 1900 (Fig. 5.1, Chap. 5), where it was also pivotal in the ongoing confrontation between Te Urewera hapū and Ngāti Rongo hapū. Whereas in the case of Whaitiripapa block Kahuwī's rights had been bestowed on him by his father's younger brother Tamawhai (and passed on to Ngāti Rongo as *pākūhā* in exchange for a Ngāti Rongo woman in marriage), in the case of Manawarū in Ruatāhuna block the key issue was whether or not Kahuwī had gift rights bestowed on him (as distinct from birthrights) by Arohana as his adoptive father (Fig. 8.1).

In Numia's case for the internal division of Manawarū, he and Te Whenuanui II's supporters agreed at the outset that Arohana had been gifted his right to Manawarū by the widow Whakaroto in return for avenging her husband's death (unrelated to Kahuwī's father's death) (221–2). Both sides also came to agree that Arohana had 'gifted' the southern part of Manawarū to Kahuwī as his adopted son, while retaining the larger, northern part of Manawarū for his own offspring. However, Numia and Paora Noho (Mihaka's witness) differed crucially regarding the specific form of Arohana's gift to Kahuwī: while Numia claimed the gift was "absolute" (NACMB 1: 240; i.e., a gift of the land itself, in perpetuity or "perpetual"), Paora claimed the gift was only for use as a food resource for Kahuwī and his descendants, and intended eventually to "revert to the donor" (228–9; 231–2). Although in the minutebook these phrases appear in the legal terms of European property, their expression in Māori would have been in the equally subtle terms of traditionally established forms of *take tuku whenua*, quite familiar to the court.[2]

Numia's insistence that Arohana's gift of land to Kahuwī was absolute may have anticipated a further issue that appears never to have been raised by either side. It was probably well-established among Tūhoe that the birthrights of natural children could be extended to *whāngai tamariki* if they were sufficiently closely related, as was normally the case in Māori adoption (Milroy 2000). With the help of Best's genealogical plates (1973, Vol.II plate 27 p. 2), I found that Kahuwī was Arohana's second cousin "twice removed" and, furthermore, that with Murakareke their common ancestor, they were both potential members of Te Urewera hapū (Fig. 8.1). Nowadays, according to Milroy (himself a contemporary Tūhoe leader), four generations removal from a common ancestor is considered by Tūhoe to be close enough kinship to assure equal birthrights to land or its production. If Numia had felt that the decision was going against him, he might have been planning to give up his argument that Kahuwī's rights were stronger than his adoptive siblings' rights in the disputed portion of Manawarū, and argue for something less. However, for whatever reason, this issue was apparently not raised by Numia, Te Whenuanui II, or his supporters.[3]

The hearing regarding Manawarū was organized loosely in terms of appellants, conductors, one or two witnesses, and cross-examiners of witnesses for each side (NACMB 1: 220–41). Mihaka Matika's case for the ancestor Arohana and all of Manawarū was supported by Whenua Tahakawa as conductor and Paora Noho as witness (all implicitly supporting Te Whenuanui II's position); Numia's opposing case for the ancestor Kahuwī and the southeastern portion of Manawarū was apparently conducted entirely by himself, also acting as witness and cross-examiner of the others. Mihaka's case was probably given priority because both Numia and Te Iriwhiro were challenging the southern boundary of Manawarū (Numia for what would become the Kahuwī partition and Te Iriwhiro for the Waiiti partition). After Paora Noho had laid out the general history, boundary, and *whakapapa* for all of Manawarū, Te Iriwhiro's challenge for Waiiti's northern boundary was briefly considered and the court's decision reserved (Fig. 9.1; NACMB 1: 220–7).

Numia had submitted boundary descriptions of all five subdivisions on 6 December, reporting that all were agreed on except that between Kahuwī and Arohana (208). Again, he pointedly took the opportunity to remark that 'one party'—clearly Mihaka's—had not yet written out their boundary claim to the disputed area. The boundaries of Manawarū as claimed by Paora, Numia's dispute with sectors of it, and Numia's boundaries for the Kahuwī subdivision were detailed by them on 9 and 10 December (222; 227–8; 236 confirmed by the court at 250–1). The typical difficulty in following these descriptions accurately on available maps was aggravated by fragmented recording of verbatim statements in the Native Appellate Court minutes. Especially in cross-examination, it was often unclear whether a statement is a question asked or a reply given, because one or the other is not recorded; this also obscured who it was who made the statement.

As mentioned in Chap. 8 the *whakapapa* presented in Fig. 8.1 are primarily adapted, respectively, from parts presented by Paora (NACMB 1: 223; 228) and from several parts presented by Numia Kererū in the earlier Whaitiripapa block case as well as the Manawarū case (UMB 1: 337–9; NACMB 1: 231; 235–6). It is important that both Paora's and Numia's *whakapapa* were apparently accepted by each other as well as others on the opposing sides. Although the *whakapapa* did not directly contradict one another, as was characteristic in confrontations before the commission or a court (and probably traditionally as well), each side often avoided inclusion or recognition of the other's key ancestors by choosing lines of descent that instead supported their own case. While Paora's *whakapapa* evidence appears primarily on the left side of Fig. 8.1 traced from Arohana, Numia's appears primarily on the right, traced from Kahuwī. Especially Numia's 1912 *whakapapa* appeared to be presented tactically in successive parts, probably carefully to guide the court's clearer understanding and also to lend impact to his arguments. The *whakapapa* given by Paora, on the other hand, appeared to be either poorly recorded by the court clerk or less well-prepared.

Paora's evidence seems generally less coherent, perhaps because the recording of it was more fragmentary but also because, as described earlier, some pages from the preliminary hearing in August may have inserted in the December minutes. He appears to have given the boundary of Manawarū twice (the first described as the gift to Arohana), both on 9 December, and each time followed by a commentary describing occupation by Arohana or his descendants (NACMB 1: 222–4; 227–31). Most of the place names used in the second account differed from those used in the first. Numia responded to Paora's second account by disputing several of its numbered locations, and he later presented the boundary of Kahuwī (227; confirmed 336). Only a few of the place names enumerated in the three accounts can be identified on the maps and plans examined, and many that appear in one account do not appear in the others. Little contiguity between points can be discerned in any of the accounts, nor in the points disputed by Numia, that coincide with the boundaries of Manawarū or its subdivisions of Arohana and Kahuwī as they appear on subsequent plans.

However, some place names are common to the three accounts and several do appear in one or another plan or map: Opuhou Stream (misspelled 'Opuho' by the clerk), Pukerimu, Pokopoko a Hakianina, Pakopako, Manawarū hill, Te Roto, and the Mahakirua, Ruataniwha, Waitawa, and Taurekarekarua streams (roughly from west to east in Kahuwī partition). One helpful consistency is that both of Paora's accounts commenced at Opuhou Stream (although the following points differ) and Numia's boundary began at Pokopoko a Hakianina, which follows or precedes Opuhou Stream in both of Paora's accounts. Not far from the locations of Opuhou Stream, Pukerimu hill, and (perhaps) Pokopoko a Hakianina is the contemporary *kāinga* (settlement) and *marae* of Mātaatua, which was frequently referred to in the evidence of both parties and will be further discussed below. The Mātaatua area was probably located at or near the southwest end of the boundary between Arohana and Kahuwī where it joins with the Huiarau subdivision boundary, and would have been contentious for this reason among others.

Early in Paora's evidence he seemed surprisingly ready to admit Arohana's descendants' occupation of "the disputed portion" of Manawarū (i.e., on what Numia had declared as Kahuwī) had been brief and limited to visits for cultivation, and furthermore to admit that his familiarity with the area was limited and often second hand (222–4). At this point in Paora's evidence it would have appeared that Te Whenuanui II's claim to recent occupation on the disputed portion was very weak, limited to descendants of Arohana's *mātāmua* daughter Te Matau and not continued after her son Aihurangi, and based only on cultivation and temporary shelters (Fig. 8.1). Paora's own line of descent was from Te Matau and Aihurangi (and being through Te Arahe, included all the other Taratoa cousins), but because he admitted cultivation in the disputed area had ceased since Aihurangi's time, his claim appears to have fallen well short of the general requirement of continuous occupation at least since the third generation before the oldest living claimant. Furthermore, this evidence would appear to exclude all descendants of Arohana's two younger begotten children Ihukarira and Hukipoto—the latter of which was Te Whenuanui II's own line from Arohana.

However, later the same day following his second account of the Manawarū boundary, Paora's evidence for occupation appeared much stronger, although apparently inconsistent with the earlier evidence (NACMB 1: 228–30). Referring explicitly to "the overlap" between his and Numia's boundaries from Opuhou Stream to Pukerimu hill (at the eastern end of the disputed area), he stated that "occupation there commenced with Aihurangi and Hukipoto – and continued by Takahi and Te Umuariki" (his earlier testimony reported that cultivation had ceased with Aihurangi). As can be seen in Paora's *whakapapa* (Fig. 8.1, left side), while Aihurangi was great-grandparent of the Taratoa sibling group through Te Arahe, Hukipoto was Aihurangi's father's younger brother and, through his child Takahi and grandchild Te Umuariki, were Te Whenuanui I's immediate predecessors. Paora then named several permanent buildings belonging to these persons, described Mātaatua and the 'very large' meeting house named Te Whai a te Motu also owned by Te Whenuanui I (and II) and built 'for all the hapus'. He then concluded with a description of a *pa* (fortified village) at Pukerimu hill where his father Noho Taratoa and a close relative Te Ao were currently living.

The importance of the Mātaatua area was reflected in the frequent references to it (227; 228–30; 232; 238–9). The apparent contradiction between Paora's earlier evidence that there had been no occupation on 'the disputed portion' after Aihurangi's time, and this later description of permanent occupation in the Mātaatua area down to his own time, might be explained if he was defiantly refusing to consider this 'overlapped' area around Mātaatua as part of 'the disputed area'. In Paora's second account of occupation he also extended his claim to continued occupation by Arohana's descendants in the disputed area well outside Mātaatua, to a *kāinga* named Toi that he claimed was built and occupied by Aihurangi, his son Matiu, and others (NACMB 1: 230; probably at the northwest corner of Kahuwī partition). While giving these details, Paora emphasized that occupation had been carried on by descendants only of Arohana, but admitted that descendants only of Kahuwī had often lived among them. He concluded that 'we were practically one people and lived together', and that he had 'heard' that Te Amo (a descendant only of Kahuwī) still lived at Mātaatua.

These admissions implicitly raised the key issue of *take tuku whenua*: Did the gift of this disputed portion of Manawarū from Arohana to his adopted son Kahuwī give his descendants the right to continue living there even if they were not also descended from Arohana? And if so, were these rights limited or perpetual? To put this issue in customary terms as Numia later did: From whom did the dominant *mana* over this portion of Manawarū come, and through whom was it passed down? (231).

3 Numia Kererū Builds His Case

At this point, Paora's statements begin to appear more like cautious answers, suggesting that Numia's cross-examination of Paora may have begun informally (NACMB 1: 230–1). Numia would have known that such continuing acceptance of cohabitation over generations between descendants of Arohana and Kahuwī would be of interest to the court in its concern with the specific nature of the *tuku whenua*. Some tentative conclusions can be drawn despite the ambiguous way that questions and answers were recorded. Perhaps following up on Paora's concessions, Numia apparently asked him if any of Kahuwī's people lived at Toi along with Aihurangi's son Matiu. Paora apparently answered cautiously that he did not know. However, when Paora reported that a certain building called Mataraua was built by Te Matau (Arohana's first-born child and Aihurangi's mother) and her brother, Numia apparently asserted that Kahuwī had helped them build it. Again, Paora denied any knowledge of this, but went on to admit that 'we were practically one people and lived together', adding that 'the reason Arohana cut off this land for Kahui was lest his children should show ill feeling' against his adopted child. This could well have been taken by the court as evidence that the gift was intended to protect a permanent bond between siblings regardless of Kahuwī's adoption, strengthening the possibility that the gift had been intended to be absolute or perpetual.

Formal cross-examination began at this point. Numia apparently began by asserting that 'I understand Te Matau and others agreed to Arohana laying down boundary' and was not contradicted by Paora. Because it was not denied, this assertion would also strengthen the implication that Arohana had not only sought to avoid ill-feeling by dividing the land, he had also sought agreement from his begotten children for what was a more 'absolute' gift to their elder adopted brother, and not intended to 'revert to the donor'. Numia then went on to ask if Paora knew that 'Kahui accompanied Arohana to fight at Oputara' and, again, Paora could only say that he had no knowledge of this (this was typically a way in which denial was nevertheless implied). Between the spontaneous exchange and the cross-examination, Numia had probably succeeded in establishing that where Paora's evidence had substantiated occupation by Arohana's children, Kahuwī or his descendants had often been closely involved and perhaps accepted in terms of permanent occupation. However, Numia was about to take further advantage of Paora's implicit concessions and uncertainty to raise the possibility that rights to the disputed portion were *stronger* through Kahuwī than they were through Arohana.

As had Te Whenuanui II in 1902, Numia claimed dual rights or descent from both Kahuwī and Arohana. As pointed out in Chap. 8, the chances that such claims could be made were limited because the ancestral source of rights being argued in Manawarū was only five or six generations before these spokespersons, and the Tūhoe restriction on marriage between relatives usually extended back at least three generations. Consequently in this case the issue of *dual* rights, by recent occupation as well as ancestry, was probably sensitive but much more important than it appeared to be in the minutes. Early in the hearings (apparently in the preliminary hearing on 9 August) Numia had asserted that "Mihaka claims from one source. Te Arohana only – My party claim from two sources Te Arohana and Kahui" (219–20). However, on 10 December he described the situation more carefully: "I claim under both Kahui and Arohana myself – some of my party [Te Amo, for one] only claim under Kahui [.] Those on Paora's side [including at least Paora's Taratoa cousins Mihaka and Whenua] claim under Arohana only" (236). Significantly, this assertion was not challenged by 'Paora's side'.

Although Numia apparently did not explain his claim, the *whakapapa* evidence before the court regarding the predecessors of Numia, Te Amo, and the Taratoa cousins can confirm it (Fig. 8.1). As shown on the left side of the composite *whakapapa* (primarily Paora's evidence), Puritoroa was probably the wife of Tangataiti and grandmother of Numia and his sibling group, and the source of their rights from Arohana. However, because she was a descendant of Arohana 'by another wife', she was not closely related to Kahuwī's descendants and there would be no impediment or incest stigma to prevent her marriage with Tangataiti. However, it may be significant that this crucial information had been furnished in Paora's *whakapapa* rather than Numia's, whose case benefitted from it.

Consequently, unless 'Paora's side' could demonstrate descent from Kahuwī as well as Arohana in their claim to the disputed portion (as Numia presumably could), any evidence that descendants of Kahuwī had an equal or stronger right there than descendants of Arohana left them in a vulnerable position. Probably as a tactical effort to emphasize only Arohana's descendants and ignore Kahuwī's, Paora's *whakapapa* had even neglected to show how Te Whenuanui II and his full siblings came by their dual right to all of Manawarū, which was through their mother Turaki II and her father Pouwhenua, who was a grandson of Kahuwī (Fig. 8.1). Surprisingly, although the Taratoa cousins' role was to defend Te Whenuanui II's case against Numia's attack, Paora's *whakapapa* (or the record of it) had not even included Turaki II, Te Whenuanui I's wife and mother of Te Whenuanui II and his full siblings—and furthermore mistakenly reported the *mātāmua* sibling as Te Whenuanui II rather than his elder sister Te Mauniko (NACMB 1: 223). Ironically, it was Numia's *whakapapa* that had reported Turaki II's crucial role, along with his emphasis on Kahuwī's descendants.

After Numia had established Kahuwī's probable occupation of the disputed portion along with Arohana's birth-children, he next presented the part of the *whakapapa* shown in Fig. 8.1 that traced Pouwhenua's descendants to the cousins Whenuanui II and Te Amo Kokouri, revealing that Pouwhenua was himself a descendant of Kahuwī (231). Tactically, he probably intended to focus the court's attention on the implications of this straight-forward fragment, reserving for the following day his presentation of the fuller *whakapapa* showing more of Kahuwī's descendants (235–6). The fragment may have simply been intended to show his supporter Te Amo's descent from Kahuwī, and by the way displayed the source of Te Whenuanui II's own claim to dual rights. It is tactically significant that in this *whakapapa* fragment Numia specified 'Turaki II' because later, when he presented the fuller *whakapapa* from Kahuwī, the namesake relationship of Te Whenuanui's wife from Turaki I (Kahuwī's birth-mother) would be dramatized for the court. Although Numia's own more senior line and *mātāmua* sister (and mother of the eminent Tupaea Rapaera) had been named Turaki, possibly as Turaki III, he did not raise this implication, perhaps displaying *whakaiti* ('humility').

However, Numia probably also intended an immediate impact of the earlier *whakapapa* fragment upon the court. If it could be shown that a stronger or exclusive gifted right to the disputed portion of Manawarū came from Kahuwī through Pouwhenua, then the strength or exclusivity of these rights held by Te Whenuanui I's children (the fragment showed only 'Te Whenuanui II') as well as Te Amo came from their mothers (Pouwhenua's two daughters)—*bypassing* Te Whenuanui I himself. Unless Te Whenuanui I could claim descent from Kahuwī as well as Arohana, the rights he himself passed on would be weaker or excluded in the disputed portion of Manawarū. Numia next bluntly posed the following questions to Paora:

> Is it not a fact that mana over this portion [of Manawarū] originally came from Pouwhenua to Turaki II?....Was it not because Whenuanui [I] *married* Turaki [II] that they lived on this land?... Did your father [(Noho Taratoa) *also*] occupy in his *wife's* right? (NACMB 1: 231–2; my brackets and emphases)

Because of the key role of *take tūpuna*/ancestral descent (or *take tuku*/gifting) in rights to land, it is a potential stigma for a spouse, especially a male leader of *mana*, to raise a family or reside on land to which his or her only right is through the other spouse (and their children). The term *whakapapa whakamoe* describes a descent claim of this sort, but can imply such a stigma when a claim to land rights relies exclusively upon it (Webster 1975: 140–1; an alternative line of descent from the same founding ancestor is usually found or claimed to avoid the stigma). Paora did deny both of Numia's insinuations regarding his father's and Te Whenuanui I's reliance on their wives' rights. However, surprisingly he apparently did not take the opportunity firmly to correct them by asserting that the ancestral source of both Te Whenuanui I's and Noho Taratoa's right to all of Manawarū came from Arohana (through Te Umuariki and Te Arahe, respectively)—as was shown in the *whakapapa* Paora himself had presented earlier that day (NACMB 1: 223; Fig. 8.1).

Responding to Numia's challenge that *mana* over the disputed portion originally came from Kahuwī through Pouwhenua, Paora answered that Pouwhenua "was occupying under a dual right – Eventually he abandoned his Kahui claim" (231). Perhaps Paora felt he had to avoid legitimizing claims through Kahuwī, but in neglecting to describe how Pouwhenua was also a descendant of Arohana, he was also foregoing the chance to show that Numia's 'party' were not the only ones besides Te Whenuanui II and his siblings to enjoy a dual right to the disputed portion of Manawarū.

So apparently in default of any effective counter-argument, in this way Numia was able to imply that descendants of Kahuwī but not Arohana (specifically, Pouwhenua's descendants) had at least a sustained right and perhaps a stronger or more exclusive right to the disputed portion than descendants of Arohana but not Kahuwī (specifically, Te Whenuanui I, Paora, his father Noho, and the other descendants of Taratoa and Te Arahe). Such a right, whether stronger or merely sustained over generations, would furthermore support the implication that Arohana's gift of this portion of Manawarū to Kahuwī was of the more permanent nature suggested in some of the previous exchanges.

Later, at the conclusion of his own testimony and just before the court retired to consider its decision, Numia apparently flatly stated that "Whenuanui I claims only from Arohana" (241). Paora and Whenua Tahakawa apparently both accepted Numia's bold assertion and so probably strengthened his insinuation that although Te Whenuanui I had rights in the rest of Manawarū, he had been occupying the disputed portion only in virtue of his wife Turaki II's stronger or exclusive right. On the other hand, according to Numia's later evidence at least one of those in his own party who claimed only under Kahuwī was Te Amo Kokouri (240, 241), whose right was from Pouwhenua through his mother Maria. Numia emphasized that Te Amo continued to live in the disputed portion, implying that his right to do so had never been challenged.

At one point Paora attempted to take the offensive, raising a point to which Numia's case was vulnerable: "...when the case set up This is not shown in the minutes It was you and Te Amo who set up Te Kahui. Whenuanui [II] apparently claimed whole of Manawarū -" (231). It is likely that Paora was referring to the commission's minutes in 1902, which did raise this issue in response to Numia's first effort to gain Te Whenuanui II's recognition of Kahuwī. However, Paora's point could have been made more strongly: in 1902 the commission itself pointed out that neither Numia nor Te Amo had made any claim for Kahuwī in 1899 when such claims should have been made, but neither of them had offered an explanation for their tardy claim in 1902. The implication was clear that they were opportunistically 'setting the case up' between themselves. Paora could also have gone on to suggest—as Te Whenuanui II had probably suspected—that Numia had been encouraged to set up a case in Ruatāhuna by the relative success in 1900 of his claim against Te Urewera hapū in Whaitiripapa block, also through Kahuwī.

However, Numia successfully side-stepped Paora's challenge, instead shifting attention to Paora's earlier admission of the limitations of his first-hand knowledge by asking a series of detailed questions about the history of Manawarū: Paora admitted that he didn't know if some *poupou* posts of the Te Whai a te Motu meeting house at Mātaatua were named after descendants of Kahuwī or even of Arohana; he could not deny that although he "used to live on Manawarū" it had been "five years since I was there"; he did not deny that he or at least his father had lived in Waikaremoana for years; and he also admitted that his knowledge of Manawarū was based on infrequent visits and learned from others (232).

Later that day, after clearly laying out the fuller *whakapapa* from Kahuwī included in (Fig. 8.1, primarily right side), it was Numia's turn to display his own detailed knowledge of the disputed portion of Manawarū (NACMB 1: 235–40). Significantly, this *whakapapa* showed several prominent Tūhoe *rangatira* were descended from Kahuwī's children, including Numia's own sibling group, Tamaikoha's extensive hapū branch, and Te Iriwhiro, as well as Te Whenuanui I. Perhaps with the humility appropriate to a *rangatira*, Numia Kererū Te Ruakariata apparently let his diagram speak for itself without pointing out the relative *mana* of these leaders as descendants of Kahuwī's children—and that his own Ruakariata sibling group was the surviving *mātāmua* line while Te Whenuanui I was the *pōtiki* (last-born sibling) line.

Numia devoted most of his testimony to locations in Manawarū occupied by Kahuwī's third child's descendants Wiremu (father of Te Iriwhiro) and Mika (Numia's first cousins). However, implicitly with regard to himself, he also outlined occupation, probably in the disputed portion, by descendants of Kahuwī's second child Tangataiti (Numia's father's father), Tangataiti's descendants, and those of his "nephews and nieces" (probably Tawhakamoe II, Rangipa, or Aurarehe) (Fig. 8.1; NACMB 1: 238). The most dramatic part of his account of Tangataiti's occupation was his establishment with 'his people' of a 'big kainga' called Horahora on Manawarū hill (he also called it a 'mountain'), which is located on the Huiarau ridge 2–3 kilometers east of contemporary Mātaatua *marae*. Numia said that Tangataiti was "left as a sort of arbitrator among the Tūhoe people", and later

> *sent word to* Umuariki to come to him. Te Umuariki *came and lived* at Kaharahi [?] and they between them tapu'd Manawarū mountain – hence the expression "Manawarū is the mountain, – Tangataiti is the chief". On Tangataiti's death [this] saying was changed to "Manawarū is the mountain, Te Umuariki is the chief". Descendants of these two persons are – Kererū [Numia's deceased eldest brother] from Tangataiti and Whenuanui [I] from Te Umuariki. No attempt to disturb this land in their time – they adhered to the boundaries given by me to the court. (NACMB 1: 238–9; my emphasis)

Like many of Numia's questions and statements, this story implied the long-established dominance of Kahuwī's descendants over Arohana's descendants in the disputed portion of Manawarū—but also their established cooperation—and thus at least the intended permanence of Arohana's gift of this portion to Kahuwī. His account of how the saying attributing the *mana* of Manawarū mountain was transferred from Tangataiti to Te Umuariki upon the former's death (i.e., from his grandfather to Te Whenuanui I's father) may have been intended to explain (or impugn) the assumed dominance of Te Whenuanui II's *mana* throughout the area.

In concluding his testimony Numia pointed out that Paora's evidence had claimed only that Noho Taratoa and Te Ao were living on the disputed land, whereas Whenua Tahakawa and his family had lived only on Paraeroa block (about 25 kilometers northeast on the lower Tauranga River) and Ohiwa (on the Bay of Plenty coast north of the Urewera). Whenua Tahakawa was about to cross-examine Numia on his testimony, and this was probably an intentional derogation of his credentials in terms of recent occupation. Contrasting Whenua Tahakawa's occupation and knowledge with his own, Numia asserted that he and his family had lived on the disputed land and the last-born child of his family was born there (Best recorded Numia as the last-born of his siblings, 1898: 33). On the other hand, Numia reported that he had never seen Noho or Te Ao living on this land, only Pouwhenua's family (again implying the stronger occupational right of the latter as a descendant of Kahuwī). Numia then concluded his testimony with the blunt claim:

> I say [Arohana's] gift [to Kahuwi] was an absolute gift. This is shown by the strength of the occupation of Kahui's descendants. Te Amo and his descendants exercise acts of ownership [although] they claim only from one side – Kahui.

4 Conclusion

Numia's account of his descent and occupation left at least two or three obvious weaknesses that could have been challenged in cross-examination. The *whakapapa* that Paora himself presented gave details of Numia's (as well as Tamaikoha's) main descent lines from 'another wife' of Te Arohana's beside Turaki I (Fig. 8.1). On the other hand, Numia's *whakapapa* had left out Tangataiti's probable wife and grandmother of Numia's sibling group: Puritoroa. Numia may have done this to avoid raising the crucial possibility that Numia's father Ruakariata and his family could have been occupying Manawarū on the strength of Arohana's rather than

Kahuwī's *mana* over the disputed portion. After all, Numia himself had emphasized his dual right and that of others in his party. Most compromisingly, this possibility could have countered Numia's insinuation regarding Te Whenuanui I's and Noho Taratoa's reliance on their wives' rights by raising the possibility that Tangataiti's own rights to occupy Manawarū mountain relied on those of his wife Puritoroa! However, this implication was apparently never raised by Paora in response to Numia's cross-examination, nor by Whenua Tahakawa in his cross-examination of Numia.

Similarly, Numia's account of his descent group's occupation of Manawarū had gaps that were apparently not pursued by his opponents. While Kahuwī's own occupation of the disputed portion would be sufficiently recent ancestral occupation (within three deceased generations) to minimally establish his descendants' claims, Numia's account of Tangataiti's and his 'nephews and nieces' occupation of Manawarū mountain probably strengthened this claim for descendants of all four of Kahuwī's children. His fuller account of the Aurarehe siblings Wirimu's and Mika's families' occupation probably also accomplished this. However, insofar a *continuity* of occupation strengthened this evidence, Numia's account had left open the possibility that, after birth of Numia's youngest sibling in Manawarū, his father Ruākariata and his family had taken up primary residence elsewhere. Certainly by 1899, Numia and probably most of his sibling group had probably left Manawarū and resettled permanently further south in Ohāua or even Rūātoki: they were leaders in Ngāti Rongo hapū, which in 1899 Numia himself reported to be located primarily in those locations and Te Houhi (on the southwestern boundary of the Urewera). After all, Numia's own closing testimony intended to fault both Paora's and Whenua Tahakawa's families' occupation of Manawarū for similarly recent changes of primary residence. However, apparently none of these gaps in Numia's own account were probed by Paora or Whenua.

Whenua Tahakawa, who was the conductor of the case for Te Whenuanui II's supporters and Paora's father's older brother's son, cross-examined Numia (NACMB 1: 240–1). The record of this cross-examination is even more perfunctory than previous ones, with no indication of who was speaking. If one can assume the first part was Whenua's surprisingly neutral summary of Numia's argument, the second part appears to have furnished Numia with an opportunity to drive home rather than weaken some of his key points regarding *whakapapa* and relative rights: while Te Whenuanui II's claim was from Kahuwī as well as Arohana, Te Whenuanui

I's claim was only from Arohana (again raising the possibility that the father's right was through his wife); Te Amo's continuing occupation of the disputed portion even though a descendant only of Kahuwī; and finally that "before the first Comn" Te Whenuanui II, while supplying a list of names but specifying no internal boundaries, had given "Kahui and Arohana amongst takes – and that was right" (241).

Whether this last claim was Numia's or Whenua's, it was misleading and—because it was not corrected—was probably damaging to Paora and Whenua's' (and so to Te Whenuanui II's as well as the Taratoa siblings') case. All that was actually recorded in the 1902 case when Numia and Te Amo had first requested Te Whenuanui II's recognition of Kahuwī as a *take tūpuna* was that the commission noted Kahuwī's descendants had already been included in Te Whenuanui II's list of names, and that "Whenuanui admits they have a claim" (Chap. 8; UMB 6: 109–10). This admission of *a claim* for his descendants was far short of accepting Kahuwī as a *take tūpuna*. Nevertheless, if this was Numia's bold claim, Whenua Tahakawa apparently left it unchallenged. In any case, Whenua may have been offended by what he took to be the derogatory or patronizing tenor of some of Numia's responses. In conclusion, apparently taking an opportunity to emphasize his continuing respect for the *mana* of the deceased *rangatira*, Numia even displayed the *noblesse oblige* or *whakaiti* ('humility') characteristic of a leader: "Whenuanui [II,] I admit[,] was the chief of Ruatāhuna people -" (NACMB 1: 241).

Numia's testimony and cross-examination had taken most of the morning of 10 December 1912, but the court then retired and, before adjourning for lunch, returned with their decisions. They (1) found 'very much' in favor of Te Iriwhiro's boundary between Waiiti and Manawarū and (2) declared 'the weight of evidence in favor of the boundary given by Numia' between Arohana and Kahuwī (241). Insofar as Numia and Te Iriwhiro (another prominent descendant of Kahuwī) had already agreed to the boundary between Kahuwī and Waiiti, the court had thereby implicitly dispatched two cases with one decision.

The other boundaries of Parahaki and Huiarau as well as Waiiti partitions had earlier been settled, but the redistribution of Ruatāhuna's relative shares among its five new partitions (including those of Manawarū, named Arohana and Kahuwī) was to take several more weeks of detailed and patient hearings. As was usually the case with Tūhoe land rights, 'relative shares' meant nothing at all like European property rights in land, but instead meant the intricacies of generations of ancestors, intricacies of histories, and precarious balances of *mana*, all embedded deeply in the history of the land itself. Consequently every 'share' of 'ownership' was loaded with these important implications, and worth a battle nearly to the death. *He kotahi a Tūhoe, ka kata te Po* ('If there is but one Tūhoe warrior present, the goddess of death laughs with anticipation'; quotation from Brenda Tahi's oral evidence 28 June 2004; my translation).

It is unlikely that the final establishment of Ngāti Rongo hapū rights in Ruatāhuna against Te Whenuanui II's *mana*, let alone Kahuwī as a founding ancestor, was fully accepted among the other hapū recognized to control the block in 1902. Even a decade after the 1912 decision there is evidence that some leaders of the migrant marriage alliance refused recognition of Ngāti Rongo's rights in Manawarū, instead recognizing only those of Arohana and Te Urewera hapū, as had Te Whenuanui II. As will be described in Volume II, in 1923 Wahia Paraki (Fig. 7.1; Pareihe Rangimatuatini's sister's grandson) recorded both Arohana and Kahuwī partitions to be under the *mana* of Te Urewera hapū alone, although he recognized some rights of Ngāti Rongo in Huiarau partition. In this position he opposed Te Amo Kokouri's (Numia's passive ally in 1902 and 1912) dramatic testimony only a few days earlier before the hostile UCS commission, echoing Te Whenuanui II's opening statement for all the hapū of Ruatāhuna in 1902, but recognizing Ngati Rongo's control in Kahuwī.

The unpredictable but profoundly historical ironies of the Ruatāhuna partition had only begun. As will be described in Chap. 8 of Volume II, in 1917 the Crown's campaign to purchase throughout the UDNR had been extended to Ruatāhuna, but it turned out that the Chief Judge's records and decision had been lost. Several months' delay in finding them occasioned a further irony: the Tūhoe were able to play the Crown's surprise to their own advantage, and minimise further loss of Ruatāhuna lands.

Notes

1. Figure 9.1 is a composite made from five sketches that were drawn up in the 'Memoranda of Transfer' to support the Crown's unsuccessful efforts to purchase all shares in each of the five partitions 1919–1920 (Bassett and Kay 2002, S.P. Vol. 3: 180–290). These sketches include important details such as streams and place names, and were almost certainly drawn up from the map used in 1912–1913, upon which the final legal decisions were made. I

used these sketches together with survey plans 6873, 227, and NZMS 170 (see the bibliography for these sources) and plans 6852 and 11408 (in LINZ, Hamilton archives) in an attempt to locate the boundary between Arohana and Kahuwī partitions more accurately, roughly depicted in Fig. 1.2. It will be noticed in Fig. 9.1 that the relative proportions and boundaries of Arohana (partition 1, mis-spelled 'Arahana' here) and Kahuwī (partition 2, mis-spelled 'Kahui' here) are less extensive than their representation in Fig. 1.2. As is often the case in Native Land Court records as well, many of the place names and references were impermanent (e.g., particular named trees, bends in a river), forgotten, or no longer readily identifiable, but were located at the time on a sketch map kept before the court but usually archived separately from the minutebooks. Although these sketches can sometimes be located in surveyors' logs or archives, they were often lost when replaced by surveyed plans revised to accord with new boundaries.

2. Furthermore, *tuku whenua* could be intentionally ambiguous: Numia himself, as chairman of the Komiti Nui of the reserve, had in 1908–1909 attempted to placate the Crown's demand that Urewera lands be sold by offering short-term leases that would 'revert to the donor'. It was probably Apirana Ngata's understanding and impatience with Numia's subterfuge that led to Ngata's subversion—as the Crown's representative—of Numia's control of the Komiti Nui by forcing inclusion of Rua Kenana's faction, which favored outright sale to the Crown (Webster n.d. ([1984–5]).
3. Indeed, that Te Whenuanui II had raised his objection on this basis may suggest that Milroy's evidence reflects a relaxation of the exclusion of *whāngai tamariki* from such rights over the intervening century.

References

Bassett, Heather and R. Kay. 2002. "*Ruatāhuna: land ownership and administration c. 1896–1990.*" With Supporting Papers (S.P.) Vols 1–3. WAI 894 #A20. Wellington, N.Z.: Waitangi Tribunal.

Best, Elsdon. 1898. "Tuhoe genealogies 1898" (spine title); "Genealogies of the Tuhoe tribe. Also includes all living members of the tribe in 1898, as given before the Urewera Commission set up under the act of 1896." Manuscript qMS [172]. Wellington, N.Z.: Alexander Turnbull Library. [The author can supply a digital index for this resource.]

Best, Elsdon, 1973. *Tuhoe, Children of the Mist.* Vols. I and II (genealogies). Second edition. Wellington, N.Z.: A.H. and A.W. Reed Ltd. (first published 1925 as Vol VI of the Memoirs of the Polynesian Society).

Milroy, J. Te Wharehuia 2000. Expert opinion in the case of Waimania Hohua. Appeal 2000–8, Minute Book 10, APRO 49–51. Rotorua, N.Z.: Waiariki Maori Land Court District.

NACMB 1. Native Appellate Court minute book 1, Jackson Palmer, Rawson, (13Nov1912–Feb1913), index 9 pp., 386 pp.; NA Wgtn: Waiariki, Urewera Appelate MB 1, CD 3518/2, 397pp.; NA Ak: AREPRO 4711/1450. Acronym: NACMB 1.

UMB 1. Urewera District Native Reserve Commission minute book 1 (identified as Urewera Commission minute book '3'), Smith, Butler, et al, (1Feb1899–8Mar1900), in Māori, Index 22pp., 382pp. NA Wgtn: Urewera MB 3, MLC 13, W3518, CD2, Vol 3, 397 pp.; NA Ak: AREPRO 4711/1445. Acronym: UMB 1.

UMB 6. Urewera District Native Reserve Commission minute book 6, Butler, Scannell, et al. (16May1901–26Apr02) in English, index 9 pp., 382 pp.; NA Wgtn: Waiariki, Urewera MB 6, CD W3518/2, 398 pp.; NA Ak: AREPRO 4711/1448. Acronym: UMB 6.

Webster, Steven. 1975. "Cognatic Descent Groups and the Contemporary Māori: a Preliminary Reassessment." *The Journal of the Polynesian Society* Vol.84(2): 121–152, 1975.

Webster, Steven. n.d. (1984–5) "Urewera Land 1895–1926; a tentative historical survey of Government and Tuhoe relations as reflected in official records." Unpublished manuscript, 50pp. Held in the University of Auckland Library. Auckland, N.Z.

Webster, Steven. 2004. *The Urewera Consolidation Scheme: Confrontations between Tuhoe and the Crown, 1915–1925*. Vols I, II. Report commissioned by the Waitangi Tribunal. WAI 894 #D8. Wellington, N.Z.: Waitangi Tribunal.

CHAPTER 10

Some Plausible Explanations

1 Introduction

Led initially by the problem of the Ruatāhuna-Waikaremoana amalgamation proposal in 1902, the previous chapters of Part II have identified and traced the intricate history of a particular confrontation that appears to have involved major Tūhoe leaders and continued for some decades. One Tūhoe leader recently assured me that there were many other stories about such notorious conflicts of *mana* in the past.

In Chap. 7 a developed and extensive marriage alliance was reconstructed as it stood about 1898 between leaders of relatively recent migrant families with rights in both Waikaremoana and Ruatāhuna blocks but few others of the reserve. In Chap. 8 different confrontations in Waikaremoana and Ruatāhuna 1899–1907 involving leaders of this alliance were examined. The confrontation over northern Waikaremoana block was primarily between Tamakaimoana hapū of nearby Maungapōhatu and the migrant marriage alliance. The confrontation over the Manawarū area of Ruatāhuna block was primarily between Numia Kererū for Ngāti Rongo hapū and Te Whenuanui II for Te Urewera hapū, whose resistance by 1903 was backed by the entire migrant marriage alliance. Several unresolved aspects of these confrontations were silent or ignored before the UDNR appeals commission 1906–1907 but emerged again in the 1912–1913 partition of Ruatāhuna block, which was examined in Chap. 9. That chapter described the triumph of Numia Kererū's long campaign to establish Ngāti Rongo

© The Author(s) 2020

S. Webster, *A Separate Authority (He Mana Motuhake)*, Volume I,
https://doi.org/10.1007/978-3-030-41042-1_10

rights in Manawarū, following upon the death of Te Whenuanui II and the weakening of resistance by the leaders of the migrant marriage alliance.

Each of the above chapters has sought to stick to the documented facts, but historically reconstructing this fragmentary information has often had to rely on probabilities, possibilities, and guesswork. Attempting further explanation of the many gaps and inconsistencies remaining in the above account must be more speculative and might be seen as presumptuous. Any such speculation must go further in 'reading between the lines' of the official record, and also probably further in possible trespass and offense of contemporary sensitivities. On the other hand, it will be even more vulnerable than the previous chapters to corrections or challenges from the long memory and *mana motuhake* of Ngāi Tūhoe who, as should be obvious, have long been able to fend for themselves.

2 Behind the Scenes of the Ruatāhuna and Waikaremoana Hearings, 1900–1903

The Ruatāhuna-Waikaremoana migrant marriage alliance described in Chap. 7 had developed over several generations, and is itself probably sufficient explanation of the 1902 proposal and presumably wide support of the Ruatāhuna-Waikaremoana amalgamation. If so, then most of the two apparently different confrontations fought out in and behind the investigation and appeals of each block, and the final partitioning of Ruatāhuna and expropriation of Waikaremoana, might be seen more coherently as further developments of this same alliance in confrontation or cooperation with other Tūhoe leaders or the Crown. Although the ground of the earlier confrontations shifted when in 1908 Crown benevolence began its transformation into subversion, continuities can be traced through to the Consolidation Scheme and relocation of Tūhoe 'non-sellers' surviving shares to fragments of land scattered throughout the 'Crown award' by 1926.

The commission hearings in which the very different Waikaremoana and Ruatāhuna confrontations were recorded were generally approached in the previous chapters as independent developments. However, while dealing with adjacent blocks and overlapping hapū, the two cases were often closely concurrent as well as being heard in the same location. Behind-the-scenes negotiations and confrontations among the participants and observers of the different cases were likely. In 1902 the final stage of both the Waikaremoana investigation and all of the Ruatāhuna investigation described in Chap. 8 was heard in Rūātoki at Tauarau *marae* between 3 February and 3 March (although other cases intervened). Perhaps in an effort to pre-empt or mollify mounting appeals, the proposal to amalgamate all 34 blocks of the reserve into just ten titles, including the amalgamation of Ruatāhuna and Waikaremoana blocks, emerged at the end of that season's sittings in May 1902, also in Rūātoki and probably at Tauarau *marae*.

In 1907, although the Waikaremoana appeals hearing began in Wairoa on the East Coast the previous December, the settlement of the appeals for both Ruatāhuna and Waikaremoana blocks described in Chap. 8 occurred during only five days 1–5 February 1907 in Whakatane, just north of Rūātoki (see Fig. 1.1). With regard to the partition of Ruatāhuna in 1912, all the hearings described in Chap. 9 were held in Taneatua even closer north of Rūātoki, and at least one of the five descent groups of the Ruatāhuna-Waikaremoana migrant marriage alliance was fully involved. Similarly, a decade later in the wake of the Crown's purchase campaign the early hearings held by the consolidation commissioners in Waikaremoana and Ruatāhuna both occurred within a few days of February 1922, and although the occasional meetings 1923–1925 were usually brief and all but one held only in Ruatāhuna, it is clear that at least some of the old or new leaders of the migrant marriage alliance were able to attend along with leaders of the Apitihana ('opposition') to the consolidation scheme.

Although it was not clear in either of the two confrontations examined separately, in retrospect it became obvious that Numia Kererū was the missing link in the confrontation between Waikaremoana and Maungapōhatu leaders, and the migrant marriage alliance was the missing link in the confrontation over the Manawarū part of Ruatāhuna. The obscured but central role of Numia in the Waikaremoana confrontation between Tutakangahau and leaders of the marriage alliance, and the obscured but central role of leaders of the migrant marriage alliance in the Ruatāhuna confrontation between Te Whenuanui II and Numia, did not begin to emerge in the commission records until the 1907 appeals hearings. In retrospect, the situation was actually more straightforward: if Te Whenuanui II is not assumed to stand alone in his pre-eminent *mana* in Ruatāhuna but is simply seen as a leader in the migrant marriage alliance (at least because two of his children had married into three of its descent groups), Numia Kererū's confrontation with the leaders of the marriage alliance in both blocks is thrown into clearer perspective. Numia's role as a *rangatira* of Ngāti Rongo hapū and Tauarau *marae* in Rūātoki would have been studiedly low-key but nevertheless influential, because that is where the crucial hearings of both these cases, as well as the amalgamation proposal, were hosted in 1902, and the appeals for both cases were settled in 1907 at Whakatane, not far away.

The concurrence of both the hearings on Waikaremoana and Ruatāhuna in February 1902 in Rūātoki suggests that Te Whenuanui II's supporters in the migrant marriage alliance became aware of Numia Kererū's key role in both cases long before the alliance's mobilization became obvious in their 1903 appeals and the 1907 appeals commission hearings. The notorious Whaitiripapa case settled through proxy hapū for Ngāti Rongo, and Te Urewera hapū in 1900 might have been an early warning. As the confrontation between the migrant marriage alliance and Tutakangahau's and Paora Kingi's claims to Waikaremoana approached deadlock in Te Whaiti in 1901, Tutakangahau's pleas to adjourn the case to Rūātoki to look into "the interests of the different families" must have aroused their suspicions regarding Numia's role behind the scenes. After all, Tutakangahau's claim was primarily for nearby Maungapōhatu and his own Tamakaimoana hapū and, as Te Mapu pointed out, 'all Tamakaimoana are here and so are the Waikare[moana] people'. Numia, himself a claimant in both cases, had been stood down from the commission, but had written out and submitted the list of Tutakangahau's claimants through Te Wao Ihimaera who, ironically, led the determined resistance against it with Te Mapu. Whatever was going on behind the scenes would have been of wide interest to other leaders in the migrant marriage alliance.

Tutakangahau's predicament and failing case in Te Whaiti in 1901 might be understandable if Numia was not there, having remained in Rūātoki because stood down from the commission and not needing to argue cases in the southern blocks in which he had interests. Tutakangahau may have pressed for an adjournment of his case to Rūātoki to benefit from Numia's greater expertise in the history of 'the interests of the different families' in Tutakangahau's own Tamakaimoana hapū or, more likely, Numia's familiarity and skill with the procedures of courts and commissions (as well as hosting of the commission at Tauarau marae in Rūātoki).

However, examination of the Maungapōhatu hearings showed that Numia was in Te Whaiti 7–9 May 1901 in order to argue a claim for his hapū Ngāti Hā *against* Tamakaimoana hapū for an increase of shares in a small western portion of Maungapōhatu bordering on Ierenui-Ōhāua (UMB 5: 339, 344). (Ngāti Hā was recognized to have sole rights to the adjacent Te Ranga a Ruanuku block, but was also associated with

Tamakaimoana hapū (Kruger 2004).) On 3 May Numia had also conducted the case *for* Tamakaimoana claiming parts of Paharakeke and Manuoha blocks, just to the east of Maungapōhatu (UMB 5: 329, 343). However, Te Oti (Tahakawa) Tutakangahau, conducting for Tamakaimoana hapū, cross-examined Numia on his claim for Ngāti Ha to the small western portion of Maungapōhatu, catching him in a significant boundary over-reach and perhaps evasions of several other questions, and the decision went unanimously against Numia's claim (UMB 5: 346–8, 351).[1] He was not mentioned in any further hearings until 16 May when it was noted that he was absent due to illness (UMB 6: 1). The intervening hearings were all concerned with Waikaremoana block where he was also stood down, and it is plausible that he returned to Rūātoki soon after the decision on his claim against Tamakaimoana went against him on 9 May. It was on 13 May that Tutakangahau first asked that the Waikaremoana case be adjourned to Rūātoki.

It may be significant that the day after the decision against Numia's claim in Maungapōhatu, Te Oti reported that "there is a great disturbance about my objecting to certain shares. Tamakaimoana [hapū] are angry with me for doing so" and demanded that Maungapōhatu be divided up among the many hapū with rights in it (UMB 5: 351). It is plausible that Te Oti had overplayed his hand against Numia who, after all, was conducting Tamakaimoana's claim to part of Paharakeke and Manuoha blocks as well as writing up their claim to Waikaremoana for Tutakangahau. If this were the case, Numia's indignation might have aggravated an illness that excused his return to Rūātoki, depriving Tutakangahau of the advice he urgently needed to defend the claims list Numia had drawn up for him for Waikaremoana. Tamakaimoana (and Te Oti's father Tutakangahau) might have been angry at Te Oti because he had not sufficiently recognized Numia's services to them in his opposition to Numia's own claim in Maungapōhatu. The 'great disturbance' Te Oti reported on 10 May 1901, or his demand that Maungapōhatu be divided up by hapū, may have also had something to do with the agreement 'among all the parties interested' in Waikaremoana to reverse their earlier decision and give its northern part over to Maungapōhatu and Tamakaimoana hapū, announced *later that same day* by the commission.

Another paradox in the 1901 record regarding Waikaremoana might be resolved by another plausible explanation. Te Wao's revelation in 1907 that he had submitted the claimants list of 92 persons being appealed against, but that Numia had written it out, raises new questions about the five original claimants lists that were submitted in 1901 and the immediate objections to them.

It was pointed out in Chap. 8 that with the exception of Paora Kingi's list most of the objections were made by three leaders of the migrant marriage alliance against lists submitted for Waikaremoana by one or another of themselves, and that the only list that was largely accepted by all three objectors was the one recorded as submitted by Numia Kererū. The closing of ranks among leaders of the migrant marriage alliance that was evident by the time of the four 1903 appeals, and by 1907 was directed against the list of 92 persons admitted to Waikaremoana, implies that the claimant's list submitted under Numia's name in 1901 was quite different from the offending list of 92 persons. Its ready acceptance by the three leaders of the alliance may have indicated that it was only for descendants of Numia's sibling group (AJHR 1903, WM# 533–542) and a few others of Ngāti Rongo hapū, and quite separate from the one that Te Wao said he had submitted but that Numia had written out for Tutakangahau and Tamakaimoana hapū. But the claimants list recorded as submitted by Te Wao in 1901 was not widely objected to at that time: apparently Te Mapu objected only to 'certain names' on this list. How could this be the same list that was admitted to the title despite dismissal of Tutakangahau's case and appealed against by Mahaki Tapiki and other leaders of the alliance by 1907?

This paradox might be resolved by a fuller appreciation of Te Wao's strategy regarding the northern portion of Waikaremoana. It may be significant that Te Wao himself signed onto none of the four appeals, and hung back at the 1907 hearing until called to appear. It will be remembered that Te Wao's hurried arrangement when he arrived at the 1901 hearings was that the northern boundary of Waikaremoana should remain 'as surveyed'. Presumably, this boundary was in accord with the 1899 agreement at the meeting in Waimako between Tutakangahau and leaders of the migrant marriage alliance that Waikaremoana would not be divided and its northern portion given up to Maungapōhatu as urged by Paora Kingi. In the 1901 hearing in Te Whaiti Te Oti immediately confirmed this agreement for Tamakaimoana, while perhaps provocatively identifying the northern part of Waikaremoana as 'Tamakaimoana land'. Then the very next morning Te Rahui angrily reported to the commission that Te Wao was nevertheless cutting Tamakaimoana names out of this northern part as well as what Te Rahui termed 'the conquered land', apparently those lands further south in the block.

It was suggested in Chap. 8 that Te Wao's certainly provocative disregard of the agreement to leave what Tamakaimoana considered to be their own land in Waikaremoana block was his considered strategy on behalf of Ngāti Ruapani allies of the Tūhoe conquest (Te Wao was a leader in Ngāti Ruapani hapū of Tūhoe). In this way, Te Wao or Te Mapu could force Tamakaimoana to demonstrate the *sustained* occupation as well as ancestral rights required among Tūhoe as stigmatized *intermarrying immigrants* in this northern part of the block, as well as the 'permanent' occupation (explicitly required by the commission) of any claims for conquered land further south in the block. If the commission's punitive decision to shift the boundary south and give Tamakaimoana 'their' land as part of Maungapōhatu (presumably a reaction to Te Wao's provocation) was finally disregarded—as it was in practice if not officially—Te Wao's strategy turned out to be resoundingly successful. Such a strategy was furthermore vindicated when Tutakangahau's as well as Paora Kingi's case was heard and both were dismissed.

In this way, fuller appreciation of Te Wao's strategy might explain the otherwise surprising degree of acceptance of the list he submitted in his own name for Numia. While Te Mapu's objection only to 'certain names' may have been hesitant in deference to the agreement not to divide Waikaremoana, Te Wao had known this list was drawn up by Numia for Tutakangahau and Tamakaimoana hapū and, rather than confront this covert alliance between two powerful *rangatira*, quietly resolved to challenge it in negotiation outside the commission or, if necessary, before it. Tutakangahau may have also known this would be Te Wao's strategy, and sought Numia's support against it. Again, if this was indeed his strategy, it would have been entirely successful if the list had not somehow been included in the title contrary to the commission's decision. Even so, Te Wao's unobtrusive victory over the two leading *rangatira* must have resounded to his *mana*. After watching Tutakangahau's case deflate without Numia's close support in 1901, the unofficial disregard of the official decision to move the northern boundary of Waikaremoana south may have even been the commission's unspoken apology to Te Wao and the other leaders of the migrant marriage alliance.[2]

Although the commission remained in Te Whaiti in 1901 and Tutakangahau had to present his case for Waikaremoana there (and see it dismissed), the allocation of shares was left to be settled the next year. When in February 1902 the hearings on Waikaremoana and Ruatāhuna blocks were reconvened, it was on Ngāti Rongo hapū's Tauarau *marae* in

Rūātoki, where Numia was the leading *rangatira*. Tauarau's meeting-house Rongokarae had been used for the commission hearings in 1899 and 1900, but it was not formally opened until 1901–1902 (Binney 2002: 136); in any case, the *mana* of Ngāti Rongo as host hapū would have been quietly pervasive.

Both Numia and Tutakangahau were formally stood down as commissioners due to their interest in the cases being heard. However, as well as Numia's role as host, Tutakangahau was almost certainly there as a claimant and, as it turned out, probably continued (through his sons) to insist on inclusion in the Waikaremoana shares despite the dismissal of his case. Te Mapu arrived in Rūātoki from Waikaremoana on 14 February to settle the shares for that case, probably accompanied by others in the migrant marriage alliance, including Te Wao Ihimaera. Te Wao's position may have been ambiguous, insofar as it was he who had delivered Numia's list for Tutakangahau's claim to Waikaremoana, still in deadlock and undeterred by its dismissal. All of this, including Numia's central role, would have been out in the open at Tauarau *marae* although invisible in the records. Also perhaps in the air at this time would have been the 'agreement' the previous May to divide Waikaremoana, probably done by the commission to appease Tutakangahau or Te Oti and still not officially rescinded because it had become an embarrassment when Paora Kingi's and Tutakangahau's claims for conquest and occupation of Waikaremoana collapsed for lack of Numia's guidance.

A few days later during the 20 February 1902 sitting in Rūātoki, first the Waikaremoana case and then the Ruatāhuna case reached a crisis involving Numia. Regarding Waikaremoana, the commission's impatient reply to Te Oti's protest for his brother made it clear that at least the portion of Numia's list including Tutakangahau's family had been included in the block order despite the dismissal of Tutakangahau's case. The draft order may also have shown that, contrary to the commission's assertion, many other Tamakaimoana hapū members had been admitted as well as more than merely token shares awarded to members of Tutakangahau's whole *whānau*. On top of this, it may have been widely assumed that the division of northern Waikaremoana to Maungapōhatu's and Tamakaimoana's benefit was still in effect (as it was, at least officially). Somewhat later *that same day* the hearings for Ruatāhuna were resumed, and Numia himself asked Te Whenuanui II for the second time to recognize Kahuwī and thus Ngāti Rongo hapū's rights in Manawarū—thus more on the order of a public demand than a respectful request. Again, Te Whenuanui II refused without deigning to offer an explanation—thus more on the order of a public rebuff of Numia's *mana*, even on his own *marae*. If not alerted to it since 1900, Te Whenuanui II certainly realized by then that Numia's similar case for Kahuwī and Ngāti Rongo hapū had been successful against Tamaikoha and Te Urewera hapū for inclusion in Whaitiripapa block, and that Numia was pressing such a case in Ruatāhuna too—in the middle of Te Whenuanui II's domain and against the *mana* of Te Urewera hapū.

Perhaps having just experienced their own frustration in the admission of a part or all of Numia's list for Tutakangahau to Waikaremoana, Te Mapu and other leaders of the migrant marriage alliance were probably witnesses to this rising confrontation over nearby Manawarū in Ruatāhuna. Several days later on 3 March 1902, Te Iriwhiro—probably as Numia's proxy—put the request to Te Whenuanui II a third time, but more in the form of a demand that 94 of Kahuwī's descendants be allocated a full 20 shares each (those in the senior generation) even though none were descended from Arohana. Again, Te Whenuanui II refused but this time raised an argument: he explained that while he had allotted 20 shares to Arohana's descendants because his rights had been exclusive over the whole of Manawarū, Kahuwī's descendants had no rights beyond mere *aroha* because he was only an adopted son of Arohana and therefore had no birthrights at all in Manawarū.

The decision of the commission immediately followed this exchange and, while sounding superficially like a compromise, actually favored Numia's case by granting Kahuwī rights *equal to* Arohana: a full 20 shares only to descendants of both Arohana and Kahuwī, and 10 shares to descendants of only one or the other of them. Strangely, this decision was apparently announced without requiring Te Iriwhiro or Numia to answer Te Whenuanui II's argument regarding Kahuwī's adoption. Even if the decision was misguidedly in the spirit of compromise, and unadvised by the only formally sitting Tūhoe commissioner (Te Pou Papaka), it was implicitly a public insult to Te Whenuanui II's *mana*.

Whether or not Te Mapu Pukeiotu and others of the migrant marriage alliance had stayed in Rūātoki after conclusion of the Waikaremoana case and witnessed this, they would surely have soon heard about it. They probably suspected that Numia had also supported Tutakangahau's persistent demand for shares in Waikaremoana block, and would have closed ranks in support of Te Whenuanui II's defense of Manawarū against Numia's demands for recognition there. Te Whenuanui I, as well as having held the dominant *mana* of Ruatāhuna, had also been a prestigious leader among the alliance, having married two of his children into two or three of their descent groups (Fig. 7.1). Even if Te Whenuanui II had not fully realized the implications of the commission's 'compromise' decision, he would have soon been advised by his supporters. The alliance would have found common cause with him regarding Numia's role behind the incursions of Tutakangahau and Tamakaimoana hapū in Waikaremoana block and his resistance to Numia's and Ngāti Rongo's incursions in Ruatāhuna.

After all, the migrant marriage alliance remained vulnerable: the division of the northern portion of Waikaremoana block to the gain of Maungapōhatu block, the anathema emphasized by the elders of Waikaremoana at the start of the investigation on 3 May 1901, was still not rescinded on the books; the block orders were still only provisional and apparently subject to arbitrary decisions of the commission; and the appeals were yet to be heard by another commission. The Ruatāhuna-Waikaremoana amalgamation was proposed in May 1902 just before the conclusion of that year's sittings. If the long-standing migrant marriage alliance was not itself sufficient to support the proposal, such a mobilization against a common threat would have reinforced it.

Examination of shares allocated in the 1903 provisional order for Ruatāhuna block suggests that the 'compromise' decision of 3 March 1902 was followed, although probably not by Te Whenuanui II. The enforcement of the commission's decision to grant 20 shares only to descendants of both Arohana and Kahuwī would account for the unusually low proportion of descent groups, sibling groups, and individuals who were allocated strong shares in the 1903 provisional order for that block. Only 29 of 884 persons were allotted 15 or 20 shares (this included the 3 children of Te Whenuanui I at ranks 1–3, and Numia and his elder sister at ranks 206–7). Because most or all descendants of Arohana and Kahuwī were only 4–5 generations removed from a common ancestress in Turaki I (Fig. 8.1), and marriage between cousins was generally forbidden out to the third generation, there would still have been very few marriages between their descendants. (Te Whenuanui I's parents were apparently second cousins but, as discussed in Chaps. 6 and 7, this was either a rare exception or a Tūhoe adaptation of what Ngata described as a mark of 'highly prized lines' in East Coast hapū.) Te Whenuanui I's children by Turaki II were probably among the first to be descended from both ancestors.

The enforcement of the 1902 decision might also account for the way in which the appeals by Te Whenuanui II and his supporters continued to avoid reference to it and, in the 1907 appeals hearing as well as the original appeals, simply protested that shares of 'permanent residents' had been reduced and those of 'emigrants' or small rights had been increased. While relying on both the *mana* of Te Whenuanui II and the promise of the appeals process, this strategy could also avoid the risk of drawing the attention of the appeals commissioners to the insulting decision only to confirm it.

As described in Chap. 8, by 1903, when Te Whenuanui II, Mahaki Tapiki, and Te Mapu submitted four appeals protesting unjust reduction of some shares and increase of others in the provisional order for Ruatāhuna block, the mobilization of most of the descent groups of the migrant marriage alliance was displayed in the signatures or names of their leaders on these appeals. Meanwhile, Mahaki and other Waikaremoana leaders had also submitted their appeal against the inclusion of 92 persons from Tutakangahau's and Paora Kingi's lists in the provisional order for Waikaremoana block despite the dismissal of their cases. An abiding paradox of all these appeals and their eventual hearings 1–5 February 1907 is the studied disregard of several key issues, not only in the appeals themselves and even by the new set of commissioners, but also by the appellants, defendants, and observers in the hearings.

3 The Emergence of Numia Kererū's Strategy, 1903–1907

Several different aspects of the situation may converge to explain this paradox of the appeals hearings: (i) the concurrence of the two hearings; (ii) the redistribution of 1903 shares accepted by the appeals commission; (iii) additional details of Te Whenuanui II's death. Examination of each of these implications below suggests that Numia was devising a strategy for his claim to Ngāti Rongo rights in Ruatāhuna.

It will be helpful to begin with a brief preview of the main issues apparently left unaddressed in the 1906–1907 appeals hearings for each block. In the case of Ruatāhuna, while both Te Whenuanui II's appeals had explicitly raised the key issue of Kahuwī's rights relative to Arohana's rights, apparently neither this issue, nor the commission's decision in 1902 to award them equal shares without requiring Numia or Te Iriwhiro to rebut Te Whenuanui II's argument, was ever raised—by Te Whenuanui II's supporters, the appeals commissioners, or Numia. Instead, the issue appeared to remain merely unforeseen decreases and increases of shares in the block order, and when Numia finally admitted he had made the reductions and offered to resolve the matter outside, the settlement was simply turned over to him and results approved with no questions asked.

In the case of Waikaremoana, while Mahaki Tapiki clearly described the inclusion of 92 claimants to the block order despite the dismissal of the cases made for them, the appeals commission ignored this issue, instead of repeatedly asking who had put these names into the order in the first place, and adjourning the case from Wairoa to Whakatane "to afford opportunity for those objected to appear before us" (AJHR 1907 G-4: 12). However, when this case was reconvened and Te Wao reported that the list of 92 claimants had been written out by Numia Kererū, the appeals commissioners dismissed the appeal because they could not "believe that any mistake was made in regard to the inclusion of these [92] names by the last commission"—and Mair's diary revealed that he felt the list had already undergone 'two ordeals', again ignoring its dismissal after the final 'ordeal'. If the appeals commission was even aware of the unresolved status of the northern portion of the block, they may have reasonably assumed the decision to include it in Maungapōhatu had been rescinded to compensate for the inclusion of the 92 names in Waikaremoana; but it had neither been rescinded nor raised in the hearings. Numia Kererū was likely to have been present at the Wairoa as well as the Whakatane appeals hearings on Waikaremoana but, despite the commission's repeated concerns to find out who in 1902 had put these 92 persons 'into the list of owners in the first place?', neither offered nor was asked for an explanation.

Although the Waikaremoana hearing had begun at Wairoa, its resumption in Whakatane began on Monday 4 February 1907, the same day the Ruatāhuna hearing on Manawarū appeals was concluded by approval of the lists amended outside under Numia's supervision (see Fig. 1.1; UCAMB 2: 101–5). Therefore the appeals commissioners as well as the appellants, defendants, and observers in either case who were present in the hearings Friday, Monday, and Tuesday 1, 4–5 February 1907 (or discussing it over the weekend) were likely to have been aware of the dramatic developments. The answer to the commission's frustrated effort to understand who made the apparent changes to the 1903 Ruatāhuna shares was followed by the same answer to their repeated questions regarding who had put in the list of persons included in the Waikaremoana block list despite dismissal of their case. In both cases, the answer was Numia Kererū, revealed in the 1 February hearing on Ruatāhuna, and in the 5 February hearing on Waikaremoana. And in both cases, the commissioners apparently suddenly had no further queries, approving the amendments guided by Numia outside in the Ruatāhuna case and dismissing the appeal against his list for Tutakangahau in the Waikaremoana case.

Comparison of the 1903 and 1907 Ruatāhuna block orders, the 'before' and 'after' of this opaque situation, offers some clues to explain what may have happened. First of all, the solidarity of the marriage alliance behind Te Whenuanui II might have had some bearing on Numia's admitted reduction of Ruatāhuna shares in 1902 and his negotiation of increased shares in 1907. There is some evidence that his reduction of shares for the 1903 block order anticipated the mobilization of the migrant marriage alliance and attempted to mollify some of their leaders by overlooking their lack of appropriate ancestry or occupation. This might explain the concern of the appeals with increased as well as decreased shares. There were probably more strong shareholders left in the 1903 order than would have been necessary in a strict application of the 3 March 1902 decision, that is, full shares only to descendants of both Kahuwī and Arohana. Of the 29 persons who were allotted strong shares (15–20 for the eldest living generation), 7 or about 25% held only narrow rights beyond Waikaremoana and Ruatāhuna and so might have been affiliated with the migrant marriage alliance. Because of the relatively restricted ancestry of this alliance, it is doubtful that all of them were descendants of both these ancestors, let alone to have maintained recent occupation in Manawarū. More significantly, among them were Te Mapu Pukeiotu, Te Wao Ihimaera, and Paraki Wereta, all leaders in the migrant marriage alliance and two of them leaders in the 1901–1902 investigation of Waikaremoana. Other members of the alliance who would be more likely to be able to claim descent from both these ancestors (because they were in fact descendants at least of Arohana) were the Hauwai brothers Mātaatua and Whakamoe and the Taratoa sibling group (Figs. 7.1 and 8.1). However, none of these received strong shares in the 1903 orders, instead receiving relatively small shares (5–10 for the eldest living generation).

Closer examination of the increases of shares for the 1907 Ruatāhuna final order arranged outside the commission between Numia and the supporters of Te Whenuanui II (i.e., presumably in compensation for those shares reduced by Numia in the 1903 order) similarly suggests he may have intended to mollify their resistance against his initiatives. A comparison of the several lists of objections, appeals, and provisional and final

Ruatāhuna block orders 1902–1907 shows that of the 884 persons in the 1903 provisional order for the whole block, about 174 had their shares increased in the 1907 order, and these were usually doubled (typically from 10 to 20 for the senior generation, and 5–10, or 1–3 for their children and grandchildren). About 81 different persons were also added to the 1907 order (bringing the total to 966 shareholders). Although like most other final Urewera block orders these were all added at the end of the order, unlike most other orders they were nevertheless allotted substantial shares for their age: from 5 to 20, not merely 1–2 token shares allotted in *aroha* as was often the case in other blocks.

Comparison of the names on Te Whenuanui II's, Mahaki's, and Te Mapu's 1903 appeals or their amendments with the senior generation of persons who received increased shares in the 1907 orders enabled approximate identification of the descent groups, sibling groups, and individuals appearing in both. In the 1903 Ruatāhuna block list of 884 persons, there were about 25 such groups or individuals who received increased shares in the 1907 order. Sixteen of these 25 groups or individuals or 64% could be identified with the names listed in the amended appeals regarding the Manawarū part of Ruatāhuna: 7 in Mahaki Tapiki's appeal (for Te Whenuanui II's and his own original appeals); 1 in Noho Taratoa's appeal (also for those same original appeals); and 9 in Whareturoa Hoani's appeal (for Te Mapu Pukeiotu's original appeal). The disproportionate attention shown in the share increases for Manawarū compared to the other partitions may also have been influenced by the relative ranking or implied *mana* of the groups and individuals involved. Those groups and individuals deriving from Mahaki's and Noho's amended appeals appeared in the 1907 block list mainly between #22 and #182, while individuals on Whareturoa's list appeared mainly between #224 and #779 (of 966 individual owners).

Previously in the discussion of the 1903 appeals (Chap. 8), it was pointed out that between the four appeals supporting Te Whenuanui II all five descent groups of the migrant marriage alliance were represented among the signatories. The success of all five of these descent groups in the 1907 increase of shares in Ruatāhuna is striking. The Taratoa and Hauwai descent groups occupied 54 of the 100 leading positions in the list's rank order (#35–89), although only the Taratoa siblings' were increased from 10 to 20 shares; the Whakamoe and Mātaatua (Hauwai) descent groups were increased to only 7–10 shares for the senior generation despite their leading rank, probably reflecting continuing stigma of primary occupation outside Ruatāhuna, perhaps in Waikaremoana. According to the *whakapapa* given by Paora in 1912, Mātaatua and his brother Whakamoe were first cousins of Te Arahe through their mother Hinepoto (who must have been Hauwai's wife), and so were themselves descendants of Arohana, unlike Taratoa whose children could claim that ancestry only through their mother Te Arahe (UCAMB 1: 223; see Fig. 8.1). This ancestry may explain the high rank of the Hauwai descent group despite their small shares.

The next alliance leaders allotted increases in the Ruatāhuna rank order were the deeply intermarried Tawa and Hautu descent groups of Tangira, Hurae, Manuera, and Turipa sibling groups, led by Mahiki Tapiki and including Te Mapu Pukeiotu and his daughter. This group totaled 34 persons, the senior generation of which was increased from 10 to 20 shares (#169–184) or from 5 to 10 shares (#283–302, again, probably due to primary occupation outside Ruatāhuna). The next alliance leaders allotted increases were the Pareihe descent group including Te Mataa, Pareihe, Hori, Tarei, and Hiwarau sibling groups (#470–492), the senior generation of which was increased from 10 to 20 shares. The last alliance leader in the original list was Paraki Wereta, whose shares were increased from 15 to 20, although his many descendants (#498–524) already held full (10 or 5) shares in virtue of their mother Mutu Hakopa's 20 shares (#497), so received no increases.

Descent groups of the migrant marriage alliance receiving increased (usually doubled) shares in 1907, therefore, totaled about 111 persons or 12.5% of the original 884 shareholders. However, these increases were over half of the total 214 persons whose shares were increased in the final block order for Ruatāhuna. On the face of it, this result reflects the disproportionate success of appeals originating from the migrant marriage alliance in support of Te Whenuanui II against Numia's claims to Manawarū. However, because these increases were left to Numia to negotiate outside the hearings and accepted without question by the appeals commission, it might be suspected that they were also intended to mollify supporters of Te Whenuanui II's resistance against Numia's demands for recognition of Kahuwī.

The time and manner of Te Whenuanui II's death on 2 January 1907 might have been a crucial factor in the negotiation of these share increases. The negotiation occurred during the overlapped Ruatāhuna and Waikaremoana appeals hearings 1–5 February in Whakatane, just a month after his death. Judith Binney's careful clarification of the widespread contemporary confusion between Te Whenuanui I and II, and even the succession of a Te Whenuanui III (summarized in Chaps. 5 and 7) enables a fuller appreciation of what may have been going on behind the scenes of the appeals commission. One of the letters on which Binney rests her case, previously described in Chap. 7, was sent to the Native Minister on 10 January 1907 reporting that "Te Whenuanui II (Te Haka) died unexpectedly, on 2 January 1907" (Binney 2002: 21 fn 37). Although Binney does not pursue implications regarding the 'unexpected' manner of his death, the previously published biography of Te Whenuanui by Pou Temara (whom Binney points out had mistakenly 'amalgamated' father and son in his biography) furnishes further evidence.

Perhaps drawing from family documents as well as oral history, Te Pou Temara's biography of Te Whenuanui (II) understood other parts of their ancestry better than either Best or Binney, and recounts some striking details of the oral history (Temara 1993; Fig. 8.1). According to Temara, Te Whenuanui (II) died in 1907 from injuries received in 1906 while being thrown and dragged by a newly broken horse. He had been carving decorations for a meeting house at Waimako, just southeast of Lake Waikaremoana. Binney reports that Te Whenuanui I, his son Te Haka (Te Whenuanui II) and the latter's nephew Reupene were all accomplished carvers, having completed by 1888 the famous Te Whai a te Motu meeting house at Mātaatua, Ruatāhuna, in memory of Te Kooti's escape from government forces in the Urewera. Te Whenuanui II's death from injury was probably the meaning behind the 10 January 1907 report that it was 'unexpected'.

Although he was described in that report as 'Tuhoe's paramount chief', Te Haka was apparently not yet an old man. While Temara's account misidentifies Te Haka as Te Whenuanui I rather than his son, the likelihood that Te Haka died 'unexpectedly' rather than from old age is consistent with his account of Te Whenuanui (I) as having taken a war-party (including his *mātāmua* daughter Te Mauniko among eight women) to support Maniapoto defenders at the battle of Orakau against British regulars in 1864. Temara recounts that Te Whenuanui (I), escaped after a three-day siege with his daughter Te Mauniko and, although wounded in his knee, they were among the few Tūhoe survivors who returned to Ruatāhuna. If Te Whenuanui I *and* his eldest daughter were old enough to take a war-party to Orakau in 1864, his death in 1894 (substantiated by Binney) may have been from old age; Temara also reports that Te Whenuanui (I) was given wives by two different hapū, but he was too aged to have children by them. If he was, say, in his 70s by the time of his death in 1894, his son Te Haka would have been old enough (at least 40) to succeed successfully to his chiefly title as Te Whenuanui II. By this reckoning, he would have been only in his 50s when he died of his injuries in 1907.

Temara's account of what turns out to be Te Whenuanui II's death fills out the otherwise laconic details of the 1906–1907 Urewera appeals commission minutebooks. Only weeks before his death, on 14 and again on 19 December 1906 in the hearing at Te Wairoa (on the coast 60 kilometers east of Lake Waikaremoana), Te Whenuanui II had given testimony before the appeals commission regarding the traditional boundary between Tūhoe and Ngāti Kahungunu *iwi* along what was to become the boundary between Waikaremoana and Ruatāhuna blocks (UCAMB 1: 47 from O'Malley 1996 S.P.Vol I: 294; AJHR 1907 G-4: 13). On 3 January 1907 the commission resumed its hearings in Whakatane but announced Te Whenuanui II's death and adjourned for a *tangi* ("funeral") marking this and the death of two other chiefs (UCAMB 1: 84A, 80–86). Again, this is consistent with the 10 January 1907 report by Tūhoe leaders that Te Whenuanui (II) had died 'unexpectedly'. Insofar as he had given evidence before the appeals commission in Wairoa 60 rugged kilometers east of Waimako where Temara reports he was injured, the injury probably took place after returning from the hearings to his carving in Waimako and he died shortly thereafter.

Temara's biography furthermore states that Te Whenuanui (II) was buried in a lead coffin in Waimako behind the meeting house he was carving, but that in 1910 his body was exhumed and returned to his home for re-burial at Te Whai a te Motu meetinghouse in Mātaatua, Ruatāhuna (which he had helped to carve with his father, Te Whenuanui I). In Temara's biography of Hikawera Te Kurapa, he reports that Hikawera was Te Whenuanui (I)'s great-grandson descended through Te Mauniko (Te Whenuanui (I)'s *mātāmua* daughter) and Te Mauniko's second daughter Matahera, who was Hikawera's mother (Temara 2000; Fig. 8.1). Temara points out that one of Hikawera's skills was horse-breaking, perhaps ironically redressing the cause of his grand-uncle's death. Temara also reports that Hikawera remembered as a child seeing Te Whenuanui (II)'s body being returned to Te Whai a te Motu *marae* for re-burial in 1910. Although Hikawera probably knew it, this would have been Te Whenuanui II not I, as Temara appears to assume. Insofar as Temara has close knowledge of as well as personal affiliation with this descent line in Te Urewera hapū, it is curious that his biographies did not make this distinction clear. On the other hand, I suspect that the merger or 'amalgamation' of Te Whenuanui I and his son Te Haka Te Whenuanui II has become accepted among many of his descendants and members of Te Urewera and other hapū, perhaps in the identification with common ancestral 'substance' that was well-established in accounts given before the UDNR commission as well as the Native Land Court.

The tragic manner of Te Whenuanui II's death, apparently in his prime and on the eve of the appeals that he had organized or inspired at least partly against Numia's initiatives in Ruatāhuna and Waikaremoana, may have been a factor in the paradox of the appeals hearings. The studied disregard of several key issues by all participants as well as the appeals commissioners, and Numia's silence or reserve, may have reflected appropriate mourning of such a death of whom many felt was a paramount Tūhoe *rangatira*. However, especially under such a pall of sincere respect, it may also have given Numia the opportunity that he needed to close the unresolved issues in Waikaremoana and re-open others in Ruatāhuna.

4 Arranging Succession to Te Whenuanui II's Title

Numia Kererū's 27 April 1907 report to the Native Minister regarding Reupene Mihaka's succession to the title of Te Whenuanui II, briefly discussed in Chap. 7, needs to be more carefully examined here. Binney reproduces the Māori original as well as its English translation by the Native Ministry (Binney 2002: 21–2); below is the translation, clarified by Binney in brackets with her initials, or me in brackets with my initials:

> This is to inform you that the hapus of Tuhoe have set up Reupene Mihaka as successor to his uncle Te Whenuanui [II (sw)], who is now dead. Reupene Mihaka has now been named Te Whenuanui [III (sw)]. That person is [the son (jb)] of [the late (jb)] Te Whenuanui's [II's (sw)] sister, Hinepau Te Whenuanui. Hinepau & Te Whenuanui junr [II (sw)], now decd., were [children (jb)] of one father & mother. Hinepau married Mihaka, son of Hariata, sister to Ahikaiata & Tupara [Kaaho (sw)].
>
> Reupene [sic (sw)] Te Whenuanui [III (sw)] is living at Matatua [Ruatāhuna (sw)]. That is his permanent kainga. All Govt. matters & all other business relation to Ruatāhuna & the Maoris should be forwarded to him at Matatua. Timi [James Carroll, Native Minister (sw)], he is a good man. I am his counsellor.

Before interrogation of the implications of this letter, an obvious question addressed by neither Binney nor Temara can be asked: Why had succession to Te Whenuanui II's younger deceased sister Hinepau's son been so widely supported by (all?) 'the hapus of Tuhoe'? Were there no other appropriate successors?

Between Best's 1898 census, *whakapapa* mutually accepted by Numia Kererū and Paora Noho in arguing the 1912 case (Chap. 9), information from Temara's biographies, and my fieldnotes, Te Whenuanui I's descendants were more fully reconstructed in Fig. 8.1.[3] However, a crucial confusion between these sources regarding the name of Te Whenuanui I's senior wife must first be cleared up. Like Best, Temara records his wife as 'Akiu' (Best adds that she was also known as Paaka, and adds a second wife Taiha Wahawaha). Insofar as Turaki (II) was recorded by Numia and Paora in 1912 as having had the same children and sister (Maria) as 'Akiu' was recorded by Best to have had, it is clear that 'Akiu' (alias Paaka) and Turaki II were the same person: the daughter of Te Pouwhenua. Consequently, as was described in Chap. 9, while Te Whenuanui I could probably not claim 'dual descent' from both Arohana and Kahuwī, Te Whenuanui II (Te Haka) and his full siblings could.

According to Best, Numia, and Paora, Hinepau was the daughter and third-born child of Te Whenuanui I and Turaki II. (Pou Temara only reports that Te Whenuanui (I) had two recognized children, identifying Te Mauniko but not the other.) But one must ask why any of several other descendants were not considered to be more appropriate successors to the title (Fig. 8.1): (i) their *mātāmua* daughter Te Mauniko (who was probably in her late 50s by 1907) or (ii) one of her daughters (Taraipene or Matahera), or (iii) Taraipene's daughters (age 20 and 12 by 1907), or (iv) Pirau, the son of Te Haka himself and about age 15. According to the 1907 orders, all these persons were still living (e.g., in the order for Ruatāhuna they were ranked most highly as # 1–11). According to Best's 1898 census, there were furthermore (v) two other sons of Te Whenuanui I, Kiriahuru (by another wife, Taiha Wahawaha) and his last-born by Turaki II, Te Maipi. Although Te Maipi was recorded by Best as an adult male without children, he does not appear in the 1903 block lists and may have died by then. However, Kiriahuru Te Whenuanui appears in both the 1903 and 1907 block lists and, furthermore, was sufficiently influential in 1907 to be appointed to the Tapatahi block committee (Fig. 2.1). Although Te Haka's own son Pirau may have been only 15 in 1907, he was apparently a staunch 'non-seller' through the Crown purchase campaign and by 1921 he was a leading shareholder along with his mother's siblings in one of the small reserves that survived the Crown's preemption of the Waikaremoana block (AJHR 1921 G-7: 29, grp 40).

One must wonder why Numia's letter of 27 April 1907 quoted above simply announced that 'the hapus of Tuhoe have set up' one of these likely successors while ignoring these several others. He does appear to justify selection of Reupene in terms of the full siblinghood of his mother and her brother Te Haka, Te Whenuanui II, pointing out that 'Hinepau & Te Whenuanui junr [II (sw)], now decd., were [children (jb)] of one father & mother'. Although Numia does not name either of their parents (Te Whenuanui I and Turaki II), if he intended full siblinghood of Reupene's parents to be a qualification for succession among collateral relatives, it applied equally to the *mātāmua* Te Mauniko, Te Haka, and Te Maipi as well as to Hinepau, although it may have disqualified Kiriahuru, who was another son of Te Whenuanui but born of a different mother.

Relative to Reupene (i.e., Rangiteremauri) Mihaka's apparent qualifications, what other considerations may have disqualified each of these alternative possible successors to Te Whenuanui II? Although he was only in his 20s, Reupene had been appointed to the committee for Tapatahi in 1902 and reappointed in 1907 (Fig. 2.1), so he was not without influence, probably stemming from his uncle Te Haka Te Whenuanui II who held leading shares in the block. Reupene may also have been adopted by his uncle Te Haka when his mother Hinepau died, or may have been close to Te Haka as his apprentice *tohunga whakairo* 'master carver', a prestigious status furthermore 'inherited' from Te Whenuanui I. However, these advantages would not be likely to over-ride more direct blood line continuity and seniority among males such as Pirau and Kiriahuru could claim, nor the *mātāmua* status such as Te Mauniko and her daughters could claim.

In terms of seniority as well as full siblinghood, Te Mauniko might have been considered when Te Whenuanui I died in 1894. Like younger brother Te Haka, at that time she would probably have been in her 40s. Although among Tūhoe (and most other *iwi*), apart from public political representation women suffer very little disadvantage in terms of formal status such as birth (rank) and property rights (Webster 1975: 124–6), Te Mauniko's succession to Te Whenuanui I, and her or her daughters' succession to Te Whenuanui II, may have been left out of consideration simply because it was a male's title. Te Whenuanui I's wife Turaki II is an example of a gender-specific title, used by Numia himself in the 1912 case (Fig. 8.1). Nevertheless, this leaves unexplained why Kiriahuru, an active adult male and son of Te Whenuanui I himself, and Pirau, a young male and son of Te Haka Te Whenuanui II himself, were passed over by 'the hapus of Tuhoe' for young Reupene. Reupene was probably in his 20s and not much older than Pirau. Furthermore, if the *mātāmua* Te Mauniko was unqualified because Te Whenuanui was a male's title, would this not have likewise disqualified Reupene, who would have to succeed to the title through a female, his mother Hinepau? One would suppose that although Hinepau had long been dead and her husband Mihaka had remarried, this would have been a greater impediment to Reupene's succession than it appears to have been for Te Mauniko or even her daughters who were, after all, the *mātāmua* line.

What may have disqualified Pirau Te Haka, Te Whenuanui II's own son and apparently only child, and probably not much younger than Reupene? Only a few years later in 1912 Numia's whakapapa testimony recorded 's.p.' (sin partum, no offspring) for Te Haka and Mako Mātaatua, and this was not challenged by his opponents the Taratoa cousins. So it may have been that Pirau Te Haka was adopted by Te Haka and Mako from among their migrant marriage alliance relatives with whom he had settled by 1926, and for this reason was ineligible to succeed to his adoptive father Te Whenuanui II's title. However, as well as Best's record that Pirau was born to Te Haka and Mako, the extensive land shares he still held in 1921 were much more likely to have been rights through his father than his mother (who, as a member of the migrant marriage alliance, held only narrow Urewera rights), implying that he was indeed Te Haka's begotten son.

Te Mauniko's, Te Haka's, Hinepau's, and Te Maipi's paternal half-sibling Kiriahuru, along with his nephew Reupene appointed to the Tapatahi block committee in 1907, might have been a strong contestant if Numia's emphasis on full-sibling predecessors was not meant as a pre-requisite of succession to the title between collateral relatives. In any case, he was probably a generation older than Reupene or Pirau, and respected enough to be appointed to the block committee of the important little Tapatahi block near Rūātoki where, as Ruepene's uncle, he would have out-ranked him on the same committee. On the other hand, Kiriahuru appears to have had few land rights through his mother Taiha Wahawaha, who may have been from outside the Urewera and whom Best records as married at one time to Kokouri, Turaki II's sister's husband, as well as to Te Whenuanui I (Best 1898: 96, 105; Fig. 8.1). Kiriahuru was recorded to have no children and by 1921 had apparently died or lost all his land to the Crown purchase campaign. Similarly, although Te Maipi, the youngest child of Te Whenuanui I and Turaki II, would have been fully qualified to succeed to the title, he was recorded by Best to have had no children by 1898 and apparently left the Urewera permanently or died before 1903, appearing in no block lists.

Numia's own explanation of succession by Reupene in his 27 May letter raises further questions. Strangely, after emphasizing that Hinepau and Te Haka 'were children of one father & mother', rather than naming their parents (Te Whenuanui I and Turaki II—the source of the title being passed from Te Haka Te Whenuanui II to Hinepau's son) Numia's explanation follows a genealogical tangent away from them: 'Hinepau married Mihaka, son of Hariata, sister to Ahikaiata & Tupara' (Fig. 8.1, dotted line). This two-generation divergence not only ignores the source of the title in Te Whenuanui I; it also ignores Matika Taratoa, a *mātāmua* leader of the Ruatāhuna-Waikaremoana migrant marriage alliance that had closed ranks in support of Te Whenuanui II. A third ancestral generation may have been implicitly ignored: the Taratoa sibling group's mother Te Arahe, the source of their *mātāmua* descent from the Ruatāhuna *tīpuna* Arohana and their leading mana in that block. Indeed, it was the Taratoa sibling group that in 1912 would oppose Numia's next effort to gain rights for the descendants of Kahuwī separate from those of Arohana in Manawarū.

This divergent *whakapapa* might be understandable with regard to whom Numia was writing his announcement: Timi Kara (Jimmie or James Carroll, the Native Minister). Numia's emphasis upon Matika Taratoa's wife was Hariata Kaaho, 'sister to Ahikaiata & Tupara' Kaaho, may simply have been because her brothers were Tūhoe leaders who would have been recognized by the Native Ministry, the former being *mātāmua* of the sibling group, important in earlier negotiations with government, and replaced by his youngest brother Tupara when Ahikaiata died. Binney raises the 10 January and 27 April 1907 letters as examples of Tūhoe care to keep government informed of the deaths of important leaders as part of the continuing compact between Tewhitu Tekau (Tūhoe's organization of leadership in the 1870s) and government, and points out that they were so informed when Ahikaiata, who was its founding secretary, had died in 1898 (Binney 2002: 21).

The earlier letter reporting Te Whenuanui (II)'s 'unexpected' death sent on 10 January 1907 may have other important implications. As described in Chap. 7, this letter was signed by Te Wharekotua (an important leader affiliated with Ngāti Manawa and Ngāti Tāwhaki hapū of the western Urewera blocks) and 'Mihaka Te Pouwhenua (Te Whenuanui Mihaka)'. If 'Te Whenuanui Mihaka' was Reupene Mihaka (his new title appropriately followed by his father's first name as a surname), then he was already signing the report as successor to Te Whenuanui II only a week after the latter's death. Furthermore, if as also suggested in the 10 January report, Te Whenuanui (III) Mihaka was also known as 'Mihaka Te Pouwhenua', he was probably also displaying his descent as great-grandson of Te Pouwhenua through Turaki (II) and her daughter Hinepau, Reupene's mother.[4] Because Te Pouwhenua was a grandson of the ancestor Kahuwī, as mentioned above, this name also carried important implications for Numia Kererū's claim to rights from Kahuwī in the Manawarū area of Ruatāhuna.

Although Reupene's display of this alternative name and its ancestral right might have been his or his parents' custom, it is possible that he (or his father Mihaka) had been advised to do so in the drafting of the 10 January letter by Numia Kererū as his 'counselor'. As shown in Numia's letter of 27 April quoted above, a few months later Numia was personally assuring 'Timi' (James Carroll, the Native Minister) that Reupene was 'a good man' and that he, Numia, was furthermore Reupene's 'counselor' (my translation of '*Ko au ano tona hoa hei tohutohu*' would be 'It is I, after all, who as his friend counsels him'). Ngāti Rongo hapū and Numia's own *whānau* actually had indirect links by marriage to Mihaka Matika: probably sometime after Hinepau's death Mihaka had remarried with Hiria Rangiaho, whose younger brother Pioioi Rangiaho had married Numia's mātāmua daughter Hine (Te Ariki) Numia (Fig. 6.3; Best 1898: 63).

As shown in Fig. 6.3, the marriages of the Rangiaho sibling group linked Ngāti Rongo to Tamaikoha's branch of Te Urewera hapū as well as to Te Whenuanui II's branch of that hapū and two descent groups of the migrant marriage alliance. This indirect link was furthermore of rather long-standing: already in 1898 Mihaka's daughter (Turehira) by Hiria Rangiaho was nine years old, and his children by Hinepau (Reupene and Tikina) were both adults (over 18) (Best 1898: 5, 63). Consequently, if Hinepau had died before Mihaka married Hiria, by 1907 this Ngāti Rongo/Te Urewera link might have already been established for over 15 years. In this way, Hiria, second-born of the Rangiaho sibling group of Ngāti Rongo hapū in Rūātoki, may have become a 'step-mother' to Reupene in Ruatāhuna. Furthermore, Hiria Rangiaho's *mātāmua* sister Hakurangi had married Taipeti Mātaatua, the son of Mātaatua Hauwai and Hana Pareihe whose marriage had allied two of the descent groups of the migrant marriage alliance. Taipeti's *mātāmua* sister was Mako Mātaatua, the wife of Te Haka Te Whenuanui II (Figs. 6.3 and 7.1; Best 1898: 30).

From the point of view of Numia's connections through the Rangiaho sibling group, Numia's shift of emphasis in his 27 April letter from Te Haka Te Whenuanui II to his long-deceased sister Hinepau and moreover to Hinepau's husband's mother (Hariata Kaaho) appears all the more suspicious. This might be seen as *whakapapa whakamoe* at its most presumptuous.

Whether or not Numia advised Reupene or his father Mihaka Matika in the drafting of the 10 January announcement of Te Whenuanui II's death, he may have foreseen some promise in this situation with regard to his quest for Ngāti Rongo rights in the Manawarū area of Ruatāhuna. On 10 January 1907 when the letter was sent, the appeals commission had been reconvened in Whakatane since 3 January (when it announced Te Whenuanui II's death) to hear the Ruatāhuna and continue the Waikaremoana appeals among others. If Numia had a hand in arranging the succession announced in the 10 January letter, it may have been by way of approaching Mihaka Matika or his son Rangiteremauri (Reupene) during these hearings, either directly or through his Rangiaho relatives.

Indeed, both the revelation and implicit approval of Numia's role in adding Tutakangahau's claimants to the Waikaremoana block list, and his settlement of the Ruatāhuna appeals from the migrant marriage alliance, occurred 1–5 February 1907. Numia's negotiation of increases of Ruatāhuna shares especially to leading families of the migrant marriage alliance may have facilitated such an approach to the Taratoa sibling group as well as their *mātāmua*'s son Mihaka Matika: as described above, this highest-ranking sibling group received the largest increase of shares among those distributed to the migrant marriage alliance. The two and a half months before Numia announced that 'the hapus of Tuhoe have set up Reupene Mihaka as successor to his uncle Te Whenuanui' in his 27 April letter would have been ample time for him to negotiate agreement among 'the hapu of Tuhoe' as well as the Taratoas, Mihaka Matika, and his son Reupene.

One further clue may clarify Numia's intentions and even reveal his emerging strategy finally to gain recognition of Kahuwī's and Ngāti Rongo's rights in Manawarū, rights that Te Whenuanui II would not have allowed him had he been alive. I recently learned from a descendant of Numia's that he was 'brought to' Ruatāhuna by 'contracting' or making an arrangement with Ngāi Te Riu, one of the several hapū to which Ruatāhuna had been awarded in 1902 and among which it was partitioned in 1912.

As described above, Numia's credentials for Reupene ignored both the genealogical source of his succession to the title of Te Whenuanui I and II and their supporters in the migrant marriage alliance. Instead, Numia traced Reupene's credentials to Matika Taratoa's wife Hariata Kaaho and her brothers Ahikaiata and Tupara. This bias may have reflected Numia's 'contract' with Ngāi Te Riu hapū to gain rights in Ruatāhuna. Ahikaiata and, since his death, Tupara Kaaho were well-known leaders in Ngāi Te Riu hapū and descendants of its founding ancestor Te Ruruhe (Best 1898: 62; 1973 Vol II: Table 12). In 1899 before the UDNR commission, Tupara Kaaho had claimed the Huiarau area of Ruatāhuna as spokesperson for Ngāi Te Riu, and by 1902 this hapū was among those found to have rights in that block. Although Numia does not mention it, Hariata had herself died as had Ahikaiata (Best 1898: 62–3), leaving Tupara as the only surviving sibling.

Other evidence suggests that Numia's arrangement with Ngāi Te Riu may have also extended his influence *within* the migrant marriage alliance and Te Urewera hapū itself. While Ngāi Te Riu had established rights in Ruatāhuna block, Ngāti Hinekura was one of several hapū, together identified as the 'conquering' Tūhoe, found to have rights in Waikaremoana block (Fig. 2.1). As explained in Chap. 5, Ngāti Hinekura and Ngāti Taumata were recognized to be two emergent hapū that together constituted Ngāi Te Riu hapū. In 1896 Whakamoe Hauwai, husband of Matika Taratoa's younger sister Whareti, was leading *rangatira* of Ngāti Hinekura in Te Kuha, Waikaremoana (Fig. 7.1; Best 1896 in Binney 2002: 498). In this way, Ngāi Te Riu hapū might be seen to have some direct influence over Mihaka Matika and his son Reupene Te Whenuanui III in two ways: (i) through Mihaka's father's sister (Whareti, wife of Whakamoe) and (ii) through Mihaka's mother Hariata, Matika Taratoa's wife and sister of Ahikaiata and Tupara Kaaho (Figs. 7.1 and 8.1). Furthermore, as well as claiming Ruatāhuna for Ngāi Te Riu hapū, according to Numia's own evidence given in the final hearings on Ruatāhuna block in 1902, Tupara Kaaho was also affiliated with Te Urewera hapū in Ruatāhuna along with its leader Te Whenuanui II (UMB 6: 282).

There were further inside connections to Ngāi Te Riu hapū available to Numia. Tamaikoha, who otherwise did not appear in the confrontations over Ruatāhuna and Waikaremoana and held no leading shares in either block, may have nevertheless been influential in Numia's arrangement with Ngāi Te Riu. As described in Chap. 5, Tamaikoha laid claims for Ngāi Te Riu in the Hukanui, Parekohe, and Paraoanui areas of the lower Waimana basin, and the Ngāti Taumata hapū of Ngāi Te Riu, of which he was a leader, was found to have exclusive rights to Paraoanui. As a leader of Te Urewera hapū in the lower basins, Tamaikoha had accepted Numia and Ngāti Rongo rights (under Te Urewera *mana*) in Whaitiripapa. It is plausible that his influence with Ngāi Te Riu and Ngāti Hinekura in Ruatāhuna, or even in Te Urewera hapū after Te Whenuanui II had died, may have backed those of the Kaaho sibling group in their support of Numia's strategy.

As pointed out above, Tamaikoha's daughter Pohe was also married to one of the Rangiaho sibling group that straddled Ngāti Rongo hapū (Numia's *mātāmua* daughter Hine Te Ariki was married to Pioioi Rangiaho), Te Urewera hapū, and the migrant marriage alliance (Fig. 6.3). It may be significant that Paora Rangiaho (Pohe's husband) was appointed along with Tupara Kaaho to the leading positions in the Paraeroa block committee in 1907, indicating his as well as Tupara's leadership in Ngāti Hinekura (and thereby Ngāi Te Riu) hapū, which was recognized to have leading rights in that block as well as Waikaremoana (Figs. 1.2 and 2.1). Certainly due to his mother Hariata Kaaho's standing in N.Te Riu hapū, Mihaka Matika had been appointed to the committee for Paraeroa block in 1902 but (perhaps again significantly) became the lowest-ranking member when Tupara Kaaho and Paora Rangiaho were appointed in 1907. Finally, it will also be remembered that in the 1912 case Numia denigrated Matika's as well as Tahakawa's knowledge of Manawarū in Ruatāhuna by pointing out that they had lived and even grown up primarily in Paraeroa block and even further north at Ohiwa harbor (Chaps. 7 and 9; Fig. 1.1). It is ironic that in 1907 Numia might have relied on their Paraeroa roots to make his arrangements with Ngāti Hinekura and Ngāi Te Riu hapū regarding the succession of Mihaka's son Reupene to his uncle Te Whenuanui II's title.

Might this Rangiaho/Kaaho/Mātaatua axis have been the network of influence that displaced consideration of Te Whenuanui I's other descendants from succession to his title? If Numia's 'contract' with Ngāi Te Riu involved such influential allies, his strategy for gaining rights in Ruatāhuna block in the wake of Te Whenuanui II's death was promising. But one must still ask why he would lay these details before the Native Ministry? Binney raises his 27 April 1907 letter as an example of Tūhoe's continuing care to keep government advised of the deaths of important leaders.

However, in this particular case it may have been intended to communicate much more. In the midst of the UDNR appeals proceedings, Numia's personal assurance to 'Timi' Carroll, the Native Minister, of his counselor relationship with the new Te Whenuanui III may have been intended to reassure Carroll that through Numia's influence the Ministry would be able to control the notoriously difficult Ruatāhuna leadership and finally settle the UDNR.

As mentioned in Chap. 2, in 1904 'Timi' Carroll had accompanied the governor Lord Ranfurley on a tour of the Urewera. While being hosted at the Te Whai a te Motu *marae* in Mātaatua, Ruatāhuna (certainly by Te Whenuanui II and Te Urewera hapū), he had to defend the government against Tūhoe suspicions regarding the government's motives in the UDNR and did so in a diatribe contemptuous of their concerns (Binney 2002: 298–303). In her 2004 report on Ruatāhuna for the Urewera inquiry, Brenda Tahi mentioned that a *waiata* was composed in memory of the occasion ridiculing Carroll as a whore of the Crown (Tahi 2004). The governor's tour was grandly received a few days later at Tauarau *marae* in Rūātoki, and Numia would certainly have heard about the confrontation at Ruatāhuna. In 1907 Carroll would not have forgotten this confrontation and would have been interested in Numia's emerging role with Te Whenuanui II's successor. In this way, Numia might have recruited government support of his own future goals in Ruatāhuna.

Although there is little doubt that in 1912 the Taratoa cousins Mihaka Matika, Whenua Tahakawa, and Paora Noho confronted Numia's case for Kahuwī's rights in Manawarū with sincere intention to defend Te Whenuanui II and the migrant marriage alliance's legacy of resistance to it, their opposition did appear to collapse too quickly. It may be significant that although most or all of the senior Taratoa sibling group were still living (Matika, Tahakawa, Whareti, and Noho), it was Mihaka Matika—Matika Taratoa's and Hariata Kaaho's *mātāmua* son and father of Reupene Rangiteremauri (Te Whenuanui III)—who was left to conduct the opposition case. There must have been some important reason that the senior generation of siblings left the responsibility of defending Te Whenuanui II's opposition to Numia to three of their sons. The Taratoa cousins seem to have known they were making their last stand against him for their old patrons Te Whenuanui I and II.

It may have simply been that since 1907 Numia had been able to cultivate his influence in Te Urewera hapū and the Ruatāhuna-Waikaremoana migrant marriage alliance, working through the Rangiaho and Kaaho network in Ngāi Te Riu hapū, and his nominal counselor status between the Crown and Te Whenuanui III. The most likely turning-point in the 1912 confrontation over Manawarū was Numia's co-option of the south-eastern boundary between Manawarū and Te Waiiti through his ally Te Iriwhiro, speaking for Waiiti and Ngāti Kurī hapū, enabling the court to settle two boundaries with one decision (Chap. 9). The poorly recorded court record of this early part of the confrontation inserted evidence from the preliminary hearing in August, obscuring Mihaka's and Whenua's objections to this arrangement. In any case, it appeared to be a fait accompli when in December Te Amo Kokouri, another ally of Numia since the 1902 case and resident of Manawarū, sided with Numia.

If, during the several months between those hearings, Numia's arrangement of that boundary had included an agreement with Te Iriwhiro that some significant portion or landmark both accepted to be in the disputed portion of Manawarū would be quietly included in the Te Waiiti rather than Kahuwī partition, this could have been among the terms of the 'contract' with Ngāi Te Riu even in 1907. In such an arrangement, Te Iriwhiro may have been speaking for Ngāi Te Riu as well as Ngāti Kurī hapū: in their 1923 evidence both Te Amo and Wahia Paraki agreed that both these hapū had established rights in Waiiti as well as Huiarau partitions. Consequently, the contract between Numia and Ngāi Te Riu could have also influenced the even more contested boundary between Huiarau and Manawarū in the vicinity of Mātaatua at the western end of the disputed portion (Chap. 9).

However, as will be laid out in some detail in Volume II, the solidarity of the migrant marriage alliance, even into its sixth or seventh generation by the time of the 1921 Urewera Consolidation Scheme, continued to be a major factor in resistance against the Crown's betrayal of the UDNR. Especially under the leadership of Matamua Whakamoe 1922–1925, many of the new generation of its leaders repeatedly confronted the Crown in petitions as well as hearings. The solidarity of the alliance often extended to cooperation with the Apitihana opposition to the Urewera Consolidation Scheme. This cooperation furthermore included those descendants of Kahuwī and other Ngāti Rongo who, through Numia's strategic leadership against the migrant marriage alliance, had taken a large part of Manawarū in Ruatāhuna and enforced the intrusion of Tamakaimoana hapū into northern Waikaremoana.

There is even evidence that by 1921 Numia's 'contract' with Ngāi Te Riu hapū in 1907 to support of his strategy in Manawarū had led to a nascent alliance between Kaaho/Rangiaho sibling groups on the one hand and Taratoa/Whakamoe sibling groups on the other. Although Numia himself had died during the intervening years, the network of influence that he developed may have had continuing force. In any case, one suspects that Numia's mounting frustration at the impending loss of most of the UDNR to the Crown would have been eased in the knowledge that such a defiant alliance had taken shape in the same Manawarū over which they had been fighting.

5 Conclusion

The years between Numia's triumph in the partition of Ruatāhuna in 1912 and the 1926 declaration of over 70% of the UDNR as 'the Crown award' saw the subversion by the Crown, intensified since it began in 1908, of all that the Tūhoe and the UDNR commission had worked for since 1894. Numia died in 1916 in the middle of the Crown purchase campaign that had begun by circumventing his control of the General Committee, having helplessly to witness the steady pressure upon *pupuri whenua* 'non-sellers' to give up their last shares of ancestral land in each of the original blocks of the UDNR. One can only hope that he foresaw what little victories were left to the Tūhoe: that not one of these blocks would be fully acquired by the Crown, leaving it with only an undivided share in common along with its *pupuri whenua* neighbors; that thanks to Tūhoe solidarity and fecundity, by 1921 the Crown actually faced more Tūhoe owners of the UDNR than it had in 1903; and, perhaps most satisfying to him, that solidarity between Ngāti Rongo and Te Urewera owners of the Kahuwī and Arohana partitions of Manawarū would become the backbone of an opposition movement that steadfastly refused cooperation with the Crown's Urewera Consolidation Scheme from its start in 1921 to its finish in 1926. One might argue that it was the solidarity behind these little victories that enabled *He Mana Motuhake* of *Ngāi Tūhoe* to survive nearly a century and finally to recover hopeful control of their Urewera sanctuary in the 2014 Te Urewera Act.

In Chaps. 6 through 9 of Part II, I have pursued the problem of the aborted 1902 Ruatāhuna-Waikaremoana amalgamation proposal from a reasonable explanation of it in the migrant marriage alliance, through several later developments between the same leaders and the same two blocks to the partition of Ruatāhuna in 1912. (As will be seen in the sequel Volume II, virtually all of Waikaremoana was lost to the Crown by 1926.)

While these chapters remained relatively close to the recorded facts along with all their gaps and ambiguities, in this final chapter of Part II I have allowed myself an attempt to understand in plausible terms what was going on 'between the lines' of the records and behind the official scenes. Whether or not my argument holds up, it is clear that a great deal was going on behind the scenes that can be revealed by further research, whether by Tūhoe or other historians.

In the following conclusion to both Part I and Part II, I will return to fill out the sketch of some of my and my family's personal fieldwork experiences with which I began the Preface. I will do this in terms of how I have come to see *Ngāi Tūhoe* and the confrontations between Te Urewera hapū, Ngāti Rongo hapū, and the wider hapū clusters of which they were a part. In this way I hope to approach their as well as my own present situation, attempting to span the several generations that have passed but whose *wairua* 'spirits' continue to watch over us.

Notes

1. A detail in this case adds interest to Chap. 6's account of the Tamaikoha descent group as well as hapū discipline or *utu* ('compensation') practices. Te Oti also got Numia's admission that a piece of land had been given over by Tamaikoha to Tupaea because of Pihitahi's "misconduct" (UMB 5: 348). However, Numia claimed that piece was outside the boundary of his claim for N.Hā, and that it had been given to N.Rongo, not N.Hā (i.e., included in Ierenui Ohāua).
2. I suspect that the well-known New Zealand novelist Witi Ihimaera is a descendant of Te Wao Ihimaera or his brother Wharepapa (Fig. 7.1), but am unable to demonstrate it due to the loss of UDNR land in the Waikaremoana expropriation and consequent disappearance of Te Wao, Wharepapa, or their offspring in the UCS records.
3. The appropriateness of Te Haka himself to have succeeded to the 'title' of Te Whenuanui I is questioned by knowledgeable Tūhoe. Nowadays the story is recounted that Te Haka was not the son of Te Whenuanui at all, but rather perhaps a nephew, and that the latter's two older sons both died in the battle of Orakau. This fact is commemorated in a disdainful *waiata* sung by women to Te Whenuanui when he returned to Ruatahuna as a survivor of that battle. Furthermore, efforts to enable him to have further children were fruitless due to his senility (Tamati Kruger, personal communication 2018). I have decided to discount the implication of this story that Te Haka was not the son of Te Whenuanui I and Turaki II because apparently neither

Numia nor Paora objected to each other's whakapapa as presented in Fig. 8.1. Nor can I think of a motive that might have led Numia to report or accept this if it were not true.

4. On the other hand, perhaps to mark their other key ancestor, Reupene/ Rangiteremauri's sister Tikina had probably been similarly named with special significance after her mother's father's (Te Whenuanui I's) mother Tikina, who was the wife of his father Te Umuariki (Fig. 8.1). Both Tikina (I) and her husband Te Umuariki were great-grandchildren of Arohana (adoptive father of Kahuwī) and thus second cousins. Temara reports that Te Whenuanui (I) became one of the two 'leading chiefs' of Tūhoe upon the death of Paora Kingi I, son of Te Whenuanui's elder brother Te Au, *mātāmua* son of Te Umuariki. (He does not name the other leading chief but it was probably Kererū Te Pukenui, Numia's older brother and *rangatira* of Ngāti Rongo hapū.) Best similarly reports that the Te Whenuanui (I) and Rakuraku lines 'might be said to be the principle *gentes* of the tribe', adding that 'Kererū and Paora Kingi families were also of importance' (1973 Vol. I: 223–4). As discussed in Chaps. 8 and 9, although Tūhoe probably generally considered marriage closer than fourth cousins to be incestuous (and still do), and claims to dual descent by Numia as well as Te Whenuanui II may have remained unsubstantiated because they were sensitive, close cousin-marriages like the second-cousin marriage in Te Whenuanui I's and Paora Kingi's line may have gained some acceptance as prerogatives of a developing Tūhoe aristocracy.

References

AJHR 1903. D. Scannell. 'Commissioners' Orders Under the "Urewera District Native Reserves Act, 1896."' Undated. Appendices to the Journal of the House of Representatives 1903, G-6: 1–256. Wellington, N.Z.

AJHR 1907. G. Mair, D.F.G. Barclay, Paratene Ngata. "The Urewera District Native Reserve: reports of the commissioners appointed …." Report and orders. Undated. Appendices to the Journal of the House of Representatives 1907 G-4: 1–190. Wellington, N.Z.

AJHR 1921. "Urewera Lands Consolidation Scheme (report on proposed)." 31 October 1921. Appendices to the Journal of the House of Representatives G-7: 1–39. Wellington, N.Z.

Best, Elsdon. 1898. "Tuhoe genealogies 1898" (spine title); "Genealogies of the Tuhoe tribe. Also includes all living members of the tribe in 1898, as given before the Urewera Commission set up under the act of 1896." Manuscript qMS [172]. Wellington, N.Z.: Alexander Turnbull Library. [The author can supply a digital index for this resource.]

Best, Elsdon, 1973. *Tuhoe, Children of the Mist*. Vols. I and II (genealogies). Second edition. Wellington, N.Z.: A.H. and A.W. Reed Ltd. (first published 1925 as Vol VI of the Memoirs of the Polynesian Society).

Binney, Judith. 2002. *Encircled Lands; Part Two: A History of the Urewera 1878–1912*. An Overview Report on the Urewera for the Waitangi Tribunal. WAI 894, A15. Wellington, N.Z.: Waitangi Tribunal.

Kruger, Tamati. 2004. "Ngā Hapū ō Ngā Pōtiki." Appendix to Final Report *Ruātoki; Ngā Rauru ō Ngā Pōtiki*. Anamata College, Taneātua, N.Z. 10 January 2004. Urewera Enquiry WAI 894. Wellington, N.Z.: Waitangi Tribunal.

O'Malley, Vincent. 1996. *The Crown's Acquisition of the Waikaremoana Block 1921–25*. A report for the Panekiri Tribal Trust Board, with Supporting Papers (S.P.) Vols I-III, May 1996. WAI 894 record of inquiry, doc A50. Wellington, N.Z.: Waitangi Tribunal.

Tahi, Brenda. 2004. *Ruatāhuna - Te Manawa o Te Ika*. Part II: History 1896–1980s. Waitangi Tribunal report WAI 894 #D2. Wellington, N.Z.: Waitangi Tribunal.

Temara, Te Pou. 2000. "Hikawera Te Kurapa (1907–1985), Tuhoe tohunga, horse-breaker, farmer, Ringatu leader." Dictionary of New Zealand Biography. Te Ara - the Encyclopedia of New Zealand. http://www.TeAra.govt.nz/en/biographies/5t9/te-kurapa-hikawera (accessed 13 May 2017).

UMB 5. Urewera District Native Reserve Commission minute book 5, Butler, Scannell, et al. (18Mar1901 – 16May01), in English, index 5 pp., 382 pp.; NA Wgtn: Urewera MB 5, MLC 13, W3518, CD 2, Vol. 5, 388pp.; NA Ak: AREPRO 4711/1447. Acronym: UMB 5.

UMB 6. Urewera District Native Reserve Commission minute book 6, Butler, Scannell, et al. (16May1901 – 26Apr02) in English, index 9 pp., 382 pp.; NA Wgtn: Waiariki, Urewera MB 6, CD W3518/2, 398 pp.; NA Ak: AREPRO 4711/1448. Acronym: UMB 6.

UCAMB 1. Urewera District Native Reserve Commission Appeal minute book 1, D.F.G. Barclay, Mair, Ngata, (5Dec1906–22Jan1907). 10 pp. index, ?pp.; NA Wgtn: unable to locate; NA Ak: AREPRO 4711/1133; Univ. Auck. Lib: 333.0995 N536u. Acronym: UCAMB 1.

UCAMB 2. Urewera District Native Reserve Commission Appeal minute book 2, D.F.G. Barclay, Mair, Ngata, (23Jan1907–12Mar1907) index, 382pp.; NA Wgtn: unable to locate; NA Ak: AREPRO 4711/1134; Univ. Auck. Lib: 333.0995 N536u. Acronym UCAMB 2.

Webster, Steven. 1975. "Cognatic Descent Groups and the Contemporary Māori: a Preliminary Reassessment." *The Journal of the Polynesian Society* Vol. 84(2): 121–152, 1975.

PART III

Conclusion

CHAPTER 11

A Contemporary Retrospect: Getting to Know *Ngāi Tūhoe*

1 'Kaupois' Lost in Te Urewera

Now I shall return to the more personal reflections on Ōhāua te Rangi, Te Urewera, and Ngāi Tūhoe that I briefly allowed myself at the beginning of the Preface. As hinted at there, it was my later ethnohistorical work that finally enabled me to better understand the ordinary ***whānau*** or extended family relationships in which I and my family became increasingly involved in the 1970–1980s. Even though in my social anthropological research I had unconsciously avoided these personal relationships and the ancestors we had come to take for granted in those early years, my later ethno*historical* research slowly drew me back to the same ancestors until, here in Part II, I found myself dealing with them, even too closely for comfort. In the context of Part II, I had not only to unravel the obvious confrontations between them, but to make informed guesses regarding their strategies and motives hidden behind the backs, official propriety, or biases of the UDNR Commission. By that time our original hosts in Ruatāhuna, Mātaatua, Ōhāua, and Rūātoki lay in their graves, probably giggling, because, as I suggested in the Preface, it had been 'as if they knew even in the 1970s that this would happen'.

Ōhāua te Rangi was iconic in our early experiences of Te Urewera. By the later 1970s we had hiked the 10–12 kilometers down the Whakataane River from Mātaatua and slept in the Ōhāua meetinghouse Te Poho o Pōtiki several times. Two more heroic family treks still stand out in my memory, the earlier one south up the length of the Whakataane River and the later one further north down it. From the graciously indulgent Tūhoe

© The Author(s) 2020

S. Webster, *A Separate Authority (He Mana Motuhake)*, Volume I,
https://doi.org/10.1007/978-3-030-41042-1_11

point of view, both treks were probably seen as innocent but fated adventures of naive *kaupois* who had foolishly left their horses behind in the USA but were too proud to borrow theirs and ask for a guide.

Sometime in the 1970s we had gotten to know the Rūātoki extensions of our Mātaatua whānau, and I decided to 'hike' (Kiwis say 'trek' or 'tramp') the length of the Whakataane River north from Rūātoki to Mātaatua (about 50 kilometers) with my family, delivering a box of chocolates to our *nanny* ('grandma' or, in this case, great-grandmother) Rangiwhaitiri Wharekiri Wiringi, our original host in Mātaatua. We (I, my wife Lois, and our two U.S.-born boys then aged 10–12) started out from Nanny Rangiwhaitiri's son Tumoana's home in Rūātoki on foot with frame backpacks and sleeping bags (unknown to Tūhoe, who traveled on horseback with blankets and a rifle for game) and were able to fjord the river whenever the track disappeared. We were lucky the river was low, and made it along easy river tracks as far as what was probably Paraeroa B (Fig. 1.2), where we slept on the ground in a deserted old hut the first night. However, we spent the next two days and nights fording the river arm-in-arm in rapids and searching on our hands and knees below underbrush for passable foot-tracks. I don't think we ever got more than a few miles beyond the Waikare River junction, whether toward Korouanui or Hanamahihi I do not remember (as I later found out, the latter is the especially rugged area that the roadway promised in 1921 planned to avoid). I had an excellent topographical map, compass, and long experience in using them in other countries, but it was to no avail in Te Urewera. My foot got infected and the kids enjoyed *mimi*-ing ('peeing') on the wound (Nanny Rangiwhaitiri had mentioned that is how they used to sterilize eye infections). Finally we gave up and limped back to Rūātoki and mailed the chocolates to our nanny in Mātaatua.

Years later in 1986, by then with our eight-year-old *whāngai tamariki*, his slightly older brother Tahuri, and teenage uncle Aubrey, I set out similarly with backpacks rather than horses and a knowledgeable *whānau* member as guide from Mātaatua to Ōhāua, intending to cross the Te Ranga a Ruanuku ridgeline between Tawhiwhi and the Waikare River and visit Korouanui, their ancestral land above its junction with the Whakatane River (Fig. 6.1). We stayed the first night at Ōhāua and continued on through Tawhiwhi the next day (Fig. 6.2). Young Aubrey found it strange to be on foot, crossing streams without a horse, sleeping in a sleeping bag, and living off bread and peanut butter rather than game. We made it up the ridge and through heavy brush nearly to the Waikare River, but the track had disappeared. We finally gave up and returned to spend the night back on the Whakataane River near Tawhiwhi before retreating the next day—passing through Ōhāua with dignity—back to Mātaatua.

My earlier naïve or partial understanding of the relationship between Te Urewera hapū and Ngāti Rongo hapū was built up from many personal experiences along with my family: a first summer in 1972 in Murupara, over which the Urewera ranges and stands of native timber of the National Park loom, and past which some of its deep rivers run; our first visit to Ruatāhuna and Mātaatua and the families we are still connected to; a drive with my wife Lois, our two U.S.-born boys, and her mother into the notorious Maungapōhatu, advised by a friendly but impish Tūhoe sojourner on the road that all that was necessary to part the clouds over its summit was a *whakapohane* (showing one's buttocks) in its direction; Ringatū twelfths in Te Whaiatemotu meetinghouse in Mātaatua and visits to the several other marae of Ruatāhuna, accompanying our host family as their guests; excursions to Ōhāua and later, alone with our own children, attempting the quixotic trek from Rūātoki described above; possum trapping below Pukerimu hill and lambing below Manawarū mountain and the Huiarau ranges; beginning to understand that both Te Urewera hapū and Ngāti Rongo hapū were two different hapū, and furthermore each had 'sister' marae spanning the Urewera between Mātaatua, Ōhāua, and Rūātoki; beginning to realize that the Urewera National Park had a hidden history: a whole Tūhoe history was buried in the *mōrehu* remnants of their lands scattered throughout the park; beginning to realize that these lands, long memories, genealogies, and the dead themselves were, somehow, the same thing; the sudden death of our Te Urewera nanny Rangiwhaitiri (great-great-granddaughter of Te Whenuanui I) while we were visiting back 'home' in the USA, and a comforting impromptu *tangi* ('funeral') just for us when we returned too late to help bury her; her *ōhākī* ('last wishes') to take care of us becoming a full-fledged 'Māori adoption' that would be fraught but bind us together forever; the realization that we were being handed over like beloved orphans, along with another *whānau pani*, to the Rūātoki family of the nanny's only surviving birth-child; being immediately taken in there by both Te Urewera and Ngāti Rongo hapū, sister *marae* of the same two hapū that had already taken care of us for several years of our visits to the other end of Te Urewera mountains; a reunion of survivors celebrating the re-decoration and re-opening of Te Poho o Pōtiki meetinghouse at Ōhāua *marae* half-way between Ruatāhuna and Rūātoki.

Later, there were more deaths and *tangi* in Rūātoki and Ruatāhuna: *rangatira*, other great-grandmothers, irreplaceable *kaumātua*, beloved *whāngai tamariki* dying too soon, then finally our Tūhoe 'parents' (*mātua whāngai*, even co-parents) gone before we could grow old together—and again, while we were too far away to be near when they died, irresponsible foot-loose *kaupois* 'cowboys' that we were, always too late for the *tangi*.

All this time I was becoming aware that Te Urewera hapū and Ngāti Rongo hapū were inter-related in complicated ways, as well as having sister *marae* at opposite ends of Te Urewera. In Mātaatua our nanny had hesitantly printed out a *whakapapa* of 'first-', 'second-', and 'third-cousins' for me that followed some descendants of Waewae Te Kotahitanga, the old *rangatira* of Ōhāua, to show me how the persons we had gotten to know, many her *whāngai tamariki*, were connected. OK, that was Ngāti Rongo hapū and its sister *marae* at Tauarau in Rūātoki, but where did her own hapū, Te Urewera, come in? Another of her fragmentary *whakapapa* also connecting herself to one of her many *whāngai tamariki* evidently represented Te Urewera hapū, but began with her great-grandparents without giving their predecessors. In any case, I was beginning to understand the mute tragedy behind her printed words at the end of several descent lines: 'no issue', no issue, no issue. This wasn't even written down for what appeared to be the Te Urewera fragment, but it was clear enough to me: *he whare ngaro*, or 'empty house'. The descent group had to be carried on with the help of adopted children for some generations now. But all these *whāngai tamariki* were apparently relatives too. I would understand someday.

2 *Tatau Pounamu?*[1]: Belatedly Understanding Some Marriages, 1890s–1950s

Sometime in the 1980s I re-read Raymond Firth's classic *Primitive Economics of the New Zealand Māori* (1959 [1929]) and was startled to realize that I knew about some ancestors and places shown in photos he had taken in 1924 in Ōhāua (Figs. 11.1, 11.2, and 11.3). Waewae 'Te Kotahitanga' Te Roau was the Ngāti Rongo *rangatira* who had hosted Firth. Figure 11.1 shows him standing with his wife Te Hirea Pahiri (of Ngāti Tāwhaki hapū) and some grandchildren in front of their Ōhāua *wharepuni* (sleeping house). Figure 11.2 shows him with some of the Ōhāua branch of Ngāti Rongo hapū, and probably others from Te Urewera hapū, in front of the Ōhāua *wharenui* or *wharewhakairo* Te Poho o Pōtiki. The frontispiece of Firth's classic work, not included here, also displays Waewae standing alone and holding a birding spear in front of Te Poho o Pōtiki. As mentioned in Chap. 6, the four famous brothers from whom Ngāti Rongo trace their descent are commemorated in the entryway *pou* (carved columns supporting the eves) of this meetinghouse.

Plate 4a *R. A. Falla*

DWELLING OF OLD STYLE (WHAREPUNI)

A wharepuni at Ohaua-te-rangi. In front are Te Kotahitanga and his wife Te Hirea, dressed to receive visitors, and several of their grandchildren

Fig. 11.1 Waewae Te Roau and Te Hirea Pahiri at Ōhāua *wharepuni*, 1924. (Firth 1959: 284 facing Plate 4a)

Plate 3b *Raymond Firth*

THE PEOPLE OF THE VILLAGE

Ngati-Rongo hapu *of Ohaua-te-rangi in front of their meeting house, named "Te Poho-o-Potiki"*

Fig. 11.2 Waewae with some of Ngāti Rongo hapū in front of Ōhāua *wharenui* Te Poho o Potiki, 1924. (Firth 1959: 253 facing Plate 3b)

Fig. 11.3 Ōhāua village in 1924, looking south up Whakatāne/Ohinemataroa valley. (Firth 1959: 253 facing Plate 3a)

Waewae, Te Hirea, and some of their predecessors and descendants have been depicted genealogically in Fig. 6.3 and discussed in Chap. 6. Although I became aware of the significance of these photos in the 1980s, it was not until some 20 years later when I had developed a fuller understanding of Urewera history that they began to 'speak' to me, to evoke innumerable questions that I had not realized remained unanswered. The past had brought the present Urewera more fully to life, and perhaps not merely because, from the Māori point of view, the past is ancestral.

In Fig. 11.3 I sentimentally recognized the familiar landscape behind the old village of Ōhāua and noted that there was already no sign of most of the buildings that were there in 1924. (Is that a partly denuded Miromiro ridge standing over the Whakatāne River? Was an ancestral *urupā* 'cemetery' located on it, perhaps named 'Roau' as in the 1901 survey plan (Fig. 6.2)? Is that the Tuhituhi Stream where Te Whiuwhiu is said to have run down Kereopa to turn him over to the authorities?) However, beyond the array of ***kauta*** ('cooking houses') in the middle-ground of the photo, one can glimpse the old ***wharenui*** Te Poho o Pōtiki to the east and the old ***wharepuni*** to its west; while the former had been restored by 1983, no sign of the latter was left. Another of Firth's photos not included here shows another view of the ***wharenui*** in the background, with food-storage gourds and implements (and unidentified person, perhaps Firth himself) in the foreground (1959 [1929]: plate 9b, 349 facing). Excitingly, over 50 years after Firth had published the photos in his classic work, I was able to correspond with the aging author in England and relay copies of some of his original field notes (mainly on 'material culture') to the descendants of his hosts. This happened to also be the time in the early 1980s when the Ōhāua meetinghouse Te Poho o Pōtiki was being restored and redecorated, later to be celebrated in the 1983 reunion described below.

However, only recently have I realized that the other tall angular-faced man in Fig. 11.2, apparently standing on the meetinghouse *pae* ('bench') behind Waewae and also wearing a ***rangatira***'s feathered cape, was probably Waewae's ***mātāmua*** son Te Hata Waewae who married Te Whenuanui I's ***mātāmua*** granddaughter Taraipene (Figs. 6.3 and 11.4, below). Or was he Wharekiri Paparatu, husband of Waewae's elder daughter Hera? Wharekiri was also a leader in Ngāti Tāwhaki hapū and so could wear such a cape; indeed, the cape may have been the same one worn by Te Hirea (also of Ngāti Tāwhaki hapū) in Fig. 11.1. As will be described in Volume II, in 1924 Te Hata had refused to cooperate with the Apitihana opposition to the Urewera Consolidation Scheme, in which Ngāti Rongo as well as Te Urewera hapū were central, and so might well have been disaffected from Ōhāua and living in Rūātoki. Was Firth oblivious to the tumult and pain of land-loss lying behind all these solemn faces and across these valleys?

Who were the two younger men standing to the left of these two ***rangatira***, one proudly holding the bird spear? The other one in black with a white hat is said to be Pakitu (Hieke) Wharekiri, son of Wharekiri Paparatu. Although he is not holding the bird spear, he is almost certainly the "Paki of Ōhāua" mentioned by Firth who explained the details of bird-snaring to him (1959 [1929]: 158). It was this young man who married Hikawera Te Kurapa's older sister Meriaira (also known as Hauauru, Fig. 11.4); is she in the photo? In the 1980s (by which time both of them had died), Pakitu's ***whāngai tamariki*** and ***mokopuna*** ('grandchildren') would say admiringly of him that 'when he ate eels, no bones came out!' Pakitu and Hauauru were the parents of Rangiwhaitiri Wharekiri (their only living birth-child) who took me and my family in as our hosts in Mātaatua in 1972. That pert little girl in the white dress, on the left side of the photo

(Fig. 11.2) in front of the *wharenui*, was little Rangiwhaitiri nearly 50 years before she took us into her home at Mātaatua. Although she had many *mokopuna*, she too had had only one birth-child.

The bird spear and *taiaha* (fighting staff), displayed by different people in the 1924 photos, may have been in response to Firth's interest in material culture, but they were also heirlooms and symbols of leadership. The bird spear was held by Waewae himself in the frontispiece photo of Firth's 1929 book, while the *taiaha* was held by his wife Te Hirea Pahiri in Fig. 11.1 and a young boy standing beside Waewae in Fig. 11.2. Who was this boy (he was likely to have been important in some way!)? By the 1980s my family and I had probably met some of the other young people in this photo as old men and women. Perhaps because Pakitu and Hauauru had died by 1972 (she not long before), their daughter Rangiwhaitiri took us in with special warmth. She later explained her affection for us in terms of her *mokemoke* 'loneliness' for her parents. This is also how *whāngai tamariki*, adoption typically works among Māori; 'lonely' grandparents take in and raise as their own children new-born *mokopuna* grandchildren of their own or their cousins' children. It is often assumed and deferred to as their right, especially by parents who have plenty of birth-children or find themselves pregnant too soon, and children are indeed thought of as 'raised by a village'. As 'Americans' far from our own family and home, we were seen as *mokemoke* and homeless ourselves. The intrusion of Pākehā law and social class prejudice into this tradition of 'Māori adoption' has recently been historically documented by Maria Haenga-Collins (2011).

Firth's photos also prompted me to have more questions and some answers about Te Waewae's younger brother Te Pouwhare Te Roau. Firth apparently visited the famous meetinghouse Te Whai a te Motu on Mātaatua marae, which is located just below Rangiwhaitiri's home in Ruatāhuna where we were first hosted in 1972. Plate 5a is a photo of the ancestor Toroa carved into the main supporting post of the meetinghouse roof-beam in Te Whai a te Motu. Firth reports that in 1924 an *uhunga* or mourning party of visiting "relatives" from Rūātoki was being hosted in this meetinghouse on the occasion of Te Pouwhare's death (Firth 1959 [1929]: 100; 285 facing). At Tauarau marae in Rūātoki, a stone obelisk standing before the meetinghouse Rongokarae commemorates Te Pouwhare's leadership of Ngāti Rongo hapū. This apparent *heremate* ('drawing together of the dead' or circuit of *tangihanga* 'funerals' among other hapū to which a deceased person is importantly affiliated) implies that Te Pouwhare's *mana* was recognized by Te Urewera hapū, the *tangata whenua* ('people of the land') of Mātaatua marae in Ruatāhuna.

Strikingly, then, whether he knew it or not, Firth was witness not only to the agonies of Urewera Consolidation Scheme in Ōhāua but also to the solidarity between Ngāti Rongo and Te Urewera hapū that had been maintained in the Apitihana opposition against the Scheme despite previous decades of confrontation between these two hapū.

An even older photo than Firth's taken in 1917 beholds the front of Te Whaiatemotu meetinghouse in Mātaatua, Ruatāhuna. Its mounted enlargement now looks down onto my desk in Ponsonby, Auckland.[2] It is a revealing close-up of two middle-aged women holding two children, sitting on the *pae* ('bench') along the front of the meetinghouse. Both women have *kanohi waikauri* (tatooed faces). Their workaday old dress clothing is stained and tattered, bespeaking either an impromptu photograph or the grinding poverty of *pupuri whenua* in the ninth year of the Crown's predatory purchase campaign and the eve of the 1918 flu epidemic (of which the campaign took advantage). Neither of the women is smiling. Both sit beside equally somber children, holding them protectively. Might these children be our nanny Rangiwhaitiri and her uncle Hikawera? Are these solemn, mildly alarmed women our nanny's mother Hauauru and Hikawera's mother Matahera? I like to think they are. But the children are relatively young, so probably are their grandchildren or *whāngai tamariki*. Whoever they all are, they were surely relatives of theirs and, like ancestral photographs along the walls of *wharenui* ('meetinghouses') in Te Urewera, all four of them are gazing purposefully at me. Might this photographer have been aware of what was going on then? In any case, I am thankful for his as well as Firth's efforts.

Rangiwhaitiri herself died unexpectedly in 1977 from hepatitis. I and my family were on leave in Peru and the USA, but she had written endearingly to us from Mātaatua *kākahu māuku* (which she translated as 'all dressed in wet ferns'). I went right to Mātaatua marae and her grave when I returned to N.Z. and, although it was too late for her *tangi*, was supportively given a little *pōwhiri* ('welcome') and exchanged *aureretanga* ('groans' of grief) with her survivors. She had passed her care of us on to her only birth-son Tumoana Tumoana, who lived in Rūātoki, born of her first marriage to Kunare Tumoana, great-grandson of Numia Kererū's *mātāmua* sister Turaki (III? Figs. 6.3 and 11.4). By 1980 we had vaguely realized that as 'guests', *manuhiri*, or *whānau pani* ('orphans'), we had been passed from the care of Te Urewera hapū in Ruatāhuna to the care of Ngāti Rongo hapū in Rūātoki, but only now am I beginning to understand some of the implications of this gesture.

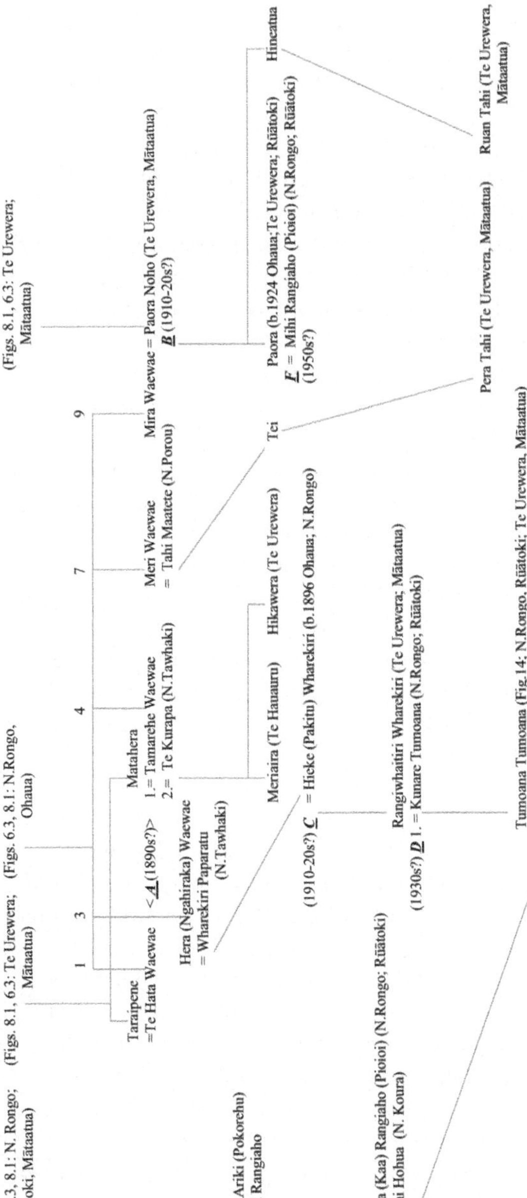

Fig. 11.4 *Tatau pounamu*: Ngāti Rongo/Te Urewera marriages 1890s–1950s

Only recently, furthermore, have I fully realized that both of these marriages (Pakitu and Hauauru, and their daughter Rangiwhaitiri and Kunare Tumoana, 'C' and 'D' in Fig. 11.4), and moreover the succession of one upon the other, were extraordinary. Each of them was a marriage between a young leader of Ngāti Rongo hapū and a young leader of Te Urewera hapū. Their predecessors, furthermore, had been young leaders of these same hapū in their own day. As painstakingly printed out for me by Rangiwhaitiri in my notebook in about 1975 on her (cleared) kitchen table, her mother's mother Matahera and Matahera's older sister Taraipene, as daughters of Te Whenuanui I's *mātāmua* daughter Te Mauniko, had both married, respectively, the brothers Tamarehe and Te Hata, the fourth and *mātāmua* children of Waewae Te Roau and Te Hirea (double marriage 'A' in Fig. 11.4). This earlier double marriage had therefore already firmly allied the Ōhāua branch of Ngāti Rongo and the Mātaatua branch of Te Urewera hapū.

Rangiwhaitiri's *whakapapa* sketch also made it clear that while her mother Hauauru was born of one of these two marriages, her father Pakitu had been born of a third marriage between Wharekiri Paparatu and Hera (Nga Hiraka) Waewae, yet another child of Waewae and Te Hireas', further consolidating this alliance. Matahera had furthermore also married Te Kurapa (Fig. 11.4), yet another representative of Ngāti Tāwhaki hapū, and their son Hikawera Te Kurapa was the leading *rangatira* speaking for Te Urewera hapū at the Mātaatua marae until he died in 1985. It was Paora Noho's son Paora who, in 1983, told me that Matahera was 'one of the most famous persons in Tūhoe'. I did not think to ask him what, beside the *mana* of her ancestry and offspring, was implied by her fame. That Matahera's children sometimes went by either Tamarehe or Te Kurapa as surnames, and Hauauru and Hikawera were considered sister and brother, suggests that, indeed, she might have had two husbands concurrently, officially or not.

And sitting there beside Rangiwhaitiri at her kitchen table while she carefully sketched out these details I vaguely knew, but had not yet clearly understood, that her own first marriage (and source of her only living birth-child) had been to Kunare Tumoana (marriage 'D' in Fig. 11.4). But only later did I slowly realize that Kunare was *mātāmua* grand-son of Tupaea and Pihitahi, whose marriage had marked the alliance between the *mātāmua* line of the Rūātoki branch of Ngāti Rongo and the *mātāmua* branch of Te Urewera led by Pihitahi's father, the great war leader Tamaikoha (Fig. 6.3; Webster 2010).[3] By the time I understood all these,

Rangiwhaitiri had died, and we had long since been passed on to her only birth-child Tumoana Tumoana in Rūātoki.

But furthermore, Tumoana's wife, our hostess Kui (Ngā Hirata) Hohua, was a great granddaughter of Numia Kererū himself. The marriage between Kui and Tumoana ('E' in Fig. 11.4) can be seen as sealing the succession of marriages that led to them, indeed, as sealing the alliance—or the reconciliation—between Ngāti Rongo and Te Urewera hapū. Kui described to us how, when they decided to marry, Tumoana took her to Mātaatua to meet his mother Rangiwhaitiri's parents Pakitu and Hauauru: in grand but mock indignation, Kui recounted that 'they looked me over like a side of beef!...but when they heard my name, and who my parents were, they looked at each other and nodded... so I guess it was OK with them!' In retrospect, it occurs to me that Pakitu might have misheard Kui's formal name 'Ngahirata' as his own mother's name 'Ngahiraka', and assumed some common ancestry. When Kui died we might ourselves have mistakenly had her bronze tombstone plate engraved with the name Ngahiraka rather than Ngahirata—and her survivors were too gentle to tell us. In any case, Pakitu and Hauauru would have enjoyed the irony.

When Tumoana died with many *whāngai tamariki* but no birth-children, again and again it was said by his mourners that he was the 'the last of his kind', that is, the last person so fully representative of leading predecessors who in themselves had personified marriage alliances between Ngāti Rongo and Te Urewera hapū. His mother's painful awareness of the infertility of too many of their predecessors as well as herself had come home to rest. Of course, we were never told about all these important marriage alliances in such grand words as I have used here; the *mana* of *rangatira* does not need to announce itself, least of all to innocent yankee *kaupois*, *whānau pani* lost in the Urewera.

A more recent photo of Te Poho o Pōtiki meetinghouse in the Ōhāua settlement that I had taken in 1983 now looks back at the photo Firth took of Waewae Te Roau and his people in front of the same meetinghouse in Ōhāua in 1924 (Fig. 11.5, below). Three generations had passed, but the two photos can now speak to each other, just as old photos hung in *wharenui* always do. In 1983 we had been invited to join a reunion in Ōhāua of Waewae and Te Hireas' descendants to mark the re-decoration and re-opening of that meetinghouse with a *tekaumārua* ('twelfth'), a traditional Ringatū church ceremony. Without being aware of it yet, I had taken a photo of the reunion in front of Te Poho o Pōtiki that would echo the photo taken in 1924 by Firth.

Fig. 11.5 Gathering after *Tekaumarua* and re-opening ceremony for Ōhāua *wharewhakairo* Te Poho o Pōtiki, February 1983

As well as descendants of Waewae and Te Hirea, my 1983 photo includes Te Whenuanui I's great-grandson Hikawera himself (male, seated in the middle in dark shirt, a leader of Te Urewera hapū in Ruatāhuna), Numia Kererū's great granddaughter Kui Ngā Hirata Hohua (seated just to Hikawera's left, of Ngāti Rongo and Ngāti Koura hapū in Rūātoki), and Paora Noho's son Paora Kruger of Te Urewera hapū in Rūātoki (standing behind and to the left of Kui). As described in Chap. 9, Paora's father Paora Noho was the Taratoa cousin who in 1912 had unsuccessfully opposed Numia's claim for Kahuwī in Manawarū, just south of Ōhāua. At the 1983 reunion it was Paora Kruger who had sat me down in Ōhāua beside an old shed, as our nanny Whaitiri had several years earlier in Mātaatua at the cleared kitchen table of her home. Carefully printing names with his pencil stub, Paora drew up several *whakapapa* in my notebook, patiently explaining to me how some of the persons at the reunion were related to each other and to others that we knew. Of course, most of the implications of the momentous marriages in Fig. 11.4 were still invisible to me.

Te Poho o Pōtiki meetinghouse had been occupied ('kept warm') for some months and redecorated by a *whānau* under the leadership of Kui's birth-son, who was also the *whāngai tamariki* or adopted son of Paora (whose wife was Mihi Rangiaho, another granddaughter of Numia's as was Kui). Although the adoptive father was a *rangatira* of Te Urewera hapū in Rūātoki, it turned out that his father Paora Noho (Numia's main adversary in 1912) had married Mira Waewae, youngest child of the Waewae sibling group (Fig. 6.3), yet another marriage between Te Urewera hapū and Ngāti Rongo hapū (Fig. 11.4, marriage B)! Their son Paora had grown up in Ōhāua, and he might have been among the children in the 1924 photo (but said he had moved to Rūātoki in that year). The young *tohunga whakairo* (master carver/decorator) of Te Poho o Pōtiki in 1983, Paora's adopted son, was affiliated with Ngāti Rongo hapū through his birth-mother and Te Urewera hapū through his adoptive father in Rūātoki. Before initiating his work on Te Poho o Pōtiki in Ōhāua, he had also wisely sought tutelage from Hikawera Te Kurapa, *rangatira* of Mātaatua marae and Te Urewera hapū in Ruatāhuna (again in Fig. 11.5, seated beside Kui).

As guests of Rangiwhaitiri we came to know her 'uncle' Hikawera as the slim, stooped, and aging male leader presiding over ceremonies in Te Whaiatemotu meetinghouse. In his younger days he was known to have outwitted an Urewera Park game-warden who accused him of hunting *kererū* (protected native 'wood pigeons') by hinting that he would be doing just that the next morning, but then successfully evading him as the warden ran after one distant shot-gun report after another, finding only feathers for his effort. Our youngest son (then five–six years old) will not forget his encounter with the old man when the two of us dropped by to visit him at his home: Uncle Hikawera was wandering absent-mindedly in his backyard, *hūpē* ('mucus') dripping unnoticed from his nose, but in full awareness he placed his hand gently on the boy's head to give him a Ringatū blessing. Perhaps in the same generous spirit, Hikawera's photo fell and broke as my wife Lois approached his casket to say good-bye at his *tangi* at Te Whaiatemotu some months later.

Another young man on the left end of the 1983 group photo at Ōhāua appears to be Paki Haumate, grandson of the *mātāmua* marriage between Te Whenuanui I's granddaughter Taraipene and Te Waewae's son Te Hata (Fig. 6.3). As was mentioned in Chap. 6, Paki's predecessors were thus a senior line in Te Urewera hapū. While in Mātaatua, where he was raised as a *whāngai tamariki* by Rangiwhaitiri, this young man would lovingly hold our hands while he translated Māori expressions for us, and was known among his ***whānau*** as mentally slow but also as the most expert in both 'old' Māori and English languages. Upon his adoptive mother's death, he was passed to her son Tumoana Tumoana's care in Rūātoki (and us along with him). Paki died unexpectedly from pneumonia only a few years later in the arms of Tumoana, fittingly the ***mātāmua*** as well as only birth-son of Paki's adoptive mother Rangiwhaitiri. It was said that Paki had gone around on his motorbike and visited each of his friends before he took sick and died. As his little brother's ***mātāmua***, Tumoana looked utterly bedraggled at Paki's tangi. Tumoana himself died suddenly from a heart attack only a few years after that, and his wife Kui died a few years later. She was found in the yard, with 'Yankee' waiting beside her.

Yankee was the old pure-bred Pekingese dog we had clumsily gifted Tumoana's mother Rangiwhaitiri years before, joking about his expensive ***whakapapa***! Later she gently advised us that as ***manuhiri*** in her care, it was not for us to be generous with her. Similarly, when we accompanied her ***whānau*** as visitors onto another marae but lay down our own ***koha*** ('contribution') for the occasion, she later gently corrected us: her ***koha*** was to be for us as well her ***whānau***. Rangiwhaitiri named the dog 'Yankee' to gently put us in our place and, incongruously but notoriously, carried him everywhere she went on Te Whaiatemotu marae in Mātaatua, Ruatāhuna until she died (after which, like us, he was passed on to her son Tumoana and Kui).

Enough of deaths. ***Ka nui tonu te aureretanga; takoto mai raa aaku matua***. I will always feel that we have not been able to live up to these deaths.

Anyway, by way of review, these marriages can be traced chronologically through Fig. 11.4, which should be seen as a continuation of both the wider Ngāti Rongo hapū ***tīpuna*** ('ancestors') in Fig. 6.3 and the wider Te Urewera hapū ***tīpuna*** in Fig. 8.1. In Fig. 11.4, these more recent marriages are marked A through F, in approximate chronological order:

A. Taraipene Te Hira and Te Hata Waewae; Matahera Te Hira and Tamarehe Waewae (1890s?);
B. Paora Noho and Meri Waewae (1910s?);
C. Meriaira (Hauauru) Te Kurapa and Hieke (Pakitu) Wharekiri (1920s?);
D. Rangiwhaitiri Wharekiri and Kunare Tumoana (1930s?);
E. Tumoana Tumoana and Kui Ngahirata Hohua (1950s?);
F. Paora (Paora) Kruja and Mihi Rangiaho (1940s?)

The more recent marriages may have occurred when the difference between these two hapū had begun to blur, partly as a result of these marriages. Working 'backwards' through them and emphasizing their role in this alliance: Paora II and Mihi Rangiaho were probably affiliated primarily with Te Urewera and Ngāti Rongo, respectively, and probably married sometime in the 1940s; Tumoana Tumoana and Kui Hohua, who were probably married sometime in the 1950s, were probably both affiliated primarily with Ngāti Rongo, but Tumoana was also affiliated closely to Te Urewera through his mother (and Kui to Ngāti Koura hapū through her father). Rangiwhaitiri Wharekiri and Kunare Tumoana, who were probably married sometime in the 1930s, were probably primarily affiliated with Te Urewera and Ngāti Rongo, respectively. Hauauru Te Kurapa and Pakitu Wharekiri, who were probably married sometime in the early 1920s, were primarily affiliated with Te Urewera and Ngāti Rongo, respectively (Fig. 8.1). Paora Noho and Meri Waewae, who were probably married by 1912, were primarily affiliated with Te Urewera and Ngāti Rongo, respectively. The two sisters Taraipene and Matahera Te Hira and the two brothers Te Hata and Tamarehe Waewae, who (respectively) probably had their double marriage in the 1890s, were primarily affiliated with Te Urewera and Ngāti Rongo, respectively (Te Hata's other marriage was with Te Unupo, a daughter of Tamaikoha, primarily affiliated with Te Urewera hapū).

I have emphasized that this early double marriage appears to have been especially significant. It may have been importantly associated with the final settlement in 1900 by the UDNR commission of the long-running confrontation over Whaitiripapa block between Tamaikoha for Te Urewera hapū and Numia Kererū for Ngāti Rongo hapū, discussed in Chap. 5. As described there, apparently a still earlier *pākūhā* marriage of a Ngāti Rongo woman to a Te Urewera man, marking a reciprocal gift of land, had been an issue in the confrontation over that block since the 1860s. The double marriage in the 1890s may even have been another such *pākūhā* or *tatau pounamu* or peace-making between Te Urewera hapū and Ngāti Rongo hapū, but more successful.

Nevertheless, as traced in Chaps. 7, 8, 9, and 10, this peace-making apparently did not prevent the confrontation between these two hapū breaking out again over Waikaremoana as well as Ruatāhuna blocks and running at least from 1902 to 1912. Might the marriage 'B' between Paora Noho of Te Urewera and Mira Waewae of Ngāti Rongo have been intended to finally reconcile these two hapū? Rather than a victory for

Numia Kereru, the passing over of part of Manawarū to the descendants of Kahuwī may even have been seen by some as marked by this marriage, another *pākūhā* marking the *tatau pounamu*. As will be shown in Volume II, the solidarity of these two hapū in the Apitihana opposition movement, throughout the entire crisis of the Urewera Consolidation Scheme, speaks well for the finality of such a reconciliation. Certainly the prominent series of marriages since then should have established a lasting *tatau pounamu* or even, as some now say, the indistinguishability of the two hapū.

On the other hand, the confrontation between them described below, and perhaps even continuing to emerge in the present, suggests that any such reconciliation has again fallen short of the ideal of *tatau pounamu*.

3 The 1983 Tekaumārua at Ōhāua

Once again, review of my old fieldwork notebooks has only recently revealed to me that what I then took to be ordinary *mihi-mihi* evening 'discussions' in the meetinghouse were instead profound echoes of this history of confrontation and reconciliation. There in Te Poho o Pōtiki in December of 1983, descendants of that common history were again implicitly raising more than a century of confrontations between Ngāti Rongo and Te Urewera hapū, flashes of indignation again being soothed by sincere words of calm *mana*.

Tensions had probably been building up since Tumoana's death in December 1981 and especially since the unveiling of his tombstone in April 1983 (Webster n.d. [1983] UNB 2: 1). As the last survivor of leading predecessors uniting the two hapū, he had succeeded to extensive ancestral rights in many of the new blocks surviving the UCS. Later that year, his wife Kui expressed her sense of the rising confrontation in dramatic stories she told us. With reference to Best's *whakapapa* plate on Ngāti Rongo hapū, she pointed out how both Ngāti Rongo and Te Urewera hapū were descendants of Rongokarae by his primary and secondary wives, respectively, and because of this Te Urewera had always been subordinate to Ngāti Rongo (Best 1973 [1925] Vol. II, plate 8: 1–2; Webster n.d. [1983] UNB 2: 23). When I pointed out to her that Best's plate 27 p. 1 for the Te Urewera hapū displayed Ngāti Rongo as junior rather than senior to Te Urewera hapū (due to the birth-order of ancestral siblings rather than the rank order of polygamous marriages), Kui disdainfully replied, 'Oh well, that's the whakapapa they like to use!'

With similarly skeptical humor, Kui often dismissively referred to Rongokarae's secondary wife as 'defacto', reinforcing the subordination of her Te Urewera descendants to Ngāti Rongo. She may have been implying a strategy she had been told by her aristocratic grandmother (Hine 'Te Ariki', Numia Kererū's *mātāmua* daughter) to use when needed to assert her more extensive rights in ancestral lands if she were bullied by her husband's mother Rangiwhaitiri. At that time these two *kuia* (woman elders), Hine te Ariki Numia and Rangiwhaitiri Wharekiri, were leaders of Ngāti Rongo and Te Urewera hapū, respectively (Fig. 11.4). While this may appear like Pākehā 'mother-in-law' humor, in this case it clearly reflected traditional confrontation between hapū, and was furthermore centered on *mana whenua*, the ancestral rights to land use upon which hapū leadership is often based.

Over the preceding few years since the 1970s, representatives of Te Urewera hapū in Mātaatua and nearby Ruatāhuna had been working hard to organize a challenge against the Tūhoe-Waikaremoana Trust Board by all the owners of the Tuawhenua region in the upper Whakatāne River basin (see Fig. 1.3). This initiative had been mobilized against the Board's plan to amalgamate the hundreds of surviving blocks of *pupuri whenua* land scattered throughout the National Park under a trust devoted to their protection and productive use. In August 1979, accompanying our Mātaatua *whānau*, I had attended a Māori Land Court hearing in support of Te Urewera hapū's protest against the amalgamation of the Tuawhenua blocks. (I spoke out against the judge's patronizing manner and, apparently expecting that I would be disciplined, he wrote to my professor at U. of Auckland; thankfully, my professor laughingly shrugged it off!) Although it took several years of litigation, the amalgamation orders were finally quashed (the history is told from a Tuawhenua Trust leader's point of view in Tahi 2004, 2017; also see Fraser 2004).

These representatives of Te Urewera hapū had also been working to organize enterprises in the Tuawhenua lands under their own control, including 'safari' tours for European and Pākehā tourists down the Whakatāne River to and past Ōhāua, deer-culling for export meat and trucking live deer to commercial farms, and experimental farming of 'Māori' potato varieties, as well as continuing the old business of possum trapping (to eat as well as to market the skins). The old Ōhāua settlement was being revitalized not only by the restoration of the Te Poho o Pōtiki meetinghouse: two or three of its old *kauta* were being used again for feeding, housing, and entertaining tourists who were coming from all over the world to see the wilderness wonders and birdlife of Te Urewera. While the persons leading these efforts were primarily affiliated with Te Urewera hapū of Ruatāhuna, it was a *whānau* primarily affiliated with Ngāti Rongo of Rūātoki who had gotten the blessing and tutelage of the Te Urewera *rangatira* Hikawera Te Kurapa and begun resurrection of Te Poho o Pōtiki, moving in and living at Ōhāua—and even giving birth to one of their children there.

The quiet confrontation between the two hapū over their relative rights in Ōhāua came to a climax at the re-opening of the *wharenui* meeting-house *tekaumārua* Ringatū Church gathering there 11–13 December 1983. Figure 11.5 is only one of several wonderful photos that I have found among my old field notes. I still see nothing in them suggesting the tensions I can now feel regarding one evening's *mihi-mihi* in Te Poho o Pōtiki.

During that discussion in the meetinghouse Pera Tahi (Fig. 11.4) had stood to assert the prior rights of Te Urewera hapū of Ruatāhuna to Ōhāua. Young Tamati Kruja immediately responded to defend the prior rights of Ngāti Rongo. Pera was in his 40s while Tamati was only in his 20s, but it was Tamati who had led the restoration of the meetinghouse the re-opening of which was being celebrated.[4] Pera then asked Paora Kruja (who had been born in Ōhāua and had come from Rūātoki, where he was affiliated primarily with Te Urewera hapū) for his clarification of the *whakapapa* for Ōhāua. At this point Hikawera Te Kurapa gently intervened (as *tohunga whakapono* or spiritual leader guiding the Tekaumarua ceremony) to demure that Ngāti Rongo's prior rights were long-established in Ōhāua but he wished to defer to Paora Kruja (as had Pera Tahi) as the appropriate *tohunga whakapapa* ('genealogical expert'). Paora then stood and, in his *whakaiti* (humble) way, explained that his mother-in-law (Hine 'Te Ariki' Numia; see Fig. 6.3) knew far more than he did, but proceeded to dramatically enunciate a *whakapapa*. It was probably significant (and a factor in Hikawera's deference to him) that while Paora was affiliated primarily with Te Urewera hapū at Te Totora marae in Rūātoki, his mother-in-law Hine te Ariki had been a *rangatira* of Ngāti Rongo; on the other hand, Paora's father Paora Noho had affiliated primarily with Te Urewera hapū in Ruatāhuna, but married Mira Waewae, youngest daughter of the Ngāti Rongo descent group at Ōhāua (Fig. 6.3).

Paora's *whakapapa* began with Rongokarae, the ancestral founder of Ngāti Rongo, but traced descent through Tamahore, one of the four brothers commemorated in the entryway *pou* posts of Te Poho o Pōtiki, slowly 'throwing' each name at the meetinghouse (lest it be forgotten!), concluding it by naming Reuben Tahi but also gesturing toward Pera Tahi, a 'nephew' of Reuben's. In Fig. 11.5, I think that is Reuben standing fourth from the left, probably smiling and with spectacles. It had been Reuben whom I had met in the Murupara pub in 1972, and who brought me and my family up to Mātaatua to meet Rangiwhaitiri for the first time. He worked in Murupara as a laborer for the local timber industry but visited Ōhāua often, trapping possoms and eels for skins and food while he was there. He was nearly blind, wearing thick glass spectacles that were usually opaque with *hinu* (meat fat), and he seemed always cheerful. On one of our visits to Ōhāua he showed us his eel catches drying on a fence line, and showed me how to knock the maggots off them once they stiffened and were ready for a boil-up with watercress from the nearby stream. Yes, it would have been these eels that Pakitu had eaten generations before, '...and no bones came out'.

I had been unable to follow most of the Paora Kruja's whakapapa, but was helped by his son Tamati's translation. Paora probably traced descent from Tamahore to the Tahis by way of Meri Waewae's husband Tahi Matete, Pera's grandfather (see Fig. 11.4). Reuben Tahi was an older 'uncle' of Pera's and so was a more appropriate stand-in for the ancestral rights that Pera was claiming. When Pera stood to reply to Paora (Reuben was probably too shy, and deferred to him), Pera calmly said '*ake, ake, ake, ko tātou marae...*' ('forever, forever... it is our marae'); this was apparently meant as an inclusive rather than exclusive claim, but nevertheless included Te Urewera hapū while probably accepting Ngāti Rongo's stronger claim, and it was met by approving murmurs throughout the meetinghouse. Paora then stood again to respond, emphasizing that he had meant no offense to Pera by implying his right to Ōhāua came from Ngāti Rongo rather than Te Urewera. Nevertheless, along with Hikawera's earlier judgment, this was also the implication of Paora's whakapapa—and (so far as I was aware) no alternative had been offered by any spokesperson for Te Urewera hapū.

However, this confrontation (or reconciliation) had already been aired at an earlier ceremonial gathering, and apparently more provocatively. Either at the *hurahanga kōhatu* ('tombstone unveiling') for Tumoana Tumoana at Rūātoki on 22 April 1983 or at an earlier *tangi* for Reg Nikora (my family and I were present at the former but only heard about the latter; a brother of Reg Nikora is the tall man on the left in Fig. 11.5, with Paki Haumate on his right side and, I think, Reuben Tahi on his left side).

At this earlier gathering Pera Tahi had stood to welcome visitors from Ngāti Porou iwi of the nearby East Coast, pointing out that his wife Brenda was one-quarter Ngāti Porou and remarking that they always had good piss-ups (drinking parties) when Tūhoe visited them. Joining in the laughter, Paora Kruja had stood to speak, pointing out that Pera himself was really Ngāti Porou, his predecessor Tahi having come from that iwi on the East Coast.[5] My old notes innocently recorded that Pera was angry and embarrassed by this assertion. His explicit deference to Paora at the Ōhāua hui for clarification of the whakapapa suggests there had been no offense between them. I am unsure whether or not Pera appears in the photo of Fig. 11.5, perhaps having left the gathering earlier. Some others of his *whānau* at Mātaatua had apparently not been able to come at all.

The grounds of Pera's staunch defense of Te Urewera hapū's rights to Ōhāua had already strengthened for several years through the pre-requisite of *noho* (literally 'sitting'), active occupation, or use of the land and its resources. Reuben Tahi and others' prolonged stays in their family *kauta* or kitchen there may even have qualified as *noho tuturu* ('true sitting') in the sense of residence rather than only use of the resources of the land. Insofar as Te Urewera hapū use was backed by descent from founding *tīpuna* of Ōhāua lands, the occupation or use increasingly established by Tuawhenua and other Te Urewera hapū undertakings on those lands had grown stronger. Through continuing activities of the thriving Tuawhenua organization in the upper Whakatāne River basin since 1983, Te Urewera hapū rights to Ōhāua have continued to grow still stronger. After all, Rūātoki and most of Ngāti Rongo members are now located much further away from Ōhāua than are Ruatāhuna and Mātaatua. Yet, if significant Ngāti Rongo occupation or use is continued, the ancestral history of the hapū can always emerge again to trump Te Urewera claims.

Surprisingly, current evidence suggests that the causes of the 1983 confrontation in Ōhāua have emerged again, and that factions of each hapū remain unreconciled. On the one side is the new leadership of Te Urewera hapū in Mātaatua and Ruatāhuna pressing for the *mana* of Tuawhenua enterprises that began to develop in the 1970s in confrontation with the Tūhoe Trustboard and the threat of an amalgamation of the Tuawhenua blocks under its control. Ōhāua and the Ōhāua te Rangi block of Tuawhenua was a rallying point for them by 1983 and perhaps continues to be regardless of the outcome of that gathering. On the other side is the new leadership of Ngāti Rongo hapū in Rūātoki and Ōhāua whose mana over Ōhāua was defended by their elders, including Hikawera as well as Paora, in 1983.

In current terms, the public statements that probably best represent this confrontation between these two sides (of both hapū!) are, on the one hand, the Tuawhenua website cited above and, on the other hand, Tamati Kruger's 'Koia Mārika' address described in the Preface, determined to recover *mana motuhake* for Te Urewera but avoid the entrapments of neoliberal business enterprise that had fettered the Trust board. In the Preface I recalled how already in the early 1980s young Tamati (speaking into the starlit darkness of Ōhāua where I and my family were visiting his family and sleeping together in Te Poho o Pōtiki) was already emphasizing that 'money and *mana* are irreconcilable'.

The 13 blocks of the Ōhāua te Rangi pupuri whenua land 'shares' that survived the Crown's predation 1915–1926 were actually scattered between the northern extensions of Tuawhenua and the southern extensions of Te Pae o Tūhoe (Figs. 1.2, 1.4 and 6.1). This Ōhāua te Rangi *whānui* ('widespread') can actually be traced in some detail as the *morehu* ('remnants') of the Ōhāua te Rangi amalgamation planned in 1902, relocated as individual shares of 'ownership' in the false promises and chaos of the Urewera Consolidation Scheme (Webster 2019, Fig. 8). Along with the rest of the over 200 *pupuri whenua* blocks scattered by the UCS inside what was to become the Urewera National Park, these remnants of the old Ōhāua te Rangi hapū cluster developed divergent title histories between 1926 and 2014, including the quashed amalgamation plan of the 1970s (Fraser 2004; Tahi 2017). Most of these blocks continue under jurisdictions (usually that of the Māori Land Court) that differ radically from the surrounding Te Urewera land under the new 2014 statutes. The Ōhāua marae and settlement now lie in the middle of six of the thirteen Ōhāua te Rangi *whānui* blocks that by 1926 ended up in the Tuawhenua region. These six blocks have been under pressure to join the Tuawhenua Trust since the 1980s, but two of them, including the large Ruahine block that surrounds the Ōhāua marae, still have not joined.

The *tīpuna* lie patiently where they were buried, but tug at us from different directions. Only a few months ago I found myself having to choose between loyalty to old friends aligned with Mātaatua and Te Urewera hapū and loyalty to the encompassing *mana motuhake* of the new Te Urewera as it is represented by its council Te Uru Taumatua. I take the ambivalent confrontation over Ōhāua described above to explain my personal predicament. Confronted by my little crisis, I stood on a busy footpath in Rotorua looking up into the shadows of Te Urewera toward Mātaatua where I had intended to continue my journey from Auckland for a visit with old friends. Instead, I decided it was best to return to Auckland. On the way out of Rotorua I stopped to soak my feet in the hot springs, as I had some years ago when I was searching the archives of the Waiariki Māori Land Court and sleeping nights in the car.

At the present moment, caught in what appears to be a very old but ambivalent confrontation, my *manawa* or heart tends to side with our nanny Rangiwhaitiri and her ancestors from Te Whenuanui, but my *whakāro* or mind tends to side with my *tuakana* Tumoana Tumoana, Numia Kereru, and their ancestors. May their reconciliation be a true *tatau pounamu*, albeit a *pokaikaha* or fraught sort of *tatau pounamu*. And may they forgive me for my *kaupoi* sort of presumption to join in their common struggle for *he mana motuhake* in Te Urewera. *Koia mārika*, indeed![6]

E te atua
tahuri mai ōu taringa ki tā mātou īnoi
hei whakangaro atu koe inā tangi atu mātou.
Anga mai, titiro mai hoki koe
ki a mātou e pokaikaha noa nei,
tangi nei hoki,
koi mātou e whakakorōria nei
ki tōu ingoa tapu.
Āmine.

('O Lord
turn your ear to our prayer
lest our cries be lost to you.
Turn to us, look at us
see our turmoils,
our cries of anguish,
so that we may glorify
your sacred name.
Amen')

Notes

1. *Tatau pounamu.* Timoti (Sam) Kāretu, from Tūhoe and Ngāti Ruapani of Waikaremoana, translated this as "the door of greenstone", defining it as a "figurative expression for an enduring peace, which was often cemented by the exchange of valuable greenstone heirlooms" (Kāretu 1987: 106). He cites two *whakataukī* ('proverbs') as examples: *Me tatau pounamu, kia kore ai e pakaru, ake, ake.* Let us conclude a permanent treaty of peace, that

may never be broken, for ever, for ever and *He whakahou rongo wāhine he tatau pounamu.* Peace brought about by women is an enduring one, adding that 'Normally, in times of crisis, high-born women, puhi, were married to the victors to cement the peace and to ensure there would be no more warfare'. In response to a version of this chapter, Robert Rapata Wiri, also from Tūhoe and Ngāti Ruapani, translated *tatau pounamu* as "reconciliation" among Tūhoe (personal communication). Hirini Mead of Ngāti Awa discusses peace-agreements including *tatau pounamu* along with several other traditional accounts (Mead 2016).

2. Poster advertising an exhibition of Auckland Museum collection 'Whakaahua; photographic images of Māori Life 1860s–1930s,' shown 1987–1988.
3. I have recently learned that the marriage between Rangiwhaitiri Wharekiri and Kunare Tumoana was considered a *tomo*, an "arranged" marriage in the special sense that it was widely recognized as bringing together two leading descent lines of Te Urewera and Ngāti Rongo hapū (Tamati Kruger, personal communication 25May2019). Rangiwhaitiri's father Pakitu had furthermore come to Rūātoki and built a house at Tauarau for Kunare and his daughter to live in. Pakitu was primarily affiliated with Ngāti Rongo of Ōhāua but in his marriage to Hauauru had come to be seen as also representing Te Urewera hapū of Mātaatua. However, Rangiwhaitiri had confided in us that after a few years she had left Kunare because he had brought another wife into their home in Rūātoki. Furthermore, when her parents Pakitu and Hauauru came to Rūātoki to take her back home to Mātaatua, it was considered a *taua*, a hostile expedition avenging the betrayal of the *tomo*. Kunare's assumption of a second wife would not have been considered merely an infidelity, but a grave insult to the *mana* of the arrangement of the first marriage. Te Urewera hapū of Mātaatua furthermore demanded restitution from Ngāti Rongo of Rūātoki in the form of heirlooms, a *muru* for the shame that Ngāti Rongo had brought upon Te Urewera. Kunare would know that because of this shame he would never be accepted as a leader of Ngāti Rongo.
4. It was young Tamati's assertion at the Ōhāua reunion in 1983 that "…Tamahore was great-grandfather of both Waewae… and Kereru…" which enabled my recent correction of Best's genealogies, shown in Fig. 6.3 as Pahi and her daughter Patu (Webster n.d. [1983] UNB 2: 54).
5. The implied stigma in this apparently good-humored reminder appears to be of the same order that led me to an explanation of why generations of migrants between the "conquered" Waikaremoana lands and adjacent blocks who had gained only narrow rights to a few of the Urewera blocks had formed the Ruatāhuna-Waikaremoana migrant marriage political alliance in order eventually to gain acceptance and wider rights to Urewera lands through intermarriage with longer-established Tūhoe (Webster 2017, 2019).

6. This is my own variation of the traditional Ringatū liturgy (perhaps more appropriately: ***karakia*** 'prayer-chant' or ***inoi*** 'prayer-plea') by Te Kooti. It is adapted from Judith Binney's *Redemption Songs: A Life of Te Kooti Arikirangi Te Turuki* (2012: 297–8; fn 118; Bridget Williams Books, Wellington, New Zealand), but differs importantly in ways for which I am indebted to the Tūhoe but for which only I am responsible.

   This ***karakia*** is known as the 'Pokaikaha' in the Ringatū church tradition. My version presented here in Māori is adapted from the original 1995 edition of Binney's book, from which it varies by changing ***Atua*** to ***atua*** to avoid the monotheist assumption that Jeffrey Holman's critique of Elsdon Best's influence on traditional Māori concepts has called into question (Holman 2010), by marking the long vowels with macrons, and by changing ***kei*** to ***hei*** to reflect Tūhoe pronunciation. My translation also diverges significantly from Binney's due to my interpretation of the Tūhoe ***tohunga whakapono*** ('expert on truth') Hikawera Te Kurapa's advice on the meaning of ***pokaikaha***. In 1983 I was told that he considered the concept to be central to the Ringatū church (but rejected by Rua Kenana's ***Iharaera*** version of Ringatū) and that he translated it as "winding in, involution, even confusion of strength ***in face of Pākehā oppression***" (Webster n.d. [UNB 2 (1983): 45]; my emphasis). Similarly, Williams translates ***pōkaikaha*** as "confused, at a loss, in doubt" and ***pokai*** as a "ball…roll…swarm…" (1957: 289). The addition of ***kaha*** 'strong' implies, to me, the tension of a coiled spring. Williams' example of ***pōkaikaha*** also uses the phrase …***pōkaikaha noa***… or '***ordinary*** pokaikaha'.

   Although Binney recognizes Ringatū concern "with the problems of the colonised" and regard to God in the spirit of Exodus rather than Christ (2012: 297–8), her interpretation leans more toward piety than mine. In the context of Te Kooti's ***karakia***, I think 'turmoil' best straddles all these meanings. Similarly, while Williams translates ***koi*** (in the sixth line) as "whilst" or "lest" (1957: 127), in the context of ***tatau pounamu*** "reconciliation" as raised in Chap. 11 of Volume I and my recent essay (Webster 2019), I feel that '…so that we may…' best conveys an appropriate sense of defiance or tension as well as pious entreaty or plea (which I also see in the second line ***hei whakangaro atu***…). I, of course, must bear all responsibility for my rendition and this interpretation of Te Kooti's ***karakia***.

References

Best, Elsdon. 1973. *Tuhoe, Children of the Mist.* Vols. I and II (genealogies). Second edition. Wellington, N.Z.: A.H. and A.W. Reed Ltd. (first published 1925 as Vol VI of the Memoirs of the Polynesian Society).

Binney, Judith. 2012. *Redemption Songs: A Life of Te Kooti Arikirangi Te Turuki.* (First edition, 1995.) Bridget Williams Books, Wellington, New Zealand.

Firth, Raymond. 1959. *The Economics of the New Zealand Maori*. Second edition. Wellington, New Zealand: Government Printer. (1st edition 1929).

Fraser, Clementine. 2004. *Amalgamation of Urewera Lands 1960–1980s*. WAI 894, #F3. Wellington, N.Z.: Waitangi Tribunal.

Haenga-Collins, Maria. 2011. *Belonging* and *Whakapapa: the closed Stranger Adoption of Māori Children into Pākehā Families*. MA thesis, Massey University, Palmerston North, N.Z.

Holman, Jeffrey Paparoa. 2010. *Best of both worlds: the story of Elsdon Best and Tutakangahau*. Auckland, N.Z.: Penguin.

Kāretu, Timoti. 1987. *The Reed Book of Māori Proverbs* (Te Kohikohinga Whakataukī a Reed). 2d edition, revised by Timoti Kāretu. Reed Books, Auckland, New Zealand.

Mead, Hirini. 2016. *Tikanga Māori (Revised Edition): Living By Māori Values*. Huia Press, Wellington, N.Z.

Tahi, Brenda. 2004. *Ruatāhuna – Te Manawa o Te Ika*. Part II: History 1896–1980s. Waitangi Tribunal report WAI 894 #D2. Wellington, N.Z.: Waitangi Tribunal.

Tahi, Brenda. 2017. 'History of the Tuawhenua Trust' and 'List of Blocks in the Tuawhenua Trust'. www.tuawhenua.biz.

Webster, Steven. n.d.[1983–4]. UNB 2 (Urewera Notebook #2. February 1983–January 1984).

Webster, Steven. 2010. "He kaawai hapuu Tuuhoe no te ao o mua: An ethnohistorical reconstruction of one hapuu branch of Ngai Tuuhoe in the Urewera District Native Reserve 1899–1903" *Sites*, (N.S.), 7(1): 1–43.

Webster, Steven. 2017. "Māori Kinship and Power: Ngāi Tūhoe 1894–1912." *Journal of the Polynesian Society* 126 (2): 145–180.

Webster, Steven. 2019. "Ōhāua te Rangi and Reconciliation in Te Urewera, 1913–1983." *Journal of the Polynesian Society* 128 (2): 191–224.

Williams, H.W. 1957. *A Dictionary of the Maori Language*. Sixth edition. Wellington, N.Z.: Government Printer.

References

AJHR 1895. The Prime Minister's visit to the Ureweras. Undated. Appendices to the Journal of the House of Representatives, 1895 G-1, Vol II: 48-79.

AJHR 1899. Smith, S. Percy. "The Urewera District Native Reserve Act, 1896." Undated. Appendices to the Journal of the House of Representatives 1899, C-1: x–xi. Wellington, N.Z.

AJHR 1902. Butler, W.J. "The Urewera District Native Reserve Act, 1896." 6 August 1902. Appendices to the Journal of the House of Representatives 1902, G-6: 1. Wellington, N.Z.

AJHR 1903. D. Scannell. 'Commissioners' Orders Under the "Urewera District Native Reserves Act, 1896."' Undated. Appendices to the Journal of the House of Representatives 1903, G-6: 1–256. Wellington, N.Z.

AJHR 1907. G. Mair, D.F.G. Barclay, Paratene Ngata. "The Urewera District Native Reserve: reports of the commissioners appointed ...." Report and orders. Undated. Appendices to the Journal of the House of Representatives 1907 G-4: 1–190. Wellington, N.Z.

AJHR 1921. "Urewera Lands Consolidation Scheme (report on proposed)." 31 October 1921. Appendices to the Journal of the House of Representatives G-7: 1–39. Wellington, N.Z.

Anderson, A.J. 1980. "Towards an explanation of protohistoric social organisation and settlement patterns amongst the southern Ngai Tahu." *New Zealand Journal of Archaeology* 2: 3–23.

Ballara, Angela. 1995. "Porangahau: The Formation of an Eighteenth Century Community in Southern Hawke's Bay." *New Zealand Journal of History* 29(1):3–18.

© The Author(s) 2020
S. Webster, *A Separate Authority (He Mana Motuhake)*, Volume I,
https://doi.org/10.1007/978-3-030-41042-1

Ballara, Angela. 1998. *Iwi: The dynamics of Māori tribal organisation from c.1769 to c.1945*. Wellington, N.Z.: Victoria University Press.

Bassett, Heather and R. Kay. 2002. "*Ruatāhuna: land ownership and administration c. 1896–1990.*" With Supporting Papers (S.P.) Vols 1–3. WAI 894 #A20. Wellington, N.Z.: Waitangi Tribunal.

Berghan, Paula. 2001. "Block Research Narratives of the Urewera, 1870–1930; A resource document for Urewera District Treaty Issues." WAI 894 #A86. Wellington, N.Z.: Waitangi Tribunal.

Best, Elsdon. 1898. "Tuhoe genealogies 1898" (spine title); "Genealogies of the Tuhoe tribe. Also includes all living members of the tribe in 1898, as given before the Urewera Commission set up under the act of 1896." Manuscript qMS [172]. Wellington, N.Z.: Alexander Turnbull Library. [The author can supply a digital index for this resource.]

Best, Elsdon, 1973. *Tuhoe, Children of the Mist*. Vols. I and II (genealogies). Second edition. Wellington, N.Z.: A.H. and A.W. Reed Ltd. (first published 1925 as Vol VI of the Memoirs of the Polynesian Society).

Binney, Judith. 1995. *Redemption Songs; A Life of Te Kooti Arikirangi Te Turuki*. Wellington, N.Z.: Bridget Williams Books.

Binney, Judith. 1997. "He Mana Tuatoru: the Rohe Pōtae of Tūhoe." *New Zealand Journal of History* 31(1): 117–131.

Binney, Judith. 2002. *Encircled Lands; Part Two: A History of the Urewera 1878–1912*. An Overview Report on the Urewera for the Waitangi Tribunal. WAI 894, A15. Wellington, N.Z.: Waitangi Tribunal.

Campbell, S.K.L. 1997. *Urewera Overview Project: Land Alienation, Consolidation, and Development in the Urewera 1912–1950*. A report commissioned by the Crown Forestry Rental Trust. WAI 894, A55. Wellington, N.Z.: Waitangi Tribunal.

Dougherty, Wirimu. 2014. "Mātauranga ā-Iwi as it Applies to Tūhoe – Te Mātauranga o Tūhoe." *Enhancing Mātauranga Māori and Global Indigenous Knowledge*. Wellington: N.Z. Qualifications Authority/Mana Tohu Maatauranga o Aotearoa.

Edwards, Cecilia. 2004. *The Urewera District Native Reserve Act 1896, a report for the Crown Law Office*. Parts I–III. WAI 894, #D7. Wellington, N.Z.: Waitangi Tribunal.

Firth, Raymond. 1959. *The Economics of the New Zealand Maori*. Second edition. Wellington, New Zealand: Government Printer. (1st edition 1929).

Firth, Raymond. 1962. "Book review of *Maori Marriage: An Essay in Reconstruction*" by Bruce Biggs (Polynesian Society Monographs, No. 1. Wellington, New Zealand: The Polynesian Society Incorporated, 1960). *American Anthropologist* 64: 193–4.

Fraser, Clementine. 2004. *Amalgamation of Urewera Lands 1960-1980s*. WAI 894, #F3. Wellington, N.Z.: Waitangi Tribunal.

Haenga-Collins, Maria. 2011. *Belonging* and *Whakapapa: the closed Stranger Adoption of Māori Children into Pākehā Families.* MA thesis, Massey University, Palmerston North, N.Z.

Holman, Jeffrey Paparoa. 2010. *Best of both worlds: the story of Elsdon Best and Tutakangahau.* Auckland, N.Z.: Penguin.

King, Michael. 1975. *Te Ao Hurihuri; the world moves on: aspects of Maoritanga.* Wellington, Hicks-Smith.

Kruger, Tamati. 2004. "Ngā Hapū ō Ngā Pōtiki." Appendix to Final Report *Ruātoki; Ngā Rauru ō Ngā Pōtiki.* Anamata College, Taneātua, N.Z. 10 January 2004. Urewera Enquiry WAI 894. Wellington, N.Z.: Waitangi Tribunal.

Laurie, John. 1995. "Annotated index of Urewera and Whakatane Minutebooks." University of Auckland Library. Auckland, N.Z.

Marr, Cathy. 2002. *The Urewera District Native Reserve Act 1896 and Amendments.* A report commissioned by the Waitangi Tribunal. WAI 894, A 21. Wellington, N.Z.: Waitangi Tribunal.

Metge, Joan. 1967. *The Maoris of New Zealand.* London: Routledge & Kegan Paul.

Miles, Anita. 1999. *Te Urewera.* A report for the Waitangi Tribunal Rangahaua Whanui Series. WAI 894, A 11. Wellington, N.Z.: Waitangi Tribunal.

Milroy, J. Te Wharehuia 2000. Expert opinion in the case of Waimania Hohua. Appeal 2000–8, Minute Book 10, APRO 49–51. Rotorua, N.Z.: Waiariki Maori Land Court District.

Murton, Brian. 2004. *The Crown and the People of Te Urewera, 1860-c2000: The Economic and Social Experience of a People.* Research report commissioned by the Crown Forestry Rental Trust. 2 vols., 1,791 pages. Wai 894 H12, Te Urewera inquiry. Wellington, N.Z.: Waitangi Tribunal.

Ngata, Apirana. n.d. MS. Not dated; probably 1929. "The genealogical method as applied to early history of New Zealand." ATL qMS NGA. Alexander Turnbull Library, Wellington. (A copy also held in Special Collections mss 2 archives A-135, University of Auckland Library, Auckland, N.Z.).

NZMS 170 n.d. "Urewera National Park" (3rd Edition). New Zealand Map Service. Wellington, N.Z.: Dept. of Lands and Survey.

Oliver, Steven. 2002. "Ruatoki Block Report." A report commissioned by the Waitangi Tribunal. WAI 894 record of inquiry, doc A6. Wellington, N.Z.: Waitangi Tribunal.

O'Malley, Vincent. 1996. *The Crown's Acquisition of the Waikaremoana Block 1921–25.* A report for the Panekiri Tribal Trust Board, with Supporting Papers (S.P.) Vols I–III, May 1996. WAI 894 record of inquiry, doc A50. Wellington, N.Z.: Waitangi Tribunal.

Pouwhare, Te Iki. 1959. "Genealogies from Tūhoe, by Te Iki Pouwhare." *Journal of the Polynesian Society* Vol.68(3): 215–218.

Ryan, P.M. 1995. *The Reed Dictionary of Modern Māori.* Auckland, N.Z.: Reed Books.

Shore, Cris and M. Kawharu, 2014. The Crown in New Zealand; Anthropological Perspectives on an Imagined Sovereign. *Sites*, vol 11 no 1.

Sissons, Jeffrey. 1991. *Te Waimana, The Spring of Mana: Tuhoe History and the Colonial Encounter.* Dunedin, N.Z.: Otago University Press.

Sissons, Jeffrey. 2002. "Waimana Kaaku: A History of the Waimana Block." A report commissioned by the Crown Forestry Rental Trust, June 2002. Wellington, N.Z.: Waitangi Tribunal.

Sissons, Jeffrey. 2010. "Building a house society: The reorganization of Māori communities around meeting houses." *Journal of the Royal Anthropological Institute* (N.S.) 16: 372–86.

Sluka, Jeffrey. 2010. "The Ruātoki Valley 'Antiterrorism' Police Raids: Losing 'hearts and minds' in Te Urewera." *Sites* N.S. Vol 7(1): 44–64.

Sorrenson, M.P.K. 1956. "Land purchase methods and their effect on Māori population 1865–1901." *Journal of the Polynesian Society* 65 (3): 183–199.

Sorrenson, M.P.K. 2015. "The lore of the judges: Native land court judges' interpretations of Māori custom law." *Journal of the Polynesian Society* 124 (3): 223–242.

Stokes, Evelyn, J. Te Wharehuia Milroy, and Hirini Melbourne. 1986. *Te Urewera; nga iwi, te Whenua, te Ngahere; People, Land and Forests of Te Urewera.* Hamilton, N.Z., University of Waikato. WAI 894 record of inquiry, doc A11. Wellington, N.Z.: Waitangi Tribunal

Tahi, Brenda. 2004. *Ruatāhuna – Te Manawa o Te Ika.* Part II: History 1896–1980s. Waitangi Tribunal report WAI 894 #D2. Wellington, N.Z.: Waitangi Tribunal.

Tahi, Brenda. 2017. 'History of the Tuawhenua Trust' and 'List of Blocks in the Tuawhenua Trust'. www.tuawhenua.biz.

Temara, Te Pou. 1993. "Te Whenuanui (?–1907), Tuhoe chief, builder, and carver." The Dictionary of New Zealand Biography. Te Ara – the Encyclopedia of New Zealand. http://www.TeAra.govt.nz/en/biographies/2t33/te-whenuanui (accessed 13 May 2017).

Temara, Te Pou. 2000. "Hikawera Te Kurapa (1907–1985), Tuhoe tohunga, horse-breaker, farmer, Ringatu leader." Dictionary of New Zealand Biography. Te Ara – the Encyclopedia of New Zealand. http://www.TeAra.govt.nz/en/biographies/5t9/te-kurapa-hikawera (accessed 13 May 2017).

Te Urewera Act 2014. Public Act 2014 No 51. Date of assent 27 July 2014. N.Z. Parliament. http://www.legislation.govt.nz/act/public/2014/0051/latest/whole.html

Tūhoe Claims Settlement Act 2014. Public Act 2014 No 50. Date of assent 27 July 2014. N.Z. Parliament. http://www.legislation.govt.nz/act/public/2014/0050/latest/whole.html.

Urewera Minutebooks Series, 1899–1926

Arranged chronologically by acronym. Copies held in various archives noted (NA Wgtn: National Archives, Wellington, N.Z.; NA Ak: National Archives, Auckland, N.Z.; Waiariki MLC: Waiariki Māori Land Court Archives, Rotorua, N.Z. (also holds most copies and some originals); Univ.Auck.Lib: University of Auckland Library (also holds many on microfilm).)

UMB 1. Urewera District Native Reserve Commission minute book 1 (identified as Urewera Commission minute book '3'), Smith, Butler, et al, (1Feb1899–8Mar1900), in Māori, Index 22pp., 382pp. NA Wgtn: Urewera MB 3, MLC 13, W3518, CD2, Vol 3, 397 pp.; NA Ak: AREPRO 4711/1445. Acronym: UMB 1.

UMB 2. Urewera District Native Reserve Commission minute book 2, Smith, Butler, et al., (8Mar1900–20Feb1901), in Māori, Index, 350 pp. NA Wgtn: Urewera MB 2, MLC 13,W3518, CD2, Vol.2, 358 pp.; NA Ak: AREPRO 4711/1442. Acronym: UMB 2.

UMB 3. Urewera District Native Reserve Commission minute book 3 (identified as '3A'; English translation of last part of UMB 1), Smith, Butler, et al, (9Feb1900–8Mar1900). 189 pp., index, NA Wgtn: Urewera MB 3A, MLC 13, W3518, CD 2, Vol 3A, 191 pp.; NA Ak: AREPRO 4711/1444. Acronym: UMB 3.

UMB 4. Urewera District Native Reserve Commission minute book 4 (English translation of UMB 2), Butler, Scannell, et al, (9Mar1900–May1900), index 12 pp., 344pp.; NA Wgtn: Urewera MB 4, MLC 13, W3518, CD 2, Vol. 4, 357 pp.; NA Ak: AREPRO 4711/1446. Acronym: UMB 4.

UMB 5. Urewera District Native Reserve Commission minute book 5, Butler, Scannell, et al. (18Mar1901–16May01), in English, index 5 pp., 382 pp.; NA Wgtn: Urewera MB 5, MLC 13,W3518, CD 2, Vol.5, 388pp.; NA Ak: AREPRO 4711/1447. Acronym: UMB 5.

UMB 6. Urewera District Native Reserve Commission minute book 6, Butler, Scannell, et al. (16May1901–26Apr02) in English, index 9 pp., 382 pp.; NA Wgtn: Waiariki, Urewera MB 6, CD W3518/2, 398 pp.; NA Ak: AREPRO 4711/1448. Acronym: UMB 6.

UMB 7. Urewera District Native Reserve Commission minute book 7, Butler, Mair, et al. (28Apr1902–14Oct02), in English, 70 pp.; NA Wgtn: Waiariki, Urewera MB 7, CD, W3518/2, 63 pp.; NA Ak: AREPRO 4711/1449. Acronym: UMB 7.

UMB 8. Urewera District Native Reserve Commission minute book 8, ("Urewera Commission Minute Book 1896" in Waiariki MLC archives, bound xerox copy), probably by Elsdon Best. draft orders, annotated with share modifications, mothers, etc., for 20 blocks (UMB 9, covering the other blocks, appears to be lost since 1984). No copies in NA. Acronym UMB 8.

UCAMB 1. Urewera District Native Reserve Commission Appeal minute book 1, D.F.G. Barclay, Mair, Ngata, (5Dec1906–22Jan1907). 10 pp. index, ?pp.; NA Wgtn: unable to locate; NA Ak: AREPRO 4711/1133; Univ.Auck.Lib: 333.0995 N536u. Acronym: UCAMB 1.

UCAMB 2. Urewera District Native Reserve Commission Appeal minute book 2, D.F.G. Barclay, Mair, Ngata, (23Jan1907–12Mar1907) index, 382pp.; NA Wgtn: unable to locate; NA Ak: AREPRO 4711/1134; Univ.Auck.Lib: 333.0995 N536u. Acronym UCAMB 2.

UCAMB 3. Urewera District Native Reserve Commission Appeal minute book 3, D.F.G. Barclay, Mair, Ngata, (12Mar1907–10June1907); NA Wgtn: unable to locate; NA Ak: AREPRO 4711/1135; Univ.Auck.Lib: 333.0995 N536u. Acronym UCAMB 3.

NACMB 1. Native Appellate Court minute book 1, Jackson Palmer, Rawson, (13Nov1912–Feb1913), index 9 pp., 386 pp.; NA Wgtn: Waiariki, Urewera Appelate MB 1, CD 3518/2, 397pp.; NA Ak: AREPRO 4711/1450. Acronym: NACMB 1.

NACMB 2. Native Appellate Court minute book 2, Jackson Palmer, Rawson, (1Feb1913–20Aug1913), index 5 pp., 136pp.; NA Wgtn: Waiariki, Urewera Appelate MB 2, CD 3518/2, 140pp.; NA Ak: AREPRO 4711/1451. Acronym: NACMB 2.

UCMB 1. Urewera Consolidation minute book 1, Carr, Knight, (7Dec1921–5Jul1923), index 33 pp., 372pp.; NA Wgtn: Urewera MB 1, MLC 13, W 3518, CD 2, Vol1, 403pp.; NA Ak: AREPRO 4711/1441. Acronym: UCMB 1.

UCMB 2. Urewera Consolidation minute book 2A, Carr, Knight, (27Apr1923–18Dec1926), index 33pp, 246pp.; NA Wgtn: Urewera MB 2A, MLC 13, W 3518, CD2, Vol.2, 284pp.; NA Ak: AREPRO 4711/1443. Acronym: UCMB 2A.

UCMB 2B. 'Urewera Consolidation minute book 2B' (probably Carr, revised groups and draft orders, loose unfiled papers found in Waiariki MLC archives; not a closed file. Acronym: UCMB 2B.

UCS Group Book 167 (an index of names alphabetised by first name; cover missing). *Urewera Consolidation Group Book series*, Waiariki District Māori Land Court archives.

UCS closed file 630 (1921–1926). Summary of groups, alphabetical index, consolidated group lists, consolidated successions. Urewera Consolidation Scheme files, Waiariki District Māori Land Court archives, Rotorua, N.Z.

Wai 2445. July 2014. "Memorandum of counsel for Tūhoe Te Uru Taumata opposing application for urgent hearing by Vernon Winitana on behalf of Ngāti Ruapani." Te Rōpu Whakamana i te Tiriti o Waitangi. Wellington, N.Z.: Waitangi Tribunal.

Webster, Steven. 1973. "Māori Adoption." University of Auckland, Department of Anthropology Working Paper No. 21. Held in University of Auckland Library. Auckland, N.Z.

Webster, Steven. 1975. "Cognatic Descent Groups and the Contemporary Māori: a Preliminary Reassessment." *The Journal of the Polynesian Society* Vol.84(2): 121–152, 1975.

Webster, Steven. 1983–4. UNB 2 (Urewera Notebook #2. February 1983–January 1984).

Webster, Steven. n.d.-a (1984–5) "Urewera Land 1895–1926; a tentative historical survey of Government and Tuhoe relations as reflected in official records." Unpublished manuscript, 50pp. Held in the University of Auckland Library. Auckland, N.Z.

———. 1997. "Maori hapuu and their history" in *The Australian Journal of Anthropology* 8:3:307–335. University of Sydney, Sydney, Australia.

Webster, Steven. 1998a, "Maori Hapu as a Whole Way of Struggle: 1840–50s Before the Land Wars." *Oceania* 69(1):4–35.

Webster, Steven. 1998b. *Patrons of Maori Culture: Power, Theory, and Ideology in the Maori Renaissance*. Dunedin, N.Z.: Otago University Press.

Webster, Steven. 2004. *The Urewera Consolidation Scheme: Confrontations between Tuhoe and the Crown, 1915–1925*. Vols I, II. Report commissioned by the Waitangi Tribunal. WAI 894 #D8. Wellington, N.Z.: Waitangi Tribunal.

Webster, Steven. 2010. "He kaawai hapuu Tuuhoe no te ao o mua: An ethnohistorical reconstruction of one hapuu branch of Ngai Tuuhoe in the Urewera District Native Reserve 1899–1903" *Sites*, (N.S.), 7(1): 1–43.

Webster, Steven. 2013. "Are Maori Hapu 'Houses'? Are Whakapapa 'Strategic Improvisations'? The Ethnohistorical Evidence From Ngai Tuhoe." *Sites* N.S. Vol 10 (1): 30–50.

Webster, Steven. 2017. "Māori Kinship and Power: Ngāi Tūhoe 1894–1912." *Journal of the Polynesian Society* 126 (2): 145–180.

Webster, Steven. 2019. "Māori indigeneity and the ontological turn in ethnography." *Sites, N.S.* 16 (2): 11–36.

Webster, Steven. 2019. "Ōhāua te Rangi and Reconciliation in Te Urewera 1913–1983." *Journal of the Polynesian Society* 128 (2): 191–224.

Williams, H.W. 1957. *A Dictionary of the Maori Language*. Sixth edition. Wellington, N.Z.: Government Printer.

Wiri, Robert. *Te Wai-Kaukau o Nga Matua Tipuna: Myths, Realities, and the Determination of Mana Whenua in the Waikarmoana District*, M.A. Māori Studies thesis, University of Auckland, 1994.

Index[1]

[1] Note: Page numbers followed by 'n' refer to notes.

© The Author(s) 2020

S. Webster, *A Separate Authority (He Mana Motuhake)*, Volume I,
https://doi.org/10.1007/978-3-030-41042-1

S

T

The manufacturer's authorised representative in the EU is Springer Nature Customer Service Centre GmbH, Europaplatz 3, 69115 Heidelberg, Germany. If you have any concerns regarding our products, please contact ProductSafety@springernature.com

Printed and bound by CPI Group (UK) Ltd, Croydon, CR0 4YY
21/05/2026
02116082-0001